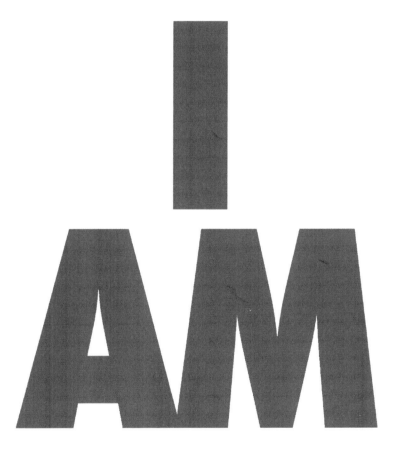

A Oneness Pentecostal Theology

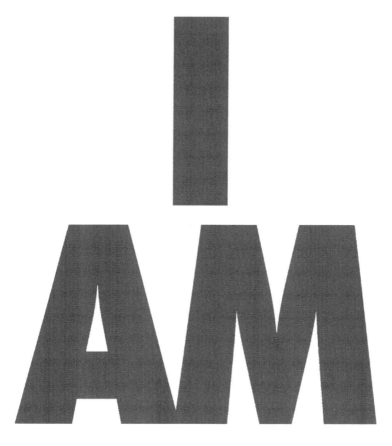

A Oneness Pentecostal Theology

David S. Norris, PhD

I AM
A Oneness Pentecostal Theology

by David S. Norris, PhD

Cover Design by Laura Jurek

©2009 David S. Norris
Hazelwood, MO 63042-2299
Printing History: 2009

Unless otherwise indicated, all Old Testament passages are taken from the New Jerusalem Bible (NJB) and all New Testament passages from NKJV.

All rights reserved. No portion of this publication may be reproduced, stored in an electronic system, or transmitted in any form or by any means, electronic, mechanical, photocopy, recording, or otherwise, without the prior permission of Word Aflame Press. Brief quotations may be used in literary reviews.

Printed in United States of America

WAP ACADEMIC
A Division of Word Aflame Press
8855 Dunn Road, Hazelwood, MO 63042
www.pentecostalpublishing.com

Library of Congress Cataloging-in-Publication Data

Norris, David S., 1954-
   I am : a oneness Pentecostal theology / by David S. Norris.
   p. cm.
Includes bibliographical references.

   ISBN 978-1-56722-730-7
   1. Oneness doctrine (Pentecostalism) 2. Trinity--History of doctrines--20th century. 3. Oneness Pentecostal churches--Doctrines. I. Title.
BX8763.N67 2009
230'.994--dc22   2009007453

To my wife,
Nancy Abshire Norris

Table of Contents

DEDICATION.................................... v

ACKNOWLEDGEMENTS............................ xi

SECTION I: THE GOD WHO IS 1
Chapter 1: Oneness Pentecostalism......................... 3
   Introduction.. 3
   Oneness Pentecostal Theology in the Twenty-First Century 6
   The Possibility of an Apostolic Hermeneutic.................. 8
   Methodology... 10
   Some Final Thoughts 12
Chapter 2: The God Who Is................................ 15
   Creation: A Study in Relationship 15
   Humanity—Created in the Image of God.................... 17
   Yahweh as "I AM" 19
   The Presence of Yahweh................................. 22
Chapter 3: The God Who Is Not............................ 25
   Introduction.. 25
   Hellenistic Influence..................................... 26
   The God of the Philosophers 26
   How the Jewish Conception of God Changed 28
   Philo and the Allegorical Method.......................... 30
   Philo and the "I AM" 32
Chapter 4: The God Who Is in Covenant 35
   God's Covenant with Adam 35
   Restoration of Covenant.................................. 36
   Yahweh's Covenant with Israel 37
   Invoking Yahweh's Name in the Covenant Community 40
   Yahweh's Universal Covenantal Love 42

SECTION II: THE MAN WHO IS 45
Chapter 5: Discovering the Man, Christ Jesus 47
   Introduction.. 47
   Confronting Objections to an Apostolic Hermeneutic 48
   The Obstacle of Plurality in the New Testament 55

   The Challenge of a Oneness Christological Argument.......... 60
Chapter 6: The Man Who Preexisted 63
   Introduction.. 63
   The Man before Bethlehem 64
   New Testament Passages 66
   First-Century Language of Incarnation 69
   The Prologue of John 70
   Conclusion 73
Chapter 7: The Man Born in Bethlehem...................... 75
   The "Name" and the Incarnation 75
   The Only Begotten 77
   An Anthropological Understanding of Jesus 80
   Implications 84
Chapter 8: The Man on a Mission........................... 85
   Jesus: A Man Who Believed in Yahweh.................... 85
   Jesus at Age Twelve 86
   At the Jordan River..................................... 87
   Temptation and Its Purpose............................... 91
   Jesus at Nazareth....................................... 92
   The Philippian Hymn (Philippians 2:6-11).................. 93
Chapter 9: The Man Who Taught about Yahweh 97
   Introduction.. 97
   Jesus' Language about the Father......................... 102
   Jesus' Language about the Holy Spirit 105
   Jesus' Language about "Divine Origins" 107
   Jesus' Language about the Son of Man 109
   Jesus' Language about the "I AM" 111
Chapter 10: The Man Who Was Crucified 113
   In the Shadow of the Cross.............................. 113
   Jesus and the Glory of God.............................. 115
   In the Garden of Gethsemane 118
   Jesus Condemned to Die................................ 119
   Jesus on the Cross..................................... 121
   The Victory of the Cross................................ 122
Chapter 11: The Man Who Was Glorified..................... 125
   Introduction... 125
   Jesus as Priest 126
   Jesus as King... 129
   Jesus as Mediator 132
   Working toward the Eschaton............................ 133
   Jesus in the Eschaton 135
Chapter 12: The Man with the Saving Name 137

The Apostles' Language Regarding Jesus 137
The Theology of Jesus' Name 140
Jesus as *Kurios* 141
The Saving Name Is Invoked 142
Answering Objections 145
Conclusion 147

SECTION III: THE MAN WHO IS NOT 149
Chapter 13: Moving Away from Orthodoxy 151
A Redefinition of Orthodoxy 151
Oneness Christology in a Jewish Milieu 155
Ebionism in Its Jewish Christian Context. 158
Ignatius: Christology in a Gentile Milieu 160
Summary. 162
Chapter 14: Apologists and the Hermeneutical Shift 163
Introduction. 163
The Advent of Christian Philosophers 164
Justin Martyr. 165
Oneness Christology in the Second Century 168
"Exceptions" to the Rule 171
The Beginning of Change. 172
Chapter 15: Displacing Oneness Christology 175
Introduction. 175
Normative Oneness Christology: Praxean Modalism. 175
The Developing Trinitarianism of Tertullian 177
Noetus and Sabellius. 178
Origen's *Logos* and the Developing Trinity 179
Oneness Christology in Opposition to the Fathers 180
The Success of Athanasius over Arius 181
Augustine 182
Oneness Christology in the Age of Augustine 185
Evaluating Historical Trajectories 186

SECTION IV: THE MAN WHO IS IN COVENANT 187
Chapter 16: The Place of Baptism in Covenant Initiation. 189
Introduction. 189
What the Bible Says about Baptism 190
The Baptismal Formula 192
Answering Objections 194
Abraham and Initiation into Covenant 196
Summary. 199
Chapter 17: The Covenant and the Spirit 201

Introduction. 201
Oneness Pentecostals and the Baptism of the Spirit. 202
The Relationship between Baptism and the Holy Spirit. 204
Initiation into Covenant in Acts 206
Speaking in Tongues. 209
Paul and "Abba". 211
An Invitation of the Spirit. 213
Chapter 18: Rediscovering Covenant 215
Introduction. 215
Theological Roots of Pentecostalism 216
Pentecostalism Beginnings. 219
The Advent of Oneness Pentecostalism 221
Conclusion 224

EPILOGUE 229
A Lesson from History 229
Covenantal Soteriology 233
Recovering a Covenantal Emphasis 236
Covenantal Christology 238

ENDNOTES. 243

ABBREVIATIONS 313

BIBLIOGRAPHY 315

SUBJECT & AUTHOR INDEX. 351

SCRIPTURE INDEX 371

INDEX FOR ANCIENT WRITINGS 381

Acknowledgments

Special thanks to Word Aflame Press and Robin Johnston who encouraged me to trim this text from being a Oneness Pentecostal theology (where I give my opinion about everything) to a Oneness Pentecostal christology (where I just give my opinion about Jesus Christ). While this tome might still be big enough to be utilized as a doorstop, the book is better for condensing it.

Thanks to the United Pentecostal Church International for allowing me to teach at Urshan Graduate School of Theology; thanks as well to my students who have put up with the varying and amorphous versions of this text. Although I am indebted to suggestions from colleagues, students, and others, any historical, biblical, or theological errors are strictly my own.

I am very appreciative for the leadership of UGST's president, David Bernard. I have been enriched by both his formal lectures and by informal discussion related to the systematic theology class where we team teach. My understanding of God is very much influenced by my grandfather, S. G. Norris. My understanding of the man Christ Jesus has been informed by studying under Robert Sabin. Numerous seminary and graduate school professors have all left their mark on me. It will very quickly be apparent to the reader which academics and christologians I tend to read and follow.

SECTION I:

THE GOD WHO IS

Chapter 1

Oneness Pentecostalism

Introduction

In the last decade, Oneness Pentecostalism has arguably grown from fifteen to twenty-five million adherents,[1] largely an indigenous growth that shows little sign of abating. Still, most academics have focused little on what Oneness Pentecostals really believe, and those who study the movement have often viewed the Oneness perspective through a faulty lens. The difficulty begins when scholars readily categorize Oneness Pentecostals as a subset of Evangelicals or more narrowly as part of the larger Pentecostal-Charismatic movement. Oneness Pentecostalism has significant distinctives from both of these groups and is unique christologically, soteriologically, and pneumatologically. Further, in an attempt to categorize this movement, academics often start with their own particular idea of orthodoxy, and then attempt to discern how Oneness Pentecostals either fit or do not fit within this preconceived construct. Such a method prevents Oneness Pentecostalism from telling its own story in its unique perspective. Consequently, even those who are sympathetic miss important nuances of the Oneness movement, often writing with little more than paternalistic sympathy.[2]

The writings of those earliest modern Pentecostals who became "Oneness" in 1913-1915, those whom academics believe capture the essence of Oneness christology in its formation,[3] reveal that these Oneness proponents argued in a particular way. They did not offer a systematic approach to theology in the usual sense. But then, some current attempts by Trinitarian Classical Pentecostals[4] to create a systematic theology have not been altogether fruitful, and for similar reasons.[5] Historically, Evangelical theology, which provides a particular template for a methodology, has leaned toward a rationalistic approach to theology, a particular kind of "propositionalism." That is, Evangelicals typically start with specific theological propositions about God and about theology proper; and only then is the biblical text marshaled for proof in a kind of ancillary role, demonstrating the "correctness" of the stated propositions. Terry Cross may be representative of Pentecostals at large when he critiques this pervasive Evangelical tendency, charging, "Systematic theology has followed this direction by positing propositional truth revealed in Scripture and setting forth dogma from on high."[6]

Historically, Oneness Pentecostalism was born out of the same impulse that spawned modern Pentecostalism in the first place. Pentecostals are by birthright restorationists. Thus, when at the beginning of the twentieth century Pentecostals deduced from the Book of Acts that speaking in tongues is the consistent biblical evidence for receiving the baptism of the Holy Spirit, they expected that God would in fact restore this gift to the church.[7] This simple hermeneutic, one insisting that church tradition retreat in the face of the biblical narrative—that Scripture should speak on its own terms—is the very milieu out of which Oneness Pentecostalism was born. Consequently, when in the second decade of the twentieth century, a number of Pentecostals exploring the scriptural mode of baptism in the light of the Book of Acts began baptizing in Jesus' name, their focus on the name of Jesus caused them to critique the doctrine of the Trinity. Ultimately these same people understood the Father, Son, and Holy Spirit in a way that others deemed unsound or even heretical, for it challenged a christological definition that stood, arguably, for fifteen hundred years.

In the writings of Frank Ewart, G. T. Haywood, and Andrew Urshan, it is readily apparent, at least to an insider, that not only do current Oneness Pentecostals have the same confession as these early Oneness Pentecostals; they argue in a similar way as well. By way of clearing the ground, we offer the following nomenclature for this study. Oneness Pentecostals are sometimes wrongly called modalists by their detractors,[8] an appellation we avoid. Even though Ewart, Haywood, and Urshan were called "Apostolic" by their own self designation,[9] for the sake of consistency, we utilize "Oneness" or "Oneness Pentecostal" as the preferred label for the movement that arose, in part, because of these men. Further, there was a particular way in which these men argued—an underlying set of presuppositions and way of studying the Bible that we designate as an "Apostolic hermeneutic." Briefly, we are defining an Apostolic hermeneutic as an attempt to privilege the Old Testament declaration of God in the way it was understood and interpreted by the apostles, particularly with respect to their understanding of Jehovah (we use Yahweh)[10] and their lived experience with Jesus. The assumption is that the Gospels and the Book of Acts give an accurate portrayal of the apostles' experience. An Apostolic hermeneutic has two significant methodological distinctions that largely separate it from Evangelical Christianity. Biblically, such a hermeneutic makes normative the Old Testament teaching of the unicity of God (God in His absolute oneness) while empowering the Luke-Acts narrative to interpret various didactic texts.[11] Historically, an Apostolic hermeneutic rejects a triumphalistic reading of church history, privileging what Oneness Pentecostals believe to be the teaching and praxis of the earliest church. It was the application of this Apostolic hermeneutic by the early Pentecostals that resulted in a proclamation of Jesus Christ that has little in common with christological definitions offered by the Catholic Church of the fourth and fifth centuries.

While simplistic definitions of a Oneness Pentecostal christology generally lead to misunderstandings, a few things should be stated as a preliminary working understanding about Oneness beliefs. Oneness Pentecostalism has commonalties and differences with both Evangelicals and other Pentecostals. For instance, Oneness Pentecostals hold a high view of Scripture, they believe in the virgin birth, the imminent return of Christ, the deity of Jesus, and typically pass other litmus tests conservative Evangelicals as well as Pentecostals generally utilize for assessment. On the other hand, Oneness adherents decry any ontological distinction between persons "in a Godhead." They do not ascribe to Unitarian thought, merely stripping Jesus of His divinity. Rather, a Oneness christology teaches that the God of the Old Testament was the Father of Jesus, the very Spirit that overshadowed Mary. Further, while Jesus was absolutely human in every sense, the very life of Jesus is the life of God, the fullness of God in Christ. Additionally, since there is no ontological distinction of persons, Oneness Pentecostals necessarily baptize in Jesus' name and see what other Pentecostals believe to be the empowerment of the baptism of the Spirit as really a part of initiation into the covenant relationship. It is these claims that create significant dissonance, which at once labels Oneness adherents as both a subset of the larger Pentecostal and Evangelical community while being at the same time assessed as "other-than-orthodox."

But the intent of this book is not merely to offer an apologia for those inside the Oneness movement. Our aim is to provide a cogent study for theologians utilizing a heuristic model to accurately present a Oneness construal. The primary source of theology for early Oneness writers was Scripture. It was Scripture used in a specific way, with a logic that made sense in its historical context.[12] Only then might they appeal to an extra-biblical source in support of their argument.[13] We argue in kind, primarily utilizing Scripture; secondarily, we are in conversation with current theologians, arguing in a way that makes sense in our current context.

Oneness Pentecostal Theology in the Twenty-First Century

In the last twenty-five years, a plethora of new approaches has begun to be utilized in studying the biblical text, such as canonical criticism, deconstructionism, and reader response criticism. From a Pentecostal perspective, canonical criticism has been helpful, as well as certain kinds of narrative criticism that allow for a theological reading of the narrative of Luke-Acts.[14] Various narrative approaches have been offered by the works of Hans Frei, George Lindback, and Robert W. Jenson.[15]

While Oneness Pentecostals in large part avoid post-liberal readings of the text, they do have some theological agreement with those who propose that the biblical text itself is a theology; for example, in the case of the narrative of Luke-Acts, one should respect the author's original intent: to teach theology through the narrative. An allowance for the legitimacy of new methodologies has worked in tandem with another theological development. Meta-systems that were once safely ensconced into the warp and woof of Christendom are now coming under scrutiny. For Oneness Pentecostals, a postmodern critique of dogma has cracked open the door for conversation in a way that was not possible before.

Oneness Pentecostals welcome voices that are suspicious of the way in which the church solved the "problem" of the Incarnation. We would agree with New Testament scholar Oscar Cullmann's complaint that christology came to be defined in ways that strayed from the manner in which the New Testament speaks.[16]

Old Testament scholars have also weighed in on this issue. John Goldingay critiques Trinitarianism as "two steps away from most of the NT narratives" and "three stages removed from most [Old Testament] biblical narrative." Indeed, for Goldingay, a Trinitarian perspective "seriously skews our theological reading of Scripture."[17] Thus, while most of the theologians who are cited in this book do not agree with a Oneness reading of the biblical text, they are sufficiently suspicious of the status quo for us to engage them in conversation. For instance, Emil Brunner, in seeking to demonstrate the sources of historical theology, states of the "mystery" of the Trinity, "There is no trace of such an idea in the New Testament. This *'mysterium logicum'* . . . lies wholly outside the message of the Bible."[18] Oneness adherents are encouraged that the twenty-first century birthed an era that supports those willing to return to a biblical understanding in constructing our Christian beliefs.[19]

The earliest Oneness Pentecostal pioneers had a particular way in which they read the Bible. For them, the Bible tells a panoramic story of redemption.[20] These men did not separate the Old and New Testaments as two antithetical stories. Rather, there was one biblical story, that of the redemptive victory of Jesus Christ. They read Adam's fall as a prelude to Christ's redemption; they did not spend a lot of time reflecting on how fallen Adam was or on the limits of what God could or could not do. Rather, the Bible was a celebration of relationship. While they did not utilize the word "covenant" to describe this relationship, we have chosen this word as a kind of umbrella term to talk about God's redemptive relationship with humanity in an optimistic reading of Scripture.[21] While one might argue that the concept of "covenant" has too many theological presuppositions attached to the use of the word, this should not necessarily prevent its use.[22] In fact, the extensive biblical use of covenant language suggests it is a core biblical concept. Walther Eichrodt is typical of those who affirm the centrality of covenant in the Old Testament.[23] For Eichrodt, the word "covenant" is the premiere concept used to define the relationship between Yahweh and the people of Israel.[24] Eichrodt is correct insofar as he goes; he simply does not go far enough. Not only is covenant the primary thematic designation of God's relationship with Israel; we would argue that the fully restored covenant relationship between God and humanity is the essence of the biblical story, and that in a truly biblical sense, "covenant" extends from Genesis to Revelation.[25] Echoing the basic theological premise of these early Oneness adherents, we utilize covenant as a term that describes an ongoing thread, a reciprocal relationship between God and His people. This covenant relationship was not abrogated with humanity's fall. Rather, it continued unabated. Certainly there was a significant loss when Adam and Eve were expelled from Eden, but it was not a loss of covenant. God was faithful in offering covenant to them still, anticipating a fully restored relationship that would be possible through Jesus Christ. Thus, in the Old Testament, God continued to extend covenant to His people based upon both the future promise of redemption and current reciprocal relationship with those who were willing to live their lives in obedience to Yahweh. With this kind of covenant theology as a backdrop, we attempt to tell the Oneness christological story of how the man Jesus restored covenant relationship with God on behalf of humanity. Further, we attempt to demonstrate biblically how such an understanding is woven into the fabric of the New Testament and in first-century understanding.

The Possibility of an Apostolic Hermeneutic

From the very beginning of Oneness Pentecostalism, Oneness adherents called themselves Apostolic. What they meant by this was that they held to both the doctrine and experience preached by the apostles. What we call an Apostolic hermeneutic demonstrates not only how they understood the belief of the apostles, but additionally, what scholars can add to such an assessment; specifically, we explore historical elements of the understanding of and experience of the writers of the New Testament in their Jewish Christian identity, attempting to see the Old Testament through the eyes of Jesus and the apostles. That is, since both Jesus and His apostles were Jews, the assumption should be (but often is not) that they believed in, practiced, and lived out lives squarely in keeping with their received Jewish tradition.[26] The Old Testament must not be discounted, particularly as it informs our understanding of christology.[27] Therefore, what the Old Testament says about the unicity of God is not to be redefined by the New Testament; rather, the interpretation of the New Testament must in fact be controlled by this Old Testament foundation.[28]

There is a commonalty to the way the writers of the New Testament speak, particularly the ways in which they dealt with the Hebrew Bible. These men knew nothing of form criticism, nor did they consider important issues of genre and authorship, at least not in post-enlightenment terms. They could readily quote from one or another of the prophets, blending together their sources to support christological claims. We approach the Old Testament similarly. In some ways echoing Brevard Childs's canonical approach, the presumption is that since Old Testament theology is a Christian enterprise, the text should be viewed in its canonical context "as a continuing interpretative activity by that community of faith which treasures its Scriptures as authoritative."[29] While we do not prescribe to Childs's method whole cloth,[30] the attempt is to read the Old Testament in a manner faithful to the way the apostles understood it. In this way, an Apostolic hermeneutic does not differentiate theologically between a presentation in the Torah and what is written, say, in the Prophets or from the Wisdom Literature.[31]

An Apostolic hermeneutic should be applied to the New Testament as well. Since the presumption is that the apostles commonly heard the teaching of Jesus and were in fellowship with one another, there should be a certain theological "sameness" among the New Testament writers. That is, while there are certainly different styles, and there are unique presentations by these New Testament authors, one need not distinguish between them.[32] Further, an Apostolic perspective knows nothing of the later church controversies, definitions imposed by a later church, or categories that were not part of the first-century Apostolic world.[33] Thus, Oneness Pentecostalism seeks to identify what the first-century church believed, even if it is different than what the historic Christian church came to believe.

The objection might be raised that one cannot merely rely on what the apostles wrote but must also accept the authority of the historic church. After all, it was during the same century that the church formulated an orthodox Trinitarian approach that it "canonized" the New Testament. A Oneness christological response is that such an argument is misplaced, merely reading the Reformation concern of "canon" back into the early church. The churches to which Paul wrote hardly needed a church council or later tradition to accept his letters as authoritative. The question was never whether these writings that would later become books of the New Testament had authority. Later tradition essentially confirmed an evolving consensus, and where traditions among groups varied, the issue tended to be settled by working toward inclusiveness related to specific disputed books, so long as they were consonant with the other books.[34] Further, that God used the church to preserve the text is not in itself a guarantor of the church's doctrinal purity. After all, did not God use the Jewish people to preserve, collect, and arguably "canonize" the Old Testament? Yet it would be impossible to put any sort of *carte blanche* Christian imprimatur on developing "Jewish theology" in the centuries prior to the Christian era, much less in those centuries that follow it. Indeed, the very basis of Protestantism is that one cannot just assume without question that "because the church is the church" it remained faithful and consistent in its interpretation of the biblical text.

In a related argument, someone might suggest that it is simply not possible to leave christology in the hands of the first century, for the New Testament as well as first-century leaders were focused on other issues and had not worked through all the principles that would define christology. That is, the apostles did not yet have the advantage of time to systemize and define important concepts into a theology; theirs was "a primitive christology," one that would only later be fully explained. Yet, such an argument simply echoes the triumphalism of later Christian centuries. Ironically, when someone charges that a New Testament christology is primitive, in reality, the claim is really that it is *not like* later christology that would be developed by the church.

The implication seems to be that this early christology was in some sense not yet articulated in clear terms. But this objection is a bit strained, for it presumes that Christians who are centuries removed may historically assess that the apostles—who knew Jesus better than anyone—were only beginning to work toward a correct understanding of who He was. Once again, such a statement only thinly veils an operating premise that the evolving thought of the church truly came to the correct interpretation: that people several centuries removed from Jesus had more complete insight into the ontological identity of Jesus Christ than did the men who knew Him best. In what amounts to a great irony of history, if the apostles were somehow magically dropped into a christological discussion by church leaders of the fourth or fifth centuries—ostensibly those whose very lineage was based upon the teaching of the apostles—it seems altogether certain that the apostles themselves would not have the least clue as to what was being argued.[35]

Methodology

While the argument of our study is singular, the methodology varies throughout the book. Part theology, part declaration, part historical survey, there is a chronological and logical flow to the book that deconstructs while it builds. The book consists of four sections that provide a theme for individual chapters. Section I is entitled "THE GOD WHO IS" and consists of chapters 1-4. In this section, we work to define God's covenant relationship with His people in the Old Testament. This is a necessary prolegomenon, for the principles of covenant relationship established in the Old Testament function in continuity in the New Testament. Section II is entitled "THE MAN WHO IS" and turns to christology proper. After a chapter that revisits methodology (chapter 5), we build on the Old Testament patterns to begin talking about covenant christologically. Of course, it is impossible to explain christology in a single chapter; so we have parsed "THE MAN WHO IS" into six chapters (6-12). Under this aegis we introduce such chapters as "The Man Who Preexisted"; "The Man on a Mission"; "The Man Who Was Crucified," and so on, in a kind of chronological flow while at the same time dealing with significant ontological issues relating to Jesus Christ.

Academics largely recognize the historiographical dilemma in sorting out legitimate sources.[36] Admittedly, we come to this project with the bias that one can deduce a coherent christological confession from the biblical text. We assert that for the apostles, the eschaton turned on Jesus, the faithful covenant partner with Yahweh, who, before the foundation of the world was envisioned by Him. Further, while the apostles personally knew this man Jesus as their messiah, they also had another significant confession as well—this *man* whom they came to know was the very *I AM* of the Old Testament. We argue that such a christology is apostolic, understandable biblically, and verified historically in the early church. Understanding that the christology of the apostles was framed in the context of late Second Temple Judaism, we assert that it was expressed in such a way as to be fully understood in its first-century Jewish context.[37]

In Section III, entitled "THE MAN WHO IS NOT" (chapters 13-15), there is a methodological shift. In these three chapters we demonstrate how the christology expressed by the apostles ultimately became historically untenable when in the second century and beyond there was "a transition from Jewish to Hellenistic religious and subsequent Hellenistic philosophical categories."[38] It is beyond the scope of this book to track in detail the development of the doctrine of the Trinity; but where its development is considered, we demonstrate the specific ways in which philosophical presuppositions influenced how it evolved.

Section IV, entitled "THE MAN WHO IS IN COVENANT" (chapters 16-18), works to pragmatically define the covenantal implications of the identity and work of the man Jesus. In so doing, we endeavor to demonstrate the relationship of Oneness christology with soteriological and pneumatological themes. It is not until chapter 18 that we begin to explore the historical place of Ewart, Haywood, and Urshan and their Oneness confession. Finally, the epilogue serves as a kind of implied direction derived from the book.

The question may well be asked what difference any of this makes, or whether a Oneness construal may be just a matter of semantics. Oneness Pentecostals insist otherwise. Considering the broad theological application of a correct methodological approach, it may well be argued that what is at stake is an entire biblical worldview. In praxis, one's understanding of christology affects every aspect of a relationship with God. A Oneness metanarrative is that of God's relationship with humanity, one inextricably woven into the fabric of the biblical text. We are proposing that from Adam onward, the presence of God is experienced in covenant worship, even as the invoked name of God becomes guarantor for this same covenant relationship. In continuity with what has gone before, and in fulfillment of it, the New Testament allows for experiencing God in a way that is both like and surpasses Old Testament experience. The further argument of the book is that related to God covenanting with His people, there is a centrality to the name of Jesus, particularly in baptism, and the importance of being baptized in the Holy Spirit. Last, there is a focus on covenantal proclamation, one that is not merely doctrinal but relational as well. Oneness christology can hardly be reduced to syllogisms; thus, the distinctives of the Oneness proclamation will be explored from both the biblical narrative and from the historical inception of Oneness Pentecostalism.

Some Final Thoughts

It would not be correct to say that tradition does not play a part in an Apostolic hermeneutic. First, as we have begun to suggest above, while the broad sweep of church tradition is not central to an Apostolic hermeneutic, early church tradition is vitally important. Second, Oneness Pentecostalism itself has evolved. As a restorationist movement begun in the early part of the twentieth century with the writings of Ewart, Haywood, and Urshan playing a part, it is more recent Oneness construals that are studied as a basis of Oneness doctrine. Nonetheless, the writings of these men do play a foundational role in what constitutes the ongoing development of the Oneness Movement. This book recognizes almost a hundred years of tradition, and we make every attempt to remain faithful to the core tenets of Oneness proclamation passed down during the past century.

The reader will notice a certain unevenness about the method and presentation of the materials in the book. The reasons for this unevenness are varied. Part of the problem, I must confess, stems from a simple lack of interest or ignorance of particular authors or theologians. More important, I tend to utilize scholars whose work I believe in some fashion propels the argument of the book. Perhaps the greatest reason for the unevenness of the book has to do with what Ewart, Haywood, and Urshan deemed to be most important theologically. The book makes an effort to be faithful to represent both the tenor and content of how those Oneness Pentecostals argued, an intensity most evident when pressing specific points relating to christology and New Testament covenant initiation. Certainly there are points where I may not have it quite right, for I am trying to link twenty-first century issues with those of a century ago, and I bring as well my own situatedness as an author. Yet, every effort is made in making my own presuppositions visible. Furthermore, this text is not meant to be the last word. The attempted scope of this book is in itself an invitation to theological conversation, both from inside and outside the Oneness Pentecostal movement.

Chapter 2

The God Who Is

Creation: A Study in Relationship

We begin our study of God with an important assumption: God can only truly be known "relationally." That is, just as there is a difference in speaking *about* someone and speaking *to* someone, so it is not possible to really know about God without moving from a third-person perspective to a second-person perspective. God cannot be studied as an "indirect object."

Consider how it is that the third-person perspective speaks of another as an "it," while a second person speaks *to* the other. For example, if Moses spoke to Aaron about the Red Sea, he would have been speaking of the Red Sea as an "it." Yet, the specific relationship between Moses and Aaron themselves as they talked was that of an "I-you" relationship. Further, Moses had one kind of "I-you" experience when speaking with Aaron. He had another kind of "I-YOU" experience when speaking with God. Indeed, all biblical writers were writing about God as the overflow of their own relationship with Him, in what Martin Buber calls an "I-Thou" relationship.[1]

Relationship with God must begin by understanding biblically the distance between divinity and humanity. God is infinitely higher than we are; He does not share a category with any other. In attempting to express such an idea of this "otherness," God's ultimate uniqueness, the Bible describes God as "holy."[2] Theologians should neither limit this understanding of God's holiness to particular aspects of goodness nor His ethical purity. Indeed, God's holiness is the aspect of God that separates Him from the mundane, and is the thing that invites awe. As such, an ordinary usage of words hardly seems to suffice in definition. Thus, Rudolph Otto plays with language a bit when he describes "the holy" as an "overplus of meaning."[3] Otto suggests that an experience of the holy cannot merely be taught. Such an awareness comes "out of the spirit."[4] He describes this as the consciousness of the "wholly other."[5] The point we wish to draw is that discovering and communing with the Holy, that is with God, is something that cannot be learned intellectually; it can be done only in relationship. And what is more, we are changed by such a relationship with the Holy so that in an ongoing relationship we can be said to be holy as well.

In order to understand the theological freight of the creation narrative, one has to shift from the perspective of neutral observer to celebrant, one who truly discerns the reason for the Creation. It is precisely because the writers of the Bible are involved in what Buber calls this "I-Thou" relationship that they are able to write as they do. These writers celebrate the mighty acts of God for what they really are—testimonies of the holiness and glory of God. For instance, the psalmist sings of creation, "The heavens declare the glory of God, the vault of heaven proclaims his handiwork."[6] Creation itself testifies to God's goodness. Isaiah revels in Yahweh's ability to create from absolutely nothing, proclaiming Yahweh alone is God. So that Judah would know that idols of the nations were not gods, Yahweh Himself mocks these so-called gods for their inability to call things into existence. Isaiah 44:24 records, "Thus says Yahweh, your redeemer, he who formed you in the womb: I, Yahweh, have made all things, I alone spread out the heavens. When I hammered the earth into shape, who was with me?" The idols, of course, have no defense. God taunts their failure and by implication the spiritual poverty of those who worship them, charging, "Taken altogether they are nothingness, what they do is nothing, their statues, wind and emptiness" (Isaiah 41:29). Thus, for Judah, creation is a declaration that Yahweh is present, that He alone has power to deliver from bondage.[7] These Jewish authors can offer this celebratory writing because God is not only their Creator; He is *their* God who creates—a God in relationship.

It is not too much to say that we only know our story, the story between God and us. Consider that we know virtually nothing of God's activities before Genesis 1:1. God chooses to tell us the creation story because it begins the story of relationship. This is why Genesis 1:1 begins with the phrase, "At the beginning of God's creating . . ."[8]

In the song of Genesis 1 that celebrates God's creative voice, verse 2 offers a picture of chaos where the *ruach* [translated variously Spirit or wind] did something;[9] it *merachephet* [possibly was hovering or blowing],[10] but then the focus quickly moves from chaos[11] to celebrating the creative acts of God. Because the genre is poetry, one cannot be too dogmatic as to whether the Hebrew *ruach* is "wind" or "Spirit." However, if indeed this is speaking of the Spirit of God, it is important to note this is not a different hypostasis than the Creator, but God Himself.[12] The use of the Spirit of God in the text is a circumlocution, an alternate way of speaking of God Himself in His active power. Let us think about how the apostles would have understood the creation narrative. As Jews, they believed that the God with whom they were in relationship created the cosmos alone, by Himself.[13] Just as no plurality may be deduced from the use of the Hebrew word translated God (*Elohim*),[14] neither does the word Spirit imply a plurality in God.

Humanity—Created in the Image of God

It is no accident that the creation of humanity takes longer to unfold in the biblical text than does the creation of the cosmos. From a literary and theological perspective, the creation account in Genesis 1 serves largely as a backdrop for God's creation of humanity. In Genesis 2, the story slows down to relish this act. God fashions. He gets His "fingernails dirty." God breathes life. The New Jerusalem Bible offers, "Yahweh God shaped man from the soil of the ground and blew the breath of life into his nostrils, and man became a living being." This man, (*Adam* in the Hebrew), was constructed from the dust of the earth (*adamah*).[15] In this play on words, the intended implication is the difference between so much dirt and a human being, the highest of God's creation, is simply God's hand and God's breath! There is an intimate involvement based on God's love, God's special concern for those to whom He would be in relationship. Nor was the creation of woman any less startling. From Adam's rib Yahweh fashioned a partner, a helper and companion. The implicit wonder of this special creation is captured by the eighth psalm, where the psalmist proclaims in wonder: "What are human beings that you spare a thought for them, or the child of Adam that you care for him?" Explaining the exalted state of the creation of humanity, the psalmist goes on to say, "Yet you have made him little less than [angels],[16] you have crowned him with glory and beauty, made him lord of the works of your hands, put all things under his feet, sheep and cattle, all of them, and even the wild beasts, birds in the sky, fish in the sea, when he makes his way across the ocean."[17] Not only is the act of creating in view here. The psalmist is celebrating the considerable care involved as well, for when God created humanity, He called them into relationship.

In Genesis 1:26, God said, "Let us make man in our own image." No plurality of God is intended in the text. God made Adam in His likeness. The consensus of Jewish interpreters is that God alone, singularly, was Creator; there are a number of opinions as to whom He was referring when He said, "Let *us* make man." Suggestions include God speaking "with His own heart, with Angels, with the Torah, with Heaven and earth."[18] Others suggest that the "us" constitutes a literary plural.[19]

While not dogmatic about it, we would suggest that the text has angels in view. Although Genesis gives no record of it, there was a prehistory with regard to angels, and arguably to Satan as well.[20] Like the angels, Adam and Eve were created with a choice in the matter of whether or not to obey God.[21]

Angels participated with Yahweh not merely in the creation of the material world; they were specifically involved in the creation of humanity. Thus Yahweh pronounced: "Let us make man in our own image."[22] Angels knew virtue, for they had witnessed the lack of it in Satan—thus they shared this commonalty with Adam and Eve. Unlike the animals who had been created before them, Adam and Eve truly had power to choose. They could experience virtue by doing what was right, or they could learn of virtue by knowing the guilt that resulted from doing wrong. It is for this reason that Yahweh could say to the angels, "Humans are become one of us, to know good and evil" (Genesis 3:22).

Covenant relationship with the Creator is constituted and sustained by human response. Unfortunately, Adam and Eve, created in the image of God, did not choose to keep covenant. There were certainly consequences of their disobedience—the loss of Eden, thorns, pain, death, and more—consequences that are still with us. The question remains, then, just what sort of brokenness occurred in humanity as a result of Adam and Eve's fall? We consider this further in chapter 4, but one thing is vital to understand: humans still retained the image of God, and this allowed for human reasoning, choice, and the possibility for virtue.[23] Consequently, in every generation humanity must make the same choice made by Adam and Eve, whether or not to be in relationship with God. The Bible consistently reaffirms God's image as a part of humanity's inheritance. Consider Genesis 9:6, which makes the claim without equivocation that murder is wrong because humanity is in the image of God. Nor is the New Testament without corroborating proof. First Corinthians 11:7 offers no qualifiers when it reports that we are created in the image of God. James 3:9 rebukes people who bless God but curse people, who are made in His likeness.[24]

Yahweh as "I AM"

In polite society, for two people to get to know each other in a meaningful way, names must be exchanged. These same two people then intuitively associate particular qualities of the other individual with the name of that person. In human/divine relationship, it is not enough for God to know our names; we must know God's name. But one's understanding of the name of God cannot merely be a cognitive knowing (an "I-it" relationship). In the Old Testament, one "knew" Yahweh's name in a face-to-face covenantal worship, a concept that we shall deal with more in chapter 4.[25]

The covenant name of God in the Hebrew is four consonants: יהוה; also referred to as the Tetragrammaton.[26] Although this Hebrew name has sometimes been transliterated into English as Jehovah, and some versions of the Bible (such as KJV) translate it into all caps (LORD, or GOD), it should more aptly be written Yahweh.[27] A number of scholars are correct to reject the greater part of attempts to find the etymology of Yahweh;[28]

William Albright rightly links the meaning of the name of Yahweh with Exodus 3:14.[29] This verse, more than any other verse in the Old Testament, is the key to understanding what the name Yahweh proclaims. In this verse, Yahweh, who has called Moses to deliver His people, tells Moses why He should not be fearful to go down into Egypt. The reason given in Hebrew is "*ehyeh asher ehyeh*," a phrase that is translated variously into English. Translators work with a wide possible range of meaning for this phrase. Many versions translate the proclamation in capital letters, implicating a divine title, and possibly indicating its association with Yahweh. The New International Version (NIV) hedges just a bit by including a marginal reference with the translation: "I AM WHO I AM [Or, I WILL BE WHAT I WILL BE]." The original New Living Translation was incorrect in its translation, as it took the verse as stative: "I AM THE ONE WHO ALWAYS IS."[30] Nor is the *Tanak* helpful by leaving the Hebrew: "Ehyeh-Asher-Ehyeh."[31] The claim "I AM" cannot be missed in Exodus 3, for it is repeated four successive times—once recorded in verse 12 and three times in verse 14; each time, Yahweh repeats the thematic "I AM." The declaration "I am" or *ehyeh*, (אֶהְיֶה in Hebrew) is related to the verb, "to be," *hayah* (הָיָה), sharing largely the same consonants as Yahweh (יהוה).[32]

When Moses asked, "Who shall I say sent me?" Yahweh responded, "*ehyeh asher ehyeh*," a proclamation offered in the Hebrew imperfect, that in this case represents potential of what will occur.[33] As readers of the narrative, we can now look back on the events of Exodus 3 and know what is about to happen. God *is about to do* what His name *means*. There will be a contest between the so-called deities of Egypt and Yahweh Himself. Yahweh will free the slaves from bondage, those He calls officially into relationship. In doing so, He will confound Pharaoh. When Yahweh says, "I AM," He makes a challenge to every empty idol, particularly to the so-called Egyptian deities, but as well to every false god that would make a claim against His people in the future. His pronouncement, "I AM" is a declaration that "*they are not!*", a confession that came to be a part of the very fabric of Israel's understanding from this time forward.[34]

There are other instances where I AM is significant in the biblical text. Not only does it occur in Deuteronomy,[35] but its usage is replete in Isaiah.[36] Perhaps one of the most significant demonstrations of Yahweh's name occurs in the I Kings narrative. When Elijah confronted the prophets of Baal, Yahweh was calling His people back into an active relationship with Him. A contest was set up and the prophets of Baal were challenged to demonstrate his power. The contest demonstrated two important truths. First, Baal could not be summoned by his prophets, for he was a god who *was not*.[37] Second, Yahweh demonstrated His name by sending fire on the water-drenched altar and everything surrounding it. The people rightly cried out " 'He is (There)! He is God!' meaning, 'Yahweh, He is Present, He (is) God.' "[38]

The name Yahweh was not newly revealed in the time of Exodus; rather, His name was known from the very beginning of Genesis.[39] On the surface, Exodus 6:3 seems to indicate that Yahweh was not known to the patriarchs, for it reads, "To Abraham, Isaac and Jacob I appeared as *El Shaddai*, but I did not make my name Yahweh known to them." Some have suggested that the apparent discrepancy in Exodus 6 is due to bad editing by a later redactor of the Torah. For those holding this evolutionary perspective of the text, Genesis would not need to be reconciled with the Exodus narrative. The presumption is that in one tradition, the patriarchs knew Yahweh by name; in another, they did not. Over time, these traditions became amalgamated into the text, and both traditions are thought to be visible in this instance. But this should be rejected out of hand. To consider whether *El* or *Elohim* had a certain *vorlage*,[40] or to explore what tradition knew the name Yahweh misses the point.[41]

There are other interpretive solutions that do not do violence to the text. For example, some read the Hebrew in the Exodus text as interrogative. Thus, rather than suggesting that Yahweh was not known to the patriarchs, it may be asking, "Was I not known to them?"[42] Still another viable solution is that Yahweh was not known to those earlier patriarchs in the way that He will now reveal Himself to Moses. This makes particular sense in the context of the subsequent events of the Exodus narrative. God is preparing Moses for an experiential revelation of His identity, one where He would demonstrate His power to save, to redeem, to bring into covenant a group of slaves and make them His own special people. It is this redemptive aspect of Yahweh's name that is for Moses a new revelation. There is in the Exodus narrative for the first time in the Old Testament a narrative definition of the power of God to redeem a people. Nor is this just deliverance by creative fiat—but God once again gets His fingers dirty in the deliverance of His people, just as He did in the Creation.

For some theologians, this personal language of God cannot be taken seriously. They would reject the construal that we have thus far presented as it requires more interaction than their notion of God will allow. For them, any speaking of this kind is not a metaphysical reality; it is just a way of the divine accommodating Himself to human language and thought process. Yet the biblical portrait of God should be our starting place, not preconceived notions of what God can or cannot do. Yahweh is both personal and passible; no amount of anthropomorphizing can remove these characteristics of Yahweh from the biblical text.[43] Consider just a sampling of Scriptures: God has sympathy (Psalm 103:13);[44] God is jealous, not petty, but jealous (Deuteronomy 5:9);[45] God hurts with grief (Judges 10:16);[46] God hates wrong (Psalm 5:5);[47] God has joy (Isaiah 62:5);[48] Isaiah 63:9 insists that it was no messenger, no angel who saved them. Yahweh personally became involved. They were saved because of "his presence . . . his love and pity." God hears, answers, acts, and reacts.

God listens to the cries of those in need. It was just such cries of Abraham's descendents that prompted Yahweh to deliver them from their bondage. Ten plagues later, Egypt and its gods were defeated, and the armies pursuing the people were no more. There is only one proper response to redemption: praise! The people celebrated that "the horse and the rider are thrown into the sea" (Exodus 15:1); "Yahweh carried the people on eagle's wings" (Exodus 19:4); "Yahweh is warrior!" (Exodus 15:3). When Israel praised the name of Yahweh, they included in this praise the works of Yahweh and their relationship with Him. Others may have heard the name Yahweh. But it was Israel who was delivered; thus, in terms of I-Thou relationship, it was only Israel who "knew" Yahweh's name.

The Presence of Yahweh

While God is not confined to human experience, there are three primary ways in the biblical narrative that Yahweh is experienced by humanity.[49] First, even the absence of God illustrates that God is transcendent, greater than what humans can conceive. Second, God demonstrates His very real presence with His literal presence. God is immanent. Thus, Adam and Eve literally walked with God in the cool of the day. The third primary way in which humanity experienced the very real presence of God was in the context of worship. While God can be known indirectly, say, through nature only, these latter experiences speak to knowing God relationally.

Let us first consider how Yahweh revealed His transcendence.[50] Even in the Garden of Eden, because Adam and Eve experienced God as absent, they knew that God did not live there; He was somehow *other* than His creation, beyond it, and above it. How much more they knew is difficult to say, but as the Old Testament progresses, a fairly normative way of talking about the dwelling of God developed. God lives in Heaven (*shamayim*).[51] That is His abode. The Scripture says that He both rules from and dwells in heaven.[52] As James D. Tabor notes, "To describe God as dwelling in heaven is to recognize the transcendence of God, God's separateness from the creative order."[53]

Throughout the Old Testament, God's people learned about Yahweh not only from His presence, but also from His absence. What it taught them was related to their understanding of the holiness of God. Eichrodt notes it is in this very absence that God is known. He notes that God is "unapproachable because of his complete 'otherness' and perfection when compared with all created things."[54] While it is true that there is a semantic range as to the use of Heaven in the Hebrew Bible,[55] our focus here is to speak of Heaven as the abode of God. Thus, as Eichrodt notes, "At all periods, it is accepted as a matter of course that God's dwelling-place is heaven."[56] Further, while numerous texts make it clear that God has locale, there is also a way in which it can be said that Yahweh fills the universe. He is not the cosmos, nor is He contained by the cosmos, yet He can rule every part of His creation at any time and in this sense fills the cosmos.[57]

The second way God revealed Himself to Adam is something that occurs very few times in the Old Testament; nor is it is ever a long-term phenomenon. Adam experienced Yahweh in this way in the Garden of Eden. God was present, literally. In the narrative, God has locale. He comes from heaven and communes with Adam in His very person. God spoke to Moses in a similar way from the burning bush. Moses experienced God literally, and there could have been no other simultaneous burning bush experience, for what Moses experienced was specifically God speaking at the locale where He was. That is to say, while there may be any number of revelations where there is a phenomenological presentation of God, and while it is true God in some sense is everywhere sustaining the entire cosmos, what Adam and Moses experienced was God—period. Theologians have coined the word "theophany" for this phenomenon, although it is variously understood. We can allow the word theophany if we understand this is literally God, albeit cloaked in some way, manifesting His singular presence to an individual or group.[58]

There is a third way Yahweh manifests Himself, and this is of primary importance as a focus of this book. There is a unique way in which Yahweh is present in covenant relationship. A whole set of language relates to this communing; one of the principal ways to speak about experiencing Yahweh in covenant relationship is that one in covenant experiences "His presence." In Eden, Adam fled from the presence of God when he disobeyed. The Hebrew word that is translated "presence" is *panim*, literally "face."[59] The *panim* of God may be used in a number of contexts. It can simply mean God is in proximity with a person; it can denote God's active force in the world;[60] and it can be used variously to denote both pleasure and anger;[61] further, there is a special understanding of the *panim* of God in covenant worship.

Consider the language of Yahweh's covenant relationship after Adam and Eve were expelled from Eden. Yahweh was not present in the same way as He was in Eden, but it is clear that He was present. The narrative begins in a covenantal act of sacrifice,[62] one where Yahweh had respect (*sha-ah*) unto Abel's offering from the flock, in contrast with the rejection of Cain's offering of "farm produce" (NLT).[63] There was an expectation by Cain that his sacrifice would be accepted in context with this covenanting community, but it was not, for it was not the prescribed worship. God gave him a chance to repent,[64] but he did not and was driven from the place of worship.[65] That is, he was distant from the place where Yahweh made Himself known.[66] Covenantal worship, then, is the place where Yahweh can be known. As we have suggested, Israel came to "know" Yahweh's name because they discovered Yahweh's "face." While the name Yahweh was known from the very beginning, He was experienced in a new way as God called them into relationship. We discuss in detail the further significance of the name in its covenantal context in chapter 4. But before that, we must explore concerns as to what is not true about God—what He is not like. This is essential to understand, for a syncretic understanding of God not only influenced Jewish thinking, but also later Christian theologians who struggled with these same syncretic beliefs.

Chapter 3

The God Is Not

Introduction

It is quite possible for people to forget their own story, to disown their history, and even to reinterpret meaningful relationships. This is exactly what happened to the Jewish people. In the time after Malachi was penned, cultural pressure influenced them to reinterpret their history and even their understanding of God. While their history is inextricably woven together with the God who *speaks* and *acts*, sometime during the late Second Temple Period,[1] their narrative began to be understood in a new way. In this new telling of the story, the active God of the covenant people came up missing, replaced by a static notion of God. In this new understanding, God did not speak. He did not mitigate. He did not act. Indeed, the history of God's covenantal relationship with them was essentially reduced to allegory. Any descriptions of the works of God were no longer factual; they were, indeed, just a metaphoric way of speaking. As a matter of course, the entire Hebrew Bible came to be viewed as anthropomorphic.[2] Things devolved so badly that the very name of Yahweh, which the Jewish people were to praise, lift up in worship, and call upon in invocation could no longer be uttered out loud; it was forbidden to speak that name. This chapter is offered to trace how such an incredible phenomenon took place. Further, we show how the allegorical method of interpretation distorted the covenant relationship Yahweh had with His people.

Hellenistic Influence

In the wake of the various powers that invaded Israel/Judah up to and including the Babylonian exile, Jewish people were scattered throughout the Ancient Near East. Settlements could be found across the Mediterranean, in Egypt, and in Assyria. While in some cases the Jews assimilated with local populations, compared to other ancient people groups, the Jewish people showed a remarkable resiliency to sustain their identity and their fealty to God. The survival of the Jewish faith to the present, and the inclusion of Judaism as a modern world religion can readily be contrasted with the boneyard of gods long gone, with religious devotions relegated to the past.[3] Even the exile proved to be a time for the Jews when many beliefs were codified, and they became absolutely certain of the power and place of Yahweh. Institutions were developed to sustain the Jewish religion and practice, securing the identity of the Jewish people.[4]

It was primarily after Alexander the Great conquered Persia and began ruling over lands where Diaspora Jews made their home that Jewish faith was challenged in a new way. Because of the pervasiveness of Hellenism, (Greek culture and a Greek worldview), a gradual shift in beliefs by many Jews was practically inevitable.[5] The reconstituted state of Judah remained politically insignificant,[6] while the majority of Jewish people lived elsewhere. Because Greek became the universal language throughout the Mediterranean world, Diaspora Jews no longer needed their facility in Hebrew. Yet, such a loss had religious consequences. In Alexandria, Egypt, where a large population of Jewish people lived who could no longer speak Hebrew, the Scriptures were translated into Greek, a translation that came to be known as the Septuagint (*LXX*). We will deal with the ways in which Greek understanding and perspective influenced this translation later in this chapter, but in order to tell this story, we must first explore what we call a Hellenistic conception of God, an understanding of the divine contrary to the received understanding of Israel.

The God of the Philosophers

The foundation of Western civilization is said to have its beginning when an arguably ordered understanding of the divine and the universe unseated a mythological worldview. This new worldview was established by a sometimes competing set of Greek philosophies.[7] From the perspectives of their historical contributions, the most important philosophers were Aristotle and Plato.[8] Particularly important are the contributions offered both by Plato and Plato's interpreters,[9] though Aristotle played an ancillary role as well.

While in many ways epistemological planks offered by Plato and Aristotle are foundational in Western civilization, their contribution is mixed. One may liken the contribution of Plato to a train that arrives at the station pulling a hundred railroad cars, most of which contain goods that are useful, but some of which contain noxious poison. Although Greek philosophy is rarely described in this way in any history book, considering the theological categories that ultimately resulted from Platonic/Aristotelian epistemological definitions of the divine, for me, at least, this is not overstating the Greek influence. The application of Hellenistic notions of God ultimately became incorporated into the very fabric of Judaism (and ultimately in Christianity). In this regard, the lesson of the Trojan horse may well be applied: Beware of Greeks bearing gifts.

Though the study and interpretation of Plato is an ongoing enterprise, there are general principles upon which scholars agree. First, because of his definition of "God," Plato speaks at once of God and gods, in the singular or plural, without danger to his system. His notion of the deity is far removed from the contemporary mythology of his day. For Plato, there are two different "worlds." The material world is an object of lower passions of humanity. Objective philosophy is of necessity grounded in objective reality derived from the immaterial world. Whereas the material world is a world of appearances, the immaterial world is actually the place where the "form" or "idea" exists. That is, standing behind every particular thing in the material world is the idea or the form of the thing. These ideas or forms are ultimately related to the Form of the Good. For Plato, the Form of the Good may be compared to the sun—that is, it "not only gives visibility to objects but sustains them and causes living things to grow, without itself being a part of the earthly process."[10] Thus, like the sun, one could say that "God" is behind the process—but not actually part of the process. Aristotle, the student of Plato, furthers this distancing of God when he frames God as the "unmoved mover."[11] As Plato came to be interpreted, God is beyond that which can change, that which can be known in the physical universe. Thus removed, God is unknowable. Any attempt to talk about the deity in a corporal manner or by making comparisons to any part of the creation is to be rejected. One cannot even know how to speak of the divine. As Hans Bietenhard summarizes Plato, "the true names of the gods are those which the gods call themselves: since we cannot know these, we must be content with the names which we are wont to call on the gods in prayers."[12] Thus removed, God is not an object of inquiry as much as a necessary construct, a necessity when understanding the cosmos. Interpreters of Plato may debate the way in which Plato's God was involved in the creation;[13] what is not debated is that for Plato God is distant, hardly a proper subject of personal inquiry.

The Greek philosophers had a problem. The common populace lacked understanding of things philosophical and readily held on to their mythological perspective. They had gods aplenty, gods who could sometimes behave like very bad people writ large. As a strategy for change, philosophers mediated a way to let the people still identify with their gods while integrating their mythological motifs with a higher truth. Philosophers worked toward helping the common people "reread" these myths so that the deeper meaning was consonant with the view of the philosophers. That is, if one could understand the stories about the gods as primarily conveying some noble truth, both the philosophically astute and the ignorant listener could enjoy the same telling of the story. Thus, when Homer and Hesiod were allegorized in this way, those schooled in philosophy did not need to be embarrassed by the crude behavior of the gods. As early as 520 BC, Theogenes of Rhegium allegorized Homer; this methodology was soon picked up by other philosophers such as the Stoics, Chaeremon, and Cleanthes. In this way, they could "promote their own ideas while still claiming to be faithful to the writings of the past."[14] As Greek philosophy became more and more pervasive in the centuries just prior to Christ, the allegorical method was not merely applied to Greek mythology; unfortunately, it began to be utilized in interpreting the biblical text.

How the Jewish Conception of God Changed

There were a number of factors that influenced the way the Jews spoke and thought about Yahweh. One should not be simplistic when defining the dynamics of the time period. While the Diaspora Jews were not unaffected by the current thinking of the Hellenistic world, neither was the world unaffected by Judaism.[15] It is certainly true that Jews attempted to convert Gentiles, and there was considerable literature devoted to this endeavor. The Jewish people became a viable force in the Greco-Roman period; estimates as to their population vary, but it no doubt numbered in the millions.[16]

One of the effective tools the Jewish people utilized in influencing their world was the Septuagint.[17] In Alexandria, Egypt, where the Septuagint was translated, there was a great emphasis placed on reaching out to Gentiles.[18] Consequently, when translating the biblical text, scholars rendered the Scriptures into Greek in such a way as to be least offensive to a Hellenistic mindset.[19] That is, language of God acting, working, showing emotion, and the like was softened wherever possible. Regrettably, in an unfortunate rendering of the Septuagint, some passages were translated in a way that suggests that the name Yahweh should not even be spoken.[20]

Allegory is not the same as metaphor. Certainly biblical writers readily use metaphor. They can speak of God as covering someone with "His feathers," of God "riding on a swift cloud" to bring deliverance, of "God's arm" saving, or any number of other phenomena,[21] metaphors readily understood as a particular kind of speaking. Such usage is a legitimate use of an anthropomorphic (or zoomorphic) vernacular. But it was not these metaphors alone that were at issue in the Old Testament from a Hellenistic perspective. First and foremost it was the whole narrative presentation of Yahweh. Hellenistic thinking could not tolerate a God who acted volitionally in the cosmos. It ruffled Greek sensibilities to speak of the divine except in the most distant of terms. Perhaps it is not surprising then, that in translating the Ten Commandments into Greek, there was an overt change in meaning that differed considerably from the Hebrew text. As it was translated, the *LXX* text did not merely prohibit speaking the name of Yahweh "in vain"; rather, it prohibited the name of Yahweh from being spoken at all, a translation that would certainly have been more palatable to the Greek inclination not to ascribe a name to the divine.[22]

Any time books are translated from one language to another, there are sometimes unwitting changes in meaning, for no two languages are exactly equivalent. Further, translators often have to make choices according to their own biases. In the Septuagint, going from Hebrew to Greek, some biblical texts suffered worse than others at the hand of the translators. Significantly, when the Hebrew text of the third chapter of Exodus was brought over into Greek, translators gave Yahweh's proclamation of Himself an altogether different emphasis than it had in the original language. As Raymond Brown notes, "The Hebrew reads 'I am who causes to be,' or perhaps more originally in the third person, 'I am He who causes to be.' "[23] This reading shows Yahweh as volitional. Unfortunately, when the Hebrew got translated into Greek, the phrase was turned into a passive statement of existence. As Brown points out, it comes over in the *LXX* as, "'I am the Existing One,' using a participle of the verb 'to be,' and thus stressing divine existence."[24] Further, this does not only occur in the Book of Exodus. In the prophets, the Hebrew of "I am he," a phrase suggesting the unicity of Yahweh, gets translated *ego eime*, again, a statement of existence. In certain cases in Isaiah, there is a way that the Septuagint actually seems to make "*I AM*" a name.[25] Hence, in going from Hebrew to Greek, the tenor of the translation merely affirmed Yahweh's existence. Thus, Greek language and philosophical thinking both worked to subtly shift the Jewish worldview.

By the third century BC,[26] it became normative not to speak the name Yahweh, but instead substitute the more generic *Adonai*.[27] Because the name Yahweh was itself entrance into an "I-Thou" relationship, not speaking His name distanced the Jewish people from Yahweh Himself; His name was integrally connected to His communion with Israel and essential to His very being.[28] In a further regression, for Jews in educated circles, it was not even acceptable to talk about the deity by using the more generic *Adonai*.

Relentlessly, a Hellenistic worldview continued to chip away at the perceptions of the Jewish people until their normative understanding of Yahweh became something of an embarrassment, especially to those learned in Greek philosophy. The God of the Jews is very earthy. He acts, reacts, and is literally in communion with the people of Israel. The Scriptures command the people of God to orally praise Yahweh, to rejoice in His name every day, proclaiming that He alone is God. Since the Hellenistic view of the deity put the divine beyond what could be known or named, the Jewish people were not merely being accommodating by acquiescing to not mentioning Yahweh; they were unwittingly changing their view of what their God was like and what He would do.

Philo and the Allegorical Method

One of the most important historical figures as a change agent in the late Second Temple period was a Jew of Alexandria by the name of Philo, born in about 20 BC. Overtly Hellenistic in his worldview, he applied the allegorical method that had been used by philosophers in revisioning Greek mythology to his own interpretation of the Old Testament. Philo suggested that every Old Testament text had a double reference.[29] The second sense of the text, the allegorical meaning, was governed by the dictates of a Greek philosophical worldview; the obvious sense of the text, the literal meaning, was for Philo one that was "fit only for weaker minds."[30] Philo's method, then, was to continually refer to the biblical text and in great detail explain it. His explanations were always guided by Hellenistic sensibilities. Inevitably, his interpretation of each Old Testament reference was based upon one central hermeneutical key: God is transcendent.[31]

Almost any page of Philo's writing demonstrates such a method, but we briefly offer an excerpt derived from Philo's *On the Unchangeableness of God*. In this work, expositing loosely from Genesis 6, Philo explains why God had changed His mind about humanity and would now destroy them with the flood. Genesis 6:6 reads, "Yahweh regretted having made human beings on earth and was grieved at heart." Philo's surprising interpretation is that the text actually means that it is impossible for Yahweh to change at all. The kind of proof that Philo uses for such a construal is simply that any other reading of the text does not square with what is known of God (i.e., a Hellenistic understanding). Further, in explaining Genesis 6:7 where God changed His mind about humanity and said that He would destroy wickedness from the earth, Philo offers (for no apparent reason) that the wickedness of humanity (the wickedness that caused God to decide to destroy them) was in fact the wickedness of thinking that God could change! As rationale for such pummeling of the biblical text he offers: "For that those, who have studied philosophy in a sincere and pure spirit, have derived as the greatest good arising from their knowledge, the absence (in God) of any inclination to change with the changes of affairs, and the disposition with all immovable firmness and sure stability to labor at every thing that it becomes to pursue."[32] Only when the God of Moses began to look like the God of Plato could Philo rest easy. By definition, then, any time the Bible spoke of Yahweh operating, moving, or working, this was nothing more than an anthropomorphism, just a human way of speaking—God accommodating Himself to human language. In the end, Philo's understanding of the entire Old Testament turned out to be a kind of anthropomorphism! This notion has been described as Philo's "negative theology"[33] because of his attempt to extract from the language anything that would make the deity accessible.

For Philo, it is not God, but intermediaries who interact with the cosmos. It was in this sense that Philo spoke of the *Logos* (Word). God Himself did not appear on earth; it was the *Logos*.³⁴ While Philo's construct of the *Logos* follows Plato's *Timaeus,* Philo utilizes it in interpreting the biblical account of Creation and adapts the *Logos* to replace the concept of the world soul so central in *Timaeus*. Further, Philo mixes the notion of the *Logos* with that of *Sophia* (Wisdom), and in some sense regards them as equivalent.³⁵ Various intermediaries were involved in acting on God's behalf,³⁶ utilizing both the currency of personification and ultimately allowing for hypostatization of intermediaries.³⁷

Not everyone in the late Second Temple Period was affected by Hellenism in the same way. There were, in fact, any number of Jewish groups who opposed the encroachment of Hellenism, some of whom were specifically formed to fight Hellenistic influence. In the centuries just prior to the time of Christ, the *Hasidim* and later, the Pharisees fought against Hellenism. At the time of Jesus (with whom Philo is contemporary), one finds a kind of Philonic gestalt more readily among the educated elite, such as the Sadducees, than, say, the men Jesus chose for His apostles.

Philo's influence may hardly be confined to the time in which he lived. His methodology ultimately found a home in the historic Christian church, a subject we will explore in detail in chapter 14. Church historian Henry Chadwick makes the rather bold claim: "The history of Christian philosophy begins not with a Christian, but with a Jew, Philo of Alexandria, elder contemporary of St. Paul."³⁸ Our particular concern will focus on the influence of Philonic interpretation on particular formations of christology. As we shall argue in chapters 13-15, there was a gradual redefinition of God in the church that began in earnest sometime in the middle of the second century where Christian theologians made normative Philonic methodology in their interpretation of the biblical text. This methodology was arguably the single most decisive factor in the theological drift that led *Logos* Christologians to the eventual formation of Trinitarian christology.³⁹

Philo and the "I AM"

In conclusion, let us revisit Exodus 3:14, one of the most defining Scriptures in the biblical text. In the passage, Yahweh proclaims to Moses, "I AM"; Philo, in reinterpreting the text, is aided in his Hellenistic gestalt by the rather tepid translation of the Septuagint: "I am who is."⁴⁰ Not surprisingly, for Philo, the text proves God's transcendence and actually means that God *is*, but one *cannot* truly speak His name.⁴¹ Whereas for the

Jewish faith, Yahweh is the high and lofty one,[42] for Philo, God may be referred to as "the most generic one."[43] By this Philo means that "God belongs to no class and hence we do not know what He is."[44] In this way, Philo takes the Old Testament understanding of the power and presence of the God who is in covenant and turns it on its head.

In the next chapter we revisit in some detail a biblical picture of the God who actively concerns Himself with His people; such an understanding stands in stark contrast with the presuppositions and methodology of Philo and his ilk. In privileging Plato over Moses, Philo destroys the hope of those who long for real covenant relationship, offering instead a God who cannot hear, cannot feel, and cannot save—in other words, a God who is not! We return to Philo again when we focus on the church fathers; but now, we pick up the biblical story where we left off, in celebration of the God Who is in Covenant.

Chapter 4

The God Who Is in Covenant

God's Covenant with Adam

While there were different kinds of covenants current in Old Testament usage,[1] typically covenant was "an arrangement between two unequal partners."[2] Further, as the word covenant is commonly used, "the more powerful partner binds himself to a certain attitude toward the less powerful if certain conditions are fulfilled by the less powerful."[3] Though Genesis does not specifically use the language of covenant for the relationship between Yahweh and Adam, it certainly was that.[4] Adam and Eve were given a choice of freedom to be in covenant in the Garden of Eden. In the Garden, God gave Adam and Eve work to do, limits to observe, all the while communing with them, bringing them into the inner sphere of the holy. It was in this sphere that God walked with them "in the cool of the day."[5] Such was their face-to-face relationship with the One with whom they were in covenant. God it was *certainly*—and appear He did *actually*—and learn of Him they did *personally*.

The Genesis narrative is the relational account of humankind as a whole; consequently, when Paul wrote about the fall from Eden, he utilized Adam as the referent.[6] When we speak of this initial transgression, we may suggest that when Adam[7] succumbed to the serpent's lies, the real sin was that Adam was guilty of attempting to be like God in a way that bypassed what was clearly circumscribed.

By definition, relationship must be based upon truth. When Adam and Eve willfully violated the clear command of God, they diminished the word and identity of their Creator, the One who made them stewards of the Garden of Eden. Consequently, they broke their relationship by authorizing for themselves the right to circumnavigate God's clear directives.[8] They were no longer telling the truth about God. On the face of it, God should have destroyed them and started over with a new creation, for the pronouncement had already been made, "But as for the tree of knowledge of good and bad, you must not eat of it; for as soon as you eat of it, you shall die" (Genesis 2:17, *Tanak*). Though there were consequences, mercy was granted to Adam and his descendents based upon another man who would come, one who would ultimately die in the place of Adam and his progeny. As we shall discuss in chapter 6, in the plan of God, redemptive provision had already been made.

Restoration of Covenant

Cain's failure was worse than that of his parents, for he added murder to the sin of disobedience to Yahweh, and he was not merely deceitful but obstinate when challenged.[9] Cain's rebellion ultimately produced generations after him whose hardness only intensified and whose rebellion only increased.[10] By contrast, Seth's descendents were godly, and it is with this group in particular that the text celebrates restoration.

Genesis 4:26 makes a curious statement when introducing descendents of Adam and Eve who kept covenant with Yahweh: "At that time men began to invoke the name of the LORD" (NRSV). The phrase that is translated "to call upon the name of Yahweh" comes from the Hebrew "*liqroh beshem* Yahweh."[11] Indeed, it is quite likely that the Hebrew phrase is an idiom, one captured by a marginal reading of the original KJV: "Men began *to be called by* (italics mine) the name of the LORD [Yahweh]."[12] This language is significant, for it is the first pronouncement of initiation into covenant.

D. Preman Niles argues that the meaning of the name of Yahweh can best be understood in covenant worship. Niles proposes that in certain instances, while *yiqrah beshem* Yahweh is sometimes descriptive of people in covenant worship calling out in prayer *to* Yahweh, there are certain instances where the reverse is taking place; that is, as this is an idiom, it is the name of Yahweh that is actually invoked *upon* the worshiper. Though worshipers invoking the name of Yahweh might do so in distress[13] or thanksgiving,[14] the phrase may also be used in another way, that of a "liturgical pronouncement of Yahweh" over His people.[15] For Niles, this is an important way in which covenant was affirmed.[16] Further, such a pronouncement was made in the context of initiation into covenant, and it is this initiation that is going on in Genesis 4:26.[17] The name of Yahweh was pronounced over those who chose to be in covenant relationship with Him. Whether this invocation of the name of Yahweh was pronounced by the head of the family or some other intermediary, as the priests who functioned on behalf of Yahweh in the context of worship,[18] or whether on occasion Yahweh manifested His physical presence to confirm this covenant,[19] we cannot say. We have no report of a ceremony, a particular worship venue, or how they experienced the presence of the Lord in this covenant relationship; but we do know that they experienced Yahweh's presence in this initiatory act, for where Yahweh is in covenant, His people experience Him in face-to-face relationship. Those who were being initiated into covenant were entering with Yahweh into an "I-Thou relationship." They would truly know His name in experiencing His presence.

As we have begun to suggest previously, covenantal language was relational, and each new mention of covenant in Scripture is not descriptive of a new way for Yahweh to soteriologically manage His people. Thus, God's covenants with Noah, Abraham, Isaac, and Jacob were not new covenants but a continuation of covenantal relationship. We deal with the implications of God's covenant with Abraham in some detail in chapter 16; for now, though, we would suggest that there is more continuity in covenant relationships than discontinuity. For example, because the language of covenant is so prominent in the flood narrative, many mistake God's covenant with Noah as a new and different covenant. Genesis 6:9 begins, "This is the story of Noah: Noah was a good man, an upright man among his contemporaries, and he walked with God." Further, the text says, "Noah won Yahweh's favour."[20] After the flood, what is sometimes called "the Noahic Covenant" was enacted; this should more accurately be understood rather as the renewal of what was already an established covenant, for it confirmed the relationship Yahweh already had with His people.[21] Victor Hamilton points out that the Hebrew word used for Yahweh's covenant with Noah after the flood may well point "not to a new situation, but to the implementation of a previous word, or promise, or action."[22] As Eichrodt notes, the Noahic narrative demonstrates that the whole of humanity stands in covenant relationship with God.[23]

Yahweh's Covenant with Israel

We have started with the premise that it would be wrong to suggest a new covenant was made after Eden, or with Noah or any of the patriarchs;

that is, we must not see each pronouncement of covenant in the biblical text as a turning point or necessarily as describing some completely different salvific arrangement between God and humanity. The story of covenant is singular; it is the telling of covenantal relationship between Yahweh and those who respond in obedience. Thus, it was a continuation of Yahweh's covenant with the patriarchs in which He pronounced to Abraham's descendents in Exodus 19:4: "You have seen for yourselves what I did to the Egyptians and how I carried you away on eagle's wings and brought you to me." When Yahweh heard the cries of the people who were enslaved and delivered them from their bondage, He "redeemed" these slaves. By this saving act, Israel "belonged" to God. At the formal covenanting of Sinai, the invitation from Yahweh was that "if you are really prepared to obey me and keep my covenant, you, out of all peoples, shall be my 'personal possession' "[24] God loved Israel, certainly; but not Israel alone. It was God's ideal that through Israel He would minister to the rest of the world; for when He constituted them as a nation, He said in the following verse it was His intent that the Israelites be a "kingdom of priests."

The people of Israel needed no king but Yahweh. With this in view, when He covenanted with them, He utilized kingly language that they would understand. In the Ancient Near East, kings would often make suzerainty treaties with their vassals. There was a prescribed way in which this was done.[25] In the Hittite Suzerainty treaties, for instance, when a king offered covenant, he would start such a covenant proclamation by saying "I am such and such king." Then he would list all the many titles that he possessed. This would be followed by a long list of the king's accomplishments, effectively offering reasons why the people should serve him. This kind of treaty made by a ruler with the people was considered to be a sacred covenant; in the presence of the gods a nation pledged their loyalty solely to this suzerain—they became "his" people.

In the incredible narrative of Exodus 19–20, Yahweh speaks thus to the people, covenanting with them in this language that was known to them. He wanted Israel to understand that they were no less a nation than any other. However, Yahweh did not need subordinates or witnesses or gods in order to ratify a covenant relationship. As Exodus chapter 20 opens, the people stood in awe as the very voice of God made an audible declaration over them. The words were in some fashion like those of a king making covenant with a people; but when Yahweh spoke, His words rumbled and roared, thundering in an audible voice loud enough for all of Israel to shake in the holy presence of the divine as He pronounced over them, "I am Yahweh your God!"[26] And because Yahweh was greater than any king, no matter what their accomplishment, He needed no list of accomplishments to recommend Himself. His portfolio was that He "brought you out of Egypt, where you lived as slaves" (Exodus 20:2). In this Ancient Near Eastern context, the statement "I am Yahweh your God" was thus similar to but greater than any form used in Hittite Suzerainty treaties. Yahweh had claimed His people by speaking His name audibly over them!

The pronouncement of the covenant between the king and his people was followed by stipulations of the treaty. Yahweh gave similar stipulations—points of obedience for the people to practice. We know these as the "Ten Commandments."[27] When Yahweh spoke His name over the people along with the stipulations, it mirrored what a king might do for those over whom he was suzerain. Any other ratification ceremony pales when compared to God speaking at Sinai. An Ancient Near Eastern king might speak with the authority of an army or riches, but Yahweh spoke with credentials as the Creator of cosmos. His most recent accomplishment was declaring victory over an Egyptian army by rolling back the waters and drowning them. Now, Yahweh's voice was accompanied by "thunder pealing, the lightning flashing, the trumpet blasting and mountain smoking" (Exodus 19:18). Yahweh needed to call no other gods to witness such a covenant, for He was God alone.[28] The sight and sound were fearful, and the people, though in awe, felt as if danger was a potential, so powerful was Yahweh. They decided they would rather live in a safer circumstance, suggesting that it might be better if they just spoke to Moses. Moses replied that Yahweh had manifested Himself in this way so that they would fear Him, and that they would keep from sinning. (See Exodus 20:20-21.) The people responded by acknowledging and accepting whatever Yahweh might ask them to do. They replied with one accord, "Whatever Yahweh has said we will do" (Exodus 19:8). Yahweh uniquely possessed Israel, a fact that was not burdensome to them.

In summary, in Exodus chapters 19–20, the people officially covenanted with Yahweh, promising to keep the stipulations of His covenant. Principally, the covenant consisted of the Decalogue, spoken audibly to all the people, accompanied by lightning and thunder.[29] The great irony, then, was that within days of promising faithfulness, the people of Israel worshiped a golden calf that they themselves had fashioned, breaking the very first stipulations of the covenant. Like Adam and Eve before them, they resisted at the pivotal point of obedience. Within forty days of Yahweh miraculously pronouncing an invitation to covenant they acted with volition in counting as worthless the tenets Yahweh had uttered. When Moses came down from the mount and found the people naked before a golden calf, he broke the tablets in disgust.

Moses told the people, "Perhaps I can secure expiation for your sin" (Exodus 32:30). It was in this context as intermediary for the forgiveness of the people that Moses asked to experience the face of God, not conditionally,[30] but in actuality.[31] Moses hid himself, receiving the renewal of the covenant on Sinai and experiencing Yahweh's glory. Yahweh said, "I shall make all my goodness pass before you, and before you I shall pronounce the name Yahweh; and I am gracious to those to whom I am gracious and I take pity on those on whom I take pity" (Exodus 33:19). The supreme way in which Yahweh demonstrated His glory was to invoke His name over Moses;[32] He overshadowed Moses in a profound exhibition of ownership and covenant relationship, invoking His name upon Moses. God spoke His own name upon this man who stood alone on behalf of all of the people of Israel: "Yahweh, Yahweh"—in this way Yahweh's name became a guarantor of His presence. James Plastaras notes that the Hebrew construction in the text mirrors the wording of the Hebrew when Yahweh revealed Himself to Moses as the "I AM"; this certainly was no accident.[33] This invoking of His name over Moses signified His renewal of the covenant with Israel—He was their "I AM," and He was willing to forgive.[34] Niles rightly suggests Yahweh's calling His name over Moses was an act "by which Yahweh binds himself in a covenant with Moses and through him with the people."[35]

Invoking Yahweh's Name in the Covenant Community

Jewish children understood they were born into covenant community. While there would come a time when the children would become adults that they would personally have to affirm that covenant, they lived their lives with an assurance that Yahweh was their God. At the beginning of each year, Israel would officially renew their covenant, and in this regard, the name of Yahweh was also connected with forgiveneess of sins. Once a year, on the Day of Atonement, God prescribed that the high priest should offer a sacrifice for the sins of the nation. In the context of offering for the people, the high priest functioned in a mediatorial role. It was only on this day that he could enter behind the veil to approach the ark and mercy seat. Not only did he offer the blood upon the mercy seat, history records that on this day the high priest orally invoked the name of Yahweh. Indeed, even after Jewish people stopped uttering the name of Yahweh, on the Day of Atonement, the high priest spoke the name of Yahweh in connection with the forgiveness of their sins.[36]

Priests generally had an important function in the Old Testament. On the one hand, they went to God on behalf of the people. On the other hand, they represented God to the people. As representatives of the people to God, priests participated when the people offered sacrifices to the Lord. As representatives of God to His people, they participated in rites of blessing. In this regard, it was not merely that the priests were blessing the people on their own behalf. They were representing God to the people in a worship setting. The biblical text demonstrates that they represented the very identity and name of God and were set apart for this purpose.[37] Yahweh cautioned circumspect behavior by each priest, for he "bears the consecration of the anointing oil of God. I am Yahweh." Further, they had the special and unique privilege of actually imputing Yahweh's name by speaking orally over the people the blessing that was prescribed in Torah. Such speaking over the people was a guarantee of Yahweh's presence. This was an official act, a necessary rite in their covenant relationship.

Numbers 6:23-27 is very specific as to how the priests were to orally pronounce the covenant upon the people. Verse 27 says, "This is how they must *call down* (emphasis mine) my name on the Israelites, and then I shall bless them."[38] To invoke the name was to invoke the blessing. Yahweh said, "Speak to Aaron and his sons and say: 'This is how you must *bless* the Israelites.' " There are three stanzas to this blessing: The first charges: "Yahweh will bless you and keep you." The second implores for Yahweh to "let his face shine on you" (He will let His presence light you up, illuminate you), and "Yahweh will be gracious (full of the greatest mercy) to you." The third stanza is a command for the presence of Yahweh to be operative for it blesses, "Yahweh show you his face and bring you peace (*shalom* or wholeness)." This is not merely a ritualistic benediction; rather, the name of Yahweh is spoken over the people in covenantal worship. This is how they *"called down"* Yahweh's name upon the people. To say Yahweh's name was to call upon the very Sovereign of all of the universe, and to claim it as their guarantee.[39]

Niles, who posits such a rite as an ongoing part of Israelite covenant,[40] suggests that it is essentially in this specific context where the name of Yahweh can be understood experientially. Sigmund Mowinckel goes so far as to say that "all worship reached its culmination in the priestly words of blessing."[41] The priest, speaking on the behest of Yahweh, promised that Yahweh's presence would attend the people because Yahweh's name was invoked in this way. When Yahweh pronounced the blessings of covenantal relationship, it would be guaranteed by I AM—the God who creates, the God who acts, the God who redeems. God did not act "magically." Speaking the name of Yahweh was not an incantation. Covenant was confirmed as Israel worshiped from their hearts. Brueggemann calls this praise a "constitutive act," an event in which worshipers do not merely describe what is, but evoke what is not yet until they act or speak.[42] That is, it was simply not enough for Israel to rest on the initiation of covenant that happened in the past. Nor were the priestly rites on the Day of Atonement or in the context of congregational worship enough; it was their sincere worship that declared covenant relationship in the present tense! Worship celebrates "genuine newness"; a worshiper experiences anew the redemptive power of God, so that, in the words of Brueggemann, "The claim is real as it has never been real before this moment of articulation."[43] It was in this relational sense of speaking, that to say "Yahweh" was to experience Him in an "I-Thou" bond of love.

Yahweh's Universal Covenantal Love

From the very beginning, Yahweh not only wanted the people to be in covenant, but He wanted to extend the covenant through them to the entire world. The prophets continued Yahweh's message of just such a universal covenant. Isaiah, Ezekiel, Zephaniah, and Amos all promise universal hope for the world. Also prophetic was a prophecy of Amos that offered universal invitation to covenant utilizing a specific structure from the time of King David. When David brought the ark to Jerusalem in anticipation of building the temple for Yahweh, he built a kind of tent, waiting for the completion of the temple.[44] This tent became a kind of open place of worship where whoever wanted to come could worship freely.[45] There were no restrictions for women, for foreigners, or for those who were not of the priestly line. Worship was joyful and free, offered by those whose hearts went beyond ceremony. This same tent of

David provided an important picture in a prophecy by Amos; this freedom of worship in the tent of David became a theme for a future time when Yahweh would include anyone to worship, and as it was interpreted, it made room for Gentile worshipers as well. As we shall discuss later, this tent becomes a symbol in both Amos and Acts 15 for the inclusion of Gentiles in covenant relationship.[46] It was in this tent that unmitigated song and worship became a backdrop of hope. In the same prophecy in which Amos promises the reapers will virtually come on the heels of those who planted, Yahweh promises to raise up again this tent (*succah*) of David.[47] The covenant promise of Israel would be extended upon all nations "over whom my name has pronounced."[48] Amos 9:12 is particularly instructive. The text suggests the people (*goyim*), those outside the covenant relationship, will be called by the name of Yahweh. The Hebrew in this Scripture literally means the name of Yahweh would be pronounced on them.[49] And in doing this, they would become Yahweh's special possession.

The prophecy of Amos does not stand alone, for both Ezekiel 36:24-28 and Zephaniah 2:11-15 are other eschatological texts that promise the same thing, that those who are not Jewish—those who are not part of the covenant people—they too shall become Yahweh's people.[50] Thus, it is the plan of Yahweh to extend His covenant to those who are not His people, so they too will be called by His name. In the next chapters, we begin our study of how such prophecy is accomplished through the work and ministry of Jesus and begins to be actualized with His ascension and glorification. In this regard, the Old Testament is not a story with an ending. Nor is it a story of failure. To be sure, it is a story of mercy and grace, and an offer that continues to expand to all who will listen and respond. Yet, just as Yahweh pursued covenant in the Old Testament, so the advent of the New Testament is the continuation of that same pursuit.

SECTION II:

THE MAN WHO IS

Chapter 5

Discovering the Man, Christ Jesus

Introduction

Christian theology is held together by a man. Whoever, or whatever else He was, He was a man—not apparently, but actually. This was understood by the apostles; they talked with Him, shared His food, and saw Him asleep in a boat during the middle of a storm. But they had witnessed other things as well. They tasted of fish He produced miraculously, rejoiced with a woman whose fevered brow had been instantly cooled; and after His resurrection, they saw Him ascend from a mountain into Heaven. It was only then they reflected about His words to them when He had washed their dirty feet in an upper room. He had told them He was going to die. But He told them something else; He was telling them this ahead of time. He said, "so that you may believe 'I AM.'"[1] Certainly Jesus was a man who told about God. But they now realized with certainty that He was also something else, the very "I AM" who spoke to Moses.

An apostolic understanding of Jesus began to be left behind when in the second century philosophical definitions became the starting place for theology generally and for christology specifically.[2] A number of factors precipitated this change. Importantly, there was a demographic tipping point, when a critical mass in the leadership of the church were Gentiles and drew more from their epistemological understanding than from Scripture. This precipitated a theological shift as to the starting place for reflection about God. The new orientation of those in leadership specified limits as to what God could or could not do, limits that nuanced the way in which the Incarnation could be articulated. All told, instead of beginning with what Hendrikus Berkhof terms "the way of Israel,"[3] and which for simplicity we will call the Old Testament, Christian theologians began their presentations of God by employing Greek ontological categories. Richard Bauckham rightly suggests that one cannot merely propose an evolutionary trajectory from the apostles to Nicea in a story of the evolution of christology. Rather, one must bracket a first-century understanding of the church in order to faithfully capture a biblical presentation of Jesus apart from later confessions. As we suggest in chapter 1, this is exactly what we mean by an "Apostolic hermeneutic." But before we focus on the biblical text, we need to revisit some assumptions that we are making. In the first four chapters of this work, we attempted to demonstrate a covenantal presentation of Yahweh's identity and work. In these next eight chapters we specifically focus on how this same understanding of Yahweh informs the apostles in their insight as to the covenantal identity and work of Jesus Christ.

This chapter serves as a kind of necessary clearing the ground to demonstrate once again how an Apostolic hermeneutic is not only possible but viable.[4] For some, this chapter will not be enough. Entire books have been written addressing the limits of determining meaning from a text, questions of genre, authorship, and authority of the biblical text, not to mention how to determine what, if any, sources underlie the text. These issues will only be dealt with in a cursory manner, and thus for some the chapter will not carry enough weight to establish our approach. For others, what is most important in this book is analyzing a modern presentation of Oneness theology, and this chapter does little to further that presentation. Still, the larger argument of this book demands such a chapter. We are attempting to lay a foundation that demonstrates that Oneness christology is both biblical and logical; specifically, we are arguing that such a construal best fits what the apostles understood about Jesus Christ.

Confronting Objections to an Apostolic Hermeneutic

We suggest in chapter 1 that it is possible to read the biblical text as the apostles did. In this chapter, we work to tease that methodological concept out a bit more as we prepare to focus on christology proper. Let us begin by revisiting what we mean by "apostolic." Certainly, not all the books of the New Testament were written by the apostles, and a number of New Testament books are debated as to their provenance, authorship, and even the dating of the book. Further, there has been a propensity in certain circles of New Testament scholarship to push forward the dates of the New Testament books, thus allowing any number of generations between the apostles and the books themselves; concomitant to this, there is a considerable effort to vie for the very early dating of certain noncanonical materials and to even question the relevance of what the apostles themselves may or may not have believed. We would suggest that such a rereading of the earliest Christian community is intentionally revisionist. Arguably, from the very beginning, the apostles sought unanimity in doctrinal teaching. These were the men who walked and talked with Jesus, and they were as well the earliest adherents of the Christian community.[5] Indeed, when later controversies arose as to which books might be excluded as "noncanonical," acceptance of a book into the canon was in part facilitated by whether a book or its author was directly associated with the apostles and their teaching.

We are not merely suggesting that the apostles read what each other wrote and consequently came up with a consensus of how and what should be written. Rather, their commonalty largely consisted in their shared experience of Jesus. Though there were evidently times when they had to work at coming to a common voice of their teaching,[6] their association was not so much ecclesiastical as it was one forged by the bond of their fellowship. It was this *koinonia* that worked to form consensus. Although to suggest the apostles saw no difference between themselves doctrinally flies in the face of any number of contemporary interpreters who seek for diversity of Christian communities wherever it can be alleged; nonetheless, this is the consistent historical record. As Adolf Harnack demonstrated over a hundred years ago, the earliest church desired "a common faith."[7] Raymond Brown is instructive as well; he rightly notes that although there were times when Peter, Paul, and James disagreed among themselves, "these issues did not cause a break in *koinonia*, so far as anyone can prove."[8] Indeed, where controversy among the apostles is recorded, it is not related to the identity and work of Jesus. Rather, it largely involved issues relating to the Gentile mission and the place of Torah.[9]

Based upon this confidence in the witness of the apostles and those associated with them, one should not discount the New Testament as the primary source for how the early church understood christology and initiation into covenant. Methodologically, then, we will not make an effort to find diverse source material in either the Gospels and Acts, nor will we assume they necessarily offer different construals than the teaching of the epistles. While we will in an ancillary way utilize Jewish constructs of the period, we will not depend on the church fathers as a starting place, nor will they be considered authoritative, but will be explored in a secondary manner. Thus, an Apostolic hermeneutic as it relates to the New Testament assumes that one should start by letting the text itself speak, and take as a reliable source the testimony of the men who provide the closest written witness to Jesus.

At least four objections may be offered to this sort of methodology. First, some may suggest that the genres of the New Testament disallow any real accurate information about the historical Jesus. Second, some have suggested that what is portrayed about Jesus is for the most part a later invention of the church, sayings largely made up. A third and different sort of objection is that an Apostolic hermeneutic as we describe it disallows the framing of christology in its ecclesiastical context, thus mirroring recent liberal attempts to turn an orthodox interpretation on its head. A fourth objection is that an Apostolic hermeneutic seeks for a pristine christological primitivism that never existed historically. Each of these objections will be dealt with in order.

An initial difficulty some may have in saying anything substantive about Jesus Christ is that they have disallowed the New Testament as a valid source for information based upon the genre of the material. The charge is that the Gospels contain only a hazy incomplete biography of Jesus and that the epistles are more "faith statements" than historical record. For instance, Paul, who wrote a considerable portion of the New Testament, never really knew Jesus, and his presentation of the earthly Jesus is sketchy at best. But such objections are not so telling as they once seemed. Now, while it is true that the Gospel record of Jesus is told only through specific events and individual speeches that are representative, this does not mean the record is necessarily suspect. Rather, the events and speeches intentionally present specific revelation offered by Jesus, important moments designed to present the theological import of the person and work of Christ. As D. A. Carson, Moo, and Morris point out, while moderns in the West presuppose the necessity of a particular chronological telling of a biographical story, the first-century construct would be a portrait likely focusing on certain relationships the person had, painting a "biographical sketch" by relating specific things the person said or did.[10] In other words, a first-century telling would look something like the Gospels. Further, when assessing whether or not Paul was a reliable source, one only needs to consider that he was writing a mere twenty years after the cross, and there is considerable evidence that he makes use of received tradition. Indeed, Paul utilizes hymns, tradition from the apostles, and confessions of the church that predate his epistles. Allegations from the beginning of the twentieth century that it was Paul who created the notion of the Incarnation or that he was innovative have been largely been put to rest.[11]

A second objection is that in fact little objective material can be found about Jesus in the Gospels. The presupposition is rather that the Gospels are the work of the church of a later generation, that they are merely representative of the *Sitz im Leben* of the church. In this regard it has been common to assume that Christian prophets perhaps "accidentally" made up sayings about Jesus. Again, the presupposition is that there were some significant differences between the spoken word of Jesus on earth and what these alleged prophets received through revelation of the Spirit. But such reconstruction is highly speculative. Wayne Grudem argues that there is no evidence of inspired prophetic speech being transformed into historical narratives, either in the New Testament, or extant Jewish writings.[12] Further, as Ben Witherington points out, "It is no longer necessary nor sufficient simply to assume that historically there must be a radical difference between the way Jesus viewed and presented himself and the way the early church interpreted him."[13] The Gospels are what they claim to be: the faithful record compiled of a person about whom the historical data is given, one who lived in a particular place, cultural milieu, at a specific time in history. Such a presentation is not ahistorical. In *The Christology of Early Jewish Christian Christianity*, Richard Longenecker acknowledges that there was in fact a historical setting (what he refers to as *Sitz im Leben Kirche*), from which the church wrote. But Longenecker would also recognize that there was a historical setting in which Jesus lived, in which He taught, and from which He Himself shared revelation (what he calls *Sitz im Leben Jesu*). Longenecker offers, "Both are proper and necessary considerations for the historian. But to understand the early church [*Sitz im Leben Kirche*], that of Jesus must take priority over the church."[14] In other words, Longenecker, though a critical scholar, takes seriously the New Testament as our best source of information about Jesus Christ.

A third objection to utilizing this sort of Apostolic hermeneutic is that the privileging of the canonical text and epistemologically divorcing it from corroborating evidence in later church tradition essentially allows the interpretation of the New Testament to be turned on its head. Indeed, one only has to look at the plethora of reconstructions of Jesus to know that we live in a time when interpretative method is largely out of control. Given this, such an objection at first seems viable. Yet, our approach hardly divorces the text from being anchored in first-century tradition; rather, it is primarily this first-century tradition that drives our argument. Further, we would argue the tradition that comes *after* the earliest Christian community is not nearly so important for our understanding as the tradition *that leads up to* the formation of the earliest teachings about Jesus. Just as a rabbinical tradition centuries after the time of Jesus cannot be uncritically considered an authoritative source for first-century Judaism, so the church fathers, centuries removed from the events of the first century, can only testify of what the church *came to believe*. Oscar Cullmann captures the difficulty of studying the christological "problem" by critiquing the church fathers:

> The later so-called christological controversies refer almost exclusively to the *person* or *nature* [emphasis his] of Christ. They refer on the one hand to the relation between his nature and that of God; on the other hand, to the relation which exists in Christ between His divine and human nature. If we are to avoid the danger of seeing the christological problem of the New Testament in a false perspective from the very beginning, we must attempt first of all to disregard these later discussions.[15]

While Cullmann's perspective seems valid, some might argue that if one divorces christological understanding from the safety of the historical interpretation of the Christian church, the loss of this anchor allows for a significant distortion in interpretation. Once again, at first glance, this seems to be confirmed by the plethora of recent reinterpretations of Jesus that do not consider church teaching about Christ as methodologically significant.[16] For example, one popular reinterpretation of Jesus is that He was a kind of neo-Marxist, one whose ministry was primarily in usurping the notions of the socioeconomic upper class in His day. Another popular construal of Jesus sketches Him as a kind of cynic sage. Dozens more interpretations could be listed, but these may be considered as representative. Yet, one needs to ask just how these construals are related to the biblical text. In exploring a neo-Marxist approach, for instance, the question needs to be asked whether or not this kind of interpretation results from merely divorcing the biblical text from church history, or if in fact there was something else going on with the interpreters. A cursory look at the so-called neo-Marxist model of Jesus demonstrates that, in fact, the biblical text is not the starting place of this construal. But neither is church history the starting place. In actuality, this sort of reinterpretation starts with a specific heuristic model and only subsequently comes to the text or to church history for hints that substantiate that, in fact, such a model is plausible.[17] Thus, the biblical text is clearly secondary to the specific heuristic model itself.

Those who propose that Jesus is a kind of cynic sage operate by privileging, not the New Testament, but specific parts of the New Testament that seem to favor their interpretation. That is, in order to get to the "truth" about the historical Jesus, the text is strip-mined one layer at a time until the researcher finally gets to the "original layer" of the story being presented, generally the information that the exegete was hoping to recover! Thus, effort is expended to find the earliest (and presumably the most human material) about Jesus in the Gospels. The presumption of researchers in allowing Markan priority is to invalidate much of the rest of the Gospels; further, in the other allegedly earliest source, "Q" (the hypothetical source used by Matthew and Luke containing mostly sayings of Jesus), one finds what amounts to just an echo of what may truly describe the historical Jesus.[18] In tandem with this, because it is now in vogue to utilize noncanonical gospels as "primary source material," some, in arguing for a very early date of the Gnostic *Gospel of Thomas* and in conjunction with a late dating of the Gospels, allow Thomas as a source for the biblical Gospels![19] This revisionist reading of sources cannot be sustained.[20] All of this should not be an unexpected turn when interpreters have decided purposely to move epistemologically away from letting the text speak on its own terms.[21] But we will have none of this. Such parsing of the text has no controls, and is in fact guided by a specific agenda (each year in "Q" scholarship, adjustments are made to this hypothetical document to make it sound more and more like Thomas). We may be accused of having presuppositions; but the presuppositions that we offer are not merely a faith statement. They are in keeping with valid historical method.

This leads to a fourth objection, that the kind of "Apostolic method" about which we speak is naïve, for christologically, what amounts to a developmental stream can never be traced to some sort of pristine moment of understanding; that is, there was always changing perspective, even in the biblical text. In this regard, it is normative to suppose there was christological development among the various books of the New Testament so they each tell a different story.[22] Nils Dahl's view is typical when he writes, "The christology of Paul is higher than that of Luke/Acts, and christology of the Pastoral Epistles appear to be lower than that of Colossians and Ephesians."[23]

Several points need to be considered in response to this objection. First, those who criticize the kind of methodology we are proposing often come across as objective and sound; but what remains invisible is that an alternate set of presuppositions drives their critique in the first place. That is, there is in scholarship a singular distaste for any sort of harmonization that seems to come up with a largely single reading of an event. Thus, to suggest that all the apostles taught essentially the same christology flies squarely in the face of the postmodern necessity to prove that there cannot be a single position, there was no "normal christology," and any attempt to propose a singular teaching of the early church that sprung from Jesus and the apostles is groundless. Against this critique, we would summarize the points we have begun to raise. The leadership of the earliest Christian community consisted in large part of those men who traveled with Jesus for several years, men who remained in fellowship, collaborating on new challenges as they arose. One cannot take as necessity the presupposition of broad diversity among the leaders of the early church. Richard Longenecker points out that the earliest biblical records, the letters of Paul, actually demonstrate a singular approach in leadership and doctrine by those Galilean apostles who were in fact over the Jerusalem church.[24]

As to the charge that the New Testament only gradually developed its christology and that it took the entire first century to ascribe divinity to Jesus, the historical and biblical necessity for this claim is now being challenged. Richard Bauckham, for example, has worked to demonstrate that from the very beginning, Jesus was considered divine in the earliest Jewish Christian milieu.[25] Bauckham's assertion of an early understanding of high christology effectively challenges an evolutionary approach to christological development and takes the text seriously as a source.

If Bauckham is correct, then one needs to rethink presuppositions that demand a particular christology of Paul, say, or of Mark, or a Lukan Peter be assessed as to whether it is either "higher" or "lower" than that of another biblical construal. Once this presupposition of an evolving stream of diverse christologies is expunged, a closer reading of the biblical text undermines what some have termed a "high" or "low" christology in the same book. For instance, as Hendrikus Berkhof notes, sometimes God seems to be acting in Jesus, and other times it appears that Jesus is acting over against God. He writes, "Statements of this kind, which are contradictory in terms of substantialistic thinking, are regularly found in the same writer. Cf. e.g. Rom. 1:3f. with Phil. 2:6f.; Heb. 1:1-4 with 5:1-10; John 10:30 with 14:28."[26] There are indeed different ways of speaking about Jesus Christ in the New Testament. Specific texts may seem to present Jesus as distant from God while others make an absolute identification with Yahweh.[27] Still, this is not the same as a biblical contradiction. The apostles were comfortable with different ways of speaking about Jesus, easily utilizing a variety of language, not in a contradictory but complementary sense. One needs to reflect on the christological concerns of the apostles, not on those of later centuries. We seek christological definition from biblical categories inherent in the text itself. Recovering first-century language and constructs that were useful in speaking of the Incarnation is sometimes difficult; in some cases, this language went completely out of use after the first century. Fortunately, there are a number of scholars who worked in this area and whose research has been foundational in this study.[28]

The Obstacle of Plurality in the New Testament

Some who know only what amounts to a caricature of Oneness beliefs have sometimes dismissed Oneness christology out of hand because of the clear language of plurality in the New Testament. Further, because passages that distinguish the Father and Son proliferate and the New Testament inaugurates the age of the Spirit, some will presume an insurmountable "threeness" in the New Testament. Certainly, with regard to the outpouring of the Spirit, it is a bit more complex to clearly define the Spirit as a person in conjunction with, say, the persons of the Father and Son, but there are at least some texts that can be helpful in this regard. And even if threeness is not an abundant confession of the New Testament, certainly one cannot discount the considerable weight of the passages that indicate the very real relationship between the Father and the Son. The answers to these objections can only be considered fully within the purview of the next seven chapters. However, let us briefly consider whether or not these objections must at once overwhelm any sort of defense we make for a Oneness perspective in subsequent chapters. In the remainder of this chapter, we attempt to do three things. First, we survey Scriptures that demonstrate threeness in such a way that some suggest declare a Trinity, particularly texts that include the Holy Spirit. Second, we define a Oneness perspective with regard to passages that demonstrate presence of both Father and Son. Finally, we outline how it is that we will be arguing in greater detail in subsequent chapters.

Let us begin our discussion by focusing on whether New Testament writers understand the Spirit to be a distinct person of God. As we demonstrate below, there are only a handful of New Testament texts that in some fashion seem to differentiate between the Father, Son, and Holy Spirit. By contrast, there are scores of passages where both Father and Son are present but the Spirit is absent. Indeed, upon reflection, it is the momentous absence of the Holy Spirit in salutations, benedictions, doxological praises, and hymnic material that is startling, particularly if the Trinity were a first-century confession. As we have discussed, in the Old Testament the Spirit is either a circumlocution for God or a way of expressing God's actions; by contrast, the New Testament is the age of the Spirit. Yet, despite this, there is very little one can uniquely say about the Spirit. For instance, in the New Testament, while Jesus was begotten of the Father, yet it was the Spirit that overshadowed Mary in an act of paternity.[29] It was at once the Father and the Spirit that both uniquely raised Jesus from the dead.[30] In fact, Jesus said He would raise Himself from the dead. (See John 2:19.) In the Book of Revelation, seven times the Spirit is said to be speaking to the church, and yet at the close of the book, we see that it was Jesus speaking.[31] A number of other examples could be cited, but it is easy to see the fluidity with which the New Testament speaks. Some demand that all such language refers to *perichoresis*, or the doctrine of the interpenetration of persons. Yet, such a doctrine is absent in the earliest centuries of the church.

A number of interpreters posit it is not the absence of the many texts but the presence of a few texts that can establish the Spirit as a person. For example, one might argue that it is at the Last Supper where one finds a clear depiction of the Spirit as a distinct person apart from either the Father or the Son.[32] Yet, if this were true, it is curious why the relationship of the Spirit with the Father and Son is so terribly muddled. Six times in the Gospels and Acts Jesus is said to be the one who baptizes with the Spirit;[33] yet, at the Last Supper discourse it is the Father who gives the Spirit. (See John 14:16, 26.) Further, at one point during this discourse, Jesus makes the Spirit equivalent to the Father *and* the Son! Finally, after Jesus speaks at length about the Spirit, He then identifies Himself with the Spirit, proclaiming, "I will not leave you orphans; I will come to you" (John 14:18). In reality, as we discuss in the following chapters, the biblical text can just as readily interchange the speaking of the Spirit with Jesus' speaking. Paul can without embarrassment equate the two, offering: "Now the Lord is the Spirit; and where the Spirit of the Lord is, there is liberty" (II Corinthians 3:17). In Hurtado's study of this biblical phenomena, he finds this fluidity of language pervasive throughout the New Testament.[34]

Admittedly, the academic studies from which we largely draw in subsequent chapters have little to say about the Spirit. Historically, it was only after christology began to be framed with philosophical underpinnings that christological development began its long and winding road that ultimately framed Christ unambiguously as a person co-equal with the Father.[35] This took centuries. It took even longer, when the church, almost as a historical afterthought, defined the Spirit as a co-equal person, largely as a corollary to the place of the Son.

The question remains, then, regardless of our critique of the Spirit in biblical presentation and in church history, how a Oneness construal makes sense of verses that do indeed proclaim threeness in the New Testament, no matter how small their number. There are indeed some passages from which one can derive the Trinity, but only when dogmatic presuppositions are allowed to inform the texts. Dahl notes there are "formulations that mention God, Jesus Christ in syntactic coordination or parallelism (e.g., Matthew 28:19; II Corinthians 13:14; I Corinthians 12:4-6; 1 Peter I:1-2)."[36] But as Dahl also points out, the New Testament may also speak of threeness in a way that could hardly be deemed to relate to persons of God. For example, the text may speak of "God, Christ, and the holy angels (I Timothy 5:21; cf. I Thessalonians 3:13; Luke 9:26), or the name of God, the name of the city of God, and the name of Jesus himself (Revelation 3:12)."[37] Much of this speaking is a stylistic form of emphasis, a kind of Hebraism repeated for emphasis.

Lest we dismiss threeness out of hand, let us at least acknowledge important passages where those who typically seek a Trinity go for corroboration. We will treat the first two passages in only a cursory manner. The first is I John 5:7: "For there are three that bear witness in heaven: the Father, the Word, and the Holy Spirit; and these three are one." I John 5:7 cannot be found in an increasing number of modern translations;[38] the reason for this is that there is absolutely no attestation for this verse in the earliest Greek manuscripts.[39] Thus, it should be given no weight in a discussion of first-century christology. A second passage we mention only briefly here is the baptismal scene of Jesus. On first glance, this passage does indeed demonstrate a visible representation of the Trinity; yet, a Oneness construal suggests that a first-century audience would never have taken this event to mean any such thing. The importance of this scene's biblical and christological significance is so great that it is given much fuller consideration in chapter 8.

Third, let us consider a specific text that might on the face of it be seen to offer a clear Trinitarian construal. Second Corinthians 13:14 reads, "The grace of the Lord Jesus Christ, and the love of God, and the fellowship of the Holy Spirit *be* with you all. Amen." By reading the text with creedal assumptions, one could certainly find the Trinity. It is interesting that of all salutations, this is the only one that references the Spirit. In contrast, approximately twenty salutations praise both God and Jesus, while the Holy Spirit receives no mention.[40] As Harry Austryn Wolfson demonstrates, the salutation of "grace and peace" is adapted from an Old Testament priestly blessing, where, as we discussed in chapter 4, priests literally called down the name of Yahweh upon the people.[41] The addition of Jesus to the original blessing offered from Yahweh reflects the lived experience of the apostles. First, they knew God; second, they came to know the redemptive work of Jesus Christ. It made sense to invoke the blessing of the covenant, which they knew all their life while at the same time celebrating the identity and work of Christ, something they came to know. Further, the priestly blessing itself invoked the presence of God. As we shall discuss in the following chapters, for the apostles, an invocation of divine presence would not take place without actually naming the name of Jesus. Thus, II Corinthians 13:14 is for Wolfson a kind of Hebraism, and while reflecting the "tripartite priestly blessing," he suggests that in fact, the mention of the Father, Son, and Holy Spirit is not ontological, but economic (God's revelation in time). In this regard, the phrase, "the fellowship of the Holy Spirit" can hardly be thought to introduce a person. Rather, the Greek syntax suggests that the correct interpretation means "a participation in the Holy Spirit"[42]—that is, their lived experience in Christian community. Just as a salutation from God and Jesus represents the chronology of revelation, so Paul's inclusion of the Spirit points to the way in which the Spirit is operating in this eschatological era. It is in this same economic treatment that one should consider I Peter 1:1-2.[43]

Finally, we offer only a brief mention of Matthew 28:19, a verse that we shall consider in some detail in chapter 16. Briefly, the triune baptismal formula in this verse does not reflect the earliest baptismal practice of the church; this will be demonstrated both biblically and historically. We would be reticent to suggest that this text is merely a variant tradition of the Matthean school, say, or that it was introduced as a later addition to the biblical text. Rather, Matthew 28:19 should be understood as the same kind of Hebraism as suggested above by Dahl, the repetition being offered for emphasis. Further, it is the same sort of Hebraism that occurs in I Corinthians 12:4-6: a repetition for emphasis.[44]

In the salutations of the epistles, just because there is a mention of both "God and the Lord Jesus Christ" or something similar, this does not necessitate that there are two persons. In some cases, at least, the Greek conjunction *kai* often joins two proper nouns when there is no distinction of persons intended. Certainly, when the Epistle of James offers that "pure and undefiled religion before God and the Father is this" (James 1:27), the intent is not to suggest that there is one person of God and another person of the Father. In this verse, "Father" and "God" do not represent a different person, but they do represent a different identity. The term Father further identifies aspects not offered by "God." Grammarians allow that the "and" (Greek *kai*) can readily refer to the same person.[45] The Father and Son are not different persons but, like the text in James 1:27, they describe different identities. A Oneness construal recognizes the logic of Harry Wolfson's explanation. In celebratory praise, the writers of the epistles call down blessings at once from God, a God with whom they delighted in relationship. Yet the apostles saw neither conflict nor competition in appropriating that covenant to the man, Jesus Christ. It is in this way that plurality in language is useful. The Old Testament is about one—Yahweh. The New Testament is about two—Yahweh and Jesus Christ.

The apostles were a part of the larger Jewish culture that remained firm in their belief in Yahweh and no other. Ferdinand Hahn notes that the *Shema* "was recited several times every day by every God-fearing Jew at the time of Jesus and the primitive church."[46] For the apostles, Yahweh was their God, Yahweh alone. But their lived experience, their revelation of the redemptive work of Christ, caused them to rethink the *Shema.* They could agree with Paul who affirmed "For there is one God and one Mediator between God and men, the man Christ Jesus" (I Timothy 2:5).[47]

Yet, it is not enough to say that the apostles knew the man Christ Jesus. One of the earliest confessions of the church is "Jesus is Lord" (*Kurios*). As we shall discuss in later chapters, this confession went a long way toward unmitigated identification of Jesus with Yahweh. There is a "two-ness," certainly, in the New Testament. The apostles knew Yahweh, and they came to know Jesus Christ. The apostles saw no confusion in the words of Jesus at the Last Supper, "And this is eternal life, that they may know You, the only true God, and Jesus Christ whom You have sent" (John 17:3). In these next seven chapters, we will work out in significant detail how the apostles came to a confession of Jesus both as a man with whom they became acquainted and as the mighty God.

The Challenge of a Oneness Christological Argument

The remainder of this book constitutes a singular argument by employing several methods. First, in chapters 6-12, we work to view christology through the eyes of the apostles. We concentrate primarily on a study of the life of Jesus, focusing on when and how it was that the apostles framed their identity of this man. Thus, we subsume these chapters under the aegis of "THE MAN WHO IS." Under this heading, we explore "The Man Born in Bethlehem," "The Man on a Mission," among other pivotal moments in Jesus' life and ministry. In this study, we want to carefully explore the apostles' gradual process of discovery that led to their understanding.

After these chapters addressing christology proper, we then modify our method, moving from biblical theology to a specific christological survey of church history. If what we say about first-century christology is accurate, then there ought to be a historical remembrance of it in the ensuing centuries. In chapters 13-15, "THE MAN WHO IS NOT," we track two things. First, we demonstrate how the first-century remembrance of christology was present in ensuing centuries; second, we survey an alternate trajectory, offering a study of the steps required in order for an evolving Trinitarian christology to become "orthodox."

After this historical survey, we then seek to demonstrate the theological implication of Oneness christology as it informs covenant initiation. Chapters 16-18 are employed to do this work: "THE MAN WHO IS IN COVENANT." Methodologically, we argue first from the biblical text in chapters 16 and 17. In chapter 18 we attempt to historically demonstrate the relationship of christology and covenant initiation as it is framed in the modern Oneness Pentecostal Movement. The final chapter is in the form of an epilogue, containing observations, synthesis, and suggestions as to direction for the future.

Chapter 6

The Man Who Preexisted

Introduction

On the face of it, the title of this chapter, "The Man Who 'Preexisted,' " is simply nonsense; it is a logical fallacy. It is impossible; indeed, something cannot *exist before it exists*. Yet, this turn of phrase is helpful in understanding a Oneness construal. Trinitarian christology presupposes an eternal Son, one who in His preincarnate state existed in eternal fellowship with the Father. From the perspective of Oneness adherents, such a confession makes nonsense of the *Shema*: "Hear, O Israel! The LORD is our God, the LORD alone" (Deuteronomy 6:4, *Tanak*). Yet, for Oneness christology to reject any actual preexistence of the Son, certain problem passages must be addressed, biblical texts that at first blush ascribe some sort of preexistence to Jesus Christ. In this chapter, we deal with two kinds of texts. The first category is Old Testament texts that mention the Son. The second category involves New Testament texts that seem to project the Son into eternity past. A correct understanding of these two kinds of biblical passages is integral to establishing a Oneness position. As we shall argue below, rather than demonstrate the existence of the Son prior to the Incarnation, these Scriptures in different ways demonstrate how God not only spoke the cosmos into existence; He also creatively spoke forth redemption, words that would find their fulfillment in the man Christ Jesus. It is only in this way, and precisely in this way, that Jesus Christ may be said to "preexist."

The Man before Bethlehem

When Philip met the Ethiopian eunuch returning from Jerusalem, the latter was in his chariot reading from the scroll of Isaiah. The eunuch was puzzled about the text and asked Philip the interpretation of the passage. What was confusing to the eunuch was that in the reading (Isaiah 53), a servant was being wounded and flailed for the iniquities of others. Because the eunuch took the passage as speaking of past events, he could not discern whether the prophet was speaking of himself or someone else. The eunuch had reason to be confused, for Hebrew prophets showed a propensity toward writing their predictions in the perfect tense (often translated in the English past tense), so certain were these prophets of the fulfillment of their prophetic word. Philip quickly explained how that in Isaiah 53, even though the prophet spoke as if the Servant had already died, in reality this scriptural passage was predictive of Jesus Christ. Philip went on to explain how that Jesus had only recently been "wounded for our rebellions, crushed because of our guilt"; further, Philip defined for the eunuch what it implied spiritually that "the punishment reconciling us fell on him, and we have been healed by his bruises."[1]

In light of such startling Old Testament predictions it is no wonder that New Testament writers reveled in the prophetic certainty of God's redemptive Word. I Peter offers that Jesus was "destined before the foundation of the world" (I Peter 1:20, NRSV) to accomplish this redemptive task. Depending on the translation of Revelation 13:8, it is either the church or most probably "the Lamb slain" from the foundation of the world. Thus, in comparison to proclamations by God, human proclamations seem very feeble indeed.

There are only a few times when humans speak that it is possible for the words themselves to be equivalent to an action.[2] For instance, when someone christens a ship, she may smash a bottle on it and call down a name upon it. Or when the minister at a wedding intones, "I pronounce you man and wife," the deed is done. But even these words may misfire. With humans, words are always contingent.[3] If, for example, the minister were not licensed properly, or if the person christening the ship had merely walked out of the crowd with their own bottle and made up a name, then these words would have no authority. Yet, with God, "misfiring" is impossible. God's creative Word is the same as the event, even if the actual fulfillment of the event does not occur for thousands of years.

The reason that New Testament Christians could see Jesus Christ in the reading of the entire Old Testament was simple. If God from the very beginning had a plan for redemption, it was no great difficulty for Him to offer a blueprint in the biblical text. It is just because of this presupposition that New Testament writers mined the Old Testament text for every "shadow" or a "type" that prefigured God's redemptive plan. For example, the writer in Hebrews focuses on elements from the Tabernacle in the wilderness and makes application to Jesus Christ. Most important were historical and sacral events in the life of Israel that were deemed to be patterns of the work that Christ would do, particularly feasts such as the Passover and the Day of Atonement. Both the paschal lamb and sacrificial animals on the Day of Atonement worked to paint a redemptive foreshadowing of the work of Christ. Pauline epistles are replete with citations; the Book of Revelation offers more Old Testament allusions and metaphors than any other New Testament book, confidently harvesting them from the scrolls of holy writ whose predictive symbols enabled the seer to complete a panorama of Jesus in the eschaton. It is no wonder that Paul in writing to the Galatians pronounced, "Therefore the law was our tutor to bring us to Christ, that we might be justified by faith."[4]

Let us now consider how the Old Testament spoke of Jesus Christ. As we have begun to suggest, when the eunuch read from the Isaiah scroll, the prophet's use of the perfect tense was stylistic, demonstrating the certainty of the voice of God. In this sense, the Crucifixion "preexisted" in the Old Testament, though it would be hundreds of years before it occurred in reality. It is in this same sense of predictive prophecy that Jesus could pray in the Old Testament, say, to be strengthened on the cross; further, in the same predictive sense Yahweh could speak hope to the man Christ Jesus. Thus, even a "divine conversation" in the Old Testament does not negate the proleptic nature of such discourse; it is a prophecy. A number of psalms that seem to be recording a conversation concurrent with the life of the psalmist are actually predictive of redemptive events.

Briefly, two psalms that we will return to in later chapters, Psalm 2 and Psalm 110, offer just such "divine conversations." At first glance, Yahweh is addressing a Son in the Old Testament. In Psalm 2:7 Yahweh declares, "You are My Son, Today I have begotten You." Yet, we know from the New Testament fulfillment that these words penned by the psalmist were yet to be spoken. Further, like other Old Testament prophecies, Psalm 2:7 can be made to do considerable work. Certainly, the psalm has a prophetic reference to the birth of Christ. It alludes as well to Jesus' baptism, where the voice of God speaks a prophetic promise to the man standing in baptismal waters that Jesus' sacrificial work will be followed by resurrection and ascension.[5] Paul confirms such an understanding of the psalm when in Antioch he applies this psalm to the resurrection and specifically to the official pronouncement made to Jesus at the Ascension.[6]

What is vital to understand is that the words of Yahweh recorded by the psalmist cannot be understood in any other way than proleptic—they are predictive of an event that will surely happen. Treated in other ways, the psalm adds to the impossible christological tangle that attempts to explain how an "eternally begotten" Son was in fact begotten in punctiliar fashion, especially since the psalm spoke of a particular day when the Son was begotten, one that had already taken place in the Old Testament.

While any number of psalms could be addressed, the above psalm is suggestive of how the others should be interpreted. Briefly, though, let us refer to one additional psalm that is central to understanding christology. The most oft quoted Old Testament text by New Testament writers is Psalm 110:1: "Yahweh declared to my Lord, 'Take your seat at my right hand, till I have made your enemies your footstool.' "[7] This passage prophesies of an official declaration made by God at the Ascension.[8] Because of its significance, we will focus on this psalm in considerable detail in chapter 11. The point here is only to note that no actual Son need exist prior to Bethlehem in order for this kind of prophetic speaking to occur. In actuality, there is no other sense that this psalm can have meaning; it was precisely the man Christ Jesus who was raised from the dead, who ascended, and who was in a place of divine prominence. Thus, it was only in this way that the man Jesus can be said to have "preexisted" in the Old Testament. He was envisaged as central to the eternal redemptive plan of God.

New Testament Passages

There are any number of passages in the New Testament, which, if one came to the text with a Trinitarian perspective and wanted to read preexistence into the texts, one could find it. For instance, Jesus made a claim to have existed before the Incarnation when He said, "Before Abraham was, I am." A Trinitarian reading might understand that the text teaches the Son was co-eternal with the Father. An important consideration, though, is to understand the proclamation as the Jewish listeners would have heard it. They rightly understood Jesus' statement of "I AM" as a claim to be Yahweh. This is evidenced in the immediate response by some who gathered stones to kill Jesus for making what they deemed to be a blasphemous assertion. (See John 8:58-59.)

Other texts which may seem to indicate Jesus' preexistence are those texts which can be interpreted as Jesus speaking of the Son descending from a heavenly realm to an earthly realm. While we will deal further with these texts in chapter 9, we would suggest briefly that this kind of language which Jesus utilized is intentional. In some cases, Jesus was making reference to His divine origins; in other cases, He was highlighting His mission and the ultimate eschatological triumph that would ensue upon His ascension. What these texts have in common is that they epitomize the unique way in which Jesus spoke. By both direct and indirect reference, He worked to illuminate the understanding of those who had ears to hear.

There is one category of New Testament texts that we wish to highlight in some detail, for it is in these texts that many seek for proof of the preexistence of the Son. These are texts that have been identified as poetry, and are thought to be songs sung by the earliest church in celebratory praise of the work of Christ. Jack Sanders has identified a half dozen of these christological hymns. They are Philippians 2:6-11; Colossians 1:15-20; I Timothy 3:16; I Peter 3:18-22; Hebrews 1:3; and the prologue of John. [9]

We begin an exploration of these hymns by acknowledging their genre: songs that marshal metaphors and stretch stanzas into doxological delights of praise. As such, their playful and creative use of phrases is meant to capture the majesty of the Incarnation. Further, all of the hymns have certain commonalties in terms of flow and direction. For instance, they all commemorate Jesus' life and mission and praise Him for His work; with the exception of the prologue of John, they all celebrate His ascension and glorification. Beyond this, each hymn must be understood in its own context and integrity. The two hymns that are both the most integral and most universally misunderstood are the prologue of John and the Philippian hymn. Consequently, we will deal with these passages in considerable detail. While the Philippian hymn will be addressed in subsequent chapters, the remainder of this chapter will largely explore issues related to John's prologue. Before embarking into our study of the prologue, though, let us briefly survey the other hymnic material, particularly with an eye as to whether these songs demonstrate that the Son existed before the Incarnation.

We may at once dispense with the hymn in I Peter, for it cannot be said to even hint at a "preexistent Christ." Similarly, one would be hard pressed to call on I Timothy to support any notion of a pre-incarnate Son. The hymn begins: "God was manifested in the flesh" (I Timothy 3:16); other versions have "He" instead of "God" at the beginning of the hymnic material."[10] Although the majority of late Greek texts begins the verse with θεός (God),[11] the textual evidence is in favor of the relative pronoun "*hŏs*," typically translated "He."[12] It is not at all unusual for a hymn to start with this relative pronoun *hŏs*. Indeed, the use of the relative pronoun is one of the normative markers to begin a hymn.[13] More to the point, neither "Christ" nor "the Son" can be found as an antecedent. While God is referenced in the preceding verse, this is not absolute evidence that "God" is in fact the referent. Consequently, without reading dogmatic presuppositions into the text it cannot demonstrate any sort of preexistent Son.

More problematic for a Oneness construal are the hymns from Hebrews and Colossians that appear to ascribe the Creation to Jesus Christ. Oneness authors typically respond to these passages by suggesting that when the text says that Creation was "by the Son," it simply means that cosmos was created with the Son in view or that this in some way blends the notion of Son in view with God's creative word.[14] Certainly for God the Son was in view at Creation. Yet, it was not merely the cosmos. When Hebrews 1:2 says of the Son, "by whom He created the worlds," the Greek *aiōnas* has reference to periods of time in the eschatological sense. That is, God did not merely construct the cosmos with the Son in view; He mapped out the eons! Hendrikus Berkhof agrees with this when he offers of Colossians 1:15-20, "There it is precisely the man Jesus who, as 'the firstborn of all creation,' has become preeminent in everything, and for whose sake the world was made as it was."[15] Again, Berkhof notes that it is the same for Hebrews 1:1-4 in which he sees the "obedient son and mediator . . . these texts know nothing of a separate preexistent life, apart from and different from the earthly and glorified life of Jesus."[16] Berkhof interprets the prologue of John similarly, but we would suggest the Prologue is a bit more complex. In order to fully appreciate this hymn, we need to first discuss certain language and constructs that serve as a background for Jewish Christians in the first century.

First-Century Language of Incarnation

It may not be too much to suggest that the Incarnation cannot be fully understood without a Jewish understanding of covenant. In chapter 4, we have suggested that in the Old Testament, when God made a covenant with His people, such a covenant was initiated by Yahweh calling His name upon the individual or group. Thus, when God called down His name upon the people in Exodus 20 and on Moses in Exodus 33, he was initiating and renewing His covenant respectively.[17] Further, covenant renewal functioned in Jewish worship, evidenced by a particular rite in congregational worship. During the service, priests would literally call down the name of Yahweh upon the people. This priestly profession on behalf of God served as a reminder of His faithfulness. Further, such an invocation was a guarantor that Yahweh's face (*panim*), that is His presence, would be resident with the people, and His people would be holy unto Him.[18]

Not only did Yahweh put His name on the people; by extension, places where covenant was practiced were also a place upon which Yahweh placed His name. Thus, Jerusalem, the Temple Mount, and the Temple itself were all holy for the same reason. Specifically, God singled out the city of Jerusalem where He would keep covenant and demonstrate "His face" in a special relationship. Although there had been other places that were utilized for the worship, Yahweh promised that Jerusalem would be the official place of worship, and He had chosen this place to put His name. Yahweh's presence would guarantee this, and they were to rejoice in this promise. Deuteronomy 12:11 records this charge: "To the place chosen by Yahweh your God as a home for his name, to that place you must bring all the things that I am laying down for you: your burnt offerings and your sacrifices, your tithes and offerings held high, and all the best of your possessions dedicated by you to Yahweh."[19] Not only does the Old Testament teach that the Temple was "the place which he has chosen to establish his name" (II Samuel 7:13; I Kings 3:2), it was "the place where Yahweh's name is present" (Isaiah 18:7). Such a biblical phenomenon was recognized by Gerhard von Rad and labeled, "Theology of the Name." That is, Yahweh's face is where His name is.[20] The challenge that the prologue is posing is the question as to where Yahweh's name now dwells.

By the first century, the Jewish people no longer spoke the name of Yahweh, but would rather utilize a number of circumlocutions. While in the synagogue Yahweh was replaced with *Adonai* (the more generic Hebrew word translated Lord), it was also common for people to generally utilize *HaShem* (the Hebrew for "The Name"). Colloquially, God was often referred to as "the Most High," or something similar.[21] An attribute of God that sometimes served as a circumlocution for Yahweh was "glory." To speak of the glory of Yahweh was to speak of Yahweh Himself. Yahweh's glory was understood to be with the Jewish people because of His covenantal promises. The Septuagint takes the house of Yahweh as the "dwelling place" of His glory.[22] When the Hebrew word translated "glory" (*kabod*) was translated into Greek (*doxa*) there followed an intensifying of meaning to speak of the very essence of God. As Gerhard Kittel notes, the translator gave *doxa* a change in meaning, the sense of which hardly could be surpassed. "He made it express something absolutely objective, i.e., the reality of God."[23]

Because both Yahweh's name and glory were connected with the Temple, the Temple took on an incredible symbolic status such that for the Jewish people, the structure itself functioned as the most significant representation of the divine; indeed, for many, this is where the Most High dwelt. It is just this question of where Yahweh "dwells" that serves as the hinge upon which the prologue turns. In a direct challenge to many among his Jewish audience, John makes what would have been to many a startling claim: Yahweh's dwelling place is no longer in the Temple. Rather the place where Yahweh uniquely dwells is in Jesus Christ. In doing so, John stakes a christological claim, arguing that Yahweh now dwells in Christ. John's claim could not be misunderstood by his Jewish audience, for, as Jean Daniélou asserts, for Jewish Christianity, "dwelling is the Semitic category best suited to express the incarnation."[24]

The Prologue of John

We are now ready to consider the prologue in its Jewish context. We will not treat the hymn apart from John's Gospel, but rather as an introduction to themes of the Gospels as a whole.[25] In this regard the Book of John is unique. Whereas the Gospel of Mark begins Jesus' story with His ministry, Luke begins with His birth, and Matthew takes the narrative of Jesus all the way back to Abraham, it is John's prologue that takes the redemptive work of Jesus Christ to eternity past.

The prologue begins with the familiar words "In the beginning," a phrase not lost on John's primarily Jewish audience.[26] "In the beginning was the word (*logos*)" offered a phrase that echoed Genesis 1:1.[27] John's use of the *Logos* is not meant to be Philonic, nor is it meant to answer the sort of metaphysical questions imposed on it by later interpreters.[28] Rather, it was intended to revisit the creative word of God. Just as the emphasis of Genesis 1:1 is that God, absolutely alone, called the creation into existence, so John has no intention of introducing any sort of additional hypostasis to the Person of God at the beginning. John 1:1 says both that the "*Logos* was with God, and the *Logos* was God."

Theologically, God's speaking cannot be separated from God Himself. The psalmist sang of the army of stars that Yahweh called into existence: "By the word of the LORD (*debar* Yahweh) the heavens were made, and all their host by the breath of his mouth" (Psalm 33:6, NRSV). In Psalm 147, when the creation account is celebrated, God's word is credited with making changes in the world (verses 15-19). In these verses Yahweh's word "runs swiftly," "it melts the ice . . ." The psalmist says, "He sent his word, and healed them."[29] Yet, the psalmist was not celebrating "word of Yahweh" in any sense an intermediary or a hypostasis. The celebration was in the power of Yahweh speaking.

For John, at the same time God was creatively speaking "Let there be light!", He was creatively pronouncing something else. Before He dug into the dust of the earth to create Adam, He had in view another man, a man who would effect redemption, an obedient Son whose covenant with His Father would redeem a people who had lost their way. Further, John wanted his audience to know one more thing about this man who was in view before the Creation, no matter how awkwardly it stretched the language: this man is God.[30]

John's prologue begins, "In the beginning was the Word (*Logos*), and the Word (*Logos*) was with God, and the Word (*Logos*) was God." The Word, the *Logos*, has been interpreted variously. Some have taken the Greek to mean "the Word was "face-to-face" with God."[31] But such a translation is hardly demanded by the Greek text. The semantic range of the Greek *pros* does not demand such an interpretation. Indeed this is not the usual way of suggesting a face-to-face encounter.[32] Oneness author David Bernard suggests that "pertaining to God" would be a viable translation based upon a similar translation of *pros* in the accusative in other passages.[33] The context itself ought to warn us against imposing this kind of dogmatic import into the Prologue's celebratory language. In order to utilize this verse to define a plurality of some sort, one would need to change the meaning of the words right in the middle of the verse. When the text says that the *Logos* was God (*Theos*), this cannot merely mean that the *Logos* was divine. Exegetes have rightly determined that it can only mean that the *Logos* is God (*Theos*).[34] Consequently, whatever it means to say that the Word was *Theos* must also inform the phrase, the Word was with *Theos*. If taken literally to mean that the preexistent Son was with the Father (face-to-face or otherwise), then the third phrase must be: "The Preexistent Son was the Father." No one would opt for such an interpretation. Nor can "God" be read to mean "Trinity" for then, "The Preexistent Son was the Trinity." Fortunately, there is a fairly simple way for this passage to makes sense; that is, if we understand that John has reference to Yahweh's creative speaking about redemption.[35]

Four verses are key to understanding how it is that the prologue argues: John 1:1, which introduces the *Logos*; John 1:14, which says the *Logos* "became flesh" and "tabernacled (*skenoo*) among us"; and finally, the comparison between Moses and Jesus in verses John 1:17-18. Let us consider first verse 14: "And the Word became flesh and dwelt among us, and we beheld His glory, the glory as of the only begotten of the Father, full of grace and truth." Although this *skenoo*, literally, tenting, of God in His plan can refer to "a temporary dwelling," it may also refer to a "unique dwelling," and of course, the Incarnation is one of a kind—it is unique,[36] as it is expressed in the rest of the verse. But the claim could not be missed by Jews who challenged Jesus' role as the unique revelation of Yahweh because of their conviction that Yahweh dwelt in the Temple. In the face of this John proclaimed that Yahweh was not "tenting" in the Temple; He was "tenting" in Jesus!

As we have suggested above, "dwelling" is an incarnational verb.[37] This way of speaking is utilized in John as well as other parts of the New Testament.[38] Paul could say, "God was in Christ reconciling the world to Himself" (II Corinthians 5:19) and God was "manifest in the flesh."[39] As Colossians 2:9 offers, "For in him all the fullness of Deity dwells in bodily form." Nor is the Incarnation represented as a "temporary" dwelling. The word "dwells" implies permanency,[40] not only in the New Testament, but in the Old Testament as well. This verb is normative in the *LXX* to express the way Yahweh dwells in heaven.[41] The words of Jesus themselves speak to this understanding. In John 14:8-10, Jesus says that those who had seen Him had "seen the Father." He goes on to say that it was the Father who dwelt in Him that did the works. That is, the Father permanently resides (μένων) in Jesus.[42] In Christ, God is permanently dwelling among men.

In John 1:14, the language of "glory" gets linked to the notion of dwelling or tabernacling. As we suggested above, "glory" also became for the Jewish people a circumlocution for God. Gerhard Kittel puts it this way: "In reality, the term always speaks of one thing. God's power is an expression of the 'divine nature,' and the honor ascribed to God by man is finally no other than an affirmation of this nature."[43] As Berkhof notes, "The exclusive sphere of God, the 'glory,' passes in Jesus to *one* man."[44] Paul could speak in the same fashion, as in II Corinthians 3-4.[45] Indeed, although such normative Jewish Christian language went out of use in the early second century, the language of "glory" was the language of divinity, the language of Incarnation.[46] It was in this way that a first-century Jewish Christian would be able to speak of God ontologically being in Christ without violating the culturally prescribed requirement to speak of God in circumlocutions.[47] The claim of the prologue, then, is that while God's covenantal relationship with His people was previously confirmed in the Temple/Tabernacle, it is now made manifest in Jesus Christ. Jesus is the unique revelation of God, where both the name and presence of God dwells.[48]

Verse 15 and the following verses build on the previous theme of glory and develop it until the prologue reaches a climax in verse 18.[49] In contrast with Moses (who was unable to see God), Jesus (who is the very revelation of God) distributes God's covenantal blessings. Elizabeth Harris points out the deliberate progression from Jesus as "only begotten" in verse 14[50] to Jesus as the "only begotten God" in verse 18.[51] Verse 18 then not only provides a climax for the prologue but something of an inclusio as well. It combines the *Logos* of verse 1 who became incarnate in verse 14 and explains in verse 18 that this is in fact the unique revelation of God; Jesus is in the bosom of His Father,[52] and God Himself, begotten. The Old Testament promises reach their acme in this verse, for present in the verse is both the man who was promised throughout the text and another confession, one that stretches the language of the text incredibly—that man was God!

Conclusion

In this chapter, we have sought to address biblical texts that have been purported to find the Son before the Incarnation. From a Oneness perspective, this is not strictly possible. There are only two ways in which the

Son may be said to have "preexisted" prior to the time of Bethlehem's baby. First, because ontologically Jesus was God who was manifested in flesh, He had existence as God. This is the only way to make sense of Jesus' claim, "Before Abraham was, I am." Second, any mention of the Son in the Old Testament is proleptic. In the mind and plan of God, the Son was envisioned. So certain was this creative speaking by God that it could be said that Jesus' blood was shed "before the foundation of the world" (John 17:24). In God's redemptive plan, Yahweh spoke salvation before there was ever a sin to be forgiven. He spoke healing before there was ever a wound. He spoke of a restored covenant relationship before there was ever a breach.

The very term Son "implies" a beginning, and both the Old Testament and New Testament are consistent in this affirmation. When the psalmist prophesied, "You are my son, today have I fathered you," it would take considerable wresting of the text to come up with any other conclusion than that the Son came into existence through an act of paternity. The clear confession of the New Testament is that "Jesus Christ our Lord . . . was born of the seed of David according to the flesh" (Romans 1:3). Jesus had a beginning. It is this ontological beginning, then, that we now turn to explore.

Chapter 7

The Man Born in Bethlehem

The "Name" and the Incarnation

In what has been termed "salvation history," there are specific events which, when once they occur, nothing can ever be the same again. While these events span to the eschaton, the most crucial events involve the Incarnation. Throughout the next chapters, we will parse key moments in the life of Jesus significant in this regard; in this chapter, we explore the Incarnation as it relates to His conception and birth, events upon which the eschaton turns. Importantly, we will ask one very difficult question, one that is the basis of a significant amount of christological controversy: what does it mean to say that Jesus is both human and divine? Our answer is specific and utilizes a first-century understanding to demonstrate the viability of Oneness christology. While a historical defense of a Oneness position will have to wait until subsequent chapters, we do seek to answer certain objections biblically in this chapter.

Before pursuing ontological questions, we offer a few observations about names, titles, and the notion of covenant generally. First, while there is significant covenantal import in the Incarnation, it would be wrong to suggest that through it God was dissolving one covenant relationship in order to begin another. Rather, covenant should be understood holistically; God's covenant with His people in the Old Testament anticipated the work of Jesus Christ. Further, while there are privileges for the people of God not available before the cross, it is not too much to say that it is not even possible to fully discern the significance of the Incarnation without understanding Old Testament constructs and promises.

Integral to understanding this divine covenant relationship is an understanding of divine names. Recall that in anticipation of the covenant God was to make with Israel, God gave special revelation to Moses by speaking out of a burning bush. God told Moses in Exodus 3:14 (NKJV) "I am who I am (*ehyeh asher ehyeh*)," a Hebrew affirmation etymologically related to the name Yahweh. As we suggest in chapter 2, this Hebrew phrase is in the imperfect verb tense and is an affirmation of the potential of what will occur. By telling Moses His name, Yahweh was not merely offering a definition. Based upon what His name meant, He was proclaiming to Moses that He would soon bring salvation to the people of God.[1]

Analogously, the name of Jesus functions covenantally much the same as Yahweh. The name "Jesus" originally derives from the Hebrew *Yeshua*. Like other Hebrew names, *Yeshua* contains a portion of the divine name, Yahweh.[2] Significantly, an angel instructed Joseph to name Mary's baby "Jesus," explaining that this name was descriptive of what Jesus would do and be. The angel said, "And she will bring forth a Son, and you shall call His name JESUS, for He will save His people from their sins" (Matthew 1:21). Thus, the angel's explanation as to how the name Jesus relates to salvific actions is based upon the first-century meaning of *Yeshua*: "salvation of Yahweh."[3] New Testament writers celebrated the fact that the appellation "Jesus" not only included the identity of Yahweh but also declared what Yahweh would do in the person of Jesus Christ. Just as the name "Yahweh" inherently claims that Yahweh would redeem Israel, so "Jesus" means that He would be a savior, a title normally ascribed to God. As an explanatory aside, Matthew's Gospel offers that all of this was done in fulfillment of the prophecy of Isaiah, " 'Behold, the virgin shall be with child, and bear a Son, and they shall call His name Immanuel,' which is translated, 'God with us' " (Matthew 1:23).

Not only is the name of Jesus important; titles ascribed to Jesus also proclaim His identity. The Lukan celebration of the birth of Christ is unambiguous. Angelic pronouncements offered to shepherds were a clear ontological affirmation of deity. The angel declared: "To you is born this day in the city of David a Savior (*Soter*), who is the Messiah (*Christos*), the Lord (*Kurios*)" (Luke 2:11). Each one of these titles is significant in identifying Jesus with Yahweh. While focus on the title Lord (*Kurios*) will be a recurring theme in subsequent chapters, it should be noted that *Kurios* is a central title in identifying Jesus with Yahweh. As we have begun to suggest, in a first-century Jewish context, both the titles "Savior"[4] and "Lord"[5] are appellations that denote Yahweh. Christ (*Christos*) is a bit more complex, but primarily relates to Jesus and His fulfilling of the mission

God called Him to do.[6] Thus, both Jesus' name and titles describe Jesus' identity and mission.

The Only Begotten

In the Luke 2 birth narrative, Mary was visited by Gabriel, an angel who pronounced the Incarnation. Gabriel promised her, "The Holy Spirit will come upon you, and the power of the Highest will overshadow you."[7] The passage offers few details beyond this cryptic pronouncement about the actual way in which God's Spirit would overshadow Mary. The manner in which Luke handles this scene is with reverence; in truth, it is almost delicate. Some have suggested that in describing his act of paternity, Lukan language is reminiscent to the creative acts of the Spirit of God in Genesis 1.[8]

Though the Incarnation is mystery, there is a way in which, as in any act of paternity, something of the Father must be represented in the offspring. Nor, as we suggested above, is there any ontological distinction between God and His Spirit who overshadowed Mary.[9] It was Yahweh and no one else who was Father. Thus, when the angel pronounced that the Spirit would overshadow Mary, Gabriel went on to say, "Therefore, also, that Holy One who is to be born will be called the Son of God."[10]

Again, while acknowledging there is much we do not know, we affirm that scripturally, Mary truly was the mother of Jesus. For several reasons, we must insist that the biblical narrative cannot mean anything other than that Mary contributed half of the chromosomal material that resulted in an embryo. This is confirmed in the Greek phrase underlying Elizabeth's words of blessing pronounced prophetically to Mary: "blessed is the 'fruit of your womb.' "[11] Further, the reference to Jesus as "the son of David," has literary relationship to the Lukan genealogy where Mary's lineage is traced back to David. Thus, it is only by ignoring the text that one can claim that the connection of Jesus to David was only in a legal or in (an adopted) familial sense. Rather, the biological implication is that Mary's genetic material had ultimately been passed down from David and was transmitted to Jesus through her. Mary was no mere incubator; she lived out every maternal function in nurturing Jesus in His prenatal growth.

In the strictest sense of the word, it was only in an act of paternity and not before that Yahweh became "Father,"[12] for one cannot rightly speak of being a father without progeny. Further, procreation requires that half the genetic material be contributed by the mother and half by the father. We cannot entirely understand how it was that half of the genetic material was supplied by God. Certainly the biblical presentation is that Jesus was both humanly and genetically complete as every person born before Him. We may only presume that in the act of paternity, God supplied *de novo* the genetic material to complete the embryo.[13] Further, there is a way in which the Spirit indwells Jesus that is entirely unique. It is not enough to say that Yahweh merely ignited the life of Jesus or that Jesus was born of divine origin. If the Incarnation means anything at all, it means that the very life of Jesus is the life of God and that Jesus is Yahweh's unique dwelling place.

The difference between a Oneness and Trinitarian christology becomes clear precisely at this point. In chapter 2, we suggested that there were three ways in which the Old Testament spoke about the presence of God. First, God's abode was Heaven; second, He would temporarily make appearances as a theophany; third, God was present in His covenant community, particularly in the process of covenantal worship. Principally, though, we insisted that the abode of God is Heaven. As we began to suggest above, Oneness christology suggests that at the moment of conception, when the Spirit overshadowed Mary, something significant took place with regard to God's dwelling place. At that moment, God took up new residence. Although the Incarnation stretches our limits to conceive of it, in actuality, God's dwelling place was now in that tiny embryo. Think of it! The One who ruled the cosmos lived in a fetus. The affairs of time and eternity were controlled by the One whose residence was a babbling baby. And while the boy worked in a carpenter's shop and even before He answered the call of the Spirit at Jordan, God was in Christ. It is for this reason that Jesus could speak of having the Spirit without measure. (See John 3:34.) This is also why, too, that in a rare moment of revelation, Jesus told his apostles, "For where two or three are gathered together in My name, I am there in the midst of them" (Matthew 18:20).

It will not do to think in terms of a universe filled with an amorphous presence of God in which the divinity in Jesus merely constitutes one part of that larger being that is called God. Nor will it do to think of multiple centers of divine consciousness and that one or another of these centers of consciousness became incarnate. The Lukan confession could not be simpler. Jesus was the Son of God for one reason: because the Spirit overshadowed Mary. The biblical record is consistent throughout the New Testament. Paul would write, "For in Him dwells all the fullness of the Godhead bodily" (Colossians 2:9).

Apart from whatever specific questions of biblical interpretation one may have, there are at the outset two very difficult hurdles that those who have been trained in classical theology must overcome to begin to consider the viability of a Oneness christology. The first is that implicit in a Oneness construal is the necessary claim that God changed.[14] Related to this is a second claim, that in the Incarnation God has truly become passible in the man Christ Jesus. He feels, hurts, acts, and interacts in the person of Jesus Christ just as He did in the Old Testament. This second assertion was particularly offensive historically, and was pivotal in the historical development of Trinitarianism. Indeed, because of many centuries of established church dogma, many will not begin to listen to another theological voice. Whether or not these objections should stand, though, should not rest solely on what the church came to believe; let us consider both of these objections from a biblical perspective.

There are several passages of Scripture that upon first reading do seem very plain in their proclaiming that God cannot change.[15] Malachi 3:6 is typical and is probably utilized more than any text. It states: "I, Yahweh, do not change." Now, if one begins with the notion that God by definition cannot change, then the passage does indeed prove that inherently it is impossible for any change in God. Yet, as in other texts where ontological strictures are artificially imposed, we ought to dig more deeply into the context of this prophet. A cursory reading of the book reveals that Yahweh was reaching out to people whose passion for genuine covenant worship had waned. It is in this regard that God was proclaiming His covenant faithfulness. He was reminding Judah that He had not changed with reference to them even though they had been unfaithful to Him. Yahweh continued: "So you, O descendants of Jacob, are not destroyed." That is, although Yahweh was certainly threatening judgment upon the people (Malachi 2:2-4; 9), it had not come as yet because of His covenant faithfulness. It is in this way we are to understand that God's character cannot change; if it had, based upon their own behavior, they would have already been judged. We certainly must affirm with Malachi that God will not change with regard to His character. But to ascribe a divine limitation of ontological unchangeableness is to hang a very large theological presupposition on a very small scriptural hook.

A second objection to a Oneness construal is that it demands that if Yahweh were incarnate, then the Father would be a fellow-sufferer with Christ. Particularly in chapter 15, we will track how this objection owes more to philosophical presuppositions than to biblical ones.[16] We have demonstrated already that an Old Testament understanding of Yahweh presumes that God could act and react, feel and respond.[17] Further, as we shall demonstrate, once this Old Testament truth about Yahweh was disallowed, the second- and third-century church absorbed certain Hellenistic truisms with reference to God, ones that placed further strictures upon divinity. But in so doing, God was redefined. Just as the people of Israel distanced themselves from biblical proclamation, so the church began to move away from its Old Testament roots. The biblical record demonstrates that there was ontological change that allowed for the Incarnation. If Immanuel means anything at all, it means that God has literally come near.

An Anthropological Understanding of Jesus

A necessary implication of the claim that Jesus was a man is that whatever it means to be human has application to Jesus Christ. Thus, to be human, Jesus had to have independent reasoning, and in reality He had to have been able to experience all the appetites of the flesh. When defining Jesus in terms of His psychological or inner makeup, a bit of caution is required. First, we should speak with biblical understanding. That is, an Old Testament perspective informs a first-century Jewish concept as to what it means to be a "person." In this regard, we should treat as suspect later discussions that had as their starting place in the study of the anthropology of Jesus the post-biblical language of a "dual nature" of Christ. The term "nature" is fraught with difficulties and the term "dual" starts by parsing Jesus rather than considering Him holistically. As Catholic theologian, Hans Küng, offers, "The two-natures doctrine, using terms and ideas which bear the imprint of Hellenistic language and mentality, is no longer understood today."[18]

While it was typical of Greek thought to make ontological distinction between component parts of a person, as we have begun to suggest, this strays from normative Hebrew understanding. In a Jewish conception, a person was typically seen as a whole. That is not to suggest that the Old Testament has no conception of an "inner person"; only that one proceed carefully. For instance, in the Old Testament, while reference could be made to different component parts of an individual, these were never inflexible definitions. Indeed, while an author could refer to specific parts of the body, like in English, for example, "heart," "spirit," and "soul" could have considerable metaphorical latitude. Further, the mentioning of different parts often served as a circumlocution or for added emphasis. For example, the *Shema* commanded Israel to love Yahweh "with all your heart, with all your soul, with all your strength." While the specific mention of these human aspects did have meaning, the text is not meant to suggest that one is to love Yahweh with just these specific elements. Rather, the repetition here serves as parallelism to heighten emphasis. In keeping with Hebrew construction, the repetition functions to suggest that one should love Yahweh with everything that is within you. In this sense the poetic repetition of specific parts serves as a superlative.[19]

Christologically speaking, this Jewish perspective should caution us against attempts to parse exclusively human or divine functions in Jesus' body, soul, and spirit. The New Testament does indeed use a number of different terms that describe the inner workings of a person, but their meaning should be framed cautiously. The flesh (*soma*, but primarily *sarx*) is often contrasted with the spirit (*pneuma*); the soul (*psuche*) may also be contrasted with the flesh; and, on occasion, the soul can be contrasted with the spirit. The difficulty of offering a specific theology based upon these New Testament texts, however, is that there does not seem to be one technical meaning for these terms; even within the same author, usage seems to vary according to the particular context. Further, there are times when these terms are utilized metaphorically and no ontological definition is supposed by their use. Thus, in the synoptic Gospels, while there are specific mentions of Jesus' spirit, soul, flesh, and mind, one is limited as to the extent to which one may parse Jesus ontologically. Recalling an Old Testament anthropological construal, it may be that what appears to be a component part of Jesus may well be a circumlocution for Himself, or may pertain to His thoughts or motives.

Let us consider specific Scriptures as they relate to Jesus' flesh, His spirit and His soul. Several times Jesus mentions His soul,[20] but again, the uses in the synoptic Gospels are ambiguous.[21] Nor are the mentions of the "spirit" without difficulty. John 6 makes sharp distinction between flesh and spirit, but this is not ontologically oriented toward Jesus Himself. Rather the text attempts to distinguish in a more generic sense that which is spiritual from that which is natural.[22] Even in the narrative of the death of Lazarus, where it is quite likely that the mention of spirit is intended to demonstrate Jesus' inner self, the usage is metaphorical, for otherwise the statement that Jesus "groaned in the spirit" becomes nonsensical.[23]

When we analyze the inner workings of Jesus, the most significant challenge is to explain how it is that He is both God and man—divine and human. As we have insisted, attempts to label certain of these component parts of Jesus as divine or human or to separate deity from humanity readily distorts the Incarnation. For example, let us consider the concept of "mind." In order for Jesus to be human, He had to have a human mind—a center of consciousness that is like other persons'. Further, it is obvious that God has reasoning and cognition. In this ordinary understanding of the word "mind," then, God has a mind. Clearly, if the Incarnation is meaningful at all, it must mean that in the person of Jesus Christ God functions, reasons, and sustains the cosmos. Yet the question as to where the mind of God ends and the mind of Jesus begins is one that is beyond us. The same is true for Jesus' will. Jesus certainly had a human will, and this will was in submission to the will of His Father and He could speak of it as such. Yet, we need to be cautious about attempting to set up two competing wills in Jesus. God was in every cell of Jesus' body, in every internal organ, and in every part of Jesus' inner workings. We must not ever think in terms of Jesus being "half God" and "half man" nor is He two persons. On this the biblical record is very careful in how it speaks. Jesus Christ is no schizophrenic—now acting as God, now acting as human, as if He could not quite fit all that identity into His person. What we can say is that in the miracle of incarnation Jesus was at once truly human and truly divine.

The question is sometimes asked as to whether Jesus had a "fallen nature"; a corollary question is then proffered: if Jesus did not have a fallen nature, how could He be representative of humanity? Such a discussion is fraught with presuppositions. Talking about a fallen nature is a little bit like talking about a "dual nature." It is the kind of language and construct that developed post-biblically. Indeed, much of what is described as a fallen nature owes more to Augustine than it does to the Old Testament, say, or the apostle Paul.

We must not deny the consequences of the fall from Eden; the world is broken. Death and suffering abound. Yet, when talking about fallenness, a typical Pentecostal confession is that humanity now has a propensity toward sin. Further, as to the anthropological question as to what tendencies Jesus did or did not have, we can find direction in the epistles, particularly in Paul. As we shall discuss in subsequent chapters, theologically, Jesus answers to Adam. That is, whatever it is we can say in terms of anthropological tendencies reflected in Jesus correlate to those tendencies that were in Adam as he was in Eden. Certainly in Eden, God created Adam whole, not soiled or sullied in any way. The same could certainly be said of Jesus.

Part of the confusion regarding the anthropology of Jesus relates to the different ways of speaking in the New Testament particularly as it pertains to Jesus' divinity.[24] Some passages make overt identification of Jesus with Yahweh, while others demonstrate Jesus as other than and less than God; still other texts emphasize His being sent from God. We will deal with this variety of texts in some detail in subsequent chapters. Certainly Jesus grew naturally, just as every other child grows. We should consider as heretical narratives in the Gnostic *Gospel of Thomas* that have Jesus speaking overtly as God, demanding obeisance, and making clay pigeons fly.[25] There is no record that the child Jesus spoke with the divine "I." To say otherwise distorts the biblical portrayal of the boy Jesus; the clear presentation of the canonical Gospels. While we know little of the years prior to age thirty, the New Testament record is consistent in suggesting that it was in conjunction with the advent of His ministry that His identity was proclaimed. It was a very human Jesus who made startling claims of divinity. In Jesus there is a permanent coalescing of the human and divine. We agree with Hendrikus Berkhof that one should not speak of two subjects in Jesus, "but his human 'I' is, out of free will, fully and exhaustively permeated by the 'I' of God; and in virtue of this permeation he becomes the perfect instrument of the Father."[26]

Consider this analogy. Pentecostals believe that people can speak under the unction of the Spirit, and because the Spirit is in them, there is a way they may speak with the divine "I," where God Himself speaks prophetically. Yet, this is only an analogy, because this man, Jesus Christ, was given the "Spirit without measure" (John 3:34). He wasn't merely speaking on behalf of God. He was divine.

In conclusion, we would suggest that this is not merely a Oneness issue; it is an incarnational issue. While a number of Trinitarian Christologies have affinity with a Oneness construal by not emphasizing three specific centers of consciousness nor radically separating the human from the divine within Jesus, yet there is a basic ontological difference in their confession. Oneness believers start with the affirmation that it is Yahweh who became incarnate. The typical starting place for Trinitarian Christologies is that the *Logos* became incarnate. We admit that there are challenges of language that must be addressed for Oneness christology to be sustained. A key question, for instance, is how to make sense of Father/Son language which, upon first reading, calls for a clear plurality in understanding. By contrast, though, Trinitarian construals have a whole litany of obstacles to overcome. For instance, was it God the Son praying to God the Father, say, or the human Jesus praying, or some blending of the two? Further, if it was the *Logos* who is incarnate, why are the Spirit, say, and the Father so active in the work of Jesus Christ? While such questions are often answered in terms of the language of *perichoresis*, an "interpenetration" of the Persons of the Godhead, a further set of difficulties is thus introduced in discerning how each Person act(s)/interact(s) within Jesus. While it is possible to offer answers, in the end the answers given begin to resonate less and less with the simplicity of the biblical text.

Implications

Regardless of one's christological perspective, the question of Incarnation must affirm the ontological reality of both the human and the divine in the person of Jesus Christ. The mystery, where it exists, has nothing to do with natures or persons. The question is how it is that God became a man. The question of incarnational anthropology is the question as to how Jesus could be wholly and completely human while being wholly and completely divine. Any christological profession that does not allow for both assertions to be true does not do justice to the identity of Jesus. In chapters 7-12, we will continue to explore this key question as we follow along in the life of Christ. In chapters 13-15, we will explore how a first-century understanding of the anthropology of Jesus was discarded and the church fathers began with a different starting place. We will demonstrate as well how this change in the epistemological starting place ultimately evolved into what came to be fourth- and fifth-century ontological definitions. Unfortunately in the history of the evolving christological pronouncements, far from making the Incarnation more understandable, creedal confessions tended toward the opposite result, the loss of genuine biblical presentation of the true humanity and divinity of Jesus.

Chapter 8

The Man on a Mission

Jesus: A Man Who Believed in Yahweh

Jesus was the unique Son of God by procreation. But there was another equally important way in which He was the Son of God. Like every other son of Adam, He was called by God into covenant, and He had to decide to walk in that covenant. Jesus was God's Son by accepting this covenant. Further, a covenantal relationship is one that requires continued obedience. This was particularly significant for Jesus; Yahweh asked Jesus to accomplish a task unique from every other son of Adam. Jesus' work was to restore completely that which Adam had lost. Thus, while others had been chosen for various tasks as they fulfilled their covenant obligations to Yahweh, no one had been asked to do what Jesus was required to do. Kings had been anointed to reign; priests had been anointed to minister. Yet, their roles paled compared with what Jesus was anointed to accomplish. His mission as a son of Adam was to open the door to a fully restored covenant, and to restore to all humanity what Adam had lost. It is because of the remarkable mission to which He was called that Jesus is named the Anointed One (Greek *Christos*/Hebrew *Meshiach*). In this chapter, our focus is on Jesus' response to His call. We first view Jesus at age twelve but then quickly move to explore Jesus' anointing at His baptism. Finally, we work to understand some of the unique aspects of of Jesus' ministry by investigating the christological hymn from Philippians 2, all in an attempt to explore the mission for which Jesus was called.

Jesus at Age Twelve

The question may be asked as to how old Jesus was when He understood His identity and mission. As we suggested in the previous chapter, despite apocryphal stories that appeared later, the biblical text says virtually nothing about His childhood. We get the first glimpse of Jesus when He was twelve years old and visited the Temple in Jerusalem. Yet, it would be a mistake to deduce that the experience of the twelve-year-old Jesus in Luke 2 should be ascribed to His childhood. Rather, the narrative occurs at the approximate time when in that culture, individuals were understood as moving from the innocence of childhood to the accountability of adulthood.[1] Indeed, the Lukan purpose of the Temple pericope is offered to demonstrate that as Jesus was entering into adulthood, He was living out His covenantal obedience to Yahweh. The exact circumstances surrounding Jesus' visit to the Temple are not clearly stated in the biblical text. It has been suggested that in the background of the narrative is a miscommunication between Jesus and His parents as to which group of family members Jesus would travel with in a return to Nazareth upon leaving Jerusalem after His *bar mitzvah*.[2] Whether this is true or not is not so significant as understanding that Jesus was entering into a time of responsibility as an adult individual.[3] When Joseph and Mary ultimately discovered Jesus after accidentally leaving Him, they found Him sitting among the teachers, who were themselves astounded with His knowledge.[4] In Luke 2:48, though Mary was amazed to find her son among the learned teachers, she asked, "Son, why have you treated us like this? Look, your father and I have been searching for you in great anxiety." Jesus responded, "Why were you searching for me? Did you not know that I must be concerned with what is my Father's [meaning either 'the things of my Father' or 'the house of my Father']?"[5] Although I believe Gottlobb Schrenk to be wrong in his emphasis of Jesus as a child, he is correct insofar as he applies christological significance to the words: "These, [the words 'my Father'] which are plainly Palestinian in origin like those of Matthew testify to the christological precision of the deliberate 'my Father.' According to Luke 2:49, this saying on the lips of the boy Jesus can even presuppose a sense of His unique relation to the 'Father.' "[6] The point of this narrative piece is that at age twelve, Jesus both knew of His identity and mission; what is left unsaid but is implied is that even in the eighteen years that passed between this moment and the inception of His formal ministry, Jesus was obedient and in covenant relationship. This submission to Yahweh manifested itself in submission, as well, to His family at Nazareth. Jesus, though capable at age twelve, was deferent to Mary and Joseph. Luke 2:51 significantly offers that Jesus "was obedient to them" (NLT).

Just like every other person, for Jesus to believe and obey God required faith.[7] If faith was not required, then it would be meaningless for Hebrews to celebrate that Jesus can "sympathize with our weaknesses" for the simple reason that He "was in all points tempted as we are, yet without sin."[8] Further, Jesus had to have faith for His unique origin and mission. How much Mary told Him we cannot know. When it was that He received direction of the Spirit to begin His mission we cannot say. But when the curtain rose at the Jordan River as Jesus was ready to formally begin His ministry, He already knew His mission was to die for humanity's transgression.

When Galatians 2:16 describes the "faithfulness of Christ," it is the faith of the man Jesus—it has reference to His covenant faithfulness.[9] As Bruce Longenecker rightly affirms, the faith of the man Jesus is not merely a Pauline invention; rather, it is a "central component of early Christian understanding about God's covenant righteousness."[10] It is incredible to consider that the man Jesus had to believe that His life made sense, and not merely in context of His birth. The Spirit was calling upon Him to believe that from the foundation of the world, His life was destined to have eternal consequence for every son of Adam. It is in the context of that eternal plan that we shall now consider the biblical proclamation of that mission.

At the Jordan River

Just as the birth of Jesus was a significant moment in salvation history, so too was His baptism, for it was at the Jordan River that Jesus' official mission was publicly offered and accepted. In the Gospel narrative, the events transpire suddenly and are breathtaking. Whether or not His coming that day had initially been a surprise to John, the text does not say; but in any case, the One of whom John had preached, the coming Messiah, stared John in the face. As Jesus came down the muddy slopes of the Jordan to be baptized, John prophetically introduced Him to the crowd: "Behold the Lamb of God who takes away the sin of the world!"[11] It was those words that would be affirmed in the water, for Jesus' call to ministry was two things. It celebrated the majesty of restored covenant while at the same time calling for the ultimate sacrifice for sin.

In a very real way, everything after this point was a denouement in John's life, for He had on this day prepared the way for the man Jesus Christ, the Lamb of God. John's very identity was tied up in the moment, for he described his purpose in connection to a self-identification as Isaiah's voice crying in the wilderness; in this way, he was the voice "preparing the way of Yahweh."[12] In a paradox of incarnation, Jesus is at once identified as Yahweh while at the same time coming to the river to respond to Yahweh's call. For this is the whole point of Jesus' baptism. For though "God was in Christ, reconciling the world to himself," (II Corinthians 5:19) in plunging into Jordan's muddy waters, it was as a man reconciling the world to God that Jesus was commencing specific roles that were uniquely prophesied of Him before He was ever born.

While it was normally only Gentiles who underwent baptism to be born anew and join with the Jewish people as proselytes in covenant relationship,[13] John demanded of the Jews that they too repent and be baptized. For John, there was a new eschatological order, and the Jewish people had to volitionally choose to be a part of it.[14] John only awaited the Messiah, and it was in anticipation of the appearance of the Christ that John baptized. When John recognized Jesus as the Messiah, he had no intention of acquiescing to Jesus' request to be baptized. But Jesus insisted this was necessary to "fulfill all righteousness."[15] Importantly, Jesus was not baptized because of sin or because of His need to turn from a particular path, but He was baptized to be anointed—to inaugurate the mission of which John spoke, one that would ultimately result in His being the "Lamb of God."

That Yahweh chose Jesus at His baptism as the man to fulfill the mission as the "Lamb of God" is not strictly the same as suggesting that the baptism of Jesus is an adoptionist text.[16] Rather it is a "covenant text," the point in time where Yahweh speaks and uniquely commissions.[17] There is in the baptism of Jesus a calling of God, a calling that empowered Jesus for the work He had to do.[18] While Jesus had answered the call of covenant prior to this time, covenant commitment demands continued obedience. John plunged Jesus under the water, and in the context of this baptismal scene two elements appeared that were not a part of any of the other baptisms with which he was involved: a voice, and a visible sign of the dove landing on Jesus. Who all saw the dove and who heard the voice may be argued, but the celebratory nature of this text acknowledges that this was not merely a private sign to the Baptist or a secret vision of Jesus.[19] Nor was this an ontological demonstration of various Persons of the Trinity.[20] While interpreters vary as to the meaning of the dove, commonalty among most interpreters is that the dove as well as the voice are thought to indicate the advent of the eschatological epoch.[21] One thing is certain; this act of initiation gives Jesus authority throughout His entire ministry. [22]

Let us now consider the words of the voice: "You are my beloved Son in whom I am well pleased."[23] This was the voice of Jesus' Father, the One who, though present in Him, and who, though having begotten Him, was now calling Him for a special purpose. To understand this more fully, let us revisit the three principal ways in which one can speak of how God dwelt with humanity. In the Old Testament, the principal truth is that Heaven is the abode of God. There were unique occasions, though, when Yahweh would tangibly and literally be present at times on earth. But these instances were the exceptions, and they were always temporary in nature. Besides dwelling in Heaven or coming as a theophany, a third way in which one could understand God as being present was in a covenant relationship, particularly in the context of worship. Further, as we have offered, to suggest that the abode of God was in Heaven did not limit Him at the same time from ruling the cosmos, controlling, ruling, operating, and sustaining His creation. Because of His power, God could at once rule in the heavens, hear prayer from limitless petitioners, and even demonstrate divine phenomena that emphasized His very presence. Even at the Incarnation, Heaven was still to be considered the abode of God, the permanent dwelling place of God, even while the Creator resided as a man among men. It was Yahweh who became uniquely manifest in the human being Jesus Christ, inextricably integrated into the makeup of this human being from the moment of conception. And from the very first, Jesus understood both His divine origins and His heavenly destination upon accomplishing His work. Thus, while "God was in Christ," Just as God in the Old Testament manifested various phenomena beyond His abode in Heaven, so now God could continue to demonstrate His power and purpose beyond His dwelling place in Christ. It is for this reason that the manifestation of the voice of the Father does not require a separate hypostasis outside of God who was in Christ.

The Gospel narrative does not allow the reader to be privy to the inner conversation in the deepest part of Jesus—the calling as it was delivered and received. But there was an eschatological call in the message; the words offered inaugurated a new age.²⁴ Those who heard would have immediately recognized the source of these words. "You are my beloved son" echoes the prophetic voice of Psalm 2 that we considered in the last chapter, while "in whom I am well pleased" recalls the words of Isaiah 42.²⁵ Further, the words of both Psalm 2 and Isaiah 42 would have been recalled in their original prophetic contexts. We will deal with the Isaiah text in some detail, but let us briefly suggest that Psalm 2 is a royal psalm. This psalm was evidently utilized at coronations of Old Testament kings, and was pronounced as a special blessing of Yahweh's favor. Ben Witherington writes of the use of this psalm: "What is significant is that an individual, when assuming the tasks and functions of the king, is at that point called 'my Son' by the authorizing voice, who perhaps was the priest speaking *vox dei*."²⁶ Thus, Jesus would have had good reason to rejoice at the implied promise of that utterance. As we suggested in chapter 6, there are a number of other points at which this psalm is fulfilled; but here the promise to Jesus is what He ultimately understands to be an eschatological one. Jesus has already been challenged by God's calling on His life as articulated by John to be the Lamb of God. This psalm promises that ultimately the "glory" He already possesses will find full expression in the Ascension—in that despite the cost of restoring covenant between God and man, He must believe that there are rewards of eternal import.

Oscar Cullmann argues convincingly that the phrase "in whom I am well pleased" in John's Gospel is derived from a translation of Isaiah 42:1.²⁷ It is one of the "Servant Songs," those prophetic psalms from Isaiah that called for an individual to be the "Servant of Yahweh" in a unique way. The Servant of Yahweh (*Ebed Yahweh*) was to give His life for the nation.²⁸ Cullmann goes on to say, "Jesus therefore became conscious at the moment of his baptism that he had to take upon himself the Ebed Yahweh role."²⁹ The prophecy of Isaiah is that Yahweh would lay "the iniquity of us all," upon one man who would be stricken "for the transgressions of My people."³⁰ Not only was there the call to suffer, but again, there was intermingled in the same call, a commission to believe that this same suffering would lead to glory. This was not only promised in the portion of the text citing Psalm 2,³¹ but also in the Servant Songs themselves.³²

The dove further confirmed Jesus' anointing. While kings and priests were ordained with anointing oil, and this oil was a demonstration of the imprimatur of their office, so the physical presentation of the dove was the same sort of physical reminder of Jesus' anointing of the Spirit, but it announced a clear eschatological proclamation. This man is the Christ! Jesus was heralded as a man empowered of the Spirit for ministry, called to proclaim a new age where the Spirit will be available to every person. The dove certainly was not a "person." The language of Jesus as Spirit-endowed is the language of mission. It was not the third person of the Trinity who had been resident in Heaven descending to empower the second person of the Trinity. It was the Spirit of God, the very life of Jesus, who was now empowering Him to accomplish the purpose for which He had given Himself, the redemption of the world.

Temptation and Its Purpose

As we shall now begin to explore, Jesus theologically answered to Adam. That is, we shall in the subsequent chapters seek to demonstrate the theological necessity for Jesus' sacrificial work to redeem humanity. Part of that work included temptation, and it began in earnest soon after Jesus' incredible Jordan River experience. Indeed, Jesus left the baptismal scene and went to the desert for a season of fasting and preparing Himself for the challenges of the mission that lay in front of Him. It was during this time of fasting that Satan tempted Jesus. This temptation was not in any sense preliminary to the mission of Christ. It was integral to it. Hebrews 4:15 teaches the man Jesus was "tempted in all points as we are" and yet did not sin. While this series of temptations in the wilderness was one evidence of Jesus being tempted, it does not stand alone. As Cullmann points out, the Greek in Hebrews 4:15 is really quite strong and hardly limits temptation to the time after the baptism of Jesus and Gethsemane. Cullmann offers of Hebrews 4:15, " 'In every point as we are' refers not only to form but also to content."[33]

Recall that the first humans tempted were Adam and Eve; their failure resulted in their expulsion from perfect communion with God. It was that specific loss that was being redressed through the work of Christ. Ultimately, because Jesus never did succumb to temptation but rather fulfilled His sacrificial mission, He was able to begin to "undo" the consequences of the Fall, the ultimate benefit of which will be realized in the eschaton. This theological truth is made plain in a number of biblical texts. One of the most important passages is found in Romans 5, where an extended theological comparison is offered between Adam and Jesus. Paul suggests that while death made its entrance into the world through Adam, it is in

Jesus that "life" is now available.[34] In reference to Adam's sin Paul wrote, "For as by one man's disobedience many were made sinners,[35] so also by one Man's obedience many will be made righteous."[36]

Recall that Adam's sin was his disbelief in God's prohibitions and promises. All of the trees of the Garden were available to the first human couple, but they were prohibited from eating of the tree of the knowledge of good and evil. Satan called this restriction into question, suggesting that God was holding out on them—that, in fact, if they ate from the tree they would actually become like God. He offered Adam and Eve "a shortcut to divinity" that did not require absolute surrender to God. It was theirs, according to Satan, if only they would take that which God claimed as His prerogative alone. And in this act of claiming something that rightfully belonged to God, Adam and Eve made themselves culpable, breaking covenant with Yahweh; though covenant was renewed, it was done so anticipating another human who could reverse the curse and bring complete restoration.

In Satan's several attempts to tempt Jesus in the wilderness, he likewise offered to Jesus the same chance he offered to Adam, that of circumventing the required covenantal directives. Jesus had already accepted His mission to "become the Lamb of God" and suffer for the redemption of the world. But Satan offered Jesus "a shortcut," one that would enable Him to bypass the cross. Satan said, "All these things I will give You if You will fall down and worship me." Jesus' response was to cite Deuteronomy to Satan. "Away with you, Satan! For it is written, 'You shall worship the Lord your God, and Him only you shall serve.'"[37]

Jesus at Nazareth

After Jesus' victory over Satan in the wilderness, He was prepared to officially inaugurate His ministry. He chose to do this in His hometown synagogue in Nazareth on the Sabbath. He was offered a position of honor in reading from the Isaiah scroll, evidently the prescribed reading for that particular day. The passage was messianic. The Messiah, that is, the Anointed One, would accomplish ministry through the power of the Spirit. Jesus read:

> The Spirit of the LORD is upon Me, Because He has anointed Me to preach the gospel to the poor; He has sent Me to heal the

brokenhearted, To proclaim liberty to the captives and recovery of sight to the blind, To set at liberty those who are oppressed; To proclaim the acceptable year of the LORD (Luke 4:18-19).

While there was nothing offensive in the reading of those words, it was the explanation of the text that called for a decision by those who attended synagogue that day. Jesus said, "Today this Scripture is fulfilled in your hearing." This was an incredible claim. Jesus seemed to be announcing both the commencement of the eschatological Year of Jubilee[38] and personally claiming to be Yahweh's Anointed One, the Messiah.

As Jesus predicted in His message, the crowd did not respond favorably to this young man they all knew. In the ensuing uproar, Jesus quietly thwarted their effort to kill Him, and He began in earnest to do the things He announced were His mission. From the very beginning Jesus was opposed in both the spiritual and natural realms from accomplishing His work, but He succeeded in the face of all adversity.

The Philippian Hymn (Philippians 2:6-11)

We have now surveyed two important concepts that are essential in understanding the mission of Jesus and that are the necessary backdrop for understanding the language and concepts undergirding the christological hymn in Philippians.[39] The first concept is the understanding of Jesus as the "suffering Servant of Yahweh." That is, Jesus would suffer, not just for the sins of a nation, but for the sins of the world. The second important concept is that theologically and christologically, Jesus answers to Adam. That is, the mission of Jesus included undergoing the same kinds of temptation Adam did.

Before proceeding to the Philippian hymn, let us focus a bit more on this second concept. There are numerous Pauline texts where Jesus is theologically compared with Adam. First Corinthians makes a comparison between Adam and Christ that is tied to the eschaton. (See I Corinthians 15:22.) Further, throughout Romans Adam is referenced, even at times when it is only a passing allusion to humanity.[40] C. K. Barrett puts it aptly: "Whenever in Paul we meet the word *man* (or other words, as *image*, used in Gen i–iii), we may suspect that Adam is somewhere in the background."[41]

It is this understanding that is important when coming to the opening stanza of the christological hymn in Philippians. The hymn begins with the phrase "Who being in the form of God." Some take this to mean that Jesus had a divine nature in a preexistent heavenly existence, from which He would become incarnate.[42] But to read the text in this way is to begin by presupposing that specific interpretation into the text.[43] As Jerome Murphy-O'Connor points out, to interpret this passage as a *kenosis*[44] by Jesus from a heavenly realm results from a particular doctrinal presupposition, "an acceptance that is facilitated by the dogmatic understanding of Christ as the Second Person of the Trinity."[45] In point of fact, far from being a description of Jesus' divine essence, "Who being in the form of God" recalls the language of Genesis and the creation of Adam. Thus, it is a declaration of Jesus' humanity, one that draws its language from Adam.[46] In this regard, a number of scholars have worked to demonstrate that the word translated "image" could not have reference to deity but must refer to humanity.[47] Murphy-O'Connor points out that the text does not say Christ was in fact in the *form* of God. For Murphy-O'Connor, the Greek disallows "equality" in the strict sense of the term.[48] Thus, like Adam, Jesus was made in the image of God; yet, unlike Adam, He was sinless. As Bakken puts it, "He is the man God intended man to be."[49]

The second phrase of the stanza reads, "did not regard equality with God a thing to be grasped" (NAS). While some translations presuppose the text to mean that the preexistent Son did not suppose that equality with God was a thing He was not afraid to lose,[50] the text means something else altogether. Indeed, the text has reference to the man Jesus, who, like Adam, was tempted. Yet, unlike Adam, He did not grasp at divine prerogatives.[51]

Verse 7 begins, "but made Himself of no reputation" (NKJV). Some translations, those that read the text as a preexistent Son becoming incarnate, translate the phrase: "but emptied Himself" (NAS).[52] The underlying Greek verb (*kenoo*) has been the basis of incredible amount of historical speculation. *Kenosis*, then, has been historically defined as the "lowering" that took place when the preexistent Son underwent some sort of self-limiting of divine attributes in the Incarnation. While the majority of scholars still see this sort of *kenosis* in the Philippian hymn, many scholars have rejected this reading of the text. Charles Talbert, for instance, finds what he deems to be "obvious difficulties" in interpreting the text with reference to the preexistence of Christ.[53] Rather, for Talbert, the text is about the man Jesus who did not succumb to temptation. Unlike Adam, He did not vie for divine prerogatives but rather He humbled Himself.

We have waited until now to introduce this hymn, for it reflects the theological purpose of the mission of Jesus Christ. Jesus willingly accepted the anointing God gave Him to be the Lamb of God that would take away the sin of the world. Further, by overcoming temptation, Jesus knew His work would work toward the complete restoration of humanity marred by Adam's transgression. Yet to be the representative man had certain complications. It affected Jesus' thoughts and actions. It restricted Him as to what He could do and say. We will explore these implications further in the next chapter, "The Man Who Taught about Yahweh."

Chapter 9

The Man Who Taught about Yahweh

Introduction

The way a person speaks is often dictated by the role in which that person is placed. For instance, a statesman might speak one way while giving an official speech to a large audience. That same statesman would speak differently giving instructions to an administrative assistant, and still yet another way while at home eating supper with his family. The statesman does not cease being a statesman when he goes home; yet his demeanor is different when he is with his wife and children than it is when he is acting in official capacity. When considering how it was that Jesus spoke, we must first understand that He was both human and divine. There were instances when Jesus spoke as only God can speak. For example, it is not possible for any man but Jesus to pronounce while healing a paralytic, "Son, your sins are forgiven you."[1] Still, most of Jesus' speaking was different in kind than this. Indeed, most of the time Jesus sounded like a man who was pointing people toward God. Let us consider briefly the various roles that Jesus was fulfilling, for they greatly influenced the way He taught.

Recall that theologically, Jesus' mission entailed succeeding in the same areas where Adam failed. Although the physical and cultural location was different, still there were important commonalties between Jesus and Adam. Whereas covenant faithfulness required Adam to properly tend the garden, covenant faithfulness for Jesus required Him to live an exemplary life within culture, and to learn, to grow, and to obey. While obedience was primarily to His parents in His early life, when Jesus started His ministry, He was called to be in constant obedience to Yahweh. Hebrews makes the powerful statement that "though [Jesus] was a Son, yet He learned obedience by the things which He suffered" (Hebrews 5:8). The verse does not mean that Jesus was first disobedient and then became obedient; rather, Jesus learned obedience experientially by His faithful living even when in specific instances, His faithfulness was in the face of suffering.

Further, because Jesus theologically answers to Adam, then the same human limitations that were on Adam had to apply to Jesus Christ.[2] Consider the temptation of Jesus in the wilderness. No matter what Satan tempted Jesus to do, Jesus' response to the temptation was to answer him back from Scripture. How was it that Jesus offered just the right scriptural passage back into the teeth of Satan? Some suppose the Spirit that indwelt Jesus prompted Him with the correct response. But there is yet another possibility. Indeed, it was as a boy that Jesus was instructed in the Torah and committed vast portions of it to memory. In one of the great paradoxes of incarnation, though the Spirit in Him inspired the text, yet it was up to Jesus to learn it by rote, to study it, and no doubt contemplate its meaning.[3] Jesus answered Satan in the same way Adam should have answered: He rebuked him with the known commands of Yahweh.

Further, when at His baptism Jesus received the official call to a mission that would end in death, He did not refuse. Willingly, Jesus took on the role of the Servant of Yahweh as prophesied by Isaiah. There were some aspects of this Servant's role that offered the promise of incredible rewards to Jesus. In what amounted to an astonishing prediction, Isaiah prophesied that the Servant of Yahweh would ultimately be glorified.[4] Regrettably, though, before the Servant would be glorified, He had to willingly choose to suffer, humble Himself in self-abasement, and ultimately give up His life. Further, before His glorification, the Servant's role was to reflect Yahweh's character and direct attention to God. Thus, two roles Jesus had to fulfill were the role of the Servant of Yahweh and the role of a Son who in obedience to Yahweh and unlike Adam did not grasp at divine prerogatives.

A central component of Jesus' mission was to teach about Yahweh, both by His words and by His actions. Looking back at how Jesus fulfilled this requirement, the christological hymn in Hebrews 1 rejoices in the character of Christ. The writer of Hebrews declares in verse 3 that Jesus is the "express image of [God's] person"; that is, Jesus in His humanity is "an exact representation" of what God was like.[5] Both by His words and actions Jesus Christ succeeded; for as an obedient Son, this man, whose very life was Yahweh, in His humanity averted attention from Himself in order to reveal Yahweh to the world. Further, not only did Jesus demonstrate God's virtue; He also revealed the awe and power of God as well. Hebrews 1:3 further declares of the man Jesus, "who being the brightness of *His* glory." That is, Jesus as a man was called upon to shine forth the brightness of God's glory.

One way Jesus demonstrated Yahweh's glory was through miracles. These miracles were selective and had a specific purpose. That purpose was not to entirely rid the world of sickness or of death. Indeed, the world will not be free of its brokenness until the eschaton. Rather, Jesus did miracles to teach about Yahweh and to demonstrate His glory. This mission is confirmed elsewhere in the New Testament. Second Corinthians 4:4 suggests that Satan, as the god of this world, works diligently to blind those who do not believe, "lest the light of the gospel of the glory of Christ, who is the image of God, should shine on them." That is to say, God reveals His message of salvation through the "light" of Christ Jesus. In II Corinthians 4:6, Paul teaches that God commanded the light "to shine out of darkness" and furthermore, God has "shone in our hearts to give the light of the knowledge of the glory of God in the face of Jesus Christ." These passages demonstrate Jesus' unique role in speaking and acting as an obedient Son such that He would shine forth God's power and reveal God's virtue, yet demanding no accolades for Himself.

The question may well be asked as to how Jesus could, on the one hand defer glory to God, while on the other hand teach people about His real identity. One only needs to read the Gospel account to see how Jesus worked to accomplish this. For example, despite the fact that crowds followed Him, Jesus was not a crowd pleaser. He often ran from the multitudes. Further, not only did Jesus not always answer questions that were asked; sometimes He seemed downright rude to people. For instance, consider the very troubling passage where a man sincerely asked Jesus, "Good Teacher, what shall I do that I may inherit eternal life?" Jesus responded with a question of His own. He asked, "Why do you call Me good? No one is good but One, that is, God" (Mark 10:17-18). Taken as a proof text, the passage strips Jesus not only of His deity but also of His goodness, yet the Gospels cannot be read in this way. This passage underscores a method Jesus utilized to challenge people to receive revelation. It was the desire of Jesus that the man who asked the question go beyond rules and regulations; Jesus invited him into relationship. But this could only happen if this man were to grapple his way toward truth. It was in this manner of teaching that Jesus was at once able to answer to Adam theologically, maintain the Ebed Yahweh role, and still speak in a way that let people understand His identity and mission.

In attempting to address such speaking, I wrote an allegory where a Commander secretly takes on the role of a private in the army to root out evil and corruption.[6] In the novel, the "private" speaks about the character of the Commander in the third person. Even when the other soldiers in his platoon do not comprehend what he is doing, the Commander/private rescues them from any number of difficulties. After discreetly giving word that a young man should be saved from the sergeant's wrath by being sent to sick bay, the Commander (incognito as Private Christopher Adams) is approached by one of the men in the platoon whose name is Butch Peterson. Peterson begins:

> "Hey, Adams, you need to level with me about something. I'm not the smartest guy in the world, but even I know that it is impossible to get anyone to listen to you in this Army. You couldn't have been gone five minutes; but when you came back, it was all settled. What's the deal?"
>
> "Butch, I asked you to trust me, remember? Let's not talk about it."
>
> Peterson challenged, "You've got pull then, huh?"
>
> "Butch, let's not talk about it."
>
> "Chris, if you've got so much pull, why don't you get yourself transferred to another platoon?"
>
> "I suppose I could do a lot of things," Adams said. "But, Butch, what if I told you that I was in this platoon for some purpose? What if I told you that there was a very great difference between the Commander and the others? What if, in fact, the Commander was good, and others were not good? What if the difference was as great as night and day?"
>
> Peterson responded honestly. "I hate to say it, Adams, but I'm confused."
>
> "All right, then, let me get as plain as I can. Did it ever occur to you that the Commander was really concerned about his troops; not that he was just trying to put down rebellion, but that he was really concerned? What would he do if he wanted to make his presence known to the worst platoon in the military?"

A sparkle of revelation began to lighten Peterson's eyes. "Do you mean to tell me that he sent you to our platoon because he is actually concerned about us?"

Adams smiled, "In a manner of speaking . . . yes."

Peterson rubbed his chin and made an honest reply. "You know, Chris, I want to believe that . . . but it sounds too good to be true!"[7]

Later, Butch is concerned that Adams is going to be killed by the sergeant and takes matters into his own hands. Adams confronts him, saying:

Did you really think that you could influence the Lieutenant?"

Peterson turned, startled. "But how did you know that I . . ." he began, forgetting his anger.

"You're pretty self-righteous, aren't you Butch?" Adams was upset. Peterson could see it in his face.

"But I was only trying to . . ."

"I know exactly what you were trying to do. You want it all your way, Butch. You'll follow the Commander only if he uses your plan and gets rid of all the problems out of your life. Do you think for one minute that he owes you anything?"

"But, Chris, I did it for you," complained Butch.

"You did it because you don't trust the Commander. In fact, you don't trust anyone."

"That's not true," argued Peterson in his own defense. "I trust you, but how can I trust a Commander who willfully plans your death?"

Christopher Adams was more reconciling now. "Butch, you don't understand it all now, but someday you will. You need to believe me when I tell you that I'm acting of my own free will. I tell you Butch, the Commander is no ogre. I promise you that. I know him like no one else does."

"Chris, I believe in you!" said Peterson in a voice thick with emotion. "I don't always understand you, but I trust you. I've watched you. The sergeant is evil, but I know that you're good."

"Butch, it's not enough to believe that Private Christopher Adams is a good man. I came from the Commander, and I'm going back to the Commander. If he's not a good man, then I'm not a good man."

"But, Chris..."
"There's only one way to follow the Commander; it's all or nothing. Anything else is not really following. Butch... don't lead—follow."
Peterson didn't understand everything, but he knew he was ready. Maybe he would never understand everything. He began his profession slowly, *"If the Commander... is anything like you... then I'll trust him and serve him totally."*[8]

Jesus' Language about the Father

In the book, the Commander (a.k.a. Christopher Adams) reaches out to those in the platoon with what seems at times to be rather convoluted and confusing language. He does so because he seeks to have a genuine relationship with the men in the military; one not based upon the authority of his office, but on their understanding of his authentic goodness. Thus, as we have continued to suggest, though it is true that "God was in Christ, reconciling the world to himself," yet Jesus often spoke as if God were remote from Him. Sometimes Jesus' language was misunderstood; sometimes it was understood perfectly, but the claims that it called for were rejected. In either case, Jesus seemed quite settled with the ambiguity and was willing to let revelation seep in to His audience gradually. Jesus' words were sometimes gentle; other times harsh. In His attempt to reveal the character of Yahweh He did not mind speaking in ways that were confusing or that broke convention. Let us consider briefly how Jesus challenged the sensibility of culture when He taught His disciples to speak to Yahweh.

As we have noted previously, Jesus lived at a time when the name of Yahweh was not spoken.[9] Instead circumlocutions that made Him more distant were employed. Yahweh was "the Most High," or "the Name," or "*Adonai*." Yet, despite this, Jesus taught His disciples to call God "*abba*." *Abba* is an Aramaic word, for conversationally and in teaching, Jesus spoke Aramaic.[10] When Jesus spoke of God as *Abba*, He was speaking the Aramaic equivalent of "Daddy." "*Abba*" (daddy) and "*imma*" (dear mother) were generally the first words a Jewish child uttered.[11] In that culture, to call Yahweh "*abba*" would have generally been viewed as offensive and sacrilegious. "Daddy" was a strange way to talk about the deity, for it was an expression of a close and dependent relationship. Thus, when Jesus taught His disciples to pray in words rightly translated as "Our

Daddy who is in heaven," (Matthew 6:9) it is no wonder Jesus' audience was often puzzled.

Another example of language difficult to understand is found in John 8. From a Oneness perspective, at first reading, it is very challenging to understand. The Pharisees accused Jesus: "You bear witness of Yourself; Your witness is not true." Often, when challenged to defend His authority, Jesus refused.[12] Yet, on this occasion, He made an extended defense. Jesus offered, "It is also written in your law that the testimony of two men is true. I am One who bears witness of Myself, and the Father who sent Me bears witness of Me." Because Jesus appealed to Deuteronomy from passages that called for at least two people who actually witnessed something in order to establish truth (Deuteronomy 17:6; 19:15), one could readily understand His words as an appeal of a person who existed apart from and independent from Himself. Taken at face value, this undermines a Oneness perspective. Yet, there is more to this challenge than an affirmation of two persons in the Godhead. Indeed, Jesus' language was utilized purposely to challenge His accusers to deal with the question as to who Jesus' Father actually was. At that time, there was a rumor floating around that Jesus was illegitimate (John 8:41), so no doubt his hearers were taken aback that Jesus would dare appeal to His Father as witness. As an itinerate rabbi, the whole situation could have been potentially embarrassing for Him.

In actuality, Jesus did not need to refer to His Father. Jesus' initial response to the accusation was that He did not require two witnesses; He said, "Even if I bear witness of Myself, My witness is true, for I know where I came from and where I am going; but you do not know where I come from and where I am going." In this, Jesus was making an enigmatic statement predicting His crucifixion and glorification. Further, while they couldn't quite understand Him, Jesus was also uttering a riddling threat of God's judgment. Then, in an interesting turn of phrase, Jesus offered, "You judge according to the flesh; I judge no one. And yet if I do judge, My judgment is true; for I am not alone, but I am with the Father who sent Me." Note that Jesus chided them for judging only by what they could see. Then, He challenged them to understand how it was that even at that very moment He was not alone. His Father was with Him in some way. From the perspective of His accusers, He certainly looked alone. Yet, He stubbornly professed otherwise. Obviously, they saw no father. It was only at this point that Jesus quoted the Torah with regard to the need for two witnesses. Finally, Jesus got what He sought for all along. Their curiosity was piqued. They asked, "Where is Your Father?" Jesus challenged, "You know neither Me nor My Father. If you had known Me, you would have known My Father also." Amazingly, Jesus enigmatically claimed His divinity even while being faithful to His role as Servant of Yahweh.

It is no wonder that even Jesus' most intimate followers were confused at times. Jesus stated, "I am the way, the truth, and the life. No one comes to the Father except through Me." He continued, "If you had known Me, you would have known My Father also; and from now on you know Him and have seen Him." This was simply too much for Philip, who insisted, "Lord, show us the Father, and it is sufficient for us." Jesus responded, "Have I been with you so long, and yet you have not known Me, Philip? He who has seen Me has seen the Father; so how can you say, 'Show us the Father'? Do you not believe that I am in the Father, and the Father in Me? The words that I speak to you I do not speak on My own authority; but the Father who dwells in Me does the works" (John 14:7-10). Even though Jesus explained this to them, for the time being His disciples remained confused. It was only later that revelation would come.[13]

Typically, Jesus refused to offer a direct answer to the question as to His messianic identity.[14] For instance, in John 10, the Jews surrounded Him and badgered Him to answer whether He were the Christ. John records that Jesus answered them, "I told you, and you do not believe. The works that I do in My Father's name, they bear witness of Me." In this instance, Jesus took no credit for Himself. There is an oblique reference to His divinity (My Father's Name),[15] but He made them work to figure it out. They were not inclined, so He continued to challenge them to search for understanding about His Father. First, He attributed the safety of the "sheep" He was calling to Himself, for He held them in His hand. Then, abruptly, He said that these sheep were in His Father's hand. Then Jesus said, "I and My Father are one." The Jews would not at all have thought that Jesus was claiming to be a second divine person. They were furious because they recognized He was claiming to be Yahweh. Consequently, they picked up stones in preparation to stone Him for what they deemed to be blasphemy. In this case as in other cases we have surveyed, Jesus made the declaration of His divinity in a way that gave glory to God.

Jesus' Language about the Holy Spirit

Compared with Father/Son language, there is very little mention in the Gospels regarding the Spirit. Jesus was filled with the Spirit and was led by the Spirit. (See Luke 4:1; 4:18.) But these allusions are sparse in narrative, and where they do occur, the Spirit serves as a circumlocution for God. When Jesus speaks of the Spirit, He typically speaks enigmatically, for He is introducing the age of the Spirit, one which is closely tied with His own identity. No one had yet been filled with the Spirit, nor would they be until Jesus was glorified,[16] yet Jesus proleptically invited people to be filled with the Spirit.[17]

There are some references in the Gospel where the Spirit does seem to be separate and independent. For instance, we may at first be tempted to draw a distinction in persons when Jesus mentioned blasphemy against the Holy Spirit. Jesus said in Matthew 12:32 that someone speaking against the Son of Man could be forgiven, but speaking against the Holy Spirit could not be forgiven. This passage certainly sounds as if Jesus were making a clear distinction between Himself and the Spirit. Yet, in Jesus' teaching about the Holy Spirit, no distinction of persons need be implied. Jesus, in His role as the Servant of Yahweh, was only gradually revealing His work and purpose. It is this kind of oblique speaking that has direct relationship with what Jesus said about blasphemy against the Holy Spirit. As Procksch notes, it is possible that "sin against the Son of Man is committed in ignorance and may be pardoned. In the πνεῦμα ἅγιον [Holy Spirit] of the Pentecostal age, however God manifests Himself through Christ." Because of this, *TDNT* explains that only one who is "apprehended" by the Holy Spirit, and resists His power has the possibility of blasphemy.[18] Hence, blasphemy of the Spirit has more to do with the time in which it occurs than any distinction between Jesus and the Spirit.[19] As Schweitzer notes, the exaltation of Christ "sets Christ in the realm of the Spirit, and that union with Him ensures believers spiritual life, which is life in the community."[20]

Another potentially problematic text for Oneness adherents revolves around Jesus' discourse at the Last Supper. On the eve of His crucifixion, Jesus attempted to prepare His disciples for the age of the Spirit. In a number of ways He spoke enigmatically of His death and glorification; yet the disciples did not understand because they had no basis of experience from which to make sense of what He was saying. Everything Jesus said was new to them. It is for this reason that Jesus framed His language in a variety of ways; just as one must turn a diamond carefully in the light to see all the beauty in the various facets, so Jesus wanted them to reflect and consider. It is in this way that Jesus spoke of the phenomenon of the Spirit. The Spirit would come and teach of Him; Jesus would send the Spirit; Jesus Himself would come; Jesus would have the Father send the Spirit.

The challenge, of course, was for Jesus to get His disciples to understand that He would no longer physically be present with them, but that in reality He would be with them in some other fashion. In another place, Jesus offered, "For where two or three are gathered together in My name, I am there in the midst of them" (Matthew 18:20). But, of course, though Jesus would literally be with His disciples, they could not readily understand how this was to be accomplished. Jesus explained in John 14:16-18:

> And I will pray the Father, and He will give you another Helper, that He may abide with you forever—the Spirit of truth, whom the world cannot receive, because it neither sees Him nor knows Him; but you know Him, for He dwells with you and will be in you. I will not leave you orphans; I will come to you.

In this passage, Jesus works to reveal Himself as the Spirit of Truth. The apostles seemed to think that Jesus was already at that moment fulfilling what He said was the promise of the Spirit. One of them asked, "Lord, how is it that You will manifest Yourself to us, and not to the world?" But not only would the Spirit be available to them; it would be open for everyone. The difficulty in teaching this new truth was that the apostles "knew too much" about the Spirit already. They understood that the Spirit moved on the waters in Creation. To speak of the Spirit was to speak of Yahweh in action. Thus, their experience disallowed their understanding. Jesus needed to convey that while the reception of the Spirit involved Yahweh, it also involved Him. Further, He tried to help them see that this experience was yet future, and that this encounter with the Spirit would be universal. Jesus offered, "If anyone loves Me, he will keep My word; and My Father will love him, and We will come to him and make Our home with him."

For some, Jesus' use of "we" as well as the other language from this discourse necessarily demonstrates a plurality of persons in the Godhead. After all, in anyone's estimation, a "we" cannot be made to be one person. Yet, let us consider more specifically how Jesus defined the Spirit in this passage. Speaking of believers (whom He had just spoken about receiving the Spirit), He said that it would be both the Father and the Son who would be making their home in an individual. Certainly Jesus was not speaking substantively, for if so, He was in fact equating the Holy Spirit as being the ontological equivalent of both the Father and Son together! What Jesus was trying to challenge His disciples to understand was that because of the work of the cross, the Spirit would be available in a new and different way.

Jesus was explaining to His disciples that they would receive the Spirit in a way they did not yet understand, that there would be a way the Spirit was different than the Spirit who hovered above the waters in Creation. Robert Sabin suggests that Jesus' words demonstrate how the post-resurrection Spirit is invested with a "christological hue."[21] That is, just as the tint of a glass in a window or in sunglasses casts a hue related to the color in which the glass is tinted, so, analogously, the Spirit we receive is necessarily "tinted" by Calvary's sacrifice. There is, then, an experiential difference between the working of the Spirit in the Old and the New Testaments. The Spirit we receive is the resident Spirit of Christ. Analogously, like astronauts' space suits, whose value is enhanced because they have been worn to the moon,[22] or like clothes that now have added value because Lincoln wore them, so the Spirit of God is now forever the Spirit of Christ, inextricably "colored" by the Incarnation. While Jesus was speaking enigmatically, He wanted His disciples to know that the Spirit would soon be available in a way no one had yet experienced. Yet His use of the "we" is not to explain that Father and Son are together standing in for the Spirit. It is Jesus' attempt to demonstrate the new way in which God's Spirit will be available to all, colored with a hue inextricably linked to the Incarnation and "washed by blood of Calvary."

Jesus' Language about "Divine Origins"

The biblical truth is that the abode of God is Heaven. This truth was demonstrated throughout the Old Testament and will remain true throughout eternity. The Jews understood Heaven to contain the throne of God. Prayers were answered from Heaven. It was to Heaven that appeals were made in times of crisis. Further, when Jesus ascended, the biblical truth is that Heaven will be His permanent abode. There was, in fact, only one brief period of time when Heaven was not in actuality the "dwelling place of God." That occurred during the thirty-three years that spanned the life of Christ on earth. Like a king who has put on commoner's clothes could speak in the third person of the love that the king had for his people, so God came near in the Incarnation. Thus, when Jesus in modeling prayer taught His disciples to pray to "Our Father in heaven" (Luke 11:2) this was entirely proper, for Heaven was, and would continue to be the permanent abode of God.

There is further reason why Jesus would speak of God as if He were remote from Him. Jesus as a man had a specific mission to fulfill. He was Yahweh's Suffering Servant. And perhaps more significantly in terms of how He spoke, He was the representative man, theologically answering to Adam. His speech had to be such that it did not go beyond language and conduct that was proper for any son of Adam. As we have suggested, this colored His speaking, His actions and His very thoughts, and explains in part the *kind* of speaking Jesus did. Thus, just as Adam had a God who was "other," so Jesus spoke of God at times as if He were remote. Just as every other son of Adam referred to Heaven as God's dwelling place, so Jesus did as well. And while He may have been present as "a king in commoner's clothes," only with the greatest caution did He declare His deity.

Jesus, in explaining His mission or divine origin, could rightfully and enigmatically use language that described His coming from the Father. Thus, when John 3:16 records Jesus saying "For God so loved the world, that he gave his only Son," the confession does not mean that Jesus was sent from a heavenly to an earthly world. Rather, this has reference to Jesus' mission as well as the fact that His existence derived of divine origin.

Even when Jesus claimed these divine origins, it was not done so in the context to awe His audience. As we have suggested, He ran from any such exhibitions or attempts to exalt Himself. Consider the sequence of events in John 6. After He miraculously fed the people Jesus reached the pinnacle of His popularity. The crowd wanted to make Him a king by force, so Jesus simply fled.[23] The next day, Jesus talked about bread in a way that made His audience need to reach more deeply to understand Him. He expressed it by saying "I am the living bread which came down from heaven. If anyone eats of this bread, he will live forever; and the bread that I shall give is My flesh, which I shall give for the life of the world."[24] When they questioned such a claim, He offered further, "Most assuredly, I say to you, unless you eat the flesh of the Son of Man and drink His blood, you have no life in you." These statements enigmatically revealed His divine origins, but in a way that required no easy commitment from His hearers. Jesus used bread as a metaphor for His identity. In so doing, He said that His flesh (the bread) came down from heaven. (See John 6:51, 58.) This, of course, was not literally true, for the clear teaching of the New Testament is that Jesus was a Jew, descending from both David and Abraham.[25] However, while Jesus was neither a preexistent Son nor did He have preexistent heavenly flesh, He was speaking both of His mission and of His identity. Biologically, half of Jesus' chromosomes came from God, and the very life that was in Him was Yahweh. Jesus was inviting the hearers to move beyond the miracles He did for them and work toward revelation as they participated in genuine relationship. Nonetheless, the audience could not go beyond an easy answer, and the Gospel writer reports, "From that time many of His disciples went back and walked with Him no more" (John 6:66).

Jesus' Language about the Son of Man

It is not uncommon when reading theological works on christology to find various studies on the numerous titles ascribed to Jesus in order to demonstrate His true identity.[26] We have largely avoided such an approach for a number of reasons. Donald Juel does not miss the mark when he suggests, "Titles frequently overlap in meaning to a considerable extent, and the alleged construct to which the titles refer may prove to be the product of scholarly creativity in the present."[27] There are, however, certain titles that are important to our focus. We have dealt briefly with "Savior" and "Lord" and "Christ." We will revisit these titles and functions in chapter 11 when we speak of the glorification of Jesus. Briefly though, we need to address the title, "Son of Man," for it is arguably Jesus' primary self-designation, one utilized throughout the pages of the Gospels. While the church later came to declare a kind of dialectic profession where "Son of Man" refers to Jesus' humanity and "Son of God" refers to Jesus' deity, this was not the first-century understanding of these titles. There is a significant and varied tradition as to the usage and meaning of the "Son of Man." Indeed, it is the very enigmatic nature of the title that no doubt allowed Jesus to utilize it as a teaching tool. "Son of Man" is a title that was utilized by Jesus in several different ways, some of which were rather remarkable.

One source as to the identity of Son of Man was understood to derive from Daniel 7, where there is a vision of the "Ancient of Days" who gives a scroll to the "Son of Man," one then empowered with authority and glory. (See Daniel 7:7-14.) Interpretations as to the identity of this "Son of Man" from the passage are varied. As with other books written in an apocalyptic genre, figures that appear in Daniel are often symbolic of peoples and events. Thus, a fairly common interpretation as to the identity of the Son of Man comes from the text itself; the "Son of Man" is identified as the elect among the Jewish people.[28] Yet prophetic tropes can be made to carry considerable weight, and because Daniel 7 uses the language of the Son of Man "coming on the clouds of heaven," having an "everlasting rule" and that "his kingship will never come to an end" (Daniel 7:13-14), and because Enochic tradition more fully develops an understanding of the Son of Man as a heavenly redeemer, the title came to have eschatological import. For some, the "Son of Man" was a coming heavenly redeemer. Thus, when Jesus used "Son of Man" to refer to Himself, He elicited considerable curiosity.[29] Indeed, there were points in Jesus' ministry where His use of "Son of Man" compelled people to wonder whether He was claiming to be a "heavenly redeemer," operating in cosmic power.[30]

There was another way in which the title "Son of Man" was utilized around the time of Christ. A rabbi might employ the term "Son of Man" as a circumlocution to speak of himself,[31] something Jesus did as well. For the most part Jesus did not utilize the title in a way that would make people think of heavenly power and glory; although Jesus used the term in rather fluid ways, a good number of times He seems to link the usage of the "Son of Man" with His identity as Yahweh's Suffering Servant.[32] As we have begun to suggest, the title was thus consonant with Jesus' propensity to speak in riddles, challenging His listeners to contemplate His identity. While Jesus could proclaim that the Son of Man had power to forgive sins[33] and power over the Sabbath,[34] none of this was to overtly grasp divine prerogatives. In one particular instance, He said, "Foxes have holes and birds of the air have nests, but the Son of Man has nowhere to lay His head."[35] In short, Jesus furthered His mission by the use of this title, arguably offering it as a kind of tease. Additionally, as we shall see in the next chapter, Jesus could utilize this title in a key moment of revelation. Finally, as we shall explore in chapter 11, the use of Son of Man in the Book of Revelation ultimately works towards a full-orbed understanding of the identity and work of Jesus Christ.

Jesus' Language about the "I AM"

Given that the primary role of Jesus was to demonstrate to people the love Yahweh had for them and not take to Himself divine prerogatives,

Jesus' use of "I AM" sayings,[36] seems to contradict His mission. After all, such statements can communicate nothing less than His absolute identification with the God of the Old Testament.[37] Raymond Brown demonstrates that while most of these occur in the Gospel of John,[38] there are "I AM" statements in the Synoptic Gospels as well.[39] But these should not be understood as Jesus broadly proclaiming His identity. These were not common proclamations delivered regularly to the masses. Rather, Jesus seems to have delivered these pronouncements in two ways. First, Jesus delivered "I AM" sayings in situations where not only did He not glorify Himself but rather put Himself in harm's way. That is, He delivered these claims as challenges to the Jewish leaders just precisely because those words would be such an affront. Thus, when in John 8:58 Jesus said, "Before Abraham was, I am," His claim of absolute identity was delivered into the teeth of His enemies. It required a response and challenged these folks to seriously consider His claims. But rather than give these religious leaders pause, their response was to reject Him. They picked up stones to stone Him.

A second way Jesus utilized the "I AM" sayings was to privately open up a more intimate understanding of Himself to a few individuals. An example of this is found in John 4, where He was seeking to demonstrate His identity to a Samaritan woman. At Jacob's well at midday Jesus gently reached out to a woman who in so many ways had no claim to the truth He was sharing. Her conception of the Torah was muddled, her religious views were syncretic, her own personal life seemed to be in shambles, and her understanding of the Messiah was flawed. Yet, when she confessed hope that some day a messiah would come who could teach her right doctrine, Jesus responded, "I who speak to you am He" (John 4:26). Underlying this proclamation in the Greek is His profession: "I AM." Like God speaking His very name to Moses at the burning bush in a covenantal invitation, so Jesus, too, offered covenant relationship to this woman. His was not a proclamation to a crowd, just His personal invitation to a forlorn woman alone at a well: "I AM." And while her conception of the Messiah was different than normative Jewish understanding,[40] Jesus took this private moment to reveal to her the most significant truth He could share.

Another place where there begins to be a profusion of "I AM" statements was in the hours Jesus spent with His disciples just prior to the Crucifixion. As the cross loomed larger, and Jesus' life and ministry progressed, He revealed more of His identity to those closest to Him.[41] Indeed, it was in the shadow of the cross that Jesus worked to give His apostles their deepest understanding. The Bible gives us entrance into the sacred hours leading up to Calvary, a study we will pursue in the next chapter.

In this chapter, we have focused on the way in which specific roles and capacities influenced the words of Jesus. It amounted to a brief survey, an overview that could not address every situation where Jesus spoke in a unique circumlocution or in a particularly enigmatic way. Still, the verses addressed were offered to be suggestive of other verses of the same kind. That said, some of the most significant ways in which Jesus spoke and acted are related to the crucifixion and glorification of Christ. Thus, in the next chapters we turn our focus from specific idioms and sayings related to Jesus in order to focus on particular salvific events. We will still continue to highlight some of the unique language and perspective offered by Jesus Christ when speaking, particularly as His language relates to these unique moments in salvation history.

Chapter 10

The Man Who Was Crucified

In the Shadow of the Cross

The Gospel narratives are uneven in presentation, moving swiftly from Jesus' birth into His adulthood; weeks and months are represented by a few sermons, specific conversations, and specific miracles along with summary statements. Only when the narrative approaches the cross does the story move with deliberate exactness. The last week of the life of Christ is given in considerable detail. Time ticks even more slowly in the hours just prior to the cross. The reader feels the intense struggle, hears the words of love, and senses the impending betrayal and ultimate abandonment of Jesus. Certainly the earliest church celebrated these events leading up to the cross in preaching, confessional proclamation,[1] and in partaking of the Lord's Supper. Because the cross is in fact God's eternal redemptive focus, the narrative emphasis itself is a kind of theology.

As we have suggested, Jesus taught in such a way as to require those seeking to discover His work and identity to consider everything He said in the context of the events that would transpire. Particularly as He spoke of the meaning of the cross, Jesus was difficult to understand. It was difficult for the disciples to distinguish a specific chronology or even to measure the importance of the startling things Jesus was sharing. Compounding this was that for Jesus, the closer He got to the cross, the more future eschatological hope blended together with present reality; He seemed to live in two worlds at once.

Consider that in one intimate conversation Jesus told His disciples that "in the regeneration, when the Son of Man sits on the throne of His glory, you who have followed Me will also sit on twelve thrones, judging the twelve tribes of Israel."[2] So real was this promise that the disciples inquired further. James and John requested to sit "one on Your right hand and the other on Your left, in Your glory."³ Jesus challenged them, "You do not know what you ask. Are you able to drink the cup that I drink, and be baptized with the baptism that I am baptized with?" Jesus, of course, was referring to the suffering of the cross.

In this instance, Jesus spoke to the disciples about a future eschatological promise (that they took to be imminent) and layered on this the suffering of the cross (that they did not understand at all). What is perhaps most interesting is the very metaphor Jesus used for the suffering of the cross—baptism. It is an allusion to the call that came to Jesus at His baptism. Understood in this way, from the very beginning of Jesus' ministry, from His baptism on, we may say that the cross was a reality for Him: Jesus lived in the shadow of the cross. So vivid was the calling of Jesus at Jordan, the anointing that called Him to glory and suffering, that this baptism became in itself a metaphor to Him for His death and put the cross in view. Jesus offered in Luke 12:50, "But I have a baptism to be baptized with, and how distressed I am till it is accomplished!"

Jesus' anointing at Jordan was at once a promise of eschatological glory, and a call to suffer. While Psalm 110 uses both kingly and priestly language for the exalted Messiah, a word picture constituted by "sitting on the right hand of God,"⁴ this promise could not be divorced from the Servant psalms of Isaiah, prophetic songs that promised both exaltation and vicarious suffering for the Servant of Yahweh. The Epistle to the Hebrews offers of Jesus, "Who for the joy that was set before Him endured the cross, despising the shame, and has sat down at the right hand of the throne of God."⁵ In John's Gospel in particular, the cross looms as large as the glory that will follow it. Jesus' celebration of "glory" in John's Gospel is, in the words of Richard Bauckham, "riddling." It was in this same double reference that Jesus could speak of being "lifted up" (John 3:14; John 8:28; 12:32-34); indeed, the word translated "lifted up" (*hupsoo*) has an intentional double meaning.⁶ As Bauckham notes, "It refers both literally to the crucifixion as a lifting up of Jesus above the earth (as 12:33 makes clear) and figuratively to the same event as Jesus' elevation to the status of divine sovereignty over the cosmos."⁷ Further, while most of the references to the cross were in terms of their language speaking of a man over against God, on occasion, Jesus offered another perspective, one where He is not merely acted upon but is Himself the Actor. On one occasion, He said in the first person, "Destroy this temple and in three days I will raise it up."⁸

Although it may be said that all of the Gospels have the cross as a focus, the narrative of Luke utilizes a literary form that expresses Jesus' ministry as a journey toward Jerusalem (and toward the passion of Jesus). En route, numerous events foreshadow the cross.[9] In Luke 13:32, when warned about going to Jerusalem because Herod sought to kill Him, Jesus responded, "Go, tell that fox, 'Behold, I cast out demons and perform cures today and tomorrow, and the third day I shall be perfected.'" Rather than focusing on the threat of death, Jesus' reference to being perfected is really a statement of faith suggesting that He will finish His task. Oscar Cullmann points out that the special verb (*teleioumai*) translated "perfected" in verse 32 may well indicate that "he ascribes to himself a special divine mission that consists of death."[10] Jesus' reference to death in this way is both a certain proclamation and a statement of faith. It was a prophetic claim that He believed the suffering on the cross would be efficacious. His statement in the next verse is that "Nevertheless I must journey today, tomorrow, and the day following; for it cannot be that a prophet should perish outside of Jerusalem" (Luke 13:33).

Jesus and the Glory of God

John's Gospel as well focuses on the Cross linguistically throughout the text. For instance, as we have suggested previously, "glory" is a theme portrayed throughout John's Gospel. The usage of "glory" and Christ is expressed in many ways, "and the whole dynamism of the relationship of God and Christ is reflected in the use of the term."[11] This theme is used throughout the Gospel and takes on growing significance. The playful use of "glory" (*doxa*) and its verbal counterpart "glorify" (*doxăzō*) often presents difficulty for the modern interpreters. At times, Jesus' use of glory seems to be in some sense a circumlocution, or something purposefully offered ambiguously. When the whole question of authority arose, for instance, Jesus said "I do not receive honor (*doxa*) from men." In this instance, translators chose the word honor, and it could mean honor, but it seems to have as well the nuance of God's glory. Jesus asked these religious leaders, "How can you believe, who receive honor (*doxa*) from one another, and do not seek the honor (*doxa*) that comes from the only God?"[12] There is a double reference in this rebuke, for the *doxa* that came from God was not just God's authority; it was for Jesus a self reference. John's Gospel delights in this ambiguity. Then, in John 9:24, the Jewish rulers told the blind man who had been healed by Jesus, "Give God the glory! We know that this Man is a sinner." The narrative irony is that not only was Jesus not a sinner, but the blind man *was* giving God glory by acknowledging Jesus. That the person of Christ demonstrates God's glory could not be misunderstood, for it was a claim of divinity. Indeed, first-century Jewish Christians would seize upon the word "Glory" and make it a circumlocution for Jesus.[13] As Kittel notes, in John, various shades of meaning of *doxa* "are abruptly set aside one another in apparently strange fashion."[14] Thus, just as Jesus glorified God in His obedience,[15] so God glorified Him in His obedience; while this ultimately included the Glorification at the Ascension,[16] because the promise was so certain, it could include the suffering of Jesus on the cross[17] or any aspect of that ministry that anticipated the cross and ultimate glorification of Jesus Christ.[18]

It is in this context, then, that we must come to Jesus' use of glory at the Last Supper. In John 17:3 Jesus speaks to God of the men who stand in His hearing. He says, "And this is eternal life, that they may know You, the only true God, and Jesus Christ whom You have sent." They had known God, and Jesus prayed they had come to know Him, the man obedient to God. At the very threshold of the cross, Jesus then said to His Father, "I have glorified You on the earth. I have finished the work which You have given Me to do." It was in faith Jesus prayed—faith that He would fulfill the mission of the next hours, faith that His sacrifice would indeed be efficacious.[19] It was the human faith of a man facing death, believing there was eternal meaning in that death. Jesus, in anticipation of the glory that would follow the cross, cried, "And now, O Father, glorify Me together with Yourself, with the glory which I had with You before the world was" (John 17:5). Jesus was not suggesting He was co-eternal with the Father and had somehow temporarily displaced this glory in an act of *kenosis*. Rather, Jesus had reference to the fact that from the very beginning, God had not only envisioned Jesus' death; He had also envisioned the glory that would follow. As Jesus offered this prayer in the shadow of the cross, it was made as a statement of faith! Nor was this a selfish prayer, for the glory that the ascended Christ would receive would accomplish the full restoration of Yahweh and humanity, and permanently reestablish a full-orbed relationship lost in Adam's transgression. Jesus' prayer in John 17 was that "they also whom You gave Me may be with Me where I am, that they may behold My glory which You have given Me; for You loved Me before the foundation of the world" (John 17:24). If one were to trace the thematic thread in verses 10, 22, and 24, it would be apparent that the eschatological glory Jesus is envisioning is so real the apostles are said to already have possessed it in the decree of God and are now in possession of it.[20] Certainly the apostles were not preexistent, nor did they in actuality possess the glory that would be theirs in the eschaton.[21] Just as Jesus was not of the world—the world had no claim on Him—so He could say that the disciples were not of the world. In the same way that the Father sent Him into the world, so Jesus sent His disciples into the world.[22] This is a man praying for men—a man praying for men in the shadow of His own cross.

At the same time as this obedient man was washing the feet of His disciples in the deepest humility, there was resident in His identity a divine claim, a claim to be Yahweh. In John 13:19, Jesus said to His disciples, "Now I tell you before it comes, that when it does come to pass, you may believe that I am *He*."[23] In the text, "he" is italicized; Jesus actually said, "you may believe 'I AM' (*ego eime*)."[24] It is here, girded with a towel and washing dirty feet that Jesus offered His greatest revelation to His disciples. Kneeling on the floor before them, the God who spoke the cosmos into existence, the One who covenanted on Sinai—He was present. From a safe distance, we see how this proclamation only further added to the irony of that night. But real revelation for the apostles would come only in remembrance of the things Jesus told them once the Crucifixion and Ascension took place. So difficult was it for them to conceive of eternity past or of the redemptive future that it was necessary that Jesus speak "in parables"; even when He was "speaking plainly" they struggled. That same night, Jesus spoke eschatologically of the Spirit. "But the Helper, (*parakletos*) the Holy Spirit, whom the Father will send in My name, He will teach you all things, and bring to your remembrance all things that I said to you" (John 14:26). As we have suggested, He was trying to tell them that they would be experiencing Him in a different way, for in verse 16 of the same chapter, interpreters have adduced that Jesus' reference to the *parakletos* was a reference to Himself.[25] Nor is there any ambiguity in I John 2:1: "My little children, these things I write to you, so that you may not sin. And if anyone sins, we have an Advocate (*parakletos*) with the Father, Jesus Christ the righteous." Again, this kind of speaking was an attempt to help the disciples to begin to understand the chronology of what would happen. Jesus could offer, "But when the Helper (*parakletos*) comes, whom I shall send to you from the Father, the Spirit of truth who proceeds from the Father, He will testify of Me" (John 15:26). Yet, in the same teaching, as we have suggested, Jesus could say, "I will not leave you orphans; I will come to you."[26] Yet despite this teaching, events were swirling too quickly for the apostles, and revelation would have to wait.

In the Garden of Gethsemane

After Jesus shared the Last Supper with His disciples, He went with them to the Garden of Gethsemane to pray. This was the time when He offered Himself fully to the will of God. Hebrews 5:7-8, seems to have this in view. Looking back from the present of Christ's glorification, the writer of Hebrews, says,

> Who, in the days of His flesh, when He had offered up prayers and supplications, with vehement cries and tears to Him who was able to save Him from death, and was heard because of His godly fear, though He was a Son, yet He learned obedience by the things which He suffered.

Several things are significant in the passage; first, the human cry and the very real suffering and genuine prayer of Jesus. As we have begun to suggest, when the writer of Hebrews offers that Jesus "learned obedience," this relates to how Jesus had to choose to suffer throughout His ministry; here we specifically focus on Jesus' intimate petition to be kept from the severity of suffering He knew would come. This is not to suggest that He was before this time disobedient. Rather, it is to demonstrate that Jesus learned obedience experientially.[27] Here we share one of the most intimate moments of communion in the entire Gospel. Jesus prayed, "Abba, Father, all things are possible for You. Take this cup away from Me; nevertheless, not what I will, but what You will" (Mark 14:36). As we have suggested in chapter 9, Jesus' use of *Abba* was meant to convey God's intimate relationship. And while He could teach the apostles to pray to *Abba*, such teaching was proleptic of the relationship that would be theirs once He won back whole and complete covenant relationship by His sacrifice. In a very real way, it was only Jesus who could properly speak the words *Abba* with reference to God. That is why Mark recalls Jesus' use of *Abba* in the original Aramaic during Jesus' prayer in the Garden. Jesus' use of *Abba* is not unique to Jesus' prayer in the Garden of Gethsemane;

Mark offers the original Aramaic because of its importance here. There were two things Jesus could be claiming when He used *Abba*. The first was that He was literally begotten by Yahweh. The second is that He was an obedient Son.[28] While it is in both senses that the title is employed here, the emphasis is on Jesus' willing covenant obedience. Futher, Jesus' redemptive work opened fellowship for the church so that Yahweh would be their *Abba* by adoption. Indeed, this *Abba* relationship would become a kind of soteriological claim made by Christians in the earliest Christian communities.[29]

It was in the Garden of Gethsemane that Jesus would in actuality own His role as the Ebed Yahweh. Mark records the prayer of Jesus: "Abba, Father, all things are possible for You. Take this cup away from Me; nevertheless, not what I will, but what You will" (Mark 14:36). In the christological hymn from Philippians, the early church celebrated that Jesus "taking the form of a bondservant . . . humbled Himself and became obedient to the point of death, even the death of the cross" (Philippians 2:7-8). The humbling that Jesus underwent occurred throughout the context of His life and ministry. But it was in the Garden of Gethsemane that Jesus gave His final assent to be wounded, flailed, and to ultimately give His life as a ransom for many.[30]

The disciples slept while Jesus prayed. Yet, Jesus' hour of prayer was soon interrupted as Judas entered the garden with the soldiers. John's Gospel offers a snapshot of this revelatory moment. "Jesus therefore, knowing all things that would come upon Him, went forward and said to them, 'Whom are you seeking?' They answered Him, 'Jesus of Nazareth.' Jesus said to them, 'I AM (*ego eime*).'"[31] Whether or not Judas was sensitive to this moment, or whether or not the soldiers or Temple representatives understood Jesus' claim is not certain. It seems more likely this was an intimate revelation for His apostles. Almost certainly, the weight of the confession was lost on them in the hubbub, only to be recalled later. But what happened next confirmed Jesus' profession. "Now when He said to them, 'I AM (*ego eime*),' they drew back and fell to the ground" (John 18:6). In this incredible display of power and purpose, Jesus, the I AM come in flesh, spoke revelation in the first person. No doubt, this revelatory moment was only recalled later and formed part of the christological construct of the apostles.

Jesus Condemned to Die

During the remainder of the night, Jesus offered revelation to the rulers of His time, sometimes by His words, sometimes by His silence. One of the most significant moments was when before the high priest, confounded by the discrepancy among the witnesses, the high priest asked Jesus out of desperation to convict Him: "Are you the Christ, the Son of the blessed?" (Mark 14:61). Jesus needed only to stay silent in order to escape entrapment. Instead, He spoke, absolutely accepting the charges that were leveled at Him. Jesus said, "I am. And you will see the Son of Man sitting at the right hand of the Power, and coming with the clouds of heaven" (Mark 14:62). In making these claims, Jesus brought together significant prophetic claims of His identity and work. The most immediate claim is "I AM."[32] Second, there is an allusion to the "Son of Man sitting," an anticipation of the Ascension. Third, Jesus confessed that the Son of man will be "coming with the clouds of heaven." In this declaration He focused on the climactic moment of the eschaton, when He would return, culminating in His reign in power and judgment. This single statement of Jesus draws biblical texts from the past in order to speak of the anticipation of the future. Donald Juel sees in this statement an allusion to Psalm 110:1, Daniel 7:13, and possibly to Zechariah 12:10.[33] Thus, in a single claim of Jesus the entire plan of redemption is collapsed so that the hearers are challenged to fully hear this claim of the man who sat before them on trial.

There is some mystery involved as to why Jesus said these things just at this time. From a human standpoint they could not have so readily condemned Him if He had kept quiet. And as we have suggested, He wasn't prone to say these things to crowds. It could be that He spoke these things so that prophecy would be fulfilled or as a final proclamation so that in judgment these priests could not claim ignorance of His identity. But there is another possibility, one which stretches the notion of grace pretty far. Recall that it was when God gave Moses a revelation of His name that He both called Moses to mission and allowed Moses to know the name of Yahweh in an experiential way. That is, at the burning bush, Yahweh was calling Moses to an "I-Thou" relationship unknown since the time of Adam. Moses heard the call and knew the name, not merely cognitively, but in constituting a face-to-face relationship of significant magnitude. It could well be that while His accusers were plotting how to get rid of the menace that they took Jesus to be, Jesus was offering the same kind of relationship that was proffered at the burning bush. They only had to hear Him. Sadly, though they did on one level hear Him, they rejected His claim, for the high priest immediately assessed that Jesus spoke blasphemy, a decision that was quickly agreed upon by all who were present. (See Mark 14:63-64.)

At the baptism of Jesus, Psalm 2 was spoken audibly by the very voice of God, and this prophetic promise, "You are my beloved Son," included the collateral promise alluded to in this royal psalm, His ultimate enthronement. In an irony that is apparent to the readers but not to the participants, the charge that Jesus is the King of the Jews echoes across the various scenes that played a part in the hours just prior to the cross. Before Pilate, the question of kings and kingdoms becomes prominent. While Jesus continued to assert that "My kingdom is not of this world" (John 18:36), He never denied that He was a king, something not apparent by His humiliation, yet a truth that was integral to His salvific purpose, and one that He spoke by faith.[34]

Jesus on the Cross

Throughout the Crucifixion, Gospel writers connect the dots, demonstrating how each aspect of His suffering had been foretold. Juel offers a study of the sayings of Jesus on the cross, demonstrating not only the importance of each saying; Juel also demonstrates how the words of Jesus had been predicted in detail in the Psalms. Some of the allusions are self-evident and some are left to the evangelists' audience to discern. Psalm 22 in particular foreshadows Jesus' suffering. In verses 7–8, the psalmist wrote, "All those who see Me ridicule Me; They shoot out the lip, they shake the head, saying, 'He trusted in the LORD, let Him rescue Him; Let Him deliver Him, since He delights in Him!'" Mark 15:29 recalls the kind of verbal abuse of Jesus prophesied in the Psalm.[35] The parting of His garments (Mark 15:24) was spoken of in Psalm 22:18 [*LXX* 22:19]; Mark 15:29 has in reference Psalm 22:7 [*LXX* 22:8]. Juel suggests that Psalm 69:21 [*LXX* 69:22] stands behind Mark 15:36 where they offered Jesus vinegar to drink. In sum, Juel would argue these allusions to Old Testament texts do not intrude into the story; rather they do make an argument.[36]

Jesus quoted from Psalm 22:1 when He said, "My God, My God, why have You forsaken me?"[37] The question may well be asked whether or not God had forsaken Jesus on the cross. If this was the case, it presents an ontological dilemma. For if Jesus were actually forsaken by God, then Jesus had ontological existence apart from God; thus, Jesus was not divine. But let us revisit the psalm in its original context. The genre of the psalms is a poetic genre of passionate feeling. David cried, "My God, My God, why have You forsaken Me? Why are You so far from helping Me, And from the words of My groaning?" (Psalm 22:1, NKJV). But the fact is that while David expressed his feeling of being forsaken, he was still in covenant with Yahweh when he uttered this cry. The psalm is not about a theological reality—it was about a feeling of aloneness. When Jesus quoted the psalm, He was certainly still in covenant with Yahweh, but He utilized this psalm to describe His feelings. Jesus was, as the suffering Servant and obedient Son, offering to God the depth of His soul. Though He felt the "aloneness" of the moment, it is not possible that Jesus was forsaken in actuality; Hebrews 9:14 says of Jesus, "Who through the eternal Spirit offered Himself without spot to God." It was in submitting Himself to the Spirit within Him that Jesus accomplished this redemptive act. Further, there is some evidence to suggest that Jesus specifically had the whole of Psalm 22 in mind; this psalm may at once speak of the suffering of Christ while at the same time declare the benefits of this suffering. In the psalm, verse 22 switches from the mode of humiliation to the mode of celebratory praise; moving from speaking from suffering in the first person, the psalm begins to speak of praise in the second person. Whereas verse 21 closes the cry of prayer, "Save Me from the lion's mouth and from the horns of the wild oxen! You have answered Me," verse 22 begins the celebration, "I will declare Your name to My brethren; In the midst of the assembly I will praise You." It seems clear that Jesus, in contritely offering Himself in faith, saw beyond the suffering to victory that was being won.

The Victory of the Cross

When Jesus died, God did not die. Yet, He who was God died. It was this offering of Himself that was in fact salvific; New Testament authors use a wide variety of metaphors to describe the atoning work of Christ, indicating that more important than "how" the cross forgave their sin was their very realization of this forgiveness.[38] In this regard, when Jesus said "It is finished!" there was a sense of completion over evil powers.[39] Indeed, Hebrews 2:14-15 says Jesus partook of flesh and blood because the "children" [descendents of Adam] did, so that "through death He might destroy him who had the power of death, that is, the devil, and release those who through fear of death were all their lifetime subject to bondage." There are militaristic sounding verses throughout the New Testament that work to describe the struggle that occurred surrounding the cross. In Matthew 16:18; Jesus declares that the gates of Hell would not prevail against the church. Certainly, it is on the cross where this victory begins to take place.

In the epistles and in Revelation, there is a celebratory backwards look at Christ's victory over Satan. While there is some discussion on the interpretation of Ephesians 4:8-10, there is good reason to believe that this has reference to the descending of Jesus after He died, that He stripped Satan of His powers, and that He elevated those who prior to this time had been distant to the presence of God.[40] This disarming of Satan is also in view when the resurrected Christ appears to John on the Isle of Patmos to declare, "I am He who lives, and was dead, and behold, I am alive forevermore. Amen. And I have the keys of Hades and of Death" (Revelation 1:18). Colossians reports this same victory as a "public triumph, [one] in which the defeated foes are led captive in the train of a triumphant general";[41] "He has stripped the sovereignties and the ruling forces, and paraded them in public, behind him in his triumphal procession" (Colossians 2:15, NJB). And although the victory of Christ over Satan was epic, the church anticipates the final eschatological victory that is recorded in Romans 8[42] and I Corinthians 15[43]; it is here the church will share in the ultimate eschatological victory of Jesus Christ. Further, because of Jesus' victory over Satan and His subsequent ascension, there is a whole new heavenly reality. It is this reality that we will explore in the next chapter.

Chapter 11

The Man Who Was Glorified

Introduction

The change that occurred in the apostles between the last pages of the Gospels and the first pages of the Acts of the Apostles is nothing less than startling. When in the last hours of His life, Jesus sought the support of the apostles, He could not count on them. They could not grasp the truths He attempted to share with them but were rather thickheaded. Yet, at the beginning of the Acts of the Apostles, the apostles are powerful and articulate. It is particularly on the Day of Pentecost when this radical change becomes apparent. There were several things that led to this change. First, they saw the resurrection side of Calvary. Jesus appeared to them and taught them in post-resurrection appearances. Second, there was an incredible change when they were filled with the Spirit. Jesus had told them that the Spirit would illuminate them with regard to His identity and work.[1] In any case, the world was different after the victory of the cross. In this chapter we explore the theological meaning of the resurrection, the ascension, and glorification of Jesus. Further, the Scripture teaches us of a future hope, an eternal reality we will share because of the work of Christ. This chapter concludes with a synopsis of a Oneness christological understanding of eternity.

On the Day of Pentecost, after having been filled with the Spirit, Peter was able to explain to the crowd the ontological reality of Jesus' ascension. He quoted Psalm 110 and said that is what occurred when the man Jesus ascended into the heavens: "The LORD said to my Lord, 'Sit at My right hand,[2] Till I make Your enemies Your footstool.'" (Acts 2:34-35). Let us now consider the meaning of Psalm 110, for as we have suggested, it is a key moment in salvation history.

Psalm 110 is a psalm of enthronement and should be understood in its entirety even when only verse 1 is quoted. In its original context, Psalm 110 was a promise to a monarch that he would reign in Yahweh's favor.[3] Yet, like other prophetic texts, it can have secondary and even tertiary applications.[4] The understanding of Psalm 110:1 is nuanced by additional information found in verse 4, where Yahweh prophesies to this king, "Yahweh has sworn an oath he will never retract; you are a priest for ever of the order of Melchizedek." Thus, not only is there a reference to this man as a king, He is also a priest—a particular kind of priest. Messianically, then, Jesus is prophesied to be a king/priest, a man enthroned in divine glory.

The psalm is not at all suggesting that Jesus is literally at God's right hand. F. F. Bruce aptly points out the Christian use of this psalm: "No literal location was intended was as well understood by Christians in the apostolic age as it is by us; they knew that God has no physical right hand or material throne where the ascended Christ sits beside Him; to them, the language denoted the exaltation and the supremacy of Christ as it does to us."[5] Bruce is correct, of course. While the text clearly uses language of Jesus as a man over against God, such language is to be taken metaphorically. If Jesus were literally at the right hand of God, then He would not be God. Yet it is just such metaphorical language that explains Jesus' salvific work, accomplished in His office as King/Priest. The pronouncement that Jesus is made "Christ" is related to His ongoing eschatological office as priest. Let us consider the meaning of the unique blending of metaphors that describe Jesus as priest.

Jesus as Priest

New Testament writers blend word pictures together to suggest a fuller picture of Jesus' identity. In the Epistle to the Hebrews such blending regularly occurs in working to define the priesthood of Jesus. In Hebrews, the priesthood of Jesus is depicted with a confluence of word pictures supplied by allusions to the Melchizedekian and Aaronic priesthood, priestly acts, and the prophetic role of Suffering Servant. These all get blended together in a celebration of Jesus' victory on the cross and His ascension into heaven.

For the writer of Hebrews, disparate priestly metaphors are all legitimate word pictures in the redemptive panorama. Melchizedek is marshaled out by the author, not only to serve typologically as a king/priest, but because

Melchizedek did not require a priestly lineage to function in the office. He only needed to be called by God. In like manner, Jesus was able to function as a priest because Yahweh called Him.[6] The writer of Hebrews also uses the lack of genealogy in Genesis[7] to typologically signify that Melchizedek foreshadowed Jesus Christ's priesthood "without end."[8]

Further, the writer of Hebrews also employs the Aaronic priesthood as typological where it was useful.[9] The Day of Atonement employed, captures the imagery of the high priest taking the blood of the sacrifice to offer it for the sins of the nation. On other days, the high priest would not go beyond the veil, for behind it was the holiest earthly place known to Israel. People had died in the presence of the Ark of the Covenant, Dagon was destroyed in its presence, and plagues occurred as a result of not reverencing it an appropriate way. The veil was a thick curtain, and it was only with fear and trepidation that on the Day of Atonement the high priest carried the blood into the most holy room of the Temple to apply blood to the mercy seat. When Jesus ascended, metaphorically, He entered into the heavenly "inner sanctum." Hebrews allows a blending of imagery; for the Servant of Yahweh, it wasn't the blood of an animal that was offered but His own blood.

In contrast with the high priest who entered into the holiest part of the Temple and then left quickly in awe of God's power, Jesus not only "offered His own blood" in "God's inner sanctum"; He stayed. That is, He sat down in an official way, fulfilling the proclamation of Psalm 110:1, part of this same blended imagery where Yahweh officially pronounces to Jesus to sit on His right hand. As F. F. Bruce notes, "A seated priest is the guarantee of the finished work and an accepted sacrifice."[10] Further, as one author proclaims, our High Priest is one "who can boldly and permanently pull back the great curtain that shuts us out from God and can invite us all, as brothers and sisters, to come in, to enter into intimacy with the living God."[11]

The principal role of a priest was to go to God on behalf of the people, to function as a mediator between them and God. This priestly function was fulfilled in Jesus, which is why He says, "No one comes to the Father except through Me" (John 14:6). Thus when Jesus completed His sacrificial work on the cross of Calvary, He ascended, opening a way for every son of Adam to be in fully restored covenant relationship with God. Ontologically, of course, God was in Christ, but functionally, Jesus was a "go-between" between humanity and God. He Himself became the de facto guarantee of this restored relationship. First Timothy 2:5 speaks of this in a slightly different way, "For there is one God and one Mediator between God and men, the man Jesus." In the text, the Greek word for mediator is *mesites*, a word that is used of Jesus throughout Hebrews as well.[12] Cullmann writes that it is "a *terminus technicus* of legal language designating an arbitrator or guarantor."[13] In the context of Hebrews, *mesites* is translated "mediator" (8:6; 9:15; 12:24), and in each case that it is used it has reference to Jesus Himself being the guarantor of the New Covenant. As a man, Jesus was called to this mission. It was a divine command that gave Him this place of power. As Simon Kistemaker notes of Jesus' enthronement, "He was fully entitled to that place, as the priest who has fulfilled his task of removing sin and as a king who has conquered sin and death."[14]

A priest did not merely go to God on behalf of the people. Recall that besides going to God on behalf of the people, a priest also went to the people on behalf of God. That is why the priests in Numbers could invoke the name of Yahweh over the people and God's blessings would come. The power and presence of Yahweh would be constituted in that act of worship and people would experience Him in communal worship. As good as that was, Jesus anticipated something even better once His sacrifice was complete. As a priest, it was Jesus' role to pour out the priestly blessing of the Holy Spirit. At the Feast of Tabernacles, He invited, "If anyone thirsts, let him come to Me and drink. He who believes in Me, as the Scripture has said, out of his heart will flow rivers of living water" (John 7:37-38). John explained in the next verse that while Jesus was speaking of the Holy Spirit, no one could receive the Holy Spirit until Jesus was glorified. Indeed, in the beginning of all four Gospels Jesus' ministry was defined, comparing it with John's. In each instance, John's ministry was described as baptizing with water, while Jesus would baptize with the Holy Spirit.[15] Yet it was not until the Day of Pentecost that anyone was baptized with the Spirit. Peter recognized this linkage and said in regard to the glorification of Jesus: "Therefore being exalted to the right hand of God, and having received from the Father the promise of the Holy Spirit, He poured out this which you now see and hear" (Acts 2:33). When on the Day of Pentecost they were filled with the Holy Spirit, they entered into an "I-Thou" relationship in a way not possible before.

Jesus as King

At the Ascension, Jesus received an identity that no man had ever possessed before. Some have wrongly suggested that it was at the Ascension that Jesus became divine. This is absolutely not the case. Yet, while there was no ontological change in Jesus at the Ascension, there was a change in function. Consider once again the hymn in Philippians 2:9-11:

> Wherefore God also has highly exalted Him and given Him the name which is above every name, that at the name of Jesus every knee should bow, of those in heaven, and of those on earth, and of those under the earth, and that every tongue should confess that Jesus Christ is Lord, to the glory of God the Father.

This last portion of the Philippian hymn occurs after Jesus willingly took upon Himself the form of a servant, and sacrificed Himself on the cross. It begins by describing the incredible way in which God exalted Jesus. The enthronement of Jesus is described by the words "highly exalted." The Greek (*huperupsosen*) that stands behind these words is in fact a declaration that absolutely stretches language. This Greek superlative could only be accurately understood as a kind of super-exaltation, that in fact Jesus was now in a place where no human being had ever been before.[16] In this same context, Jesus receives a "name which is above every name." Incredibly, this exaltation of the man Christ Jesus is derived from Isaiah 45:23 where Yahweh is the speaker. Yahweh says of Himself: "All shall bend the knee to me, by me every tongue shall swear."

Consider what the Philippian hymn does. It takes a "Yahweh text" from Isaiah that calls for praise to be applied only to Yahweh and celebrates this text by applying it to Jesus—every knee will bow to Him. It is Jesus who is the One to whom they shall now swear in fealty. Thus, while there was a way in which Jesus could be called Lord in His earthly ministry, this was in some sense anticipating the official eschatological act of enthronement. That is to say, at the Ascension, one may now look at Jesus the man and declare that He is Kurios-Yahweh.[17] Because one may speak of the enthroned man Jesus as Yahweh, subsequently, this makes Jesus greater than the angels, and places Him higher than any human has ever been. There is a way in which the Philippian hymn anticipates the final eschatological act, one that has not occurred as yet; a future point in time when every knee will bow to the man, when universal confession will be made of this man that He is *Kurios*.

At the baptism of Jesus, Yahweh's voice pronounced Jesus' calling based upon two Old Testament passages. The voice proclaimed: "This is My beloved Son, in whom I am well pleased."[18] As we have suggested, "in whom I am well pleased" is derived from a "Servant Song," where the Servant of Yahweh would suffer redemptively for the people. "This is My beloved Son" derives from a psalm that lauds the enthronement of a king in celebratory language. At first glance, these passages do not seem to belong together at all. Yet, as we have begun to suggest, there is not so much a thematic disconnect as one would suppose. Indeed, this Servant Song not only prophesies of a servant who would suffer; it also prophesies that this same servant will be glorified. It reads, "His visage was marred more than any man." (See Isaiah 52:14.) Isaiah also prophesies, "He shall be exalted and extolled and be very high" (Isaiah 52:13, NKJV). As Richard Bauckham demonstrates, this can only mean glorification.[19] That is, the Servant who suffers is subsequently celebrated as divine.

But there is another point. When the Philippian hymn says that Jesus was "highly exalted" (*huperupsosen*) the Greek is unusual. In a style that is almost linguistically redundant, the verb conveys the sense that Jesus was uniquely brought to the highest place to which anyone could be brought! Clearly the hymn cannot refer to a preexistent Son returning to the place where He already was before. Rather, it makes sense only if someone were going where they had never been, if the hymn were in fact celebrating a man who was now being enthroned.

Let us consider briefly how John's Gospel also makes the same claim—that there will be One on the throne, and that One is Jesus. John 12:38-41 blends together two portions of Isaiah, chapter 6 and chapters 52-53, in offering a reason as to why the Jews did not believe in Jesus. In doing so, John says that Isaiah foresaw Jesus' glory. In other words, John claims that what Isaiah saw when he viewed the Lord (*Adonai*) "high and lifted up" on the throne was not simply a scene of Yahweh in His glory. Rather, what he saw proleptically was the man Jesus Christ on the throne![20]

Bauckham explains how it is possible in the context of Jewish exegesis for Isaiah 52:13 and Isaiah 57:15[21] to be linked with Isaiah 6:1. Bauckham takes several pages to demonstrate how the vocabulary that calls for glorification in the Servant Psalms is the same vocabulary used in Isaiah 6.

Bauckham notes a Jewish interpretive principle called *gezera shava*, an interpretive system employed where texts with similarity of verbs are deemed to be related. As Bauckham offers, "This is why, in John 12:38-41, Isaiah 53 and Isaiah 6 are brought together, and Isaiah is said to have seen Jesus' glory, meaning that he did so when he saw the glory of the Lord in his vision in chapter 6."[22] Thus, when Isaiah said in chapter 6:1: "In the year of King Uzziah's death I saw the Lord seated on a high and lofty throne,"[23] he was not merely speaking of Yahweh. Because the subject is the same subject as in Isaiah 52-53. John's Gospel rightly notes that Isaiah was looking forward to the eschaton, and proleptically seeing Jesus Christ on the throne.[24]

The Servant Psalms really are a study in paradox. As we have suggested, Isaiah 52-53 could at once prophesy of a Servant who was "bruised" for us while at the same time celebrate the glorification of this same Servant. As we have worked to demonstrate, one of the foundational claims of the New Testament is that both Jesus Christ and His followers applied this title and psalm to Jesus. But there is another point that should be considered from this Servant Psalm. As Raymond Brown has demonstrated, the same Servant psalm of Isaiah that speaks of the glorification of Jesus makes another declaration. Brown notes that when Isaiah 52:6 pronounces "In that day . . ." (NKJV), it has reference to Jesus in His eschatological glory. Then he focuses on the first part of the verse, where the servant says, "Therefore My people shall know My name; Therefore they shall know in that day That I am [*ego eime* in the *LXX*!] He who speaks: 'Behold, *it is* I.' "[25] This is a prophecy of the supreme moment of revelation. There is One who is "I AM." It is Isaiah's Servant, the same one who walked the dusty roads of Palestine, and further, there is a point in time when people will celebrate this, calling Him by name. It is no doubt the same moment from Isaiah when "every knee shall bow." In the glorification of Jesus, it is not so much that Jesus ontologically becomes Yahweh. As we have suggested, if the Incarnation means anything, it means that Jesus could not have ontologically existed apart from Yahweh who was His very life. Yet, what begins to occur at the Glorification and which will be even more prominent in the eschaton is the collapse of language.

Because the man Jesus is glorified, something significant happens. When one sees the man, one can rightly say Yahweh. One can rightly say "I AM." This is the meaning of Hebrews 1:4, "Having become so much better than the angels, as He has by inheritance[26] obtained a more excellent name than they." The name that the man Jesus could now be called was *Kurios*; when one looks at the glorified man, one can rightly say: Yahweh! Hendrikus Berkhof writes of the glorified Christ, "This completed covenant relationship signifies a new union of God and man, far beyond our experience and imagination."[27] Berkhof goes on to say, "God does not push the human person of Jesus aside, but He permeates it entirely with his Spirit, that is, with himself."[28]

Jesus as Mediator

While ontologically, Jesus is *Kurios*, there is still a functional need of a mediator. And this is exactly the point of Psalm 110 in blending the king/priest imagery. Jesus is still the "guarantor," fulfilling what can best be understood in the metaphor of priestly functions. The author of Hebrews, in contrasting the durative priesthood with that of the Levitical priests, says that Jesus "always lives" (Hebrews 7:25) to make intercession. But just as Jesus did not literally bring His blood to a heavenly mercy seat, neither is He now actually pleading for sinners, nor are prayers being offered by Him in a heavenly realm. Hebrews 10:12 celebrates that when Jesus died on the cross He offered "one sacrifice for sins forever"; and in contrast now sits enthroned. His own singular sacrifice is efficacious; no more are needed. Jesus does not prostrate Himself as a man to God continually, nor does He suffer again, nor does He pray as a man who would now pray to God. Rather, it is the ontological place of the man Jesus in Heaven that in effect makes intercession for us. We might liken this to the blood of the paschal lamb that the Israelites daubed on the lintels and doorposts. It was the single act of a lamb being slain that was necessary. Whenever it was during the night that the death angel passed over to pronounce judgment on the firstborn male in the household, the blood interceded against that judgment. Analogously, because there is a man seated on the throne, there is metaphorical "blood on the doorposts of Heaven" for us. Indeed, only when the whole Old Testament set of metaphors and word pictures comes into play can we even begin to comprehend what the glorification of Jesus Christ means for us. To summarize, while ontologically Jesus is Yahweh, functionally, He is Mediator. This will be the case until the eschaton.

Working toward the Eschaton

The Book of Revelation very much portrays the role of Jesus as that of a Lamb, but not merely as a mediatorial sacrificial Lamb. Rather, as the eschaton approaches, Jesus is ultimately the Lamb who metes out judgment. It is significant as well that in this last book of the Bible, there is no language of the "person of the Son" in Heaven.[29] Nor is there a "person of the Spirit."[30] They simply are not there. One would think that if any book made eternal reality clear, it would be the Book of Revelation. In the imagery of John the Revelator, for instance, there is one who sits on the throne; a Lamb receives a scroll from the One on the throne, a document that authorizes the unfolding of the narrative in subsequent chapters in the Book of Revelation. (See Revelation 5:1-7.) Praise is then offered to the One on the throne and to the Lamb: "Blessing and honor and glory and power Be to Him who sits on the throne, And to the Lamb, forever and ever!"

In apocalyptic imagery such as one finds in the Book of Revelation, an image can be an event, a theological truth, a historic era, or a person. Imagery is not intended to literally describe physical reality. Thus, the work and identity of Jesus is in one sense depicted in the figure of "a Lamb as though it had been slain, having seven horns and seven eyes, which are the seven Spirits of God sent out into all the earth" (Revelation 5:6). That is to say, the imagery delights in Jesus' life, death, and in His role as the One who gives His Spirit to the seven churches. Revelation's Lamb has been "slain from the foundation of the world" (Revelation 13:8); martyrs "overcame . . . by the blood of the Lamb" (Revelation 12:11) and who alone as the Lamb is worthy to mete out judgment" (Revelation 5:5-6). This Lamb cannot be made to be another person of God, certainly, for there is nothing in the language to suggest this. The Lamb is the celebratory symbol of the man Christ Jesus, whose death on the cross restored covenant relationship for all humanity. Throughout the Book of Revelation, praise is offered to both God and the Lamb. Ultimately, though, the Marriage Supper of the Lamb occurs and then final judgment is meted out. John is newly introduced to "the throne of God and of the Lamb" (Revelation 22:1) where it now becomes clear that distinctions between God and the Lamb are in fact a celebration of God and of the Incarnation. At this point, the passage brings clarity. Describing a vision that includes the tree of life and healing waters, John writes: "The throne of God and of the

Lamb shall be in it, and His servants shall serve Him" (Revelation 22:3). Thus, as John approaches the eschaton, we begin to understand that God is not a different person than the Lamb. "They shall serve Him (not them). The text goes on, "They shall see His face (not faces), and His name (not their names) shall be on their foreheads" (Revelation 22:4). Thus. in this final picture of the throne, there is no more need of distinction. Jesus Christ may be worshiped as God without any functional language of separation.

There is one additional place where one finds what could be deemed as plurality in the Book of Revelation. While there is no reference to God the Son, there are two references to "Son of Man" (and a single reference to the "Son of God" who is described exactly as the Son of Man). In order to explore this further, though, we need to refer back to Daniel's vision of the Ancient of Days and the Son of Man. In Daniel 7, the "Son of Man" came in the clouds to receive incredible authority from the "Ancient of Days." He is given

> dominion and glory and a kingdom, That all peoples, nations, and languages should serve Him. His dominion is an everlasting dominion, which shall not pass away, and His kingdom the one which shall not be destroyed" (Daniel 7:14, NKJV).

In Revelation 1, John does not see the Ancient of Days and the Son of Man. Rather, John sees in His vision one described as the Son of Man. Yet surprisingly, where in Daniel it was the Ancient of Days whose "garment was white as snow" and whose "hair of His head was like pure wool," now these are descriptions that are applied to John's Son of Man! In Revelation, John's Son of Man had "eyes like a flame of fire; His feet were like fine brass, as if refined in a furnace" (Revelation 1:14-15). Further, it is clear that whoever the Son of Man is, it is the same person as the Son of God in Revelation 2:18; for the Son of God is described in exactly the same terms: "who has eyes like a flame of fire, and His feet like fine brass." The description of the Son of Man, then, is once again similar to Daniel's Ancient of Days whose "throne was a blaze of flames, its wheels were a burning fire."

In summary, John's Son of Man has the distinct features of the Ancient of Days. Thus, in John's prophetic vision, we are beginning to see a celebratory collapse of imagery. That is, as one approaches the eschaton, in playful celebration, the Ancient of Days cannot be readily distinguished from the Son of Man. It seems probable that John's vision in chapter 1 is a vision of the eschaton, where there is no more necessary distinction of roles. Indeed, this vision functions in a similar way to Isaiah's vision where he saw One seated on the throne; and that one was Jesus Christ.[31] This further recalls the prophetic declaration of Jesus before His accusers when He not only claimed to be the Son of Man; at this crucial moment in salvation history, Jesus also claimed to be the "I AM."[32] While it is important that we keep understanding Jesus' mediatorial role, it is also good to reflect on what is the clear picture of eternity.

Jesus in the Eschaton

The climax of the Book of Revelation draws from a blend of Old Testament language of the Day of the LORD[33] in depicting the cosmic judgment that culminates in the triumphal appearance of Jesus as King of Kings and Lord of Lords, and then ultimately when He sits on a throne in Revelation 20, meting out judgment. Until this ultimate end, Jesus will still function as priest, savior, and mediator. First Corinthians 15:24-28 talks about this end. Verse 24 offers, "Then comes the end, when He delivers the kingdom to God the Father, when He puts an end to all rule and all authority and power." Gordon Fee writes that while it is true that this is the "end" (*telos*), it is an end "that has two sides to it."[34] Fee notes further, " 'Then the Son himself is subjected to the One (God) who subjected all things (death) to him (the Son)' is the new way of saying, 'when he hands over the kingdom to God the Father.' "[35] That is to say, when the last sinner is saved, and the last enemy is destroyed, the age that required the necessity of salvation will be over. There will be no further need of a Savior. What then happens eschatologically is this: Christ's final obligation as Savior, in terms of salvation history, is to turn the kingdom to the Father. This is His last work as "Savior."[36] Thus, when the end comes, the Son will deliver the kingdom to God, the Father, that God may be all in all. C. K. Barrett suggests that this is meant to be understood soteriologically, not metaphysically.[37] F. W. Grosheide offers, "The Mediator will lay down His office at the feet of the Father, when He has finished the former's work as such."[38] However, I Corinthians 15 does not in any case teach the eternal subjection of the Son. Psalm 110:4 says that the Messiah would be king/priest "forever." In the Hebrew, this is literally, *la'olam*, "to the age." Thus, Jesus as man will be priest while there is one sinner left to save, but will release that role when the last enemy is destroyed. At this point, it is not that God has no more need for the man Jesus. God in Christ is ontologically one with humanity, inseparable.

I recall my grandfather, S. G. Norris, illustrating the meaning of this passage from I Corinthians 15 by telling a kind of parable. In his telling, there was a single doctor who serviced a town. The doctor was so incredibly proficient that he, in fact, cured every sickness. He did this with such effectiveness that no one ever got sick again. My grandfather then offered, "Would the people of the town expel the doctor because they had no more need of him? No, they would elect him mayor, honoring him for his significant accomplishment."[39] In the Philippian hymn, Jesus has already fulfilled His role as a servant who willingly lowers Himself to the point of the death of the cross. He as man already has been "superexalted," as we offered above. Now, it only remains for every knee to bow to Him. This will happen at the White Throne Judgment in Revelation 20:11-15. It is not that salvation will be universal, but even those who continue to rebel against His control will, awed by His glory, bend their knee. And when the work and identity of the man Jesus is understood and He is worshiped as God, this gives glory to God, who in an act of paternity fathered this man and who, from eternity past, spoke this redemptive plan into existence. It is for this reason that we have suggested Hebrews 1:8 is proleptic and likely refers to the ushering in of eternity. The author of Hebrews appropriates a psalm about Yahweh and applies it to Jesus: "But to the Son He says: 'Your throne, O God, is forever and ever; A scepter of righteousness is the scepter of Your Kingdom.'"

Chapter 12

The Man with the Saving Name

The Apostles' Language Regarding Jesus

On more than one occasion the Gospel of John offers that it would be only after the Resurrection that the apostles would understand the identity and work of Christ.[1] In describing what was ahead, Jesus said, "When you lift up the Son of Man, then you will know that I am *He,* [*ego eime*]." (See John 8:28.) In saying this, Jesus not only had in mind the divine phenomena surrounding the Crucifixion;[2] He was thinking as well about His ascension and glorification,[3] Indeed, for the Spirit would give them illumination after Pentecost.[4]

There were, in fact, a number of important christological implications that dawned upon the apostles when they received the Spirit. First, the apostles readily understood that when they spoke of the Spirit, this was no different than speaking of Jesus. Second, although the apostles could ontologically speak of Jesus as God, there was a certain hesitancy to do so. In their lived experience, they first knew Yahweh; and in time they came to know Jesus Christ. Although ontologically Jesus was the *I AM*, it was of the utmost importance to the apostles to celebrate the work of the man Jesus, particularly in relation to their fully restored relationship as the children of God. Third, while linguistically the apostles hesitated in equating Jesus with God, they had no hesitancy in focusing on biblical texts that referred to Yahweh and delightfully appropriating them to Jesus Christ. Fourth, it was in this same regard that they readily understood that the invocation of the name of Yahweh was now accomplished when the name of Jesus was invoked. Although scholars suggest that Jesus only gradually came to be viewed as divine, we will work to demonstrate that the only consistent way to read the biblical text is to understand that this high view of Christ was the confession of the church from its very inception.

An important starting place in studying the proclamation of the apostles is to address how they understood and celebrated God as Father, particularly in relation to the work of Jesus Christ. Before doing so, however, recall that these same apostles did not in the same way celebrate the work of the Spirit. For the apostles, so closely was the work of Jesus' glorification tied together with the work of the Spirit that this language was used interchangeably. Indeed, for the apostles, the working of the Spirit was the working of Jesus.[5] Just as the Spirit was utilized as a circumlocution for Yahweh in the Old Testament, so, it now became a circumlocution for the work of Jesus in the church. For instance, in Acts 16:7, it is the Spirit of Jesus that prevented Paul and His companions from going to Bithynia. In verse 6, a similar act is attributed to the Holy Spirit. As any number of commentators of Luke will allow, "The Spirit who exists in the Old Testament (Acts 28:25) and whom God gives believers (Acts 5:32) also is the Spirit of Jesus."[6] Further, it was not uncommon in the Pauline corpus to equate the Christ with the Spirit. For instance, Paul writes to the Corinthians, "Now the Lord is that Spirit; and where the Spirit of the Lord is, there is liberty" (II Corinthians 3:17). Again, Paul will use the expression *en Christou* and *en pneumati* interchangeably. Note especially Romans 8:9–11 where the Spirit of Christ is indistinguishable from the Spirit in any sense. It is no stretch to say that in the Book of Romans, there is no material distinction between the Spirit and Christ.[7] The early Christian community allowed that when the resurrected Jesus spoke, it was the Spirit that was speaking to them.[8]

Let us now consider the Father/Son language utilized by the apostles. The New Testament is the result of the apostles reflecting about Jesus. They do so not merely in the Gospels, but in Acts and the epistles as well. As we have begun to suggest, they were reluctant to refer directly to Jesus as God. Certainly their overt confession of Jesus as God is present in the text,[9] yet, their lived experience demonstrated that in a very unusual sense, Jesus was "more than God" to them. That is, while it was true that Jesus was the "I AM," He was also a man, the obedient covenant partner who restored what Adam lost. As Paul offers, "For if by the one man's offense many died, much more the grace of God and the gift by the grace of the one Man, Jesus Christ, abounded to many" (Romans 5:15).

The apostles were witnesses of Jesus' redemptive accomplishment and celebrated it. It is for this reason that the epistles contain the salutations that invoke blessings in a priestly manner from both God and the Lord Jesus Christ, such as "Grace to you and peace from God our Father and the Lord Jesus Christ." In a number of epistles, the opening greeting often includes some variation of a blessing from "God our Father and the Lord Jesus Christ." Since the writing of Brent Graves, Oneness advocates have sometimes stressed that the Greek conjunction translated "and" (*kai*) can have reference to the same person.[10]

As I write this, I just received a paper from a student working to demonstrate a Oneness christology in the Book of James.[11] Granville Sharp's rules were referenced freely to demonstrate that James links God with Jesus Christ as the same person.[12] As with most grammars, though, rules are not absolute. Thus, even though Sharp's rules do not strictly apply in this case, Sharp himself argues in his exegesis of James 1:1 that "it is thought probable, and by some proofs much confirmed, that the Apostle meant to style himself, 'a servant of our God and Lord, Jesus Christ.' "[13]

While neither arguing with Granville Sharp or of the Oneness authors who seek to demonstrate that in these greetings God and Jesus are the same person,[14] consider that the apostle's use of both God and Jesus is intending to convey something significant. As we suggested previously, the salutations are drawn from what was originally a priestly invocation of the name of Yahweh.[15] Before the Incarnation, God could be known in covenant relationship. Priestly blessings called down the name of Yahweh in covenant worship.[16] But now, they are celebrating the redemptive work of Christ and calling down the blessings as well that were accomplished on the cross.[17] To offer any less would be an insufficient celebration of the redemptive identity of Jesus.

The apostles were Jews in covenant before they met Jesus, and initially, when the Spirit was first poured out, they saw themselves as leaders of the Jewish people who would direct all the Jewish people to accept the identity and work of Jesus Christ.[18] Further, all initial evangelism took place to Jews, and it was the expectation because it was the turn of the eschaton and Yahweh would bring the revelation of Jesus Christ to the Jewish people. When Peter preached, he often identified Jesus as a prophet. Such an identification has messianic import, for the Torah prophesied that the Messiah would be a prophet—*the* prophet—like Moses. By making this identification for his Jewish audience, Peter would then begin to segue to bring them further understanding. Acts is not offering a different christology than other parts of the New Testament. Rather, it frames the Incarnation through language and constructs understood by first-century Jewish listeners.

The Theology of Jesus' Name

There are two complementary associations with the name of Jesus that inextricably testify to His deity. Unfortunately, one cannot understand the claims of the biblical text until one attempts to return to a first-century way of speaking of the Incarnation. We will deal with how it was that an understanding of *Kurios* affected christology. But first, and in a complementary fashion related to this, we must consider how "The Name" became a significant concept in talking about incarnation.

In chapter 7, we began to talk about how "The Name" was important in the context of the Prologue. John readily used it as a category that the Jewish people understood. Gerhard von Rad, in his "Theology of the Name," posits that Yahweh dwells where His name is.[19] Thus, in Deuteronomy 12:5, when Yahweh instructed that when Israel possessed Canaan, they should worship at the place He chose "as his habitation to put his name there," they should go there. In verse 11, not only did Yahweh say He would put His name there, but He also says that he will *dwell* there.[20]

HaShem (The Name) began as a circumlocution for Yahweh. While utilized broadly, it was most prominent in the synagogues.[21] After a time of speaking this way, that is, *HaShem* as a substitute for Yahweh, *HaShem* began to be thought of as a way of speaking of the very essence of God. Quell writes, "The nature of God is compressed in the name of God. The name is both the quintessence of His person and the vehicle of His power. To name His name is to give concrete form to all that is perceptible in God."[22] Jean Daniélou writes, " 'The Name' is used to designate Yahweh in his ineffable reality, and is therefore a Semitic equivalent of what the divine οὐσία [*ousia*] was to be for the Greeks."[23] Jewish tradition suggests a high priestly usage of *HaShem* in the Temple in lieu of Yahweh.

It was natural then, for Jewish Christians, especially when communicating with their fellow Jews, to construct christology in terms that would be readily understood. From the very outset of the church, the "Theology of the Name," a Jewish construct, became appropriated at the very initiation of Jewish Christian community as "the Theology of Jesus' Name."[24] Because "The Name" was a theological construct utilized to speak of the very essence of God, every time the "Name" of Jesus was spoken, there was an "ontological wash of deity," a secondary claim that Yahweh was present in Jesus Christ. This way of speaking occurs not only in Acts, but in the epistles as well, where the Name of Jesus is both shorthand for Yahweh as well as for the salvific work of the man Jesus. As we shall study in the next chapter, it was found as well in a number of the church fathers. Hans Bietenhard finds this same sort of usage in III John 7 as well, "where it said of the missionaries that for the name (ὑπὲρ γὰρ τοῦ ὀνόματος) they went forth."[25] For Bietenhard, this is consonant with the message of Acts; "ὄνομα Ἰησοῦ [name of Jesus] is to be understood as the presence of Christ."[26] But again, it is not merely the presence of Christ; it is Yahweh acting salvifically in the work of Jesus Christ. Such an understanding is evident in covenant initiation. Whereas, in the Old Testament, it was Yahweh's name that was invoked in covenant initiation, in the New Testament, it is the name of Jesus. In James 2:7, in his challenge to the church not to be partial to the rich, he charges of that group: "Is it not they who blaspheme the excellent name that was invoked over you?" (NRSV). The "excellent name" that was invoked has reference to baptism, and how it was that the name of Jesus was orally invoked over them in covenant initiation. But what we should not miss is that in the use of "Name," there is an implicit claim that Yahweh is present.

Jesus as *Kurios*

As we have suggested above, by the first century Yahweh was a "too-sacred-to-use" name. By far, the most common circumlocution for Yahweh in the synagogues was *Adonai*. In a service where Scripture was read aloud, a reader would see the name Yahweh but then read aloud *Adonai*. An interesting development occurred when the Hebrew text was translated into Greek.[27] Because in the Greek text both Yahweh and *Adonai* were translated as *Kurios*, and because the Greek word has a considerable semantic range and was not in itself a sacred word, *Kurios* was considered safe to be spoken in the Greek-speaking synagogues as a generic way of saying Yahweh.[28] Perhaps we can understand this better when we consider that there is something analogous between the Greek word *Kurios* with the English word "Lord." As with *Kurios*, so "Lord" may refer to either a human authority or king or could actually refer to divinity. Thus, it was an apt term in denoting both respect and honor, yet it didn't offend Jewish sensibilities that someone saying it might take the divine name "in vain." Over time, this *Kurios* language became entrenched in the Jewish Diaspora.

From the very earliest years of the church, *Kurios* was one of the premiere titles of Jesus. Further, there was no hesitation in linking Jesus as *Kurios* in the present with eschatological images of Yahweh.[29] Jesus was pronounced *Kurios* at His birth, and Paul took *Kurios* as a normative title for Jesus.[30] Further, because it immediately suggested itself to the apostles, Old Testament texts that had been applied to Yahweh began to be consistently applied to Jesus Christ.[31] Arguably, the earliest confession of the church is "Jesus is *Kurios*." To confess that Jesus is *Kurios* was effectively equating Jesus with Yahweh, and this effectively broke down verbal barriers to that of equating Jesus with God. Raymond Brown sees this connection and argues, "In this formula Christians gave Jesus the title *kyrios* which was the standard Septuagint translation for *YHWH*. If Jesus could be given this title, why could he not be called *theos*, which the Septuagint often used to translate *elohim*? The two Hebrew terms had become relatively interchangeable, and indeed *YHWH* was the more sacred term."[32]

The Saving Name Is Invoked

Apostolic christology was not a process of long reflection, though they did have three years to hear Jesus teach and to gradually come to an understanding of who He was; nor did they have a long time before they began taking texts referring to Yahweh and applying them to Jesus. But they did not need much time. As Richard Longenecker notes, "Jesus Himself was for the earliest Christians both the source of their basic convictions and the paradigm in their interpretation of the Old Testament."[33]

Historically, taking the Lukan presentation of Peter seriously, it was on the Day of Pentecost, at the inception of the church, that Peter first linked Yahweh and Jesus. We deal with this more in chapter 16, but briefly, Peter identified the phenomena in the upper room with the fulfillment of Joel's prophecy that the Spirit would be poured out on all people. Peter continued to quote Joel, not so much because he was interested in the attending cosmic phenomena predicted by Joel; rather he wanted to get to "and it shall come to pass that whoever calls on the name of the LORD shall be saved."[34]

In a pivotal interpretive turn, after citing Joel, Peter immediately preached about Jesus. As we suggested in the last chapter, when Peter spoke of the ascension of Jesus, he applied the prophecy to Jesus, and added that God made Jesus, whom they crucified, both *Kurios* and *Christos*. This immediately recalled the Joel prophecy, and when asked what they should do, Peter asked them to repent and to undergo baptism as a way to be a part of the turn of the eschaton. The way in which the Joel text is appropriated further reflects the idiomatic invocation of Yahweh. Only now it was the name of Jesus that was invoked over them in covenant initiation. Commentators agree that when Peter was calling for people to be baptized in the name of Jesus Christ, he was appropriating Joel's prophecy that whoever calls upon the name of Yahweh shall be saved.[35]

It is significant that Diaspora Jews from "every nation under heaven" are attending the Feast of Pentecost, and that they are in Peter's audience, for they represent all of the covenant people. At this eschatological juncture, the invoking of the name of Jesus has incredible theological significance. It was a guarantor that Yahweh's presence would be with them. When the first Jewish members of the audience were plunged into baptismal waters and the name of Jesus was invoked over them, what happened was nothing less than the birth of Christianity, for it was not Yahweh who was the covenant partner, but it was Jesus Christ. In the minds of the apostles, there was only one possible revelatory explanation, for it was not that Yahweh's place as covenant partner was superseded by Jesus Christ. There was no betrayal of Yahweh, as every Jew knows that Yahweh will not share His glory with another. It must be that, in Jewish ontological speaking, the Name of Yahweh had saved. Yahweh's Name had now become integrated in the identification of Jesus Christ. It must mean that calling upon the name of Yahweh is realized when one calls upon the name of Jesus. It must mean as well that the idiomatic fulfillment for this covenant initiation occurs in the Name of Yahweh when the name of Jesus is uttered in covenant initiation. It must be that when someone speaks of the "Name of Jesus," this is an ontological affirmation that the very essence of Yahweh dwells in Jesus; that Jesus is the abode of Yahweh.

Stephen had no qualms about offering prayer to Christ, nor did Matthew consider it blasphemous for Jesus to allow that where two or three gathered in His Name, He would be there. Implicit in the mention of the name of Jesus was the recognition that God was present. Just because the word "name" is on a certain level a confession, and "Name" recalls an ontological identification of Jesus with Yahweh, Peter did not consider it an affront to Yahweh to appropriate the place of Isaiah's language of salvation to Jesus Christ when he told the Sanhedrin concerning Jesus Christ: "Nor is there salvation in any other, for there is no other name under heaven given among men by which we must be saved" (Acts 4:12).

This understanding also explains the outcome of the council in Acts 15. When the council met to determine whether Paul's converts would be required to keep the Torah, the following question was revisited: With whom are these people in covenant? If the answer was Yahweh, then Paul was wrong to ignore the Torah, for keeping the Torah demonstrated covenantal faithfulness to Yahweh. Further, Paul was particularly in error for not insisting on circumcision of his converts, for circumcision demonstrated a willingness to take the sign of the covenant that identified Jewish men as part of the covenant with Yahweh. It is clear from the narrative that the discussion was quite heated, and there were proponents of strict adherence to Torah that were in attendance. For them, the issue amounted to covenant faithfulness.

In the end, it was James who spoke authoritatively.[36] James recapped how Simon Peter had declared how God at the first visited the Gentiles to "take out of them a people for His name" (Acts 15:14). At first blush, it appears that James might have had in mind that these people were really converts of Yahweh, but that Jesus played some sort of intermediary role. But that was not James's point at all. He cited the prophets for support, drawing from Amos 9 as the primary referent. But the Amos text was not alone in suggesting that the Gentiles would become the people of Yahweh. The phrase, "a people for his name," besides referring back to the Amos passage, may also refer to Ezekiel 36:24-28 and Zechariah 2:11-13, eschatological texts which offer that the Gentiles shall become a people of the Lord.[37] Whether these texts were specific referents, they were known by the people at the council. Zechariah 2:11 prophesies: "And on that day many nations will be converted to Yahweh. Yes, they will become his people, and they will live among you." Obviously, Yahweh had a claim upon the converts from Paul's mission.

In specifically referencing Amos, though, James reminded his audience of the prophetic promise that when the eschaton turned, God would rebuild "the tabernacle of David," and by this citation James implied that spiritually, such an event had occurred.[38] That this had happened is confirmed by the rest of the Amos passage: "So that the rest of mankind may seek the LORD, Even all the Gentiles who are called by my name." As we suggested in a previous chapter, the Hebrew in Amos means that Yahweh will literally invoke His name upon these peoples.[39] It is the same with the Greek construction of the text as offered by James. The name of God was literally to be invoked upon the people.[40] But then James linked this with what he previously said, and his conclusion in essence was that this has already happened. In the context of the Book of Acts, James could have only one thing in mind. F. F. Bruce rightly translates the phrase as " 'all the Gentiles over whom my name has been invoked' (i.e., in baptism)."[41] That is to say, when converts were baptized in Jesus' name, this fulfilled the prophecy of Amos that the nations would enter into covenant by having Yahweh orally invoked upon them. The practical result was that the council proclaimed that Gentiles do not have to keep Torah to be a part of the covenant; they entered convenant when the Name of Jesus was invoked in fulfillment of Amos's prophecy. By this application of a Yahweh text to Jesus, not only do Gentiles not have to be circumcised; the theological freight is much greater. Baptism becomes an ontological claim. The name of Jesus Christ is now the saving name of Yahweh. And Yahweh is present when Jesus' name is called over those being initiated into covenant.

The christological significance of such a scene cannot be overstated. It is not that Yahweh has not gained members to a covenant relationship through Jesus as an intermediary, nor is it that Yahweh has lost members of a covenant community because they now belong to Jesus, the consequence of covenant initiation in His name. Rather, inherent in the saving name of Jesus is a confession understood by the earliest church. In baptizing converts in the name of the Lord Jesus Christ, missionaries were implicitly acknowledging identification of Yahweh with Jesus Christ. Yahweh received glory when Jesus was glorified, for blended into the saving name of Jesus was Yahweh Himself.

Answering Objections

While our presentation demonstrates the earliest understanding of a high christology, there are any number of scholars who would disagree. Even among those who suggest that christology evolved very early, such as James D. G. Dunn, this is not the same as reading the New Testament with a high view toward christology. Dunn would argue that even though Jesus did receive worship and had prescribed roles that identified Him with the divine, Jesus actually did not so much receive praise as God but as one who was "functioning" as God.[42] That is, early Christians did not actually ascribe deity to Jesus in a formal sense. Yet, Richard Bauckham (in contradiction with his own earlier position),[43] suggests that it is problematic "to say that for early christology Jesus exercises the 'functions' of divine lordship without being regarded as 'ontically' divine." He goes on to note that such a distinction is highly problematic, from "the point of view of early Jewish monotheism, for in this understanding of the unique divine identity, the unique sovereignty of God was not a mere 'function' which God could delegate to someone else."[44] In this regard, Bauckham is quite right; Jewish monotheism did not allow the unicity of God to be threatened by someone who "functioned" as God. But Bauckham's solution, in the end, is no better than that of Dunn.

The thesis of Bauckham is that before one book of the New Testament was ever written, in the earliest believing Christian community, "the inclusion of Jesus in the unique divine identity was central to the early church."[45] Bauckham is correct, at least in as far as he goes. Yet, what he ultimately decides upon is a kind of binitarian scheme. When he suggests that Jesus be included "in the divine identity," this is with the clear presumption that Jesus is "another" beside God. In what amounts to an anachronistic confession of faith from a later century, Bauckham seems content to import another Person back into the first-century confession of God. Further, it seems inconceivable that his construal would satisfy Jewish sensibilities in any sense. That is, given the tenacity to which Jews held to the *Shema*, it is baffling how they would immediately allow for another. It is inconceivable that Jesus could join Yahweh as a partner "in the unique divine identity."

Not surprisingly, not everyone is satisfied with a binitarian inclusion of Jesus as a partner with Yahweh. As Paul Rainbow points out, such a position hardly solves the issue of christological origins. Indeed, because the Jews were so strict in their monotheism, how could they, in the words of Rainbow, "accommodate veneration of Jesus alongside God while continuing to see themselves as loyal to the fundamental emphasis of their ancestral tradition on one God?"[46] Rainbow's answer, of course, is that they simply could not. By contrast, consider that a Oneness construal does not merely allow for the "inclusion of Jesus in the divine identity." Rather, it insists that the divine identity, The Name, is in Jesus. The Old Testament confession was, "Hear, O Israel! The LORD is our God, the LORD alone."[47] In the New Testament, the *Shema* is nuanced in a number of texts, not the least of which is I Timothy 2:5: "For there is one God and one Mediator between God and men, the man Christ Jesus." It is precisely because God is working in Christ that Jewish monotheism is not threatened by this construal. Arguably, this is the only satisfactory explanation as to how monotheistic Jews were not threatened but rather exalted in entering into covenant with the Lord Jesus Christ.

Conclusion

No one comes to Jesus Christ for the first time. Christology does not spring from the biblical text without presuppositions. Given the diversity of speaking in the New Testament, it is possible for someone to make an apologetic for a strictly "human Jesus," an "Arian Jesus," and a "Trinitarian Jesus." What we have attempted to demonstrate in these last eight chapters is that a Oneness reading of christology makes sense if one understands the New Testament in its first-century Jewish Christian setting. Because we were in the main attempting to address concepts and paradigms, we have not been exhaustive in our treatment of scriptural texts that could be brought to bear christologically. That said, we did attempt to address a full complement of "kinds" of Scriptures that seem to challenge Oneness christology: passages that might have been deduced to ascribe a place for the Son prior to the Incarnation, passages that speak of Jesus' heavenly origins, passages where God seems to be remote from Jesus, and passages where some kind of plurality seems to compromise a Oneness position. What we have resisted doing is marshaling an endless string of proof texts that demonstrate absolute identity of Jesus Christ with God. We have made reference to such passages, but our method has rather been to focus instead on certain thematic passages. We spent a considerable time in the christological hymns, for they are among the earliest confessions of the church. Further, we treated as thematic the "I AM" passages; all of these as suggestive of other kinds of texts that do the same sort of work. Ultimately, it will be up to the reader to decide the effectiveness of our argument, but the intent of this work is to present Oneness christology as logical, biblical, and historical. In so doing, we have thus far attempted to lay a biblical foundation in logical sequence. In the next three chapters, we attempt to demonstrate the historical integrity of Oneness christology.

SECTION III:

THE MAN WHO IS NOT

Chapter 13

Moving Away from Orthodoxy

A Redefinition of Orthodoxy

If what we have argued thus far is true, then Oneness christology represents the profession of the apostles, based both upon their intimate knowledge of Jesus and their common communion with each other. This is a different argument, say, than suggesting that Oneness christology merely was represented in the first century or that it was an important historical voice or even that it was the dominant voice among Jewish (or Gentile) Christians. Yet, if the claim of the apostolic origin of Oneness christology is true, then there should be two sets of historical evidence readily available to verify such a contention. The first set of evidence would show a record of a broadly held Oneness construal. The second set of evidence would demonstrate how and in what way the historical church turned from such a belief. This is exactly the kind of argumentation we offer in the next three chapters.

In suggesting that Oneness christology may be found broadly and very early on, let us begin by offering what we are not saying. We are not saying that Christians in the first century held only to a Oneness christology. Certainly, even during the time of the apostles, there were those who were preaching a heretical view of Christ.[1] Nor are we suggesting that all Oneness adherents were part of some sort of monolithic pristine stream of belief. Certainly there are presentations of some kinds of Oneness christology that we would suggest are not quite right, or in some cases, are completely wrong.[2] But the fact that there came to be diverse presentations of Oneness christology at all is just the sort of historical phenomenon that one would expect to see if our thesis were true; that is, if these construals, while differing in their trajectories, could all be traced in some way to the first century—branches of the same tree that unwittingly turned this way or that, but which can nonetheless be tracked back to their first-century trunk. A suggestion of diversity, however, should not be understood in the wrong way. We will, in fact, argue for a considerable populace who held to the kind of Oneness christology we have already discussed. Indeed, we will attempt to demonstrate that up until the beginning of the third century AD, this specific kind of Oneness christology was the dominant view of the church.

The second part of our argument works to establish just how a developing trinitarianism became dominant. Primarily, we follow Harry Austryn Wolfson, who has alleged such evolutionary development.[3] He suggests that a progression to full Trinitarian belief was enabled by several metaphysical jumps in thinking. In a view not dissimilar to Bauckham, Wolfson sees the embracing of Hellenistic philosophy during the second century as pivotal in this evolutionary process. Wolfson demonstrates how it was that Justin's (Middle) Platonic use of the *Logos*, arguably mediated through Philo, was furthered by the Hellenistic speculation of Irenaeus and Origen. In mapping the evolutionary development of Trinitarianism, we show how Tertullian created the language necessary for further adaptation, how Athanasius continued this philosophical evolution, and how that ultimately such a Hellenistic understanding of God was made official, theologically codified in Augustine. Significantly, Justin, Hippolytus, Origen, and Tertullian all framed their particular *Logos* christology with Oneness christology in view, and in the case of the last three men, they constructed a good deal of their positions over against Oneness christology.[4] Further, their argumentation was increasingly informed by philosophical presuppositions. Indeed, by the time Augustine authoritatively presented a western Trinity, Plato had arguably contributed more to the epistemological strictures that defined christology than had any church council.[5] Augustine applauded church fathers for their use of philosophers. He contended that appropriating these Hellenistic constructs in defining God was not only appropriate; it was equivalent to the Israelites plundering the Egyptians of their riches![6]

Before we start our historical survey, we must confess a certain bias in reading church history, one made clear by the following question: what is the difference between a "slave rebellion" and "The War of Independence"? The answer is simple. The slave rebellion failed; otherwise it would not be called a "rebellion." Clearly the winner named that event. The label itself passes judgment on the slaves; they were not worthy of freedom. Their effort to get free was nothing but an unfortunate "rebellion." In contrast, "The War of Independence" succeeded, and the winners celebrate this triumphally; the label trumpets the worthiness of their cause. Given, then, that labels are themselves arguments, we begin by rejecting certain labels traditionally assigned to those who have held a Oneness christology.

In the past thirty years, historians have been increasingly concerned with letting groups tell their own story, of not imposing the meaning of another's story upon them. While this is a noble ideal, church historians have not yet caught up with such a strategy. When one reads about Oneness christology, it is universally couched as "heresy" or as a "heretical group." What is particularly distressing about such a portrayal, though, is that historically, those holding Oneness christology were not merely a little group that was readily marginalized. Both Origen and Eusebius used the term "mass" in connection with those who believe this.[7] At the time Tertullian writes, he acknowledges that those who believed Oneness christology were, in fact, a majority of the church.[8]

It is not only in labeling events that historians make arguments. It is also by ignoring them. What may be the most significant christological turning point in the history of the church is universally glossed over by church historians. At the end of the second century, leaders who held to Oneness christology, the dominant confession in the church, battled against evolving *Logos* christology to reaffirm Oneness christology as the only position that should be held by church.[9] It was a battle they lost. Additionally, what started as a political defeat subsequently led to a loss of influence, resulting in the presence of Oneness adherents in ever decreasing numbers.

Pierre Bourdieu, in attempting to demonstrate how groups contend with other groups for dominance, suggests that once a group reaches a dominant position, the next logical step is for the group to take control of the language in order to portray competing groups as heterodox.[10] If the ascendant group succeeds on this front, they then work toward a complete domination of the language. Historically, this explains the fate of a Oneness construal. Once control was wrested from those church leaders who held to Oneness christology, language was made to ally against their cause.[11] Therefore, although J. N. D. Kelly is typical in regarding a Oneness christological tradition as ancient,[12] Tertullian alleges (against historical evidence to the contrary) that it was recent.[13] At the same time Tertullian (in a negative way) charges that the christology of his opponents went back to a Jewish way of thought![14] Because they are generally assumed by the church to hold the "orthodox high ground," Tertullian and Origen have uncritically been allowed to charge their opponents with being simple;[15] a charge that was to stick and is still commonly assumed by church historians. Ironically, what Tertullian and especially Origen meant by "simple" and "uneducated" is that these Oneness adherents could not accept a christology as philosophically abstract as *Logos* christology and that they were uneducated in the sense that they were not able to understand how such an extrabiblical notion could be true. Further, the Oneness attempt to retain the christology held by the majority was framed by Hippolytus as a controversy that "agitated the whole church."[16] Yet, while a kind of *Logos* christology ultimately won out politically, it was less successful with these same "simple people." Adolf Harnack charges that the christology of Hippolytus and Tertullian could not compete with Oneness christology, for "their theology did not correspond to the wants of men."[17] For Harnack, it had to fail because it "conflicted with tradition as embodied in worship to see God Himself in Christ."[18]

Despite this, church historians are too often complicit in a portrayal that paints Oneness adherents as heretics against whom noble Christian champions of orthodoxy battled. It strikes one as odd, though, that the men against whom these Oneness adherents fought were not yet fully Trinitarian and could not themselves have fully ascribed to the Nicean/Constantinople Creed. Origen, whose writings were integral in the development of the Trinity, was later condemned for not being orthodox. Tertullian, who provided the language necessary to formulate a Trinitarian construal is largely given a pass for his incipient Trinitarianism; historians couch this middle ground as Tertullian still "reflecting" on things christologically.

In this study of history, we do not draw from secret sources or from speculative evidence. We utilize standard sources recognizable to theologians and church historians. Despite this, the reason Oneness christology is largely invisible is that its history has been told from the perspective of those who "came to be orthodox." Analogously, this triumphal presentation of Trinitarianism tells the story of the "War of Independence" by explaining how the majority view with regard to Christendom's christology was overturned because it was (analogously) merely a "slave rebellion." Some theologians sincerely argue for the validity of the evolution of christology mediated by Hellenistic philosophy, claiming that there was divine initiative at work in incorporating "MiddlePlatonic/Stoic/NeoPlatonic thought" into christological formation. Perhaps; but for me, such a baptism of Plato strains credulity.

Oneness Christology in a Jewish Milieu

The different ways Oneness christology was expressed in the first and second centuries sometimes had to do with whether that expression was offered in the context of a Jewish or Gentile milieu. Typically, a Jewish construal would more indirectly refer to the divinity of Christ. A Gentile construal might have less reticence in proclaiming Jesus God. Yet, such statements hardly do justice to the whole christological narrative, for they do not take into account a number of historical subtleties. In our survey we do not attempt to ignore exceptions to our construal; yet, we do work to offer how they would fit into our telling of the story. Thus, while some christology of the period is considerably muddled, we offer a few possibilities as to how this christology may or may not be a part of the kind of trajectory for which we are arguing. Before overviewing the earliest christological confessions among Gentile believers, let us consider the known Jewish confessions.

As we discussed in the previous chapter, Jewish christology inherited vocabulary useful to speak of incarnational language. "The Name" (*HaShem*) functioned to talk about the essence of God in the late Second Temple Period.[19] Further, as we noted, Richard Longenecker confirms how that just as "the name" was "a pious Jewish surrogate for God, so for early Jewish Christians, it became a designation for Jesus."[20] Indeed, this Name christology is typical among all early Jewish construals of Jesus Christ. The earliest Jewish Christian Church baptized in Jesus' name. Further, they spoke of this event as "bearing the Name."[21] As we have suggested in chapter 7, other metaphors were useful in describing the Incarnation. Jewish christology utilized the vocabulary of "dwelling" and "glory."[22] Certainly still, it would be wrong to suggest that this Jewish christological proclamation was amorphous or that christology simply did not matter. Such may well be a later reading of christology back onto the first and second centuries. We would suggest, rather, that Jewish christology did not utilize constructs so much as a variety of recurring metaphors that were empowered to speak of Jesus as divine without offending Jewish sensibilities.

In surveying the literature demonstrating this Jewish christology, one has to go beyond reading the church fathers. A whole collection of Jewish Christian *testimonia*, Scriptures from the Old Testament that prove a Oneness christology, is said to have originated in Asia Minor and was widely used by the end of the second century.[23] Further, Jean Daniélou finds a Oneness position, (elements of monarchianism),[24] in an extant Jewish Christian book, *De Montibus* represented in Africa. This is exactly the same kind of Oneness-Jewish christology Tertullian opposes in *Against Praxeas*, known not only in Africa, but also in Rome.[25] The nature of this Jewish christological confession is confirmed by other church historians as well.[26] A first-century Jewish foundation rested first and foremost upon the unicity of Yahweh, and only then did one speak christologically to determine how it is that Yahweh became incarnate.

A Oneness-Jewish Christian theology may also be found in the second century *Paschal Homily* of Pseudo-Hippolytus,[27] and in the third-century poems of Latin Judaeo-Christian Commodius.[28] Indeed, despite the lack of Jewish Christian sources, the sources that we do know about historically are consonant with Oneness christology. *First Clement*, written at the same time, also uses "the Name" as a circumlocution for Jesus. In *1 Clement*, LVIII, people are to "be obedient unto His most holy (παναγίῳ) and glorious (ἐνδόξῳ) Name."[29] This recalls the way the Epistle of James in the New Testament uses "Name" in the context of baptism in Jesus' name being called over the believers.[30] *First Clement* 58.1 says, "trusting in the most holy name of his majesty"; in 59.2, God has "called us . . . from ignorance to the full knowledge of the glory of His name"; and in 59.3, "that we may set our hope on Thy Name, which is the primal source (ἀρχέγονον) of all creation." What is missing in all of these Jewish Christian christological writings, particularly here in *1 Clement*, is any kind of christological focus on Jesus as *Logos*.[31]

We will unpack the evidence relating to the *Shepherd of Hermas* a bit more slowly, for at first consideration, the book stands in contrast with what we have presented thus far as a Jewish christological confession.[32] We allow Hermas among these other Jewish Christian writings, for one can see a particular way in which Name theology was articulated. Yet, there is a kind of syncretic and popularized mixing of Jewish and Hellenistic understanding in the book.[33] Pneumatology is more important than christology in Hermas and while the Father/Son/Holy Spirit are mentioned, the Spirit is really a polymorphous presence and distinctions between the

Son and Spirit are blurred.[34] Further, though there is even a kind of "angel christology" operating,[35] the text is more properly adoptionist; as such, it is the "only work preserved entire which gives clear expression to adoption christology."[36] Adolf Harnack broadly interprets Hermas to show that Jesus "is in the Divine sphere, and one must think of him as of God. But there was no unanimity beyond that." What Hermas does share with all other works of the earliest epoch is that there is a unanimity expressed that "we must think about Christ as we think about God . . ." based upon His redemptive work.[37]

While we seek for some sort of tentative connection with Oneness christology in Hermas, there is little from which we may draw. Still, one can at least find a connection with Name christology.[38] That is, in the Jewish-Christian Hermas, the name Jesus is never actually used, but "The Name" is used everywhere as a circumlocution, indicating that Jesus is not just a man, but that Jesus functions as divine, analogous to the way in which circumlocutions are used for Yahweh. Jean Daniélou cites Hermas (*Vis.* III, 3:5): "The Tower (i.e., the Church) has for its foundation (θεμέλιος) the word (ῥῆμα) of the Almighty and Glorious (ἔνδοξος) Name, and is strengthened by the invisible power of the Master." Daniélou continues, "Thus *Sim.* IX, 14:5 speaks of those 'who bear (φορεῖν) the Name', and in *Sim.* IX, 13:2f. the same phrase appears to be synonymous with 'receive' the Name, *Sim.* VIII establishes a connection between 'bearing the Name' and 'confessing the Name': 'They never denied God, but bore (ἐβάστασσαν) the Name gladly' (*Sim.* VIII, 10:3)."[39] Throughout there is an identification with the "Name" theme and baptism.[40] What we may ultimately say about Hermas was first offered by Daniélou. He contends that the book offers a Jewish way of reckoning Christ; further, there is in Hermas an attachment to a belief system removed from its original understanding.[41] Scholars universally acknowledge the syncretic nature of Hermas; even so, we would posit, following the lead of Daniélou, in Hermas we find the possibility of a remembrance of an earlier Oneness christology.

There is an evident lack of sources to explore this early Jewish christology, in part because by the close of the first century, the leadership and constituency of the church largely passed into Gentile hands. Consequently, those in leadership were less concerned about preserving this literature than would be helpful. But in our brief survey of the extant Jewish Christian literature there are reasons to link a Jewish confession on some level to Oneness christology. Baptism is significant in covenant relationship, and the name of Jesus functions in an important defining capacity. One readily notes the absence of the *Logos* as a construct. And the christology as we have presented it is "high christology." Ironically, this flies in the face of what most people think about Jewish christology; what informs many people's understanding of Jewish christology are Jewish groups who held what is known as "Ebionism." While on first glance, the Ebionites did not hold a high christology, the historical picture is not so simple as some have supposed.

Ebionism in Its Jewish Christian Context

When I was in seminary, my New Testament professor once suggested to me conversationally that he believed the Ebionites actually represent a remembrance of the earliest Christian community. Adolf Harnack agrees.[42] Consider that Ebionism functions as a kind of umbrella term applied to any number of construals of Jewish Christianity as it later came to be articulated.[43] What is important to note is that critiques of Ebionism are in fact critiques of Jewish groups after the first century. While a study of Ebionism is made more difficult because of the known inaccuracies of the church fathers,[44] our argument is that not everything the Ebionites *became* was necessarily representative of the earliest Jewish-Christian communities that were the earliest adherents.

Rather than starting an exploration of Ebionism with definitions of what was later normative, let us begin with some things of which we are fairly certain. We know historically that the Ebionites were "a considerable movement," one derived from orthodox Jewish Christians.[45] These were Jewish Christians who believed in the necessity of keeping Torah; but then, so did the entire church before the Pauline mission and arguably the entire Jewish-Christian community continued to hold a high view of the Torah, even after the counsel described in Acts 15. Ebionites believed in baptism in Jesus' name and that water baptism was "being born again";[46] they believed it was necessary for forgiveness of sins and entrance into the Kingdom of God.[47] This too, arguably, is what the apostles taught.[48] Some Ebionites went into Gnosticism and others held a number of varied beliefs. By the time of Epiphanius they could be termed "a many-headed monster."[49]

The Later Ebionites would speak of God dwelling in Jesus, and by that they meant that Jesus was not divine. Yet, this kind of incarnational language could also be consonant with acceptable Jewish vocabulary that does not strip Jesus of His ontological divinity. Let us consider a heuristic model as to how both an earlier high christology and a devolving christological transition could both be a viable possibility. According to some sources, at least, it was only after the Jerusalem council and the loss of the Temple that the Ebionites "began to propound views on christology and on the binding nature of the Mosaic Law which were heterodox and led to their breaking away from the Church."[50] At that time, Jesus was understood to be their Messiah. Normative language described Him as a prophet or a man in whom God dwelt.[51] Based on similarity of language to that used by Paul and John, one cannot exclude the possibility, at least, of a high christology. If this is true, four things may have contributed toward taking the Ebionites in a direction different than the earliest church: first, the Jerusalem council ruling that the Torah did not need to be kept by Gentiles; second, the destruction of Jerusalem,[52] a tragedy that contributed to their relative isolation;[53] third, the increasing number of Gentiles in the church, particularly in leadership;[54] and fourth, and perhaps the final straw—the church changed christologically as it began to focus on *Logos* speculation in the second century. Adolf Harnack does indeed confirm the marginalization of Jewish Christians as the church became more "catholic."[55]

Sociologists have demonstrated that when the identity of a group is threatened by another group becoming "normative" or "orthodox," the competing group will adjust its identity and language to further distance themselves from the so-called orthodox group.[56] Thus, when christology began to be stripped from its Jewish roots and *Logos* speculation abounded, the Ebionites may have retreated from an allowable position within their ranks—a proclamation that Yahweh indwelt Jesus in a way that defined Jesus as divine.

We are not suggesting that late second-century Ebionites held to a Oneness christology; nor are we suggesting that we can with certainty track the doctrinal development of the Ebionites. But we can posit footprints, at least, of an earlier confession. That they baptized in Jesus' name, connected this event with the forgiveness of sins and being born again; that they could speak of God dwelling in Jesus, and that they traced their roots to the earliest Christianity; these all worked toward the possibility of such a trajectory, one that is consonant with the confession of the apostles.

Ignatius: Christology in a Gentile Milieu

Our earliest writings outside the canon are arguably those who have been termed "apostolic fathers," those authors who are largely a generation or so removed from the apostles and who arguably have some sort of "linear claim" to the teaching of the apostles. Yet, by the time of the apostolic fathers, the curtain was drawn shut on any personal acquaintance with Jewish Christianity.[57] These church leaders knew little or nothing of Jewish sensibilities and did not have the historical necessity of the same christological circumlocutions. While not everyone who overtly called Jesus God was necessarily proclaiming a Oneness christology, there is, in fact, considerable Oneness material preserved from the second century.

At the beginning of the second century, at least, the difference in christology from that of the first century was probably more in language than in substance. The Gentile mission was reached largely in continuity with earlier Pauline missions in the first century and the beginnings of a broader acceptance of the Christian message. The Christian faith continued to spread and experienced charismatic leadership; expressive exuberant worship, prophetic voices, and songs in praise to Christ were the norm. We can trace such a trajectory particularly through Ignatius who wove hymns and doxologies throughout his epistles. These songs are not unique to him, but serve as a testimony to the kind of confessions that were common in the period; it was language that he inherited.[58] Adolf Harnack is typical of those who do not appreciate this sort of genre in Ignatius. He writes, "In the epistles of Ignatius the theology frequently consists of an aimless stringing together of articles manifestly originating in hymns and the cultus."[59] Although framed in a negative way, Harnack is instructive on two points. First, the material Ignatius cites is accepted material brought over from the first-century church in the context of worship. Second, Ignatius is using normative worship language of praise to describe Jesus in work and practice, a language that conveys his christology.

Ignatius could speak of "the flesh of God," "the suffering of God," "the blood of God," and so forth.[60] Although there is one biblical text that may have articulated the "blood of God" in this way,[61] this kind of language would have largely been beyond the scope of a normative way of speaking among Jewish Christians. For Ignatius and those whom he is apparently quoting, it was celebratory. He writes to Polycarp, "The Invisible, who for our sake became visible, the Impassible, who became subject to suffering on our account and for our sake endured everything."[62] While Ignatius can on occasion utilize the language of the Father, Son, and Holy Spirit,[63] he does not have three persons in mind.[64] Although any number of christological persuasions claimed Ignatius as their own, there is no doubt for Ignatius, that the Father suffered in Jesus.[65]

Ignatius has rightly been called a modalistic monarchian.[66] That is to say, Ignatius was Oneness in his christology. There is in Ignatius a christological playfulness that goes beyond the New Testament in the way that the hymnic material celebrates the identity of Jesus. Consider the hymn of Ignatius found in *To the Ephesians* 7.2, "(Jesus is) both flesh and spirit, born and not born, God in man, true life in death, both from Man and from God, first passible and impassible, Jesus Christ our Lord."[67] Ignatius then offers that Jesus is the healer[68] who was flesh and Spirit, first suffering, but now beyond suffering. Ignatius's christology certainly has nothing in common with later second-century apologists. Nor does he speak in the same way as later church fathers thought to be an orthodox understanding, for some thought it good to emend particularly troublesome portions of Ignatius.[69] Still, the fact that even these writings of Ignatius are retained and celebrated is significant, as the historic church did not always preserve writings not consonant with what came to be official doctrine.

There are at least some writings of other church fathers that are also helpful. Melito of Sardis would say in praise of Jesus Christ that the "grace [of God] has been poured out upon the uttermost parts of the inhabited world, and there the almighty God has taken up his dwelling place through Jesus Christ."[70] In *2 Clement*, an anonymous sermon attached to the epistle of *1 Clement*, there is an offering of unmitigated praise to Jesus as God[71]: "Brethren, we ought so to think of Jesus Christ as God, as of the judge of living and dead. And we ought not to belittle our salvation; if we belittle him, we expect also to receive little" (*2 Clement* 1:1-2).[72]

The lack of linguistic distinction between Jesus and the Father would hardly have pleased the apologists of the same period. For example, Melito closes this same piece by offering of Jesus,

> This is the Christ. This is Jesus. This is the general. This is the Lord. This is the one who rose up from the dead. This is the one who sits at the right hand of the Father. He bears the Father and is borne of the Father, to whom be the glory and the power forever. Amen.[73]

For Melito, this sort of playful ambiguity is allowable in doxological praise. He writes, "He who is impassible suffers and does not take revenge, he who is immortal dies and does not answer a word."[74] Melito represents a normative and ancient way of speaking. It is this way of speaking that is not substantively consistent with *Logos* christology. Clearly this kind of speaking is either "a branch" of the tree leading back to the "trunk" of a Oneness christological confession or else it is the trunk itself.

Summary

We began the chapter by beginning to deconstruct the language and triumphalistic reading of a later christology accepted by the church. Then, we proceeded under the working assumption that if Oneness christology was apostolic in origin, the broad sweep of the earliest literature would either confirm this directly or would allow for such an explanation; in either case, the evidence would not contradict a Oneness construal. Attempting to fairly represent a construal of the earliest representative material, we suggested that in fact a broad belief in Oneness christology in both Jewish and Gentile Christianity from this earliest period is consonant with the historical data. In the next chapter, we move ahead chronologically to consider a christological construal that contested this early profession of Jesus Christ as God.

Chapter 14

Apologists and the Hermeneutical Shift

Introduction

At the 2002 SBL meeting in Toronto, Richard Bauckham's book, *God Crucified*, was considered by a panel of scholars in front of an audience of over a thousand of Bauckham's colleagues and members of the Society of Biblical Literature. Bauckham broke new ground with his scholarly defense of a high christology in the earliest Jewish community. When discussion was allowed from the floor, a question was directed to Bauckham: "If christological understanding was evolving and it historically took until Nicea for the church to officially confess the full divinity of Jesus, how was it that the earliest church considered Jesus divine?" Bauckham's answer echoed the claim of his book; he asserted that in the second century, there was an epistemological shift, one in which the church moved away from approaching Jesus in the context of His first-century Jewish-Christian claims; instead, church fathers began seeing God and Christ through a Hellenistic lens. Prior to Bauckham, others have made the same claim as well; yet there is a reason that this claim has largely fallen on deaf ears. Academically, it undermines a naturalistic approach to christology. Religiously, it critiques a divinely sanctioned evolution of christology. Some balk at what they label "Bauckham's Big Bang christology." Nonetheless, Bauckham is right to bracket the belief of the earliest Christian community. Further, he provides a great service in making visible a transition that has largely been ignored both academically and theologically.

The Advent of Christian Philosophers

In the second century, not all Gentile church fathers "are created equal." While Ignatius and others might use celebratory language of Jesus as God, other, more "educated" church fathers did otherwise. Unfortunately, to be "educated" in the second century meant to be educated in philosophy. Similarly, to be "scientific" was to accept the "science" of Greek philosophy. A catalog of significant second-century fathers demonstrates that both Aristides (136-161) and Clement of Alexandria (*ca.* 185-211/215) were converted from paganism and were trained philosophers. Tatian, Theophilus, and Justin were not only trained in philosophy; they left revealing accounts of their training. Given this turn of events, it is not surprising that Christian proclamation began to take on a decidedly different tone.

Perhaps the most significant philosophical presupposition accepted by second-century apologists (an umbrella term that overlaps with the men we have mentioned),[1] one that set up the necessity for utilizing an intermediary for the Incarnation, is that of the impassability of God. The dominant philosophy of the second century was Middle Platonism,[2] the same sort of philosophy that influenced Philo in the first century. While it may be debated just how much these fathers utilized Philo, there is considerable evidence to indicate that a number were directly dependent upon him. As we began to suggest in a previous chapter, Philo certainly held stringently to the impassability of God.[3] Alister McGrath decries this inheritance. He writes, "Early Christian theologians, anxious to gain respect and credibility in such circles, did not challenge the idea. As a result, it became deeply imbedded in the Christian theological tradition."[4]

Earlier we contended that these church fathers drifted from the church's Old Testament moorings. But this claim must be understood in a particular way, for although certain Gnostic groups ignored the Old Testament and others taught that it was not inspired and should be disregarded,[5] the apologists did neither. Yet, their use of the Old Testament was problematic: allegorical interpretation in a manner analogous to Philo. Thus, while their intention was to defend the Christian faith against Jews or pagans in the most educated terms, they were deprived of the ballast of Old Testament interpretation, and the apologists began fighting philosophy with philosophy. The question then ultimately became whose philosophy was right. In the apologists' construal, they referred to their own philosophy as "our philosophy" and the opposing view as "barbaric philosophy." Speaking in these terms, the apologists did not regard Christianity as one philosophy among others but as *the* philosophy.[6]

Justin Martyr

A. Justin and the *Logos*

Of all the apologists, the most influential was Justin Martyr. Hailing from Alexandria, Egypt, Justin actually lectured in a philosopher's robe, teaching that God had been accurately defined by the classical Greek philosophers.[7] Significantly, it is through Justin that christology moved into the realm of what Harry Austryn Wolfson calls "philosophized Christianity."[8] The starting place for Justin Martyr with regard to God was that He was omnipotent, unmovable, and thus unchangeable.[9]

Justin was compelled with the same allegorical necessity as Philo to allegorize a very active God in the Old Testament, no small pedagogical shift.[10] Yet, Justin had a problem beyond that of Philo: the problem of incarnation. Since God was essentially removed from the realm of human affairs, Justin needed *another* to act—this, Justin found in the *Logos*.

The use of the *Logos* by Justin was an effort to utilize a term that was in currency for any number of philosophical systems. At some point the *Logos* had been seen as the rational power of calculation by which humanity reasoned; in the second century though, the concept of the *Logos* developed further until it could be a hypostasis of deity, a *"deuteros theos"* [second god].[11] The *Logos* thus supplied a key for Justin as it not only provided an intermediary between God and the created world, but "it also provided the bridge between pagan philosophy and Christianity."[12] For Justin, it was not Yahweh represented in various theophanies in the Old Testament; it was the *Logos*. Yet because the *Logos* was effectively an apologetic device, one clearly not thought through, Justin's presentation was uneven and forced at times.[13]

It seems logical to assume that Justin's notion of God would be hard for Christians to allow, for the God of the philosophers was nameless and ineffable. Yet, despite opposition in the church, this is exactly what Justin taught. He wrote, "To the Father of all . . . there is no name given."[14] Justin worked to convince Christians that earlier Greek philosophers were in fact correct in their understanding of God. For Justin, Plato and the Stoics shared claims that the Word (λόγος) was in Jesus.[15] But this was a stretch for most Christians. Most difficult to allow was the implication that since the *Logos* guided philosophers like Heraclitus and Socrates, they were actually "Christians" before Christ.[16]

While for Justin the Son is unique and special, there is a way in which the Son as intermediary gets removed from God and more identified with the creation. Justin writes in *1 Apology* 6, "The Son who came from him . . . and the host of other good angels who follow him and are made like him, and of the prophetic Spirit, we worship and adore."[17] Thus, the Son is just one among others to whom secondary worship is offered. Justin's appropriation of a Platonic construct to Christianity thus resulted not only in a worship of Yahweh as the Supreme God in the ultimate sense; but his system allowed for worship of all derivatives, including both Jesus and angels. According to Bauckham, "A Jewish understanding was open to the inclusion of Jesus in the divine identity. But Greek philosophical—Platonic—definitions of divine substance or nature and Platonic understanding of the relationship of God to the world made it extremely difficult to see Jesus as more than a semi-divine being, neither truly God nor truly human."[18]

B. Justin and the "I AM"

In Justin, God was formally constructed as beyond the cosmos, distant from His creation. Already in Philo, Exodus 3:14, which identified Yahweh as the "I AM," became a proof text for God as ineffable and unknowable.[19] For Justin, it was no longer Yahweh who spoke from the burning bush but another. Since one of the names of Jesus Christ, the *Logos* of God, is angel, and since Exodus references an angel, for Justin, it must be that Christ spoke from the bush.[20] Exodus was seen to define God in a passive way and the *Logos* was understood as God's active agent; any use of the Hebrew "Word of God" [*debar* Yahweh] was then appropriated to the actions of the Hellenistic *Logos*.[21] Indeed, Justin's position on Exodus 3:14 suggested a particular interpretation of the verse, one which became a significant proof text for Clement of Alexandria[22] and Origen.[23] C. R. Seitz has suggested that the very nature of the christological question has come from the reading of the Greek—the I AM of Moses that got turned into the "*ego eimi ho on*" [I am THE BEING] in Greek.[24] For Seitz, the Greek language changes the focus. "It is a very small leap to see how *ousia* dominated rather than personality."[25] Beginning with the work of Justin, christologians moved to questions of "being," clearly a path in the wrong direction.

C. How Justin Approached Oneness Christology

Justin was certainly aware of Christian communities that called Jesus God and he didn't care for it.[26] Indeed, Adolf Harnack notes, "From Justin's dialogue that the direct designation of Jesus as θεὸς [God] (not as ὁ θεὸς [the god]) was common in communities." Justin complained against those Christians who suggested that there was no metaphysical difference between Jesus as divine and the God of the Old Testament. Among such Christians, the common way of understanding the *Logos* was as a difference in name only.[27] In contrast, Wolfson offers, "Justin Martyr maintains that the *Logos* is distinct from the Father 'in number' (ἀριθμῷ) and not 'in thought' (γνώμη); in number and not 'in name (ὀνόματι) only.' "[28] Arthur Cushman McGiffert suggests that Justin has reference to what *we* would term a Oneness christology when he ridiculed, "For those who say the Son is Father are proved neither to be acquainted with the Father nor to know that the Father of the universe has a son, who being *Logos* and first born of God, is God."[29]

Part of the driving force of second-century fathers was their focus against things Jewish, and this no doubt included a Oneness hermeneutic. Even though these apologists didn't really understand the Jewish worldview,[30] anti-Jewish rhetoric was widespread. Harnack suggests that those "who resisted the advancing hellenizing of Christianity, with regard, for example, to the doctrine of God, eschatology, christology" were charged as "Judaizers," a charge that was considered a reproach.[31] As we suggested in chapter 13, *Logos* christologians employed such labeling as an argument in itself, for only by getting a Oneness position to abandon their hermeneutic could they hope to make headway; for, as Claus Westermann explains, "The question of the relation of the persons of the Trinity to one another and the question of the divinity and humanity in the person of Christ as a question of ontological relations could only arise when the Old Testament had lost its meaning for the early church."[32]

Oneness Christology in the Second Century

A. Apocryphal Acts

Justin was one voice of the second century, a representative of a larger group of apologists; but there were many other voices as well. For instance, common literature, such as the *Apocryphal Acts*, taught that Jesus is God. Although some have categorized the christology of the *Apocryphal Acts* as naïve, it is clearly Oneness christology. Consider the *Acts of Andrew*. What can be deduced is that "it is not possible to distinguish between divine persons."[33] So too with the *Acts of Paul*, where "the most important statement for the author is that Christ is Lord, not only the Lord of his Church, but also of life and death." *Acts of Paul* readily reflects "early Christian christology as a whole. Of a well-marked *Logos* christology there is in the *APL* [Acts of Paul] hardly any trace."[34] In the *Acts of John*, prayers can be found addressed to Christ both as King as well as the Lord of the Universe,[35] while Thomas addresses prayer to Jesus in a similar way in the *Acts of Thomas*.[36] In the *Acts of Paul and Thecla*, Paul prayed, "O God, who knows the heart, Father of our Lord Jesus Christ,"[37] while Thecla would pray, "My God, Son of the Most High, who art in Heaven."[38] In her martyrdom she plunged herself into a reservoir of water, saying, "In the name of Jesus the Messiah, I baptize myself on my last day."[39] The book closes by her praying, "Jesus Christ, Son of God, my help in prison . . . you alone are God and to you be glory for ever. Amen."[40] In the *Acts of Peter* as well, which is rightly assessed to be monarchian,[41] one finds Oneness christology. For though Peter baptizes the shipmaster in the titles of the Father, Son, and Holy Spirit, he responds to an appearance of Jesus, "Most excellent, the only holy one, it is thou that hast appeared to us, thou God Jesus Christ; in thy name hath this man been washed."[42] Throughout the *Acts of Peter*, it is Jesus Christ who is divinely acting, and it is to His name that appeals are made.

B. Testamentary Literature

Another example of the way in which Jesus was celebrated as God among the common people was the Jewish Testamentary literature edited for Christian purposes. Testamentary literature demonstrates this same simple monotheism, particularly the *Testaments of the Twelve Patriarchs*.[43] Harnack suggests that a Christian editor interpolated christological offerings in the *Testaments of the Twelve Patriarchs*. In his translation, H. C. Kee puts what he believes to be a Christian interpolation in brackets. After the *Testament of Benjamin* suggests that "the Most High shall send forth his salvation through the ministration of the unique prophet . . .," Kee then offers that the following interpolation was added: "[He shall enter the first temple, and there the Lord will be abused and will be raised up on wood.]" The *Testament of Dan*, 5, offers, "The Lord will be in her (Israel's) midst [living as human beings]."[44] The *Testament of Naphtali* prophesies, "Through his kingly power God will appear [dwelling among men on the earth]."[45] The *Testament of Asher* 7 records that "the Most high shall visit the earth. [He shall come as a man eating and drinking with human beings.]"[46] In the *Testament of Judah* 24, the prophecy is offered of God speaking in the first person: "My rule shall be terminated by men of alien race until the salvation of Israel comes, until the coming of the God of righteousness."[47] In the *Testament of Simeon*, 6.5, the author offers, "Then Shem shall be glorified; because God the Lord, the Great One in Israel, will be manifest upon the earth [as a man]. By himself he will save Adam . . . [because God has taken a body, eats with human beings, and saves human beings]."[48] While Oneness christology is not universal in this literature,[49] it comes close.

C. Confessions of Martyrs

Other confessions that can be linked to Oneness christology are the various confessions of martyrs. It was not uncommon for martyrs to speak doxologies, literature that reflects a Oneness christology as well. These martyrdom doxologies contrast "the divine rule of Christ, to whom worship is due, with Caesar's idolatrous pretensions of divine worship."[50] The early *The Acts of Christian Martyrs* seems always to have ended with a doxology to Christ alone. Thus, in their dying prayer, martyrs, like Stephen, expected that it was Jesus whom they would see and Jesus who would receive them.[51] Some who read such martyrologies were not pleased, as evidenced by later glosses added to "correct" these texts. As Bauckham notes, "In some cases, the later expansion of an original christological doxology into a later Trinitarian form can be clearly seen."[52] Bauckham continues, "Here the Trinitarian doxology is the post-Nicene development; the purely christological doxology is the early form." By contrast, there is very little in the way of doxologies that gives glory in "coordinated" form to the Father, Son, and Holy Spirit; and those few that do are disputed as to how early a date may actually be ascribed to them.

D. Marcionites, Montanists, and Others

So widespread was Oneness christology that it was represented in a variety of movements, even ones that were considered marginally or overtly heretical by the church of the second century. For instance, there is some evidence that Marcion, who in the middle of the second century created his own canon and set of churches, had a Modalist christology.[53] While Adolf Harnack did not think that Marcion himself was of this opinion, there are others who think otherwise. Thus, though it may be argued that Marcion leaned toward Oneness christology, it is likely that there was a representative affinity to Oneness christology among his followers; for the Marcionite system was fairly fluid and would allow Marcionites various conceptions of Christ as God.[54]

Further, there were impulses toward spiritual restoration of the earliest church, such as the one represented in a movement called the Montanists. While Montanus himself may not have believed in Oneness christology,[55] it is certain that among the followers of Montanus there were those who held no hesitation in speaking clearly of Jesus as God.[56] The confusion comes in assessing whether Montanus himself and the prophetic women taught Modalism, for they certainly used formulas that had a modalistic sound; but they also had others that could afterwards be interpreted "economically."[57]

Not only Montanists and Marcionites, but widespread acceptance of Oneness christology is represented in a number of diverse groups in the second and third centuries.[58] For instance, there were among the Simonians as well those who exhibited a Oneness christology.[59] Further evidence for its centrality is the way in which it becomes a foil for Justin and his inheritors over against which to frame their own particular christological scheme. Thus, there is evidence of pervasive Oneness christology in the second century, one which may well be "branches on the tree" connected to a first-century christological trunk.

"Exceptions" to the Rule

A. The *Didache*

Even among books that do not strictly teach a Oneness christology, there is an echo of it. For instance, let us consider the *Didache*. Scholars certainly are right to note a certain unevenness about the text. It may be that there were Trinitarian additions made to it,[60] or it could be that it was merely "written in a time of transition" where an unknown author sought to harmonize "revered traditions of the church with new ecclesial necessities." Whatever the case, the *Didache* was utilized as a liturgical catechism for a local assembly. The book cannot be construed as a universal attempt to "regulate the behavior of the entire church" but was rather written with a local situation in view.[61]

In chapter 7 of the *Didache*, there is instruction about baptism using a Trinitarian formula. Yet in chapter 9 of the *Didache*, the text clearly states of those baptized that they "have been baptized in the name of the Lord...." It is for this reason that some posit different recensions in the *Didache* reflecting earlier and later tradition; at minimum, the least one can say about it is that there are different traditions within the document. There are definite Jewish elements in the *Didache* that demonstrate an early stream of Oneness christology. Considering "Name" as a substantive way of speaking of God in Christ, it is informative that the prayer is offered, "We give thee thanks, O Holy Father, for thy holy Name which thou hast made to tabernacle (κατεσκήνωσας) in our hearts." Jean Daniélou sees this as a reference to Yahweh texts in the Old Testament being appropriated to Christ.[62]

B. Dynamic Monarchianism

One of the difficult things to unravel is how one should consider second-century "Dynamic Monarchians," those Christians who, as they are generally described, defined their belief in the solitary nature of God by suggesting that Jesus was, in fact, not God. Christologically, this position would be akin to confessions of certain Ebionites. Yet, there is reason for caution on this score. Those who wrote against them were themselves singularly attempting to be change agents; *Logos* Christologians readily lumped together those who would consider themselves to be polar opposites, believers who made Jesus God (Modalistic Monarchians) and those who did not in any sense make Him God (Dynamic Monarchians). Because both groups denied that it was the *Logos* who became incarnate, that is, the *Logos* as a second person of God, they were both considered to be equally wrong. For those holding to a *Logos* christology, it was moot as to how much of God was alleged to be incarnate by these "simple" people. They were wrong for not affirming the *Logos* in a substantive manner. This lack of interest in defining the real position of the opponents may have led to some of the confusion in the textual evidence. Consider the case of Theodotus. He is often identified with second-century Dynamic Monarchians; however, he is also included among those who definitely had a high christology and could rightly be included in those whose christology was Oneness.[63] This makes one suspicious of categories and classifications offered by those who deemed the *Logos* as a second god.

The Beginning of Change

While Justin and the apologists were attempting to change the way the masses thought, they themselves struggled for consistency in their speaking. For although Justin tried to rid the church of hymnic accolades to Jesus, it was not so easy to dispose of his own inherited praise to Jesus. Seemingly, *Logos* Christologians and their inheritors could not help speaking in this way. Irenaeus, an inheritor of Justin, could still say, "*Deus impassabilis* has become *passible*."[64] Such phrases as "God is born," "the suffering God," or "the dead God"[65] could readily be made by Tatian!

Still, change was in the air. From the perspective of the evolutionary development of the Trinity, doctrines were "advancing." Education and science seemed to be on their side in allegorical interpretation. Harnack rightly captures the spirit of the time when he suggests that "to find the spiritual meaning of the sacred text, partly beside the literal, partly by excluding it, became the watchword for the 'scientific' Christian theology."[66] Further, on the strength of argument and education, Justin's view became normative for those whom he taught. Rather, as Harry Wolfson notes, "And this view of Justin Martyr from then on constitutes the orthodox view."[67] Yet not all church theologians are happy about such a development. Adolf Harnack, reflecting on its Philonic origins, does not spare judgment for those who were inheritors of Philo. He notes that "Philo was the master" of dogmatic deception.[68] If this is true, it is not a deception that ends in the second century, but it is one that continues to evolve.

Chapter 15

Displacing Oneness Christology

Introduction

The second century closed by bringing into conflict the christological views held by the majority of Christians and the evolving trajectory that sprang from the introduction of Justin's *Logos* christology. On the side of the inheritors of *Logos* christology were some of the most influential teachers in the church, but on the other side were influential teachers as well. On both sides of the issue, key positions were held by dominant leaders. Historically, the theological label generally ascribed to those who opposed the *Logos* christologians is modalistic monarchians, or simply, modalists. The terminology is more properly an umbrella term representing some variety of christological expression. While one may also call these Oneness christologies, we will refrain, as we have thus far attempted to reserve the nomenclature of Oneness christology for what we deem to be a biblical construal. That said, there was among these modalists a majority who held to just such a first-century perspective. The purpose of this chapter is to demonstrate how *Logos* christology first became dominant in the church and ultimately evolved to full Trinitarianism. Because of our specific concerns, we largely focus on theological argument rather than teasing out related history that politically assesses reasons for the change.

Normative Oneness Christology: Praxean Modalism

Specific construals of Jesus Christ, which largely represented the majority opinion, were in the third century termed modalism. As we have begun to suggest, Modalism is actually an umbrella term and incorporates a number of different approaches. While the names Sabellius and Noetus are the ones most often linked with modalism, the position of these men represents only one small segment of modalists. An earlier form of modalism may be deduced from Praxeas;[1] although we have to tease out his beliefs because of the hostility of Tertullian in his *Against Praxeas*, his was a simple (we would suggest normative) Oneness construal. For Praxeas, there is no plurality of Persons in the Old Testament.[2] Rather, it was the power of the Highest that overshadowed Mary, and this was none other than God Himself. It is God who is in Christ, and the distinction for Praxeas, where distinction should be made, is between the man and God. Further, although some commentators want to argue otherwise, this kind of modalism had nothing to do with Stoicism, Gnosticism, nor was it Neoplatonic in its origin. Nor was this kind of modalism confined to Africa; it was in Rome, in Asia,[3] and throughout the East. It was pervasive.

Tertullian called Praxeas a pretender of yesterday and an innovator[4] while at the same time representing himself with the cloak of orthodoxy.[5] There are at least several very good reasons to be suspicious of this depiction. First, in defending what he had taught, Tertullian says that they have believed this "especially since they have been instructed of the paraclete." If Tertullian is just now teaching what either others or himself (this implies a change of position) have been "instructed of the paraclete," this smacks of a recent development. Further, in an effort to explain himself, Tertullian resorts to neologisms. Alister McGrath has noted that Tertullian is responsible for creating "509 new nouns, 284 new adjectives, and 161 new verbs in the Latin language."[6] Many of these neologisms have to do with christology. Further, in his *Against Praxeas*, Tertullian struggles in ways that are not apparent in his other writings, redoubling his argument, back-pedaling to insist what he is or is not saying; Harnack contrasts this doctrinal uncertainty with Tertullian's more certain style in other books.[7]

Although Tertullian situates himself against philosophy,[8] he held to certain presuppositions that were based on the culture in which he lived. As a convert to Christianity, for Tertullian, Justin was normative.[9] Thus, taking as normative Justin's assertion that Plato had contact with Moses,[10] Tertullian inherited both a syncretic set of Platonic notions about God and absorbed a good deal of Stoicism as well.[11]

Tertullian had come to accept a view of God that disallowed the God of the Old Testament from physically being present and participating in human affairs. Tertullian's antipathy with Praxeas seems to stem from the fact that the Praxean party was large and not above mocking the position of Tertullian as that of polytheists. Tertullian writes,

> The simple, indeed, (I will not call them unwise and unlearned,) who always constitute the majority of believers, are startled at the dispensation (of the Three in One), on the ground that their very rule of faith withdraws them from the world's plurality of gods to the one only true God; not understanding that, although He is the one only God, He must yet be believed in with His own μοναρχια. The numerical order and distribution of the Trinity they assume to be a division of the Unity; whereas the Unity which derives the Trinity out of its own self is so far from being destroyed, that it is actually supported by it. They are constantly throwing out against us that we are preachers of two gods, while they take to themselves pre-eminently the credit of being worshippers of the one God.[12]

For Tertullian, the Praxean position was wrong by definition, for it was the *Logos* only who could become incarnate. This was the operating presupposition that drove his own argument. Because Praxeas allowed that it was God who literally became incarnate, there was an obvious corollary: Praxean christology allowed that the Father suffered. Tertullian was enraged by this possibility and in his ire framed an epitaph for Praxeas: "Patripassian."[13] In so doing Tertullian betrays his indebtedness to philosophy. As church historian Jaroslav Pelikan notes, Tertullian, for all of his hostility to metaphysics, freely accepts the notion of the impassability of God without either biblical support or theological proof.[14]

The Developing Trinitarianism of Tertullian

It was Tertullian who in Latin first constructed God in terms of "persons," the term *Trinitas* coined over against Praxeas. For Tertullian, the *Logos* was a second person,[15] and though "person" did not mean to Tertullian what it would later come to mean,[16] threeness was fully intended; Tertullian offered building blocks with regard to the Father, Son, and Holy Spirit, suggesting they were

> three, however, not in status (*statu*), but in degree (*gradu*); not in substance (*substantia*), but in form (*forma*); not in power (*potestate*), but in species (*specie*); yet of one substance, and of one

status, and of one power, inasmuch as He is one God from whom these degrees and forms and species are reckoned under the name of the Father, and of the Son, and of the Holy Spirit.[17]

It is this statement as much as any other that convinces church historians that Tertullian was not in fact arguing against innovators, but the rank and file of Christianity. As Arthur Cushman McGiffert notes, "Those to whom Tertullian refers as 'the simple, who are always the majority of believers' were certainly not innovators."[18] Tertullian was neither particularly convincing nor consistent. His terminology is drawn unevenly from Hellenistic categories,[19] and in the end it would all be reshuffled by later church fathers. Nonetheless, Tertullian's contribution to language and the beginnings of definition for Trinitarianism cannot be denied. Though Tertullian would in the end of his life argue against the church that he worked to build, during these christological debates, he would assume the high ground as orthodox.[20]

Noetus and Sabellius

Besides the modalism of Praxeas, there are two other more well-known representatives of modalism at the beginning of the third century, Noetus and Sabellius.[21] In later lists by heresiologists, it would be Noetus and Sabellius who are most notably spoken against, whose very names are attached to modalism. While one reads of "the heresy of Noetus" or "the heresy of Sabellius," Praxeas slips in under the wire. Noetus has been variously represented, but he appears to have the simplest christology of the modalists, if in fact what has been written about him is not a caricature: Jesus equals God and God equals Jesus.

Certainly Noetus had no problem confessing Jesus as God. Noetus said, "For Christ was God, and suffered on account of us, being Himself the Father, that He might be able to save us. And we cannot express ourselves otherwise, he says, for the apostle also acknowledges one God, when he says, 'Whose are the fathers, (and) of whom as concerning the flesh Christ came, who is over all, God blessed forever.'"[22] Yet, Noetus could speak of the Father in a way similar to Praxeas.[23] Thus, Noetus certainly would have been guilty of the claim that the Father suffered; Epiphanius, writing a century later, writes that Noetus said that the Father died.[24] Two things cloud the issue, however. First, the evidence of whether Noetus actually said this is mixed.[25] Second, if Noetus did say that the Father died, he may have been making such a statement in the same manner as Melito or Ignatius; offering in praise a doxological paradox.

The name of Sabellius is used in connection with modalism more than any other. Though we know nothing of Sabellianism from friendly sources or from his own writings,[26] if sources are correct, Sabellius falls prey to the idea that he has to fight philosophy with philosophy. Since the *Logos* Christologians could explain the way in which the rays of the sun are like their monarchy, "one" yet streaming forth, so Sabellius turns the language of the Stoics to his own defense.[27] The Godhead, says Sabellius is like the sun; at this point Sabellius introduces the notion of dilation. The rays go out and manifest themselves as the Father; they return again as the Son; they return again as the Spirit. In such an explanation, Sabellius apparently believes in a Father who *became* a Son (ceasing to be the Father) and who subsequently *became* the Spirit (ceasing to be the Father or the Son). The system of Sabellius would hardly stand biblical or philosophical scrutiny; nonetheless, his name became synonymous with modalism. My guess is that Sabellianism is normative Oneness christology gone awry; that in trying to dialogue with theologians using their nomenclature and constructs his position became distorted in the process. Thus, while one finds the possibility of Oneness christology at its base, it is certainly not an acceptable construal of christology, for it makes nonsense of the biblical text.

Origen's *Logos* and the Developing Trinity

To Justin's *Logos* was added another feature by Irenaeus;[28] he taught the "eternal generation" of the *Logos*, a doctrine confirmed and made normative by Origen.[29] Origen works out his idea of the *Logos* in the context of the *Logos* of the Book of John and what he deems to be related passages. In this context, he holds the biblical text up to any light that might be offered by Philo, particularly exploring the Platonic notions from which Philo draws.[30] In the Platonic thought which Origen is utilizing, *Logos* stands for archetypal reason and ideas; in Philo, this notion gets mixed with the biblical metaphor of wisdom. As a consequence of his deliberate usage, Origen articulates a doctrine of the *Logos* in a way that is more convincing than anyone who had written up until this time. In this, rather than drawing from Philonic speculation, Origen now begins drawing from Plotinus.[31] Clement, the teacher of Origen, may also have affirmed that the Son is eternally generated.[32] In the third century this notion, propelled by these Alexandrian fathers, was received unevenly.[33] Still, Harry Wolfson rightly suggests that with a few exceptions, from Origen on, this theory became normative in the last half of the third century.[34]

Utilizing Middle Platonic interpretation,[35] Origen taught that only the Father was divine in the strict sense of the term.[36] For Origen, the Father, Son, and Holy Spirit are not equal but should be understood in descending terms with respect to their power, the Father being properly called God. In summarizing the teaching of Origen, Justinian notes that God the Father, "in holding together all things, extends his power to every level of being, imparting to each from His own store its being what it is." By comparison, "the Son, in a lesser degree than the Father, extends only to rational beings [for he is second to the Father];" the Spirit is divine "to a still lesser degree . . . and against that of the Holy Spirit is superior to the other holy agencies."[37] This doctrine of God also relates to the way in which each of the three interacts with humanity. Origen says that God the Father's power extends to all things that exist, God the Son's as extending only to living beings, and the Holy Spirit's extending only to the "saved."[38]

Oneness Christology in Opposition to the Fathers

For Origen, a Oneness christological position represented the "mass of believers," who know only "the Christ according to the flesh." He writes, "They do not wish to seem to affirm two gods; they do not wish to deny the divinity of the Savior; then they end by admitting two names, and one single person."[39] According to Jaroslav Pelikan, it was over against the position of modalism that for Origen, the *Logos* would become both eternal and external from the Father, so none could "dare to lay down a beginning for the Son, before which he did not exist."[40] Origen believed that those with a Oneness christology were "uninstructed and simple" (Cels. 16:1). While Origen's view, building on Justin, began to gain momentum in certain circles, for many it seemed too much intellectualizing of the faith.

Further, Adolf Harnack suggests that neither Tertullian nor Hippolytus were very successful in any sort of acceptance of their christology, for "their theology did not correspond to the wants of men." For Harnack, it had to fail, because it "conflicted with tradition as embodied in worship, which taught men to see God Himself in Christ."[41] According to J. N. D. Kelly, it wasn't that this doctrine was novel that caused the conflict. He regards modalism as "a fairly widespread, popular trend of thought."[42]

Harnack argues that in the end, it was Oneness christologians who caused their own demise. While this doctrine was "embraced by the great majority of Christians,"[43] it was when teachers in the movement turned from a christology that was "markedly monotheistic, and had real interest in Biblical Christianity"[44] to a defense that was "scientific" (philosophical) that it "lost its *raison d'être*" (reason to exist).[45] Thus, while a turn to a Stoic style defense of its christology seemed to be a good strategy, it failed. The masses could not follow it. Ultimately a political victory in Rome was assured and turned the tide in favor of developing Trinitarianism.

The Success of Athanasius over Arius

The third century closed with some specific developments toward Trinitarianism. As Harry Wolfson rightly notes, there were specific epistemological stages, each of which were necessary to reach what would later be the orthodoxy of the fourth and fifth centuries.[46] As we have sought to demonstrate, the first stage was accomplished by the apologists, who utilized a Philonic conception of the *Logos* to explain the Incarnation in a Hellenistic milieu. Second, Irenaeus and Origen moved from Philonic notions of Plato to a more Plotinian interpretation in their understanding of the *Logos* as both less than and being eternally generated from God. The question as to how the *Logos* could be less than God and equal with God was the next problem to be dealt with, one which dominated the beginning of the fourth century. The key positions proposed are known by the historical figures who served as spokespersons in the debate, Athanasius and Arius.

When Constantine converted to Christianity at the beginning of the fourth century, such an alliance mutually furthered the fortunes of Constantine while giving significant power to the church. Because Christianity was an important vehicle for solidifying Constantine's empire, he was concerned the debate between Athanasius and Arius might fracture the unity of the church. He therefore had a vested interest in the outcome of the debate.

There were two positions on which Arius was called into question. First, in an interpretation of Proverbs 8, he deduced that there was a time when the *Logos* did not exist.[47] Also, Arius retained what had been a fairly normative position for church leaders at that time, espousing that the *Logos* was less then God. Yet, as Arius articulated it, there was a distinction between the *Logos* and the Son such that while God made the *Logos*, it was the *Logos* that made the Son.[48] Though Arius sounded orthodox in his celebratory praise of Christ,[49] what he actually taught was in conflict with what had become codified in Origen and what was now developing into orthodoxy through Athanasius.

Because of the potential disunity in the empire, Constantine worked toward a solution. In AD 325, a regional council in Antioch condemned the position of Arius with its decisions confirmed later in the year by the Imperial council at Nicea.[50] Most readily signed on to this new orthodoxy; only Arius and two other bishops declined.[51] Still, the matter was hardly settled. In fact, by the official act of writing it all down, the Nicene Creed itself became an object of suspicion and criticism.

Athanasius also condemned those who held to a Oneness christology, particularly Sabellianism in its various forms; in a sense, it hardly mattered whether or not Athanasius's arguments were good ones or not. He could freely make normative his assumptions of God and the world just by writing them. The consequences were considerable for those who opposed the monopoly of orthodoxy. But it certainly did little to diminish what had come to be understood as heterodox christologies.

The language of Nicea would need further refinement; something that occurred largely in the work of Basil and the Council of Constantinople in 381. Basil used language suggested by Origen, that the Father, Son, and Holy Spirit shared one *ousia* but were different in hypostasis. This language was enacted with an anathema clause at the Council of Chalcedon. Indeed, the first martyr of the church—that is, the first one that was *martyred by the church* was Priscillian, a believer in Oneness christology in the latter part of the fourth century.

Augustine

We have now begun to move beyond what has been the historical focus of our inquiry. However, we will consider one last church father; indeed, he should be considered in a category by himself: Augustine of Hippo. It was Augustine who would largely become the norm for finding the church's position on arguably every major position of theology, and it was Augustine's view of the Trinity that would become the normative model for Western Christianity. Epistemologically, Augustine argues for the view of the philosophers, not as examples or as useful for analogy, but rather as a normative way of doing business doctrinally. Augustine, by his own admission in his *Confessions*, insists that "in the works of the Platonists God and His Word are introduced in all manners. . . ."[52] How much Augustine read Plato, Plotinus, or Porphyry has been debated. Although some insist that Augustine was a Neoplatonist before becoming a Christian,[53] the reality is probably a bit more complicated.[54] Other influences on Augustine were the earlier church fathers, but how much came from Ambrose, Origen, and other Greek or Latin Fathers may never be known.[55] Nonetheless, Augustine argues that church tradition recommended the use of philosophers to construct doctrine![56] What can be agreed upon is that Augustine conflated understandings from both Greek thought and church fathers in constructing his theology.[57]

In Augustine, what formerly occurred was a hermeneutical divorce between the church and its Old Testament roots. This is not to say that Augustine does not utilize the Old Testament in his construal of the Trinity.[58] Rather, it is in the particular way that Augustine utilizes the Old Testament that actually demonstrates his method. The Augustinian hermeneutic credo is widely known: "The New is in the Old concealed, the Old is in the New revealed."[59] Thus, Augustine read his philosophical constructs back into the New Testament and then utilized this understanding to read his position back into the Old Testament. Hendrikus Berkhof finds fault with Augustinian methodology because of "its implied suggestion that everything in the Old Testament is found in much clearer form in the New Testament. So it has promoted a neglect of the Old Testament in the Christian Church."[60]

Two presuppositions drive Augustinian christology. The first has to do with divine immutability. While the Hellenistic notion of divine immutability was presupposed by church fathers since the time of Justin in the second century, it was in Augustine that this doctrine formally became the doctrine of the church. Immutability is associated with the notion of simplicity in Augustine. For Augustine, as the simple good, God is ontologically unique and incommunicable.[61] Simplicity is expressed in the following way: All that God has, God is. God does not have attributes, but *is* His attributes. There are no properties that are not substance. It follows not only that God cannot be part of another being, but that God is all of His attributes. Where having an attribute is equivalent to being that attribute, the attribute in question cannot change or be lost.[62] Any loss or change contradicts divine simplicity. Consequently there are no accidents or contingent properties in God, and the possibility of change must be entirely excluded. Conversely, whatever lacks such simplicity, namely the identity of being and having, is capable of change and dissolution, and is the bearer of contingent or accidental features, and so on. Any change in God would have to be a change for the worse.[63] As a consequence, the Christian understanding of God generally gets defined as "timeless, changeless, passionless, unmoved, and unmovable."[64] This became standard for the church, not only for the medieval church,[65] but the modern church as well.[66]

Augustine's understanding of God as Creator has implications that go beyond the interpersonal relations of the Trinity. Jaroslav Pelikan notes that "Neoplatonic elements" in Augustine's Creator cause that which comes from God—*God's entire creation*—to be set, certain, and unchangeable. Augustine defined predestination as "God's arrangement of his future works in his prescience, which cannot be deceived or changed."[67] Thus, God predestines one group to be in covenant and thus saved while another group is predestined to be lost.[68]

The second presupposition that drives Augustine relates to the way in which Augustine codifies the Trinity as community; thus, "when one of the Three is mentioned as the author of any work, the whole Trinity is to be understood as working."[69] For Augustine, then, Genesis 1:26 demonstrates that humanity was created in the image of the entire Trinity.[70] In pursuing the question as to how the Trinity is "one *ousia*, three *hypostases*," Augustine deduces that there is a kind of substratum of "godhood" of which the *ousia* consists. This godhood is something that all of the members of Trinity possess commonly, not just in relationship to the Father. Thus, it is the Trinity in relation rather than the Trinity by procession.[71] In the Augustinian Trinity, there are other features that are relational as well. Having identified the Son as wisdom, He identifies the Spirit as "love" that binds the persons of the Trinity together and binds believers to the Trinity.[72]

Trinitarianism continued to develop in its understanding of persons of the Godhead, in part because the introduction of one Hellenistic construct called for another to buoy it up. For instance, in attempting to understand how the "Lord of glory," mentioned in I Corinthians 2:8 could be said to have been crucified, church theologians had to work through how it was that God could have suffered. One solution was the development of the fourth-century enigmatic formulations of mutual interpenetration (Greek:

perichoresis/Latin: *circumincessio*); this development continued until the seventh and eighth centuries.[73] This, along with "appropriation," working toward a notion of God as a "community," largely became a normative way of talking about the Trinity.[74] In some ways, this was more pronounced in the East, where for Alister McGrath, it is represented by an "understated form of tritheism which is often regarded as undergirding the understanding of the Trinity found in the writing of the Cappadocian fathers—Basil of Caesarea, Gregory of Nazianzus, and Gregory of Nyssa—writing in the late fourth century."[75] In the West, an Augustinian approach worked toward limiting such tendencies toward tritheism, but the Trinity could still be thought of as a "community."

Oneness Christology in the Age of Augustine

Oneness christology apparently existed through the fourth and fifth centuries, but when it appeared, it was largely labeled for its most prominent recent spokesperson, one who had been repeatedly condemned, Sabellius. Eusebius included Oneness christology as a major belief still extant in the fourth century.[76] For Basil, it is alive and well, a measuring stick of his own christological position.[77] In later centuries, other appellations and distinctions would largely disappear from the language of the church; Sabellianism would be the general term for any sort of Oneness christology. For instance, the Council of Alexandria stated, "But let the impiety of Sabellius and of Paul of Samosata also be anathematized by all."[78] Interestingly, both extremes of monarchianism were condemned in one fell swoop: on the one hand, dynamic monarchianism because with Paul of Samosata they denied the deity of Christ so they could claim to believe in one God; on the other hand, modalistic monarchianism because with Sabellius they believed that Jesus is God.

Pelikan confirms that although modalism was officially condemned by the church it did not quickly go away. For instance, it continued to be formally condemned by the sixth-century Synod of Braga. Pelikan offers that though Priscillian (a legitimate Oneness believer) and Sabellius were anathematized, this did not settle the matter. He writes, "The very late date of that synod, however, indicates that though the monarchian position may have been anathema, the question it raised and the intuition it represented could not be dismissed so easily."[79]

Evaluating Historical Trajectories

For many, Trinitarianism is an allowable expression of God both because it largely utilizes the language of the Bible as it has been transformed by the creeds and further, because for the vast majority of the Christian Church, it is now normal, orthodox, and understood as correct. Thus, although people would have liked to have seen a less bumpy history of the church . . . *well, that is just the way it is. It is the church, after all, warts and all.* But this very statement betrays an acknowledgment that the teaching of the church stands *because it is the teaching of the church.*[80] Pierre Bourdieu offers that once the language of orthodoxy is established, the *de facto* claim of the language is that "orthodox leadership" not only speaks for their own group, but they should speak for every one; they speak for what ought to be.[81]

The real question, though, is to what extent our relationship with Jesus Christ is affected by what we believe about christology. It would be easy to summarize how church history went out of control; the church fathers went awry when they could no longer see Jesus Christ as a man who prayed to God and as the man in whom God dwelt. The New Covenant is possible only because Jesus is absolutely a man. And it is possible only because Jesus is a man in whom God dwelt absolutely. Unfortunately, church history made Jesus a "man who is not."

Although it would be a mistake to try to condemn others' relationship with the Lord as deficient simply because they accepted the received knowledge of the church, on the other hand, it would be a mistake not to take advantage of new information offered. Genuine relationship is always enhanced when we say what ought to be said, what needs to be said. That is, while understanding covenantal identity is not mere formal acknowledgement of God in a doctrinal sense, yet, right understanding is an ally to right relationship. In the beginning of our study of christology, we spent seven chapters focusing on the identity of Jesus in the first century context. These past three chapters have worked to confirm the rightness of such an interpretation by historically demonstrating both the historical place of Oneness christology while at the same time discovering how it was that the church came to believe something different. The next two chapters will revisit what covenant initiation means biblically; the final chapter and epilogue will deal with the way in which Oneness christology has once again found a place in church life and practice.

SECTION IV:

THE MAN WHO IS IN COVENANT

Chapter 16

The Place of Baptism in Covenant Initiation

Introduction

The first four chapters of this book focused on the proper understanding of God, particularly on God as relational. Indeed, in calling people into covenant, Yahweh called them into relationship. Yet, as we have suggested, Old Testament covenant with God was only really possible because it anticipated the work of Jesus Christ, who fully restored the covenant relationship forfeited by Adam. In chapters 5-12, we explored both the identity and the work of Christ. In chapters 13-15, we worked to discover how it was that the church got it wrong—how that somewhere along the way they left behind a biblical understanding of Jesus Christ. If what we have said about Jesus is correct, then there are a number of necessary corollaries; our christology affects how we read the Bible, how we "do" church, and as a matter of application, it affects both covenant initiation and covenant relationship. In the remaining chapters of this book, we pursue these very practical implications.

Some years ago, I completed my dissertation entitled "No Other Name," a study on the covenant significance of the name of Jesus in the Book of Acts. In that study, for the sake of comparison, I focused on a Jewish group that was in existence at the same time as the founding of the church: the Qumran (arguably Essene) community. My intent was to examine the common religious values of the larger Jewish culture in the first century. What I discovered was intriguing. One thing that became apparent was how much the Qumran community greatly treasured the name of Yahweh. Their foundational documents contained passages that proclaim the great power of the name of Yahweh.[1] Further, they believed that God would record in "a book of remembrance" those who fear Yahweh and honor his name.² Most significantly, they deemed the name of Yahweh as foundational to their very existence. They confessed that the validity of their community was in fact certain for one reason: Yahweh had called them by name.³

Some have questioned the importance of baptism in Jesus' name as practiced by the apostles. In chapter 12 above, we demonstrated how that on the Day of Pentecost, Peter's christological understanding enabled him to apply a "Yahweh text" to Jesus. Consequently, this validated the apostles who invoked the name of Jesus, and not the name of Yahweh, in covenant initiation through baptism.⁴ Given that the Qumran community was functioning at the very time the New Testament Church began, their understanding of the importance of the name of *Yahweh* in connection with their very existence as a covenant community is significant. It serves as a backdrop to how the teaching of Jesus and the christological understanding of the apostles informed what they proclaimed about covenant initiation.

While we have thus far taken a considerable time exploring how it was that Jesus restored covenant, we now focus on how this restored covenant is constituted. Although it would take more than the next two chapters to tease out a full biblical understanding, nonetheless we present important points to consider with the goal of navigating in the right direction. In this chapter we trace the Apostolic teaching on baptism, addressing both the meaning and formula for baptism. After a biblical survey of this subject, we consider possible objections to our understanding, working in particular to present a correct understanding of the place of faith in covenant initiation. In the following chapter we explore the place of the Spirit in covenant initiation.

What the Bible Says about Baptism

At some time in the late Second Temple Period, there began a normative use of the *miqwah* in the conversion of Gentiles. While there is some question as to when exactly proselyte baptism began, the general consensus is that this ritual bath predated the baptism of John.⁵ The difference between this kind of proselyte baptism and John's baptism was that John invited not just Gentiles to be baptized, but the Jewish people as well, those already deemed to be in covenant.⁶ John insisted on baptizing the Jewish people, proclaiming that he was offering entrance into a new eschatological era marked by anticipation of the Messiah. In this context, John preached both hope and judgment. For those who rejected his message, there was judgment, but for those who accepted, there was expectation of a new era. Further, not only John, but Jesus' disciples baptized,[7] and though little information is given about their activity in the Gospels, the Book of Acts tracks their baptisms in considerable detail.

Consider that John's baptism was not merely the outward symbolic manifestation of good works, but rather one of conversion. The Gospel writers offer different testimonies as to the relationship of John's baptism with repentance. In some cases it appears people were baptized who were obedient with works of repentance and in other instances it seems baptism actually affected repentance. As G. R. Beasley-Murray notes, "It is now generally agreed that μετάνοια [*metanoia*] and μετανοεῖν [*metanoein*] can only be rightly represented by terms that connote *turning* or *conversion* [italics his]."[8] Further, as Albrecht Oerke suggests, "The basic concept both of Paul and of the New Testament generally in relation to baptism is that of a cleansing bath, (1 Cor 6:11, Eph 5:26, Heb 10:22; cf. Acts 2:38 and 22:16). The significance of baptism thus depends on the fact that it is a real action of the holy God in relation to sinful man. Hence both a superstitious and also purely symbolic meaning are excluded."[9]

Arguably, one key passage to consider is John 3:5, where Jesus told Nicodemus, "Verily, verily, I say unto thee, Except a man be born of water and of the Spirit, he cannot enter into the kingdom of God."[10] In John 3, when Jesus told Nicodemus he had to be "born again," he had to be "born of the water," Nicodemus would already have been cognizant of the use of water as a part of initiation into covenant for Gentiles. In John's narrative, the contextual evidence is strong that being born of the water is related to baptism. Indeed, Lars Hartman does not consider any other context for this verse.[11]

Although dogmatic considerations have caused some to suggest otherwise, the baptismal context of the first chapters of John is not ambiguous. John came preaching baptism in John 1, linking baptism both to conversion and initiation into the remnant eschatological community. This baptism anticipates both the appearance of the Messiah and the expectation of the commencement of the age of the Spirit.[12] Thus, the baptism of John forms a theological continuum with the baptism offered by Jesus and the apostles. Still in John 3, at the climax of the baptism of John and the beginning of the baptism of Jesus and His disciples, both Jesus and John are baptizing concurrently (3:22).[13] Jesus is so successful that John's disciples report "everybody" is going to the baptism of Jesus (3:26); this is no small claim, for as Beasley-Murray notes, since John's preaching was so widespread that "all the country of Judea and all the people of Jerusalem" (Mark 1:5) were in attendance, "this represents a far-reaching claim for the success and importance of the baptizing work of Jesus."[14] Thus, to suggest the statement of Jesus that "born of the water" could not textually be referring to baptism seems to largely be controlled by theological bias before considering the larger context.

The Baptismal Formula

The question of the baptismal formula is an important one, particularly as the church has baptized in the name of the Father, Son, and Holy Ghost for centuries. Further, this practice appears to follow the scriptural command of Jesus. What complicates the issue, as we discuss below, is that the biblical and historical records are consistent; the earliest church universally baptized in Jesus' name. Even after *Logos* christology gained supremacy in the church toward the end of the second century, baptism in Jesus' name continued to be regularly practiced in some fashion even until the time of Cyprian.[15]

A number of academics charge that Matthew 28:19 is largely an interpolation and was not part of the original text. While the historical record might support such a conclusion, the textual evidence against the passage is not compelling. Certainly it does not occur in its present form in some sources cited by Eusebius. Nor does it occur in later Hebrew texts that may have continuity with an original Hebrew *vorlage* of Matthew.[16]

Yet, there are no major variants in the earliest manuscript record available to us. Still, if in fact Matthew[17] accurately records the words of Jesus to His apostles, we must work toward discovering why it is that the apostles did not baptize in this way.

There are important keys within the text itself as to how the apostles interpreted these words of Jesus. In this regard, let us review some of the things that we have said thus far about "Name" theology. We have noted that in Jewish Christianity, there were specific ways of using "name" that must be recovered to understand the original context of specific Scriptures.[18] Thus, there were ways of speaking that made considerable sense to the ears of the hearers that we have to work to understand. We have suggested there are times in the biblical text when "the Name of the Father" actually functions as a kind of circumlocution for Jesus, particularly as "Name of the Father" may have reference to the man Jesus.[19] Further, as we have demonstrated above, there are specific times in the text when the "Name" is offered as a kind of a way to speak of divinity itself.[20] To be baptized in the "Name of the Father" was Jesus' indirect reference to Himself. To be baptized in the name of the Son is certainly to be baptized in the name of Jesus. As we have suggested above, the textual repetition serves as a kind of Hebraism, a repetition for emphasis.[21]

Some have suggested that in Acts, they were merely baptizing in the "authority" of Jesus' name. But as we explain below, the Greek cannot be made to do such gymnastics. Further, the apostles certainly understood the commands of Jesus with regard to baptism. Consider that in another record of a post-resurrection appearance by Jesus, He told them "that repentance and remission of sins should be preached in His name to all nations, beginning at Jerusalem," a clear reference to baptism, and baptism in the name of Jesus.[22] Historically, it was only when a second-century epistemological shift made *Logos* christology more prominent that both the meaning and rituals associated with baptism were devolved from a biblical understanding.[23]

As we have begun to suggest, there is a strong scholarly consensus that the earliest Christian baptism was practiced in Jesus' name. Both Hans Bietenhard and Lars Hartman argue that the various uses of Greek prepositions with regard to baptism in Jesus' name in Acts demonstrate that the material in the Lukan narrative seems to be translated from a rite that was original with the earliest Aramaic-speaking Palestinian community of believers.[24] Norman Fox rightly understands that Acts 2:38 has reference to orally invoking the name of Jesus over the person being baptized. He writes, "The Greek phrase *baptizein en* or *epi toi onomati Iesou* means that the act of baptism takes place with the utterance of the name of Jesus."[25] Even the formulaic evidence of orally presenting "in the name of" was in religious use among Jews. The Mishnah denotes a similar formula used where a person verbally spoke the name of the kind of offering that was given.[26]

Throughout the Book of Acts, the name of Jesus was consistently employed in baptism. Thus, the Jews were baptized in Jesus' name in Acts 2, the Samaritans in Acts 8, and the Gentiles in chapter 10. As we suggested above, the climax of Luke-Acts then comes in Acts 15,[27] when it is decided that because Gentile converts were baptized into Jesus' name, they were not to be bogged down with following the Torah, for they were deemed to already be in covenant. Similar usage of this invoking language is found in the very early Book of James; James 2:7 indicates that the name of Jesus was called over someone in baptism.[28] In some ways, the decision could have been anticipated, for it was not only baptism that took place in Jesus' name throughout the Book of Acts. Acts is replete with references to the power of the name of Jesus.[29] Bonnie Thurston notes that the apostles used the name of Jesus for a number of reasons, not the least of which being that they were aware "of the name as it was used of Yahweh's self-manifestation, to designate God's ineffable reality, the power by which God's work, and as the place where God 'dwells.' "[30]

Answering Objections

For some, baptism could not truly be as significant as we have suggested, for it would fly in the face of biblical passages that suggest that one is saved by faith alone. Yet, notice how even in the stating of such an objection to baptism, the language and emphasis carries with it certain presuppositions. Consider that since the time of the Reformation, the starting place for Evangelicals in talking about salvation has been in asking the forensic question: how exactly is one justified? This question arose out of a particular historical argument, a disagreement with the Roman Catholic Church that claimed the right to grant salvation or to withhold it. Evangelicals responded that an individual's salvation was not dependent on an institution but rather on their faith in Christ. While this historical victory was a significant milestone in working toward recapturing a biblical perspective, we should not be too quickly satisfied with historical answers, even those won by the Reformation. Consider that in the heat of struggle, particularly if a doctrinal plank is framed in opposition to an extreme position, it is possible to bring sixteenth-century conflicts back into a reading of the biblical text.

Robert Stein surveys the Acts narrative to determine the relationship of baptism and what he deems to be other components involved in becoming a Christian.[31] He suggests an interrelationship between five different components in conversion: "repentance, faith, and confession by the individual, regeneration, or the giving of the Holy Spirit by God, and baptism by representatives of the Christian community."[32] What Stein demonstrates is that in the narrative of Acts there is no set order for these to occur, but each one of these components is identified with the whole experience of becoming a part of the Christian community. John Polhill confirms such an assessment of the Acts narrative, allowing, "There is no set, mechanistic pattern by which the various components come into play, particularly baptism and the receipt of the Spirit."[33]

Paul could say, "For by grace you have been saved through faith" (Ephesians 2:8). Yet, he could say, "For as many of you as were baptized into Christ have put on Christ" (Galatians 3:27). He could also say, "If anyone does not have the Spirit of Christ, he is not His" (Romans 8:9). While all of this may be problematic in the twenty-first-century analytic mentality, in the first-century world, this did not present a conflict. F. F. Bruce notes that repentance, faith, baptism, and reception of the Spirit are among the elements that "constituted one complex of experience of Christian initiation."[34] Bruce goes on to say that "what is true of the experience as a whole can in practice be predicated of any element in it."[35]

Stein offers this useful analogy:

> If I were asked when I was married, I could respond, "When I said 'I do' " or "When I put a ring on her finger and she put one on mine" or "When the pastor pronounced us 'man and wife' " or "When the witnesses and pastor signed the marriage certificate" or "When we sexually consummated our marriage." If asked as to exactly which one of these caused me to become married, I would reply, "You cannot separate them. They were all part of my becoming married. When I mentioned any one of these, I assumed the others!"[36]

Against such a position is the challenge that to deemphasize the particular moment of faith in which one confesses Christ muddies the very meaning of conversion. After all, one might protest, how can a person argue with the clear proclamation of Scripture: "For with the heart one believes unto righteousness, and with the mouth confession is made unto salvation ... for 'whoever calls on the name of the LORD shall be saved'" (Romans 10:9; 10:13)? Yet, while such a protest is well intentioned, recall that the text Paul is citing is from Joel: "Whoever calls on the name of the LORD shall be saved." It is the same one Peter quoted on the Day of Pentecost and which was fulfilled when the people responded to the message by being baptized in Jesus' name.[37] That is why there is good reason to believe that the "life-setting" of Romans chapter 10 is a baptismal service,[38] where the name of Jesus is called upon those being initiated into covenant.

Certainly in developing catechisms believers confessed their faith to the community in the context of that baptism; prayer was offered both by the one being baptized and the one doing the baptizing.[39] A number of different practices developed in the earliest centuries connected to baptism. The essential element of baptism, though, is the oral invocation of the covenant name of Jesus over the person who is entering covenant relationship in the context of baptism.

Again, for those recalling a Catholic approach to baptism, any sort of emphasis on baptism seems to diminish the place of faith. After all, does not Paul effectively establish that it was faith that justified Abraham and not works? Further, because Abraham experienced this conversion experience prior to the institution, does that not demonstrate that faith precedes "New Testament circumcision" effected in baptism? These are valid questions, and ones that deserve to be addressed. Before examining them in detail, let us offer a brief caution: we must be careful not to read back our own presuppositions into the text but examine more closely what it is that Paul is saying.

Abraham and Initiation into Covenant

In Romans 4:3, Paul declares that Abraham "believed God" and as a consequence, "it was accounted to him for righteousness."[40] In this verse, Paul is citing Genesis 15:6, and his point seems to be that because Abraham believed, he was declared righteous (before he was circumcised). At first glance, it seems as if what we are looking at is a record of Abraham's "conversion." Yet, it doesn't take long to reflect on how the historical narrative does not bear this out, for Abraham had already been faithfully following in covenant for a number of years. Nor can one merely suggest that Abraham's faith prior to this time was incomplete or imperfect. Hebrews 11 supplies the beginning of the story for the Genesis account of Abraham. It was in Ur of the Chaldees where Abraham[41] first heard the voice of Yahweh, and it was in Ur that Abraham answered this call. Indeed, in what is arguably the most important chapter on faith in the Bible, Abraham is singularly celebrated for his faith—faith demonstrated well before Genesis 15:6. It strains credulity to suppose that Abraham would hear God's voice, follow God unwaveringly for years, and yet because of imperfect faith would only finally be justified in Genesis 15.

It is Genesis 15:6 that Romans cites: "Abram put his faith in Yahweh and this was reckoned to him as uprightness." The question as to what it means that Yahweh reckoned Abraham's faith for uprightness must be seriously considered. While some insist that this was the true moment of Abraham's conversion, Lloyd Gaston is not sure. He points out that claiming Abraham had, as it were, a conversion experience in Genesis 15:6, reads something into the narrative that is not there and demonstrates lack of awareness of covenantal relationship in the Old Testament.[42] When speaking of Abraham's uprightness, the text is not suggesting that this was the first point in time where Abraham could be called righteous. Rather, the Hebrew text underlying the translation denotes a confirmation of his righteousness,[43] "his right-standing," which interpreters correctly understand to be a function of an ongoing covenant that was once again confirmed at this point. Covenant is a living relationship and as such can only be sustained by obedience. Eichrodt is correct in the fact that covenant "bound up with conditions already implies the possibility of annulment."[44] It was Abraham's faithfulness in the face of the difficulties that caused Yahweh once again to declare Abraham's covenant faithfulness.

Let us now consider the question of circumcision. Some have suggested that since this practice was established after Abraham was already initiated into covenant, then circumcision has nothing to do with covenant initiation. The corollary is that since baptism is "New Testament circumcision," then baptism can't have anything to do with justification. Justification comes through faith alone. While this sounds right, let us first recall the perspective of Gaston. Remember that throughout his lifetime, Abraham had to continue to obey the voice of Yahweh to maintain his covenant relationship. After some time, Yahweh instituted circumcision and called for it to be implemented. Circumcision had been practiced in various rites and clans, but by elevating this ritual to a place of privilege, Yahweh allowed the human and divine to become enmeshed in their commitment one to another. When Abraham circumcised his household, he was continuing to comply with Yahweh's voice—continuing in obedience.[45] In point of fact, covenant was neither initiated in Genesis 15:6 nor with circumcision; what can be said is that in both instances, Abraham continued in covenant faithfulness.

In the life of Abraham, the story of covenant faithfulness continued. Indeed, the Book of James applies justification to an event forty years after Genesis 15. James asks, "Was not Abraham our father justified by works when he offered Isaac his son on the altar?"[46] There are, of course, different uses and nuances of the word translated justification (*dikaiosune*).[47] As E. P. Sanders notes, "In some cases, the translation of the Greek *dikaiosune* can be misleading, for the meaning is not "that one is made to be righteous," but "it actually refers to the establishment of right relationship."[48] Sometimes the verb *dikaiosune* means "to reconcile," sometimes "to sanctify," while other times "justify" is "a perfectly good translation." Sometimes, *dikaiosune* is "equivalent to having, attaining, or being given *dikaiosyne*, righteousness (cf. Phil 3:9, 'having righteousness'), in which case 'make righteous' or 'become righteous' is a more adequate translation."[49]

It is reading into the New Testament to decide that "faith" is momentary and that covenant initiation may not happen over time. Further, to understand baptism as "New Testament circumcision" also reads more into a Pauline metaphor than he is trying to say.[50] Baptism is not New Testament circumcision. While it answers to circumcision in a certain way, baptism is so much more than circumcision. In conjunction with circumcision, an infant was named. By contrast, at baptism, the name of Jesus is invoked upon the one initiated into covenant. While circumcision involved a physical ritual, the element stressed in New Testament baptism is spiritual. Thus, although Ananias could command Saul to be baptized to "wash away your sins" (Acts 22:16), he had no illusions that it was merely the water that was accomplishing this. Yet it was in the water that this experience was accomplished. New Testament baptism affords spiritual cleansing and a clean conscience.[51]

Not only in Acts, but throughout the entire New Testament, baptism is linked with forgiveness. Consider that in the paradigmatic message at the inception of the church, Peter charged the people, "Repent, and let every one of you be baptized in the name of Jesus Christ for the remission of sins." The preposition that stands behind the word translated "for" is the Greek word "*eis*." Some have understood this preposition to mean "because of the remissions." That is, because sins were already remitted, then people should be baptized; yet, as Carl Judson Davis notes, "The whole case for 'causal' (*eis*) in Acts 2:38 and baptism 'because of the forgiveness of sins' is left without real foundation either in Greek grammar or biblical theology."[52] While there are those who would suggest that the Greek demands that remission of sins only be related to repentance,[53] Ashby Camp has confirmed that both repentance and baptism in Jesus' name are related to the forgiveness of sins.[54] Lars Hartman, citing Old Testament Jewish texts, and the New Testament itself, confirms the gift of remission of sins as it is related to baptism.[55] Indeed, the weight of the evidence favors grammarians who concur that "for the remission of sins" as a prepositional phrase "denotes purpose. For as Mikeal C. Parsons and Martin M. Culy offer, "It is likely that repentance and baptism were viewed as a single complex act leading to the forgiveness of sins (cf. 2:41, 18:8, 22:16)."[56]

Summary

While the Reformation brought with it an important restoration of the centrality of faith, the application of faith is made in the numerous components of covenant initiation. The first-century church did not think of faith in terms of a punctiliar moment but rather saw faith working in tandem with other components of initiation into covenant. We can recapture the first-century confession of baptism by moving the starting place for the discussion from that of forensic justification to covenantal initiation. We must be cautious to not let a sixteenth-century historical debate reframe the clear reading of the biblical text.

People reject baptism in Jesus' name for a variety of reasons. Some might reduce the premise of this chapter to a certain kind of choice, arguing, "I would rather be baptized by using the words Jesus prescribed rather than the words of the apostles." Yet, the apostles heard the words of Jesus and they baptized in Jesus' name. Further, the apostles wrote the New Testament. Matthew was present both for the words of Jesus and the words of Peter. Although scholars shy away from interpretive solutions that harmonize one text with another, yet one should not discount a common confession if in fact that is what the apostles had. The fact is that the same people who heard the words of Jesus recorded in Matthew baptized in Jesus' name. We have good reason to expect that the apostles, who had no historical distance from the words of Jesus recorded in Matthew 28:19, were in a better position to understand the command in context than we are from this distance. Indeed, the first-century church viewed baptism in Jesus' name as incredibly significant in covenant initiation and in relation to forgiveness. The question should not be, "Do I have to get baptized in Jesus' name?" Rather, one should ask, "Could I be baptized in the name of the One who died for me and made possible a restored covenant relationship with God?"

Chapter 17

The Covenant and the Spirit

Introduction

If what we have suggested about Oneness christology is true, then there are certain necessary implications. Not only is it important for us to be baptized in the name of the One who died for us; when we receive the Spirit, we are not receiving "Another." As we have suggested, the New Testament utilizes "Spirit of God" and "Spirit of Christ" interchangeably and even celebrates: "Now the Lord is the Spirit."[1] As we have also discussed, the reception of the Holy Spirit in the New Testament must be nuanced in a way that is different than the operation of the Spirit in the Old Testament.[2] Further, both the epistles and Revelation demonstrate that the writers of Scripture regularly utilized "Jesus" and "the Spirit" interchangeably without any sort of substanive change in thinking.[3]

Experiencing the presence of God is a normative part of covenant relationship. Above, in chapters 1-4, we explored how God covenanted with His people in the Old Testament. When, after Eden, God renewed covenant, it was at the place of covenant worship where the "face" or "presence" of God was encountered.[4] Further, the presence of Yahweh was experienced when God initiated covenant with Israel[5] and when He renewed covenant through Moses.[6] In addition, in the context of their worship experience, the priests invoked the name of Yahweh over Israel while at the same time calling down His presence (*panim*).[7]

As good as the Old Covenant was, Yahweh promised that He would enact a New Covenant where His Spirit would be experienced in a new measure. It is no accident that the antitype of the covenant God gave to Moses was given on the very day Moses received the Law.[8] Consider how Old Testament prophets prophesied of this new eschatological age, one that they came to understand would be initiated by a Messiah.[9] Jeremiah spoke of this new covenant in terms of a closer and abiding presence of Yahweh. (See Jeremiah 31:31-34.) Joel prophesied that there would be covenantal access for whoever would "call upon the Yahweh," an idiom that meant Yahweh would call His name upon them.[10] Amos extended this promise of relationship to the Gentiles, so they too could have the name of Yahweh called upon them.[11] For centuries this new access to God's presence was anticipated; finally, on the Day of Pentecost, the Spirit was poured out.

In chapters 5-12, we explored the identity and work of Jesus Christ. From the very beginning, Jesus was introduced as the One who would baptize with the Spirit. In all four Gospels and in the Book of Acts, baptizing with the Spirit is lauded as the identifying feature of Jesus' ministry.[12] Indeed, it was Jesus' renewal of covenant relationship with Yahweh that allowed for the possibility that people would experience the fullness of the Spirit. Although no one would receive the Spirit until after He was glorified,[13] Jesus proleptically invited people to experience the Spirit throughout His entire ministry. He told the woman at the well that He would give her the gift of God,[14] living water (John 4:10), a metaphor He repeated in John 7, one equivalent to the reception of the Spirit. (See John 7:38-39.) For Jesus, the Spirit was not difficult to receive; all a person had to do was ask. (See Luke 11:11-13.)

In this chapter we explore the implications of Oneness christology as it relates to the infilling of the Spirit. We begin by suggesting how a Oneness Pentecostal understanding of the infilling of the Spirit is different than that of others. In this regard, we work to demonstrate the New Testament connection between baptism in water and baptism in the Spirit. Further, utilizing a narrative theological approach, we argue for a single experience of the Spirit connected to covenant initiation. Finally, we focus on how a Oneness Pentecostal understanding illuminates a biblical understanding of speaking in other tongues.

Oneness Pentecostals and the Baptism of the Spirit

The question of how to understand the baptism of the Holy Spirit is one that divides many Evangelicals. Some have suggested that the baptism of the Holy Spirit belongs to the age of the apostles and that Scripture teaches that the experience, at least the way it occurred in Acts, has ceased.[15] Others suggest that an individual receives the Spirit at a particular moment of faith but the baptism of the Spirit in Acts is theologically a *donum superadditum*, an additional gift that is given to believers.[16] Those who hold this position typically suggest that one initially receives the Spirit at the point of "saving faith"; while the baptism of the Spirit is a second experience with the Spirit, and that is what is largely tracked in the narrative of Acts.

By contrast, James D. G. Dunn rejects the notion of two experiences, arguing for a single experience of the Spirit, one that initiates the New Covenant.[17] For Dunn, there is no record of any unique language for conversion apart from receiving the Spirit in the way that Acts variously expresses it. While Acts may say that the Spirit "falls," they were "baptized with the Spirit," or that they were "filled with the Spirit," there is absolutely no distinction between initial reception of the Spirit and a later baptism of empowerment.[18] While not altogether agreeing with all of Dunn's conclusions, Oneness Pentecostals also understand the baptism of the Holy Spirit as a part of initiation into covenant. While we would agree with Dunn as to the importance of faith and repentance, contrary to Dunn, for example, we would see a much greater importance for baptism. It was for this reason that we focused in the last chapter on the centrality of baptism as it relates to covenant initiation.

There is a biblical pattern of initiation into covenant that is consistent. For instance, in the Old Testament, when the priests called down the name of Yahweh, they at once experienced the "face" of Yahweh.[19] Further, as we suggested, when covenant was renewed on the Day of Atonement, the high priest spoke the name of Yahweh.[20] At the same time, not only the high priest but the people as well expected to enter into relational experience with God.[21] So too in the New Testament, there is a clear connection between the oral invocation of the name of Jesus in baptism and receiving the Spirit. While it is true that the Spirit is experienced in the New Testament in a much greater way than it was in the Old Testament, still, the biblical pattern is to experience the "face," that is, the presence of God in covenant. Not only is this borne out in the record of the early church in Acts; such a record is consistent with the rest of the teaching of the New Testament.

Before we begin a scriptural survey, let us consider what it is that we are not saying. We are not saying that baptism equals the receiving of the Spirit. Nor are we suggesting that either baptism or receiving the Spirit may simply be reduced to formulaic ritual. Nor is there a specific prescribed order in which these events must necessarily occur. Biblically, it is possible to receive the Spirit before baptism or to be baptized before receiving the Spirit. In either case, both are necessary components of initiation into covenant. And finally, we are not merely trying to reduce biblical praxis to the initial reception of the Spirit. If being filled with the Spirit is anything at all, it is walking in a relationship with the Lord that is spiritually alive and vibrant.

The Relationship between Baptism and the Holy Spirit

The remainder of the chapter now largely focuses on an exploration of the Book of Acts. In this context, we are going to track a specific relationship between baptism in water and the baptism of the Spirit and its relationship to initiation into covenant. However, before proceeding, it is important to suggest that such an interpretation is not merely found in Acts but other biblical texts as well. Briefly, let us consider how both the apostle John and Paul make a theological link between baptism and the Spirit. In the several texts that we will survey, it is certainly possible to read the passages in more than one way; yet, taken together, and in conjunction with the Acts narrative, they represent a unified apostolic confession, though articulated in a variety of ways. We begin by returning to the passage that we addressed in the last chapter, that of Jesus teaching Nicodemus. Whereas, in the last chapter, we explored John 3 as it relates to baptism, let us now reconsider the words of Jesus to Nicodemus in John 3:5, particularly as they relate to the Spirit.

As we have suggested in the previous chapter, there is no reason to disallow that to be "born of the water" refers to baptism.[22] Jesus told Nicodemus, "Except a man be born of water and of the Spirit, he cannot enter into the kingdom of God." Very few will challenge the charge of Jesus that an individual should be born of the Spirit. The point, here, though, is to suggest its connection to baptism. Recall that John 3:5 is both a repetition and an expansion of what Jesus told Nicodemus in John 3:3, that it was essential to be born again to enter the kingdom of God. In doing so, Jesus offered the relationship between the two when prescribing covenant initiation to Nicodemus.

In the last chapter we sought to demonstrate that the flow of John's Gospel demonstrates the centrality of baptism. In this same regard, the theme of the Spirit is equally central to John. The Gospel of John begins with John the Baptist announcing there would be One who will baptize with the Spirit.[23] That promise of the Spirit was already associated with the preparatory baptism of John, thus forming a theological continuum of the Spirit with the baptism as it later appears in chapter 3. Thus, when Jesus told Nicodemus he needed to born of the water and the Spirit, Jesus was codifying this link into a kind of singular initiation experience. As Barnabas Lindars notes, the linking of water and the Spirit "refers to an act, and that act can only be water-baptism and the Spirit which it conveys."[24] Lindars is not alone in this interpretation. For instance, Don Willeford suggests that to be "born of the water and Spirit," represents one single act or event. Others agree, and it is clear that being born of the water and Spirit could be two parts of initiation into covenant.[25] Some have suggested that Paul would say otherwise; that for Paul, conversion is justification pure and simple. Yet, a Pauline understanding works to make this same association as well.

In I Corinthians 6:11, when Paul told the Corinthians they were "washed, justified and sanctified in the name of the Lord Jesus," he was making a reference to baptism. The verbs describing this event, which include baptism, are in the aorist and thus likely refer to a single happening. However, the text is not about baptism alone. Conjoined to the phrase "in the name of Jesus" is "and by the Spirit of our God." Gordon Fee notes that I Corinthians 6:11 is not just about conversion effected *only* through baptism. He is correct to associate this verse with reception of the Spirit as well. He writes, "These two prepositional phrases together modify the verbs, washed, sanctified, justified," and "both prepositions [*in* the name of the Lord Jesus and *by* the Spirit of our God] modify all three verbs."[26] Thus both elements are important in this verse. A Oneness Pentecostal reading would generally concur with Fee's interpretation, at least as far as it goes. A Oneness position sees Christian initiation as including both baptism in water and by the Spirit.

Titus 3:5 offers, "Not by works of righteousness which we have done, but according to His mercy He saved us, through the washing of regeneration and renewing of the Holy Spirit." Carl Judson Davis links this verse with Acts 2:38, noting that it refers to baptism and infilling of the Spirit.[27] Gordon Fee, too, would suggest the "washing of regeneration" has reference to baptism, and that in the same context, it is clear that what is being done is a work of the Spirit, for conjoined with the statement "washing of regeneration" is "renewing of the Spirit."[28] In this same regard, Fee argues that interpreters of Pauline theology have unduly focused on a particular aspect of Paul, but that "becoming a believer in Christ is not simply that one is given a new 'objective standing' with God—redeemed, forgiven, cleansed, 'justified.' " Rather, for Fee, "rebirth" and "renewal" are words that more aptly speak of the transforming power of the Spirit.[29] In Titus 3:6, Paul writes that this renewing of the Holy Spirit was "poured out on us abundantly through Jesus Christ our Savior." Indeed, it is no accident that the language of Titus 3:5-6 echoes the outpouring of the Spirit in Acts 2.[30]

Further, Paul offers in I Corinthians 12:13, "For by one Spirit we were all baptized into one body—whether Jews or Greeks, whether slaves or free—and have all been made to drink into one Spirit." This is a clear allusion to both being dunked in water (baptism) while drinking in the Spirit. Commentators tend to see in this text either baptism or being filled with the Spirit; yet James D. G. Dunn is correct to allow for both baptism and the Spirit in this verse.[31] Dunn suggests that Paul is alluding to the oft repeated utterance by John the Baptist: "I baptize you with water, but he [the Coming One] will baptize you with the Holy Spirit (and fire)."[32] Paul was not the first one to liken receiving the Spirit to drinking in water. Jesus told the woman at the well, "Whoever drinks of the water that I shall give him will never thirst. But the water that I shall give him will become in him a fountain of water springing up into everlasting life."[33]

Initiation into Covenant in Acts

As M. D. Goulder points out, while the actions of the Holy Spirit are pivotal throughout Acts, "there are four occasions which stand on their own, four times, and four only, when the Spirit descends and takes possession of individuals."[34] These specific instances are in Acts 2, Acts 8, Acts 10, and Acts 19. Acts 2 is critical, for it is here that the Spirit is first poured out; it is the marker and sets the standard for what it means to be initiated into the New Covenant.

In the Book of Acts, Luke set out to teach theology through the narrative. In his account of Acts 2, as the people gathered to see the apostles and those with them speaking in tongues, Peter took the occasion to preach to them about Jesus. He offered that though Jesus was put to death, He was now raised from the dead and had ascended to Heaven. Based on the exaltation of Jesus "at the right hand of God," Peter could now report that it was Jesus who is now "baptizing with the Spirit," and this was evidenced by the people speaking in tongues.[35] When the people responded and asked what to do, Peter told them to repent, be baptized in Jesus' name, and they would receive the Holy Spirit.

Richard F. Zehnle, writing of Peter's discourse in Acts 2, states that it "presents in a nutshell the Lukan notion of what it means to be saved that is maintained consistently throughout the book."[36] Zehnle goes on to say, "The hearers must repent and make profession of the name of Jesus (by baptism); then they will receive the Holy Spirit and enter the community of the saved."[37] In conjunction with this, there is a significant emphasis on being joined to the community of believers as the locus of the covenant community.[38] Dunn is correct to suggest that the presentation of Luke-Acts is that Peter's pronouncement in Acts 2:38 is meant to be normative for what he calls "conversion-initiation": repent, be baptized in Jesus' name, and receive the gift of the Holy Spirit.[39] Thus, Peter specifically addresses this message to the audience at Jerusalem, but the implications go far beyond this incident. Jerusalem is a literary focal point for Luke,[40] a chiasmus at the end of Luke and at the beginning of Acts. It is the place from which the Spirit spread "to the ends of the earth."[41] It was this message that would be proclaimed for "as many as the Lord our God will call."[42]

Consider the significant subsequent conversion experiences mentioned in Acts 8, 10, and 19, and note the commonalties with Acts 2. First, they demonstrate that baptism and the reception of the Spirit were both a part of initiation into covenant; second, in Luke, while people may receive the Spirit at the same time as they are baptized, they might not, yet it was this reception of the Spirit that is both expected and necessary; third, when the Spirit was given as a component of initiation into covenant, it was accompanied by the sudden and miraculous expression of speaking in tongues.

In Acts 8, the Samaritans believed, were baptized, and desired to be part of the church. Yet they had not received the Spirit. Many Pentecostals use Acts 8 to demonstrate that the baptism of the Holy Spirit is subsequent to conversion—that the converts at Samaria were merely waiting to be empowered. But a plain reading of the text easily refutes this claim. Acts 8:16 says emphatically that the Spirit "had fallen upon none of them." Dunn is correct to insist, "The fact is that Luke envisages *only one* coming of the Spirit to or upon the Samaritans."[43] Since this is the case, neither the explanation that this was further empowerment, nor that the Samaritans were not truly converted,[44] nor that one necessarily receives the Spirit at the point of initial faith can suffice as an explanation.[45] What the passage does suggest is that the Spirit comes suddenly in a way recognized by all, and that it was necessary—so important that Philip was compelled to send for Peter and John from Jerusalem. That is to say, initiation into New Testament covenant has component parts, including baptism in Jesus' name and receiving the Spirit.

The question may be asked as to how everyone universally knew that the Samaritans had not yet received the Spirit. Consider that Simon had already seen demons cast out, the inspired preaching and miracles of Philip, and had witnessed universal rejoicing after conversions. Yet when Peter and John laid hands on the Samaritans, something so unique happened that Simon offered money to be able to replicate the same thing. Dunn offers, "It is a fair assumption that for Luke, the Samaritan 'Pentecost,' like the first Christian Pentecost, was marked by ecstatic glossolalia."[46] What was common in Acts 2, Acts 10, and Acts 19 is that they spoke in tongues, and this is what is strongly suggested as normative in this text as well.

In Acts 10, the pattern is repeated. It would require an angel, a vision, and considerable divine prompting before Peter would break convention and be the one to open the soteriological door to the Gentiles. Acts 10 records that while Peter "was still speaking these words, the Holy Spirit fell upon all those who heard the word" (Acts 10:44). There can be no doubt this is a conversion experience. Peter preached Jesus and they believed; consequently the Spirit fell suddenly upon them.[47] When recounting the incident in Acts 11, Peter said in verse 17 of the house of Cornelius, "God gave them the same gift as He gave us when we believed on the Lord Jesus Christ." The Greek demonstrates that it was their faith that caused this to occur.[48] Indeed, this was the first time they had heard of Jesus, and their unconverted state was demonstrated by the fact that the angel told Cornelius to send for Peter "who will tell you words by which you and all your household will be saved" (Acts 11:14). But faith, repentance, and reception of the Spirit, while component parts of initiation into covenant, were still not enough. It is for this reason that Peter "commanded them to be baptized in the name of the Lord," something that was most certainly expected, now that God had demonstrated to Peter and those that had traveled with him the Holy Spirit was "poured out" on the Gentiles; it was clear, for "they heard them speak with tongues and magnify God" (Acts 10:44-48).

The narrative of the Ephesian disciples in Acts 19 further demonstrates the normative experience of initiation into covenant. While some suggest that these disciples were believers in Jesus prior to their contact with Paul and that their receiving the Spirit was merely empowerment for mission, this seems doubtful. At issue is Paul's question, "Did you receive the Holy Spirit when (after) you believed?"[49] The question as to whether or not Paul was speaking temporally has gotten rather heated;[50] Robert Menzies is correct that "the potential separation of belief from reception of the Spirit is implicit in the question." He then goes on to charge that "in the face of every evidence, Dunn will not let Luke be Luke."[51] Where Menzies is incorrect though, is that he presumes there was a prior experience of "believing" where the men were justified and now a second experience where they were being empowered. This can hardly be the case. These "disciples" had not even heard of the gift of the Spirit, and Paul treated them as those in the process of conversion.[52] Thus, their baptism and receiving the Spirit were component parts of initiation into the New Covenant. Paul first baptized them in the name of the Lord Jesus, and then the "Holy Spirit came upon them, and they spoke with tongues and prophesied" (Acts 19:6). Both of these events were essential components of initiation into covenant.

These four narratives from Acts demonstrate the common elements of initiation into covenant that included the components of both baptism and being filled with the Spirit. From a literary perspective, Peter's actions are foundational. Jesus proclaimed the theme of Acts: that the Spirit would be poured out "in Jerusalem, and in all Judaea, and in Samaria, and unto the uttermost part of the earth" (Acts 1:8). It is Peter whose proclamation brings entrance of the Spirit in Jerusalem, Samaria, and to the first Gentile. While Paul continues the Acts narrative "to the uttermost part of the earth," the pattern for the Book of Acts has already clearly been set. Dunn is correct to see Peter's message on the Day of Pentecost as paradigmatic, and the invitation of Peter that ties together baptism and the Spirit to covenant initiation.

Speaking in Tongues

One of the things consistently present in each of the events in Acts where the narrative celebrates initiation into covenant is that the experience of being filled with the Spirit is accompanied by the recipients speaking in tongues. Again, from a literary perspective, Acts 2 is paradigmatic. When on the Day of Pentecost the crowds heard the people speak in languages they could not have possibly known naturally, they inquired what it meant that these people were speaking in tongues. Peter identified their speaking with the reception of the Spirit, offering "This is that which was spoken by the prophet Joel." Joel's prophecy was clearly of the eschatological age of the Spirit, an age where the Spirit was universally available to all, where "in the last days" God would "pour out of His Spirit on all flesh."[53]

Against Dunn, Robert Menzies argues as to the empowering nature of the Spirit in Acts to allow for the Spirit as charismatic but not soteriological; that is, Menzies claims that Luke has a completely different pneumatology than Paul.[54] Yet, in this, Menzies seems to be stretching Lukan pneumatology to the breaking point. Indeed, Luke's language of the Spirit is a language of insistence. In Acts, the apostles needed the Spirit and were commanded to wait for it. The Samaritans were deficient without it. The falling of the Spirit in Acts 10 and its subsequent explanation in Acts 11 connects the coming of the Spirit in Acts 10 on the house of Cornelius with the very words whereby they would be saved. None of the narrative reads like a secondary spiritual experience of empowerment. While there is not the same sense of urgency in Acts 19, there is a definite sense that the initiation of Ephesian believers is not complete until Paul lays his hands upon the believers and they receive the Spirit. In all these instances recipients initially receive the Spirit, and in all these instances, the coming of the Spirit makes a marked change. The Spirit comes suddenly. Nor is there any ambiguity in the coming of the Spirit. Although there is fluidity in the way the reception of the Spirit is described, yet there is no ambiguity in its meaning. Of the first experience where people received the Spirit, Lukan language allows that they were baptized (Acts 1:5); filled with the Holy Spirit (Acts 2:4); Jesus poured it out (Acts 2:33); and it fell on them (Acts 11:15).[55]

When Peter was asked by the crowd what it meant that these people were speaking in tongues, Peter responded "This is that . . .", referring to Joel's eschatological promise of the Spirit. Peter was not suggesting that speaking in tongues *is* the Spirit, but rather that their speaking in tongues was so closely tied with the coming of the Spirit that it demonstrated a new spiritual reality. The eschatological age of the Spirit had commenced. Assessing that the Samaritans spoke in tongues, James Dunn offers the following summary of the intent of Luke in Acts. He concludes, "The fact is that in *every case* [italics his] where Luke describes the giving of the Spirit it is accompanied and 'evidenced' by glossolalia. The corollary is then not without force that Luke *intended* to portray 'speaking in tongues' as the 'initial physical evidence' of the outpouring of the Spirit."[56] According to Luke, those who are filled with the Spirit speak in tongues. Don Juel, in his explanation of the Lukan strategy to teach, puts it aptly: "Luke's history of Jesus and of the spread of 'the way' intends not simply to describe but also to prescribe."[57] It is in this way that Luke *does* theology. Further, there is evidence beyond Luke that the expectation of speaking in tongues was deemed a normative expression upon being filled with the Spirit. In this regard, let us survey Paul's convention of utilizing the language of "*Abba*" as it relates to initiation into covenant.

Paul and "Abba"

As we have begun to discuss, the *Abba* language embraced by the apostolic church arose out of the teaching and practice of Jesus. In the Garden of Gethsemane, Mark leaves untranslated the intimate word that Jesus spoke to Yahweh in the most critical challenge of His life. Jesus cried "*Abba*," a term of endearment that children would use for their father, something equivalent to "Daddy."[58] The reason Mark allows the Aramaic *Abba* in this account is not because this term of endearment was so unusual on the lips of Jesus. As we have offered above, Jesus spoke conversationally and taught in Aramaic.[59] Rather, it is the meaning of the word *Abba* that is so significant. In a milieu where Yahweh could not be spoken, and where the mention of Yahweh's immanence defied cultural sensibilities, Jesus intimately spoke of God as His Daddy. This testified of two things. First, Yahweh literally was His Father. Second, and just as important, because Jesus was the first son of Adam who lived in perfect covenant obedience, and covenantally, Yahweh was His Daddy. Further, because of the work Jesus would do on Calvary, He would not be the only one who would be able to enjoy this intimate relationship with God. The reason for the Incarnation was so that others could have this same access. While fulfillment of this promised hope would have to wait until the Spirit was actually poured out, this did not prevent Jesus from offering people such a relationship during his earthly ministry. Just as Jesus invited people to be filled with the Spirit all the while knowing that such an invitation was proleptic (John 7:38-39), so Jesus taught His disciples to pray using the same words that only He could rightfully use: "Daddy, who art in heaven."[60]

The word *Abba* not only had significance on the lips of Jesus. It had incredible significance to those in the earliest church. We find it used by Paul, but scholars are agreed that his use of it is not innovative. Like other Aramaic words Paul utilized when writing, his use of *Abba* was a received tradition, one going back to the confession of the earliest church.[61] In this regard, Paul, too, uses *Abba* as a term of celebration.

Paul says that those who receive the Spirit cry *"Abba*/Father." In this context, the academic consensus is that for Paul, *Abba* is a metaphor of utmost significance. Kittel notes that this kind of speaking "shows how this Father-child relationship to God far surpasses any possibilities of intimacy assumed in Judaism, introducing indeed something which is wholly new."[62] Fee offers that the language of *Abba* marks the beginning of a Christian's life. That is, a new believer experiences the "indwelling Spirit's crying out Abba."[63] In Romans 8:15, Paul writes, "But you received the Spirit of adoption by whom we cry out (*krazo*), 'Abba, Father.'" As lexicographers agree, the use of the Greek *krazo* is noteworthy. It denotes "the loud irrepressible cry with which the consciousness of sonship breaks from the Christian heart in prayer."[64]

Romans 8:16 explains, "The Spirit Himself bears witness with our spirit that we are children of God." Of this verse, James Denney explains that although it is the believer who is speaking out of his spirit, "the voice with which it speaks is, as we know, prompted and inspired by the Divine spirit itself."[65] So too, when commenting on Galatians 4:6, Marvin R. Vincent renders the meaning of *krazo* principally as "an inarticulate cry," but one that is made dignified in the New Testament. He writes, "The Spirit is represented as uttering the cry, because the Spirit gives the inspiration of which the believer is the organ."[66]

While E. A. Obeng suggests that this cry was one uttered at a baptismal service,[67] this can hardly be the whole story. Ben Witherington, who offers that *Abba* in this context involves speaking in tongues, writes, "The use of *abba* is seen as a sign that the speaker is an heir of God, a joint-heir with Christ, a child of God."[68] This miracle of speaking in an unknown tongue could only come from one place, Heaven. Consequently, it signaled both the inception of the Spirit and signaled as well a new intimacy in the Spirit with God. Those receiving the Spirit could now in reality call God their Daddy, for they enjoyed initiation into a full and complete covenantal relationship with God not possible before the cross.

There were, of course, other ways to speak of the miraculous manifestation of the Spirit in initiation into covenant. Dunn cites I Corinthians 1:5, 7; Galatians 3:5; Hebrews 2:4, and 6:5 as passages that demonstrate this common expectation of the early church with regard to the working of the Spirit.[69] As McDonnell and Montague note, biblically the baptism of the Spirit was accompanied by "charismatic expression on the part of the receiver."[70] Yet, as we have suggested in the previous chapter, the various components of initiation into covenant do not have to occur in a prescribed mechanistic order.[71] Still, it was not uncommon for believers who were baptized to, at the same time, confess Christ, have Jesus' name orally invoked over them, and receive the baptism of the Holy Spirit.[72] For this reason, Obeng is not so far wrong to suggest that the cry of *Abba* was one that occurred in a baptismal setting.[73] Because profession of faith, baptism in Jesus' name, and receiving the Spirit were all components of initiation into covenant, each one sometimes becomes a kind of shorthand for the whole experience of initiation into covenant.

In just this way, because the expectation that tongues would be concomitant to receiving the Spirit, it is not surprising that this expectation stands behind some of the earliest biblical confessions. So Paul, in I Corinthians 12:3, utilized the same Joel text from which Peter drew to preach baptism; but in this case, Paul has something else in mind. In I Corinthians 12:3, Paul offered, "Therefore I make known to you that no one speaking by the Spirit of God calls Jesus accursed, and no one can say that Jesus is Lord except by the Holy Spirit." Paul's statement is a confessional one. To say that "Jesus is Lord" is to be initiated into covenant. Cullmann links this text with the Spirit in Romans 8 and with glossolalia as well, given the context of I Corinthians 12. Indeed, a number of scholars are in agreement that for Paul, then, saying that "Jesus is Lord" integrally relates to being filled with the Spirit.[74]

An Invitation of the Spirit

Even though no one was actually baptized with the Spirit during the earthly ministry of Jesus, His message was consistent. His work on the cross would enable a new and deeper relationship, one not available before.

Jesus particularly appealed to those who were hurting, alone, or marginalized in their world. He offered hope, peace, and contentment, crying, "Come to me, all who labor and are heavy laden, and I will give you rest."[75]

Initiation into covenant is an invitation into relationship. It is amazing that the disciples never wanted to go back. There is no record of them wanting to once more walk the dusty shores of Galilee with Jesus. In receiving the Spirit, the apostles actualized words of Jesus in a way they could not heretofore have understood. Jesus said, "For where two or three are gathered together in My name, I am there in the midst of them." Now they knew. Jesus had promised "water springing up into everlasting life." Now they tasted it. He offered, "I will not leave you orphans; I will come to you." Now they experienced it. One only needs to read the Book of Acts to capture the incredible excitement of living on the cusp of the miraculous. It is to just such a place of privilege that the Lord invites His church to return.

Chapter 18

Rediscovering Covenant

Introduction

For almost a century now, people have been asking the question as to how the modern Oneness Pentecostal movement actually began. Too often, people who have been attempting to respond to this question have offered simplistic answers. Analogously, when we ask, "How did Christianity come to be?", this is not the same thing as asking, "What do Christians believe?" The former question requires historical data while the latter question may be an invitation to share important beliefs. Further, when any sort of historical investigation occurs, it is never a neutral inquiry. For example, a Roman Catholic historian would likely come to a study of the Reformation with a far different perspective than a historian who was Protestant. Beyond this, certain kinds of socio-historical investigations bring with them some fairly significant presuppositions. Often, by definition, God is not allowed to participate in historical events; sociological inquiry typically demands that events have causes that are not related to the supernatural. The question as to how the modern Oneness Pentecostal movement began is a question that deserves an answer. Yet, we are only now prepared to offer such an answer. For seventeen chapters we have been seeking to answer the alternate question: what do Oneness Pentecostals believe? We did so in anticipation of this chapter, for we have offered the beliefs of Oneness Pentecostalism while looking over our shoulder at the early Oneness Pentecostals whom we consider as representative.

Certainly Oneness Pentecostalism has a set of historical factors that led to its inception, but we track the "causes" of modern Pentecostalism with a good deal of caution. By comparison, some of the historical "causes" offered for the existence of Christianity include "economic or political oppression," the "failure of Greco-Roman religions," the "failed apocalyptic understanding of the Rabbi Jesus," or "Paul's misguided notions of what Jesus actually claimed." Depending on a particular professor's bent in a university setting, any one of these may be the chief "cause" for the existence of the Christian faith. Yet, there is another possible cause for Christianity: God. Such an answer is neither allowable to the historian or the sociologist. But it is one that is worth considering.

What "caused" modern Oneness Pentecostalism? In this chapter we track a number of historical antecedents, some predating the movement by over a hundred years, while others were apparently directly related to its development. Still, while there was a historical confluence of factors that created the soil out of which Oneness Pentecostalism grew, this is not the same as saying they are the cause. It could well be, as the early Pentecostals believed, that God is at work in the church today and the historical events we survey are in fact a part of that work.

Theological Roots of Pentecostalism

If one focuses only on the historical figures and events that were the visible cause of the birth of Oneness Pentecostalism, it is difficult to get the full sweep of influences that gave rise to it. In order to understand the impulses that led up to the beginning of the Pentecostal movement generally and the Oneness Pentecostal movement specifically, one needs to consider the religious climate toward the end of the nineteenth century.[1] Additionally, to understand the theological gestalt of the specific groups most prominent in the formation of the Pentecostal movement, one needs to go back even further, to the theological contribution of John Wesley.

John Wesley (1703-1791) was an Anglican priest whose path toward piety led him on a quest that ultimately influenced the religious landscape even to this day. As a good Anglican, Wesley believed that Adam's fall affected humanity from the neck down—the heart but not the head.[2] Further, Wesley was somehow able to baptize the British empiricism of John Locke into his theological method,[3] believing that one could inductively study the Bible and come to theological truth as well as personal application. Wesley saw that tradition was important, but only a particular slice of tradition; he believed the first few centuries of church life provided a model for the Christian life. Theologically, this is understood as primitivism, but

Wesley's was a different kind than what would evolve later among Pentecostals. While Wesley allowed for theological creeds and confessions from the first four centuries, Pentecostals believed that truth sprang from the pages of Scripture and that one could find patterns for life by studying the experience and practice of the apostolic church.[4]

John Wesley's Methodism effectively crossed from England and found fertile religious soil in which to flourish in nineteenth-century America.[5] Methodism mixed with revivalism and other religious streams into the rather optimistic Evangelical alliance that made up the dominant substrata in American religious culture. Americans not only believed in experience; they liked the notion that anyone could come to the Bible and interpret it. Philosophically, Francis Bacon was highly regarded as mediated through Scottish Common Sense Realism. With this philosophical and cultural backdrop, popular religion in nineteenth century America confirmed that God is very pragmatic; a religious climate went hand in glove with the common sense American psyche.[6] Eschatologically, there was a broad expectation that it was America's calling to Christianize the world, and that at some future point, upon the completion of such a task, Jesus Christ would return.

During the last half of the nineteenth century, however, there was a confluence of events that created a crisis in this American religious perspective. The tension that preceded the Civil War brought an end to a number of religious coalitions;[7] the Civil War itself was a terrible tragedy and the carnage did little to suggest that Christian civilization was advancing. At the same time, American shores welcomed an influx of immigrants whose presence challenged the dominant advance of Protestant Christianity. Other evils were lurking, including Marxism, Darwinism, and suspect theologians from Germany who taught higher criticism.[8] Worst of all, Christianity had become for many merely a cultural heritage. Sadly, conservative church denominations that had once been beacons of truth now embraced liberalism; indeed, numbers of churches were admitting members with no true conversion experience at all.[9] Rather than American churches Christianizing the culture, America was less rather than more Christian than it had been. Missionaries were seemingly losing rather than gaining ground. All of this flew in the face of the accepted understanding that America would Christianize the world, ultimately ushering in the triumphal return of Christ.

Recognizing the spiritual lethargy for what it was, the Holiness movement was formed in part as a quest toward reaffirming sanctification as a significant experience in a Christian's life. Revivalists came to the fore, among them Dwight L. Moody and R. A. Torrey. During Moody's travels in England, he became impressed with premillennialism. It seemed to answer significant questions about the crisis in America. Understood correctly the Bible not only taught that Jesus was coming; it taught that He was coming very soon.[10]

The shift in eschatological thinking to a more apocalyptic approach to prophecy had unintended consequences in thinking about Christian creeds and traditions. If in fact God was revealing new light on prophecy *just because* it was the end of the age, the implication was two-fold. First, received tradition must now of necessity come under the scrutiny of prophetic revelation; indeed, the pendulum began swinging to the point where church tradition had less and less say in determining truth. A second implication was that if God was in fact revealing fresh understanding of His eschatological plan, then it was likely that He would reveal other things as well. As William Faupel suggests, "As the movement neared the turn of the century, expectations arose that God was about to restore apostolic authority and power to the church to enable it to accomplish his end-time purposes."[11]

Theologically, Pentecostalism is most indebted for its theological gestalt to two sources: the second work of grace promoted by the Holiness movement and the kind of "Higher Life" theology that was promoted at conferences in Keswick, England. Both perspectives preached the eschatological significance of a second work of grace with fervency. For the Holiness movement, this experience provided cleansing. Keswick theology taught this experience was the empowering of believers with the Holy Spirit. Since preachers from both perspectives shared pulpits and platforms, there was in the years just prior to the twentieth century competing tension between purity and empowerment.[12]

As early as John Fletcher, John Wesley's colleague, one could readily speak of receiving the baptism of the Holy Spirit as a normative way of talking about the Spirit's second work of grace.[13] While there were a number of opinions as to its meaning and purpose, it was during the last decade of the nineteenth century that the language "baptism of the Holy Spirit" became normative to describe this experience.[14] Over against tendencies of the Holiness teachers to frame the one-time experience of the baptism of the Holy Spirit as the pivotal point at which the sin-nature was in some sense "eradicated,"[15] Keswick teachers tended at first to avoid such specifics but rather would speak of "repeated emptying by consecration and 'fillings' with the Holy Spirit, or the 'Spirit of Jesus.' "[16] Coincidentally, the way in which focus turned to Jesus among some revivalists was in itself divisive, and strained the Holiness/Keswick coalition. Further, that there was a crest of interest and passion related to the Spirit is confirmed by C. I. Scofield, who in 1899 offered, "Indeed, more has been written and said about the doctrine of the Holy Spirit than in the preceding eighteen hundred years."[17]

Pentecostalism Beginnings

The advent of the modern Pentecostal movement can be traced theologically to Charles Parham in 1901 and numerically to William Seymour and the Azusa Street revival in 1906.[18] The following decade saw the advent of modern Oneness Pentecostalism, springing from the broader Pentecostal movement[19] as a result of allowing the Bible to speak on its own terms. As we have begun to suggest, a key historical factor in the advent of Pentecostalism relates to how the doctrine of the Spirit was very much linked to eschatological concerns. Dispensational premillennialists increasingly viewed the coming of the Lord through a pneumatological lens.[20] While not everyone in the Holiness movement was of the same opinion on this point, it was among those who looked for an imminent return of Jesus that the baptism of the Holy Spirit was experienced in what is now normative Pentecostal understanding of the experience in the first year of the twentieth century.

The theological progenitor of modern-day Pentecostalism, Charles Parham, began Bethel Bible School in Topeka, Kansas, in the latter part of 1900, to train ministers. At this faith-based school, no tuition was charged. Parham writes, "Its only text-book was the Bible; its only object utter abandonment in obedience to the commandments of Jesus."[21] For Parham, there were a number of issues of theological import. Of specific concern to him was a focus on the baptism of the Holy Spirit. Not only was there a variety of teaching about the Holy Spirit that was current; there was a diversity of opinion about tongues, which had recently begun to manifest itself.[22] When students under Parham's direction determined that the biblical evidence of the baptism of the Holy Spirit was speaking in tongues, they prayed for this experience and received it. The theological advent of modern Pentecostalism occurred when Parham made official that the initial infilling of the "baptism of the Holy Spirit" was accompanied by the biblical evidence of speaking in other tongues.[23] For Parham, a person was first saved, then sanctified; subsequently an individual was eligible to receive the baptism of the Holy Spirit.

The Pentecostal movement framed this experience of the baptism of the Holy Spirit in eschatological garments. The church was preparing itself as the bride of Christ. Not only did Charles Parham teach that the baptism of the Holy Spirit "should be seen as a part of every Christian's experience";[24] the reception of the baptism of the Holy Spirit indicated to those who received it that they were in fact in the bride of Christ.[25] The same claim was made by William Seymour, under whom the Pentecostal fire ignited into a global phenomenon.[26] The broadly held teaching of many associated with the Azusa Street revival was that it was only those who were baptized in the Spirit that were in the bride of Christ.[27] William Faupel states, "Virtually all the early Pentecostal adherents believed that those who had received Spirit-baptism became part of the Bride of Christ, a company that was called out from, and separate from the church."[28]

Vinson Synan rightly states that the Pentecostals from Azusa viewed denominations as "mere human constructions"[29] to be swept away. These believers held a conviction that God was using them to "bring life to an overorganized and spiritless body."[30] While Pentecostals anticipated that the Holiness movement would universally embrace this new understanding of the baptism of the Holy Spirit, it was not to be. Ironically, the movement that in part turned their back on them had provided a full compliment of language and songs about the Spirit, a theological taxonomy that became instrumental in the launching of the Pentecostal movement.[31]

Cast aside by almost all established churches, Pentecostals adopted a sort of "in-your-face" attitude toward denominationalism. But condemning organizations was not the same as condemning all Christians who were not yet Spirit-filled. Azusa Street adherents initially thought that a relatively small number would make up the bride of Christ.[32] While there were other Christians aplenty, full salvation required a person to be saved, sanctified, and filled with baptism of the Holy Spirit.[33] Interestingly, Oneness Pentecostals would soon experience this same sort of cognitive dissonance, attempting to make sense of those who did not follow in a new understanding.

The Advent of Oneness Pentecostalism

In the main, the impulses that gave rise to the Oneness Pentecostal movement were not so different than those that gave rise to Pentecostalism generally.[34] The advent of Oneness Pentecostalism from 1913-1915 is arguably the result of three ongoing and interrelated theological streams that coalesced. The first stream had to do with the utmost significance attached to the name of Jesus. An emphasis on the name of Jesus began in the Holiness movement and as Grant Wacker notes, there was continuity in emphasis on the name of Jesus that permeated the entire early Pentecostal revival.[35]

While an initial impulse that helped propel Oneness Pentecostalism was a focus on baptism in Jesus' name, this practice was hardly new. Parham himself had baptized in Jesus' name;[36] as we shall see, what began to be added was the revelatory element, one that insisted on the necessity of baptism in Jesus' name. A study of the Acts of the Apostles confirmed that baptism in Jesus' name is a biblical teaching. If the apostles did it, then the issue was settled. This kind of searching for revelation in the biblical text was in itself a Pentecostal inheritance. Robert Mapes Anderson writes, "The extreme literal biblicism of the Pentecostals led them to concentrate on reproducing in detail life of the New Testament church."[37] While framed in a negative perspective by Anderson, it was indeed this focus that allowed for a rediscovery of the celebratory biblical proclamation of the name of Jesus.

The second important theological stream was related to christology. Since the Bible was to be interpreted by the Bible, and since the Bible does not contradict itself, then there was of necessity a theological meaning to baptism in Jesus' name. That is, there had to be a way in which baptism in Jesus' name theologically fulfilled the command to be baptized in the name of the Father, Son, and Holy Spirit. The immediate point of revelation came during a camp meeting in 1913 near Los Angeles where one R. E. McAlister preached incidentally on how baptism in Jesus' name was practiced in Acts. During the course of the meeting, God revealed to a man by the name of John Scheppe that biblically, baptism in Jesus' name fulfilled Matthew 28:19, because Jesus is the saving name of God.[38] While there was some initial excitement about this in the camp, the broader implications of this truth were realized over the course of months as McAlister, Frank Ewart, Glenn Cook, and G. T. Haywood reflected on Jesus' name. Ignoring what they had come to know from creeds and church tradition, they went first to the Old Testament to see what it taught about plurality in God. God was revealed as absolutely one. Then they went to the New Testament, and realized that Jesus was the God of the Old Testament who had become incarnate. Only then was this understanding utilized to critique the historic belief of the church on the Trinity; it was found wanting. The articulation of Jesus as the mighty God was based on a specific hermeneutical shift, one that had as its starting point, a theological definition of God that was oriented toward an Old Testament reading of the *Shema*. While the interpretation was new, the motivation was consonant with Pentecostalism generally, that of drawing back the curtain to an apostolic presentation of truth.[39]

The third stream of confluence was ultimately the understanding that baptism in Jesus' name and receiving the baptism of the Holy Spirit constituted the new birth. Theologians have rightly argued that the interrelationship between the oneness of God and the new birth was foundational in the formation of Oneness Pentecostalism.[40] It is a matter of debate as to how these streams coalesced; even before any public confession of the oneness of the Godhead, there was an impulse to see baptism and the Holy Spirit as components of the new birth. In 1913, a year before he was rebaptized in Jesus' name, G. T. Haywood would say, "Now, if we are brought into the body by the new birth, then we conclude that the *new birth* and the *baptism* of the Holy Spirit are *synonymous*."[41]

In all of this, one should not overlook the hermeneutics of eschatological restoration that was the lived experience of Pentecostalism. Change was in the air. In 1910, Durham declared that because of the finished work of Calvary, one need not look for a second work of grace as taught by the Holiness movement. That is, one should not expect a conversion experience and then a subsequent experience of sanctification. Full entrance into the Bride only required being saved and then Spirit-filled. Though it was not realized without struggle, the position of Durham became the normative Pentecostal position of all organizations formed after 1910. Durham's teaching became the fertile soul that allowed an even closer look at the significance of the baptism of the Holy Spirit. Frank Ewart and Glenn Cook, men who played important roles in framing Oneness christology as it relates to the new birth, both served under Durham.[42] Talmadge French offers, "Finished work sanctification, while removing one 'step' in the work of salvation, provided the necessary catalyst linking Spirit baptism with the one 'plan of salvation.' "[43]

The very week the Assemblies of God was being formed, Frank Ewart and Glenn Cook preached that God was restoring biblical truth by revealing the christological meaning of the saving name of Jesus. Like the eschatological restoration of the gift of the Spirit, and like the understanding that sanctification was not a separate experience, they taught that the baptism of the Holy Spirit was not separate and distinct from the new birth. That Jesus was revealing the importance of His name in this way was to be celebrated, for it was an integral part to what God was doing in the last days, fulfilling a prophetic promise to "give light in the evening time."[44]

The epistemological jumps required to formulate Trinitarianism, essentially the work of centuries, were undone by the logic of three simple discoveries, all made in quick succession. The first key was in understanding the logic of Jesus Name baptism as it was compared to Matthew 28:19. When interpreting Acts 2:38 as fulfillment of Matthew 28:19, these Pentecostals began focusing on Jesus as the saving name; this led to the second key that the Father, Son, and Holy Spirit in Matthew 28:19 no longer needed to be understood as Persons. In one fell swoop, hundreds of years of church history toppled; Jesus was not one Person of three, but Jesus was the *I AM*, Jehovah incarnate.

The third hermeneutical key in the advent of Oneness Pentecostalism was also related to the name of Jesus. The original Pentecostal profession had been that to be ready for the bride of Christ, one needed to be saved, sanctified, and filled with the baptism of the Holy Spirit (three experiences ultimately reduced to two by William Durham). Just after putting Durham's issue to rest, some lamented that a "new issue" arose,[45] decrying this new emphasis on Jesus' name. But arise it did, and it would not go away. Oneness Pentecostals now saw baptism in Jesus' name as integral, and, utilizing Acts 2:38, they taught that preparation to be a part of the bride of Christ included taking on the name of the Bridegroom. While still framing this experience eschatologically, Oneness Pentecostals simply added that baptism in Jesus' name was as well a necessary requirement to be in the bride of Christ. As Robin Johnston accurately notes, "When the dust cleared sometime around 1915, the New Birth message was attached to the 'New Issue' of Jesus' name baptism and the oneness of God."[46] Thus, in less than twenty years of dynamic and sometimes tumultuous upheaval, a group was birthed whose christological and soteriological confession was some considerable distance from the perspective of Evangelical Christianity. Further, because this group, who would be called Oneness Pentecostals, made what were deemed to be extreme epistemological jumps, they were no longer welcome to fellowship with other Pentecostals.

Like other Pentecostals before them, Oneness Pentecostals had offered hope for those who were not a part of the Bride.[47] That is, they created systems whereby someone who might not have all truth, may be judged according to the light they knew. There was no standard profession as to how this all worked, but various options for those who had not experienced Acts 2:38 functioned as a theodicy, making sense of why others did not follow suit and join with the Pentecostals. This is not to suggest that Oneness Pentecostals were soft or did not care about their distinctive message. On the contrary, they were unyielding. God had at last pulled back the curtain to the first century and their understanding of Scripture was unencumbered by dogma.[48] In conjunction with baptism in Jesus' name, the baptism of the Holy Spirit framed the normative biblical experience for Christians coming into relationship with Jesus Christ; for it was the Spirit that indwelt Jesus and not another that one received upon experiencing new birth. Faupel, on the theological significance of the developing Oneness Pentecostalism writes "that it was the logical and inevitable development of Pentecostal theology."[49]

Conclusion

It is only now, after looking at this history of the advent of modern Oneness Pentecostalism, that we can now speak of the various aspects of a Oneness proclamation as a unified whole. It seems to me that in order to be open to what someone presents about the identity and work of Jesus Christ, that presentation must be biblical, logical, and historical. In chapter 1, we proposed that a Oneness analysis of Jesus Christ meets all of these criteria. We have worked to make such a presentation. Yet, in order to accurately understand the arguments we have offered, it is not only important to be clear as to what we are saying; we need to assess as well what it is that we are not saying. Indeed, arguments are often won or lost by the way they are framed, even before one stitch of evidence is marshaled.

In this context, let us begin by reviewing what claim we are not making when we say that Oneness Pentecostalism is historical. What we do not mean is that modern Oneness Pentecostalism as it currently exists has followed some uninterrupted stream of pristine belief that flows from the earliest church. Rather, we as Pentecostals rest in a common Protestant confession; that is, where the historic Christian church got it wrong, it is absolutely essential to make a conscious historical jump. We must look to the biblical text and the early church for a model of belief and practice.

Conversely, what we do mean to suggest by saying that Oneness christology is historical is that it is biblical; that is, it was the normative understanding of the earliest church. In chapters 5-12, we worked to offer a presentation of christology that is not a caricature, but rather, a fair represention of the meaning of the Father/Son language in its New Testament context. Then, in chapters 13-15 we tracked Oneness literature of the second and third centuries, some of which usually gets passed over. We looked at *Testimonia, Apocryphal Acts*, martyrologies, and a broad variety of popular literature. What we determined is this: academic historians are correct to assess that what we are defining as Oneness christology was the opinion of the majority of Christians up through the second century, particularly those not educated in philosophy.

One genre of literature that we treated extensively, both biblically and historically is that of the christological hymns. What we argued in chapters 5-12 was that these hymns imbedded in the pages of the biblical text offer a Oneness christology. Further, this same Oneness christological hymnody is consistently present in the first centuries of the church. It is not merely found, say, in Ignatius and Melito; perhaps most telling is the fact even those *Logos* christologians who themselves wrote against Oneness christology could not help but quote from these same hymns that affirmed a Oneness construal, for these songs consistituted the popular confession of the majority of the church. Adolf Harnack tells us where this same majority went wrong. He concludes that when leaders of this position resorted to arguing "scientifically" (philosophically) it signaled the eventual historical demise of this christological position.[50]

Let us now consider what it is that we are not saying when we we suggest that Oneness christology is biblical. What we do not mean is that whoever reads the Bible will without question arrive at a Oneness understanding. Certainly everyone comes to the biblical text with different presuppositions. It seems quite likely that if someone comes to the biblical text already convinced of the rightness of the Trinity, then the Trinity will be found in the text. On the other hand, as we have argued throughout this book, it is quite possible to step back from such a position, endeavoring to understand the Incarnation through the eyes of the apostles rather than through the lens of what the church came to believe. We have called this perspective an "Apostolic hermeneutic."

Recall that the apostles were Jews. Our Old Testament was their Bible. Their daily confession was the *Shema*. Translated, it reads: "Hear, O Israel! Yahweh is our God, Yahweh alone."[51] Remember that when they first met Jesus, the apostles knew Him first as a man who taught them about Yahweh. It only gradually became clear to them that Jesus claimed something else; in ways that sometimes befuddled the apostles, Jesus professed that He was the *I AM*. Yet, enlightenment came; on the Day of Pentecost, Peter quoted Joel's prophesy about invoking Yahweh's name and applied it by invoking Jesus' name in baptism. Indeed, the apostles delighted in applying Old Testament passages about Yahweh directly to Jesus Christ. As christologians are now telling us, the church considered Jesus divine from the very beginning. Indeed, it was only when the epistemological curtain was drawn in the second century that the Old Testament was excluded as foundational to an understanding of God. At the same time, the philosophical sensibilities of newly converted church fathers mandated that God must remain remote from the cosmos and must necessarily send another. Sadly, the further the church got away from their Old Testmaent moorings, the less biblical and the more Hellenistic the confessions of Christ became.

Finally, we have suggested that Oneness christology is logical. Let us consider what we do not mean by such a claim. We do not mean that Oneness adherents should attempt to compete in the syllogistic grappling that occupied the church fathers related to parsing the "nature" of Jesus Christ. Further, modern Pentecostals do right by not following the bent of certain Reformed theologians who created logical systems built on reason, for these systems require nothing of experience. Indeed, Pentecostalism has its own logic. It did not begin, as some have charged, by Pentecostals exegeting their own experience. Rather, these early modern Pentecostals believed that it was their inheritance to read the biblical text and make application to their lives. It was just such a common-sense reading of Scripture that allowed Pentecostals to believe for the miraculous in the face of theological systems that told them not to bother. Further, it was the debunking of systems and the openness to the biblical text that worked toward the advent of Oneness Pentecostalism.

There have been a number of proposals offered as to what historically "caused" the Oneness movement in the early twentieth century, some less flattering than others. Given the vitriolic feelings that attended the expulsion of Oneness Pentecotals from the newly formed Assemblies of God, it is particularly poignant that Edith Blumhoffer, Assemblies of God historian, offers a rather positive assessment. She writes, "If one admits the strong restorationist component at the heart of Pentecostalism's identity, oneness Pentecostals were more zealously restorationist, more doggedly congregational, and more Christ centered—in short, in some important ways more essentially Pentecostal—than the trinitarians."[52] As Blumhoffer notes, certainly there were historical influences that coalesced in the formation of Oneness Pentecostalism; yet, there is an inherent logic of Oneness Pentecostalism that goes beyond its early twentieth century historical context. Indeed, when we take the same methodological starting point as these early Pentecostals, we too may well come to the same conclusions. The first step is to seek to understand God in the same way the apostles did. That is, they acknowledged that the Old Testament accurately demonstrates the unicity of God. Amazingly, the apostles applied the covenant name of God to Jesus. For instance, Peter applied biblical texts related to the name of Yahweh by baptizing people in the name of Jesus. Further, the apostles consistently invoked the name of Jesus as the covenant name of God. Then too, given the *Shema*, the apostles did not believe they were receiving another person when they received the Spirit. Jesus said He would come to them, and in their receiving the Spirit, He did. The critical point is this: if the apostles believed and practiced this confession of Jesus Christ, then whatever the church came to believe, if there is a choice to be made, we ought to side with belief and practice of the apostles. It follows as well that we too ought to be baptized in Jesus' name and receive the Spirit in the way the apostles did.

Epilogue

A Lesson from History

In a little more than a century's time, Pentecostalism has grown from a relatively small movement to a point where it is arguably the second largest "group" in the Christian world. This growth did not occur at once; rather, it happened incrementally. It was greatly propelled in the 1960s and 1970s, with the advent of the Charismatic movement. In the 1970s, new venues of propagating things Pentecostal began proliferating; also, with gentrification, Classical Pentecostal churches moved from across the tracks to Main Street. When the 1980s brought the advent of the Vineyard movement and other such phenomena, things Pentecostal proliferated in unexpected quarters. During the 1990s Pentecostal-style worship and experience effectively crossed a broad spectrum of church tradition. The trend toward things Pentecostal in the church world has continued unabated. Prognosticators anticipate the Pentecostalization of the greater part of the Christian church worldwide in the very near future.

It is too soon to celebrate in an unmitigated fashion, though, for Pentecostalism is reaping the fruits of its own success. Those Pentecostals whose roots go back to Azusa Street are now in the minority. Indeed, because of the significant size and diversity of those embracing things Pentecostal,[1] core definitions of what it means to be Pentecostal are now being challenged. Perhaps most significantly, the place of speaking in tongues as the initial sign of a person receiving the Holy Spirit is now fairly well on its way to being negotiated away both theologically and in praxis.[2] Indeed, it is no exaggeration to say that every distinctive known to Pentecostalism is under scrutiny. Ecumenism is asking even whether the category of "Pentecostal" should not be jettisoned, for it makes other

Christians feel like second-class citizens. Speaking in tongues is seen as an ideal, one that should not be pressed too much, for it suggests that all other Christians are missing something as long as they do not have it.[3] "Pentecostalish" theologians warn Pentecostals against being too glossolaliocentric! The extent of this trend caught me by surprise when I was assigned to respond to a scholarly paper at the Society for Pentecostal Studies by a professor from a Pentecostal/Charismatic university. His paper attempted to deconstruct (utilizing a very unpentecostal-like hermeneutic) the baptism of the Holy Spirit by preferring a particular reading of Ephesians and then reading that interpretation back into the Acts narrative.[4] All of this is in stark contrast with the confessions of faith offered in the beginning years of the Pentecostal movement.

The baptism of the Holy Spirit in those early days of the Pentecostal movement was no less controversial than it is today. Those from Azusa Street were called the "vomit of Satan" and other equally unflattering sobriquets.[5] But it did not prevent them from making a bold declaration of the necessity of Spirit baptism. It is no wonder that people often considered these early Pentecostals as stubborn and intractable, for the movement was birthed in incredible struggle. Brother earnestly contended with brother even while miracles and outpouring of the Spirit occurred. But, then, revivals are often messy. While there were exceptions,[6] Oneness Pentecostals were a particularly stubborn lot. When Oneness Pentecostals followed their convictions that there was no biblical Trinity, they not only stood in the face of hundreds of years of church tradition; they were willing to lose fellowship over those same convictions. Yet, Pentecostalism was born with the mantra of truth over tradition. Douglas Jacobsen offers, "In a certain sense, the Oneness theologies of Haywood and Urshan were also more distinctively Pentecostal than anything that preceded them; at the very least, they were less dependent on previous forms of Christian theology."[7] For Oneness Pentecostals, standing alone has become a kind of habit. So it was, that when after the formative decades of the twentieth century were over, other Pentecostals, however unevenly, assimilated into the broader Evangelical movement, Oneness Pentecostals did not. And when ecumenism became even more highly prized as the religious culture evolved into its more post-denominational disposition, Oneness inheritors of Ewart, Haywood, and Urshan, largely remained stubbornly alone.

Sociologist Rodney Stark, in attempting to answer the question as to how Christianity became a world religion, offers an assertion that ought to give one pause.[8] While he lists a number of particular factors that all have relevance, in the end, he argues that it was neither the miracles nor the preaching that resulted in the success of Christianity in the face of competing claims; rather, it was what he calls the stubborn faith of the everyday Christian. It seems hard to believe, but Christians were actually called atheists(!) because they were not broad-minded enough to worship other gods.

Now, in terms of application, it is not my intent to suggest stubbornness is a universally admirable trait. Yet, for Oneness Pentecostals, I can think of at least two ways their stubbornness turned out to be a positive thing. First, as it has played out in the twenty-first century, while others with an Azusa Street inheritance are now struggling to salvage some sort of Pentecostal identity, the stubbornness of Oneness Pentecostals has in some sense insulated them from this turbulence. That is, they believe in the Holy Spirit as evidenced by speaking in tongues as a necessary experience, one that prepares them to be a part of the bride of Christ. But it is not merely that Oneness adherents have not faltered with regard to their Azusa Street profession;[9] Oneness Pentecostals have, for the better part of a century, maintained the profession of the earliest Oneness Pentecostals as it relates to Oneness christology and what is often called the new birth.

Critics see this as nothing about which to boast. They accuse Oneness Pentecostals of being judgmental, not only because of the narrow doctrinal confines and experiential expectations imposed upon their adherents, but because of their lack of acceptance of those from other perspectives. The charge of judgmentalism is an interesting one, for while it is not new, it has certainly intensified. Paradoxically, this is not because Oneness Pentecostals have changed in either approach or doctrine. Rather, it is because culture itself has changed. And although "the sun went down so gradually we didn't see the room getting dark," the Western world is adrift in cultural relativism. Indeed, the postmodern milieu in which we live abhors any strong belief system; no denomination, biblical allegiance, or conviction about morals is immune. It is not merely Oneness Pentecostals who stand accused. Ironically, we live in a time that is reminiscent of the early church. And if there were ever a time to be just a little stubborn about biblical truth and moral conviction, the time is now.

As to the charge that Oneness Pentecostals judge Christians that are outside the movement, this charge is often brought in tandem with the fact that Oneness Pentecostals have largely shunned fellowship with the broader Christian community, and in fact Oneness adherents may be sinning in this regard. John 17 is generally marshaled out as evidence for such an accusation. Oneness folk must be sinning, for Jesus prayed that all Christians be "one," and Oneness Pentecostals are certainly violating this mandate. Upon first consideration, this seems to be a valid accusation. As we have suggested, Oneness Pentecostals do tend to keep to themselves. But if Oneness Pentecostals are sinning for not being more ecumenical, the same charge could certainly be leveled at the entire Pentecostal movement in its formative years. These early Pentecostals felt they should surrender neither their doctrinal beliefs nor their experience to the altar of ecumenism. Indeed, it was their operating premise that if people wanted "oneness in Christ," the best way for that to occur was for the rest of the Christian world to embrace Pentecostal doctrine and experience.

Further, it might do well for accusers to reflect on how it is that a lack of ecumenism came to be sin. As we suggested above, we in America have developed into a postmodern culture, one that counts tolerance among its chief virtues. Religious frailty has led to the trickling away of distinctives among religious groups. Absolutes have been shown the door. Moral stands have been rejected and doctrine anathematized. Given that post-denominational Christianity struggles for identity, it is no surprise that the value of ecumenism has skyrocketed.

As to the original question, though, of judgmentalism, I would acknowledge that as Oneness Pentecostals, we, in fact, are sometimes judgmental, we show a lack of love and are unkind. I would hasten to say, though, that this is not strictly a Oneness Pentecostal failing; rather, it is a human failing. And judgmentalism is hardly a required tenet of Oneness Pentecostalism. While we may not always practice unconditional love as we should, we believe in it. Indeed, every person should be welcomed in a Oneness Pentecostal assembly and feel the unmitigated love of Christ, no matter who they are or where they are coming from. There is no place for judgmentalism in either the pulpit or the pew. Jesus and the apostles demonstrated that passionate belief goes hand in hand with compassion and that truth is not the enemy of love. Both the apostles and earliest Oneness Pentecostal adherents provide a model of how to accomplish this. We have utilized the term "covenant" as a term of relationship throughout this text. We could do no better than close the book with a practical application of how this relates to both a presentation of Jesus' name baptism in relationship to the new birth and a presentation of the oneness of the Godhead. In this regard, we would like to frame this as "covenantal soteriology" and "covenantal christology."

Covenantal Soteriology

There is something about the lived experience of the apostles that is mirrored by the early twentieth-century experience of Pentecostals. First, recall that the apostles lived in a time of expectation of a new thing. While there were different ideas of what the Messiah would be like, there was no real consensus. Psalms of Solomon 17, a pseudepigraphical work written just prior to the first century, taught that the Messiah would break the enemies of the covenant people to shivers. At the same time, the teaching of the Essenes was that there would be two messiahs, one from Aaron and one from David. The Sadducees were not intellectually opposed to the notion of messiah, so long as messianic fervor did not reallocate allegiance to the Temple. They had good reason to fear, as there had been a number of upstarts claiming to be Messiah who had riled up the Romans. The concern of the Pharisees was not so much messianic as correctly abiding by the oral tradition; and if there were one who laid claim to messianic identity, then they would test to see if the presentation of such a one fell within the normal strictures of received tradition. If it did not, they would take action. In contrast to all these groups, the apostles whom Jesus chose were pretty ignorant of all this speculation. Thus, when Jesus called them, they largely listened to what He said and received it. While it was true they were at times given to petty differences among themselves, they were committed not just to Yahweh; they were committed to Jesus as well.

For the apostles, the crux of their theology was that Jesus was bringing them into a relationship with God that wasn't available before. Further, as they came to know the one who called them from fishing nets and tax tables, revelation as to His identity overlapped in their understanding of God. They knew God; they came to know Jesus Christ. They had already been in covenant; now they came to understand that the eschatological age framed covenant in a new way. But the difference between them and most of their contemporaries was that they were not so much given to syllogistic sparring as they were to invitational necessity. Put simply, Jesus called them to the kingdom. And that call was a relational call. On the Day of Pentecost when Peter preached to Jews who had come to Jerusalem for covenant celebration, He did not begin his message by telling them what they must do as a doctrinal necessity in a formulaic fashion. He invited them into relationship with the one they had unwittingly crucified. In the context of establishing this relationship, the crowd asked what it was that they must do. Peter then told them to repent (turn from their evil ways), and they could be made new in covenantal initiation as the name of Jesus was invoked upon them in waters that symbolized this spiritual cleansing. And as they did this, they would experience God in a new and refreshing way that would absolutely change their lives forever; they would receive the Holy Spirit. This was covenantal soteriology; not an argument but an invitation; not rules but relationship. Peter did not get stuck in doctrinal wrangling; he started with Jesus. He ended with invitational necessity.

Robert Mapes Anderson, in theorizing the causal factors for the advent of Pentecostalism in the twentieth century, largely proposes that the principal motivating need for those embracing the tongues experience was economic deprivation. That is, by embracing tongues as an authenticating experience, what was an essentially lower class group could now be on par with the religious mainstream, from which they had been largely marginalized.[10]

One wonders how Anderson would nuance such a thesis thirty years later since the sweeping "Pentecostalization" of Christendom. In any case, one piece of Anderson's research was his investigation as to the level of education attained by the initial leaders of the Pentecostal movement. His conclusion was that they were largely young, inexperienced, and uneducated, and due to their lack of seminary training were theologically inept.

In retrospect, one wonders if this lack Anderson finds was really such a bad thing. Perhaps, like the apostles of Jesus, these men and women had less to unlearn. All of those who were integral to the beginning of the Pentecostal movement already perceived themselves to be in covenant. But now, a new eschatological age was upon them; they were in the "latter rain," the "evening time" of the church when God was restoring the truth and experience. While they did not understand it before, God was calling them to receive the baptism of the Holy Spirit in covenantal invitation in order to be a part of the bride of Christ. These men and women were not merely exegeting their experience to gain acceptability. It is significant that Charles Parham's group first found the experience in the Scriptures; then, in revelational response to the Spirit's call, they both prayed for and received this biblical experience. The Azusa Street revival did not start with a syllogistic platform of certainty. When William Seymour moved to pastor a Los Angeles church, he was there only a week when he declared that the Spirit was calling the church to an Acts 2:4 experience. Seymour preached that tongues was the evidence of the baptism of the Holy Spirit even though he himself had not received it as yet. He declared this to be good news. The response of the church he came to pastor was to lock the doors on him, shutting him out. After struggling for direction and provision, it was only later that Seymour and others, motivated by personal felt need, were baptized with the Holy Spirit. Revival broke out. It was an invitational urge of the Spirit and the pressing need for space that led him to a livery stable at 312 Azusa Street in order to accommodate what it was that God was doing.

In the same stream of the Spirit's call, Frank Ewart, who deemed himself already to be in covenant, began to understand the covenantal necessity of baptism in Jesus' name, even though he himself had not yet been baptized in Jesus' name. So it was that "on April 15, 1914, in a tent pitched in the Los Angles suburb of Belvedere, Frank Ewart preached his first message from Acts 2:38. Shortly thereafter he and Glenn Cook baptized each other in the name of Jesus."[11] In the cases of Parham, Seymour, and Ewart, revelation occurred incrementally. Each was required to make a confession of something that had not yet happened in their lives but to which they were invited by the Spirit.

Covenantal soteriology is hard to quantify, but there is a certain character to it. It is not that a covenantal profession is not passionate or indifferent as to whether others may follow. Indeed, there is always an urgency about proclamation, a passionate call for action. But Oneness Pentecostal pioneers did not call from the lofty rectitude of theological tradition; rather, it was the call of one fellow traveler to another. Analogously, it was the four lepers who upon satiating themselves with more then they could ever eat, returned to a starving city with a proclamation of necessity that people must come to eat. The lepers themselves did not provide the food; they only discovered it. Further, it was like the invitation given from Jesus' disciples to the disciples of John, people who already were living in some measure of revelation. There was no condemnation of the latter, only an invitation to further revelation, offering, "We have found the Messiah" (John 1:41). This was not a dogmatic assertion, but it was a necessary invitation to people who were already doing well so that these same people could have "the way explained more perfectly" (Acts 18:26).

It is in this same spirit that Oneness Pentecostals proclaimed Jesus' name baptism. In the song, "The Water Way" an invitation is offered to those who already understood themselves to be in covenantal relationship. The call did not condemn; it was an invitation to further truth made available because there was "light in the evening time." This was a song often sung when people were baptized in Jesus' name. The chorus offers:

> It shall be light in the evening time;
> The path to glory you will surely find
> Thru the waterway; It is the light today.
> Buried in His precious name,
> Young and old, repent of all your sin,
> Then the Holy Spirit will enter in.
> The evening time has come;
> 'Tis a fact that God and Christ are one.[12]

Recovering a Covenantal Emphasis

The calendar has now turned to a new century since the first Oneness Pentecostals proclaimed this invitation to covenant. Most of the shared proclamation was oral, but the message was committed to writing as well. Periodicals were published, apologetic tracts were written, and books came off the press. Bible study charts were utilized to demonstrate the theological necessity for the Acts 2:38 experience and belief in Oneness christology. In the early 1980s David Bernard wrote a book entitled *The New Birth*, a syllogistic argument that effectively marshals Scripture in a logical progression, reflecting Bernard's training as a lawyer. This book has now been translated into a number of languages and is used more extensively than any book to demonstrate the beliefs of Oneness Pentecostals.[13] Bernard's aim was to offer an apologetic to Oneness Pentecostals on how to teach about the new birth.

Because of the syllogistic style of the book, its logical progression, and its certain biblical conclusion, Evangelicals who read Bernard's *New Birth* sometimes take it as judgmental. Bernard, who frames arguments similar to the way we have in this book, offers a definition of new birth, that, as we mentioned in chapter 18, challenges Evangelical sensibilities. When Evangelicals start with the presupposition that Pentecostals ought to be Evangelical in their perspective on justification, then they can only see "works righteousness" in the pages of the book. Yet, Oneness Pentecostals are not required to fall under an Evangelical canopy at every point. Roman Catholics, the largest Christian body, believe baptism to be essential in Christian initiation. Catholic Charismatics write boldly of the necessity of water and Spirit baptism.[14] Lutherans teach baptism for the remission of sins.[15]

The last thing Oneness Pentecostals want to do is to reduce covenant initiation to wrangling, but it sometimes comes to that. If an Evangelical starts with the question, "At what point are you justified?", the question unwittingly contains its own presupposition, that justification must of necessity occur in a moment. It is precisely to this type of question that early Oneness believers professed a willful ignorance; for they had no concern for theological syllogisms constructed by either Catholics or Reformers. All they knew was what they read in the Book of Acts, and for them, that was what was normative and ought to be practiced. We have argued that in spite of their ignorance (or perhaps because of it) they were able to draw back the curtain of tradition and return to a first-century confession of the earliest church. When Evangelicals ask at what point justification takes place, they mean for the respondent to parse whether it is the moment of repentance, say, or baptism, or receiving the Holy Spirit, and whatever response is given is deemed to be either an incorrect, or "undeveloped" soteriological construct. But, as we have argued previously, first-century thinking would not fit neatly into an Evangelical construct.

As to Bernard's *New Birth*, David Bernard is a colleague of mine, and if there is anything in the world he is not, it is judgmental. I have been to the church he planted; it was begun a little over a decade ago and as of this writing numbers over seven hundred. Bernard's approach in winning people to the Lord is not to present syllogisms but to present a Person, Jesus Christ. While I am not suggesting that he does not teach doctrine, or that he doesn't preach with urgency, what he does do is to offer a covenantal invitation consonant with those early Oneness Pentecostals. It is a celebratory invitation of relationship that offers people opportunity to have the name of Jesus invoked upon them in baptism. Nor is the baptism of the Holy Spirit merely an initiatory box to check for admittance. Rather, it is the infusion of God's power and presence, a necessary privilege and inheritance as an adopted son of God.

Covenantal Christology

As Oneness Pentecostals came to their understanding of the mighty God in Christ, the immediate hurdle they had to jump was whether or not they were going to "leave orthodoxy." This jump was made inherently easier by the spirit of Pentecostalism, the conviction that these Pentecostals were part of the restoring wave that was washing over them. If Jesus were preparing His bride, then tradition was meaningless in the face of revealed truth.

There was, of course, misunderstanding from the start. Their own Pentecostal brothers issued the charge that they were guilty of the ancient heresy of Sabellianism. It is indeed possible at first blush for an outsider to believe that Oneness Pentecostals are teaching Sabellianism, particularly if the outsider has a bent toward finding it. There is a long tradition of a particular kind of speaking in Oneness Pentecostalism that would lend itself to be heard in that way, if the outsider was so inclined. This is a tradition that goes all the way back to G. T. Haywood. Haywood could say of God that He was "Father, He was the Creator, Begetter of all things." In the same breath he could say, "as Son, He was our example in the days of His flesh, from His baptism in the Jordan up to His ascension on the resurrection morning." He would continue, "as the Holy Spirit comes within and abides forever. . . ." But Haywood would say such things only in the context of a long laundry list of titles of God, a kind of poetic cadence given in laud of the praiseworthiness of God. Further, he would end with the assertion, "And the Name of our God is Jesus." Haywood is far from being a Sabellian. No one could read Haywood's *The Victim of the Flaming Sword* without understanding that Haywood's construal of Oneness christology refutes Sabellianism.

Sometimes, in a kind of echo of Haywood's profession, one will encounter a Pentecostal preacher offering a sound byte about God: "He is Father in creation, Son in redemption, and Holy Spirit in sanctification." But they do not mean (as Haywood did not) that there is some sort of "dilation" where the Father became the Son (without remainder and ceased to be the Father) and then, subsequently the Son became the Spirit (and ceased to be the Son). From the perspective of clarity for outsiders, we may do well to leave the sound bytes at home (however much response they get from the audience) and perhaps not emphasize, say, that God is (metaphorically) a Father in the Old Testament; as we have discussed earlier, the biblical witness is that God *became* a Father when He had a Son.

Another reason Oneness Pentecostals are accused of being Sabellian is because a number of Oneness Pentecostal writers claim Sabellius as a Oneness adherent. There may well be sincere motivation for this. It may be that they are genuinely ignorant of what Sabellius believed, or at least what is universally ascribed to him. Perhaps they are attempting to locate more Oneness believers historically and feel inclined to reform claims made against Sabellius. But as was stated in a previous chapter, there seems to be no question that the view of Sabellius was heretical. There may exist somewhere a Oneness Pentecostal whose view of God is actually Sabellian, but I have not met that person yet. I have met some who claim to be Oneness Pentecostal who are effectively Noetian (Jesus equals God without remainder); I have met an adoptionist or two; some with Apollinarian tendencies; some who may have been closet Arians in their attempts to make sense of the *Logos*; but Sabellians, none.

Like the Oneness Pentecostal understanding of the new birth, so Oneness christology cannot really be reduced to syllogism. On some level Oneness Pentecostals understand this because of how Oneness Pentecostalism came into existence, through biblical revelation. Still Oneness christology is often challenged with a vengeance, and it is difficult at times not to get into a heated debate. That said, argumentation is typically not the best dialogical tool. Indeed, while there are times when people have come to understand Oneness christology through heated interchange, almost always, people need to understand Oneness christology in connection to a relationship with Jesus Christ. Let me offer a personal anecdote to better explain this.

During the mid 1980s, I was privileged to travel to Wheaton College with Robert Sabin, who was at the time a leading Oneness Pentecostal teacher. Sabin had been invited to offer a lecture to a theology class because one of the students in that theology class had been in conversation with the professor about that student's beliefs as a Oneness Pentecostal. The professor issued an invitation to Robert Sabin to come and give a guest lecture on Oneness Pentecostalism. My recollection of this experience may not capture every word exactly as it was spoken, but it was one of those life-changing moments for me. In order to bring the experience into the literary present, I take the liberty of presenting remembrances as exact quotations. They are not; rather they are merely the essence of the answers and tenor of the discussion as I remember it.

Robert Sabin entered the classroom that day just a little bit guarded, for he had just come from recording a television program with John Ankerburg. Sabin had gone to that recording session thinking it would be cordial, but Ankerburg had invited guests Walter Martin and Calvin Beisner as experts to frame a kind of exposé of Oneness Pentecostal beliefs. Sabin was essentially outgunned by the collective argument of the host and two expert guests who in relentless attacks ate up most of the airtime. Camera angles and strategic music confirmed what Ankerburg intended to show all the while, that Oneness Pentecostals were not orthodox, and that they certainly weren't very smart, especially in comparison to the then self-proclaimed "Bible-Answer-Man" and his Greek expert, Calvin Beisner.

But on that day, in that Wheaton classroom, I sat in a very different atmosphere. The teacher was cordial and inviting, and when the subject of Ankerburg and "the Bible-answer-man" came up, there was both from the teacher and class a polite sigh of disapproval as to the tactics and tenor of such an approach. In his lecture, Robert Sabin first traced the history of modern Oneness Pentecostals, gave a brief synopsis of a Oneness Pentecostal position, and then took questions from the class. They were the normal sort of questions that people ask who are not exposed to a Oneness Pentecostal perspective.

"Are you saying that the Father didn't raise Jesus from the dead?" one student inquired.

"Well, certainly the Bible says that the Father did," replied Sabin. "And we would not disagree with that. But didn't Jesus also say, 'Destroy this body, and in three days I will raise it up'?"

"What about the voice and the dove at the baptism of Jesus? How do you explain that?" another student inquired.

"Well, a voice is not a person," replied Sabin. "Historically, God caused a spontaneous voice any number of times. Certainly Balaam's donkey spoke. And Jesus said, 'If these hold their peace, the rocks would cry out.' But this doesn't demand that either the donkey or the rocks are persons. In truth, God was utilizing this divine phenomenon to testify to Jesus of His mission. Nor does the dove represent a person. It was a testimony to John of God's Spirit confirming Jesus' anointing at Jordan."

"What about Jesus on the cross? Why did He pray to His Father?"

"Jesus prayed like every man prays," Sabin began to answer, as others continued to raise their hands. Sabin not only answered this question but follow-up questions as well. "No, God didn't die. When Jesus died, the

Spirit left His body. Just like when we die, our spirits leave . . . no; when Jesus said 'Why have you forsaken me?' He was not actually forsaken by God. He only felt forsaken . . . yes . . . I understand that is what the text says, but Jesus was quoting from Psalm 22, which is a psalm about David's feelings. David felt forsaken by God when in fact he was not. This too, was how Jesus felt . . . no, you are right. God cannot be forsaken by God, but it was as a man He felt these things; and yet the Spirit had not left Him. Hebrews 9:14 says that He through the Spirit offered Himself to God."

And so it went. The questions were cordial, kind, and yet direct. The answers were handled readily. But then, a question came that I think surprised Sabin, and was in fact, the last question asked during the class period. A young man asked a question that seemed to be very near the surface of all who sat in the room. "What I want to know is this: how would I be better off; what difference would it make if I believed as you do?"

Robert Sabin paused thoughtfully, contemplating what would be an authentic response. And then, after a bit, he began, at first hesitantly. He offered, "I've always believed this, so it is difficult to answer your question from a perspective I don't have. Yet, if I had to reduce it down to one thing, I would have to say that what this kind of understanding of Jesus Christ means to me as opposed to any other is that . . . well, I would say . . . that it's just not about ontological distinctions . . . making incarnational sense of the flesh and Spirit. What it comes down to is this; I love God incredibly because He did not send another; He came Himself. He felt my pain, He knows my grief, and He paid the ultimate price for my sin. And when I think about that, then, well, all I can say is that I love Him for it." There was silence in the class. The student didn't try to argue or offer a Trinitarian defense. It was apparent to this young man that the speaker wasn't trying to stuff an opposing argument, nor was he speaking in condemnation. I watched a certain illumination wash across his face; there were others who also seemed impressed with the response. They may not have fully grasped the claims of the man who stood at the front of the classroom; or if they did, they were not altogether certain they agreed. But they could not fault his motivation and authentic proclamation of Jesus Christ. The door was left open for further conversation, and some felt free to come ask questions.

By suggesting that a relational presentation is essential, I am not suggesting that doctrinal explanations are not necessary. If so, this book would not have been written. Nor am I suggesting that argumentation should never take place. Plenty of that has occurred throughout these pages. I am not even saying that people should not be passionately driven in their presentation of christology. On the contrary, because of the import of the subject matter, passion is required. My only point is that christological understanding of the identity and work of Jesus Christ should be offered in the context of an invitation to relationship. This is covenantal christology.

Oneness Pentecostal G. T. Haywood penned a song of worship that is still sung by Oneness and Trinitarian Pentecostals alike. The chorus is at once both proclamation and adoration:

> *O sweet Wonder, O sweet Wonder,*
> *Jesus the Son of God*
> *How I adore thee, O how I love thee*
> *Jesus the Son of God.*

If we as Oneness Pentecostals do not usher people closer, not only in understanding, but also adoration of Jesus Christ, then we will have failed in being faithful to the proclamation of the earliest Oneness Pentecostal pioneers. Frank Ewart, G. T. Haywood, and Andrew Urshan were certainly great men. But it is not merely enough to know what they knew; or argue as they argued, or even experience what they experienced; we must with the same passionate conviction and invitational necessity, proclaim the opportunity for unmitigated covenantal relationship with Jesus Christ.

Endnotes

Chapter 1: Oneness Pentecostalism

1. Talmadge French did considerable research on the population and demographics of Oneness Pentecostal groups around the world for his master's thesis at Wheaton College. His findings were largely reported in his *Our God is One: The Story of Oneness Pentecostals*, (Indianapolis: Voice and Vision, 1999). For that book French used self-reported numbers by only those avowedly nontrinitiarian Pentecostal groups who with purpose baptized in Jesus' name. French is generally utilized by academics seeking to be current in the population of various Oneness groups. French reported the significant growth in Oneness adherents noted above at a symposium on Oneness Pentecostalism, Ottawa Lighthouse, Ottawa, IL, April 12, 2007. While we await specific data that corroborates this claim, I assume that the numbers are accurate, so far as they can be known.
2. Here I have in mind David Reed, who has made an ongoing study of Oneness Pentecostalism. Reed is considered by some to be the leading academic authority on Oneness Pentecostalism. See his "Oneness Pentecostalism" in *The New International Dictionary of Pentecostal Charismatic Movements*, Stanley M. Burgess, ed., rev. and exp. ed., (Grand Rapids, MI: Zondervan, 2002), 936-44. Most recently, see his *"In Jesus Name": History and Beliefs of Oneness Pentecostals*, (Dorset, UK: Deo Publishing, 2008); this book reworks and adds to his "Origins and Development of the Theology of Oneness Pentecostalism in the United States," (PhD diss., Boston University, 1978). From my perspective, Reed's approach comes across as well-meaning, but paternalistic. His intent seems to be that of a scholarly uncle, making historical sense of a Oneness position while working toward reform. See also his "Oneness Pentecostalism: Problems and Possibilities for Pentecostal Theology," *Pentecostal Journal of Theology* 11 (1997): 73-93; the tenor of the article is that despite doctrinal idiosyncrasies and their foibles, Oneness Pentecostals might be helped and are not really all that heretical.
3. Douglas Jacobsen identifies three representatives of the earliest Oneness Pentecostals whose writings we possess: Frank Ewart, G. T. Haywood, and Andrew Urshan. Although Ewart is in many ways the most instrumental of these three, because much of his writing does not occur until later, it did not fit tightly in the framework to which Jacobsen restricted himself in the text—the first generation. Consequently, he largely focuses on Haywood and Urshan while acknowledging the place of Ewart. See his *Thinking in the Spirit: Theologies of the Early Pentecostal Movement*, (Bloomington: Indiana University Press, 2003), 194-96.
4. By the term "Classical Pentecostals," we refer to those who trace their lineage to Azusa Street. While some would exclude Oneness Pentecostals from the aegis, this is largely not a historical decision. Its intent is a faith-claim, that only Trinitarians are the "real" or Classical Pentecostals. In this designation, those who are typically excluded are those

embracing a form of Pentecostalism but do not hold to the same doctrinal presuppositions. Thus, the Charismatic Movement in the 1960s and following would not be considered Classical Pentecostal. Nor would the so-called "Third Wave" in the 1980s, or any "successive waves" of people claiming some sort of affinity with Pentecostal praxis.

5. There are some exceptions, but even then, the tendency has been to take commonalties between Pentecostals and Evangelicals, and simply add a postscript about the Spirit. While one could commend the effort of J. Rodman Williams, *Renewal Theology: Systematic Theology from a Charismatic Perspective, Three Volumes in One*, (Grand Rapids, MI: Zondervan, 1996), his methodology is purposefully Evangelical with a simple change in focus.

6. Terry Cross suggests that the same impulse present in Protestant Scholastics who attempted to build a rational system of theology "science" continued through the Princeton School in the 1800s and into the present. On p. 151 of his "Can there be a Pentecostal Systematic Theology?: An Essay on Theological Method in a Postmodern World" (paper for Society of Pentecostal Studies, Tulsa, OK, March, 2001), he writes, "From B. B. Warfield to Millard Erickson, from Louis Berkhof to Carl Henry, systematic theology has followed this direction by positing propositional truth revealed in Scripture and setting forth dogma from on high."

7. Vincent Synan, *The Century of the Holy Spirit: 100 Years of Pentecostal and Charismatic Renewal*, (Nashville, TN: Thomas Nelson, 2001), 43.

8. The relationship between modalism and Oneness Pentecostalism is taken up principally in chapter 15. Modalism is an umbrella term, an aegis for any number of beliefs; while there is commonalty in a Oneness Pentecostal presentation and some modalist construals, such a relationship can best be explored after a Oneness construal has been thoroughly delineated.

9. Because of the diverse nature of the movement, there is no single label that would be considered normative. Those who do utilize the appellation "Apostolic" generally mean that they believe and teach the doctrine of the apostles as it is expressed in the Book of Acts.

10. While Haywood, Urshan, and Ewart would say Jehovah, we will use *Yahweh*. For consistency sake, we will refer to יהוה (the Hebrew Tetragrammaton) as *Yahweh* throughout the book. We deal with more specific reasons for this in the next chapter. Because the use of *Yahweh* is favorable, we typically utilize the New Jerusalem Bible (NJB) for the Old Testament as it consistently translates the Hebrew name for God as *Yahweh* as opposed to Jehovah, say, or LORD.

11. While all Pentecostals privilege Luke-Acts, there is a way in which Oneness Pentecostals treat Luke-Acts differently than other Pentecostals. Principally this relates to purpose and the normative mode of baptism and the place and identity of the Holy Spirit in a believer's life. On this, see Oneness author, David K. Bernard, *The New Birth*, (Hazelwood, MO: Word Aflame Press, 1984), 156-219.

12. Kenneth J. Archer terms their rather literal approach to the biblical text the "Bible reading method," one which was an inheritance from late nineteenth-century Evangelicals; he cites particularly R. A. Torrey. See Archer's, *A Pentecostal Hermeneutic for the Twenty-first Century: Spirit, Scripture and Community* (New York: Continuum International Publishing Group, 2004), 81. While there is some truth in this, there were numerous other historical and hermeneutical influences that we explore in chapters 17-18.

13. Haywood was the most widely read of the three. On his use of sources, see David S. Norris "Creation Revealed: An Early Pentecostal Hermeneutic," in *The Spirit Renews the Face of the Earth: Pentecostal Forays in Science and Theology of Creation*, ed. Amos Young, (Eugene OR: Pickwick Press, 2009). See also Robin Johnston's "Evening Light: The Development of Early Oneness Pentecostal Soteriology," (paper presented at the annual Urshan Graduate School of Theology Symposium, March, 2005), 129-47, 134, where he argues that even in the core revelatory matters such as christology, Haywood was not averse to utilizing sources, demonstrating how in Haywood's, "A Voice Crying in the Wilderness," no. 19 (winter 1916): 4, Haywood utilized an article entitled "God in Christ." This article was written in the 1880s by English Presbyterian J. Monroe Gibson. Johnston offers, "In it, Gibson writes 'The name of God is that by which He has

made Himself known to us, especially in the course of revelation above all, the true great name of "JEHOVAH" in the Old Testament and "JESUS" in the New.' " Ewart cited from any number of sources, usually without referencing them, and he was not above marshaling out E. N. Bell's baptism and Bell's confession as corroborating evidence for believing in Jesus Name baptism. According to Ewart, Bell said of baptism in Jesus' name, "I believe that the Apostles knew how to interpret Matthew 28:19." Ewart then concludes, "We also believe and therefore have we spoken." See Ewart's *The Revelation of Jesus Christ*, (St. Louis, MO: Pentecostal Publishing House, n.d.), 16.

14. It has become more common to utilize the narrative itself as theology. Consider, for instance, Charles H. Talbert, *Reading Luke: A Literary and Theological Commentary of the Third Gospel*, (New York: Crossroad, 1982); Robert C. Tannenhill, *The Narrative Unity of Luke-Acts: A Literary Interpretation*, 2 vols., (Philadelphia: Fortress Press, 1986, 1990); Luke Timothy Johnson, *The Gospel of Luke*, (Collegeville, MN: Liturgical Press, 1991); see as well Johnson's *The Acts of the Apostles*, (Collegeville, MN: Liturgical Press, 1992).

15. Hans Frei, *The Eclipse of Biblical Narrative: A Study in Eighteenth and Nineteenth Century Hermeneutics*, (New Haven: Yale, 1974); George A. Lindbeck, *The Nature of Doctrine: Religion and Theology in a Postliberal Age*, (Philadelphia: Westminster, 1984); Robert Jenson, *Systematic Theology*, 2 vols., (Oxford: Oxford University Press, 1997, 1999).

16. Oscar Cullmann, *The Christology of the New Testament*, (Philadelphia: Westminster, 1963), 3.

17. See pp. 130–31 of John Goldingay, "Biblical Narrative and Systematic Theology," in *Between Two Horizons: Spanning New Testament Studies and Systematic Theology*, eds. Joel B. Green and Max Turner, (Grand Rapids, MI: Eerdmans, 2000), 123-42.

18. Emil Brunner, *The Christian Doctrine of God: Dogmatics, Vol. 1*, (Philadelphia: Westminster, 1950), 226.

19. More and more modern exegetes are coming to this methodological position. One important example is Ben Witherington, who writes, "We cannot start with Calvin's or Luther's or Wesley's or Aquinas's formulations or for that matter with the formulations of the Councils of Nicaea or Chalcedon or with the creeds. Exegesis must precede theologizing or systemizing, or the formulating of creeds or confessions." *The Many Faces of Christ: The Christologies of the New Testament and Beyond*, (New York: Crossroad, 1998), 6.

20. Oneness theologians did not generally concern themselves with issues that others would consider as greatly important. For instance, the closest that any of these writers comes to any sort of atonement theory is the celebratory narrative of the work of Christ by G. T. Haywood, *The Victim of the Flaming Sword*, (Indianapolis: Christ Temple book store, n.d.).

21. This is not to suggest that covenant stands alone as a necessary metaphor to the exclusion of others. There are, of course, other Old Testament metaphors that describe God's relationship with His people. For instance, "bread, light, shepherd, and vine are all used symbolically for God's relationship with Israel." Raymond Brown, "Appendix IV, *Ego Eime—I AM*," *The Gospel According to John I–XII*, Anchor Bible 29, (Garden City: Doubleday, 1966-70), 533-38, 535.

22. It may not be too much to say that the way in which one defines "covenant" provides essential keys to one's theological perspective. While Walthur Eichrodt and Gerhard von Rad come at the word in the historical context of Israel, for others, "covenant" is understood in terms of salvation history. Gerhard von Rad, *Studies in Deuteronomy*, trans. David Stalker, (Chicago: H. Regnery, 1953); Walther Eichrodt, *Theology of the Old Testament*, 2 vols., trans. J. A. Baker, (Philadelphia: Westminster, 1961). Some Evangelicals offer a "Covenant Theology," contrasting a "covenant of works" (Eden) with a "covenant of grace"; for instance, see Louis Sperry Chafer, *Systematic Theology*, vol. 1, (Dallas, TX: Dallas Seminary Press, 1947), 42ff. A dispensationalist taxonomy seeks to distinguish between four "eternal covenants" and various temporal covenants done away with in the cross; on this, see J. Dwight Pentecost, *Things to Come: A Study in Biblical Eschatology*, (Grand Rapids, MI: Zondervan, 1958), 65-128.

23. Eichrodt, *Theology*, vol. 1.
24. Eichrodt is not unique in his emphasis on covenant, but we are using him as a starting place instead of, say, Calvin, or any sort of Reformed presentation as these latter presentations come with theological presuppositions that we are working to deconstruct. Although we do not accept Eichrodt's modern critical perspective in its entirety, it does free us from certain dogmatic presumptions. Particularly helpful is Eichrodt's emphasis on mutual obligations of the covenant parties.
25. Eichrodt saw the starting place of covenant as referencing Israel. For him, the covenant in Genesis concerning Abraham and others was merely a retrojection of Israel's concept of covenant into the past—their telling a story of their present through constructed images of the past. *Theology*, 1:49. Indeed, for Eichrodt, the patriarchal narratives are successful because in this way each of the stories of a particular patriarch can embody the fortunes of the nation. The positive thing about Eichrodt is that he rightly understands that there is only one covenant, and that both faith and obedience are necessary preconditions of covenant. *Theology*, 1:36-37; see also 2:289. The work of Eichrodt motivated others to take similar theological positions, most notably, Gerhard von Rad.
26. We recognize the fact that the Jewish tradition was fluid at the time of Christ, that "Old Testament" is a term established later that presumes both an established canon of the New Testament and of the Hebrew Bible. Still, at the time of the apostles, the authority and the relative limits of what would become codified was not amorphous but was fairly well established. Jacob Neusner has popularized the nomenclature of "Judaisms" to demonstrate that one kind of Judaism was not "normative." In this way, he sought to demonstrate that a triumphal presentation of one particular portrayal of Judaism should not marginalize other traditions. See Jacob Neusner, William S. Green, and Ernest S. Frerichs, eds., *Judaisms and Their Messiahs at the Turn of the Christian Era*, (Cambridge: Cambridge University Press, 1987). But definitions have to begin somewhere. Hendrikus Berkhof may speak of "the way of Israel"; see his *The Christian Faith: An Introduction to the Study of Faith*, trans. Sierd Woudstra, rev. ed., (Grand Rapids, MI: Eerdmans, 1986), 253-54. William Horbury writes that E. P. Sanders has been successful in his defense of "catholic Judaism," by which he means a Judaism "unified by the festivals and the common hope," *Jews and Christians in Contact and Controversy*, (Edinburgh: T&T Clark, 1998), 4.
27. For Berkhof, it was possible to accurately interpret the New Testament while simply ignoring the Old Testament, the way of Israel. Berkhof writes, "The unfortunate consequences of this one-way traffic did not fail to materialize. Detached from Israel's way in the OT with its enormous tensions and drama, the NT could be forced and distorted into all kinds of other hermeneutical schemes, and the way was open to misinterpret it Gnostically, mystically, spiritualistically, individualistically, otherworldly, existentially, etc." Berkhof, *Christian Faith*, 254.
28. Epistemologically, Oneness Pentecostals insist that the Old Testament is foundational and is, as the New Testament claims, our "schoolteacher" to lead us to Christ. Galatians 3:24 teaches us that the law was our "schoolmaster" (παιδαγωγὸς), a Greek slave who served as a custodian who directed a child to school. See Walter Bauer, trans. and adap. by William F. Arndt and Wilber F. Gingrich, *A Greek-English Lexicon of the New Testament and Other Early Christian Literature* [hereafter *BAG*], (Chicago: University of Chicago Press, 1957), 608.
29. Brevard S. Childs, *Old Testament Theology in a Canonical Context*, (Philadelphia: Fortress Press, 1986), 7-15. For Childs, Old Testament theology is a Christian and not a Jewish enterprise. For him, Judaism's relationship to the text is of necessity different than a Christian approach due to their different hermeneutical emphases. See also pp. 69-83 of Brevard S. Childs's *Introduction to the Old Testament as Scripture*, (Philadelphia: Fortress Press, 1979).
30. If it is the church that has the right and responsibility to determine the meaning based on its belief, this is all well and good. But since Oneness adherents find themselves at odds with the creedal confessions of the church, they would not simply say that what the church

believes is normative. An important question to critique Childs relates to *which* historical believing community is normative. A Oneness Pentecostal approach would take as normative and seek to identify with the earliest Christian community, believing that this community defines how one should not only view the Old Testament, but the New Testament as well.

31. This is not to say that one should not look for the historical context or not invest in some textual criticism to recover what it is that might have been said originally. Typically, such a discussion may be included where it informs the broad theological understanding of Apostolic teaching.
32. There is a growing objection to the postmodern tendency to find a multitude of communities as necessarily representative of different doctrinal positions. For a critique of this kind of presupposition, see, for instance, Richard Bauckham, "For Whom Were Gospels Written?" in *The Gospel for All Christians: Rethinking the Gospel Audiences*, ed. Richard Bauckham, (Grand Rapids, MI: Eerdmans, 1998).
33. Notably absent in this work will be any significant consideration of the claims of some of the major Catholic and Protestant theologians. Only an occasional endnote or some statement that quickly brushes aside a position will be offered. Then too, theologians that may seem peripheral are given considerable consideration throughout. Some rationale for this is given on page 13.
34. Alister E. McGrath, *Christian Theology: An Introduction*, (Malden, MA: Blackwell Publishers, 3rd ed., 2001), 14-15. For Irenaeus, the church does not create the canon. "It acknowledges, conserves, and receives canonical Scripture on the basis of the authority that is already inherent to it." While this perspective certainly does not tell the whole story, it reframes the discussion.
35. As C. Kavin Rowe notes on p. 297 of "Biblical Pressure and Trinitarian Hermeneutics," *Pro Ecclesia* 11, no. 3 (2002): 295-312, "The doctrine of the Trinity is later than biblical texts and to suggest that biblical writers were consciously thinking in creedal terms is in fact a major anachronistic mistake." As we demonstrate below, christological councils had as presuppositions specific terms laden with a history of the Greek philosophical tradition.
36. During the last hundred and fifty years, theologians have sought for the historical Jesus and have taken into consideration considerable literature that has been unearthed during this time. It would seem impossible for many to consider the New Testament and christological themes without being in conversation with sources that inform the language and concepts of the New Testament. To not at least consider this data, particularly as it applies to christology, would undermine the presentation offered. The primary argument will be that the apostles primarily utilized the language, concepts, and systems found in the biblical text. That is not to say they were divorced from the language and culture around them, or they were ignorant of Jewish literature that was part of their milieu. While we will dismiss as speculation some of the popularized notions of Christ of recent years, the intent is to be soundly situated in the historical milieu of the first-century Palestinian world.
37. James D. G. Dunn's now classic *Christology in the Making: A New Testament Inquiry into the Origins of the Doctrine of the Incarnation*, 2nd ed., (Philadelphia: Westminster, 1989) excellently demonstrates how christology arose out of Jewish milieu. See also Larry W. Hurtado, *One God, One Lord: Early Christian Devotion, and Ancient Jewish Monotheism*, (Philadelphia: Fortress Press, 1988); and Richard Bauckham, *God Crucified: Monotheism and Christology in the New Testament*, (Grand Rapids, MI: Eerdmans, 1999). In many crucial ways we agree with Bauckham's construal, logic, and overall presentation of the divinity of Jesus. Bauckham breaks new ground demonstrating how Christ was considered divine in the context of Jewish monotheism.
38. Bauckham, *God Crucified*, 78. The epistemological shift described by Bauckham, whereby the church moves from its Jewish foundation to a point where the definition of God begins with Hellenistic assumptions carries great freight in this work, for it brackets the chronological limits of an Apostolic construal.

Chapter 2: The God Who Is

1. See Martin Buber, *I and Thou*, trans. Ronald Gregor Smith, (New York: Scribner, 1958). God is experienced not as object, but experientially as in an "I-Thou" relationship.
2. On the holiness of God, see Eichrodt, *Theology*, 1:270-86. On p. 273, Eichrodt highlights one Old Testament understanding of holiness as in itself descriptive of God: "Him who is unapproachable because of his complete 'otherness' and perfection compared with all created things." See also "קָדֹשׁ" in R. Laird Harris, Gleason L. Archer, and Bruce K. Waltke, *Theological Wordbook of the Old Testament* [hereafter *TWOT*], 2 vols., (Chicago: Moody, 1980), 2:787-89. God in His holiness "belongs to the sphere of the sacred and which is thus distinct from the common or profane."
3. On this, see Rudolph Otto, *The Idea of the Holy: An Inquiry Into the Non-rational Factor in the Idea of the Divine and its Relation to the Rational*, trans. John W. Harvey, (New York: Oxford University Press, 1923), 5. Indeed, he rightly notes that with regard to the concept of the holy, " 'holy', or at least the equivalent words in Latin and Greek, in Semitic and other languages, denoted first and foremost *only* [emphasis his] this overplus." See p. 6 where Otto creates the word "numinous" to describe such an idea.
4. Ibid., 7.
5. Ibid., 27ff.
6. Psalm 19:1 (NJB). On the glory of God, see Gerhard Kittel, "F. the NT Use of δόξα," *Theological Dictionary of the New Testament* [hereafter *TDNT*], 10 vols., eds. Gerhard Kittel and Gerhard Friedrich, trans. and ed. Geoffrey W. Bromily, (Grand Rapids, MI: Eerdmans, 1985), 2:247-51. Gerhard von Rad, in his "כָּבוֹד" in the OT, *TDNT*, 2:238-42, 241, cites Psalms 63:2; 138:5; 24:8; 66:2; 79:9 as examples of how the glory of God is related to Yahweh, His name, and His sanctuary. Unless otherwise indicated, all Old Testament passages will be taken from the New Jerusalem Bible (NJB) and all New Testament passages from NKJV. The choice was not entirely academic but practical and representative in part of Oneness tradition. Oneness Pentecostals generally prefer, particularly for the New Testament passages, the KJV or NKJV. For the Old Testament, I chose a version that consistently translates the Tetragrammaton as Yahweh.
7. In this contest between Yahweh and the gods of other peoples, Yahweh charges that these other gods are merely idols. Further, just as Yahweh called the cosmos into existence, so He can create and bring deliverance for Judah. Indeed, Yahweh called forth a deliverer by name for the Jewish people—Cyrus (see Isaiah 45:1 and 41:25; 46:11).
8. On this translation, see *The Schocken Bible: Volume I. The Five Books of Moses. Genesis, Exodus, Leviticus, Numbers, and Deuteronomy. A New Translation with Introductions, Commentary, and Notes*, by Everett Fox, (New York: Schocken Books, 1983, 1986, 1990, 1995).
9. Genesis is terse; however, other parts of the biblical text may shed more light on this. It is apparent that by the time of the Garden of Eden, the serpent, identified as Satan in the New Testament, arrived out of some sort of pre-history. Although the argument is largely an intuitive one from silence, Isaiah 45:18 is considered, where on the surface it seems to contradict Genesis 1:2 where it says, "And the earth was a formless void" (וְהָאָרֶץ הָיְתָה תֹהוּ). In Isaiah 45:18 *Yahweh* pronounces, "For thus says Yahweh . . . he did not create it to be chaos (לֹא־תֹהוּ בְרָאָהּ)," here the exact same word as in Genesis, which seems to be no accident. The implication, then, is that some previous creation was despoiled by Satan. This may well be true but need not be the case. As NJB translates it, the chaos could simply be a step in Yahweh's successive creation, a kind of backdrop against which He creatively speaks.
10. מְרַחֶפֶת is the feminine *piel* participial form of רָחַף; while the context does not demand the translation "hover," it could well have this meaning. What the relationship of the chaos in Genesis 1:2 to disobedient creatures has been a matter of some speculation. Pentecostalism in general is an inheritor of certain kinds of dispensationalism. Typical is Clarence Larkin; see pp. 9-12 of his *Rightly Dividing the Word*, (Philadelphia: the author, 1921). On

p. 11, Larkin suggests that the biblical inference is that "Satan and his angels were in charge of the earth" and because of their rebellion, the pre-Adamic earth was made formless and void. Such an interpretation of Genesis 1 or espousing a particular dispensational system is not typically central to a Oneness theology.
11. There is considerable discussion as to why Genesis 1:2 says "The earth was without form, and void . . . And the Spirit of God was hovering over the face of the waters" (NKJV). This verse has been variously translated. The Schocken Bible translates this, "When the world was wild and waste, darkness over the face of Ocean, rushing-spirit of God hovering over the face of the waters—."
12. As Ludwig Köhler points out, "Spirit is the nature and possession of God." *Old Testament Theology*, trans. A. S. Todd, (Philadelphia: Westminster, 1957), 111. Köhler also notes that the Bible speaks of the Spirit of Yahweh some thirty times and the Spirit of God fifteen times. Ibid., 112. On the use of Spirit in the Old Testament, see Werner Bieder, "πνεῦμα," *TDNT*, 6:359-75.
13. While in the New Testament, certain doxological texts link the man Jesus Christ with Creation, they do so in a specific way. A number of these passages will be discussed in detail.
14. *Elohim* is a uniplural noun. It may be translated either God (as in Genesis 1:1) or gods (as in Exodus 12:12) depending on the context; *Elohim* may be translated angels (Psalm 138:1 [NJB]); it may refer to a particular heathen deity such as Chemosh (Judges 11:24) or Dagon (Judges 16:23); *Elohim* may even be used of a person, such as when Yahweh told Moses that He would make him a god (*elohim*) to Pharaoh (Exodus 7:1). It does not, however, refer to an implied plurality. Usage of *elohim* is unambiguous—it can never at once be both singular and plural. The Hebrew language will not allow it.
15. Genesis 2:7 offers that God made אָדָם from the אֲדָמָה.
16. אֱלֹהִים. Above I bracket "angels" where the NJB translates "a god." Some versions offer "angels," some "God," some "god," and some "gods." The *Tanak* translates *elohim* "divine."
17. Psalm 8:4-8. This implies both creativity as well as stewardship. As Geoffrey Wainwright points out of Adam and Eve, "The power to 'name' the non-human creation (2:19f) is less the right to exploit it than the duty to give it meaning." Geoffrey Wainwright, *Doxology: The Praise of God in Worship, Doctrine and Life; A Systematic Theology*, (New York: Oxford University Press, 1980), 23.
18. Gerhard Kittel, "εἰκών," *TDNT*, 2:392-95. As Kittel points out, rabbinic interpreters approached the biblical passage in a variety of ways.
19. Typical is J. H. Hertz, who offers, "The use of the plural, 'let *us* make man,' is the Hebrew idiomatic way of expressing deliberation, as in xi, 7; or it is the plural of Majesty, royal commands being conveyed in the first person plural, as in Ezra 4, 18." *The Pentateuch and Haftorahs, Hebrew Text, English Translation, and Commentary*, 2nd ed., (London: Soncino Press, 1972), 5. Though Jewish exegesis has allowed a variety of ways to interpret such a text, I favor the interpretation that the text has reference to angels. Throughout the Old Testament angels are identified with the Creation (Job 38:7); humanity is compared to angels (Psalm 8:5); Adam was made in the moral image of God, different than the beasts. He was unique in that he had opportunity to choose—and thus have virtue. Angels as well had this same opportunity. Genesis 3:22 has reference to angels: "Now that the man has become like one of us in knowing good from evil."
20. Normative Apostolic interpretation links the serpent with Satan. Werner Foerster notes that in contrast with Judaism of their time, New Testament writers knew the "unequivocal unity of the kingdom of evil under the single head, Satan." See "Σατανᾶς," *TDNT*, 7:151-63, 159. The presumption of most Pentecostals is that Satan's fall was not connected with Genesis 6:2 but rather is pre-Adamic.
21. In Genesis 1:27, Adam (הָאָדָם) is here used as a title for the whole human race, and includes both male (זָכָר) and female (נְקֵבָה).
22. Genesis 1:26; all four "us" texts in the Old Testament refer to Yahweh and the angels. See also Genesis 3:22; 11:7; Isaiah 6:8.

23. The Jewish tradition saw "the image of God' as the basis of humanity to have a capacity for ethical living." See Jerome Murphy-O'Connor, "Christological Anthropology in Phil 2:6-11," *Revue Biblique* 83 (April 1976), :25-50, 41.
24. The Greek is not translated "likeness" universally; yet lexically, ὁμοίωσις affirms that humanity is created in the image of God.
25. D. Preman Niles, "The Name of God in Israel's Worship: The Theological Importance of the Name Yahweh," (PhD diss., Princeton University, 1974). Niles argues that one cannot know the meaning of Yahweh by seeking etymological understanding; rather, the meaning of Yahweh must be experienced in the context of a worship experience.
26. Literally "four letters," which are י (y) ה (h) ו (w) ה (h). These letters, as well as the whole of the Hebrew language, are read from right to left.
27. As we shall discuss in subsequent chapters, the correct pronunciation of the vowels is uncertain. Jehovah was used in translation, however, at a time when the "J" sound was equivalent to a "Y." The problem relates to this pronunciation of the "J" in English and cognate languages.
28. Scholars have suggested numerous cognates for Yahweh in other languages as possible sources for this elusive derivation. For instance, some believe the name Yahweh comes from Sumerian or Egyptian while other conjectures include a Ugaritic or Indo-European origin. It has been posited by some that Yahweh derives from a word meaning "to speak," while others suggest this name derives from such notions as diverse as "to destroy," "to befall," "to blow." See G. R. Driver, in his "The Original Form of the Name 'Yahweh': Evidence and Conclusions," *Zeitschrift für die alttestamentliche Wissenschaft*, (1928): 7-25, who theorized that the original form of *Yahweh* was either *Ya(h)* or *Ya(w)*. On p. 24, Driver, evidently following the sociological notions of Durkheim and others, offers that *Yah* was a primal exclamation, an "ejaculation of ecstasy." For him, such an exclamation then was lengthened over time to Yahweh. More probable is the position of S. D. Goiten in "*YHWH* the Passionate: The Monotheistic Meaning and Origin of the Name *YHWH*," *Vetus Testamentum* 6 (1956): 1-9. On p. 5, Goiten connects the name *YHWH* with Deuteronomy and Exodus 3 and finds imbedded in Deuteronomy 10:15 linkage to the Hebrew verbs אָהַב and חָשַׁק.
29. See William F. Albright's "The Name Yahweh," *JBL* 43 (1924): 370-78, for a number of the possible etymological notions about the origin of the name of Yahweh. He posits that a comparative look at Exodus 3:14 ("I am that I am") is a key to understanding the proclamation of Yahweh's existence. A number of scholars now hold to this position as well. See, for instance, Julian Oberman's "The Divine *YHWH* in the Light of Recent Discoveries," *JBL* 68 (1949): 301-23. On p. 320, he argues that the verb upon which YHWH originated was not originally a finite verb but rather "their dialect employed a causative stem of *hwy* in a sense of 'to sustain, to bring into being, to establish.'"
30. The second edition of the NLT has emended the phrase back to "I AM WHO I AM." There are theological presuppositions that come into play when making Yahweh stative, as we argue in chapters 3 and 13. Certainly the "I AM" formula is used as a declaration of the presence of deity, as in other Ancient Near Eastern sources. For instance, there is a Moabite inscription with the proud words, "I am Mesha." In a religious context, the "I AM" formula is used in such affirmations as "I am Ishtar of Arbella" and "I am the god Nabu." But Yahweh was saying something more than this. On this, see Sigmund Mowinckel, "The Name of the God of Moses," *HUCA*, 32 (1961): 121-33, 138.
31. The *Tanak* too has something at stake theologically in the name of Yahweh, which for modern Judaism has become ineffable. We will deal with these historical developments in later chapters.
32. For the translators, the relationship between the Hebrew "I AM" and Yahweh is self-evident. Compare Exodus 3:6; with verse 3 where מַלְאַךְ יְהוָה is used synonymously with Yahweh. On the identity of the angel of Yahweh as Yahweh Himself, see especially C. F. Keil and F. Delitzsch's *Commentary on the Old Testament*, 10 vols., trans. James Martin, (Edinburgh: T&T Clark, 1866-91; repr. Grand Rapids: Eerdmans, 1959), 1:285ff. While Yahweh often

used angels as messengers, in Exodus 3:2 the Angel of the Lord (or messenger; Hebrew: *malak*) is used synonymously with Yahweh, for He serves as His own messenger.
33. G. S. Ogden, "Time, and the Verb *hayah* in the Old Testament Prose," *Vetus Testamentum*, 21 (1971), 451-69, 456. The meaning of the *hyh* verb as an "imperfect" is informed by the way that the imperfect is generally understood: to "represent actions, events, or conditions that are incomplete in themselves. Temporally they may be located in past, present or future time (normally the latter two) but as it is the nature of the action that is important, the time of its occurrence takes second place."
34. Ezekiel, like Hosea, links the "I AM Yahweh" in a way that is essentially a repeated confession in worship. G. H. Parke-Taylor, יְהוָה *Yahweh: The Divine Name in the Bible*, (Waterloo, Ontario: Wilfrid Laurier University Press, 1975), 69.
35. See Deuteronomy 32:39, where Yahweh purposefully offers, "See now that I, I AM he, and beside me there is no other god. It is I who deal death and life; when I have struck, it is I who heal (no one can rescue anyone from me)."
36. The Hebrew for the declaration of "I AM" in this context is "*ani hu*," (אֲנִי הוּא). Isaiah uses this Hebrew expression and its equivalent to proclaim the absolute unicity of God. Isaiah 43:10 (*Tanak*) offers: "My witnesses are you—declares [Yahweh]—My servant, whom I have chosen. To the end that you may take thought, And believe in Me, And understand that I AM He (*ani hu*): Before Me no god was formed, And after Me none shall exist—." Isaiah 43:13 (NJB) reads, "Yes, from eternity I AM (*ani hu*). No one can deliver from my hand; when I act, who can thwart me?" Isaiah 46:4 (NKJV) declares, "Even to *your* old age, I AM He (*ani hu*), And *even* to gray hairs I will carry *you!* I have made, and I will bear; Even I will carry, and will deliver *you*." Isaiah 48:12 (NRSV) reads, "Listen to me, O Jacob, and Israel, whom I called: I AM He (*ani hu*); I AM the first, and I AM the last." In each of these cases, when the Septuagint (*LXX*) translates the verses into Greek, it is rendered by the words "*ego eime*" (ἐγώ εἰμι). As we shall come to see, this is very important christologically.
37. James Plastaras, *The God of Exodus: The Theology of the Exodus Narratives.* (Milwaukee, WI: Bruce Publishing House, 1966), 95-97.
38. Ibid., 97.
39. There is some confusion as to whether this revelation of the name of Yahweh was newly revealed at the time of the Exodus. The question largely stems from a correlated text, Exodus 6:3. Also speaking to Moses, Yahweh says, "To Abraham, Isaac and Jacob I appeared as *El Shaddai*, but I did not make my name Yahweh known to them." On the surface at least, it appears that the revelation of Yahweh was innovative in His revelation to Moses. But the name of Yahweh was certainly revealed very early on for Genesis is replete with its use. The name Yahweh is in currency as early as Genesis 2:4 and is used throughout Genesis. Abraham addresses God as *Adonai* Yahweh as early as Genesis 15:8. Corroborating this is certain archaeological evidence that suggests that the name of Yahweh was known very early, so that the presentation of Yahweh's name in Exodus could hardly be innovative. Indeed, as John Bright notes, "It is a component of numerous Amorite names at Mari and elsewhere." The form of the name Yahweh *(yhw')* also appears in the fourteenth and thirteenth centuries BC as a place-name in Egypt as well as in its abbreviated form, ya, at Ebla over two thousand years before Christ. *A History of Israel,* (1959; repr., Philadelphia: Westminster, 1983), 125-26, note 43. Although he lists objections to a number of the citations where some suggest a theophoric element, a check of the sources listed by those mentioned and other members of the "American School" offers convincing evidence for the early use of Yahweh. On this, see particularly William F. Albright's *Yahweh and the Gods of Canaan*, (London: Athlone Press, 1968), 47-95; F. M. Cross, *Canaanite Myth and Hebrew Epic*, (Cambridge, MA: Harvard University Press, 1973), ch. 1; cf. 44ff., 60ff. On the third millennium BC Ebla material, see G. Pettinato, *Biblical Archaeologist*, 39 (1976): 44-52.
40. In recent years, confidence in the certainty of such theories is "denied by biblical scholars, the same people who once gave birth to them." While the documentary hypothesis is

not altogether being abandoned, traditional interpretation is certainly being questioned. Robert K. Gnuse, "Redefining the Elohist," *Journal of Biblical Literature*, 119 no. 2 (2000): 201-20, 201. The evidence for the use of the Canaanite as a sort of precursor of *Elohim* is not considered so strong as it once was. While one can find evidence that other Canaanite cultures had a specific god named El, this in no way demands that the Hebrew notion of God was polytheistic, only that they had a shared language. Just as translators into Arabic use Allah for the God of the Old Testament because that is the generic word for God—so in the language of the culture it was *Elohim*. On pp. 55-56 of his *The Study of Old Testament Theology Today*, (Westwood, NJ: F. H. Revel, 1959), Edward J. Young acknowledges that although Melchizedek makes reference to his God as *El Elyon*, this is not necessarily a Pentateuchal supersessionism of the ancient Canaanite deity. The text is clear in calling *El Elyon* the supreme deity, and the shared vocabulary does not necessitate any sort of accommodation. Analogously, Young notes when the Bible is translated into Arabic, it uses the term Allah for God. Yet this is not the God of Islam. It is the God of the Bible.
41. On current literary studies that have undercut basic presuppositions of form critics who distinguish between *Yahweh* and *Elohim*, see Herbert Chanan Brichto, particularly chapter 1 of his "The Names of God: The Problem: A Preliminary Review," in *The Names of God: Poetic Readings in Biblical Beginnings*, (New York: Oxford University Press, 1998). As Ludwig Köhler notes, *Yahweh* is utilized as a name over 6,700 times in the Old Testament, *Old Testament Theology*, 30.
42. NIV translators allow for a marginal reading, "And by my name the LORD did I not let myself be known to them?"
43. Anthropomorphism is a human way of speaking about God, a figurative kind of language that serves as a matter of convenience. While moderns often declare as anthropomorphic a good deal of the text, one needs to be careful about such an assessment. For example, see G. W. Bromily, in his "Anthropomorphism," *The International Bible Encyclopedia*, rev. ed., (Grand Rapids, MI: Eerdmans, 1979), 1:136-39, who assesses a good deal of the Old Testament as anthropomorphic. Still, much of this modern interpretation as to what is anthropomorphic is very much influenced by the kind of interpretation that develops historically (the subject of this chapter). There are any number of things that should be taken literally about God—for Jesus and His apostles would have assessed them to be true statements of God.
44. The outline for this paragraph associating God with various emotions typically thought of as human characteristics is drawn from a paper written by a former student at Indiana Bible College, Melissa Runkle. On God having "sympathy," see Psalm 103:13. The Hebrew רָחַם is reflected in the NJB by the use of both "tender" and "treatment": "As tenderly as a father treats his children, so Yahweh treats those who fear him." The Hebrew connotes the deepest kind of compassion.
45. See Deuteronomy 5:9; God wants His covenant people to tell the truth—that He is God alone. Bowing to an idol would be antithetical to such a confession. In such a case, God would be jealous (קַנָּא).
46. Judges 10:16 states that Yahweh "could bear Israel's suffering no longer." The Hebrew, וַתִּקְצַר נַפְשׁוֹ might literally be translated, "His soul was vexed."
47. The Hebrew is unambiguous: "You hate evil-doers."
48. Isaiah 62:5 says of Judah that God would "rejoice over you" (יָשִׂישׂ עָלַיִךְ) in the same way that the bridegroom rejoiced in his bride.
49. This construal is largely informed by the teaching of S. G. Norris. See his *Mighty God in Christ*, (St. Paul, MN: Apostolic Bible Institute, n.d.).
50. Geoffrey Wainwright notes, "The sense of God's absence implies a relationship: it presupposes what has been, or it anticipates what might become, a divine presence 'for us'; it remembers a taste or betokens a desire yet unsatisfied," *Doxology*, 42.
51. On heaven, see "οὐρανός," *TDNT*, 5:497–543; in particular, see Gerhard von Rad's "Old Testament" section (502–9). Heaven may be spoken of metaphorically in any number of

ways. For instance, one cannot take as literal the "four ends of heaven" (Jeremiah 49:36; cf. Zechariah 2:6; 6:5; Daniel 7:2; 8:8; 11:4; in some cases the cosmos is divided into three parts (Exodus 20:4; Psalm 115:15-17); more often the difference is made between the heaven and the earth. Of special significance is heaven as Yahweh's abode, a theme that von Rad takes up on pp. 504-7. On p. 504, von Rad notes, "Most of the references to heaven which are important for Israel's faith speak of Yahweh's dwelling in heaven."

52. Psalm 113:5 states, "Who is like Yahweh our God? His throne is set on high." Here NJB takes לָשֶׁבֶת in the sense of ruling and supplies "throne." Isaiah 33:5 records, "Yahweh is exalted; for he is enthroned (here NJB takes שֹׁכֵן as enthroned) above, he has filled Zion with fair judgment and saving justice."
53. James D. Tabor, "Heaven," *Anchor Bible Dictionary* [hereafter *ABD*], 6 vols, ed. David Noel Freedman, (New York: Doubleday, 1992), 3:90-94, 90.
54. Eichrodt, *Theology*, 1:273.
55. There are two broad categories in which *shamayim* is used in the Old Testament: 1) the physical heavens, and 2) the heavens as the abode of God. See Harris, "שָׁמַיִם,"*TWOT*, 2:935–936.
56. Eichrodt, *Theology*, 1:104. See the note where he cites as evidence Genesis 11:5; 18:21; 21:17; 22:11; 24:7; 28:12; Exodus 19:11; 18; 20; 20:22; Psalm 2:4; 18:6; Isaiah 31:4; Micah 1:2; Deuteronomy 4:36; 26:15, etc.
57. A number of texts suggest that God can at once be at any point in the heavens. For instance, I Kings 8:27; II Chronicles 2:6; 6:18. Jeremiah 23:23 reads, "Am I a God when near, Yahweh demands, and not a God when far away?" Jeremiah 23:24 offers, "Can anyone hide somewhere secret without my seeing him? *Yahweh* demands. Do I not fill (מָלֵא) heaven and earth?" Very familiar is Psalm 139:7-8, where the psalmist declares that He will not flee from the presence of Yahweh whether he ascends up to heaven or makes his bed in *sheol*.
58. Samuel Balentine suggests that the language of theophany was ordinarily used metaphorically and attaches cult significance to it. In any case, to speak of a theophany was not a Hebrew way of speaking; it is merely a label, not a definition. *Hidden God, The Hiding of the Face of God in the Old Testament*, (Oxford and New York: Oxford University Press, 1983), 57-64.
59. On the range of meaning for "face," see Ludwig Köehler and Walter Baumgartner, "פָּנִים," *The Hebrew and Aramaic Lexicon of the Old Testament*, 5 vols., trans. and ed. M. E. J. Richardson, (Leiden, New York, Köln: E. J. Brill, 1996), 3:940ff.
60. Ibid. Under the use of "the face of God as an action," the lexicon includes Exodus 33:14, Isaiah 63:9, and Lamentations 4:16. Deuteronomy 4:37 speaks of the face of God as means of action.
61. Ibid., 940-41. The Hebrew phrase, the "'*Panim*' of God" is nuanced by prepositions and the particular context in which it occurs.
62. While the Scripture is silent as to how it was that Cain and Abel knew about sacrifice, it may well be that Yahweh spoke to Adam and Eve before they were expelled from the Garden. However it was, Genesis 4 opens with the sacrifice of Cain and Abel.
63. While one could argue that מִנְחָה in the text does not demand a literal sacrifice, there seems to be little context to suggest it was other than this. In the next specific record of a worship scene mentioned in Genesis, Yahweh was pleased with Noah's *minchah* (Genesis 9); further, the writer of Hebrews makes Abel's blood sacrifice a point of faith on his part and celebrates it (Hebrews 11:4; 12:24).
64. *The Schocken Bible* vividly captures the sense of the Hebrew in Yahweh's words to Cain: God speaks. He asks Cain, "Why are you so upset? Why has your face fallen? Is it not thus: If you intend good, bear-it aloft, but if you do not intend good, at the entrance is sin, a crouching demon, toward you is lust—but you can rule over him" (Genesis 4:6-7). Satan is certainly involved, but Cain is still culpable.
65. Cain subsequently complains to Yahweh, "Here, you drive me away today from the face of the soil, (*adamah*) and from your face (*panim*) must I conceal myself" (Genesis 4:14,

Schocken Bible). A number of translations offer that Cain left Yahweh's "presence" (*panim*), that is, Yahweh's face—His face-to-face covenanting relationship.
66. Genesis 4:16 states that Cain left the presence of the Lord to live in Nod. The implication is that he left one geographical locale where covenant was practiced and went to another place.

Chapter 3: The God Who Is Not

1. Academics generally suggest a time period for the Second Temple Period from 520 BC through AD 135; the definition is suggested by Robert A. Kraft and George W. E. Nickelsburg on p. 1 of their *Early Judaism and its Modern Interpreters*. They allow either AD 70 or AD 135 as the closing date for the period.
2. See note 43 from chapter 2.
3. Ironically, neither the most ostentatious worship of a deity, nor the most impressive religious rite guaranteed the survival of a particular god or a people, nor could such worship even guarantee lasting remembrance. For a study of various religions of the Ancient Near East, see Henri Frankfort, *Kingship and the Gods: A Study of Ancient Near Eastern Religion as the Integration of Society and Nature.* (Chicago: University of Chicago, 1948). See also James B. Pritchard, *The Ancient Near East: An Anthology of Texts and Pictures*, 2 vols., (Princeton, NJ: Princeton University Press, 1958).
4. While we can presume the origin of the synagogue and other institutions during the Exile, it is only when we begin to have literary sources in the centuries just prior to Christ that we understand the significance of these institutions. With regard to the developments in the postexilic world, Lee Levine offers, "When the curtain rises in the second century BC and onwards—that is, when our sources become more prolific—leadership models, political institutions, literary genres, and the religious ideas that were very different from those hitherto known are in evidence. Institutions such as the *gerousia,* religious doctrines such as resurrection and the Oral Law (at least as far as the Pharisees are concerned), ritual practices (i.e., the *miqwahem*—the ritual bath), burial customs, sectarian organizational forms, the genre of the apocalypse, the institution of conversion, and more (are) all crystallized during these centuries. Another important development during this time was the synagogue." "Nature and Origin of the Palestinian Synagogue Reconsidered," *Journal of Biblical Literature*, 115 no. 3 (1996): 425-48, 425.
5. On the syncretism of the Jewish people, see especially Martin Hengel's *Judaism and Hellenism: Studies in Their Encounter in Palestine During the Early Hellenistic Period*, 2 vols., trans. John Bowden. (Philadelphia: Fortress Press, 1981).
6. Bright, *History of Israel*, 386-88; a similar position is held by J. Alberto Soggin, *A History of Ancient Israel*, trans. John Bowden, (Philadelphia: Westminster, 1984), 273-80; see also Klaus Koch, who highlights Ezra's role as central. He writes on p. 195 of his "Ezra and the Origins of Judaism," *JSS* 19 (1974): 173-97, that as an imperial official, Ezra "succeeded in moving the apparatus of a huge empire for the restoration community."
7. For a sampling of the texts that affected Christianity in some way, see C. K. Barrett's *The New Testament Background: Selected Documents*, rev. ed., (San Francisco: Harper and Row, 1987). He includes selections from Heraclitus, Plato, the Stoics, Epicurus, Aristotle, etc. See also pp. 19-79 in Colin Brown's *Christianity & Western Thought: A History of Philosophers, Ideas and Movements. From the Ancient World to the Age of Enlightenment*, (Downers Grove, IL: Intervarsity, 1990).
8. While there were other philosophical schools, and though Stoicism was arguably the dominant philosophical force at the time of the writing of the New Testament, the place of both Plato and Aristotle was assured by Christian theologians whose epistemological categories were derived from a particular reading of the philosophers. On this, see p. 54ff. of Colin Brown's *Christianity & Western Thought*.
9. It is the business of scholarship to argue whether a particular position was actually held by Plato; how Plato was reinterpreted by others, including Plotinus; and what a person like

Augustine actually meant when he credited certain of his views as coming from a "Platonic school." In some sense, my use of Plato is a kind of shorthand meant to include not only his perspective, but the attending interpretations that followed.

10. Brown, *Christianity & Western Thought*, 31. Here Brown gives a summary of Plato's theory of Forms.
11. Certainly Aristotle did not agree with Plato's notion of "forms," and in the Middle Ages, Aristotelian epistemology stands alone among Scholastics. But in the framing of God by both Philo and the early church fathers, Plato is primary; other Greek philosophies are utilized in a rather syncretic manner.
12. Hans Bietenhard "ὄνομα," *TDNT*, 5:242-81, 249.
13. On p. 34 of his *Christianity & Western Thought*, Brown writes, "In *Timaeus* Plato speaks of God as the Demiurge (artisan or craftsman) who makes the world according to the model of the Forms. But it is unclear whether in Plato's thought God was ultimately the creator of the Forms or whether the Forms already existed, or indeed whether all of this was not just a highly figurative way of speaking." Brown cites *Timaeus* 27-30 in *The Collected Dialogues of Plato including the Letters*, eds. Edith Hamilton and Huntington Cairns, (Princeton: Princeton University Press, 1985), 1161-63. Brown offers that further insight might be found in William Lane Craig's *The Cosmological Argument from Plato to Leibniz*, (New York: Barnes and Noble; London: Macmillan, 1980).
14. Roy B. Zuck, *Basic Bible Interpretation*, (Wheaton, IL: Victor Books, 1991), 50. Cf. Colin Brown, *Christianity and Western Thought*, 65. While Plato did not himself use allegory, his successors certainly used it freely. On this, see J. Tate's "Plato and Allegorical Interpretation," *The Classical Quarterly* 23 (April, 1934).
15. John J. Collins, *Seers, Sibyls and Sages in Hellenistic-Roman Judaism*, (New York: Brill, 1997), 218. Collins notes that both Philo and Seneca talk about the conversion of peoples to (Philo) "honoring our laws." Seneca said, "The customs of this accursed race have gained such an influence as they are now received throughout all the world. The vanquished have given their laws to the victors." Both mentioned keeping the Sabbath. In 139 BC the Jews were expelled from Rome for attempting to transmit their sacred rites to the Romans. A later expulsion from Rome in 19 AD was probably for similar reasons: "They were converting many of the natives to their customs." Such active proselytizing is not recorded elsewhere, but it is certain that there were many who joined throughout the Mediterranean. Philo asserts that some men in Alexandria looked upon circumcision allegorically, and who, we may infer, dispensed with it. Practical monotheism and joining a synagogue were probably the essential marks of conversion.
16. Salo Baron offers that there were almost seven million Jewish people in the Roman Empire in the middle of the first century AD. See his "Population" in *Encyclopedia Judaica*, vol. 13, (Jerusalem: Macmillan, 1973), 866-904, 871. By contrast, Magen Broshi suggests that such a figure may be inflated and estimates that the figure was perhaps as small as two million. Baron's source is that of a twelfth-century Syrian chronicler, Bar Hebreus, who, based upon a census under Claudius in AD 48, reported 6,994,000 Jews. For an assessment of this, see Magen Broshi, "The Role of the Temple in the Herodian Economy," *Journal of Jewish Studies* 38 (Spring 1987): 31-37, 35.
17. Michael D. Coogan, "Septuagint," *The Oxford Companion to the Bible*, eds. Bruce M. Metzger and Michael D. Coogan, (New York: Oxford University Press, 1993), 686-87. Coogan is rightfully suspicious of the legend that seventy-two elders did the translation in seventy-two days. He seems less suspicious that such a translation was commissioned by Ptolemy II (285-246 BC). See also Burton A. Mack and Roland E. Murphy, "Wisdom Literature," in *Faith and Piety in Early Judaism*, eds. George W. E. Nickelsburg, and Michael Stone, (Philadelphia: Fortress Press, 1983), 378-79. Mack and Murphy explore Jewish tradition as it was found in the *Letter of Aristeas*.
18. Nickelsburg and Stone, *Faith and Piety*. In *Faith and Piety*, the authors note that there were various approaches with regard to Gentiles. Certain books and documents were in fact an effort to reach out to them. While *3 Maccabees* accentuated the differences between

Jews and Gentiles, books like the *Letter of Aristeas*; *Sibylline Oracles*, book 3; and *Wisdom of Solomon* actually appealed to Gentiles in an effort to attract them to Judaism. These books were all of Alexandrian provenance.

19. Zuck, *Basic Bible Interpretation*, 30.
20. The Hebrew in Leviticus 24:16 is translated, "One who blasphemes (נֹקֵב) the name of the LORD shall be put to death; the whole congregation shall stone the blasphemer. Aliens as well as citizens, when they blaspheme the Name, shall be put to death." נקב is a masculine *qal* participle with the meaning "to curse, blaspheme," and this meaning is reflected by modern translations. This is clear in the *BHS*, which reads: וְנֹקֵב שֵׁם־יְהוָה מוֹת יוּמָת רָגוֹם יִרְגְּמוּ־בוֹ כָּל־הָעֵדָה כַּגֵּר כָּאֶזְרָח בְּנָקְבוֹ־שֵׁם יוּמָת. However, the *LXX* reads differently, and the Hebrew word (נקב) translated "to blaspheme" is replaced with the Greek word meaning "to name," (ὀνομάζω), so that the effect is to forbid one from even speaking the name of *Yahweh*. An English version of the Septuagint in Leviticus 24:16 reads, "And he that names the name of the Lord, let him die the death: let all the congregation of Israel stone him with stones; whether he be a stranger or a native, let him die for naming the name of the Lord." See *The Septuagint with Apocrypha: Greek and English. Various Readings and Critical Notes*, Lancelot C. L. Brenton, (Grand Rapids, MI: Zondervan, 1970). See also Bietenhard, "ὄνομα," *TDNT*, 5:263.
21. Psalm 91:4, in the NIV offers, "He will cover you with his feathers, and under his wings you will find refuge; his faithfulness will be your shield and rampart." Isaiah 19:1 pronounces, "Look! *Yahweh*, riding a swift cloud, is coming to Egypt." Isaiah 59:1 records, "No, the arm of *Yahweh* is not too short to save, nor his ear too dull to hear."
22. On p. 1010 of his "Names of God in the Old Testament," *ABD*, 4:1001-11, Martin Rose notes that the prohibition against misusing the name of *Yahweh* in the Decalogue was originally oriented against "magical" practices. Eventually, this prohibition of speaking the name *Yahweh* in the Hellenistic age resulted in "denying *any* use of the divine name." Bietenhard explains, "The command not to utter the name is explained by the Rabbis, not as a rule of tradition, but as a biblical command. The נקב of Leviticus 24:11 and 16 was taken to mean 'to utter.'" "ὄνομα," *TDNT*, 5:269. That is, the biblical text was used as the basis for not pronouncing the name of Yahweh. So too, Exodus 3:15, which in the modern NRSV reads: "This was my name for ever, and thus will I be called upon for generation to generation." Here, a defectively written לְעֹלָם was read as לְעַלֵּם '(this is my name) to conceal it.
23. R. Brown, *John*, "Appendix IV," 536.
24. Ibid.
25. Ibid. Brown cites Hosea 13:4 and Joel 2:27 where this occurs. Brown also notes that the Hebrew of Isaiah 43:25 reads, "I, am 'He who blots out transgressions.' Brown goes on to say, "The Septuagint translates the first part of this statement by using *ego eime* twice. This can mean 'I am He, I am He who blots out transgressions'; but it can also be interpreted, 'I am "I am" who blots out transgressions,' a translation that makes *ego eime* a name." Brown points out that the same phenomenon also occurs in Isaiah 51:12 and 62:6.
26. Exactly when the name Yahweh ceased to be spoken is a matter of some debate; it certainly occurred squarely in a Jewish-Hellenistic matrix in the centuries just prior to Jesus Christ. Indications of the disuse of Yahweh in the vernacular are suggested through the less frequent use of the name Yahweh in postexilic literature. Although it is difficult to know when the substitution of *Adonai* for Yahweh was fairly well established, it seems likely that it occurred by the time of the *LXX*. The *LXX* treats the Tetragrammaton in a curious way. For instance, A and Σ keep the Tetragrammaton in Hebrew characters in their Greek rendering. On this, see Gottfried Quell and Werner Foerster, "κύριος," *TDNT*, 3:1039-95, 1082.
27. When one read the Torah, for instance, or in general practice, a substitution of *Adonai* was made. See William F. Albright, *From the Stone Age to Christianity*, (Baltimore: Johns Hopkins Press, 1940), 351, where he proposes that such a change was made by 400 BC, but offers no proof for the assertion. Others would put the date later. See also p. 1082 of

Quell and Foerster's "κύριος." Quell notes some have argued for a date as late as the first century BC, but the evidence appears weak. Although there is some usage of the Tetragrammaton in the Pseudepigrapha at this time, Quell has rightly noted such a usage is quite limited. Thus, I suspect that a date during the Hellenistic Period beginning in the third century BC is certainly arguable. For a more thorough analysis as to why the name of Yahweh was discontinued from common use, see chapter 2 of David S. Norris, "No Other Name: A Socio-Historical Approach to the Argument of Luke Acts," (PhD diss., Temple University, 2000).

28. Rose calls this a "cosmopolitan outlook," "Names of God in the Old Testament," 1010. In any case, it functioned to allow Jewish people to fit in with their culture. Two other factors played into this. First was an honest desire to keep the name of Yahweh holy. The second was a kind of political move by the high priesthood to retain the use of the name of Yahweh for their own symbolic capital. On this later notion, see my "No Other Name," chapter 5.
29. On p. 393 of "Wisdom Literature," in surveying the Philonic allegorical method, Mack and Murphy point out that Philo did not merely take over the method of Homer, applying it to the biblical text; rather, there was a "diaretic technique," a more formal appropriation of the Platonic world of ideas was applied "to the words of Scriptures taken as symbols." On this, see especially Irmgard Christiansen, *Die Technik der allegorischen Auslegungswissenschaft bei Philon von Alexandrien*, Beiträge zur Geschichte der biblischen Hermeneutik 7, (Tübingen: Mohr-Siebeck, 1969).
30. Mack and Murphy, "Wisdom Literature," 393.
31. Peter Frick, *Divine Providence in Philo of Alexandria*, (Tübingen: J. C. B. Mohr, 1999), 26ff.
32. See Philo's *On the Unchangeableness of God*, in *The Works of Philo, Complete and Unabridged*, trans. Charles D. Yonge, (Peabody, MA: Hendrickson, 1993), 22.
33. Raoul Mortley, *From Word to Silence*, vol. 2, Theophaneia: Beiträge zur Religions-und Kirchengeshcichte des Alterums 31, (Bonn, 1986), 15.
34. Robert Grant, *God and the One God*, (Philadelphia: Westminster, 1986), 109.
35. David Winston, *Logos and Mystical Theology in Philo of Alexandria*, (Cincinnati: Hebrew Union College Press, 1985), 15. Winston offers further, "Moreover, since the Jewish Hellenistic wisdom literature employed the term, 'Wisdom' synonymously with the 'word of God,' it was only natural for Philo to use that term too as equivalent to the *Logos*."
36. In the *Wisdom of Solomon*, the author (who purported to be Solomon) declared Wisdom to be the prominent actor on behalf of God. On this, see Mack and Murphy, "Wisdom Literature," 387. Here Murphy and Mack favor a date of 38-41 and provenance of Alexandria, Egypt. The writing of the *Wisdom of Solomon* was contemporary with the writing of Philo in both time and locale.
37. For example, in *Wisdom of Solomon* 10:17, it is Wisdom that guides Moses. In other places in the text God's redeeming activity is spoken of variously as the Word, angel, and Holy Spirit. Cf. Marinus de Jonge, *Christology in Context: The Earliest Christian Response to Jesus*, (Philadelphia: Westminster, 1988), 194.
38. Henry Chadwick, *The Cambridge History of Later Greek and Early Medieval Philosophy*, ed. A. H. Armstrong, (London: Cambridge University Press, 1967), 137.
39. See Philo's *On Agriculture* 51, cited in Marinus de Jonge, *Christology in Context*, 194. In chapters 13-15, we discuss Philonic language and concepts in the development of the Trinity, but suffice it to say that the seeds for this development by later church fathers were sown in the allegorizing of Philo.
40. ἐγώ εἰμι ὁ ὤν.
41. Philo offers, "It was, therefore, quite consistent with reason that no proper name could with propriety be assigned to him who is in truth the living God." Philo, *On the Change of Names* 11, in *The Works of Philo: Complete and Unabridged*, trans. Yonge, (1854, repr., Peabody, MA: Hendrickson, 1993), 342. Unless otherwise indicated, this is the edition of Philo we reference. Frick, *Divine Providence in Philo of Alexandria*, 31. Frick notes that

three notions of Philo's idea of the transcendence of God are expressed here: (1) God as a being like no other; (2) the nature or essence of God (expressed by the terms εἶναι and οὐσία) as different than ὕαρξις; (3) the idea of the unknowability and unnamabilty or ineffability of God. As Frick notes on p. 37, note 59, Philo says on one occasion that "He who IS" may be regarded as God's proper name (κυρίῳ ὀνόματι καλεῖται), but in clarifying this, Philo points out that this is not God's real name. See Philo's *On the Migration of Abraham* 120-21.

42. Philo acknowledges God as "I AM" but the meaning is a far cry from the Jewish interpreters. See Philo's *On the Change of Names* 11; *On the Life of Moses* 1-2; and *That the Worse is Wont to Attack the Better* 160. On this, see as well pp. 208-16 of David Runia's "God of the Philosophers, God of the Patriarchs: Exegetical Backgrounds in Philo of Alexandria," in his *Philo and the Church Fathers*, Vol. 32, (Leiden; New York: E. J. Brill, 1995).

43. Philo, *Allegorical Interpretation* 2, 2:86.

44. Harry Wolfson, *Philo: Foundations of Religious Philosophy in Judaism, Christianity, and Islam*. Vol. 2., (1947; repr., Cambridge: Harvard University Press, 1982), 109-10.

Chapter 4: The God Who Is in Covenant

1. Scholars have written extensively on the subject for the last century. For an overview, see especially, Ernest W. Nicholson, *God and His People: Covenant and Theology in the Old Testament*, (Oxford: Clarendon Press, 1986). A number of texts deal with covenant in marriage: Malachi 2:14; Proverbs 2:17; Deuteronomy 7:2. There exists a *berith* of friendship and love (I Samuel 18:3), and *berith achim* (Amos 1:9), and a *berith shalom* (Numbers 25:12; Isaiah 54:10; Ezekiel 34:25; 37:26). The Hebrew Bible speaks of a pact between a king and his people by which the king was elevated to the throne (II Samuel 5:3, II Kings 11:17; cf. II Chronicles 23:3, 16; cf. Hosea 6:7-11; 10:3-4.)

2. Köhler, *Old Testament Theology*, 62. Köhler offers a lengthy exposition on covenant, beginning with a sample of various nontheological uses.

3. Ibid.

4. As later Old Testament writers describe him, Adam was in covenant with *Yahweh*, even though the specific word is not immediately present in the Genesis narrative. For example, Hosea compared the unfaithfulness of Israel with that of Adam in the language of covenant. See Hosea 6:7, where the NIV rightly translates: "Like Adam (כְּאָדָם), they have broken the covenant."

5. Genesis 3:8. See our previous discussion of theophany in chapter 2. This remains a thorny issue, particularly when the Scripture says no man has seen God. See I John 4:12; I Timothy 1:17; etc. Presumably Yahweh "cloaked" Himself in some way—allowing humans to experience God's Being.

6. James D. G. Dunn, *The Theology of Paul the Apostle*, (Grand Rapids, MI: Eerdmans, 1998), 82-83.

7. In some New Testament texts, Eve is culpable for the sin of giving in to the serpent. See, for instance, I Timothy 2:14; II Corinthians 11:3. In others texts, however, Adam is specifically mentioned as the responsible party. See Romans 5:14-19, where Adam is implicated for the whole human race, no small blame to be placed upon him. See also I Corinthians 15:22. Here we follow Romans and other texts that frame the fall of humanity in the context of Adam's sin, particularly as the redemption story is framed in the New Testament.

8. Harry R. Boer, *An Ember Still Glowing: Humankind as the Image of God*, (Grand Rapids, MI: Eerdmans, 1990), 9. Boer offers, "In creating Man, God placed him in four basic and enduring relationships: to God, to fellowman, to the world around him, and to himself."

9. It is ironic that although Yahweh warned Adam and Eve that they would die in the day they ate of the fruit, He spared them for a time. The first recorded death did not come from Yahweh, but from the son of Adam and Eve who broke covenant relationship with Yahweh.

10. The genealogy of Cain is reported in Genesis 4, and it is apparent that successive generations have followed his path outside the covenant relationship with Yahweh. Consider the

boast of Lamech in Genesis 4:23-24, claiming superiority in evil to his seventh great grandfather, Cain: "Aye—a man I kill for wounding me, a lad for only bruising me! Aye— if sevenfold vengeance be for Kayin [Cain], then for Lemekh [Lamech], seventy-sevenfold!" (*Schocken Bible*).

11. Niles notes on p. 67ff. of his "Name of God" that the expression is לִקְרֹא בְּשֵׁם יְהוָה and is not found in this construction in any other extant Semitic literature. Here the syntax is controlled by the word order and the Hebrew "בְּ" that suggests the idiom. Niles argues in the larger part of his dissertation that the meaning of יְהוָה cannot be determined through an etiological study or a "magical" use of names represented in the worship of other religions. He contends that the name Yahweh must be studied in the context of Israelite worship. Hence, the understanding of this phrase is a vital part of his research and forms a plank in the major argument of the dissertation. This phrase or its equivalent is not duplicated in any of the existing writings of the languages related to Hebrew, nor is this phrase used in the context with worship of any other god.

12. This same marginal reference is reflected by the New American Standard Version. Again, in the KJV, capital letters in "LORD" signify Yahweh or יְהוָה. In the English rendering of "Then people began to be called" some have argued that the Hebrew הוּחַל translated "began" [as a third-person masculine singular] should rather be translated negatively as "profane." The negative rendering is supported by a number of later rabbinical traditions but is not preferable. On this discussion, see Gordon J. Wenham, *Genesis 1-15*, Word Biblical Commentary 1, (Waco, TX: Word Books, 1987), 115-16.

13. Niles, "Name of God," 67. One example offered by Niles is Psalm 116:4.

14. For example, see Psalm 116:12ff.

15. Parke-Taylor, drawing from both von Rad and P. Van Ishmoot, describes the way in which priestly invocation occurred. While the Hebrew phrase could refer to "pronouncing the name of the LORD with a loud voice in an act of public worship," it was also an invocation offered by a priest or king on behalf of Yahweh upon the people. On this, see pp. 13-14 of Parke-Taylor's יְהוָה *Yahweh: The Divine Name*, particularly note 68.

16. This claim is the heart of Niles's argument. See the abstract of "Name of God," 1-3.

17. Niles's methodology relies heavily on form criticism; thus any use of what he considers to be liturgical pronouncement in Genesis would be mere retrojection. He does not focus on the Genesis accounts, but rather, he is more concerned with Exodus narrative and Moses. Though I believe he is incorrect in this aspect, and I don't think he goes far enough when exploring covenant initiation, his general principle stands.

18. See Numbers 6 and the explanation we offer with regard to the blessing in chapter 4.

19. This is less likely, but it could well have happened. See for instance, Exodus 20, and Exodus 34:6, where Yahweh orally invokes His name over Israel and Moses, respectively.

20. Translations of Genesis 6:8 that read, "Noah found grace in the eyes of the Lord," (e.g., KJV, NKJV) must not be understood merely as God gifting grace to a single individual. The Hebrew word (חֵן) translated here as "grace" does not indicate a kind of theological "unmerited favor." Rather, this grace was in part a result of Noah's response to Yahweh. Grace, in this context, is descriptive of both Yahweh's invitation to and His faithfulness in covenant. Cf. Moses' appeal to this characteristic of Yahweh in Exodus 33:12; 14; 16; and 17; see especially Exodus 34:6 where חַנּוּן is used adjectivally of Yahweh as He passes over Moses, declaring/invoking His name. Like חֶסֶד, it describes Yahweh's invitation to covenant, but more often, His faithfulness to those who are already in covenant. On this, see especially Exodus 20:6. See also Nelson Glueck, *Hesed in the Bible*, (Cincinnati: Hebrew Union College, 1967).

21. Genesis 8:21 says of the sacrifice offered by Noah upon exiting the ark that "Yahweh smelt the pleasing smell." As Wenham notes, "For God to 'smell' a sacrifice implies his acceptance of it and the offerer." *Genesis 1-15*, 189.

22. Victor P. Hamilton, *The Book of Genesis Chapters 1-17*, The New International Commentary on the Old Testament, (Grand Rapids, MI: Eerdmans, 1990), 312-13. Hamilton understands Genesis 9:1 to be congruous with Genesis 1:22 and Genesis 9:2

demonstrating new material. There is further mention in this connection with humanity being made "in the image of God," repeating Genesis 1 and Genesis 5. As Hamilton notes on p. 313, "This chapter is establishing elements of both continuity and discontinuity with Gen. 1." On p. 316, Hamilton writes, "The word *establish* (here [in Gen. 9:7] and in a different form in vv. 11, 17) translates the *hiphil* of *qum* and means literally 'to make stand, to erect.' " On the possibility that this verb does not refer to a new covenant, he offers, "In these instances the verb does not mean 'to institute' but 'to fulfill, carry out, keep' (Num 23:19; Deut. 8:18; 9:5; 1 Sam 1:23; 3:12; 1 K. 2:4; Jer. 29:10; 33:14; 34:18)." While Hamilton suggests that this could be fulfilling a promise made to Noah, what is significant is the continuity of God's promises in covenant relationship.

23. Eichrodt, *Theology*, 1:58. While we would see the narrative as a whole, Eichrodt credits "P," the priestly tradition with the Noah narrative, and believes P to stand in contrast with other traditions in the Pentateuch.

24. Exodus 19:5. The Hebrew here is סְגֻלָּה. A quick check of several lexicons yields the same result. This is primarily spoken of property; *BDB* is typical, where the word is defined as "possession, property," 688. The lexicon goes on to say, "Valued property, peculiar treasure, which Yahweh has chosen to take unto himself; always used of the people of Israel."

25. George Mendenhall, "Covenant" *ABD*, 1:1179–1202. Mendenhall demonstrates that a number of elements in the Exodus account (as well as in other portions of the Pentateuch), used a "legal genre," well known in ancient times, and known to us through the Hittite suzerainty treaties.

26. Exodus 20:3. That the narrative describes Yahweh speaking in the first person is not metaphorical is demonstrated by the text itself and interpreters of the text. See, for instance, the analysis of Exodus 20 in volume 1 of Robert Jamieson, A. R. Fausset, and David Brown, *A Commentary on the Old and New Testaments*, 3 vols., (1877; repr., Grand Rapids, MI: Eerdman, 1995), 355. The commentators offer their belief that rather than supposing these commandments were given secretly or via Moses, the words were given in a divine phenomenon "spoken in sounds resembling the tones of a human voice."

27. These, too, bore a similarity to the suzerainty treaties. This is an especially fitting argument for an early date of the Exodus. On p. 1184 of his "Covenant," Mendenhall points out that in Exodus: (1) Yahweh identified Himself formally (even though contextually this is not necessary); (2) Yahweh restated what He did on behalf of Israel (again, contextually unnecessary); and (3) Yahweh gave "Ten Words," stipulations of the covenant. The Ten Words are not commands (i.e., imperative language). They are simple future indicative verbs that indicate a future action that is the expected consequence of the preceding prologue.

28. Mendenhall notes that numerous gods with whom the people were associated were called upon to witness the suzerain treaties; thus, they would be called upon to punish the people if they broke covenant. "Covenant," 1184.

29. So incredible was this experience that it was celebrated in worship by generations that followed. See Psalm 68:8; 97:5; 114:7.

30. See for instance, Leviticus 22:3, where certain sin would result in being cut off from the face of Yahweh. Compare II Kings 13:23, where the covenant with the patriarchs for a time prevented Israel from being cut off prematurely, with II Kings 24:20, where Zedekiah, the last king of the Southern Kingdom, is cast from the presence of Yahweh.

31. Moses asked to see Yahweh's glory—to really see His face. He had seen the burning bush, he had experienced the presence of God on Sinai, but now He wanted to experience the very essence of God face-to-face. Moses asked Yahweh in Exodus 33:18, "Show me your glory."

32. Concerning the Old Testament understanding of glory, Gerhard von Rad says, it is "often linked with שֵׁם [*shem*—the concept of the name] when it is desired to magnify the honour or impressiveness of the divine name (Ps. 66:2; 79:9)." See von Rad, " 'כָּבוֹד' in the Old Testament," "δόξα," *TDNT*, 2:241; to speak of Yahweh's glory is another way to speak of Yahweh Himself.

33. Plastaras, The God of Exodus, 99.
34. P. 1075 of *The Interpreter's Bible Commentary* notes, "The revelation, as anticipated (33:19), declares God's character. The emphasis is upon his power to forgive." See George Arthur Buttrick, et. al., eds., *The Interpreter's Bible Commentary,* vol. 1, (New York: Abingdon Press, 1952).
35. Niles, "Name of God," 161.
36. While we cannot be certain as to when various tradition developed, on p. 247 of Alfred Edersheim, *The Temple: Its Ministry and Services,* (Peabody, MA: 1994), Edersheim utilizes rabbinic sources to demonstrate the oral invocation of Yahweh ten times during the ritual offering. In this context, . . . as the high priest speaks to Yahweh, he is both a penitent on behalf of the people and a representative of Yahweh's promised cleansing of the people. On the passing down of the pronunciation of the name of Yahweh from father to son in the priesthood, see Bietenhard, "ὄνομα," p. 266.
37. To defile Yahweh's sanctuary was to defile His holy Name. See Leviticus 20:3 where Yahweh says, "And I shall set my face against that man and outlaw him from his people; for by giving a child of his to Molech he has defiled my sanctuary and profaned my holy name." See also Leviticus 21:12. Priests were not to profane the name of Yahweh for they were set apart to Him (see Leviticus 22:2). Again and again this is reiterated in Leviticus. Leviticus 22:32 reads, "You will not profane my holy name—so that I may be honoured as holy among the Israelites, I, Yahweh, who make you holy. . . ."
38. While some versions render וְשָׂמוּ אֶת־שְׁמִי "and they shall put my name," the NJB captures the sense of oral invocation by translating it, "they must call down my name." On this, see p. 964 of *BDB*; with reference to this verse the use of שׂם is to "appoint, give . . ." The lexicon finds the usage in the verse to be parallel to Isaiah 61:3 where Yahweh announces that he will set a metaphorical headdress of joy on the worshiper. Whether as A. R. Fausset suggests, "this double verb [to appoint (לָשׂוּם), to give (לָתֵת)] with the same accusative, is meant to impart glowing vehemence to the style," or whether the *sum* is meant to be the controlling verb in the text, the usage of *sum* (appoint) here is parallel with *natan* (give), and serves to make it official. On this see Jamieson, Fausset, and Brown, *Commentary*, 2:752.
39. Carl E. Braaten agrees with this assessment that to name the name of God is to invoke Him in all of His power in the Old Testament. He writes, "The Old Testament generally views the name as somehow mystically united with the innermost essence of personal being, divine or human." Carl E. Braaten, "Introduction: Naming the Name," in *Our Naming of God: Problems and Prospects of God-Talk Today*, ed. Carl Braaten, (Minneapolis: Augsburg Press, 1989), 1.
40. Niles, "Name of God," 159–66.
41. Sigmund Mowinckel, *Religion and Kultus*, (Göttingen: Vandenhoek and Ruprecht, 1953), 64–66.
42. Walter Brueggemann, *Israel's Praise: Doxology against Idolatry and Ideology*, (Philadelphia: Fortress Press, 1988), 12.
43. Ibid., 35.
44. David did not disparage the Tabernacle or Israel's celebration of the covenant. For David, the Torah was sweeter than honey (Psalm 19:10); and if the Torah was in one's heart, one's steps would not slide (Psalm 37:23, 24). It was just this love for the covenant that motivated joy in worship.
45. See II Samuel 6:17; "the tent which David had erected for it." Whereas the Temple restricted the common person, women, and Gentiles, this Tabernacle of David made no restrictions. All were free to worship.
46. See pp. 42-3 on the prophecy of Amos. On the interpretation of the Tabernacle of David in Acts, see p. 144.
47. Here the poetic use of סֻכָּה is thought by some to indicate the kingdom of David. Indeed, NLT goes so far as to translate *succah* of David as "the fallen kingdom of David." The context may allow such a metaphoric interpretation of the Hebrew, but the apostles interpreted this differently and thus more broadly.

48. Amos 9:12. See the literal marginal reading in the NJB, a translation deemed likely by a number of scholars. For example, Niles notes that the Hebrew וְכָל־הַגּוֹיִם אֲשֶׁר־נִקְרָא שְׁמִי עֲלֵיהֶם is exactly the same construction as Jeremiah 7:10 where the name of Yahweh is verbally pronounced over the Temple. "Name of God," 34-35.
49. Ibid.
50. The Book of Amos is clearly the primary referent. See Nils A. Dahl, "A People for his Name," *New Testament Studies* 4 (1958): 319-27. On p. 323, Dahl notes that the phrase, "a people for his name" seems to be a specific "Targumic idiom." Noting that this is particularly seen in "stereotypical phraseology" connected to the eschatological future, Dahl specifically notes its usage in Jeremiah, Ezekiel, and Daniel.

Chapter 5: Discovering the Man, Christ Jesus

1. John 13:19. On p. 533 of *John*, "Appendix IV," Brown acknowledges this text as an "absolute use" of "I AM" by Jesus, intended to clearly convey His identity. For a full list of "I AM" texts, see p. 277 note 38.
2. Bauckham, *God Crucified*, 78; cf. p. 247, note 38.
3. On this, see p. 246, note 27.
4. As such, this chapter expands upon themes first explained in chapter 1.
5. On this, see Robert R. Hahn, "Judaism and Jewish Christianity in Antioch: Charisma and Conflict in the First Century," *Journal of Religious History* 14 (1987): 341-60. Hahn establishes the way in which the church moved from a "charismatic leadership" to a more staid authority of teachers. It was these teachers who claimed authority from consistently linking their authority to the teaching of the apostles.
6. See, for instance, the consensus reached in Acts 15 and a single letter that represented the teaching of the community.
7. Adolf von Harnack, *The History of Dogma*, 7 vols., trans. Neil Buchanan, (1895; repr., New York: Russell and Russell, 1958), 1:150-52. The familial language of the New Testament and of the early church fathers demonstrated this propensity in their "brotherly disposition" (151).
8. Raymond E. Brown, *The Churches that the Apostles Left Behind*, (New York: Paulist Press, 1984), 147-48, note 201.
9. Raymond E. Brown and John P. Meier, *Antioch and Rome: New Testament Cradles of Catholic Christianity*, (New York: Paulist Press, 1983), 1-8. Brown finds four different views of how the Mosaic Law should be kept.
10. See D. A. Carson, Douglas J. Moo, and Leon Morris, *An Introduction to the New Testament*, Grand Rapids, MI: Zondervan, 1992), 47, particularly notes 7 and 8.
11. For Rudolph Bultmann, it was in Hellenistic Christianity which began at Antioch where a syncretic christological development took place. It was here that Χριστός became a proper name and the idea of κύριος as a cult deity merged with the identity of Jesus. Bultmann, in his *Primitive Christianity in its Contemporary Setting*, trans. R. H. Fuller, (London: Thames and Hudson, 1956), 176-77, proposed that Paul was influenced by Gnostic redemption myths, that Paul appropriated in his christology a "cult deity who works supernaturally in the worship of the Church as a cultic body." Bultmann articulates the typical approach of the history of religions school, which gained prominence through William Bousset's *Kyrios Christos: A History of the Belief in Christ From the Beginnings of Christianity to Iraneaus*, trans. John E. Steely, (1913; Nashville: Abingdon Press, 1970). This is a view today in part offered by Helmut Koester, who suggests in his *History and Literature of Early Christianity*, (Philadelphia: Fortress Press, 1982), that Paul gets his christology from a pre-Pauline Hellenistic *kerygma*. But despite Koester, Bultmann has largely been discredited. When one considers that Paul already had a fully developed christology in his first epistle to the Thessalonians in c. AD 50, the difficulties of such alleged syncretism in his christology become more pronounced. Paul neither ceased his Jewishness nor his Jewish perspective; certainly his perspective on the *Shema* didn't budge one *yodh* or *tittle* with his conversion.

12. W. Grudem, "The Gift of Prophecy in 1 Corinthians," (PhD diss., University of Cambridge, 1978), 230; cited in Ben Witherington, *The Christology of Jesus,* (Minneapolis: Fortress Press, 1991), 4, note 13. Witherington argues for the trustworthiness of Gospels as legitimate sources for the words and deeds of Jesus Christ.
13. Witherington, *Christology*, 2.
14. Richard Longenecker, *The Christology of Early Jewish Christianity*, (London: SCM Press, 1970), 9.
15. Cullmann, *Christology*, 3.
16. This radical skepticism did not bring any sort of consensus to christology, for the twentieth century closed with more confusion than ever. For a survey of this historical enterprise, see "Part I" of Hans Schwarz, *Christology*, (Grand Rapids, MI: Eerdmans, 1998). See also Marcus Borg, "Portraits of Jesus in Contemporary North American Scholarship," in *Harvard Theological Review* 84 no. 1 (1991): 1-22. Borg surveys five prominent "portraits" or "construals" of Jesus that are still current. A number of these representations involve using a kind of heuristic model, and place Jesus into a particular category as the interpreter sees fit.
17. See, for example, Richard A. Horsley, "Popular Messianic Movements," *Catholic Biblical Quarterly* 46 no. 3 (1984): 471–95. For Horsley, Christianity did not originate as a reform movement within Judaism; rather, economic conditions had gotten so bad for the lower class that what became Christianity started as a kind of "peasant revolt." It was conflict, not reform, that served as the underlying basis for Christianity. On p. 477, Horsley suggests an ongoing tendency for "independent-minded peasantry" to revolt because they were "committed to egalitarian social ideals." On p. 494-5, Horsley concludes that "messianic movements were reactions to socio-economic conditions" who took "collective action in a politically conscious way."
18. John S. Kloppenborg, *The Formation of Q: Trajectories in Ancient Wisdom Collections*, (Philadelphia: Fortress Press, 1987). Though hypothetical, Q is given both chapters and verses. Further, it is even privileged above the canonical Gospels as a kind of primary source for the historical Jesus.
19. See, for instance, John D. Crossan's *The Historical Jesus: The Life of a Mediterranean Jewish Peasant*, (San Francisco: Harper, 1991), where he dates the important *Nag Hammadi Agrapha* to the AD 50s. Some of the research does not pretend to be unbiased. In the very theatrical proceedings at the "Jesus Seminar," an attempt to popularize the sort of Gnostic approach to Jesus, scholars participate in a kind of public voting assessing which sayings of Jesus in the Gospels are authentic. One suspects the field is adrift by simply considering their results. When assessing the "authentic" sayings of Jesus in Mark (presumably the oldest canonical gospel), at one point they decided that the *only* certainly genuine statement of Jesus is "Render to Caesar the things that are Caesar's and to God the things that are God's." Even Q is not deemed original—there are different layers of Q! Whereas John was an ascetic prophet preaching the end of the world, Jesus was both wisdom teacher and prophet. Ben Witherington offers a healthy corrective in his *Christology.*
20. In the end, they purport to demonstrate what they have been pushing as their agenda all along, that the "original Q" supports early dating of the *Gospel of Thomas*. This is being challenged by the likes of John P. Meier. He argues in the strongest of terms that the materials are late, and have no relevance whatsoever as a source. See *A Marginal Jew: Rethinking the Historical Jesus*, vol. 1, (New York: Doubleday, 1991), vol. 2, *Mentor, Message, and Miracle*, (New York: Doubleday, 1994).
21. Not only have noncanonical sources unduly been utilized to provide the source as to the identity of Jesus, modern epistemological method has given undue emphasis on the response of the reader who comes to the text. For an overview of methods that came into vogue as interpretive models toward the end of the twentieth century, see *The New Literary Criticism and the New Testament*, eds. Elizabeth Struthers Malbon and Edgar V. McKnight, (Sheffield: Sheffield Academic Press, 1994).

22. Typical of such an approach is James D. G. Dunn or Marinus de Jonge. For the application of a sociological model to such a construct, see also p. 43ff. of Gerd Theissen, *The Religion of the Earliest Churches: Creating a Symbolic World*, (Minneapolis: Fortress Press, 1999). Theissen presents a sociological model with three essential components to Jesus being deified. He suggests first, it was the result of *the surmounting of cognitive dissonance* in a catastrophe; it gets over the discrepancy between the expectation for salvation from YHWH and the disaster that is experienced in history. Second, it is confirmation and *intensification* of a consensus, an already-existing tendency toward monolatry, which is heightened so that it becomes 'monotheism.' Third, it is the *competitive outdoing* of the other gods and the peoples who worship them. In the face of the one and only God they all become ridiculous 'nothings.'
23. Nils A. Dahl, "Jesus the Christ," in *The Historical Origins of Christological Doctrine*, ed. Donald Juel, (Minneapolis: Fortress Press, 1991), 130.
24. Richard Longenecker, *Christology*, 8; see especially note 15, where Longenecker effectively argues against the influence of a hypothetical source over against the only data presented in the biblical record.
25. I was present when Bauckham's christology was termed "big-bang christology" during the audience question and answer period on the floor of the November 23, 2002 SBL conference in Toronto, Ontario; Bauckham was defending his views outlined in *God Crucified*. I offer a fuller treatment of this on p. 163.
26. Berkhof, *Christian Faith*, 293.
27. Jaroslav Pelikan suggests, "At least four sets of Old Testament passages which, when interpreted by the proper method and combined with their counterparts in the New Testament, spoke of Christ as divine." For Pelikan, there are first, "passages of adoption" that on the surface imply there was a point in time at which the man Jesus *became* divine; second, "passages of identity," which identify Jesus with Yahweh; third, there are "passages of distinction," which speak of Jesus as Lord in a way that draws some difference between Jesus and Yahweh; fourth, and related to the others are those "passages of derivation," which for Pelikan suggest of Jesus "that he '*came from*' God and was in some sense *less than God*." See Jaroslov Pelikan, *The Christian Tradition, A History of Doctrine and Development*, Vol. 1, *The Emergence of Catholic Tradition (100-600)*, (Chicago: University of Chicago Press, 1971), 175.
28. The reader will notice an indebtedness to Richard Bauckham, James D. G. Dunn, Larry W. Hurtado. First-century christological constructs have been particularly informed by Jean Daniélou and Richard Longenecker.
29. Compare John 1:14 with Luke 1:35.
30. Compare Romans 6:4 with Romans 8:11.
31. Revelation 2:7, 11, 17, 29; 3:6, 13, 22, all ascribe the prophetic utterance to the Spirit. Revelation 22:16 ascribes this prophetic utterance to Jesus.
32. While there are other examples in the discourse, John 14:26 is significant.
33. Matthew 3:11; Mark 1:8; Luke 3:16; John 1:33; Acts 1:5; Acts 11:16.
34. On the christological import of equating Christ with the Spirit, see Hurtado, *One God, One Lord*, 114.
35. While we introduce very briefly elements of Trinitarian doctrine in this chapter, we deal more extensively with the historical development of the Trinity in chapters 13-15, following the general line of evolutionary development posited by Harry Austryn Wolfson, *The Philosophy of the Church Fathers*, vol. I., *Faith, Trinity, Incarnation*, (Cambridge: Harvard University Press), 1957.
36. Dahl, "Jesus the Christ," 165.
37. Ibid.
38. E.g., NJB, NRSV, NLT, NAB, etc.
39. See George Eldon Ladd, *The New Testament and Criticism*, (Grand Rapids, MI: Eerdmans, 1967), 60-61; Kurt Aland and Barbara Aland, *The Text of the New Testament. An*

Introduction to the Critical Editions and to the Theory and Practice of Modern Textual Criticism, trans. Erroll F. Rhodes, (Grand Rapids, MI: Eerdmans, 1987), 306.
40. Wolfson, *Philosophy,* 147. Wolfson formulates Pauline salutations variously as coming *from* God and Christ into four categories: "(1) ten salutations containing the terms 'grace' and 'peace' (εἰρήνη) and described as coming from 'God our Father and the Lord Jesus Christ'; (2) seven salutations containing again the term 'grace' and described as coming from our Lord Jesus Christ; (3) two salutations containing again the term 'grace' but without any mention of the source from which it is come; (4) one salutation containing the terms 'peace' and 'love' and described as coming from 'God our Father and the Lord Jesus.' "
41. Wolfson, ibid. *Cf.* Numbers 6:24–26; on this, see p. 41 above.
42. Victor Paul Furnish, *II Corinthians. Translated with Introduction, Notes, and Commentary,* Anchor Bible 32A, (New York: Doubleday, 1984), 584. Furnish cites scholars who read "ἡ κοινωνία τοῦ ἁγίου πνεύματος" as both objective and subjective genitive, but suggests that there is consensus in both groups as to its meaning as "participation in the Holy Spirit."
43. Thus, "the foreknowledge of God the Father" gives glory to God in His redemptive "speaking" (see chapter 6 on this); while "in sanctification of the Spirit" is analogous to "fellowship" or "participation" (as we presented above in our discussion of II Corinthians 13:14); while "for obedience and sprinkling of the blood of Jesus Christ" is giving glory to the work of Jesus Christ. On the apostles' propensity for praising Jesus in this manner, see pp. 138-139.
44. Spirit, Lord (*Kurios*), and God are terms that the New Testament epistles utilize in playful interchange. Consider that Paul's Corinthian correspondence also celebrates, "Now the Lord (*Kurios*) is the Spirit; and where the Spirit of the Lord is, there is liberty" (II Corinthians 3:17).
45. Granville Sharp offers, "If personal nouns, of the same case, are connected by the copulative, and the first has not the article, they relate to different persons." *Remarks of the uses of the definitive article in the Greek text of the New Testament containing many new proofs of the divinity of Christ, from passages which are wrongly translated in the common English version,* (Philadelphia, PA: B.B. Hopkins, 1807), 5. The exception is that is not the case to the first rule, that being when nouns are proper or plural. On this, see Christopher Wordsworth, *Six Letters to Granville Sharp, esq. respecting his Remarks on the uses of the definite article in the Greek Text of the New Testament,* (London: J. Hodson, 1802), v. Given that these blessings in the epistles do not provide an article before "God" or "Jesus," one cannot insist that these have reference to different "persons."
46. Ferdinand Hahn, "Confessions of the One God in the New Testament," *Horizons in Biblical Theology* 2 (1980): 69-84, 69.
47. Though we utilize it unevenly, unless otherwise stated, the biblical text of choice for New Testament passages will largely follow the NKJV. This is an effort to defer to Oneness Pentecostal tradition of respect for the KJV and the "majority text." That said, where a clearer translation is helpful, or if the Greek (not merely the so-called "Textus Receptus") more readily supports another translation, we will utilize other versions. Further, because our broad framework of an Apostolic hermeneutic encompasses the confession of the canonical New Testament we will not quibble as to whether, say, the Pastoral Epistles were deutero-Pauline or whether the Evangelists whose names are ascribed to the Gospels were their authors.

Chapter 6: The Man Who Preexisted

1. While the Jewish people may ascribe the suffering servant to Israel, New Testament exegesis clearly interpreted the text as messianic.
2. J. L. Austin, *How to do Things with Words,* (Cambridge, MA: Harvard University Press, 1962; repr., Oxford: Clarendon Press, 1975), 5.

3. Ibid. Austin notes that when things are officially named, such as the naming of a ship or the pronouncing of a couple as married, such an event is contingent upon doing things in the right way so that it will be recognized socially as valid.
4. Galatians 3:24.
5. On the use of this psalm with regard to the baptism of Jesus, see p. 89; with regard to the enthronement, see p. 130.
6. Acts 13:33; after speaking of Jesus' death, Paul proclaims the resurrection of Jesus. In this context he explains, "God has fulfilled this for us their children, in that He has raised up Jesus. As it is also written in the second Psalm: 'You are My Son, Today I have begotten You.'"
7. While Donald Juel suggests that the actual number of citations of this psalm in the New Testament is relatively small, Richard Bauckham finds twenty-one allusions: Matthew 22:44; 26:64; Mark 12:36; 14:62; 16:19; Luke 20:42-43; 22:69; Acts 2:33-35; 5:31; 7:55-56; Romans 8:34; I Corinthians 15:25; Ephesians 1:20; 2:6; Colossians 3:1; Hebrews 1:3; 1:13; 8:1; 10:12-13; 12:2; 1 Peter 3:22; Revelation 3:21. David M. Hay tops this by offering as many as thirty-three New Testament references to this passage. Juel cites identical wording in the Synoptic Gospels in a parallel account: Matthew 22:41-46; Mark 12:35-37a; Luke 20:41-44; in addition, he adds Acts 2:34 and Hebrews 5:6; 7:17; 21. Donald Juel, *Messianic Exegesis: Christological Interpretation of the Old Testament in Early Christianity*, (Philadelphia: Fortress Press, 1992), 135; Bauckham, *God Crucified*, 29, note 1; David M. Hay, *Glory at the Right Hand: Psalm 100 in Early Christianity*, SBLMS 18, (Nashville: Abingdon Press, 1973), 163-66.
8. In Acts 2:33-35, Peter links Psalm 110:1 with the Ascension. See also Hebrews 1:3; 10:12-13.
9. Jack T. Sanders explores the various passages of Scriptures judged to be christological hymns and discusses their place and importance in worship in his *The New Testament Christological Hymns: Their Historical Religious Background*, (Cambridge: Cambridge University Press, 1971). With the exception of Ephesians 2:14-16, all of the hymns he identifies are distinctly christological, celebrating the centrality of the salvific work of the man Jesus Christ. On christological hymnic material, see also Martin Hengel, "Hymns and Christology," in *Between Jesus and Paul: Studies in the Earliest Christian Communities*, trans. John Bowden, (London: Fortress Press, 1983).
10. See NIV, NAS, NJB, ESV, etc.
11. The Textus Receptus supports a reading of θεός, but the weight of evidence is against such a reading. See Bruce M. Metzger, *A Textual Commentary on the Greek New Testament*, (1971; repr. Stuttgart, Germany: United Bible Society, 1975), 641.
12. Most Greek texts take as authoritative the Codex Sinaiticus which has ὅς (hōs).
13. See de Jonge, *Christology in Context*, 25.
14. David K. Bernard would suggest that the Son is in view. *The Oneness View of Jesus Christ*, (Hazelwood, MO: Word Aflame Press, 1994), 56-57. See also Daniel L. Segraves, *Hebrews: Better Things. Vol. One. A Commentary on Hebrews 1-8*, (Hazelwood, MO: Word Aflame Press, 1996), 29-33. Segraves's interpretation is a bit more nuanced. With regard to the Greek prepositional phrase, Segraves interprets *dia* in the genitive case as meaning something like "by means of." In a rather lengthy discussion encompassing the *Logos* and the creative word of God, Segraves suggests that it was God as Creator and the text is apparently only nuanced by the anticipation of the Incarnation.
15. Berkhof, *Christian Faith*, 293.
16. Ibid.
17. On the initiation of Israel into covenant, see pp. 37-38. on Yahweh literally calling his name upon Moses, see p. 40.
18. On the priestly pronouncement of the name of Yahweh upon the people, see p. 41.
19. The Hebrew might rather be translated, "where Yahweh shall choose for his name to dwell." Again in verse 21, the earlier appellation of verse 5 is repeated: "If the place where the LORD your God will choose to put his name (לָשׂוּם שְׁמוֹ) is too far from you . . ."
20. Gerhard von Rad, *Deuteronomy*, 37ff.

21. As we suggested earlier, the oral invoking of the name of Yahweh went out of use in the Late Second Temple period. See p. 256-7 note 27 for Albright's conclusions.
22. Psalm 26:8 (Psalm 26:8 in the *LXX*) reads: "Yahweh, I love the beauty of your house and the place where your glory (Hebrew *kabod*; Greek *doxa*) dwells."
23. Gerhard Kittel, "δόξα," *TDNT*, 2:232-53, 245.
24. Jean Daniélou, *The Development of Christian Doctrine Before the Council of Nicea*, Vol. 1., *The Theology of Jewish Christianity*, trans. and ed. John A. Baker, (London: Darton, Longman & Todd, 1964), 156.
25. James D. G. Dunn, "Let John Be John: A Gospel for its Time," in *The Gospel and Gospels*, ed. Peter Stuhlmacher, (Grand Rapids, MI: Eerdmans, 1992), 293-322, 313-14.
26. Dunn, *Christology*; cf. Dunn, "Let John be John"; Berkhof, *Christian Faith*, 293.
27. Herman N. Ridderbos, *The Gospel According to John: A Theological Commentary*, trans. John Vriend, (Grand Rapids, MI: Eerdmans, 1997), 23. Cf. Keil and Delitzsch, referencing "and God said" from Genesis 1, "These words are deeds of the essential Word, the λόγος, by which 'all things were made.' Speaking is the revelation of thought; the creation, the realization of the thoughts of God, a freely accomplished act of the absolute Spirit, and not an emanation of creatures from divine essence" (Keil and Delitzsch, 1:30).
28. It wasn't as if John's apologetic could readily introduce a hypostasis into the deity. That is impossible, particularly as an apologetic. Larry Hurtado asserts that for devout Jews, their "monotheistic stance was more firm and characteristic in the Hellenistic and Roman era than in any previous period." Larry W. Hurtado, *Lord Jesus Christ: Devotion to Jesus in Earliest Christianity*, (Grand Rapids, MI: Eerdmans, 2003), 35.
29. Psalm 107:20 (NKJV). The *Tanak* captures the force of the word by rendering the verse, "He gave an order and healed them."
30. Otto Procksch is correct to insist that the *Logos* in verse one speaks of Yahweh Himself in His creative acts. On *logos* as a revelatory pronouncement, see p. 99-100 of Procksch's "דָּבָר" in Kittel's entry for "λέγω" and related words in vol. 4 of *TDNT*. See particularly Psalm 33:6ff. Procksch links this text with the generative power of the word of Yahweh in Ezekiel 37:4 and its revelatory power in Job 4:12, revelation is effected by the word of Yahweh.
31. A. T. Robertson is typical, commenting of ὁ λόγος ἦν πρὸς τὸν θεόν, (*pros ton theon*), "Though existing eternally with God the *Logos* was in perfect fellowship with God. *Pros* with the accusative presents a plane of equality and intimacy, face to face with each other."
32. See James N. Anderson, "Pre-Existent Christology and Certain Passages," (Paper presented at the annual Urshan Graduate School Symposium, Hazelwood, MO, 2005), 260-88, 278. Anderson cites Johannes P. Louw, and Eugene Albert Nida, *Greek-English Lexicon of the New Testament: Based on Semantic Domains*, electr. ed. of the 2nd ed., (1989; New York: United Bible Societies, 1996). Summarizing the lexical evidence, he writes, "They list '*prosopon pros prosopon*' and '*stoma pros stoma*' as more typically taken to mean 'face to face.' Although it [pros] may be related to 'prosopon' (face), 'face to face' is usually '*prosopon kata prosopon*' or possibly '*prosopon pros prosopon*,' or '*stoma pros stoma*' not just '*pros*.'"
33. David K. Bernard, *The Oneness of the Godhead*, rev. ed., (Hazelwood, MO: Word Aflame Press, 2000), 61; citing Hebrews 2:17; 5:1.
34. D. A. Carson, *The Gospel According to John*, Pillar New Testament Commentary (Grand Rapids, MI: Eerdmans Publishing, 1991), 117. Carson argues that the grammatical structure demands the translation, "the Word was God;" noting, "A long string of writers has argued that because *theos*, 'God' here has no article, John is not referring to God as a specific being, but to mere qualities of 'God-ness.' This will not do." Carson offers as corroborating Scriptures, John 8:39, 17:17; Romans 14:17; Galatians 4:25; Revelation 1:20.
35. Robert M. Grant, *Jesus After the Gospels: The Christ of the Second Century*, The Hale Memorial Lectures of Seabury-Western Theological Seminary, (Louisville, KY: Westminster/John Knox, 1989), 33. Grant writes, "The language is basically derived from the Old Testament statements about Wisdom, correlated with the creative word that God

spoke at the beginning of creation: 'Let there be Light.' We may compare Psalm 33:6: 'By the Word of the Lord the heavens were founded and by the breath [*pneuma*] of this mouth all their strength.' The 'word' is evidently the creative word of Genesis and God's 'breath' is the *pneuma* above the waters."

36. See, for instance, the marginal note of the New American Standard Version. Cf. Wilhelm Michaelis, "σκηνόω," *TDNT*, 7:385-86. In the New Testament, σκηνόω is always used metaphorically. On p. 386, Michaelis notes that its use in John is not meant to show the "temporary and transitory element." The word does not occur in the post-apostolic fathers or in the apologists.
37. See p. 70.
38. Joe O. Lewis, "The Ark and the Tent," *Review and Expositor* 74 no. 4 (1977): 537-48, 546. Lewis writes, "The Gospel of John joined the theme of 'dwelling' (tenting, tabernacling) with that of the 'glory of God' to present the incarnation (John 1:14). The transfiguration experience (Mark 9:2ff.; Matt 17:1ff.; Lk. 9:28ff.) in the synoptic gospels may also have utilized the ancient figures."
39. It is clear that God is the referent from the previous verse. The use of God need not come from a variant reading but may well be implied by the "ὅς," which is the typical introductory relative pronoun of christological hymnic material.
40. The sense of κατοικέω is permanent. On this, see Otto Michel, *TDNT*, 5:153-55.
41. In the numerous instances where the Old Testament says that Yahweh "dwells" between the cherubim, the Hebrew verb is "יָשַׁב"and is generally rendered κάθημαι in the *LXX*. The sense is clearly of being enthroned. On this, see I Samuel 4:4; II Samuel 6:2; I Chronicles 13:6; Isaiah 37:16. The Old Testament may use the same verb to demonstrate that Yahweh is enthroned in heaven (Psalm 2:4; Psalm 113:5); [here the *LXX* uses κατοικέω to indicate the sense of permanent dwelling]. While the Old Testament may use the Hebrew word in a context such as Yahweh tabernacling among them (see Psalm 26:8 where His glory is tabernacled מִשְׁכַּן כְּבוֹדֶךָ, or Psalm 135: 21 where Yahweh is tented), the normative way of expressing this permanent dwelling is captured by the *LXX* when it translates the Hebrew with a form of κατοικέω.
42. On μένειν, see Friedrich Hauck, *TDNT*, 4:574-88, 576. Here, Hauck suggests that the use of μένειν in John "seeks to express the immutability and inviolability of the relationship of immanence." There is nothing to compare to this in the Hellenistic world or even in the Old Testament. For Hauck, it is emphatic: "God dwells in Christ."
43. Kittel, "δόξα," 244.
44. Berkhof, *Christian Faith*, 291.
45. On p. 113 of *Lord Jesus Christ*, Hurtado notes Paul's usage of glory in II Corinthians 3 and 4, particularly as Paul links Jesus with Yahweh's experience with Moses on Sinai. "In II Corinthians 3:15-18 Paul's statement that 'when one turns to the Lord the veil is lifted' (v. 16) applies to Christ, the phrasing adapted from Exodus 34:34 (where God is clearly the *Kyrios* before whom Moses takes off his veil.) Paul goes on to link Christ with the divine Spirit (vv. 17-18), and refers to him as the agent of transforming glory (*doxa* = Heb. *kavod*, one of the most important attributes of God in the Old Testament, borne here of Christ)." Here, Hurtado cites Carey C. Newman, *Paul's Glory Christology: Tradition and Rhetoric*, NovTSup 69, (Leiden: Brill, 1992).
46. The "glory of God" is a powerful New Testament phrase, one in which John delights, dismissed by Christian apologists. Justin scoffs at its usage in describing those holding a simple Oneness christology, writing that they say Christ "is called Glory, because He appears in a vision sometimes that cannot be borne; is called Man, and a human being, because He appears arrayed in such forms as the Father pleases; and they call Him the Word because He carries tidings from the Father to men: but maintain that this power is indivisible and inseparable from the Father." See Justin, *Dialogue with Trypho* 128, *Ante-Nicene Fathers,* 10 vols., trans. and ed. A. Cleveland Coxe, Alexander Roberts and James Donaldson, (Grand Rapids, MI: Eerdmans, 1965), 1:264. On Justin's development of the Trinity, see also Jean Daniélou, *The History of Early Christian Doctrine Before the Coun-*

cil of Nicea, Vol. 2, *Gospel Message and Hellenistic Culture*, particularly his section "Gospel and Hellenistic Culture," (Philadelphia: Westminster, 1973).
47. Craig R. Koester, *The Dwelling of God: The Tabernacle in the Old Testament, Intertestamental Jewish Literature, and the Old Testament*, (Washington, D.C.: Catholic Biblical Association of America, 1989), 105-6. As Koester points out on p. 102, this is clearly drawn from the allusion to the Tabernacle of Exodus. For Koester, verses 15-18 are to be taken as a whole and are descriptive of God dwelling or tabernacling in flesh within the community of believers. On p. 104 he notes, "It reflects both continuity and discontinuity with the Jewish heritage." Koester goes on to say "that the Shekinah [God's revealed presence in the temple] provides an implicit link between the glory motif in 1:14 and Jesus' replacement of the temple."
48. Ibid., 103ff. Koester notes that while there is a certain reference to the theophany on Sinai, the polemic of John is that Jewish believers who are not Christians have missed God's revelation to them. See also Elizabeth Harris, *Prologue and the Gospel: The Theology of the Fourth Evangelist*, (Sheffield: Sheffield Academic Press, 1994). The position of Elizabeth Harris is consistent with that of Koester.
49. The comparison between Moses and Jesus in verse 17 suggests that Jesus surpasses Moses. In verse 18, when it says, "No man has seen God at any time," this too is an allusion to Moses. In Exodus 33:6, Moses was unable to see God while Jesus, as the μονογενὴς θεός, reveals God.
50. Harris, *Prologue and the Gospel*, 104. Harris suggests that in verse 14 μονογενής is used "with the bare anarthrous titular sense."
51. Ibid., 93ff. On p. 102, Harris notes that "μονογενὴς θεός is found in the Siniaticus (first hand), BC (first hand) and L." It seems likely that μονογενὴς θεός is the original reading as it is the more difficult of the two, as a scribe would more likely change to μονογενὴς υἱός than vice versa.
52. Although the Greek κόλπος can refer to the "bosom, breast, chest" (so *BAG*, 443), it can also have the sense of "lap," where someone is being cradled as a small child. In either case, the verse at once demonstrates that Jesus is both in intimate fellowship (and even dependence) and is in fact God.

Chapter 7: The Man Born in Bethlehem

1. See pp. 19-20.
2. In the Hebrew culture, as well as other ancient Near Eastern cultures, it was normative to name children in a way as to include some identification with God. Thus, a name could contain an element of *Elohim* or even of Yahweh. So, in speaking the name Daniel, for instance, there was identification with *Elohim* (*El*). Daniel means, "God (*El*) is my judge." Likewise, the name Israel included *El*. Yahweh also was commonly utilized. For instance, Elijah contains elements of both *Elohim* and Yahweh.
3. Bietenhard, "ὄνομα," 272, note 200; "According to Philo *Mut. Nom.*, 121, the name Joshua [Jesus] means σωτηρία κυρίου."
4. On the use of *Soter*, see Georg Fohrer, "σωτήρ," *TDNT*, 7:1003-21. On Savior (*Soter*) as a claim of divinity, see p. 10 of C. Kavin Rowe, "Luke and the Trinity: An Essay in Ecclesial Biblical Theology," *Scottish Journal of Theology* 56 no. 1, (2003): 1-26. See note 28, where Rowe notes that this title was, in fact, a normative say of speaking of divinity. Rowe notes only three exceptions, all in Judges (3:9; 15:18; 12:3) where σωτήρ refers to human judges.
5. "Lord" is a translation of the Greek *Kurios*. In particular, we focus on this title in chapter 12. Briefly, though, Lars Hartman demonstrates how that by the Septuagint translating Yahweh to *Kurios*, the very earliest Jewish confessions could readily identify Jesus with Yahweh. *Into the Name of Jesus: Baptism in the Early Church*, (Edinburgh, Scotland: T. & T. Clark, 1997).
6. There is as well an eschatological element to the title *Christos*. On this, see p. 126.

7. Luke 1:35. This is poetic parallelism: both the Holy Spirit and "the power of the Highest" refer to Yahweh.
8. Eduard Schweizer, "πνεῦμα, πνευματικός," *TDNT*, 6:396-451, 402. Schweizer writes, "In Mt. 1:18, 20, as in Lk. 1:35, πνεῦμα is the creative power of God."
9. See p. 17. Just as there was no ontological difference between Yahweh and the Spirit of God in the Old Testament, so there is none in the New Testament either.
10. Luke 1:35. The term "Son of God" can have a variety of nuances. There is the same metaphoric relationship to God as Adam (Luke 3:38); there may be claim to kingship (cf. Psalm 2:7 quoted in Acts 13:33). Like Israel, Jesus was God's obedient Son in the desert (Luke 4:1-13, Exodus 14-17). I. Howard Marshall suggests that for Luke, the term "Son of God" controls "the christology of the whole work," but this claim is largely overstated. Other titles are just as significant and all the titles have to be understood in context of each other. Marshall, "Luke and His Gospel," in *The Gospel and the Gospels*, ed. Peter Stuhlmacher, (Grand Rapids, MI: Eerdmans, 1991), 285.
11. Luke 1:42 says that Jesus is the fruit (καρπός) of Mary's womb. While καρπός can refer to literal fruit, it here has reference to human progeny; on this, see Hauck, *TDNT*, 3:614-16. Romans 1:3 says that Jesus was "born of the seed (σπέρμα) of David according to the flesh." Here σπέρμα refers to an offspring. Cf. Acts 2:30.
12. While one may say that God was Father by creation (Luke 3:38) or by theological adoption (Exodus 19:5), in the sense of specifically "begetting," God became a Father when He had a Son.
13. To declare that Jesus was human implies certain biological and psychological requirements. If He were truly human we must consider in what way His flesh was like our flesh; further, He must of necessity have been able to reason independently and make choices. Humans have forty-six chromosomes, twenty-three contributed by the father and twenty-three by the mother. The Bible taken at face value suggests that Mary was the actual mother of Jesus and thus her contribution was not merely in a surrogate sense. Rather, she contributed half of the chromosomal material making up the zygote. The Scripture teaches that Jesus had no human father. Yet for Jesus to be human, he would have had to have forty-six chromosomes, and thus paternity must have involved a divine supplying of twenty-three human chromosomes. While understanding that there is certainly mystery involved in the miracle of the virgin birth, we must conclude that God created human DNA, *de novo*.
14. As we shall discuss in the early historical formation of a doctrine that would evolve into full-orbed Trinitarianism, Justin employed the *Logos* to become incarnate so as to safeguard the deity. On this, see chapter 14.
15. Besides Malachi 3:6, James 1:17 is also employed. But like Malachi 3:6, James can be read in a number of different ways. Like the Malachi text, it can refer to God's faithfulness and certainty of His promises. It demands too much of the passage to insist that its intention is to teach "ontological unchangeability" of God.
16. As we shall discuss in chapter 15, it was this very point at which Tertullian rejected the christology of Praxeas, whose christology most closely exhibited the resemblance to first-century Oneness christology of any of the modalists.
17. See p. 21 and attending notes.
18. Hans Küng, *On Being a Christian*, trans. Edward Quinn, (Garden City, NY: Doubleday, 1976), 131.
19. This is not to say that there are not hundreds of years of traditions where various Jewish Rabbis have added varied and extensive positions which could fill volumes. See Hertz, *Pentateuch and Haftorahs*, 770-71. Rather, I have in mind the work of James Kugel, *The Idea of Hebrew Poetry: Parallelism and its History*, (New Haven: Yale University Press, 1981), that the nature of Hebrew repetition is poetic and intended to heighten meaning.
20. The usage of soul by Jesus in the synoptic Gospels and John may be one such circumlocution for Himself. Matthew 26:38 records that Jesus confided to His disciples in Gethsemane, "My soul is exceedingly sorrowful, even to death." Similarly, when refer-

ring to this internal struggle, Jesus said in John 12:27, "Now is my soul troubled, and what shall I say? 'Father, save me from this hour: but for this cause came I unto this hour?' " Peter's use of soul in Acts 2:27 is less certain but may also reflect a circumlocution for the crucified Messiah: "For You will not leave my soul in Hades, Nor will You allow Your Holy One to see corruption." On the other hand, Acts 2:31 separates the soul from the flesh: "He, foreseeing this, spoke concerning the resurrection of the Christ, that His soul was not left in Hades, nor did His flesh see corruption." All in all, it is difficult to be dogmatic about the specific meaning of "soul" within this New Testament christological context.
21. Matthew 26:41 (KJV) offers, "Watch and pray, that ye enter not into temptation: the spirit indeed is willing, but the flesh is weak." The contrast of flesh and spirit is not just for Jesus, but for the apostles as well (cf. Mark 14:38); see also Luke 23:46: when Jesus "had cried with a loud voice, he said, Father, into thy hands I commend my spirit: and having said thus, he gave up the Spirit (ἐξέπνευσεν)." But here again, whether Jesus was meaning anything more than to say that He was releasing His life may be debated.
22. Jesus is clearly speaking metaphorically when He says, "It is the Spirit who gives life; the flesh profits nothing. The words that I speak to you are spirit, and they are life" (John 6:63).
23. John 11:33 records, "Therefore, when Jesus saw her weeping, and the Jews who came with her weeping, He groaned in the spirit and was troubled." Cf. John 11:38, where it explains, "Jesus therefore again groaning in himself (in spirit; τῷ πνεύματι) cometh to the grave." See also John 13:21, where Jesus was "troubled in spirit" in anticipation of the coming betrayal of Judas. It would be difficult to prove that any of these texts were seeking to make a specific kind of anthropological claim, a distinction, say, between a part of His person defined as "spirit" and some other metaphysical or even physical part of His person.
24. Pelikan, *Christian Tradition*, 175. On the specific categories utilized by Pelikan, see p. 264, note 27.
25. For the account of Jesus making clay pigeons fly see *Infancy Gospel of Thomas* 2:1-7, *The Complete Gospels*, ed. Robert J. Miller, (San Francisco: Harper, 1994), 373.
26. Berkhof, *Christian Faith*, 291.

Chapter 8: The Man on a Mission

1. Rabbinic sources indicate that while adulthood officially occurred at age thirteen, a year or two prior two this official event "lads should be brought up to the Temple, and made to observe the festive rights." Alfred Edersheim, *Sketches of Jewish Social Life*, rev. and upd. (Peabody, MA: Hendrickson, 1994), 113.
2. This was suggested by Glenn Koch, a New Testament professor from Eastern Baptist Theological Seminary (now Palmer Theological Seminary); Koch disallows the necessity of thirteen as the necessary age of adulthood.
3. Jesus, who would naturally follow Joseph into the trade of being a carpenter would, about this time, leave the tutelage of childhood and begin to take on adult responsibilities. It is speculative to posit how young Jesus was when He knew something of His identity. He certainly knew His origin at this point in His life.
4. As we suggested above, the *Agrapha* pick up on this singular verse and offer some fairly fanciful portrayals confounding his teachers in a kind of Gnostic telling of the story. These narratives have little in common with the canonical portrayal of Jesus in Luke 2.
5. Luke 2:49; the translation is my own but is suggested in some sense by Klaus Baltzer, "The Meaning of the Temple in the Lukan Writings," *Harvard Theological Review* 58 (1965): 263–77, 272. The Greek is not specific. The question, "Τί ὅτι ἐζητεῖτέ με; οὐκ ᾔδειτε ὅτι ἐν τοῖς τοῦ πατρός μου δεῖ εἶναί με;" implies something in relationship with the Father. Translations generally choose between "house" or "business" or their synonyms.
6. Gottlobb Schrenk, "πατήρ," *TDNT*, 5:982-1014, 988.

7. On the faith of Jesus, see Richard Hays, *The Faith of Jesus Christ. An Investigation into the Narrative Structure of Galatians 3:1-4:11*, (Chico, CA: Scholars Press, 1983), 139-91. See also Luke T. Johnson, "Rom 3:21-26 and the Faith of Jesus," *Catholic Biblical Quarterly* 44 (1982): 77-90.
8. Hebrews 4:15. Cullmann notes that the Greek in Hebrews 4:15 is really quite strong and hardly limits temptation to the time after the baptism of Jesus and Gethsemane. He offers, "'in every respect as we are' refers not only to form but also to content." *Christology*, 95.
9. Bruce W. Longenecker argues effectively that πίστις ['Ιησοῦ] Χριστοῦ is, in fact, a subjective genitive reading (over against Jan Lambrecht). "Defining the Faithful Character of the Covenant Community: Galatians 2:15-21 and beyond. A Response to Jan Lambrecht," in *Paul and the Mosaic Law*. James D. G. Dunn, ed. (1996; repr., Grand Rapids, MI: Eerdmans, 2001), 80-97, 80-81. See also Morna D. Hooker, "πίστις Χριστοῦ," in *From Adam to Christ: Essays on Paul*, (Cambridge: Cambridge University Press, 1990), 165-86, 165. If the exegetical work stands for Galatians 2:20, Christ had faith, and we can in fact appropriate the faith Christ had.
10. Longenecker, ibid.
11. John 1:29; the passage seems to be an allusion, not only of the place of sacrifice in the Jewish system of worship but Jesus' place as the Servant of Yahweh. This proclamation would be repeated by John so his disciples would recognize Jesus (John 1:36).
12. Matthew 3:3; Mark 1:2-3; Luke 3:4-6; and in part, John 1:23; cf. Isaiah 40: 3 (NJB): "A voice cries, 'Prepare in the desert a way for Yahweh. Make a straight highway for our God across the wastelands."
13. J. Keir Howard, *New Testament Baptism*, (London: Pickering & Inglis Ltd., 1970), 17. Howard notes that Gentiles were said to be "born anew" through the baptismal rite when they converted to the Jewish faith.
14. Hartman, *Into the Name of Jesus*, 17.
15. Cullmann, *Christology*, 67. Cullmann points out that this plays into the statement of Jesus who told John to baptize him in order to "fulfill all righteousness." Jesus was baptized in view of His death, that on the cross He would take on Himself all the sins of the people.
16. The hermeneutic of an adoptionist would elevate the importance of texts that seem to describe Jesus as a man that became the chosen of God; i.e., Peter's speeches or sermons, Acts 2:22, 3:13, 3:19ff., 10:38ff. Further, the accounts of the baptism of Jesus, where the Spirit came upon Him, might be cited if that is the point at which an adoptionist ascribes divinity to Christ. If the Adoptionism is of the sort where divinity is ascribed at the Resurrection, texts of principal importance would include Acts 2:36, Acts 13:34, and Philippians 2:11.
17. This is my language. I do not mean by this that Jesus was not already in covenant as a son of Israel; certainly He was. Nor do I mean to suggest that He was not heretofore aware of His special relationship with His Father; Luke 2:49 makes this clear. Rather, in this text, Jesus as a descendent of Adam, as a son of the covenant, is commissioned especially for a task within the context of this covenant relationship. Further, it is this task that will result in the eschatological restoration of every son and daughter of Adam. In restoring what Adam lost, Jesus' unique covenant relationship with the Father opens up eschatological benefits for us as joint heirs in the context of this covenant relationship.
18. While Jesus as a man was already in covenant with Yahweh, it is in the baptism that Jesus recognized His authority from Yahweh, His authorization and empowerment for ministry. On this, see Witherington, *Christology*, 150. See note 16, where Witherington argues that this must be the case, especially if one takes seriously Mark 11:27-33.
19. Heinrich Greeven, "περιστερά, τρυγών," *TDNT*, 6:63-72, 68. Greeven notes that this dove, as representative of the Holy Spirit, is variously described as coming on Jesus. "Mk. links καταβαῖνον directly with εἰς αὐτόν; Luke puts ἐπ' αὐτόν first, as also Mt., who interpolates ἐρχόμενον; Jn. combines καταβαίνειν with ἐπ' αὐτόν but adds the emphatic μένειν ἐπ' αὐτόν."
20. Jewish witnesses standing on the shore, seeing the dove and hearing the voice would not be impressed to believe in an ontological Trinity. They would no doubt correctly deduce

that this was a divine visitation upon a human to connote a special demonstration of this man's purpose and calling.
21. Otto Procksch, "ἅγιος in the NT," *TDNT*, 1:100-10, 103-4. Procksch offers, "As the dove of Noah after the flood indicates the dawn of a new epoch (Gen. 8:8ff.), so the dove-like form of the Spirit indicates the dawn of a new creation rising from Christ from the baptismal waters (cf. 1 Pt. 3:19ff.)." Others disagree. Greeven suggests that the dove is in fact a representation of the Holy Spirit, and sees rather an allusion to sacrificial rite or with the "Bath Qol" (the way in which the voice of God is thought to communicate in Rabbinic tradition). "περιστερά, τρυγών," 69.
22. When asked about His authority at the close of His ministry, Jesus responded with a question, "The baptism of John–where was it from? From heaven or from men?" (Matthew 21:25). Jesus made them choose. His own claim, though, was that His authority rested in some way on John's and may well have been an allusion to His own baptism. Jeremias takes Jesus' answer to mean, "My authority rests on what happened when I was baptized by John." On this, see Joachim Jeremias, *New Testament Theology: The Proclamation of Jesus*, (New York: Scribner, 1971), 56.
23. Mark 1:11; cf. Matthew 3:17; Luke 3:22.
24. In the new eschatological age, there was to be the apocalyptic breaking in of the divine. In the baptism features of the apocalyptic, Witherington notes the similarity of baptism experience to the experience of John the Revelator (Revelation 1:10; 4:1-2, 10:1; 21:1-3). The commonalty for Witherington in all these instances is the voice speaking from Heaven, giving revelation. *Christology*, 149.
25. Witherington, *Christology*, 151, note 22. The Western text reading of Luke 3:22 is in fact a quotation of Psalm 2:7. On this, see Cullmann, *Christology*, 66. Donald Juel suggests this connection with the royal psalms as well as what came to be the messianic interpretation of II Samuel 7. *Messianic Exegesis*, 79. "Son" in this instance, is the "Son of God," the royal messianic seed of David.
26. Witherington, *Christology*, 152.
27. Cullmann, *Christology*, 66.
28. Writing from a Jewish perspective, David Flusser writes, "Heavenly voices were not an uncommon phenomenon among the Jews of those days, and frequently these voices were heard to utter verses from scripture." David Flusser and J. Steven Notley, *Jesus*, 3rd ed. (Jerusalem: The Hebrew University Magnes Press, 2001), 42.
29. Cullmann, *Christology*, 66-67. For an excellent summary of the historical interpretation of the *Ebed* Yahweh in Judaism, and how such a title is used by Jesus, ibid., 52-87. Joachim Jeremias suggests that the understanding of Jesus as the Servant of Yahweh offered a way to understand Jesus' death for both Him and His apostles. On this see his "παῖς τοῦ θεοῦ" in *TDNT*, 5:677-717.
30. Isaiah 53:6, 8 (NKJV). The familiar prophecy in Isaiah 53:4 (NKJV) was seen as christological.
31. Peter C. Craigie allows that Psalm 2 could well be a coronation hymn. *Psalms 1-50, Word Biblical Commentary* 19, (Waco, TX: Word Books, 1983), 64. See pp. 62-69 as to the place of Psalm 2:7. Anticipation of coronation was implicit in the call; but it was an expectation that also required faith.
32. This theme is picked up again throughout the book but especially in chapter 10.
33. Cullmann, *Christology*, 95.
34. See Romans 5:14-18; cf. I Corinthians 15:45ff., where the same theme is taken up eschatologically.
35. On p. 95 of *Theology of Paul*, Dunn offers, "but the causal connection implied here by 'made' (*katastathesan*) may be nonspecific and very loose, 'made' functioning simply as equivalent to 'became' (*egenonto*)." As support, Dunn cites Albrecht Oerke, "*katheistemi*," *TDNT*, 3:445.
36. The use of the word "many" seems to be a conscious effort on the part of Paul to demonstrate that the work of Christ does not lead to a *de facto* universalism, where everyone is of necessity saved.

37. Matthew 4:10, where Jesus cites Deuteronomy 10:20.
38. This is the sense of "the acceptable year of the Lord." Indeed, a considerable number of texts translate the phrase, "the year of the Lord's favor," an eschatological trope utilized by Isaiah for the Messianic age. On this, see chapter 2 of Robert Brawley, *Luke-Acts and the Jews: Conflict, Apology, and Conciliation* (Atlanta: Scholars Press, 1987).
39. There is an academic consensus that Philippians 2:6-11 is hymnic material coming from the first generation of the church. See R. P. Martin's *Carmen Christi: Phil. 2:5-11 in Recent Interpretation and in the Setting of Early Christian Worship*, (London: Cambridge University Press, 1967). For a fuller treatment of my argument related to this hymn, see David S. Norris, "Origins and Biblical Theology of Modalistic Monarchianism," (Master's Thesis, Eastern Baptist Theological Seminary, now Palmer Theological Seminary, 1991).
40. On pp. 101-7 of *Christology in the Making*, Dunn provides an overview of Paul's allusions to Adam. Dunn sees the Genesis 1-3 narrative as a background in Romans 1:18-25. It is Adam who was made in the image of God. Further, Adam's failure is reflected universally in the post-Eden world. On p. 102, Dunn argues that when Paul writes, "All *lack* the glory of God," speaking of Adam, this could well be translated, "All have *forfeited* the glory of God." So too, on pp. 103-4, Dunn suggests that Romans 7:7-11 could apply to Adam, though perhaps not uniquely to him. The creation motif resurfaces in Romans 8:19-22, and on pp. 104-6, Dunn further develops the Adamic theme of this passage.
41. Ibid., citing C. K. Barrett, *From First Adam to Last*, (London: Adam and Charles Black, 1962), 6.
42. Alois Grillmeier, *Christ in Christian Tradition*, vol. 1, trans. John Bowden, (Atlanta: John Knox, 1975), 21. Grillmeier offers a typical Trinitarian approach by formulating the meaning in this fashion: "He who was found in the divine mode of being did not wish to cling to his position in selfish exploitation. Instead he gave himself up to the condition of *kenosis*."
43. See Martin, *Carmen Christi*, 65, note 2, for a full range of meanings of ὑπάρχων. Certainly, there is nothing grammatically that prevents one from taking the position that the hymn describes Christ's abasement here on earth. Nor is there anything of necessity in the construction of the strophes that demands a pre-incarnate Son.
44. See p. 275, note 53 as to why any sort of *kenosis* should be rejected in the Philippian Hymn.
45. Murphy-O'Connor, "Christological Anthropology," 31.
46. On p. 176 of his *Christology*, Cullmann notes that Adam was the one who initially bore this stamp of the divine image. The Peshitta indicates the same connection in translating *morphe* with *demutha* here. Consequently, Philippians 2:6 is immediately related to the concept of the *eikon*, since the Semitic root word *demutha* and its synonym *tselem* can correspond to either of the two Greek words.
47. See p. 417 of W. Robertson Nicoll, ed., *The Expositors Greek Testament*, London, 1897-1910; see also Johannes Behm, "μορφῇ," *TDNT*, 4:742-52, 749ff., where he notes that *morphe* as a literal form of God is "alien and impossible" to Jewish thinking.
48. See p. 40 of Murphy-O'Connor's, "Christological Anthropology" where he suggests that Jesus' sinlessness gave Him the divine prerogative of incorruptibility. He writes, "Christ, however, did not turn this situation to his own advantage (οὐχ ἁρπαγμὸν ἡγήσατο). He did not demand the treatment that his condition merited. On the contrary (ἀλλὰ), He permitted himself to be put to death."
49. Norman K. Bakken, "The New Humanity: Christ and the Modern Age. A Study Centering in the Christ Hymn: Philippians 2:6-11," *Interpretation* 22 (1968): 71-82, 76.
50. Martin, *Carmen Christi*, 138. Martin suggests that the question as to what it was that Christ did not grasp is propelled by one's understanding of *harpagmos*. Thus, on p. 141, Martin notes that those who hold the view that Christ preexisted in a sort of heavenly realm before the Incarnation might posit, "(He was) not then the King of the universe. The choice which faced Him was whether He would aspire to the dignity in His own right

by snatching at it, or receive it from the Father by treading the path of lowly submission and obedience."
51. Especially helpful because of their clarity are Bakken, "The New Humanity"; Murphy-O'Connor, "Christological Anthropology"; Charles H. Talbert, "The Problem of Pre-existence in Philippians 2:6-11," *JBL* 86 (1967): 141-53; Dunn, *Christology in the Making*. A more complete bibliography is offered by both Talbert and Murphy-O'Connor.
52. Other representative examples include the NJB and NRSV.
53. Talbert, in "The Problem of Pre-existence," 141, note 2, points out four reasons for rejecting pre-existence in the text, noting: "(1) Incarnation is here regarded as kenosis rather than as epiphany as in most other early Christian hymns (cf. John 1:1-18; 1 Timothy 3:16); (2) only here in early Christianity would there be a reference to a pre-existent reflection and decision of Christ; (3) the exegete virtually committed to an interpretation of 'emptied himself' as the giving up the form of God (divinity) for the form of a servant (humanity); (4) only with difficulty can the conclusion be avoided that exaltation as Lord is a higher state than being in the form of God (divinity). To read the hymn as referring to the human existence of Jesus rather than his pre-existence, however, enables one to avoid these problems."

Chapter 9: The Man Who Taught about Yahweh

1. Mark 2:5. That this was speaking beyond what is humanly allowable is indicated by the criticism of the scribes who ascribed blasphemy to Jesus.
2. In this section, I am indebted to the teaching of Robert Sabin for the flow of the argument. Robert Sabin has been a prominent Oneness Pentecostal teacher who primarily taught at Apostolic Bible Institute, in St. Paul, MN, where I was his student in the early 1970s. Sabin taught at ABI from about 1964-87.
3. This must be the case; consider how Luke 2:52 records both Jesus' physical growth and spiritual development.
4. On this, see pp. 130-132.
5. Here the word image is translated from the Greek χαρακτήρ, of which *BAG* offers on p. 884, "impress, reproduction, representation." On this, see F. F. Bruce, *The Epistle to the Hebrews: The English Text with Introduction, Exposition and Notes*, (Grand Rapids, MI: Eerdmans, 1964), 48. He says, "What God essentially is, is made manifest in Christ. To see Christ is to see what the Father is like." On the exegesis of Hebrews as hymnic material, see chapter 16 of this book; cf. II Corinthians 4:4-6.
6. David S. Norris, *Operation Daybreak*, (Dover, DE: Halak Press, 1993).
7. Ibid., 144-5.
8. Ibid., 207-8.
9. See pp. 69-70 above.
10. While Jesus could no doubt speak Hebrew, Greek, and Aramaic, it is fairly certain that His teaching was largely done in Aramaic. Notable are the number of times when phrases in the Aramaic are left in the original but a Greek translation is offered in the Gospels.
11. Jeremias, *New Testament Theology*, 61-68. On a dissenting view philologically, see James Barr, "Abba isn't Daddy," *Journal of Theological Studies*, 39 no. 1 (1988): 28-47. Barr nuances Jeremias's study to suggest that *abba* could well have been spoken by adults, and he challenges some of the claims where Jeremias makes all prayer to God. All in all, Barr's is a rather tepid critique, and Jeremias's work still stands. Mary Rose D'Angelo also critiques Jeremias in "Abba and 'Father': Imperial Theology and the Jesus Traditions," *Journal of Biblical Literature* 111 no. 4 (1992): 611-30; her critique seems to be driven from a feminist perspective and some of her presuppositions are skewed. For support of Jeremias's thesis that Jesus was unique calling Yahweh *Abba*, see Dunn, *Christology in the Making*, 26-28.

12. On numerous occasions, Jesus refused to answer for Himself. For instance, in Matthew 21, Jesus refused to answer by what authority He operated, but asked instead by what authority John worked. When the Jewish leadership refused to answer, Jesus said in Matthew 21:27, "Neither will I tell you by what authority I do these things." In Mark 8:11-21, when the Pharisees demanded of Jesus a sign, He obliquely answered that no sign would be given but the sign of Jonah the prophet (cf. Matthew 16:1-12). Further, in Luke 11:16f Jesus likewise refused to give a sign but taught them instead principles as to why His kingdom was opposed to that of Satan.
13. Jesus taught the apostles that it was the Spirit of Truth that would teach the apostles (John 16:13); it is no accident then that when Peter preached on the Day of Pentecost, he demonstrated revelation that to speak of Jesus was in fact to speak of Yahweh; covenantally, Peter applied Joel's text that proclaimed for people to "call on the name of Yahweh" by instructing his audience to be baptized with the name of Jesus invoked over them. On this, see pp. 142-144.
14. Richard Longenecker struggles to make sense of the enigmatic way that Christ (Messiah) is portrayed in the Gospels. He suggests that the portrait of Jesus as Messiah is baffling, being composed of "on the one hand, a radical rejection of the current Jewish idea of the Messiah, (2) an extreme reserve toward the title itself and, (3) explicit commands to his disciples and others not to speak of him in messianic terms, (4) a messianic consciousness underlying many of his actions and statements, (5) the acclaim of others as to his messiahship, (6) an occasional acceptance of the appellative, and (7) the express explication of his ministry in messianic terms, as presented in Luke 24." *Christology*, 71.
15. In the first century, the "Name" was equivalent to the divine essence. For Jesus to come in His Father's name, therefore, was to come in His Father's divine essence. On this see pp. 140-1.
16. John 7:38-39; see chapter 11.
17. For example, see Luke 11:13; John 3:5; 4:10; 7:37-39.
18. Otto Procksch, "ἅγιος," 104.
19. Eduard Schweitzer, "πνεῦμα," *TDNT*, 6:397-99. Schweitzer suggests that the biblical understanding may well have been that the time of ignorance ends for people with the time of the possession of the Spirit. Thus, for someone whose resistance was in conscious defiance, this was against the overwhelming power of the Spirit. This is in contrast to Jesus' more veiled references to Himself as the Son of Man, one that was only more fully understood over time.
20. Ibid., 419-20.
21. So Robert Sabin. Cf. note 2, p. 275.
22. I cannot recall dates for this teaching, but it was when I was a student at Apostolic Bible Institute in the early '70s; hence the reference to the astronauts going to the moon at that time would have had immediate relevance.
23. John 6:15ff. On the understanding of the *Messiah* as a political and military leader, see Marinus de Jonge, "The Use of the Word Anointed in the Time of Jesus," *Novum Testamentum* 8 (1966): 132-48, 134-36. Although Geza Vermès allows that *Messiah* can have a number of different connotations, he explores the title in terms of the first-century expectation of triumphal kingship. Vermès, *Jesus the Jew: A Historian's Reading of the Gospels*, (Philadelphia: Fortress Press, 1981), 131-32.
24. John 6:51. Even a cursory look at John 6:51 will demonstrate that this is no ontological hypostatic claim, nor is this a kind of Gnostic claim. The flesh is human flesh. This motif is comparative. Jesus no more means that His flesh literally came down from Heaven than He means that they should literally eat His flesh. Jesus said, "I am the living bread that came down out of heaven; if anyone eats of this bread, he shall live forever; and the bread also which I shall give for the life of the world is My flesh."
25. This is the point of the genealogy in Matthew 1. See too, the genealogy in Luke 3; Romans 1:3; John 7:42; Acts 2:30. Additionally, see Vonelle R. Kelly, *Another Jesus: The Fallacy of the Doctrine of Heavenly Flesh*, (n.p., 2004).
26. Cullmann's *Christology* is an example of this kind of methodology.

27. Juel, *Messianic Exegesis*, 23.
28. The Son of Man is interpreted as the elect of Israel in Daniel 7:18 (typically translated as "saints" or "holy ones" of the Most High).
29. It is not uncommon for this kind of representation to take place. The original term "Son of Man" is *bar anasha* (בר נשא) in Aramaic and is derived from Daniel 7 where the Son of Man is offered a Kingdom. Verse 18 offers as an interpretive scheme that the "saints of the most high" are the Son of Man. On the use of the Son of Man in the pseudepigraphal 1 Enoch, see Cullmann, *Christology*, 140. Consider the use of the Son of Man in 1 Enoch in chapters 46, 48, 52, 62, 69, and 71. On p. 141 Cullmann notes the use of Son of Man as Messiah in 1 Enoch 48:10; 52:4. There is some controversy as to when the Book of 1 Enoch should be dated, particularly the portion in question, but it stands close enough to the New Testament to offer clues of the time period.
30. Matthew 16:27–28; Matthew 19:28; Matthew 24:27, 37, 39, 44; 25:13, 31.
31. See p. 320 of Geza Vermès, "The use of בר נש/בר נשא in Jewish Aramaic," Appendix E in M. Black, *An Aramaic Approach to the Gospels and Acts*, 3rd ed. (Oxford: Clarendon, 1967), where Vermès cites Madrishim, the Targums, and IQ Genesis to demonstrate בר אנש as a circumlocution.
32. Matthew 17:12, 22; Mark 9:31; Luke 9:44; Matthew 20:18; 20:28; 26:2; Matthew 26: 24; Mark 8:31; Luke 9:22.
33. Matthew 9:6; Luke 5:24.
34. Matthew 12:8; Mark 2:28; Luke 6:5.
35. Matthew 8:20; Luke 9:58.
36. The Greek ἐγώ εἰμί is especially forceful, as the verb already contains the idea of the first person in it.
37. Bauckham notes that there are two specific "*I AM*" statements (I, *I AM* He) in Isaiah 43:25 and 51:12, that further establish this language of God in His singularlity: *anokhi, anokhi hu* (אָנֹכִי הוּא); the Hebrew is translated in the *LXX* to *ego eime* (ἐγώ εἰμί). This is the form that appears in John's Gospel. *God Crucified*, 55.
38. Raymond Brown sees three different ways in which this is expressed: (1) The absolute use with no predicate. See John 8:24; 8:28; 8:58; 13:19; (2) the use where a predicate may be understood even though it is not expressed. See John 6:20; 18:5; (3) the use with a predicative nominative. See John 6:35; 6:51; 8:12; 9:5; 10:7; 10:9; 10:11; 10:14; 11:25; 14:6; 15:1; 15:5. *John*, "Appendix IV," 533–35.
39. Brown, ibid., 538. Brown points out the use of "I AM" sayings in Mark 6:50 (parallel with Matthew 14:27); Mark 14:62 (parallel with Luke 22:70); and Luke 24:36 (some witnesses).
40. The Samaritan conception of the messiah was that of the *Ta'eb* as restorer, one who would confirm the rightness of the Samaritan position. On this, see Brown, *John*, 172.
41. Bauckham notes that as the narrative progresses, this revelatory element becomes increasingly unambiguous. He cites as these "absolute" I AM sayings: John 4:26; 6:20; 8:24, 28; 13:19; 18:5, 6, 8. *God Crucified*, 55.

Chapter 10: The Man Who Was Crucified

1. Not only christological hymnic material predated the epistles; Paul wrote a received confessional statement concerning Jesus in I Corinthians 15:1ff. that Christ "died for our sins according to the Scriptures, and that he was buried, and that he rose again the third day according to the Scriptures."
2. Matthew 19:28. This was apparently a recurrent theme, for Luke 22:30 records that during the passion week, Jesus said, "You may eat and drink at My table in My kingdom, and sit on thrones judging the twelve tribes of Israel."
3. Mark 10:37. This is parallel to the account in Matthew 20:20-27.
4. We shall cover the meaning of this psalm in some detail in the next chapter.

5. Hebrews 12:2. The NIV states, "Let us fix our eyes on Jesus, the author and perfecter of our faith, who for the joy set before him endured the cross, scorning its shame, and sat down at the right hand of the throne of God." On p. 98 of his *Christology*, Cullmann notes of the writer of Hebrews, "When he calls Jesus the pioneer and perfecter of our faith, he means, according to his conception of the High Priest in the whole letter, both that Jesus himself believed and that he brought men to faith in his work."
6. Bauckham, *God Crucified*, 64-5. see also Georg Bertram, "ὑψόω in the New Testament" *TDNT*, 8:608-12, 610. In John 3:14, the allusion is meant to demonstrate that just as the brazen serpent saved lives in Numbers 21:8ff., so Jesus will save lives as well.
7. Bauckham, ibid.
8. John 2:19; in verse 21 John adds that Jesus "was speaking of the temple of His body."
9. In Luke 9, on the Mount of Transfiguration, Moses and Elijah spoke to Jesus about His death in Jerusalem (9:31). Soon after this, "He steadfastly set His face to go to Jerusalem" (9:51); cf. Luke 13:22; 31-34; 17:11; 18:31; 19:11; 19:28.
10. Cullmann, *Christology*, 62.
11. Kittel, "δόξα," 248.
12. John 5:41 and 44, respectively.
13. *Dialogue with Trypho*, 128, *ANF*, 1:264. On Justin's development of the Trinity, see also Jean Daniélou, *Gospel Message and Hellenistic Culture*.
14. Kittel, "δόξα," 248. Kittel notes that at times in the Gospel the problem is not so much John's as ours. That is, "In all attempts at translation there is an intolerable rift of meanings which the author obviously did not himself feel." For Kittel, it was the Palestinian usage of John's *doxa*, primarily of utilizing *doxa* to represent God in His glory that should be understood. Kittel summarizes, "It [*doxa*] denotes the 'divine and heavenly radiance,' the 'loftiness and majesty' of God, and even the 'being of God' and His world" (B. the NT Use of δόξα, I), 237.
15. In John 8:50, Jesus said, "And I do not seek My own glory; there is One who seeks and judges. In John 7:18, Jesus said, "He who speaks from himself seeks his own glory; but He who seeks the glory of the One who sent Him is true, and no unrighteousness is in Him." Jesus spoke again of the glory He proleptically shared with the Father from the very beginning. In John 17:24, he prayed, "Father, I desire that they also whom You gave Me may be with Me where I AM, that they may behold My glory which You have given Me; for You loved Me before the foundation of the world."
16. John 12:16 records that "His disciples did not understand these things at first; but when Jesus was glorified, then they remembered that these things were written about Him and that they had done these things to Him."
17. In John 12:23, Jesus said, "The hour has come that the Son of Man should be glorified." When Judas left from the Last Supper, Jesus said in John 13:31, "Now the Son of Man is glorified, and God is glorified in Him."
18. John 2:11 records the beginning of the ministry of Jesus by offering, "This beginning of signs Jesus did in Cana of Galilee, and manifested His glory; and His disciples believed in Him." This seems to be the sense of the prologue as well, though that could be more inclusive, perhaps of all the works of Jesus, including the cross of Christ all the way to His ascension. In John 11:4, Jesus, responding to the report of Lazarus's sickness (and ultimate death) said, "This sickness is not unto death, but for the glory of God, that the Son of God may be glorified (δοξάζω) through it." As the narrative progresses, Jesus asked the stone to be rolled away from the tomb of Lazarus, saying, "Did I not say to you that if you would believe you would see the glory of God?"
19. As Kittel notes on p. 249 of "δόξα," there is "a distinctive Johannine tendency to describe the life of Jesus from the standpoint of the exaltation. It should not be overlooked, however, that the δόξα of the earthly Jesus can be seen only in πίστις [faith]."
20. Jesus said in John 17:22, "And the glory which You gave Me I have given them, that they may be one just as We are one."

21. Kittel, "δόξα," 251. Kittel links this same interpretation in both II Corinthians 3-4 and John 17. He offers this comparison: "The disciples see the δόξα of Jesus: θεωρῶσιν τὴν δόξαν τὴν ἐμήν, v. 24. Jesus has glorified them: δεδόξασμαι ἐν αὐτοῖς, v. 10. He has given them δόξα: τὴν δόξαν ἣν δέδωκάς μοι δέδωκα αὐτοῖς, 22."
22. In John 17:18, Jesus prayed, "As You sent Me into the world, I also have sent them into the world."
23. Most translations offer "I am he." Uniquely, the NLT renders the phrase, "I am the Messiah," but here "Messiah" is interpretive, for it is certainly not in the original.
24. John 13:19. This revelation of His person was being offered to those with whom He was closest. As Raymond Brown notes, the Exodus narrative is augmented by "I AM" statements; these same kinds of statements appear in the prophets where they "came to be understood not only as a statement of divine unicity and existence, but also as a divine name." *John,* "Appendix IV," 536. Here Brown says, "The Hebrew of Isa xliii 25 reads, 'I, I am He who blots transgressions,'; but it can also be interpreted, 'I am "I AM" who blots out transgressions,' a translation that makes *ego eime* a name." This is certainly how the *LXX* translates it.
25. See p. 90 of G. Braumann, "Advocate, Paraklete, Helper," in *New International Dictionary of New Testament Theology,* vol. 1, ed. Colin Brown, (Grand Rapids, MI: Zondervan, 1986), 88-91. The reason this seems to be a self-reference is that in verse 18 He says, "I will not leave you orphans; I will come to you."
26. John 14:18. Jesus' claim recorded in Matthew 18:20 included only Himself. He offered, "For where two or three are gathered together in My name, I am there in the midst of them." Paul is not amiss when he says in II Corinthians 3:17, "Now the Lord is the Spirit; and where the Spirit of the Lord is, there is liberty."
27. It is this very human suffering that is lauded in the preaching of the apostles. Peter would preach, "Him, being delivered by the determined purpose and foreknowledge of God, you have taken by lawless hands, have crucified, and put to death." The same tenor is also echoed in Peter's charge to the people in Acts 3:13-14, "The God of Abraham, Isaac, and Jacob, the God of our fathers, glorified His Servant Jesus, whom you delivered up and denied in the presence of Pilate, when he was determined to let *Him* go. But you denied the Holy One and the Just, and asked for a murderer to be granted to you."
28. On Jesus' use of *Abba,* see pp. 102-103.
29. See pp. 212-3.
30. See p. 129 where we continue with our focus on the hymnic material from Philippians 2.
31. John 18:4-5. We have capitalized "I AM" and left the "He" off to highlight the obvious claim of Jesus in the Greek text.
32. Brown, *John,* "Appendix IV," 538.
33. Juel, *Messianic Exegesis,* 95.
34. See John 18:37: "Pilate therefore said to Him, 'Are You a king then?' Jesus answered, 'You say rightly that I am a king. For this cause I was born, and for this cause I have come into the world, that I should bear witness to the truth. Everyone who is of the truth hears My voice.'"
35. Juel, on p. 95 of *Messianic Exegesis,* points out that "derided" is a poor choice for a translation, because it really means blasphemed, and the psalm uses *ekmykterizein*. Other parallels he offers (in note 7 on the same page) include Psalms 27:12, 35:11, and 109:2 being parallel with Mark 14:56-57; Psalm 35:7 parallel with Mark 15:32; Psalm 38:13-16 parallel with Mark 14:61, and Psalm 109:25 parallel with Mark 15:29.
36. Ibid., 96.
37. In this explanation of Jesus' use of Psalm 22, I am largely indebted to Robert Sabin.
38. See p. 522 of C. M. Tuckett, "Atonement in the NT," in *ABD,* 1:518-22. As Tuckett rightly notes on p. 519, "The precise way in which an expiatory sacrifice was thought to 'work' is never clarified."
39. Theologians have identified a certain set of Scriptures they have termed "*Christus Victor*" related to a kingly overcoming of Satan.

40. While it is not without interpretative problems, Kenneth Wuest suggests that this ascent of Christ presupposes a descent, one that Wuest takes to be both *tartarosas* (the place of the unrighteous dead), and Abraham's bosom (Luke 16:22). Christ did not enter the stronghold of Satan to suffer but rather to declare victory. "Exegesis of Ephesians," *Word Studies of the Greek New Testament*, 3 vols., (1959; repr., Grand Rapids, MI: Eerdmans, 1983). 1:100. On this, see also I Peter 3:18-22.
41. Dunn, *Theology of Paul*, 231.
42. Dunn suggests that Romans 8:31-39 envisages "the heavenly court where final judgment shall be dispensed." *Theology of Paul*, 230.
43. I Corinthians 15 deals with final victory in the eschaton, when the last enemy shall be destroyed. On this, see chapter 11.

Chapter 11: The Man Who Was Glorified

1. John 16:13–14. In what amounts to a necessary circumlocution, Jesus told them that the Spirit of Truth would guide them into all truth, "for He will not speak on His own authority, but whatever He hears He will speak; and He will tell you things to come. He will glorify Me, for He will take of what is Mine and declare it to you."
2. For a functional analysis of this phrase in early Christian literature, see David M. Hay, *Glory at the Right Hand*, 52-103.
3. See p. 19, Hay, *Glory at the Right Hand*, who offers that it apparently was "composed for a Davidic monarch in Jerusalem." An Apostolic hermeneutic would attribute the psalm to David based on the introductory "לְדָוִד מִזְמוֹר."
4. Even the same writer can cite the passage in a variety of ways. For instance, as Hay points out, while the writer of Hebrews quotes from this passage three times, there are eight allusions in the space of three chapters, none of which are identical. *Glory at the Right Hand*, 37.
5. Bruce, *Hebrews*, 7. See also p. 90 of Hay, *Glory at the Right Hand*, who also suggests that it is the idea of honor and divine glory rather than a heavenly location that is inferred.
6. See Hebrews 5:4-10.
7. On this, see Hebrews 7:1-6.
8. The Melchizedekian priesthood as derived from Psalm 110:4 is overtly applied to Jesus in Hebrews 5:6; 6:20; 7:16-17; 7:21; besides this, there are numerous allusions to the "right hand place," with reference to Psalm 110:1.
9. Susan Haber, "From Priestly Torah to Christ Cultus: The Re-Vision of Cult and Covenant in Hebrews," *Journal for the Study of the New Testament* 28 no. 1 (2005): 105-24; see 112-17 where Haber demonstrates from Hebrews the superiority of Christ's priesthood.
10. Bruce, *Hebrews*, 239.
11. V. Philips Long, *The Art of Biblical History*, (Grand Rapids: Zondervan, 1994), 96.
12. *Mesites* (μεσίτης) occurs in Hebrews 8:6; 9:15; and 12:24.
13. Cullmann, *Christology*, 89.
14. Kistemaker, *Hebrews*, 281. As George Wesley Buchanan notes on p. 165 of *To the Hebrews. Translation, Comment and Conclusions*, (Garden City, NY: Doubleday & Co., 1972), the notion of Jesus "sitting" does not mean He is passive; rather, the language is used to demonstrate that He will never be removed from His position of honor.
15. Matthew 3:11; Mark 1:8; Luke 3:16; John 1:33; Acts 1:5; Acts 11:16.
16. On the Greek, see Bertram, "ὑψόω ὑπερυψόω," *TDNT*, 8:608-9; as Bertram notes, the use of the compound ὑπερυψόω "is a genuine strengthening. By the conferring of the title Jesus receives the highest position, that of cosmocrator."
17. For a detailed analysis of how Yahweh links to *Kurios*, see chapter 12 above.
18. Mark 1:11; cf. Matthew 3:17; Luke 3:22.
19. Richard Bauckham notes the integrated nature of the Servant songs of Isaiah and the ultimate promise of the eschaton, particularly as it is fulfilled in the Servant of Yahweh. Bauckham continues, "What has not been recognized sufficiently is that, behind many of

the New Testament texts lies an integrated early Christian reading of these texts as a unified whole." On p. 49, Bauckham notes that both the Hebrew and Greek are instructive. In the Hebrew the text offers some important verbs: "Behold my servant will prosper, He will be high (*yarum*) and lifted up (*nissa*) and greatly exalted (*gavah*)." The Septuagint offers the following translation from the Hebrew into the Greek: "[My Servant] shall be exalted (*hupsothesetai*) and shall be glorified (*doxasthestai*)." *God Crucified*, 48.
20. Ibid., 50ff. Of the similarity of verbs in these verses, Bauckham writes, "Early Christians would have observed the coincidence and applied the Jewish exegetical principle of the *gezera shava*, according to which passages in which the same words occur should be interpreted with reference to each other."
21. Ibid. There is a blending then of glorification and suffering, confirmed as well by the language of Isaiah 57:15. What is important to note is that the present suffering is contrasted with the future glorification.
22. Ibid., 51. Bauckham will not go so far as to actually say that one is on the throne. Here he reverts to Psalm 110 as a paradigm, where Yahweh spoke to the man Jesus, pronouncing that He should sit on His right hand. We will talk about the priestly language used here as we discuss the Ascension. Yet, the Isaiah 6 text clearly says what Isaiah saw. There was one sitting on the throne. According to John's exegesis, this was a prophecy of the glorified Christ.
23. The Septuagint translates the last portion of the verse "and the house was full of his glory." Thus, the language of Isaiah 6 in the *Septuagint* is even closer than the Hebrew.
24. It is at this point that Bauckham falters, merely leaving Jesus at what for him is the "right-hand place." We address this further in the next chapter, but the logical conclusion is not that Jesus is merely "included in the divinity" along with Yahweh. Indeed, New Testament writers regularly equated Yahweh with Jesus. On this see in particular pp. 129-30, 132, 141-2.
25. Raymond Brown, *John*, "Appendix IV," 536-37. While Brown points out that this might refer to the Day of the Lord, I suspect that it has a reference to the Ascension.
26. The word translated inheritance is κληρονομέω. Although it can mean inheritance, it can mean something given by lot as well. On this see Werner Foerster, *TDNT*, 3:767-69, 767. As we suggested above, from the foundation of the world, God planned that the man Jesus would fulfill His mediative role, and so doing would be exalted higher than any man. It was then appointed by God that He would be "named" *Kurios*.
27. Berkhof, *Christian Faith*, 291.
28. Ibid.
29. Prior to John's heavenly vision, there is one reference to the "Son of God" (Revelation 2:18), who is described exactly as the "Son of Man" (Revelation 1:13). The Son of Man is also mentioned in Revelation 14:14 meting out judgment. See 134-5 where we deal with how Revelation blends imagery in its description of the "Son of Man," as well as the implications of such blended imagery.
30. Certainly the Spirit is present speaking to the churches. But the Spirit is ultimately equated with Jesus. On this, see p. 264, note 31. The Spirit is said to have carried John to Heaven (Revelation 4:1), and there are two instances where the text says the Spirit speaks (Revelation 14:13; 22:17), but again, Revelation 22:16 equates Jesus speaking to the churches with the Spirit. There are four mentions of the seven spirits of God (1:4; 3:1; 4:5; 5:6), but these seem to refer to the Spirit working in the seven churches listed. They are at once equated with "seven lamps of fire" (4:5) and the "seven horns and seven eyes" of the Lamb who appears as having been slain (5:6).
31. See p. 130.
32. See p. 120.
33. On the way in which the eschatological Day of Yahweh is applied to Jesus, see p. 116 of Larry Hurtado, *Lord Jesus Christ*. That the eschatological Day of the Lord is applied to the return of Jesus can be seen in a number of passages, including I Corinthians 4:1-5, where Jesus is the Lord who will judge Paul and other believers; so too see Philippians 4:5; the Lord is near. Hurtado finds affinity with this in 1 Enoch 37-71.

34. Gordon D. Fee, *The First Epistle to the Corinthians*, The New International Commentary on the New Testament, (Grand Rapids, MI: Eerdmans, 1987), 754.
35. Ibid., 759.
36. F. W. Grosheide, *Commentary on the First Epistle to the Corinthians*, (Grand Rapids, MI: Eerdmans, 1953), 366-67.
37. C. K. Barrett, *A Commentary on the First Epistle to the Corinthians*, Harper's New Testament Commentaries (1968; repr., New York, Harper & Row, 1993), 361.
38. Grosheide, 369.
39. S. G. Norris was the founder of Apostolic Bible Institute in St. Paul, MN, and he taught there from 1937 until just prior to his death in 1990.

Chapter 12: The Man with the Saving Name

1. See, for instance, John 2:22.
2. On p. 445 of Arthur W. Pink, *The Exposition of the Gospel of John: Three Volumes Complete and Unabridged in One*, (Grand Rapids, MI: Zondervan, 1975), Pink suggests that the "I am He" statement may well have had to do with the divine phenomena surrounding the Crucifixion; this would then demonstrate Jesus' identity.
3. On the double meaning for the Son of Man being lifted up; cf. Bertram, "ὑψόω," 610.
4. John 13:7;13:19; 14:20;14:29; 16:12-13; 16:23-24.
5. Otto Procksch, "ἅγιος," 103-4. Cf. Schweitzer, "πνεῦμα," 418, especially note 568. For example, Schweitzer cites II Corinthians 4:10ff. and Colossians 3:4 where Christ is associated with the giving of life; this same function is ascribed to the Spirit in Galatians 5:25 and II Corinthians 3:6. Whereas in I Thessalonians 1:5, a believer is empowered by the Spirit, in II Corinthians 12:9 and Philippians 4:13 it is Christ who empowers.
6. Carl Judson Davis, *The Name and Way of the Lord: Old Testament Themes, New Testament Christology*, (Sheffield: Sheffield Academic Press, 1996), 128, especially note 91. Davis cites E. Haenchen, *The Acts of the Apostles, A Commentary*, trans. B Noble, G. Shinn, and H. Anderson; rev. R. M. Wilson, (Philadelphia: Westminster, 1971), 484; I. Howard Marshall, *The Acts of the Apostles, An Introduction and Commentary*, TNTC (Grand Rapids, MI: Eerdmans, 1980), 263; F. F. Bruce, *The Book of Acts*, rev. ed., The New International Commentary on the New Testament (Grand Rapids, MI: Eerdmans, 1988), 307; and G. Lüdemann, *Early Christianity according to the Traditions in Acts: A Commentary*, trans. J. Bowden, (London: SCM Press, 1989). For a more tentative view, see James D. G. Dunn, *Jesus and the Spirit: A Study of the Religious and Charismatic Experience of Jesus and the First Christians as Reflected in the New Testament*, (Philadelphia: Westminster, 1975), 180.
7. Schweitzer, "πνεῦμα," 433; Schweitzer notes that "in Romans 8:1-11, πνεῦμα θεοῦ ἐν ὑμῖν (v. 9) alternates with Χριστὸς ἐν ὑμῖν (v. 10), ὑμεις ἐν πνεύματι(v. 9) with τοῖς ἐν Χριστῷ (v. 1)."
8. Berkhof writes, "Often the New Testament speaks of Spirit as a power clearly distinguished from Christ as 'another comforter,' 'the Spirit of Christ,' who leads to Christ and in us prays for the coming of Christ. But the work of the Spirit is also frequently presented as the work of the exalted Christ himself; 'I am with you always,' 'now the Lord is that Spirit,' in the resurrection he becomes 'a life-giving Spirit' and therefore does not leave us as orphans but comes again to us. As a rule this second aspect has been neglected in the study of the faith, because it did not fit the classical trinitarian pattern in which the third 'person' remains clearly distinguished." *Christian Faith*, 330.
9. Geoffrey Wainwright notes on p. 48 of his *Doxology* that even Rudolph Bultmann acknowledged that what was recorded in John 20:28, "My Lord and My God" ('Ο κύριός μου καὶ ὁ θεός μου), was an absolute confession that Jesus Christ was in fact divine. This is the only affirmation of the divinity of Christ that Bultmann allowed, but he nonetheless admitted this one, although he placed it in a "'quasicultic' setting of a Sunday meeting of

Jesus' disciples." Besides John 20:28, Romans 9:5 also calls Jesus God. On p. 137 of C. F. D. Moule's *Christ and Spirit in the New Testament*, (Cambridge: University Press, 1973), Moule notes, "Quite apart from anything that may be gathered by minute considerations of early punctuation, it is syntactically odd, in that particular complex of words, to understand the phrase 'God blessed for evermore' otherwise than as applied to Christ." Cf. Titus 2:13, Hebrews 1:8, etc.
10. Robert Brent Graves, *The God of Two Testaments*, 2nd ed., (Hazelwood, MO: Word Aflame Press, 2000). Graves, along with James S. Turner, originally self published this work in 1977. See also David K. Bernard, "The Use of *Kai*" in *Oneness of the Godhead*, 207–11; and p. 17 of Daniel Segraves's "Reading Packet in Systematic Theology" (unpublished handout, Christian Life College). Segraves appeals to Granville Sharp in his focus on II Peter 1:1 to demonstrate that Jesus Christ is the same person as God.
11. Mike Hall, "Christology of James," (paper for course in christology, Urshan Graduate School of Theology, 2008).
12. Sharp, *Remarks*, 3.
13. Ibid, 95.
14. Sharp's fifth rule allows, "If personal nouns, of the same case, are connected by the copulative, and the first has not the article, they relate to different persons." Sharp, 5.
15. See p. 59.
16. See p. 41.
17. See p. 58.
18. Given the "remnant" language of Acts, it seems clear that Luke presents those on Pentecost of the representative remnant of True Israel, a theme on which Paul also situates himself. The disciples saw themselves as leaders of this remnant. On this, see J. Bernard Chance, *Jerusalem, the Temple, and the New Age in Luke-Acts*, (Macon, GA: Mercer University Press, 1988), 74ff. Cf. Robert P. Brawley, *Text to Text Pours Forth Speech: Voices of Scripture in Luke-Acts*, (Bloomington IN: Indiana University Press, 1995), 82.
19. Gerhard von Rad, *Deuteronomy*, 38-39.20. On this, see chapter 4.
20. Solomen's dedicatory prayer over the Temple emphasizes such a promise.
21. On the theology of "The Name," we are indebted to the work of Reed, "Origins and Development." It was in the Jewish religious schools that the use of *HaShem* began to be the most common. On this, see Bietenhard, "ὄνομα," 268ff. On p. 269, Bietenhard points out that according to one Rabbinic tradition at least, the high priest even began utilizing אֲנָא הַשֵּׁם in lieu of speaking Yahweh.
22. Quell, "κύριος," 1070.
23. Jean Daniélou, *Theology of Jewish Christianity*, 148. Similar themes are traced in Bietenhard, "ὄνομα," 268ff.
24. Richard Longenecker, *Jewish Christianity*, 45.
25. Bietenhard, "ὄνομα," 273. In Acts 5:41, the Greek that is translated in some versions "for his name" is actually "ὑπὲρ γὰρ τοῦ ὀνόματος," the same as III John 7.
26. Ibid., 277.
27. In this regard, see Larry Hurtado, *At the Origins of Christian Worship: The Context and Character of Earliest Christian Devotion*, (Grand Rapids, MI: Eerdmans, 2000), 33. In note 57, Hurtado cites E. Tov, "The Septuagint," *Mikra: Text, Translation, Reading and Interpretation of the Hebrew Bible in Ancient Judaism and Early Christianity*, eds. Martin Jan Mulder and Harry Sysling, CRINT 2 no. 1 (Philadelphia: Fortress Press, 1988), 161-88.
28. *Kurios* would have certainly functioned as a *qere* in Greek-speaking synagogues; that is, when reading the text, instead of speaking *Adonai* in place of *Yahweh* as was the custom in Hebrew-speaking synagogues, *Kurios* would be an acceptable and not too holy name to speak. On this, see Martin Hengel, "Christological Titles in Early Christianity," in *The Messiah: Developments in Earliest Judaism and Christianity*, ed. James H. Charlesworth, (Minneapolis, MN: Fortress Press, 1992), 425-60, 441-42. See also Joseph A. Fitzmyer, "The Languages of Palestine in the First Century A.D.," in *A Wandering Aramean: Collected Aramaic Essays*, (Chico, CA: Scholars Press, 1979), 29–56. There were Jews of

the first century who were reticent to utilize *Kurios* in speaking or writing, just because it was equivalent to the Tetragrammaton. For instance, Josephus would not use *Kurios*, and hence we have in his work very few citations of the biblical text. Cf. Bietenhard, "ὄνομα," 265.

29. See, for instance, Paul's appropriation of Yahweh's worship in Isaiah for Jesus in the hymn upon which we have focused. It is Jesus to which every knee shall bow. It is Jesus to whom every tongue shall confess. On the connection of this hymn to the Ascension, see the previous chapter.

30. See Hurtado, *Lord Jesus Christ*, 112, where he simply offers Pauline references to Jesus as *Kurios*. He writes, "So it is remarkable that, in other citations of the Old Testament passages which originally have to do with God, Paul applies the passages to Jesus, making him the *Kyrios:* Romans 10:13 (Joel 2:32), I Corinthians 1:31 (Jeremiah 9:23-24), I Corinthians 10:26 (Ps. 24:1), II Corinthians 10:17 (Jeremiah 9:23-24). In two other places, it is more difficult to be certain whether it is God or Jesus to whom Paul applies Old Testament citations: Romans 14:11 (Isa. 45:23) and in I Corinthians 2:16 (Isaiah 40:13). There are also a number of cases where Paul alludes to Old Testament passages that mention Yahweh as *Kurios* and Paul clearly makes Jesus as the referent: I Corinthians 10:21 (Mal. 1:7, 12), I Corinthians 10:22 (Deut. 33:21), II Corinthians 3:16 (Exodus 34:34) 1 Thessalonians 3:13 (Zech. 14:3), I Thessalonians 4:6 (Ps. 94:2). But the most striking example is surely Philippians 2:10-11, which appropriates Isaiah 45:23-25 (originally proclaiming universal submission to God) to portray the eschatological acclamation of Jesus as *Kyrios* "to the Glory of God the Father."

31. Hurtado, ibid. In addition to the texts mentioned in the above note, Hurtado offers these additional Pauline texts referencing Jesus which have an Old Testament referent of "God," "Romans 11:13 (I Kings 19:10), Romans 12:19 (Deut. 32:35), I Corinthians 14:21 (Isa. 28:11)." On pp. 53-54 of *God Crucified*, Bauckham points out that on separate occasions, it is both God and Christ who are speaking, making the declaration in Revelation, "I AM the first and the last." In Revelation 1:8, it is God who says "I AM alpha and omega. In Revelation 1:18, it is Christ who says "I AM the first and the last." In Revelation 21:6, it is God who says, "I AM the first and the last, the beginning and the end." In Revelation 22:13, it is Christ who says, "I AM alpha and omega, the first and the last, the beginning and the end." Of course, as Bauckham notes, all of these declarations in Isaiah are first made of Yahweh, who proclaims in Isaiah 44:6, "I AM the first, and I AM the last; besides me there is no God." The same statement is made in Isaiah 48:12, where he says "I AM he, I AM the first and I AM the last."

32. Raymond Brown is not trying to vie for Palestinian origins here, but he is insistent that "the New Testament authors were aware that Jesus was being given a title that in the Septuagint referred to the God of Israel." *Jesus: God and Man*, (New York: MacMillan, 1967), 29.

33. Richard Longenecker, *Christology*, 9. Longenecker recognizes that though the Christ event was central, (incarnation, ministry, passion, and resurrection), Jewish christology was not merely functional but also contained metaphysical presuppositions and ontological overtones.

34. Acts 2:21 citing Joel 2:28-29.

35. See for instance, Richard Bauckham, *God Crucified*, 34. He writes that calling on the name of the Lord "means invoking Jesus as the divine Lord who exercises the divine sovereignty and bears the divine name." Like others, Bauckham links the Acts 2:21 citation from Joel with baptism in Jesus' name in verse 38.

36. James is the preeminent figure in the Jerusalem church, a time in which the Jerusalem church has "a uniquely important role," particularly as it relates to the Jerusalem council in Acts 15. Bauckham, "James and the Jerusalem Church," in *The Book of Acts in its Palestinian Setting*, ed. Richard Bauckham, (Grand Rapids, MI: Eerdmans, 1995), 416.

37. Dahl provides numerous instances where in the Torah and the Prophets Yahweh promised those addressed would be a "people before me" (קדמי). He further shows where this phrase was preceded by לשמי in older Targums of the same passage. For instance, the Fragment

Targum Exod. 19:6, Cod. Par. 110. has קדמי, while fragment F and other older prints have לשמי. For Dahl then, some of the targumim get even closer to the basis for James's speech in passages from Ezekiel and from Zechariah 2:15. "A People for his Name," 321.
38. Acts 15:16, quoting Amos 9:11. James's use of the Tabernacle of David is debated. On p. 265 of his *Acts of the Apostles,* Luke Timothy Johnson takes this to mean the kingdom of David in a messianic sense, finding a similar meaning in certain Qumran materials: *CD* 7:16; *4QFlor* 1:12, 13.
39. See note 48 on p. 262, on Amos 9:12.
40. James's use of "called by my name" (ἐπικέκληται τὸ ὄνομά μου ἐπ' αὐτούς) is similar to the septuagintal use in *Baruch* and in *I Maccabees*. In *Baruch* 2:26, Yahweh's name is called upon the Temple (ἐπεκλήθη τὸ ὄνομά σου); Yahweh's name is in *Baruch* 2:15 to call over Israel and their progeny (ὅτι τὸ ὄνομά σου ἐπεκλήθη ἐπὶ Ισραηλ καὶ ἐπὶ τὸ γένος αὐ᾽του); in *I Maccabees* 7:37, the priests prayed for protection, offering to Yahweh that "You have chosen to call this house (the Temple) by your name (σὺ ἐξελέξω τὸν οἶκον τοῦτον ἐπικληθῆναι τὸ ὄνομά σου)."
41. Bruce, *Acts*, 294.
42. Everyone from Adolf Harnack in the last century to James D. G. Dunn today offers the notion that Jesus was worshiped but was essentially less than God. Harnack attributes the use of *kurios* as applied to Jesus as mere carelessness. He writes, "The carelessness of the early Christian writers about the bearing of the word [*kurios*] in particular cases, shows that in a religious relation, so far as there was reflection on the gift of salvation, Jesus could take the place of God." Harnack, *History of Dogma*, 1:183.
43. Bauckham, "Jesus, Worship of," *ABD*, 3:812-19, 815.
44. Bauckham, *God Crucified*, 41.
45. Bauckham, ibid., 27. As we have suggested above, Bauckham's claim is that Jesus was considered divine, yet this is in a kind of binitarian sense. But it is likely that Bauckham misses the mark by his Christian pre-understanding. Indeed, the confessions have everything to do with Jesus the man who may be spoken of as God; as Harnack points out, it is precisely when the confessor speaks of Jesus' suffering and death that the profession of Jesus' divinity is most avidly claimed. There is in these confessions the language of an "exalted paradox" celebrating both the humanity and the divinity of Jesus. Certainly one sees these kinds of confessions in the earliest fathers. See Ignatius, *To the Romans*, 6:3; Tatian, *Oration to the Greeks* 13; *1 Clement* 2:10. Indeed, despite his harangue against modalism, Tertullian also speaks frequently of the crucifying of God, the flesh of God, and the death of God. Harnack suggests that this kind of speaking was normative and was not even subjected to examination until the Patripassian controversy. See Harnack, 1:186-87, note 4.
46. Paul A. Rainbow, "Jewish Monotheism as the Matrix for New Testament christology: A Review Article, Jewish Monotheism and N. T. christology," *Novum Testamentum*, 33 no. 1 (1991): 78-91, 79. While it is Larry Hurtado's position that Rainbow is critiquing, his comments are applicable to either Dunn or Bauckham. Further, on p. 82, Rainbow reemphasizes the integrity of Jewish monotheism by citing the historical evidence for the use of the *Shema* as "the nearest equivalent in Judaism to a confession of faith." See note 9 on this page where Rainbow refers to Albright substantiating its use for catechism or liturgy dating back to the second century BC. In note 10, he also traces evidence for this at Qumran through the work of F. E. Volkes. On p. 83, Rainbow cites four "ancient Jewish sources" which "expressly state that monotheism or the *Shema*, or the first commandment of the Decalogue, is the 'first' item in the Jewish way of life."
47. Deuteronomy 6:4 (*Tanak*).

Chapter 13: Moving Away from Orthodoxy

1. It is generally accepted that John, say, or Paul had to address construals of Christ that stripped Him of His true humanity or were otherwise incorrect. For instance, Colossians 1-2 specifically addresses a christology deemed to be patently false.

2. Here we do not have in mind dynamic monarchianism, though that is certainly false. Yet, we would not even consider this under the aegis of Oneness christology, for it denies the divinity of Christ. Nor do we have in mind adoptionism, either at the baptism of Jesus or at His ascension. What we are suggesting are a couple of different kinds of modalistic construals, among them positions we have termed "Noetian Modalism" and "Sabellian Modalism."

3. Wolfson, *Philosophy*. Wolfson argues that philosophical constructs aided the evolutionary development of the Trinity. He tracks movement from a two-stage "Theory of *Logos*" to a one-stage theory. He then demonstrates how Platonic ideas served to propel the prototrinitarian thought of Origen and Tertullian. For Wolfson, it was ultimately the incorporation of Plotinian interpretation that allowed a full-orbed Trinity, one that allowed for the elevation of the *Logos* and the Spirit to the status of God.

4. On the way that both Origen and Tertullian framed their christology over against Oneness christology, see chapter 14.

5. On the specific development of the *Logos* as it relates to Platonic thought, see in particular Wolfson, *Philosophy*, 257-86.

6. McGrath, *Christian Theology*, 18-19; citing *On Christian Doctrine*, II.xl.60-61. Augustine analogously notes that while the Egyptians possessed both idols as well as vessels of gold, silver, and clothes; while the children of Israel left the idols, they took what was good when they fled from Egypt. Thus, the Christian can separate "these truths from their unfortunate associations." Augustine goes on to say, "Look at the wealth of gold and silver and clothes which Cyprian—that eloquent teacher and blessed martyr—brought with him out of the land of Egypt." Augustine further acknowledges Marius Victorinus, Optatus, and Hilary of Poiters as further examples of those who had taken the gold and silver and clothes from Egypt.

7. Eusebius notes, "the great mass of people not capable of understanding this conception of God," those he suggests are "afraid of seeming to introduce a second God, declaring that Father and Son are in the same." Eusebius, *Ecclesiastical Theology*, Book 1, trans. B. E. Daley, (Harvard University, unpublished, 1983). On Origen, see Jules Lebreton and Jacques Zeiller, *The History of the Primitive Church*, 2 vols., (New York: Macmillan, 1949), 2:731. They are citing *In Titum*, in vol. 14 of *Patrologia Graeca*, ed. Jacques P. Migne, p. 1304. For Origen, a Oneness christological position represented the "mass of believers," who knew only "the Christ according to the flesh."

8. We have in mind not only Justin; in particular, we reference Tertullian who acknowledged as much; further such an interpretation is confirmed by academics. On this, see chapter 14.

9. As Harnack suggests, around the end of the third century there was a significant conflict with those who held a kind of *Logos* christology by Oneness adherents who sought to exclude every christology but their own, *History of Dogma*, 3:54. See also pp. 50-51 where Harnack offers a significant number of sources that work toward establishing the extent of modalism.

10. Those in this position Pierre Bourdieu calls "orthodox," while those in the dissenting group he terms "heterodox." The dominant group works to define the language in such a way so that they and they alone are correct. Bourdieu states on p. 170 of *An Outline of a Theory of Practice*, (Cambridge: Cambridge University Press, 1977), "Because any language that can command attention is an 'authorized language,' invested with the authority of the group, the things it designates are not merely expressed, but also authorized and legitimated." Bourdieu emphasizes this fundamental censorship of those things that can be stated, and hence those things that can be "thought, and hence the universe which can be taken for granted."

11. Pierre Bourdieu analogously frames verbal competition in economic terms where words are a kind of "capital" with which to argue. Those who are empowered essentially control the capital. Capital is seen by Bourdieu to be a basis of domination (although not recognized by the participants). On this, see "The Basic Theoretical Position," in *An Introduction to the Work of Pierre Bourdieu: The Practice of Theory*, eds. Richard Harker,

Cheleen Mahar, and Chris Wilkes (London: MacMillan, 1990), 13.
12. J. N. D. Kelly, *Early Christian Doctrines*, (Hagerstown, MD: Harper & Row, 1978), 119.
13. Tertullian, *Against Praxeas* 2, *ANF,* 3:598. Tertullian states that Praxean Modalism was *new*, suggesting that Praxeas was a "pretender of yesterday." He argued that it be rejected both because of "the lateness of date which marks all heresies, and also from the absolute novel character of our new-fangled Praxeas."
14. Tertullian, *Prax.* 31, *ANF,* 3:627. See p. 287, note 25 for full text.
15. Tertullian, *Prax.* 3, *ANF,* 3:598-99. For Origen as well, those with a Oneness christology were "uninstructed and simple." *Cels.* 16.1.
16. Hippolytus writes, "At that time the Monarchian controversy agitated the whole church." Harnack, *History of Dogma*, p. 53 citing Hippolytus, *Refutation of All Heresies* 9.6
17. Harnack, *History of Dogma*, 3:71.
18. Ibid., 72.
19. Bietenhard has demonstrated that in the Jewish language and culture of the day, "the Name" was used to represent God. "ὄνομα," *TDNT*, 5:242, 694. See p. 140.
20. Richard Longenecker, *Christology*, 45.
21. Daniélou, *Theology of Jewish Christianity*, 151ff.; on p. 153, he notes that "*Sim.* IX identifies 'bearing the Name' with 'being baptized': 'If thou bear (φορεῖν) the Name, and bear not his power, thou shalt bear His name to none effect. And the stones which thou didst see cast away, these bear the Name, but clothed not themselves with the raiment of virgins' (IX, 13:2f.)."
22. Justin is certainly aware of this kind of speaking as evidenced by his *Dialogue with Trypho* 128.
23. Jean Daniélou, *The History of Early Christian Doctrine Before the Council of Nicea*, Vol. 3, *The Origen of Latin Christianity*, ed. John Austin Baker, trans. John Austin Baker and David Smith, (Philadelphia, PA: Westminster, 1977), 158. While Daniélou posits that this is a Judaeo-Christian *testimonium*, it is certainly known by Tertullian, and as Daniélou admits, he borrows from it readily.
24. Unless otherwise indicated, monarchianism has reference to Oneness christology and serves as an umbrella term for such. Historians also utilize Modalistic Monarchianism as well. The other sort of monarchianism is Dynamic Monarchianism, which preserves the oneness of God by disallowing Jesus to be divine. This is not in view unless specifically indicated.
25. This is not to suggest that Praxeas was Jewish; however, Tertullian on more than one occasion derides the Praxean construal as a Jewish way of thinking. See Tertullian, who says of Praxeas, "but, (this doctrine of yours bears a likeness) to the Jewish faith, of which this is the substance—so to believe in One God as to refuse to reckon the Son besides Him, and after the Son the Spirit. Now, what difference would there be between us and them, if there were not this distinction *which you are for breaking down*?" Tertullian goes on to charge Praxeas, "What need would there be of the gospel, which is the substance of the New Covenant, laying down (as it does) that the Law and the Prophets lasted until John the Baptist, if thenceforward the Father, the Son, and the Spirit, are not both believed in as Three, and as making One Only God? God was pleased to renew His covenant with man in such a way as that His Unity might be believed in, after a new manner, through the Son and the Spirit, in order that God might be known openly, in His proper Names and Persons, who in ancient times was not plainly understood, though declared through the Son and the Spirit." *Prax.*, 31, *ANF,* 3:627.
26. Daniélou, *The Origen of Latin Christianity*, 157.
27. Ibid.
28. Ibid., 159.
29. Ibid., 151ff.
30. On this, see chapters 11 and 15. If this is the same James that decreed in Acts 15 that the name of Jesus invoked in baptism was sufficient to fulfill the prophecy of Amos that *Yahweh's* name would be called over the Gentiles, this is particularly significant.
31. Daniélou, 151ff.

32. The *Shepherd of Hermas* was likely written in the late first century or early second century AD and is of Italian origin. On the possible range of dates and possible recensions of the *Shepherd of Hermas*, see Carolyn Osiek, *The Shepherd of Hermas*, ed. Helmut Koester, (Minneapolis: Fortress Press, 1999), 8-10; 18-20.
33. As Osiek notes on p. 21 of *Shepherd of Hermas*, "The Shepherd of Hermas in genre is not particularly literary, and belongs to 'the common people.'" On p. 56 of Robert M. Grant's *Jesus After the Gospels*, he is rightly suspect of the Muratorian list that makes Hermas brother of Pius in Rome.
34. Osiek, 36.
35. Ibid., 34–35. Osiek allows that while in fact Hebrews may be a refutation of such christology, it might also be that the language of "angelic being" may mean that Christ is the commander in chief of angels, as in the *Ascension of Isaiah*. Still, this is far from certain, for as she allows, this is difficult to interpret in light of its apocalyptic genre.
36. Harnack, *History of Dogma*, 1:191, note 1.
37. Ibid., 187; especially note 4, which continues from 186-88.
38. Daniélou notes that the earliest form of *Hermas* was not "Name of the Son of God" but the "Name of God." See *Theology of Jewish Christianity*, 151-52, where Daniélou gives a lengthy argument for the "Son of God" as secondary.
39. Ibid., 153.
40. Ibid., 155; Daniélou writes, "There are other allusions to *Hermas* in a baptismal context, but in this case they are related to the epiclesis. The writer speaks, for example, 'of renegades which were ashamed of the Name of the Lord which was invoked (ἐπικληθέν) upon them' (*Sim.* VIII, 6:4), and later of those 'who are called (ἐπικαλούμενοι) by the Name of the Lord.' (*Sim.* IX, 14:3, cf. κεκλημένοι. *Sim.* VIII, 1:1)."
41. Daniélou, *Theology of Jewish Christianity*, 153; citing Clement of Alexandria, *Excerpts from Theodotus* 86.2.
42. For this discussion of the Ebionites, I am indebted to Glen Koch. Dr. Koch served as my thesis advisor (on the subject of modalism). One clue that the Ebionites go back to the beginning is their very appellation means "poor" in Hebrew. He is not alone to suggest that Ebionites descend from the earliest Jewish Christians. See *History of Dogma*, 1:299-300, where Harnack suggests that Origen wrote that the Ebionites were believing Jews, descended from the earliest Christians. On Origen's writing, see note 1 on p. 300 where Harnack cites numerous examples. Surprisingly, a portion of these Ebionites even recognized the virgin birth, as attested by Origen.
43. Hans-Joachim Schoeps, *Jewish Christianity: Factional Disputes in the Early Church*, trans. Douglas R. A. Hare, (Philadelphia: Fortress Press, 1969), 36. Schoeps suggests that there was in fact considerable diversity as to what the Ebionites believed. The Ebionite Church continued in the area of Transjordan for three hundred to three hundred fifty years and as time went on, they came to believe not one, but many different things, along "several lines of development." Schoeps continues, "The statement of Epiphanius (*Pan.* 30.14) that 'Ebion' was a 'many-headed monster' is significant."
44. Schoeps, *Jewish Christianity*, 11. Schoeps notes that there was no one named "Ebion," as Tertullian, Hippolytus, Epiphanius, and other church fathers deduce. Rather, this was probably a name the group applied to themselves post AD 70, calling into remembrance Jesus' beatitudes concerning the poor (Hebrew *Ebion*). On p. 18, Schoeps links the Ebionites and the Nazoreans, drawing the post 70 date in part from Epiphanius's *Panarion (Adversus haereses)*, 30.27; 29.5.4. Hurtado, too, is suspicious of the lack of evidence. On p. 431 of his *Lord Jesus Christ*, he offers that "almost everything depends on how one views the various secondhand characterizations of them in patristic sources (which are usually hostile, and often seem confused)."
45. On the Ebionites, see Karl Baus, *History of the Christian Church*, vol. 1, *From the Apostolic Community to Constantine*, (New York: Seabury Press, 1980), 154.
46. See H 11 25–32; 26 recorded in *Kerygmatic Petrou, The Pseudo-Clementines*, in the *New Testament Apocrypha*.

47. Ibid; H 27 uses the language "baptized for salvation," "for the forgiveness of sins"; cf. *Recognitions* 1:55; we know this through Epiphanius's *Pan.* 30.6.9. and others.
48. That the earliest Christian community believed this is discussed at length in chapter 16.
49. Epiphanius (*Pan.* 30.14).
50. Baus, *History*, 154.
51. Ebionites had the notion that "the concept of dwelling formed the imagery of the presence of the True Prophet in Jesus: Having appeared first in an incomplete way in the prophets in the Old Testament, the True Prophet has reached completion in the Messiah Jesus and has come to rest 'for ever.' " On this, see Schoeps, *Jewish Christianity*, 72.
52. The destruction of the Temple is historically seen as significant in Judaism, but there is a way this destruction propelled a certain kind of diversity in Christianity as well. So long as Jerusalem headquartered the church and was the nominal center of Christian faith, then this Jewish Christian locale functioned symbolically. Just as there was an incredible epistemological response within Judaism itself, so Jewish Christianity would have been especially affected by such a blow.
53. Harnack, *History of Dogma*, 1:300, note 2; Harnack cites Eusebius (*Ecclesiastical History* 3 5.3) for the information that Christians fled to Pella, in Perea, before the destruction of that city. Harnack writes, "In the following period the most important settlements of the Ebionites must have been in the countries east of the Jordan, and in the heart of Syria." Harnack, citing Jerome, *De viris illustribus* 3, continues, "This fact explains how the bishops in Jerusalem and the coast towns of Palestine came to see very little of them. There was a Jewish Christian community in Beroea with which Jerome had relations."
54. Richard Longenecker, *Christology*, 8. Longenecker posits that there were already tendencies within this community toward protognosticism and incipient Ebionism. Regarding the Ebionites, it seems fair to suggest that particularly as they became more isolated, a trajectory away from the mainstream would develop.
55. Harnack, *History of Dogma*, 1:290. First-century Jewish Christians formed the majority in Palestine, and perhaps also in some neighboring provinces, but in fact, as the church grew more "catholic," their influence was left behind.
56. Pierre Bourdieu, who does work on competition between groups, suggests that an orthodox position in facts suggests an opposite heterodox position. Thus, the more Jesus became a Hellenic *Logos*, the more this would have suggested that Jesus was rather a Jewish prophet! On the use of Pierre Bourdieu for a religious argument, see my *No Other Name*, 223. Cf. Pierre Bourdieu, *Language and Symbolic Power*, ed. John B. Thompson, trans. Gino Raymond and Matthew Adamson, (Cambridge, MA: Harvard University Press, 1991); cf. Bourdieu, *Theory of Practice*, 167-69.
57. Longenecker, *Christology*, 16. Longenecker notes, "The so-called Apostolic Fathers, the Apologists . . . and others who wrote from within Gentile Christianity; and none, with the possible exceptions of Clement of Rome and the author of the Shepherd of Hermas, can be claimed to have had any type of background in Judaism personally."
58. Geoffrey Wainwright, *Doxology*, 50-51. Wainwright cites the letters of Ignatius of Antioch, "written about the year 110, contain hymns in praise of Christ which predicate things of him in the third person." Wainwright notes that while at the beginning of the second century, prayer to Christ was common in the third person, the practice grew of addressing hymns directly to Christ in the second person in the second and third centuries. Cf. Harnack, *History of Dogma*, 1:166. As Harnack notes, "Here sacred formulae were fashioned and delivered to the members." This material could at the same time praise God and Christ. See particularly note 3, where Harnack tracks the earliest Christian communities that gave expression to their faith by hymns and prayers and attested boldly to the deity of Christ.
59. Harnack, ibid.
60. Ibid., 188, note 4. Citing Eusebius, H. E. 5.28.4-6, Harnack writes, "throughout Ignatius, θεὸς appears as a designation for Christ. He is called ὁ θεὸς ἡμῶν in the Ephes. Inscript;

Rom. Inscr. bis 3.2; Polyc. 8.3. Eph. 1.1, αἷμα θεοῦ; Rom. 6.3, τὸ πάθος τοῦ θεοῦ μου; Eph. 7. 2. ἐν σαρκὶ γενόμενος θεός; in another reading ἐν ἀνθρώπῳ θεός, Smyrn. I. 1, Ἰησοῦς Χριστός ὁ θεὸς ὁ οὕτως ὑμᾶς σοφίσας. The latter passage, in which the relative clause must be closely united with ὁ θεὸς, seems to form the transition for the three passages (Trall. 7.1; Smyrn. 6.1; 10.1), in which Jesus is called θεὸς without addition."
61. See Acts 20:28; the NKJV translates this "the church of God, which He purchased with His own blood." The textual history of the Greek manuscripts that lie behind this seems to indicate that the Greek text changed *theos* to *kurios* because it became offensive as church history evolved that God could shed His own blood. Because the textual evidence on the verse is mixed, some versions read "the church of the Lord. . . ."
62. Ignatius, *To Polycarp* 3:2.
63. Ignatius, *To the Magnesians* 13.1.
64. While it is possible for Ignatius to refer on a particular occasion to the Father, Son, and Holy Spirit the occasional usage should be understood to glorify God through the work of Jesus Christ in the age of the Spirit. On this, see Harnack, *History of Dogma*, 1:80, note 1.
65. Robert M. Grant, *Gods and One God*, (Philadelphia: Westminster, 1986), 107–8; Grant has pointed out the multiplicity of ways in which Ignatius was used. The Antiochenes appealed to Ignatius as authoritative to support their "two-natures" emphasis. However, the Alexandrians promptly replied by utilizing Ignatius for the contrary position that stressed the union of natures in Christ after the Incarnation. Both Monophysites and those who held to the creedal position of Chalcedon also claimed Ignatius as an ally. On this, see Grant's "The Appeal to the Early Fathers," in *Journal of Theological Studies* 11 (1960): 13-24, 16ff.
66. William R. Schoedel, *Ignatius of Antioch: A Commentary on the Letters of Ignatius of Antioch*, ed. Helmut Koester, (Philadelphia: Fortress Press, 1985), 20. Schoedel argues that Daniélou has missed the mark in that there is nothing Jewish Christian about Ignatius. Yet the way Ignatius speaks is primarily Monarchian modalism. But as we suggested of Oneness christology and the biblical texts, Oneness christology can in fact fit more than one category of speaking. As Schoedel points out, like the biblical writers before him, Ignatius may sound subordinationist (Ephesians 3:1-2); he may use language that is on the surface adoptionist (*Smyrn.* 1.1. cf. *Magn.* 8:2). He may even speak of Christ as having existed with the Father before the ages (*Magn.* 6.1), but there is, in Ignatius, no emphasis on a "precosmic Christ." Thus, on the whole the texts freely impute suffering to Christ while overtly calling Jesus God and even reveling in the ambiguity, lending the most support to modalist leanings. Here Schoedel is agreeing with Virginia Corwin's assessment on pp. 140-41 of her *St. Ignatius and Christianity in Antioch*, (New Haven: Yale University Press, 1960). Corwin writes, "If one term must be chosen to indicate the tendency of his thought, Ignatius must be said to be monarchian, though he is very close to the point later declared to be orthodox."
67. Grant, *Jesus After the Gospels*, 57. Ignatius's *To the Ephesians* 7.2 is a hymnic piece that poetically frames christology in polar opposites of Jesus highlighting both the humanity and divinity of Jesus. On this, see also Reinhard Deichgräber, *Gotteshymnus und Christhymnus in der frühen Christenheit, Untersuchungen zu Form, Sprache und Stil der frühchristlichen Hymnen*, (Göttengin: Nadenhoeck & Ruprecht, 1967), 155ff.
68. "εἷς ἰατρός ἐστιν." While Liddell and Scott rightly note that ἰατρός is anyone who heals and that no "professional" distinction is made, the context of the hymn is to suggest it as a soteriological title. Indeed, it was common to portray Jesus as healer in the literature of the time. Henry George Liddell and Robert Scott, *A Greek-English Lexicon*, (Oxford: Clarendon Press, 1968), 691.
69. See Robert M. Grant, "The Appeal to the Early Fathers," 16-19. Ignatius was modified so that the suffering of God disappears in the longer recensions. Of the four texts described above, in all but Romans 6:3, the link is severed. "In Ephesians inscr. τοῦ θεοῦ becomes τοῦ σωτῆρος; in Ephesians 1:1 θεοῦ is changed to χριστοῦ, while in Ephesians 18:2, ὁ γάρ

θεός ἡμῶν Ἰησοῦς becomes ὁ γάρ τοῦ θεοῦ and τῷ πάθει disappears altogether." Consider as well the hymnic piece cited above.
70. See p. 121 of Melito of Sardis, (chapter 45) *On the Passover*, in *After the New Testament: A Reader in Early Christianity*, ed. Bart D. Ehrman, (New York: Oxford University Press, 1999).
71. On p. 173 of his *Christian Tradition*, Pelikan cites this as proof that Christians were sure that the Redeemer did not belong to some lower order of divine reality, but was God himself. To demonstrate this, Pelikan quotes a number of sources, among them *2 Clement*. On this, see also Harnack 1:186, note 3, which also cites Barnabas 7.2.
72. Harnack, *History of Dogma*, 1:186. Thus *2 Clement* boldly celebrates Jesus as God. Yet, while one might rightly find some affinity in *2 Clement* with Oneness christology, it would be too much to suggest that one can identify a particular christological formulation in the book.
72. Melito of Sardis, *Fragments* 13-14; cited in Pelikan, *Christian Tradition*. 177.
73. Melito, *Fragments* 105. In the same work, see as well similar language in chapters 9 and 65.
74. Ibid., 13-14.

Chapter 14: Apologists and the Hermeneutical Shift

1. The apologists were given this label for their defense of the Christian faith, particularly in the face of persecution. They included largely second-century spokesmen of Christianity, though this not a rigid demarcation.
2. Philosophically, from 80 BC to AD 220, the kind of Platonism to flourish is known as Middle Platonism. Robert M. Berchman, *From Philo to Origen: Middle Platonism in Transition*, (Chico, CA: Scholars Press, 1984).
3. To what degree there was direct influence of Philo on Justin is debated, but whether direct or indirect, an influence is certainly present. See Runia, *Philo*, 140, for various theories of dependency. Runia proposes three possible ways that Justin could have been dependent. First, it may be that Justin knew Philo and drew from him, but did so in a very free way, which makes it impossible to determine his debts with precision; second, it could well be that Justin gained acquaintance with Philo early in his career, but later lost track of his works, so that similarities are obscured by the passing of time and personal development; or third, it could be that Justin was acquainted with themes from Hellenistic Judaism, but through other channels, which differ from Philo. As more than one church historian has noted, the chief followers of Philo were not so much Jews, but Christian intellectuals of the second and third centuries. As Colin Brown rightly notes on p. 66 of his *Christianity & Western Thought*, Philo stands closer to Origen and Clement than to rabbinic tradition or say, to Jesus or the apostle Paul.
4. McGrath, *Christian Theology*, 144.
5. For instance, since the Old Testament plainly taught the participation of God fully with His creation, it could not be regarded highly as an interpretive tool for those who vied for the transcendence of God. Marcion (ca.150) actually taught that the Old Testament was the product of a "lower creator God" who could only act according to the law of retribution. He had no use for it. On this, see Berkhof, *Christian Faith*, 226ff.
6. Luise Abramowski, "The 'Memoirs of the Apostles' in Justin," in *The Gospel and the Gospels*, ed. Peter Stuhlmacher, (Grand Rapids, MI: Eerdmans, 1991), 323-35, 327-28.
7. In his *2 Apology* 10.8, Justin would offer that Christ had been "known in part even by Socrates."
8. Wolfson, *Philosophy*, 11.
9. Willis A. Shotwell, *The Biblical Exegesis of Justin Martyr*, (London: SPCK, 1965), 21. Shotwell cites *Dialogue with Trypho* 127.2, noting that since God is unmovable, "thus it is safe to assume that Justin thought of God as unchangeable."

10. See chapter 3 above for a lengthy discussion of Philo's approach and method. On Justin's allegorical method, see p. 46 of Shotwell's *Biblical Exegesis of Justin Martyr.* Shotwell suggests Justin's method on deriving this conclusion might be termed "philosophical allegory," but it could also be categorized as an argument from analogy. On the similarities between Philo and Justin's interpretive method; cf. Erwin R. Goodenough's *Jewish Symbols in the Greco-Roman Period,* (New York: Pantheon Books, 1953), 47-52. Not only did the significant methodological shift have implications for christology, but there were serious ongoing methodological consequences as well. Justin's use of Greek philosophers while still retaining a Christian worldview was the first in a string of philosophers whose influence would carry through the Middle Ages even to the present. See N. Max Wildier, *The Theologian and His Universe: Theology and Cosmology from the Middle Ages to the Present,* (New York: The Seabury Press, 1982), 30.
11. H. Kleinknecht, "λέγω" B, in *TDNT,* 77-91, 81.
12. T. E. Pollard, *Johannine Christology and the Early Church,* (Cambridge: Cambridge University Press, 1970), 38.
13. Shotwell, *The Biblical Exegesis of Justin Martyr,* 104. Shotwell notes that in Justin the *Logos* is said to be begotten as a beginning before all of God's creatures (*Dialog* 61.1). Yet in *1 Apology* 53 he speaks of the first begotten (πρωτότοκος) of the unbegotten God and in *1 Apology* 58 he speaks of the first born of God (πρωτότογονος). While he uses the analogy of the *Logos* coming from God as light from the sun, (*Dialog* 128), it is important that there is a difference in number. He uses a philosophical figure common in his day (emanations), so it may well be that Justin is the one making the philosophical distinction.
14. *2 Apology* 6.
15. Although Justin could offer in *2 Apology* 13, in an effort to incorporate philosophers in a Christian sphere, "and whatsoever things were rightly said among all men are the property of us Christians," this understanding was received unevenly.
16. Justin Martyr's work was in some way a new genre, and in it he evolved a kind of speaking that sought to incorporate the language of philosophy with the language of church teaching. On Justin's work in the context of the development of the Trinity, see Daniélou, *Gospel Message and Hellenistic Culture.*
17. This hierarchical worship is also found in Athenagoras, *Legatio pro Christianis* 10.5, or *Cels.* 8.13, Bauckham, "Jesus, Worship of," 818.
18. Bauckham, *God Crucified,* 78.
19. Whereas in Hebrew, the construction of the Hebrew "I am that I am" connoted Yahweh's power and supremacy, in Greek the meaning was much different. It was rather interpreted to mean that God is ineffable.
20. See his *1 Apology* 63. On Justin's exegetical method, cf. Shotwell, *Biblical Exegesis of Justin Martyr.* Justin largely uses the Old Testament as proof-texting to demonstrate that Jesus is the Messiah. Only when it is in his favor will he point to context; even then, it is quite selective, and always designed to propel his particular argument.
21. Paula Fredriksen, *From Jesus to Christ: The Origins of the New Testament Images of Jesus,* (New Haven and London: Yale University Press, 1988), 14. Fredriksen writes, "Similarly, when the Lord established the heavens 'by a word' (Ps 33:6), the Hebrew *davar* became the Greek *logos*: the Creator had suddenly acquired a very Hellenistic factotum." Greek concepts, in brief, did not need to be read into Scripture. They were already there, by virtue of the new language of the text.
22. Clement of Alexandria, *Tutor (Paedagogus)* 8.71.1.
23. Origen, *On First Principles* 1.3.6. *Die griechischen christlichen Schriftsteller der ersten drei Jahrhunderte,* 22:57 ; *Prayer* 24.2 *Die griechischen christlichen Schriftsteller der ersten drei Jahrhunderte,* 3:354.
24. The English reflects Brenton's translation of the Septuagint.

25. C. R. Seitz, "Handing Over the Name," in *Trinity, Time, and Church: A Response to the Theology of Robert W. Jenson*, ed. Colin D. Gunton, (Grand Rapids, MI: Eerdmans, 2000), 36.
26. Harnack notes that there are passages "from Justin's dialogue that indicate the direct designation of Jesus as θεός (not as ὁ θεός) was common in communities; but not only are there some passages in Justin himself to be urged against this, but also the testimony of other writers, θεός, even without the article, was in no case a usual designation for Jesus. On the contrary, it was always quite definite occasions that led them to speak of Christ as of a God, or as God. In the first place there were Old Testament passages, such as Ps 45:8, 110:1ff., etc. which as soon as they were interpreted in relation to Christ, led to this predicate θεός. These passages, with many others taken from the Old Testament, were used in this way by Justin." *History of Dogma*, 1:187, note 4.
27. *Dialogue with Trypho*, 128.
28. Wolfson, *Philosophy*, 310.
29. Arthur Cushman McGiffert, *The God of the Early Christians*, (New York: Charles Scribner's Sons, 1924), 80, citing Justin Martyr, *1 Apology* 63.
30. Richard Longenecker, *Christology*, 17. Longenecker offers, "There is no question but that Justin possessed only an outsider's knowledge of Judaism itself, and a far from complete understanding of early Jewish Christianity."
31. Harnack, *History of Dogma*, 1:291-92.
32. Claus Westermann, "Das Alte Testament und die Theologie," in *Theology—was ist das?* eds. Georg Picht and Enno Rudolph, (Stuttgart: Kreuz Verlag, 1977), 49-66, 50; cited in Rowe, "Biblical Pressure," 295. Cf. Berkhof, *Christian Faith*, 226, where he offers, "In the first century, when the gospel entered a world permeated by Hellenistic, Gnostic, and syncretistic ideas, many soon came to feel the relation to the Old Testament as an obstacle for a truly contemporary interpretation."
33. Wilhelm Schneemelcher, ed., *New Testament Apocrypha*, vol. 2; *Writings Relating to the Apostles; Apocalypses and Related Subjects*, Eng. vers. trans. and ed. R. M. Wilson, (Louisville, KY: Westminster/John Knox, 1992), 113. As Schneemelcher notes, "Everything proceeds as if it were the same deity who alternatively receives the predicates 'Lord' (κύριος), 'God' (θεός), 'Jesus', 'Master' (δεσπότης), 'unbegotten' (ἀγένητος), 'light' (φῶς). . . . It must in addition be emphasized that the AA [Acts of Andrew] never brings two divine persons into relation with one another."
34. Ibid., 234.
35. *The Acts of John*, Ehrman, *Reader*, 11.
36. *The Acts of Thomas* 53, Ehrman, Reader, 16. In this example, Judas Thomas prays to Jesus for a dead woman, "We beg of you and entreat that in your holy name you raise this woman lying here by your power."
37. *The Acts of Paul and Thecla* 24, Ehrman, *Reader*, 281.
38. Ibid., chapter 29, 282.
39. Ibid., chapter 34, 283.
40. Ibid., chapter 42, 284.
41. *Acts of Peter*, Ehrman, *Reader*, 263.
42. Ibid., chapter 5, 265.
43. H. C. Kee, *Testaments of the Twelve Patriarchs*, in vol. 1, *The Pseudepigrapha of the Old Testament*, ed. James H. Charlesworth, (New York: Doubleday, 1983), 777. Kee asserts that while de Jonge would argue for a Christian author, he would agree with Charles's original assessment that the christological entries are interpolations. Nonetheless, they reflect a particular trajectory of christology ca. AD 200.
44. Ibid., 810.
45. Ibid., 813.
46. Ibid., 818.
47. Ibid., 801.

48. Ibid., 787.
49. Ibid., 789–90. One exception is that in the *Testament of Levi*, 5, there appears to be a kind of angelic christology, where when the Most High was sitting on the throne, He was asked His name, and answered, "I am an angel who makes intercession for Israel."
50. Bauckham, "Jesus, Worship of," 814.
51. Ibid. Bauckham cites numerous ancient witnesses.
52. Ibid.
53. On this, see John J. Clabeaux, "Marcion," *ABD*, 4:514-16, 515. It seems to me that there are more docetic leanings in Marcion's christology. Thus, his modalism would be more like that of Sabellius, one with Stoic tendencies.
54. Harnack, *History of Dogma*, 1:196, note 1. Harnack notes that "Marcion put no value in the distinctions between Christ and God." See also 1:275-76, where Harnack demonstrates that the fluidity of the Marcionite tradition allowed for some Patripassianism in the West."
55. See Ronald E. Heine, "Montanus, Montanism," *ABD*, 4:898-902, 902. Didymus of Alexandria accuses Montanus and those who followed him of believing that "the same one is a Father, Son, and Holy Spirit" (a caricaturizing of modalism); Heine allows that while Montanus did not believe this, it is certain that those among his followers did.
56. Harnack, *History of Dogma*, 1:196, note 1. Harnack offers, "Marcion and a part [of] the Montanists—both bear witness to old traditions—put no value on the distinction between God and Christ." Harnack suggests that in Rome in 220, there were two different parties of Montanists; one which followed the teaching of Hippolytus (an anti-modalist), and another which followed Proculus.
57. Ibid.
58. Harnack, *History of Dogma*, 1:196, note 1. Cf. the Apoc. Sophon. A witness to naïve modalism is found also in the *Acta Pionii 9:* "*Quem deum colis? Respondit; Christum. Polemon (judex): Quid ergo? iste alter est?* [the co-defendant Christians had immediately before confessed God the Creator]. *Respondit: Non; sed ipse quem et ipsi paullo ante confessi sunt*; cf. c. 16. Yet a reasoned modalism may perhaps be assumed here."
59. Ibid. Harnack offers, "It is instructive to find Modalism in the theology of the Simonians, which was partly formed according to Christian ideas; see Iren. I. 231."
60. Hurtado, *Origins*, 81; see in particular the extensive documentation Hurtado brings to bear in note 44. Hurtado sees conflicting traditions in the text and thus the importance of the non-trinitarian reference to baptism in 9:5. See also Arthur Vööbus, "Liturgical Traditions in the Didache," *Papers for the Estonian Theological Society in Exile* (1968): 36-39. Vööbus suggests that the Trinitarian formula arose in the middle of the second century and was in fact an addition to both the *Didache* and Matthew 28:19; cited on p. 127, note 11 of Kurt Niederwimmer, *The Didache*, 2nd ed., trans. Linda M. Maloney, ed. Harold W. Attridge, (Minneapolis: Fortress Press, 1998).
61. Niederwimmer, *Didache*, 3. The dating of the *Didache* is complicated by the fact that it is in itself dependent on various sources, including the "Two Ways Tractate," and apparent references to the *Didache* by early church fathers are in doubt (p. 6f). Our first certain witness of the *Didache* is the *Apostolic Constitutions*, which was copied from the *Didache* in 300 (p. 17), making it a second century AD document.
62. Jean Daniélou, *Theology of Jewish Christianity*, 156; citing Jeremiah 7:12; Ezekiel 43:7; Ezra 6:12; on this see also Chapter 9 on John 1:14.
63. Daniélou, *Theology of Jewish Christianity*, 153, citing Clement of Alexandria, *Excerpts from Theodotus* 86.2. Theodotus certainly sounds Oneness in excerpts where he comments on Jesus' conversation where He noted a coin, with Caesar's image and superscription. By comparison, Theodotus offers, "So it is with the believer: he has as a superscription through Christ the Name of God and the Spirit as an image." Daniélou notes of the parallel usage that given that the two images are on par related to the coin, "suggests that the corresponding elements in reality illustrated are also on a par, that is the Name of God and the Spirit." On p. 156, Daniélou further parallels Theodotus's use of "Name" as deity standing for Christ with the Epistle of James.

64. Jürgen Moltmann, *The Trinity and the Kingdom: The Doctrine of God*, trans. Margaret Kohl, (San Francisco: Harper & Row, 1981), 226, note 5, citing Melito, who offers, "The One who cannot suffer, suffers."
65. Tatian, *Oration to the Greeks* 13.
66. Harnack, *History of Dogma*, 1:116.
67. Wolfson, *Philosophy*, 310.
68. Harnack writes, "But applied to in a pedantic and stringently dogmatic way it is a source of deception, of untruthfulness, and finally of total blindness," *History of Dogma*, 1:116.

Chapter 15: Displacing Oneness Christology

1. As we demonstrate throughout this chapter, the critique against Praxeas was a kind of caricature of what it was he actually believed.
2. Tertullian, *Prax.* 20, *ANF,* 3:615. To show the singularity of God in the Old Testament, Praxeas, quoting Isaiah 45:5, said, "I am God, and beside me there is no Saviour."
3. J. A. Dorner, *History of the Development of the Doctrine of the Person of Christ*, vol. 2, trans. D. W. Simon, (Edinburgh: T & T Clark, 1861), 26; Dorner notes several personages associated with Modalism in Asia, recognizing that it had already existed for a considerable period.
4. See Tertullian, *Prax.* 2, *ANF,* 3:598.
5. Cushman, *History*, 79-80. Cushman offers, "They were the rank and file, ordinary Christians, not theologians, and the last thing they would have done was to introduce new and radical ideas. . . ."
6. McGrath, *Christian Theology*, 321.
7. Harnack, *History of Dogma*, 3:70. Harnack offers that Tertullian's arguments in *Prax.* "are not free from half concessions and uncertainties, while the whole tenor of the work contrasts strikingly with that of the anti-gnostic tractates. Tertullian finds himself time and again compelled in his work to pass from the offensive to the defensive, and the admissions that he makes show his uncertainty."
8. Tertullian, *Prescription against Heretics* 7; cited on p. 17 of McGrath, *Christian Theology*; McGrath offers in the larger citation: "To say that the soul is subject to death is to go the way of Epicurus. And the denial of the resurrection of the body is found throughout the writings of all the philosophers. To say that matter is equal with God is to follow the doctrine of Zeno; to speak of a god of fire is to draw from Heraclitus. It is the same subjects which preoccupy both the heretics and the philosophers. Where does evil come from, and why? Where does human nature come from, and how? What has Athens to do with Jerusalem? What has the Academy to do with the church? Our system of beliefs comes from the Porch of Solomon, who himself taught that it was necessary to seek God in the simplicity of the heart. So much the worse for those who talk of a 'stoic,' 'platonic' or 'dialectic' Christianity.' "
9. Tertullian, *Prax.*, 22, *ANF,* 3:617-18. Tertullian here is consonant with the language of Justin. Cf. Schwarz, *Christology*, 140, notes 7-8.
10. Justin Martyr argued that Plato must have taken his notion of creation, his teaching on the Demiurge in the *Timaeus* from Moses. Both Augustine (354-430) and Tertullian (160-220) were convinced that Plato had at least some exposure to the writings of Moses. Cf. Jack A. Bonsor, *Athens and Jerusalem: The Role of Philosophy in Theology*, (New York: Paulist Press, 1993), 29. On Justin Martyr's linkage of Moses and Plato, see his *1 Apology*, 59-60.
11. Justo L. González, *Christian Thought Revisited: Three Types of Theology*, (Nashville, TN: Abingdon Press, 1989), 22. González notes that Emperor Marcus Aurelius who died in AD 180 was a follower of the way of the Stoics. Tertullian, who was a lawyer, was no doubt attracted to the "law" of Stoicism. González offers, "Breathing the pervasive atmosphere in which he lived, Tertullian viewed much of reality in the same fashion as did the Stoics."

12. Tertullian, *Prax.* 3, *ANF,* 3:598-99.
13. Tertullian, *Prax.* 29, *ANF,* 3:626. Tertullian introduces his classic argument against patripassianism; indeed, he gets very intense, charging Praxeas and his followers with blasphemy. "The heretics, indeed fearing to incur the blasphemy against the Father, hope to diminish it by this expedient: they grant us so far that the Father and Son are two; adding that, since it is the Son indeed who suffers, the Father is only His fellow-sufferer. But how absurd are they even in this conceit! For what is the meaning of 'fellowsuffering,' but the enduring suffering along with another? Now if the Father is incapable of suffering, He is incapable of suffering along with another; otherwise, if He can suffer with another, He is of course capable of suffering." Even when Praxeas suggested that the Father was in some sense separate from the Son, the distinction was not enough for Tertullian who said that even if the Father was only a "co-sufferer, He was still suffering with the Son."
14. Pelikan, *Christian Tradition*, 52-53.
15. Tertullian writes, "Thus in a certain sense, the word is a second *person* (emphasis added) within you, through which in thinking you utter speech, and through which also, (by reciprocity of process,) in uttering speech, you generate thought." *Prax.* 5, *ANF,* 3:601. Tertullian continues this thought in chapter 6, writing, "This power and disposition of the Divine Intelligence is set forth also in the Scriptures under the name of σοφία, Wisdom; for what can be better entitled to the name of Wisdom than the Reason or the Word of God?" Here it is apparent that Tertullian was still working out his theology and suggested that Reason play a principal role, a concept that was never developed. Indeed, in chapter 5 he writes, "The Word was in the beginning with God; although it would be more suitable to regard Reason as the more ancient; because God had not Word from the beginning, but He had Reason even before the beginning."
16. John MacQuarrie, *Principles of Christian Theology*, 2nd ed., (New York: Scribner, 1977), 14. MacQuarrie offers that a word such as person, "as used in the formulations from the patristic age, had quite a different connotation from that which it now bears."
17. Wolfson, *Philosophy*, 328.
18. McGiffert, *Early Christians*, 79-80. McGiffert adds, "They were the rank and file, ordinary Christians, not theologians, and the last thing they would have done was to introduce new and radical ideas."
19. Ibid., 323-32.
20. Elaine Pagels, *The Gnostic Gospels*, (New York: The Random House, 1979), 109-10. Pagels notes that when it is convenient, Tertullian will identify himself with the larger orthodoxy. He identifies himself as a "Catholic Christian," and makes numerous claims for such; yet at the end of his life, he complains that the church should be "a spiritual church for spiritual people" and "*not* [Pagels's emphasis] the church of a number of bishops." See note 35, citing Tertullian, *Modesty* 21.
21. There were, of course, other writings and particular Roman bishops against which we read this or that snippet of their position, but these were the men against whom books were written.
22. Hippolytus, *Refutation of Heresies* 7.
23. Hippolytus, ibid. According to Hippolytus, Noetus seems to have expressed it in similar terms: "When indeed, then, the Father had not been born, He was justly styled Father; and when it pleased Him to undergo generation, having been begotten, He himself became His own Son, not another's."
24. Although it is certain then that Noetus imputes suffering to the Father, it is less certain whether he actually taught that the Father died. The evidence is somewhat contradictory. For instance, Epiphanius records this confession of Noetus at his trial: "What have I done wrong in glorifying one God: I know one God and none other beside him, the one who was born, suffered, and died." Epiphanius, *Pan.* p. 119.
25. Hippolytus, *Refutation of Heresies* 5. There is a tension, however, in Hippolytus whether Noetus said that the Father "died" or that he was "not in reality dead." Cf. ibid., chapter

28. "And this heretic also alleges that the Father is unbegotten when He is not generated, but *Against the Heresy of one Noetus.*"
26. Philip Schaff, *History of the Christian Church*, Vol 2, (Grand Rapids, MI: Eerdmans, 1950), 581. Schaff writes, "The system of Sabellius is known to us only from a few fragments, and some of these not altogether consistent, in Athanasius and other fathers."
27. On this, see Kelly, *Early Christian Doctrines*, 122, citing Epiphanius, *Pan.* 62.1; Kelly summarizes Epiphanius, who says of Sabellius's christological system, "The Father by process of development projecting Himself first as the Son and then as the Spirit. Thus the one Godhead regarded as creator and law-giver was Father; for redemption. It was projected like a ray of the sun, and was then withdrawn; then, thirdly, the same Godhead operated as Spirit to inspire and bestow grace."
28. Wolfson, *Philosophy*, 585. Further, as Wolfson points out on p. 199, this change in understanding of the *Logos* was introduced tentatively at first, not in direct opposition to Justin. Nonetheless, the doctrine developed from the anti-gnostic formulation of Irenaeus, in *Against Heresies*, 4.20.3, "the *Logos*, namely, the Son, was always (*simper . . . erat*) with the Father."
29. Wolfson, 201; in *Princ.*, 1.2.4, Origen offers of the *Logos*, "His generation is eternal and everlasting (*aeterna ac sempiterna generatio*) as the brightness which is produced from the sun."
30. Wolfson, 274ff. For instance, on p. 279, Wolfson notes Origen accepts Philo's notion of the *Logos* as "a second God." Citing Origen's *Cels.* 5.39, Wolfson writes, "And although we speak of a second God (δεύτερον θεὸν), let men know that by the term we mean nothing else than a power (ἀρετὴν) which includes all other powers and a *Logos* which includes every *Logos* that exists in everything which has arisen naturally, directly, and for the general advantage."
31. Ibid., 202; Wolfson writes, "A view like that implied of Origen's description of eternal generation of the *Logos* from God, expressed in exactly the same terms, is found in Plotinus' description of the generation of the Nous [the universal soul] from the One."
32. Ibid., 205-7. While some have attempted to demonstrate this understanding as early as Clement, Wolfson demonstrates a "two stage theory" of the *Logos.*
33. Ibid. Hippolytus, still allowing for a kind of two-stage theory, nonetheless allows, "Even though before the incarnation the *Logos* was not yet 'perfect Son,' God still addresses Him as Son 'because He was to be begotten in the future.' " Novatian, as well, allows that "even though the *Logos* was generated or proceeded from the Father only prior to the creation of the world, still, inasmuch as he had always been in the Father, God had always been a Father."
34. Ibid., 217. While Wolfson allows that certain Latin fathers espoused the "twofold stage theory," he suggests that such an opinion was essentially cast aside, despite occasional language in the fathers that might seem to espouse this theory.
35. Middle Platonism flourished in educated circles between 80 BC and AD 220, especially in Alexandria, Egypt. On Middle Platonism, see Robert M. Berchman, *From Philo to Origen.*
36. Brown, *Western Thought*, 90.
37. John Dillon, citing Justinian in "Origen's Doctrine of the Trinity and Some Later Neoplatonic Theories," in *NeoPlatonism and Christian Thought*, ed. Dominic J. O'Meara, (Norfolk, VA: International Society for NeoPlatonic Studies, 1982), 19-20.
38. Ibid., 19ff.
39. Lebreton and Zeiller, *History of the Primitive Church*, 2:731. Cf. Harnack, *History of Dogma*, 1:735, notes 1 and 3.
40. Origen, *Princ.* 4.4.1; cited in Pelikan, *Christian Tradition*, 191.
41. Harnack, *History of Dogma*, 3:71-72.
42. Kelly, *Early Christian Doctrines*, 119.
43. Harnack, 3:54.
44. Ibid., 55.
45. Ibid., 54.

46. Wolfson, *Philosophy*, viii.
47. For Arius, the biblical text showed a beginning to wisdom, and hence a beginning to the *Logos*. Arius took three references in Proverbs chapter 8 as conclusive. In verse 23, the text proclaims that wisdom was "established"; vv. 24-26 suggest that wisdom was begotten; v. 27 says that wisdom was established; in a letter to Eusebius, Arius offered that there was a time when the *Logos* did not exist, writing, "Before he was begotten or created or ordained or established, he did not exist." Arius offered the same to Alexander, insisting that the Son had been "begotten timelessly by the Father and created before the ages and established." See Pelikan, *Christian Tradition*, 193.
48. Pelikan, ibid.
49. Ibid., 199. Nonetheless, despite the distinction between Jesus and God, and despite the insistence that Jesus not be worshiped as God, this violated the convention of the church, and the doxological tendencies of Arius prevailed over his dogmatic position. Even in churches allied to Arius, they worshiped Jesus. Athanasius attacked Arianism for this very inconsistency; he argued in *C. Ar.* 1.8, that they were according to their own christology worshiping a creature.
50. Ibid., 200-1.
51. Athanasius was successful in his attempt to get the christological position of Arius condemned. When it came time to sign the creedal profession, only Arius and two others refused to sign, thus consigning themselves to a place outside the church while the rest saluted the emperor. Pelikan, *Christian Tradition*, 203.
52. Augustine, *Confessions*, 8.2.3.
53. Gordon J. Clark, *Three Types of Religious Philosophy*, (Jefferson, MD: The Trinity Foundation, 1973, 1989), 28.
54. Lewis Ayres, "Augustine's Trinitarian Theology," in *Augustine and His Critics: Essays in Honour of Gerald Bonner*, eds. Robert Dodaro and George Lawless, (London and New York: Routledge, 2000). Though Lewis Ayers asserts that Augustine was not necessarily first converted to Neoplatonism and then later to Christianity. Rather, it is more complicated than that. He contends that Augustine's borrowing from Platonism took place in the context of some existing knowledge of faith; he had already studied some with Ambrose. Augustine himself acknowledges that he saw the interrelationship of the Father and Son in those Platonic terms (7.9, 13-14).
55. On this question, see both the text and many helpful references in *"PAUCIS MUTATIS VERBIS:* Augustine's Platonism," by Robert Crouse, in *Augustine and His Critics*.
56. See p. 152.
57. Crouse, *"PAUCIS MUTATIS VERBIS,"* 41-42. Crouse notes, "Augustine's anti-Arian formulation of trinitarian doctrine owes much to both pagan and Christian predecessors, a good deal perhaps to Porphyry (especially if he is the author of the fragmentary *Commentary of the Parmenides)* and his remarkable conflation of Platonic and Aristotelian theology."
58. As Pelikan notes on p. 67 of his *Christian Tradition*, Augustine made considerable use of the Old Testament by equating wisdom in the Old Testament with the *Logos*.
59. Berkhof, *Christian Faith*, 264, citing Augustine, *Quaestiones in Exodum* 2.73.
60. Ibid.
61. Isaac Dorner, *Divine Immutability. A Critical Reconsideration* trans. by Robert R. Williams and Claude Welch, (Minneapolis, MN: Fortress Press, 1994), 91. In offering this summary, Dorner cites Augustine, *City of God*, 50.11.10.
62. Augustine, *The Trinity*, 6.7.
63. Ibid., 5.2.
64. Clark H. Pinnock, "From Augustine to Arminius: A Pilgrimage in Theology," in *The Grace of God, the Will of Man*, ed. 64. Clark H. Pinnock, (Grand Rapids, MI: Zondervan, 1989), 23.
65. On p. 132 of *Divine Immutability*, Dorner notes of the church's debt to Augustinian use of the philosophers, "The medieval doctrine of God in large part clearly goes back to non-Christian sources."

66. Any number of theologians could be cited who take these Augustinian doctrines as standard. Here, I cite p. 83 of Henry Clarence Theissen's *Lectures in Systematic Theology*, rev. and ed. Vernon D. Doerksen, (Grand Rapids, MI: Eerdmans, 1986). He, in turn, is largely dependent on other Reformed theologians who in the end are dependent on Augustine.
67. Pelikan, *Christian Tradition*, 297, citing Augustine's *On the Gift of Perseverance*, 17.41.
68. Ibid., 302-3; on p. 298 Pelikan cites pp. 265-66 of Gotthard Nygren, *Das Prädestinationsproblem in der Theologie Augustins*, Lund, 1956: "The doctrine of double predestination, to heaven and to hell, has . . . the last word in the theology of Augustine." Pelikan goes on to demonstrate the way Augustine defends his position, citing *On the Spirit and the Letter*, 43.60; Augustine would first quote his interpretation of Romans 11:33 and then offer, "if this answer displeases someone, let him seek more learned [theologians], but let him beware lest he find [more] presumptuous ones."
69. Augustine, *Enchiridion on Faith, Hope, and Love*, 38; cited by Wolfson, *Philosophy*, 356.
70. Pelikan, *Christian Tradition*, 197; citing *Trin.*, 12.6.6-7.
71. Wolfson, *Philosophy*, 352-54. On p. 357, Wolfson further clarifies why the Augustinian teaching led to the greater perception of equality among the persons. He writes, "For according to the predecessors of Augustine, the Father was the cause of both (1) the existence and (2) the godhood of the other two persons, whereas, according to Augustine, the Father was the cause only of the existence of the other two persons.
72. Augustine admits that such an identification does not occur in Scripture but asserts that it is implied. On this, see McGrath, *Christian Theology*, 332.
73. Wolfson, *Philosophy*, 419ff. Perichoresis was utilized by Gregory of Nazianzus to describe the interpenetration of divine and human properties in Jesus. On p. 421, Wolfson notes, "Penetration is used synonymously with mixture, thus reflecting the Stoic use of penetration in their description of mixture." On p. 426, Wolfson cites eighth-century John of Damascus, *On the Orthodox Faith* 3.3, who writes, "The Word appropriates to himself all the human [properties], for all that pertains to holy flesh is his, and he imparts to the flesh his own properties in accordance with the manner of an interchange in virtue of the penetration (περιχώρησις) of the parts into one another (εἰς ἄλληλα) and the hypostatic union. . . . Hence it is that the 'Lord of Glory' is said to have been crucified, although his divine nature never endured suffering, and 'the son of Man' is declared to be in heaven before the passion." On the way that the Cappadocian fathers developed this intermingling *perichoresis* as an interpenetration of all the members of the Trinity, see James B. Walker, "Niceno-Constantinopolitan Creed," in *The Dictionary of Historical Theology*, ed. Trevor A. Hart, (Grand Rapids, MI: Eerdmans, 2000), 369-99, 398. See, as well, Alister McGrath, *Christian Theology*, 325ff., who explains how this language is appropriated to all the members of the Trinity in the sixth century.
74. McGrath, *Christian Theology*, 325-26.
75. McGrath, *Christian Theology*, 329ff. The Cappadocian fathers play a key role in insisting on the full divinity of the Holy Spirit as the third Person of the Trinity, a feature of the Council of Constantinople in AD 381. Their analogy of the Trinity to "three human beings sharing a common humanity" is what leads down the road toward tritheism. On p. 331, McGrath cites Gregory of Nyssa, in his *Quod non sint tres dii*: "Peter, James and John are called three humans, even though they share a single common humanity. . . . So how do we compromise our belief, by saying on the one hand that the Father, Son and the Holy Spirit have a single godhood, while on the other hand denying that we are talking about three gods?"
76. On this, see Eusebius, *Ecclesiastical Theology*, 1.3. Eusebius includes three major ways in which "the great mass of people, not capable of understanding this conception of God, have thought up all sorts of ways to wander off."
77. James Stevenson, ed. *Creeds, Councils and Controversies: Documents Illustrative of the History of the Church A. D., 337-461*, (New York: Seabury Press, 1966), 115; he cites Basil, who wrote, "On the other hand, those who identify essence or substance and *hy*-

postasis are compelled to confess only three Persons (προσωπα) and, in their hesitation to speak of the three *hypostases*, are convicted of failure to avoid the error of Sabellius, for even Sabellius himself, who in many places confuses the conception, yet, by asserting that the same hypostasis changed its form to meet the needs of the moment, does endeavour to distinguish persons."
78. Ibid, 53.
79. Pelikan, *Christian Tradition*, 181-82.
80. Ironically, this is the very issue that was the underlying complaint upon which the Reformation was based. In effect, because the "orthodox" position is spoken by the empowered, it is considered true. As Ivan Snook, an interpreter of Bourdieu, pointed out on p. 160 of "Language, Truth and Power: Bourdieu's *Ministerium*," in *Introduction to the Work of Pierre Bourdieu*, "Since the beginning of critical reflection there has been a well-recognized connection between language and truth, and a clear, though largely unrecognized connection between language and power."
81. On p. 125 of his *Language and Symbolic Power*, Bourdieu demonstrates how that when a heterodox group accepts that the dominant group speaks for everyone, the product of such a speaking becomes "social magic."

Chapter 16: The Place of Baptism in Covenant Initiation

1. *Damascus Document* XVI, 2-4 cites it explicitly, and it appears that the *Genesis Apocryphon* is dependent on it and considers it authoritative as well. On the latter point, see J. A. Fitzmyer, *The Genesis Apocryphon of Qumran Cave 1: A Commentary*, Biblica et Orientalia 18A (Rome: Editrice Pontificio Istituto Biblico, 1966), 14.
2. *Damascus Document* XX, 17ff. *The Dead Sea Scrolls*, trans. Michael Wise, Martin Abegg, Jr., and Edward Cook, (San Francisco: Harper, 1996), 60.
3. Ibid., *Damascus Document* II, 53; Cook translates, "He (*Yahweh*) has arranged that there should be for Himself people called by name, so that there would always be survivors on the earth, replenishing the surface of the earth with their descendants. He taught them through those anointed by the holy spirit, the seers of truth, He explicitly called them by name. But whoever He had rejected He caused to stray." For a full treatment of this comparison, see my "No Other Name."
4. See p. 142.
5. For a survey of the various opinions, see G. R. Beasley-Murray, *Baptism in the New Testament*, (London, MacMillan, 1963), 18-31. Joachim Jeremias argues for an early date as do others. While there is an absence of mention of the practice in Philo and in Josephus, there are apparent allusions to it in the *Sibylline Oracles*, and the Mishnaic reference to controversy between competing schools of rabbis clearly predates the fall of Jerusalem.
6. See Matthew 3; Luke 3; John 1. On John the Baptist, see p. 87ff.
7. See John 3:22; 4:2.
8. Beasley-Murray, *Baptism in the New Testament*, 34. See especially note 2 where he marshals evidence; cf. J. Behm's treatment of "μετανοέω, μετάνοια" in Hellenistic Jewish literature in *TDNT*, 4:989-1008; see particularly pp. 993-94 for the treatment of this word in Philo.
9. Oerke, "βάπτω βαπτίζω," *TDNT*, 1:529-46, 540.
10. Howard, *New Testament Baptism*, 15; he notes that the Hillelite rabbis likened the Old Testament Red Sea experience (i.e., passing through the water from slavery to the promised land) to the baptism that Gentiles had to experience so that they too could pass "from heathenism through baptism into the 'promised land.' " As Howard points out on p. 17, Gentiles were said to be "born anew" through the baptismal rite.
11. When dealing with the John 3 text, Lars Hartman writes, "A birth by water can hardly refer to anything but baptism." *Into the Name of Jesus*, 156-57.
12. Francis J. Maloney, *The Gospel of John*, ed. Daniel J. Harrington, Sacra Pagina 4, (Collegeville, MN: Liturgical Press, 1998), 92.

13. John E. Morgan-Wynne, "References to Baptism in the Fourth Gospel," in *Baptism, the New Testament and the Church: Historical and Contemporary Studies in Honour of R. E. O. White*, eds. Stanley E. Porter and Anthony R. Cross, (Sheffield: Sheffield Academic Press, 1999), 157-72, 120-21.
14. Beasley-Murray, *Baptism*, 67.
15. McGiffert, *Early Christians*, 76; McGiffert cites *Epistles of Cyprian* 73:4, 16; 74:5, 7ff.
16. Although there do not appear to be major variants in the Matthean text, Fred C. Conybeare, in his "The Eusebian from of the Text Matth. 28:19," *Zeitschrift für die Neutestamentliche Wissenschaft* 2 (1901): 275-88, has demonstrated that Eusebius knew of renderings of the verse compatible with baptism in Jesus' name, citing seventeen attestations of a shorter formula: "ἐν τῷ ὀνόματί μου." Hans Kosmala's "The Conclusion of Matthew," in the *Annual of the Swedish Theological Institute* 4 (1965): 132-47, defends the work of Conybeare, despite the fact that with the exception of two other references, his testimony stands alone. On p. 138, Kosmala suggests a Matthean redaction because of the "extensive liturgical use" by the church after baptism in the name of Jesus was no longer in use as a formula. Maintaining such a position would require either at least a second-century date for the *Didache* or a redaction. Either one is a possibility. Conybeare, on p. 284, notes no patristic mention of a triune formula before this. He suggests that the triune reference in 7.1 of the *Didache* may well be "suspect because of the occurrence in 9.4 of the same document of the phrase οἱ βαπτισθέντες εἰς ὄνομα κυρίου."
17. It will not do to accept "a Matthean school" writing a variant tradition so that the traditions of both Matthew and Luke-Acts are equally valid. Nor will it do to suggest that it was up to the church to later decide as to how baptism should occur. The former argument strips the Bible of its authority and the latter strips the apostles of their authority. The first argument leads to unbelief in the Bible; the latter to discrediting the practice of the men upon whom the Christian Church is founded.
18. On this, see p. 140.
19. Jesus' chaim to this Father's "Name" was a claim to Yahweh's essence.
20. See p. 140-1.
21. See p. 58.
22. Luke 24:47; Joel B. Green, *The Gospel of Luke*, ed. Gordon Fee, *The New International Commentary on the New Testament*, (Grand Rapids, MI: Eerdmans, 1997), 858. Green rightly links repentance and baptism in this text with the way Luke underscores both of these elements of covenant initiation in Acts. Green links not only the allegiance of the Christian community to Jesus' name, but highlights baptism in Jesus' name as well.
23. Michel Meslin, "Baptism," *The Encyclopedia of Religion*, Vol. 2, ed. Mircea Eliade, (New York: MacMillan, 1986), 59-63, 62. Meslin, in utilizing both Hippolytus and Tertullian, notes that by the third century there were "such additions as interrogations (like those preceding Jewish baptism), a triple renunciation of the devil (recalling Jesus' triple renunciation during His temptations), a triple immersion (representing the Trinity), the anointing of the neophyte with the holy chrism, and laying on of hands by the bishop or priest (Tertullian, *Prax.* 26; *On Baptism;* Hippolytus, *Apostolic Tradition*)."
24. See Hartman, "Baptism," *ABD*, 1:538-96, 586; cf. Bietenhard, "ὄνομα," 275-76.
25. Norman Fox, "Baptism," in *The New Schaff-Herzog Encyclopedia of Religious Knowledge*, Vol. 1, ed. Samuel Macauley Jackson, (Grand Rapids, MI: Eerdmans, 1977), 435-54, 436. Fox notes that "*baptizein eis to onama Iesou* means that the person baptized enters into the relation of belonging to Christ, of being his property. All three formulas are alike in so far as the baptized are subject to the power and efficacy of Jesus, who is now their Lord."
26. Hartman, "Baptism," 587. He writes, "It seems that when somebody presented an offering in the temple, he declared what kind of offering he was giving: cf., e.g., *b Pesach.* 60a: 'Behold I slaughter the Pesach into its name,' i.e., 'this is a passover sacrifice.' The parallel would then intimate that the purpose or the fundamental reference of baptism was mentioned at the rite and that this was done in such a way that Jesus was mentioned."

27. See p. 144.
28. Bruce, *Acts*, 294.
29. There are a number of opinions as to why the name of Jesus gets employed the way it does in Acts, particularly in the first chapters where healing, baptism, and preaching all occur in the name of Jesus. Zeisler suggests that Luke has four different usages of "the name of Jesus." First, baptism in the name of Jesus showed possession. Second, to speak in the name of Jesus meant to speak about Him. Third, he suggests that the healing that took place in the name of Jesus was borrowed from the notion represented in Hellenistic mystery cults. However, he adds the proviso that the name works only if you add the gospel with it. Fourth, the name of Jesus is used for Jesus Himself. So, for Zeisler, the phrase, "a people called by my name" in Acts 15:17, means "those that belong to me." See J. A. Zeisler, "The Name of Jesus in the Acts of the Apostles," *JSNT* 4 (1979): 28-41.
30. Bonnie Thurston, in *The Spiritual Life of the Church*, further speculates as to the origin of the use of the name. She notes, "The disciples would certainly have been aware of the tradition of the name as it was used of Yahweh's self-manifestation, to designate God's ineffable reality, the power by which God's work, and as the place where God "dwells." She cites Daniélou, *Theology of Jewish Christianity*, 147-48.
31. Robert Stein, "Baptism and Becoming a Christian in the New Testament," www.sbts.edu/Resources/Publications/Journal/Spring_1998.aspx; 6-17. Accessed May 15, 2008.
32. Stein, "Baptism," 6.
33. John B. Polhill, *Acts*, (Nashville, TN: Broadman Press, 1992), 116.
34. F. F. Bruce, *The Epistle to the Galatians, The New International Greek Testament Commentary*, (Grand Rapids, MI: Eerdmans, 1982), 186.
35. Ibid.
36. Stein, "Baptism," 13.
37. See p. 142.
38. Beasley-Murray, 103; Hurtado, *One God*, 109; Wainwright, *Doxology*, 157.
39. On early practice connected with baptism, see Oscar Cullmann, *Early Christian Worship*, trans. A. Stewart Todd and James B. Torrence, (London: SCM Press, 1953), 25.
40. Though some would cite the aorist passive utilized by Paul in this verse as evidence of a particular moment of conversion, Paul is citing Genesis 15:6 where he writes in Romans 4:3, "Abraham believed ['Επίστευσεν (an aorist active verb likely pointing to a point in time)] God, and it was counted [ἐλογίσθη (aorist passive verb likely, meaning that there was a reckoning made of Abraham)] unto him for righteousness." The Hebrew word, חשב, demonstrates in its usage a reckoning to righteousness. The *LXX* demonstrates this in the Greek λογίζομαι, for the same general meaning. It is, of course, λογίζομαι that Paul uses in Romans.
41. While Abram's name was not changed to Abraham until later in the narrative, for the sake of simplicity we will utilize Abraham throughout this section.
42. Lloyd Gaston, "Abraham and the Righteousness of God," *Horizons in Biblical Theology* 2, (1980): 39-68, 40.
43. See pp. 827-37 of Karen L. Onesti and Manfred T. Brauch, "Righteousness, Righteousness of God," in *Dictionary of Paul and His Letters*, eds. Gerald F. Hawthorne, Ralph P. Martin, and Daniel G. Reid, (Downers Grove, IL: Intervarsity, 1993), who rightly demonstrate that is informed by Paul's Old Testament heritage; that the concept "righteousness" is clearly understood as a function of covenant. Further, they nuance the diversity with which Paul utlizes *dikaiosyne* and its cognates.
44. Eichrodt, *Theology*, 1:457. He cites the words of God to Moses in Exodus 32:10 as an example.
45. The institution became an ongoing covenantal institution. Yahweh declared in Genesis 17:14, "The uncircumcised male . . . he has broken my covenant." Further, in the same verse Yahweh stipulated that such a person "must be cut off from his people."

46. James 2:21 reads, "Was not Abraham our father justified [ἐδικαιώθη (the aorist passive is the same form of verb as used in Romans, and thus can mean was made righteous at a particular point in time)] by works when he offered Isaac his son on the altar?" The Greek here is similar to Pauline usage in Romans; we may therefore conclude that the usage does not demand a one-time punctiliar moment.
47. First, it is very difficult to translate *dikai-ŏ-ō* and *dikaiŏsyne* into English. On this, see p. 444 of J. Reumann, "The Gospel of the Righteousness of God," *Interpretation* 20 (1966): 432-52. He rightly notes the difficulty of translating the verb and noun that English sometimes translates "justify," "righteous," and "justification."
48. E. P. Sanders, *Paul and Palestinian Judaism*, (Philadelphia: Fortress Press, 1977), 470.
49. Ibid., 471. Sanders goes on to admonish translators not to read doctrinal bias into the text, offering, "It is hoped that one can learn to read 'make righteous' in a neutral sense, as a translation of the verb which conforms it to the translation of the noun as 'righteousness,' a translation which seems necessary in such a passage as Gal. 2.15-21."
50. In Colossians 2:11-12, when Paul wrote, "In Him you were also circumcised with the circumcision made without hands . . . buried with Him in baptism," he was making an analogy, not a "doctrine of circumcision."
51. Colossians 2:11; I Peter 3:21.
52. Carl Judson Davis, "Another Look at the Relationship between Baptism and Forgiveness of Sins in Acts 2:38," *Restoration Quarterly* 24 (1981): 80-84, 88.
53. See, for instance, Luther B. McIntyre, Jr., "Baptism and Forgiveness in Acts 2:38," *Bibliothecra Sacra* 152 (1996) 53-59.
54. Ashby L. Camp, "Reexamining the Rule of Concord in Acts 2:38," *Restoration Quarterly* 1 (1997): 37-42. On p. 37, Camp summarizes the argument of McIntyre, offering, "The basis of his claim is that since in the phrase, 'εἰς ἄφεσιν τῶν ἁμαρτιῶν ὑμῶν', [for forgiveness of your sins] cannot be syntactically connected to the command βαπτισθήτω because the personal pronoun ὑμῶν is second person plural whereas the command βαπτισθήτω is third person singular." Camp brings a number of scholars to bear on McIntyre's argument, demonstrating effectively that syntactically, forgiveness can logically follow both repentance and baptism. He utilizes Acts 2:36 as demonstrating his point and cites numerous other texts and commentators to effectively demonstrate the truth of his argument. Note that Greek grammarian A. T. Robertson is suggestive of the ambivalence grammarians feel as to whether the text "for" means "for the purpose of" forgiveness. Although there is a doctrinal difference as to whether baptism effects remission of sins or is because of remission of sins, consistency of understanding initiation into covenant clearly favors the former understanding.
55. Hartman, *Into the Name of Jesus*, 2–3; Hartman cites Romans 6:11; I Corinthians 1:13; 6:11. In note 3 he offers further: Jeremiah 31:34; Ezekiel 16:63; *1 Enoch* 1:5; 5:6; Romans 4:4ff.; Matthew 1:21.
56. Martin M. Culy and Mikeal C. Parsons, *Acts: A Handbook of the Greek Text*, (Waco, TX: Baylor University Press, 2003), 44.

Chapter 17: The Covenant and the Spirit

1. Romans 8:9-11; II Corinthians 3:17.
2. See "Jesus' Language about the Holy Spirit" on p. 105ff.
3. See p. 56; cf. p. 138ff.
4. See p. 23.
5. See p. 38. Certainly Yahweh demonstrated miraculous manifestation of His power in conjunction with His presence when He called His name over them (Exodus 19:16f).
6. See p. 40. In one of the most incredible displays of the Old Testament, Moses experienced the glory of God.
7. See pp. 40-41.

8. Some have argued that the identification of Pentecost with giving of the Law did not occur until the second century AD. See, for example, S. Maclean Gilmore, "Easter and Pentecost," *Journal of Biblical Literature* 81 (1962): 62-66, 65. But according to James D. G. Dunn, on p. 48-49 of his *Baptism in the Spirit: A Re-examination of the New Testament Teaching on the Gift of the Spirit in Relation to Pentecostalism Today*, (Philadelphia: Westminster, 1970), the Feast of Weeks [i.e. the Day of Pentecost] was certainly seen as a renewal of the covenant based upon the second-century BC Book of Jubilees, found in relative quantity at Qumran. Dunn cites numerous sources as well to support a first-century celebration of Pentecost in this regard. Despite the argumentation of Robert P. Menzies, in *The Development of Early Christian Pneumatology with Special Reference to Luke-Acts*, (Sheffield: JSOT Press, 1991), and further confirmation by William Atkinson, "Pentecostal Responses to Dunn's *Baptism in the Holy Spirit; Luke-Acts, Journal of Pentecostal Theology* 6 (1995): 49-72, Dunn certainly does present a convincing case for the understanding of Pentecost with Sinai as a backdrop. Cf. as well excellent argumentation on pp. 278-89 of Max Turner, *Power from on High: The Spirit in Israel's Restoration and Witness in Luke-Acts*, (Sheffield: Sheffield Academic Press, 2000).
9. There is no consensus as to when and what groups among the Jews began to believe in the Messiah. Certainly by the time of Jesus, the expectation was prevalent. On messianic expectation in the centuries just prior to the birth of Jesus, see Gerbern S. Oegema, *The Anointed and His People: Messianic Expectations from the Maccabees to Bar Kochba*, (Sheffield: Sheffield Academic Press, 1998).
10. On Joel's prophecy and its fulfillment on the Day of Pentecost, see pp. 143-4.
11. See p. 43.
12. See p. 128.
13. In John 7:39, John explains that although Jesus talked about the Spirit in terms of "living water" and actually invited people to receive it, "the Holy Spirit was not yet given, because Jesus was not yet glorified."
14. "Gift of God" here is used interchangeably with "living water" and refers to the Spirit in this eschatological age. Cf. John 4:10 and John 4:24.
15. This position typically appeals to Paul's statement from I Corinthians 13:8 that tongues shall cease. As to when the tongues shall cease, Paul notes in 13:10, "When that which is perfect has come, then that which is in part will be done away." Taking "that which is perfect" to be the compilation of the Bible or something similar, those who hold this view suggest that it was after "the Apostolic age" that tongues ceased. It hardly seems likely, though, given the eschatological nature of I Corinthians that "that which is perfect" can refer to anything other than the *parousia*, especially given the fact that in I Corinthians 1:8 Paul prayed for the church "that you come short in no gift, eagerly waiting for the revelation of our Lord Jesus Christ."
16. This position is taken by Roger Stronstad, who suggests that the Spirit is given primarily for missionary efforts. See p. 52 of his *The Charismatic Theology of St. Luke*, (Peabody, MA: Hendrickson Publishers, 1984); Cf. Robert P. Menzies, *The Development of Early Christian Pneumatology with Special Reference to Luke-Acts*, (Sheffield: JSOT Press, 1991).
17. Dunn, *Baptism in the Spirit*, 40ff.
18. Dunn cites seven principal Lukan phrases used to describe the infilling of the Spirit, and suggests that there are not two infillings but one, at conversion-initiation. The phrases are: "(a) βαπτισθήσεσθε ἐν πνεύματι ἁγίῳ [baptized in the Holy Spirit] 1.5; 11.16. (b) (ἐπ) ἔρχεσθαι τὸ πνεῦμα ἅγιον [the Holy Spirit to come upon] 1.8; 19.6. (c) πλησθῆναι πνεύματος ἁγίου [to be filled with the Holy Spirit] 2.4; 4.8, 31; 9.17; 13.9, 52 (ἐπληροῦντο). (d) ἐκχέειν ἀπὸ τοῦ πνεύματός [to pour out the Spirit upon] 2.17, 18, 33; 10.45 (ἐκκέχυται). (e) λαμβάνειν ἁγίου πνεύματος [to receive the Holy Spirit] 2.38; 8.15, 17, 19; 10:47; 19.2. (f) δίδωναι πνεῦμα ἅγιον [to give the Holy Spirit] 5.32 8.18 (δίδοσθαι);

11.17; 15.8. (g) ἐπιπίπτειν τὸ πνεῦμα τὸ ἅγιον [the Holy Spirit to fall] 8.16; 10.44; 11.15." Dunn, *Baptism in the Spirit*, 70.
19. See p. 41.
20. See p. 41.
21. Traditionally, it was not only the high priest who went behind the veil who felt the presence of God; the people who were worshiping with him at the Temple also experienced the presence of God.
22. See p. 191.
23. Maloney, *John*, 92ff.
24. Barnabas Lindars, *The Gospel of John*, ed. Matthew Black, *The New Century Bible Commentary*, (Grand Rapids, MI: Eerdmans, 1972), 152.
25. Don Williford, "John 3:1-15—*gennethenal anothen*: A Radical Departure, A New Beginning," *Review and Expositor*, 96 (1999): 451-61, 455. See, as well, Linda Belleville, "Born of Water and Spirit," *Trinity Journal NS* (1980): 125-41, 134-35. Belleville cites Murray J. Harris, "Appendix: 5. Neglect of the Possible Significance of (a) the Non-repetition of the Preposition with Copulated Nouns, and (b) the Order of Nouns that follow a Preposition," *New International Dictionary of New Testament Theology*, 3 vols., ed. Colin Brown, (Grand Rapids, MI: Zondervan, 1978), 3:1178. Belleville argues, "In verse 5, ὕδωρ and πνεῦμα are governed by a single preposition (ἐκ) and conjoined by καὶ indicating that the phrase is to be viewed as a conceptual unity, viz., 'water-spirit.' We are dealing, therefore, with a water-spirit source that is the origin of man's second γένεσις (v 3)."
26. Gordon D. Fee, *God's Empowering Presence: The Holy Spirit in the Letters of Paul*, (Peabody, MA: Hendrickson, 1994), 857, cf. note 11.
27. Carl Davis, *Name and Way of the Lord*, 125, note 80.
28. Fee, *God's Empowering Presence*, 857-58.
29. Ibid., 858.
30. See pp. 53-55 of Charles L. Holman, "Titus 3:5-6: A Window on Worldwide Pentecost," *Journal of Pentecostal Theology* 8 (1996): 53-62. Holman points out that the septuagintal use combining ἐκχέω with ἐπί ("poured out upon") is found in Joel 2:28-29, the text cited by Peter to explain the supernatural phenomenon of speaking in tongues. Further, on p. 55, Holman notes that the combination of these terms in the Old Testament, the presence of "outpouring upon" or the "the Spirit coming 'upon' " is "customarily found in the Old Testament to highlight dynamic experiences of the Spirit." See note 2 on p. 54 where Holman offers considerable corroborating evidence from other sources for the interpretation that links Titus 3:5-6 with "the Pentecostal event."
31. Dunn, *Theology of Paul*, 451.
32. Dunn, *Theology of Paul*, 450-51.
33. John 4:14; see, as well, 7:37-39.
34. M. D. Goulder, *Type and History in Acts*, (London: SPCK, 1964), 76. For Goulder, each of these occasions is important as each one marks one of four specific sections, patterns of growth offered in a cyclical typology.
35. See Dunn, "Baptism in the Holy Spirit: Pentecostal Scholarship on Luke-Acts," *Journal of Pentecostal Theology* 3 (1993), 3-27. On p. 9, Dunn suggests that this refers "to the speaking in other tongues described in 2.4 and 11." This is a central application of Oneness christology. It was the glorified Christ who could now impart this Spirit in the new eschatological age. Linked together in Acts 2:33 are (1) the exaltation of the man Jesus, (2) Jesus "receiving the Spirit," (3) Jesus baptizing with the Spirit, and (4) the evidence of tongues they saw and heard.
36. Richard F. Zehnle, *Peter's Pentecost Discourse: Tradition and Reinterpretation in Peter's Speeches of Acts 2 and 3*, ed. Robert A. Kraft, SBLMS 15, (Nashville, Abingdon Press, 1971), 62-67.
37. Ibid.

38. Ibid., 64-5. Zehnle notes the technical understanding of λαός for Luke. While not every usage of λαός is depicting believers, there are important theological turning points where this is the case. Λαός is introduced in Luke 1:17, where John the Baptist is prophesied to prepare a people for the Lord. Prophecies in Luke 1:68; Luke 2:31-32 are also significant. While there are important texts where λαός represents unbelievers in Acts, there is a prophecy to Paul that God has a great people in Corinth (λαός); most important, in Acts 15:14, James applies the words of Peter and prophecy of Amos that God has chosen a people (λαός) from among the Gentiles.
39. Dunn, *Baptism in the Holy Spirit*, 90. Of course, Dunn's emphasis would be different; but his use of this verse as paradigmatic is significant.
40. Chance, *Jerusalem*, 113. Regarding the literary importance of Jerusalem, see p. 115.
41. Acts 1:8 is the paradigmatic example; cf. Acts 2:29. The emphasis is not strictly on missionary effort of the Spirit but embraces initiation into covenant.
42. Peter's message echoed the same prophecy. The promise of the Spirit in Acts 2:38 was not merely available to a select few. Rather, Peter offers in verse 39, "For the promise is to you and to your children, and to all who are afar off, as many as the Lord our God will call."
43. Dunn, "Baptism of the Spirit: A Response," 10; cf. Dunn, *Baptism of the Spirit*, 55-58.
44. This was the initial argument offered by Dunn in *Baptism of the Spirit*; he has been hard pressed to find scholars to concur, however, and on p. 10ff. of "Baptism of the Spirit: A Response," Dunn distances himself from that argument.
45. Nor will it help to suggest this was merely an "exception" having to do with some Lukan strategy related to salvation history. It is, in fact, this so-called exception that is attempting to demonstrate a norm.
46. Dunn, *Jesus and the Spirit*, 189.
47. On p. 13 of Dunn's "Baptism in the Spirit: A Response," he offers, "The most natural inference to be drawn is that on hearing these words Cornelius and his friends believed in Jesus Christ and received what had been promised—that is, in the event, the Spirit as the embodiment or transmitter of forgiveness."
48. On p. 52 of his *Baptism of the Spirit*, Dunn cites Acts 11:17, where Peter, speaking of the experience of the house of Cornelius and how they received the Spirit as evidenced by speaking in tongues, noted, "God gave the same gift to them as he did to us *when we believed* [emphasis Dunn's] the Lord Jesus Christ." Dunn goes on to note of the word believe, "now πιστεύσαι (aorist) ἐπὶ in Luke always signifies an act of faith, the decisive commitment by which one becomes a Christian." Yet, while it is true that the apostles believed in order to receive the Spirit at the inauguration of the New Covenant, they were in covenant relationship prior to Acts 2.
49. Howard Ervin, *Conversion-Initiation and the Baptism in the Holy Spirit: An Engaging Critique of James D. G. Dunn*, (Peabody, MA: Hendrickson, 1984), 62-63. Ervin takes Paul to be asking whether they received the Spirit *after* they believed; cf. pp. 191-92 of F. L. Arrington, *The Acts of the Apostles*, (Peabody, MA: Hendrickson, 1988).
50. Dunn, "Baptism in the Spirit: A Response," 23-24; cf. Robert P. Menzies, "Luke and the Spirit: A Reply to James Dunn," *Journal of Pentecostal Theology* 4 (1994), 115-138, 122-23.
51. Menzies, "Reply to James Dunn," 123-24.
52. On this issue, see C. K. Barrett, "Apollos and the Twelve Disciples of Ephesus," in *The New Testament Age: Essays in Honor of Bo Reich*, vol. 1, ed. W. C. Weinrich, (Macon, GA: Mercer, 1984), 29-39.
53. Acts 2:17. Peter said, "Your sons and your daughters shall prophesy, Your young men shall see visions, Your old men shall dream dreams." As evidenced by the parallelism in Joel's prophecy, it would not be just a few anointed prophets that would participate; but rather, the promise would be applied universally.
54. Menzies, "Reply to James Dunn," 123-24.
55. See p. 305, note 18.

56. Dunn, *Jesus and the Spirit*, 189-90. Dunn goes on to critique Luke as "crude" in his conception, and "lopsided" in his emphasis. For Dunn, Paul is a very healthy corrective for a Lukan portrayal. While Dunn does not compel any current action on the part of a scholar, he fairly assesses what it was that Luke was trying to say.
57. Donald Juel, *Luke-Acts: The Promise of History*, (Atlanta: John Knox, 1983), 87.
58. On Jesus' use of *Abba*, see p. 102; see also p. 118. As Kittel acknowledges on p. 6 of "Αββα," *TDNT*, 1:5-6, *Abba* is the "simple speech of a child to its father," essentially, one of the first words he learns.
59. See p. 102.
60. See p. 102.
61. An Aramaic saying that Paul included in I Corinthians was *Maranatha*, which Cullmann assesses to be a prayer to Christ, one that goes back to the earliet Palestinian (Aramaic speaking) church. *Christology*, 215. Thus, for Paul, this Aramaic saying was part of his received tradition. In the same way the use of the Aramaic *Abba* was no doubt likewise passed down to him from the earliest Christian community.
62. Kittel, "Αββα," 6.
63. Fee, *God's Empowering Presence*, 866-67.
64. James Denney, *The Expositor's Greek New Testament*, vol. 2, ed. W. Robertson Nicholl, (Peabody MA: Hendrickson, 2002), 648.
65. Ibid.
66. Marvin R. Vincent, *Word Studies in the New Testament*, 4 vols., (1887-1905; repr., Peabody, MA: Hendrickson, n.d.), 4:137-38.
67. E. A. Obeng, "Abba Father: The Prayer of the Sons of God," *Expository Times* 99 (1988): 363-66, 365.
68. Ben Witherington, *Many Faces of Christology, The Christologies of the New Testament and Beyond.* (New York: The Crossroad Publishing Co., 1998),74.
69. Dunn, *Jesus and the Spirit*, 190-91.
70. See Kilian McDonnell, and George. T. Montague, *Christian Initiation and Baptism in the Holy Spirit*, (Collegeville, MN: Liturgical Press, 2nd ed., 1994), 87. McDonnell and Montague would not insist on tongues as the only gift being represented. They also allow for other experiential gifts such as prophecy.
71. See Polhill, *Acts*, 116; Stein, "Baptism," 13; and Bruce, *Galatians*, 283.
72. As we have noted, this was the relative pattern of Acts. Philip was concerned when it did not occur that way in Samaria, and sent for Peter. The Spirit fell in Acts 10, interrupting Peter's message, so in Acts 10 baptism followed the reception of the Spirit. But in Acts 2 and 19, the narrative follows this order.
73. See p. 212.
74. On the calling on Jesus as Lord in I Corinthians 12:3, see also David E. Aune, *The Cultic Setting of Realized Eschatology in Early Christianity*, NovTSup 28, (Leiden: Brill, 1972), 13. See also Cullmann, *Christology*, 219, where he links I Corinthian 12:3 with Romans 8 and glossolalia. In fact, Cullmann sees speaking in tongues as likely in the background of Paul's statement that "no one can say that Jesus is Lord except by the Holy Spirit."
75. Matthew 11:28.

Chapter 18: Rediscovering Covenant

1. See Donald Dayton, *The Theological Roots of Pentecostalism*, (Metuchan, NJ: The Scarecrow Press, 1987); D. William Faupel, *The Everlasting Gospel: The Significance of Eschatology in the Development of Pentecostal Thought*, (Sheffield: Sheffield Academic Press, 1996); Robert Mapes Anderson, *Vision of the Disinherited: The Making of American Pentecostalism*, (New York: Oxford University Press, 1979).
2. Robert Tuttle, *John Wesley: His Life and Theology*, (Grand Rapids, MI: Zondervan, 1978), 71.

3. Wesley was not only a reader of John Locke; he was also a reader of Peter Browne, an interpreter of Locke, who tempered Locke's deism. See Donald A. D. Thorsen, *The Wesleyan Quadrilateral: Scripture, Reason and Experience as a Model of Evangelical Theology*, (Grand Rapids, MI: Zondervan, 1990), 58-59; see especially Thorson's chapter 6.
4. Dayton, *Theological Roots*, 41. Dayton notes that the shape of Wesley's primitivism "was then in this sense somewhat more historically nuanced than the biblicistic appeal of Pentecostalism to the Book of Acts." While Pentecostals allowed for tradition, it was not tradition beyond the first century.
5. By 1820, Methodists numbered a quarter of a million; by 1830, they numbered twice that number. See Nathan O. Hatch, *The Democratization of American Christianity*, (New Haven, CT: Yale University Press, 1989), 3.
6. Raymond A. Eve and Francis B. Harrold, *The Creationist Movement in Modern America*, (Boston: Twayne, 1990), 14. Eve and Harrold write, "One of these approaches was the epistemological philosophy of Scottish Common Sense Realism, developed by Thomas Reid and other practical-minded Scottish thinkers of the late eighteenth century. They opposed the profound and disquieting skepticism of David Hume, who had argued that we never really establish that relations of cause and effect exist in the external world." Associated with this was a kind of "Baconian" method, distrusting words like "theory" and "hypothesis" and emphasizing that a collection of facts about the natural world would lead to scientific conclusions.
7. Dayton is correct when he catalogs the significance of a number of events, including the Civil War, replacing the broad optimistic religious and cultural feeling with a kind of apocalypticism. *Theological Roots*, 76.
8. George M. Marsden, *Fundamentalism and the American Culture: The Shaping of Twentieth Century Evangelicalism: 1870-1925*, (New York: Oxford University Press, 1980), 64-65.
9. Anderson, *Vision of the Disinherited*, 30. Anderson writes, "In the last quarter of the nineteenth century, the identification of Protestantism with middle class culture was almost complete." Standards for membership in congregations were lowered and church discipline was largely abandoned.
10. As one speaker at a prophecy conference claimed, prophecy was the "photographically exact forecasting of the future." *The Inspired Word: A Series of Papers and Addresses Delivered at the Bible Inspiration Conference, Philadelphia, 1887*, ed. A. T. Pierson, (New York: Anson D. F. Randolph, 1888), 17; cited in Faupel, *Everlasting Gospel*, 113 (note 127).
11. Not only was current revelation dependent on experience, but there was an expectation of greater experiences of the Holy Spirit to come. Faupel, *The Everlasting Gospel*, 114.
12. See Steven J. Land, *Pentecostal Spirituality: A Passion for the Kingdom*, (Sheffield: Sheffield Academic Press, 1993), 95, who suggests that such tension in the late nineteenth-century Holiness movement took place in a particular eschatological framework.
13. Synan, *Century of the Holy Spirit*, 2.
14. Dayton, *Theological Roots*, 100-4; Marsden, *Fundamentalism*, 75.
15. On the tensions as how to express this second work of grace, see Dayton, *Theological Roots*, 77-78.
16. Marsden, *Fundamentalism*, 78.
17. Marsden, *Fundamentalism*, 72; citing C. I. Scofield, *Plain Papers on the Doctrine of the Holy Spirit*, (New York, 1899).
18. See Synan, *Century of the Holy Spirit*; James R. Goff, Jr., *Fields White Unto Harvest: Charles F. Parham and The Missionary Origins of Pentecostalism*, (Fayetteville, AR: University of Arkansas Press, 1988); Cecil M. Robeck, Jr., *The Azusa Street Mission and Revival: The Birth of the Global Pentecostal Movement*, (Nashville, TN: Nelson, 2006); Jacobsen, *Thinking in the Spirit*; Grant Wacker, *Heaven Below: Early Pentecostals and*

American Culture, (Cambridge, MA: Harvard University Press, 2001); Randall J. Stephens, *The Fire Spreads: Holiness and Pentecostalism in the American South*, (Cambridge, MA: Harvard University Press, 2008).

19. See French, *Our God is One*; Fred J. Foster, *Think It Not Strange: A History of the Oneness Movement*, (St. Louis, MO: Pentecostal Publishing House, 1965); Daniel L. Butler, *Oneness Pentecostalism: A History of the Jesus' Name Movement*, (San Gabriel, Cerritos, CA: n.p., 2004); Morris Golder, *History of the Pentecostal Assemblies of the World*, (Indianapolis: n.p., 1973); Arthur. L. and Charles E. Clanton, *United We Stand: A History of Oneness Organizations*, (Hazelwood, MO: Word Aflame Press, 1970); James L. Tyson, *The Early Pentecostal Revival: History of Twentieth-Century Pentecostals and The Pentecostal Assemblies of the World, 1901-30*, (Hazelwood, MO: Word Aflame Press, 1992).
20. For some, the focus on the soon coming of Jesus compelled their thinking. This too, however, became a point of tension, for not everyone held the same perspective about prophecy.
21. Charles F. Parham *Kol Kare Bomidbar: A Voice Crying in the Wilderness*, (Baxter Springs, KS: n.p., 1902), 32.
22. For instance, Benjamin Hardin Irwin, the founder of the Fire-Baptized Holiness Church, had witnessed numerous people speak in tongues. As well, Irwin could speak of multiple baptisms. For him, there were baptisms of "dynamite," "lyddite," "oxydite." Dayton, *Theological Roots*, 97-98.
23. Synan, *Century of the Holy Spirit*, 42-43. Charles Parham, the man generally recognized as "the formulator of Pentecostal doctrine" taught that tongues are the exclusive evidence of the baptism of the Holy Spirit "and should be seen as a part of every Christian's experience."
24. Ibid.
25. Faupel, *Everlasting Gospel*, 304. Faupel suggests the necessity of being part of the bride of Christ was universal for Pentecostals.
26. Frank Ewart, *The Phenomenon of Pentecost,* rev. ed., (1947; Hazelwood: Word Aflame Press, 1975).
27. Faupel, *Everlasting Gospel*, p. 26. Faupel cites several sources and notes. "We learn that the Bride enjoys the Pentecostal baptism which of necessity brings her to a place of yieldedness and suffering not realized by the great majority of believers." See A. G. Ward, *Soul Food for Hungry Hearts*, (Springfield, MO: Gospel Publishing House, 1925), 16-17. See also F. L. Crawford, "Preparing for Himself a Bride," *The Apostolic Faith* (Portland) 18 (January, 1909), p. 2; and E. A. Sexton, "The Bride of Christ," *The Bridegroom's Messenger* 3 (1 May, 1910), p. 1.
28. D. William Faupel, *The Everlasting Gospel*, 304, note 319, citing George F. Taylor, *The Spirit and the Bride: A Scriptural Presentation of the Operations, Manifestations, Gifts and Fruit of the Holy Spirit in Relation to His Bride with Special Reference to the Latter Rain Revival*, (Dunn, NC: The Author, 1907), 119-26.
29. Synan, *Century of the Holy Spirit*, 54.
30. Ibid.
31. On the way in which the emerging Pentecostal movement was able to control the language, see Wolfgang Vondey, "The Symbolic Turn: A Symbolic Conception of the Liturgy of Pentecostalism" *Wesleyan Theological Journal* 36 no. 2 (2001): 223-47.
32. As William Faupel notes on p. 25 of his *The Everlasting Gospel*, "Most early Pentecostals believed that 144,000 composed Christ's Bride whose marriage to the Lamb is described in Rev. 19:6-9." In note 22 on the same page, Faupel rightly suggests that for Charles Parham, this number was literal, citing Parham, *Kol Kare Bomidbar*, 86.
33. Faupel, *Everlasting Gospel*, 26. Faupel citing George F. Taylor, *The Spirit and the Bride*. Taylor writes on pp. 120-21: "We can never be the bride of our Lord, nor designated as His bride until the old man is dead, for that would be spiritual adultery. The death of the old man does not marry us to Jesus, nor mark us as His bride, but simply liberates us from the bondage of the law and makes us free to be married to whom we choose. After the death of the old man—after sanctification—the real courtship between Christ and the saint

begins. If that saint yields to all the wooings of the spirit, Christ will place upon that one 'the seal'—the engagement ring—which is none other than the Baptism of the Holy Ghost."
34. For a history of the Oneness Movement from a Oneness perspective, see French, *Our God is One*; cf. Fred J. Foster, *Think it Not Strange*.
35. Grant Wacker, "The Functions of Faith in Primitive Pentecostalism," *Harvard Theological Review* 77 (1984): 353-75, 356-57.
36. In *Kol Kare Bomidbar*, 21-24, Parham explains how after spending time reflecting in prayer, God led him to baptize in Jesus' name. Ethel Goss records that her husband, Howard, was baptized by Parham in Jesus' name in 1902. Ethel E. Goss, *The Winds of God: The Story of the Early Pentecostal Days (1901-1914) in the Life of Howard A. Goss*, (New York: Comet Press, 1958), 14. Cf. Foster, *Think It Not Strange*, 56.
37. Anderson, *Vision of the Disinherited*, 176.
38. Foster, *Think it Not Strange*, 50.
39. Pentecostals have consistently claimed that their theology results from a focus on restoration of the church, a theme that hails back to the time of Reformation. Even those who do not believe in a Oneness Pentecostal presentation will allow that hermeneutically, it hearkens from this same impulse. On this, see Gary B. McGee, "Early Pentecostal Hermeneutics: Tongues as Evidence in the Book of Acts," in *Initial Evidence: Historical and Biblical Perspective on the Pentecostal Doctrine of Spirit Baptism*, ed. Gary B. McGee, (Peabody, MA: Hendrickson, 1991), 105.
40. David Reed, "Origins and Development," 108.
41. G. T. Haywood, "Baptized into One Body," *The Good Report*, (1 December, 1913): 3, cited in French, *Our God is One*, 61.
42. Faupel, *Everlasting Gospel*, 293.
43. French, *Our God is One*, 61.
44. French, *Our God is One*, 52-54. French cites numerous thematic statements by Glenn Cook and Frank Ewart thanking God for "giving light in the evening time." See p. 236 where "The Water Way" demonstrates this same theme.
45. In the June 15, 1915, issue of the Assemblies of God *Evangel*, E. N. Bell wrote of baptism in Jesus' name as the "sad new issue." Because of the labeling, "new issue" became the nomenclature with which to describe baptism in Jesus' name. On this, see Butler, *Oneness Pentecostalism*, 116.
46. Robin Johnston, "Transitional Hermeneutics in Oneness Pentecostalism," (paper presented at the first annual Urshan Graduate School of Theology Symposium, May 2002), 101-13, 104.
47. For a study of the various taxonomies utilized by early Oneness Pentecostals, see Johnston, "Evening Light" and David S. Norris, "Response to Robin Johnston's 'Evening Light: The Development of Early Oneness Pentecostal Soteriology,'" (paper presented at the annual Urshan Graduate School of Theology Symposium, March 2005), 148-53. In my response, I summarize Johnston's six alternate taxonomies that made sense of the place of other Christians who were not part of the bride of Christ. These views were not formally held by distinct groups or individuals. Some held to one or more analogies to explain the fate of those not in the bride. They included (1) those who would be "saved" by walking in all the light they knew; (2) those who would not be lost even though they were not born again, due to the fact that they were "begotten"; (3) although some were not born again, they would not be lost because they had been in some sense "adopted"; (4) the soteriological status of some was explained by the Tabernacle. Perhaps they were like those worshiping in a Tabernacle still in the wilderness and not yet in the Promised Land; or perhaps the Tabernacle itself allows for Robin Johnston's "gradations," ways people could be categorized soteriologically; (5) some were in the "Kingdom of Heaven" even though they had not yet entered into the "Kingdom of God" (being filled with the Spirit and baptized in Jesus' name); (6) some Christians were "righteous" but not yet holy. They would have a place on the "new earth" and might ultimately find a place in Heaven.

48. On p. 259 of *Thinking in the Spirit*, Douglas Jacobsen offers, "In a certain sense, the Oneness theologies of Haywood and Urshan were also more distinctively pentecostal than anything that preceded them; at the very least, they were less dependent on previous forms of Christian theology."
49. Faupel, *Everlasting Gospel*, 304.
50. See p. 181.
51. As a translation of Deuteronomy 6:4, I have utilized the *Tanak* but where they translate "the LORD" I have transliterated it as Yahweh. Of course, first-century Jews would not say Yahweh. They would read Yahweh but say the more generic Hebrew *Adonai*. Nonetheless, one can hardly miss the import of this verse spoken daily in a devotional confession.
52. Edith L. Blumhofer, *Restoring the Faith. The Assemblies of God, Pentecostalism and the American Culture*, (Urbana and Chicago: University of Illinois Press, 1993), 134.

EPILOGUE

1. Synan, *Century of the Holy Spirit*, 359-60.
2. See for instance, Fee, *God's Empowering Presence*; cf. Craig Keener, *Gift Giver: The Holy Spirit for Today*, (Grand Rapids: Baker Academic Books, 2001); Keener admits his own situatedness. See as well, Max Turner in his *The Holy Spirit and Spiritual Gifts in the New Testament Church and Today*, (Peabody, MA: Hendrickson, 1996). Turner works to define the work of the Spirit as a secondary baptism but to place it under the aegis of various experiences of the Spirit.
3. Norbert Baumert suggests that "the Pentecostal-charismatic awakening is leveled down" in terms of its significance or "presented as an ideal." See "'Charism' and 'Spirit-Baptism': Presentation of an Analysis," *Journal of Pentecostal Theology* 12 no. 2 (2004): 147-79, 152.
4. Charles Holman, Professor of New Testament and Biblical Interpretation at Regent Divinity School, offered a paper that suggested Ephesians should interpret the Book of Acts, thus deconstructing the classical notion of what it means to be "Spirit-filled." See Charles L. Holman, "Ephesians and Ecumenism (or Ecumenical Pneumatology)," (presented at the 31st Annual meeting of Society for Pentecostal Studies, Lakeland, FL, March 15, 2002).
5. On critics of Azusa street, see Synan, *The Holiness-Pentecostal Tradition: Charismatic Movements in the Twentieth Century*, rev. ed., (Grand Rapids, MI: Eerdmans, 1997), 100-2.
6. In terms of seeking to retain fellowship, Andrew Urshan is often viewed as the most ameliorating. This is hardly the same as saying that Urshan did not have strong opinions.
7. Jacobsen, *Thinking in the Spirit*, 259.
8. Rodney Stark, *The Rise of Christianity: A Sociologist Reconsiders History*, (Princeton, NJ: Princeton University Press, 1996).
9. As we suggested in the previous chapter, this was the confession of Azusa Street. While Seymour, by some accounts, softened in his faith in tongues as the evidence of the Holy Spirit, what he said needs to be understood in its historical context. Further, what we are calling an Azusa Street confession is that which was proclaimed during the time of the Azusa Street revival.
10. Anderson, *Vision of the Disinherited*.
11. Robin Johnston, "Evening Light," 1; citing Frank J. Ewart, *Phenomenon of Pentecost*, 97.
12. Hattie E. Pryor, "The Water Way," copyright 1919 by G. T. Haywood, *The Bridegroom Songs*, ed. G. T. Haywood, (Indianapolis, IN: Christ Temple, 1926). The tenor of my argument follows that of Johnston's "Evening Light."
13. This observation is based loosely on statistics on how many copies of *New Birth* have been sold and into how many languages it has been translated.
14. For a Catholic approach to the relationship of the baptism of the Spirit being related to initiation into covenant, see McDonnell and Montague, *Christian Initiation*. While there are certainly distinctives with that of a Oneness Pentecostal presentation and that of McDonnell/Montague, on p. 30 Montague will go so far as to say, "There is only one

baptism, an integral rite that involves water and the gift of the Holy Spirit." For an analysis of this position, see Baumert, 151. Baumert summarizes the position by offering that for McDonald and Montague, "Spirit baptism is an unpacking of the grace of baptism, even if this experience may occur only later, and, as such, it is 'normative' for every Christian."

15. Lutherans have certain affinities with Oneness Pentecostals, at least in how they would speak of the efficaciousness of baptism. Lutherans would suggest that "holy baptism" is a "means of grace." Interestingly, on p. 411 of "Holy Baptism" in *The Abiding Word: An Anthology of Doctrinal Essays*, Vol. 2, ed. Theodore Laetsch, rev. ed. (St. Louis: Concordia Publishing House, 1975), 394-422, Theodore J. Mueller uses the same Scriptures to demonstrate the necessity of baptism as Oneness Pentecostals (Acts 22:16; Acts 2:38; John 3:5; Titus 3:5). Clearly written against a Reformed theological position, Mueller concludes his list of texts proving the necessity of baptism by offering that Lutherans believe the Word of God "whether we understand it or not" while the Reformed tradition "rationalize the doctrine" and therefore err in their understanding due to "their perverse and conceited reasons."

Abbreviations

4Qflor	*Floregium*
ABD	*The Anchor Bible Dictionary*, ed. Noel Freedman, 6 vols., (New York: Doubleday, 1992).
ANF	Ante-Nicene Fathers
BAG	Walter Bauer, *Greek-English Lexicon of the New Testament and Other Early Christian Literature*, trans. and adap. by William F. Arndt and Wilber F. Gingrich, (Chicago: University of Chicago Press, 1957).
BDB	Brown-Driver-Briggs *Hebrew and English Lexicon*
BHS	*Biblia Hebraica Stuttgartensia*
C. Ar.	Athanasius, *Orations against the Arians*
CD	*Damascus Document*
Cels.	Origen, *Against Celsus*
CRINT	Compendia rerum Iudaicarum ad Novum Testamentum
H. E.	Eusebius, *Historia ecclesiastica* [Ecclesiastical History]
HUCA	*Hebrew Union College Annual*
JBL	*Journal of Biblical Literature*
JSS	*Journal of Semitic Studies*
JSNT	*Journal for the Study of the New Testament*
KJV	King James Version
LXX	*Septuagint* (Greek Translation of the Old Testament)
Magn.	Ignatius, *To the Magnesians*
Mut. Nom.	Philo, *De mutatione nominum* [On the Change of Names]
NIV	New International Version
NKJV	New King James Version
NJB	New Jerusalem Bible
NRSV	New Revised Standard Version
Pan.	Epiphanius, *Panarion* (Adversus haereses) [Refutation of All Heresies]
Prax.	Tertullian, *Against Praxeas*
Princ.	Origen, *First Principles*
SBL	Society of Biblical Literature
SBLMS	Society of Biblical Literature Monograph Series

Sim.   *Shepherd of Hermas*, Similitude
Smryn.   Ignatius, *To the Smyrneans*
TDNT   *Theological Dictionary of the New Testament*, 10 vols., eds. Gerhard Kittel and Gerhard Friedrich, trans. and ed. Geoffrey W. Bromily, (Grand Rapids, MI: Eerdmans, 1985).
TNTC   *Tyndale New Testament Commentary*
TWOT   R. Laird Harris, Gleason L. Archer, and Bruce K. Waltke, *Theological Wordbook of the Old Testament*, (Chicago: Moody, 1980).

Bibliography

Primary Sources

The Ante-Nicene Fathers. 10 vols. Translated and edited by A. Cleveland Coxe, +Alexander Roberts, and James Donaldson. Grand Rapids, MI: Eerdmans, 1951.

Athanasius. "Four Discourses Against the Arians," Discourse 4. Translated and edited by Philip Schaff and Henry Wace. *The Nicene and Post-Nicene Fathers,* Vol. 4, New York: The Christian Lit. Co. 1892.

Augustine. *The City of God.* Translated by Marcus Dods. New York: The Modern Library, 1950.

Bettenson, Henry, ed. *Documents of the Christian Church.* New York: Oxford University Press, 1963.

Biblia Hebraica Stuttgartensia. Edited by K. Elliger and W. Rudolph. Stuttgart: Deutsche Bibelstiftung, 1967-77.

Brenton, Lancelot C. L., trans. and ed. *The Septuagint with Apocrypha: Greek and English. Various Readings and Critical Notes.* Grand Rapids, MI: Zondervan, 1972.

Charlesworth, James H., ed. *The Dead Sea Scrolls; Hebrew, Aramaic and Greek Texts with English Translations.* 2 vols. Louisville: Westminster John Knox, 1994, 1995.

———, ed. *The Pseudepigrapha of the Old Testament.* 2 vols. New York: Doubleday, 1983, 1985.

Clement of Alexandria, *Tutor* (*Paedagogus*). 8.71.1. Die griechischen christlichen Schriftsteller der ersten drei Jahrhunderte. 12:131, Berlin.

Ehrman, Bart D., ed. *After the New Testament: A Reader in Early Christianity.* New York: Oxford University Press, 1999.

Epiphanius. *The Panarion of Epiphanius; Bishop of Salamis, Selected Passages.* Translated by Philip R. Amidon. New York: Oxford University Press, 1990.

Eusebius, *De Ecclesiastica Theologia* [Ecclesiastical Theology]. Book 1. Translated by B. E. Daley. Harvard University, (unpublished), 1983.

Fitzmyer, James A. *The Genesis Apocryphon of Qumran Cave 1: A Commentary.* Biblica et Orientalia 18A. Rome: Editrice Pontificio Istituto Biblico, 1966.

Fox, Everett. *The Schocken Bible:* Vol. 1. *The Five Books of Moses: Genesis, Exodus, Leviticus, Numbers, and Deuteronomy. A New Translation with Introductions, Commentary, and Notes.* New York: Schocken, 1995.

García-Martínez F. *The Dead Sea Scrolls Translated: The Qumran Texts in English.* Translated by W. G. E. Watson. Leiden: Brill, 1994.

Gordon, C. H. *Ugaritic Textbook, Acalecta Orientalia* 38. Rome: Pontifical Biblical Institute, 1965.

Grant, Robert M. *The Apostolic Fathers. A New Translation and Commentary.* Vol 1. New York: Thomas Nelson & Sons, 1964.

Hamilton, Edith and Huntington Cairns, eds. *The Collected Dialogues of Plato including the Letters.* Bollingen Series 71. Princeton: Princeton University Press, 1985.

Hippolytus, "Against the Heresy of One Noetus." *The Ante-Nicene Fathers,* Vol. 5.

———. "Refutation of All Heresies." *The Ante-Nicene Fathers,* Vol. 5.

Irenaeus. *Against Heresies. The Ante-Nicene Fathers*, Vol. 1.

Josephus. *Complete Works.* Translated by William Whiston. Grand Rapids, MI: Kregel Publications, 1960.

Justin Martyr. "Dialogue With Trypho." *The Ante-Nicene Fathers*, Vol. 1.

Juvenal. *The Sixteen Satires [by] Juvenal.* Translation, introduction, and notes by Peter Green. Baltimore: Penguin Books, 1967.

Kee, H. C. "Testaments of the Twelve Patriarchs," *Pseudepigrapha of the Old Testament*, Vol. 1. New York: Doubleday, 1983.

Kraeling, Emil G, ed. *The Brooklyn Museum Aramaic Papyri: New Documents from the Jewish Colony at Elephantine.* New Haven, CT: Yale University Press, 1953.

Kraft, Robert. *The Didache. The Apostolic Fathers: A New Translation and Commentary.* Vol. 3. Translation and commentary by Robert A. Kraft. Toronto, New York, London: Thomas Nelson and Sons, 1965.

Melito of Sardis. *On the Passover.* In Ehrman, *After the New Testament.*

Miller, Robert J., ed. *The Complete Gospels.* San Francisco: Harper, 1994.

Niederwimmer, Kurt. *The Didache.* Translated by Linda M. Maloney. Edited by Harold W. Attridge. 2nd ed. Minneapolis: Fortress Press, 1998.

Plato. *The Republic.* Translated by Paul Shorey. Cambridge, MA: Harvard University Press, 1937.

Pliny. *Naturalis Historia.* Translated by Philemon Holland. Selected and introduced by Paul Turner. London: Centaur Press, 1962.

Pritchard, James D. *Ancient Near Eastern Texts Relating to the Old Testament.* 3rd ed. with Supplement, Princeton, NJ: Princeton University Press, 1969.

Reed, S. A. *The Dead Sea Scrolls Inventory Project: Lists of Documents, Photographs, and Museum Plates.* Claremont: Ancient Biblical Manuscript Center, 1992.

Robinson, J. M. *The Nag Hammadi Library in English.* 3rd ed. San Francisco: Harper and Row, 1988.

Schneemelcher, Wilhelm, ed. R. Mcl. Wilson, English trans. ed., *New Testament Apocrypha*, Vol. 2; *Writings Relating to the Apostles; Apocalypses and Related Subjects.* Louisville, KY: Westminster/John Knox, 1992.

Tertullian. *Against Praxeas. The Ante-Nicene Fathers*, Vol. 3.

Tov, Emanuel, ed. *The Dead Sea Scrolls on Microfiche: Companion Volume.* New York: E. J. Brill, 1993.

Vermès Geza. *The Dead Sea Scrolls in English.* London: Penguin, 1987.

Wise, Michael, Martin Abegg Jr., and Edward Cook. *The Dead Sea Scrolls: A New Translation.* San Francisco: Harper, 1996.

Yonge, Charles D., trans. *The Works of Philo: Complete and Unabridged.* 1854. Updated reprint, Peabody, MA: Hendrickson, 1993.

Secondary Sources

Abramowski, Luise. "The 'Memoirs of the Apostles' in Justin" in *The Gospel and the Gospels.* Edited by Peter Stuhlmacher, 323-35. Grand Rapids, MI: Eerdmans, 1991.

Aland, Kurt and Barbara. *The Text of the New Testament: An Introduction to the Critical Editions and to the Theory and Practice of Modern Textual Criticism.* Translated by Erroll F. Rhodes. Grand Rapids: Eerdmans, 1987.

Albright, William F. *From the Stone Age to Christianity.* Baltimore: Johns Hopkins Press, 1940.

———. "The Name *Yahweh.*" *Journal of Biblical Literature* 43 (1924): 370-78.

———. *Yahweh and the Gods of Canaan.* London: Athlone Press, 1968.

Anderson, James N. "Pre-Existent Christology and Certain Passages." Paper presented at the annual Urshan Graduate School Symposium, 260–88, Hazelwood, MO, 2005.

Anderson, Robert Mapes. *Vision of the Disinherited: The Making of American Pentecostalism.* New York: Oxford University Press, 1979.

D'Angelo, Mary Rose. "Abba and 'Father': Imperial Theology and the Jesus Traditions." *JBL* 111 no. 4 (1992): 611-30.

Archer, Kenneth J. *A Pentecostal Hermeneutic for the Twenty-first Century: Spirit, Scripture and Community.* London, New York: Continuum International Publishing Group, 2004.

Arndt, William F. and F. Wilbur Gingrich. *A Greek-English Lexicon of the New Testament and Other Early Christian Literature.* Translated by Walter Bauer. Chicago: University of Chicago Press, 1957.

Arrington, F. L. *The Acts of the Apostles.* Peabody, MA: Hendrickson, 1988.

Atkinson, William. "Pentecostal Responses to Dunn's *Baptism in the Holy* Spirit; Luke- Acts. *Journal of Pentecostal Theology* 6 (1995): 49-72.

Attridge, Harold M. *The Epistle to the Hebrews: A Commentary of the Epistle to the Hebrews.* Edited by Helmut Koester. Hermeneia. Philadelphia: Fortress Press, 1989.

Aune, David, E. *The Cultic Setting of Realized Eschatology in Early Christianity.* Novum Testamentum Supplements 28. Leiden: Brill, 1972.

Austin, J. L. *How to Do Things with Words.* 1962. Reprint, New York: Oxford University Press, 1970.

Ayers, Lewis. "Augustine's Trinitarian Theology." In *Augustine and His Critics: Essays in Honour of Gerald Bonner.* Edited by Robert Dodaro and George Lawless. London and New York: Routledge, 2000.

Bakken, Norman K. "The New Humanity: Christ and the Modern Age. A Study Centering in the Christ Hymn: Philippians 2:6-11." *Interpretation* 22 (1968): 71-82.

Balentine, Samuel E. *Hidden God: The Hiding of the Face of God in the Old Testament.* Oxford and New York: Oxford University Press, 1983.

Baltzer, Klaus. "The Meaning of the Temple in Lukan Writings." *Harvard Theological Review* 58 (1965): 263-77.

Baron, Salo. "Population." In vol. 13 (16 vols) of *Encyclopedia Judaica.* Jerusalem: Macmillan, 1973, 866-904.

Barr, James. "Abba isn't Daddy." *Journal of Theological Studies* 39 no. 1 (1988): 28-47.

Barrett, C. K. *Acts*. International Critical Commentary 1. Edited by J. A. Emerton, C. E. B. Cranfield, and G. N. Stanton. Edinburgh Scotland: T. and T. Clark, 1994.

———. "Apollos and the Twelve Disciples of Ephesus." In *The New Testament Age: Essays in Honor of Bo Reich*. Vol. 1. Edited by W. C. Weinrich, 29-39. Macon, GA: Mercer, 1984.

———. *A Commentary on the First Epistle to the Corinthians*. Harper's New Testament Commentaries. 1968. Reprint, New York: Harper & Row, 1993.

———. *From First Adam to Last*. London: Adam and Charles Black, 1962.

———, ed. *The New Testament Backgrounds: Selected Documents*. Revised edition. San Francisco: Harper & Row, Publishers, 1987.

Bauckham, Richard. *God Crucified: Monotheism & Christology in the New Testament*. Grand Rapids, MI: Eerdmans, 1998.

———, ed. *The Gospel for all Christians: Rethinking the Gospel Audiences*. Grand Rapids, MI: Eerdmans, 1999.

———. "James and the Jerusalem Church." In *The Book of Acts in Its Palestinian Setting*. Edited by Richard Bauckham. Grand Rapids, MI: Eerdmans, 1995.

Baumert, Norbert. "'Charism' and 'Spirit-Baptism': Presentation of an Analysis." *Journal of Pentecostal Theology* 12 no. 2 (2004): 147-79.

Bauer, Walter. *A Greek-English Lexicon of the New Testament and Other Early Christian Literature*. Translated and adapted by William F. Arndt and Wilber F. Gingrich. Chicago: University of Chicago Press, 1957.

Baus, Karl. *History of the Christian Church*. Vol. 1. *From the Apostolic Community to Constantine*. New York: Seabury Press, 1980.

Beasley-Murray, G. R. *Baptism in the New Testament*. London: MacMillan, 1962.

Beisner, E. Calvin. *God in Three Persons.* Wheaton IL: Tyndale, 1984.

Belleville, Linda. "Born of Water and Spirit," *Trinity Journal NS* (1980): 125-41.

Berchman, Robert M. *From Philo to Origen: Middle Platonism in Transition.* Brown Judaic Studies 69. Chico CA: Scholars Press, 1984.

Berkhof, Hendrikus. *Christian Faith: An Introduction to the Study of Faith.* Revised edition, translated by Sierd Woudstra. Grand Rapids, MI: Eerdmans, 1985.

Bernard, David K. *The New Birth.* Hazelwood, MO: Word Aflame Press, 1984.

―――. *The Oneness of the Godhead.* Revised edition. Hazelwood, MO: Word Aflame Press, 2000.

―――. *The Oneness View of Jesus Christ.* Hazelwood, MO: Word Aflame Press, 1994.

Blumhofer, Edith L. *Restoring the Faith. The Assemblies of God, Pentecostalism and the American Culture.* Urbana and Chicago: University of Illinois Press, 1993.

Boer, Harry R. *An Ember Still Glowing: Humankind as the Image of God.* Grand Rapids, MI: Eerdmans, 1990.

Borg, Marcus. "Portraits of Jesus in Contemporary North American Scholarship." *Harvard Theological Review* 84 no. 1 (1991): 1-22.

Bonsor, Jack A. *Athens and Jerusalem: The Role of Philosophy in Theology.* New York: Paulist Press, 1993.

Botterweck, G. Johannes, and Helmer Ringgren, eds., *Theological Word Book of the Old Testament.* Translated by John T. Willis. Grand Rapids, MI: Eerdmans, 1975.

Bourdieu, Pierre. *Language and Symbolic Power.* Edited and with an introduction by John B. Thompson. Translated by Gino Raymond and Matthew Adamson. Cambridge, MA: Harvard University Press, 1991.

———. *An Outline of Theory and Practice*. Cambridge, MA: Cambridge University Press, 1971.

Bousset, Willhelm. *Kyrios Christos: A History of the Belief in Christ From the Beginninings of Christianity to Iraneaus*. 1913. Translated by John E. Steely. Nashville: Abingdon Press, 1970.

Bowman, John Wick. *The Letter to the Hebrews*. The Layman's Bible Commentary 24. Richmond, VA: John Knox, 1962.

———. *Samaritan Documents Relating to Their History, Religion and Life*. Pittsburgh: Pickwick Press, 1977.

Boyd, Gregory A. *Oneness Pentecostals & the Trinity. A World-wide Movement Assessed by a Former Oneness Pentecostal*. Grand Rapids, MI: Baker, 1992.

Braaten, Carl E. "Introduction: Naming the Name." In *Our Naming of God: Problems and Prospects of God-Talk Today*. Edited by Carl E. Braaten. Minneapolis: Augsburg Press, 1989.

Brauch, Manfred. "Appendix: 'God's Righteousness' in Recent German Discussion." In *Paul and Palestinian Judaism: A Comparison of Patterns of Religion*. Edited by E. P. Sanders. Philadelphia: Fortress Press, 1977.

Braumann, G. "Advocate, *Paraklete*, Helper" in *The New International Dictionary of New Testament Theology*. Vol. 1. Edited by Colin Brown, 88-91. 1975. Reprint, Grand Rapids, MI: Zondervan, 1986.

Brawley, Robert L. *Luke-Acts and the Jews: Conflict, Apology and Conciliation*. Atlanta: Scholars Press, 1987.

———. *Text to Text Pours Forth Speech: Voices of Scripture in Luke-Acts*. Bloomington, IN: Indiana University Press, 1995.

Brichto, Herbert Chanan. *The Names of God: Poetic Readings in Biblical Beginnings*. New York: Oxford University Press, 1998.

Bright, John. *A History of Israel*. 1957. Reprint, Philadelphia: Westminster, 1981.

Bromily, G. W. "Anthropology." In *The International Standard Bible Encyclopedia*. Vol. 1. Edited by G. W. Bromily. Grand Rapids, MI: Eerdmans, 1979.

Broshi, Magen. "The Role of the Temple in the Herodian Economy." *Journal of Jewish Studies* 38 (1987): 31-37.

Brown, Colin. *Christianity & Western Thought: A History of Philosophers, Ideas and Movements. From the Ancient World to the Age of Enlightenment.* Downers Grove, IL: Intervarsity Press, 1990.

Brown, Francis, S. R. Driver, and Charles A. Briggs. *Hebrew and English Lexicon with an Appendix Containing the Biblical Aramaic.* Peabody, MA: Hendrickson, 1979.

Brown, Raymond E. *The Churches that the Apostles Left Behind.* New York: Paulist Press, 1984.

———. *The Gospel According to John.* 2 vols. Anchor Bible 29, 29A. Garden City, NY: Doubleday, 1966–70.

———. *Jesus: God and Man: Modern Biblical Reflections.* New York: MacMillan, 1967.

Brown, Raymond E. and John P. Meier. *Antioch and Rome: New Testament Cradles of Catholic Christianity.* New York: Paulist Press, 1983.

Bruce, F. F. *The Book of Acts.* The New International Commentary on the New Testament. Revised edition. Grand Rapids, MI: Eerdmans, 1988.

———. *The Epistle to the Galatians: A Commentary on the Greek Text.* Grand Rapids, MI: Eerdmans, 1982.

———. *The Epistle to the Hebrews: The English Text with Introduction, Exposition and Notes*, Grand Rapids, MI: Eerdmans, (1964) 1990.

———. *The Greek Text with Introduction and Commentary.* 3rd ed. Grand Rapids, MI: Eerdmans, 1990.

Brueggemann, Walter. *Israel's Praise: Doxology against Idolatry and Ideology.* Philadelphia: Fortress Press, 1988.

Brunner, Emil. *Dogmatics*, vol. 1: *The Christian Doctrines of God*. Translated by Olive Wyon. Philadelphia: Westminster, 1950.

Buber, Martin. *I and Thou*. Translated by Ronald Gregor Smith. New York: Scribner Press, 1958.

Buchanan, George Wesley. *To the Hebrews: Translation, Comment and Conclusions*. Garden City, NY: Doubleday, 1972.

Bultmann, Rudolph. *Primitive Christianity in its Contemporary Setting*. Translated by R. H. Fuller. London: Thames and Hudson, 1956.

Burgess, Stanley E., ed. *The New International Dictionary of Pentecostal Charismatic Movements*. Grand Rapids, MI: Zondervan, 2002.

Butler, Daniel L. *Oneness Pentecostalism: A History of the Jesus' Name Movement*. San Gabriel, Cerritos, CA: n.p., 2004.

Buttrick, George Arthur, ed. *The Interpreter's Bible: In the King James and Revised Standard Versions with General Articles and Introduction, Exegesis, Exposition for Each Book of the Bible*. 12 Vols. New York: Abingdon Press-Cokesbury Press, 1951-57.

Camp, Ashby L. "Reexamining the Rule of Concord in Acts 2:38, *Restoration Quarterly* 1 (1997): 37-42.

Carson, D. A. *Exegetical Fallacies*. Grand Rapids, MI: Baker, 1993.

———. *The Gospel According to John*. Pillar New Testament Commentary. Grand Rapids, MI: Eerdmans, 1991.

Carson, D. A., Douglas J. Moo, and Leon Morris. *An Introduction to the New Testament*.
Grand Rapids, MI: Zondervan, 1992.

Chadwick, Henry. *The Pelikan History of the Christian Church*. Vol. 1. *The Early Church*. Grand Rapids, MI: Eerdmans, 1967.

Chafer, Louis Sperry. *Systematic Theology*. 3 vols. Dallas, TX: Dallas Seminary Press, 1947.

Chance, J. Bradley. *Jerusalem, the Temple, and the New Age in Luke-Acts*. Macon, GA: Mercer University Press, 1988.

Charlesworth, James H., ed. *The Messiah: Developments in Earliest Judaism and Christianity: The First Princeton Symposium on Judaism and Christian Origins.* Minneapolis: Fortress Press, 1992.

Childs, Brevard. *Old Testament Theology in a Canonical Context.* Philadelphia: Fortress Press, 1985.

———. *Introduction to the Old Testament as Scripture.* Philadelphia: Fortress Press, 1979.

Christiansen, Irmgard. *Die Technik der allegorischen Auslegungswissenschaft bei Philon von Alexandrien.* Beiträge zur Geschichte der biblischen Hermeneutik 7. Tübingen: Mohr-Siebeck, 1969.

Clanton, Arthur. L. and Charles E. Clanton. *United We Stand: A History of Oneness Organizations.* Jubilee edition reprint, Hazelwood, MO: Word Aflame Press, 1995.

Clark, Gordon H. *Three Types of Religious Philosophy.* 1973. Reprint, Jefferson, MD: The Trinity Foundation, 1989.

Clines, David J. A., ed. *The Dictionary of Classical Hebrew.* 5 vols. Sheffield: Sheffield Academic Press, 1993.

Cohen, Shaye. *From the Maccabees to the Mishnah.* Philadelphia: Westminster, 1987.

Collins, John J. *Seers, Sibyls and Sages in Hellenistic-Roman Judaism.* New York: Brill, 1997.

Conybeare, Fred C. "The Eusebian form the the Text Matth. 28,19," *Zeitschrift Für Die Neutestamentliche Wissenschaft* 2 (1901): 275-88.

Coogan, Michael D. "Septuagint." In *The Oxford Companion to the Bible.* Edited by Bruce Metzger and Michael Coogan. New York: Oxford University Press, 1993.

Corwin, Virginia. *St. Ignatius and Christianity in Antioch.* New Haven: Yale University Press, 1960.

Craig, William Lane. *The Cosmological Argument from Plato to Leibniz.* New York: Barnes and Noble; London: Macmillan, 1980.

Craigie, Peter C. *Psalms 1-50*. Word Biblical Commentary 19. Waco, TX: Word Books, 1983.

Crawford, F. L. "Preparing for Himself a Bride." *The Apostolic Faith* (Portland) 18 (January, 1909).

Cross, Frank M. *Canaanite Myth and Hebrew Epic: Essays in the History of the Religion of Israel*. Cambridge, MA: Harvard University Press, 1973.

Cross, Terry. "Can there be a Pentecostal Systematic Theology?: An Essay on Theological Method in a Postmodern World" Paper for Society of Pentecostal Studies, Tulsa, OK, March, 2001.

Crossan, John D., *The Historical Jesus: The Life of a Mediterranean Jewish Peasant*. San Francisco: Harper, 1991.

Crouse, Robert. "*PAUCIS MUTATIS VERBIS:* Augustine's Platonism." In *Augustine and His Critics: Essays in Honour of Gerald Bonner*. Edited by Robert Dodaro and George Lawless. London and New York: Routledge, 2000.

Cullmann, Oscar. *The Christology of the New Testament*. Translated by Shirley C. Guthrie and Charles M. Hall. Philadelphia: Westminster John Knox, 1963.

———. *Early Christian Worship*. Translated by A. Stewart Todd and James B. Torrence. London: SCM, 1953.

Culy, Martin M. and Mikeal C. Parsons. *Acts: A Handbook of the Greek Text*. Waco, TX: Baylor University Press, 2003.

Dahl, Nils A. "A People for his Name." *New Testament Studies* 4 (1958): 319-27.

———. "Jesus the Christ." In *The Historical Origins of Christological Doctrine*. Edited by Donald Juel. Minneapolis: Fortress Press, 1991.

Daniélou, Jean. *The Dead Sea Scrolls and Primitive Christianity*. Baltimore: Helicon Press, 1958.

———. *The Development of Christian Doctrine before the Council of Nicea*. 3 vols. Translated and edited by John A. Baker. Vol. 1,

The Theology of Jewish Christianity. Vol. 2, *Gospel and Hellenistic Culture.* Vol. 3, *The Origin of Latin Christianity.* London: Darton, Longman & Todd, 1964, 1973, 1977.

Davis, Carl Judson. "Another Look at the Relationship between Baptism and Forgiveness of Sins in Acts 2:38." Restoration Quarterly 24 (1981): 80-84.

———. *The Name and Way of the Lord: Old Testament Themes, New Testament Christology.* Sheffield: Sheffield Academic Press, 1996.

Dayton, Donald. *The Theological Roots of Pentecostalism.* Metuchan, NJ: The Scarecrow Press, 1987.

Denney, James. *The Expositor's Greek New Testament.* 5 vols. Edited by W. Robertson Nicholl. Peabody MA: Hendrickson, 2002.

Dillon, John. "Origen's Doctrine of the Trinity and Some Later Neoplatonic Theories" in *NeoPlatonism and Christian Thought.* Edited by Dominic J. O'Meara. Norfolk, VA: International Society for NeoPlatonic Studies, 1982.

Dorner, Isaak August. *Divine Immutability.* Translated by Robert R. Williams and Claude Welch with an introduction by Robert R. Williams. Minneapolis: Fortress Press, 1994.

Dorner, J. A. *History of the Development of the Doctrine of the Person of Christ,* Vol. 2. Translated by D. W. Simon., Edinburgh: T & T Clark, 1862.

Driver, G. R. "The Original Form of the Name 'Yahweh': Evidence and Conclusions." *Zeitschrift für die alttestamentliche Wissenschaft* (1928): 7-25.

Dunn, James D. G. *Baptism in the Spirit: A Re-examination of the New Testament Teaching on the Gift of the Spirit in Relation to Pentecostalism Today.* Philadelphia: Westminster, 1970.

———. "Baptism in the Holy Spirit: A Response to Pentecostal Scholarship on Luke- Acts." *Journal of Pentecostal Theology* 3 (1993): 3-27.

———. *Christology in the Making: A New Testament Inquiry into the Origins of the Doctrine of the Incarnation*. 2nd ed. Philadelphia: Westminster, 1989.

———. *Jesus and the Spirit: A Study of the Religious and Charismatic Experience of Jesus and the First Christians as Reflected in the New Testament*. Philadelphia: Westminster, 1975.

———. "Let John Be John: A Gospel for its Time." In *The Gospel and Gospels*. Edited by Peter Stuhlmacher. Grand Rapids, MI: Eerdmans, 1992.

———. *The Theology of Paul the Apostle*. Grand Rapids, MI: Eerdmans, 1998.

Durkheim, Emile. *The Elementary Forms of Religious Life*. Translated by S. W. Swain. London: Allen and Unwin, 1915.

Eichrodt, Walther. *Theology of the Old Testament*. 2 vols. Translated by J. A. Baker. Philadelphia: Westminster, 1961.

Edersheim, Alfred. *Sketches of Jewish Social Life*. Updated edition. Peabody, MA: Hendrickson, 1994.

———. *The Temple: Its Ministry and Services*. Peabody, MA: Hendrickson, 1994.

Erickson, Millard J. *Christian Theology*. Grand Rapids, MI: Baker, 1983.

Ervin, Howard. *Conversion-Initiation and the Baptism in the Holy Spirit: An Engaging Critique of James D. G. Dunn*. Peabody, MA: Hendrickson, 1984.

Eve, Raymond A., and Francis B. Harrold. *The Creationist Movement in Modern America*. Boston: Twayne, 1990.

Ewart, Frank. *The Name and the Book*. Chicago: Daniel Ryerson, 1936.

———. *The Phenomenon of Pentecost: A History of the Latter Rain*. Houston, TX: The Herald Publishing House, 1947. Revised edition, Hazelwood, MO: Word Aflame Press, 1975.

———. *The Revelation of Jesus Christ*. Hazelwood, MO: Pentecostal Publishing House, n.d.

Faupel, D. William. *The Everlasting Gospel: The Significance of Eschatology in the Development of Pentecostal Thought.* Sheffield: Sheffield Academic Press, 1996.

Fee, Gordon D. *God's Empowering Presence: The Holy Spirit in the Letters of Paul.* Peabody, MA: Hendrickson, 1994.

———. *The First Epistle to the Corinthians.* The New International Commentary on the New Testament. Grand Rapids, MI: Eerdmans, 1987.

———. *1 and 2 Timothy, Titus.* New International Biblical Commentary. Edited by Ward Gasque. Peabody, MA, 1995.

Fitzmyer, James A. "The Languages of Palestine in the First Century A.D" in *A Wandering Aramean: Collected Aramaic Essays.* Chico, CA: Scholars Press, 1979.

Flusser, David. In collaboration with J. Steven Notley. *Jesus.* 3rd ed. Jerusalem: The Hebrew University Magnes Press, 2001.

Foster, Fred J. *Think It Not Strange: A History of the Oneness Movement.* St. Louis, MO: Pentecostal Publishing House, 1965.

Fox, Norman. "Baptism." In *The New Schaff-Herzog Encyclopedia of Religious Knowledge*, vol. 1. Edited by Samuel Macauley Jackson, 435-54. Grand Rapids, MI: Baker, 1977.

Frankfort, Henri. *Kingship and the Gods: A Study of Ancient Near Eastern Religion as the Integration of Society and Nature.* Chicago: University of Chicago, 1948.

Freedman, David Noel, ed. *Anchor Bible Dictionary.* 6 Vols. New York: Doubleday, 1992.

Frei, Hans. *The Eclipse of Biblical Narrative: A Study in Eighteenth and Nineteenth Century Hermeneutics.* New Haven: Yale, 1974.

French, Talmadge. *Our God is One: The Story of Oneness Pentecostals.* Indianapolis: Voice and Vision, 1999.

Fretheim, Terrence E. *The Suffering of God: An Old Testament Perspective.* Philadelphia: Fortress Press, 1984.

Frick, Peter. *Divine Providence in Philo of Alexandria*. Tübingen: J. C. B. Mohr, 1999.

Fudge, Thomas A. *Christianity without the Cross: A History of Salvation in Oneness Pentecostalism*. Parkland, FL: Universal Publishers, 2003.

Furnish, Victor Paul. *II Corinthians: Translated with Introduction, Notes, and Commentary*. Anchor Bible 32A. New York: Doubleday, 1984.

Gaston, Lloyd. "Abraham and the Righteousness of God." *Horizons in Biblical Theology* 2 (1980): 39-68.

Gilmore, S. Maclean. "Easter and Pentecost." *Journal of Biblical Literature* 81 (1962): 62-66.

Glueck, Nelson. *Hesed in the Bible*. Cincinati: Hebrew Union College, 1967.

Gnuse, Robert K. "Redefining the Elohist." *Journal of Biblical Literature* 119 no. 2 (2000): 201-20.

Goff, James R. *Fields White Unto Harvest: Charles F. Parham and the Missionary Origins of Pentecostalism*. Fayetteville, AR: University of Arkansas Press, 1988.

Goiten, S. D. "*YHWH* the Passionate: The Monotheistic Meaning and Origin of the Name *YHWH*." *Vetus Testamentum* 6 (1956): 1-9.

Golder, Morris. *History of the Pentecostal Assemblies of the World*. Indianapolis: n.p., 1973.

Goldingay, John. "Biblical Narrative and Systematic Theology" in *Between Two Horizons: Spanning New Testament Studies and Systematic Theology*. Edited by Joel B. Green and Max Turner. Grand Rapids, MI: Eerdmans, 2000.

González, Justo L. *Christian Thought Revisited: Three Types of Theology*. Nashville, TN: Abingdon Press, 1989.

———. *Jewish Symbols in the Greco-Roman Period*. New York: Pantheon Books, 1953.

Goss, Ethel E. *The Winds of God: The Story of the Early Pentecostal Days (1901-1914) in the Life of Howard A. Goss.* New York: Comet Press, 1958.

Goulder, M. D. *Type and History in Acts.* London: SPCK, 1964.

Grant, Robert M. *Gods and the One God.* Philadelphia: Westminster, 1986.

———. *Jesus After the Gospels. The Christ of the Second Century.* The Hale Memorial Lectures of Seabury-Western Theological Seminary. Louisville, KY: Westminster/John Knox, 1989.

———. "The Appeal to the Early Fathers." *Journal of Theological Studies* 11 (1960): 13-24.

Graves, Brent. *The God of Two Testaments.* 2nd ed. Hazelwood, MO: Word Aflame Press, 2000.

Green, Joel B. *The Gospel of Luke.* The New International Commentary on the New Testament. Edited by Gordon Fee. Grand Rapids, MI: Eerdmans, 1997.

Grillmeier, Alois. *Christ in Christian Tradition.* Volume 1. *From the Apostolic Age to Chalcedon.* Translated by John Bowden. Atlanta: John Knox, 1974.

Grosheide, F. W. *Commentary on the First Epistle to the Corinthians.* Grand Rapids, MI: Eerdmans, 1953.

Grudem, Wayne. "The Gift of Prophecy in 1 Corinthians." PhD Diss., University of Cambridge, 1978.

Gunton, Colin E. *Yesterday and Today: A Study of Continuities in Christology.* Grand Rapids: Eerdmans, 1983.

———. ed. *Trinity, Time, and Church: A Response to the Theology of Robert W. Jenson.* Grand Rapids, MI: Eerdmans, 2000.

Haber, Susan. "From Priestly Torah to Christ Cultus: The Re-Vision of Cult and Covenant in Hebrews." *Journal for the Study of the New Testament* 28 no. 1 (2005), 105-24.

Haenchen, Ernst. *The Acts of the Apostles.* Translated by Bernard Noble and Gerald Shinn. Philadelphia: Westminster, 1971.

Hahn, Ferdinand. "The Confession of the One God in the New Testament." *Horizons in Biblical Theology* 2 (1980): 69-84.

Hahn, Robert T. "Judaism and Jewish Christianity in Antioch: Charisma and Conflict in the First Century." *Journal of Religious History* 14 (1987): 341-60.

Hall, William Phillips. *Remarkable Bible Discovery, or the Name of God according to Scriptures*. 3rd ed. New York: American Tract Society, 1931.

———. *What is "The Name"? or the "Mystery of God" Revealed*. Greenwich CT: By the Author, 1913.

Hamilton, Victor P. *The Book of Genesis, Chapters 1-17*. The New International Commentary on the Old Testament. Grand Rapids, MI: Eerdmans, 1990.

Harnack, Adolf von. *The History of Dogma*. 7 vols. Translated by Neil Buchanan. 1895. Reprint, New York: Russell and Russell, 1958.

Harris, Elizabeth. *Prologue and Gospel: The Theology of the Fourth Evangelist*. Sheffield: Sheffield Academic Press, 1994.

Harris, Murray J. "Prepositions and Theology in the Greek New Testament." In "Appendix: 5. Neglect of the Possible Significance of (a) the Non-repetition of the Preposition with Copulated Nouns, and (b) the Order of Nouns that follow a Preposition" in *New International Dictionary of New Testament Theology*, Vol 3. Edited by Colin Brown. Grand Rapids, MI: Zondervan, 1978.

Harris, R. Laird, Gleason L. Archer, and Bruce K. Waltke. *Theological Wordbook of the Old Testament*. 2 vols. Chicago: Moody Press, 1980.

Hartman, Lars. *Into the Name of Jesus: Baptism in the Early Church*. Edinburgh, Scotland: T. & T. Clark, 1997.

Hatch, Nathan O. *The Democratization of American Christianity*. New Haven and London: Yale University Press, 1989.

Hay, David M. *Glory at the Right Hand: Psalm 100 in Early Christianity*. SBLMS 18. Nashville: Abingdon Press, 1973.

Hays, Richard B. *The Faith of Jesus Christ: An Investigation into the Narrative Structure of Galatians 3:1-4:11*. Chico, CA: Scholars Press, 1983.

———. "Three Dramatic Roles. The Law in Romans 3-4." In *Paul and the Mosaic Law*. Edited by James D. G. Dunn. Grand Rapids, MI: Eerdmans, 2001.

Haywood, G. T. "Baptized into One Body." *The Good Report* 1 (December, 1913).

———. *Before the Foundation of the World: A Revelation of the Ages*. Indianapolis, IN: Christ Temple Book Store, 1923.

———. "A Voice Crying in the Wilderness." no. 19, (winter 1916).

———. *The Victim of the Flaming Sword*, Indianapolis: Christ Temple book store, n.d.

———, ed. *The Bridegroom* Songs. Indianapolis, IN: Christ Temple, 1926.

Hengel, Martin. *Between Jesus and Paul: Studies in the Earliest Christian Communities*. Translated by John Bowden. London: Fortress Press, 1983.

———. "Christological Titles in Early Christianity." In *The Messiah: Developments in Earliest Judaism and Christianity*. Edited by James H. Charlesworth. Minneapolis, MN: Fortress Press, 1992.

———. *Judaism and Hellenism: Studies in Their Encounter in Palestine During the Early Hellenistic Period*. 2 vols. Translated by John Bowden. Philadelphia: Fortress Press, 1980.

Hertz, J. H., ed. *The Pentateuch and Haftorahs: Hebrew Text, English Translation and Commentary*. 2nd ed. London: Soncino Press, 1972.

Holman, Charles L. "Ephesians and Ecumenism (or Ecumenical Pneumatology)." Presented at the 31st annual meeting of Society for Pentecostal Studies, Lakeland, FL, 2002.

———. "Titus 3:5-6: A Window on Worldwide Pentecost." *Journal of Pentecostal Theology* 8 (1996): 53-62.

Hooker, Morna D. *From Adam to Christ: Essays on Paul*. Cambridge: Cambridge University Press, 1990.

Horbury, William. *Jews and Christians in Contact and Controversy*. Edinburgh: T&T Clark, 1998.

Horsley, Richard A. "Popular Messianic Movements." *Catholic Biblical Quarterly* 46 no. 3 (1984): 471-95.

Howard, J. Keir. *New Testament Baptism*. London: Pickering & Inglis, 1970.

Hurtado, Larry. *At the Origins of Christian Worship: The Context and Character of Earliest Christian Devotion*. Grand Rapids, MI: Eerdmans, 2000.

―――. *Lord Jesus Christ: Devotion to Jesus in Earliest Christianity*. Grand Rapids, MI: Eerdmans, 2003.

―――. *One God, One Lord: Early Christian Devotion, and Ancient Jewish Monotheism*. Philadelphia: Fortress Press 1988.

Jackson, Samuel Macauley, Charles Colebrook Sherman, and George William Gilmore, eds. *The New Schaff-Herzog Encyclopedia of Religious Knowledge*. 10 vols. Grand Rapids, MI: Baker, 1977.

Jacobsen, Douglas. *Thinking in the Spirit: Theologies of the Early Pentecostal Movement*. Bloomington and Indianapolis: University of Indiana, 2003.

Jamieson, Robert, A. R. Fausset, and David Brown. *A Commentary on the Old and New Testaments*. 3 vols. 1877. Reprint, Grand Rapids, MI: Eerdmans, 1995.

Jenson, Robert. *Systematic Theology*. 2 vols. Oxford: Oxford University Press, 1997, 1999.

Jeremias, Joachim. *New Testament Theology: The Proclamation of Jesus*. New York: Scribner, 1971.

Johnson, Luke Timothy. *The Acts of the Apostles*. Collegeville, MN: Liturgical Press, 1992.

―――. *The Gospel of Luke*. Collegeville, MN: Liturgical Press, 1991.

―――. "Rom 3:21-26 and the Faith of Jesus." *Catholic Biblical Quarterly* 44 (1982): 77-90.

Johnston, Robin. "Evening Light: The Development of Oneness Pentecostal Soteriology." Paper presented at the annual Urshan Graduate School of Theology Symposium, March, 2005.

―――. "Transitional Hermeneutics in Oneness Pentecostalism." Paper presented at the annual Urshan Graduate School of Theology Symposium, May, 2001.

Jonge, Marinus de. *Christology in Context: The Earliest Response to Jesus.* Philadelphia: Westminster, 1988.

―――. "The Use of the Word Anointed in the Time of Jesus." *Novum Testamentum* 8 (1966): 132-48.

Juel, Donald. *Luke-Acts: The Promise of History.* Atlanta: John Knox, 1983.

―――. *Messianic Exegesis: Christological Interpretation of the Old Testament in Early Christianity.* Philadelphia: Fortress Press, 1992.

Keener, Craig. *Gift Giver: The Holy Spirit for Today.* Grand Rapids, MI: Baker Academic Books, 2001.

Keil, C. F. and F. Delitzsch. *Commentary on the Old Testament.* 10 vols. Translated by James Martin. 1866-91. Reprint, Peabody, MA: Hendrickson, 2001.

Kelly, J. N. D. *Early Christian Doctrines.* Hagerstown, MD: Harper & Row, 1978.

Kelly, Vonelle R. *Another Jesus: The Fallacy of the Doctrine of Heavenly Flesh.* n.p. 2004.

Kenyon, Essek. *The Wonderful Name of Jesus.* Los Angeles: West Coast, 1927.

Kistemaker, Simon J. *Exposition of the Book of Hebrews.* New Testament Commentary. Grand Rapids, MI: Baker, 1984.

Kittel, Gerhard, ed. *Theological Dictionary of the New Testament.* 10 Volumes. Translated and edited by Geoffrey W. Bromily, Grand Rapids, MI: Eerdmans, 1964-75.

Kloppenborg, John S. *The Formation of Q: Trajectories in Ancient Wisdom Collections.* Philadelphia: Fortress Press, 1987.

Koch, Klaus. "Ezra and the Origins of Judaism." *Journal of Semitic Studies* 19 (1974): 173-97.

Köhler, Ludwig. *Old Testament Theology.* Translated by A. S. Todd. Philadelphia: Westminster, 1957.

———, trans. *The Hebrew and Aramaic Lexicon of the Old Testament.* 3 vols. Leiden, New York, Köln: E. J. Brill, 1996.

Koester, Craig R. *The Dwelling of God: The Tabernacle in the Old Testament, Intertestamental Jewish Literature, and the New Testament.* The Catholic Biblical Quarterly Monograph Series 22. Washington, DC: Catholic Biblical Assocation of America, 1989.

Koester, Helmut. *History and Literature of Early Christianity.* Philadelphia: Fortress Press, 1982.

Kosmala, Hans. "The Conclusion of Matthew." *Annual of the Swedish Theological Institute* 4 (1965): 132-47.

Kraft, R. A. and G. Nickelsburg, eds. *Early Judaism and Its Modern Interpreters.* Philadelphia: Fortress Press, 1985.

Kugel, James. *The Idea of Hebrew Poetry: Parallelism and its History.* New Haven: Yale University Press, 1981.

Küng, Hans. *On Being a Christian.* Translated by Edward Quinn. Garden City, NY: Doubleday, 1976.

Ladd, George Eldon. *The New Testament and Criticism.* Grand Rapids: Eerdmans, 1967.

Land, Stephen J. *Pentecostal Spirituality: A Passion for the Kingdom.* Sheffield: Sheffield Academic Press, 1993.

Larkin, Clarence. *Rightly Dividing the Word.* Philadelphia, PA: by the author, 1921.

Latourette, Kenneth Scott. *A History of Christianity*. 2 vols. New York: Harper and Row, 1975.

Lebreton, Jules and Jacques Zeiller, *The History of the Primitive Church*. Vol. 2. New York, Macmillan, 1949.

Levine, Lee I. "The Nature and Origin of the Palestinian Synagogue Reconsidered." *Journal of Biblical Literature* 115 no. 3 (1996): 425-48.

Lewis, Joe O. "The Ark and the Tent." *Review and Expositor* 74 no. 4 (1977): 537-48.

Liddell, Henry George, and Robert Scott. *A Greek-English Lexicon*. 9th ed. Oxford: Clarendon Press, 1968.

Lindbeck, George A. *The Nature of Doctrine: Religion and Theology in a Postliberal Age*. Philadelphia:Westminster, 1984.

Lindars, Barnabas. *Jesus Son of Man*. Grand Rapids, MI: Eerdmans, 1984.

Long, V. Philips. *The Art of Biblical History*. Grand Rapids, MI: Zondervan, 1994.

Longenecker, Bruce W. "Defining the Faithful Character of the Covenant Community: Galatians 2:15-21 and Beyond. A Response to Jan Lambrecht" in *Paul and the Mosaic Law*. Edited by James D. G. Dunn. 1996. Reprint, Grand Rapids, MI: Eerdmans, 2001.

Longenecker, Richard N. *The Christology of Early Jewish Christianity*. Studies in Biblical Theology 17. Naperville IL: Alec R. Allenson, 1970.

Lüdemann, G. *Early Christianity according to the Traditions in Acts: A Commentary*. Translated by John Bowden, London: SCM Press, 1989.

Mack, Burton A. and Roland E. Murphy. "Wisdom Literature" in *Faith and Piety in Early Judaism*. Edited by George W. E. Nickelsburg and Michael Stone. Philadelphia: Fortress Press, 1983.

MacMullen, Ramsey. *Christianizing the Roman Empire A.D. 100-400*. New Haven: Yale University Press, 1984.

MacQuarrie, John. *Principles of Christian Theology.* 2nd ed. New York: Charles Scribner's Sons, 1977.

Malbon, Elizabeth Struthers and Edgar V. McKnight, eds. *The New Literary Criticism and the New Testament.* Sheffield: Sheffield Academic Press, 1994.

Malina, Bruce. *The New Testament World: Insights from Cultural Anthropology.* Atlanta: John Knox, 1981.

Maloney, Francis J. *The Gospel of John.* Edited by Daniel J. Harrington. Sacra Pagina 4. Collegeville, MN: Liturgical Press, 1998.

Marsden, George M. *Fundamentalism and the American Culture: The Shaping of Twentieth Century Evangelicalism: 1870-1925.* New York: Oxford University Press, 1980.

Marshall, I. Howard. *The Acts of the Apostles: An Introduction and Commentary.* Tyndale New Testament Commentary. Grand Rapids, MI: Eerdmans, 1980.

———. "Luke and His 'Gospel.'" In *The Gospel and the Gospels.* Edited by Peter Stuhlmacher. Grand Rapids, MI: Eerdmans, 1991.

Martin, R. P. *Carmen Christi.* Cambridge: Cambridge University Press, 1967.

McDonnell, Kilian, and G. T. Montague. *Christian Initiation and Baptism in the Spirit.* 2nd ed. Collegeville, MN: Liturgical Press, 1994.

McGee, Gary B. "Early Pentecostal Hermeneutics: Tongues as Evidence in the Book of Acts" in *Initial Evidence: Historical and Biblical Perspective on the Pentecostal Doctrine of Spirit Baptism.* Edited by Gary B. McGee. Peabody, MA: Hendrickson, 1991.

McGiffert, Arthur Cushman. *The God of the Early Christians.* New York: Charles Scribner's Sons, 1924.

McGrath, Alister E. *Christian Theology: An Introduction.* 3rd ed. Malden, MA: Blackwell Publishers, 2001.

McIntyre, Luther B. Jr. "Baptism and Forgiveness in Acts 2:38." *Bibliothecra Sacra* 152 (1996): 53-59.

Meier, John P. *A Marginal Jew: Rethinking the Historical Jesus.* 3 vols. Anchor Bible Reference Library. Vol. 1, *The Roots of the Problem and the Person.* Vol. 2, *Mentor, Message, and Miracles.* Vol. 3, *Companions and Competitors.* New York: Doubleday, 1991.

Menzies, Robert P. *The Development of Early Christian Pneumatology with Special Reference to Luke-Acts.* Sheffield: JSOT Press, 1991.

———. "Luke and the Spirit: A Reply to James Dunn." *Journal of Pentecostal Theology* 4 (1994): 115-38.

Meslin, Michel. "Baptism," *The Encyclopedia of Religion*, Vol. 2. Edited by Mircea Eliade. New York: Macmillan, 1986, 59-63.

Metzger, Bruce M. *A Textual Commentary on the Greek New Testament.* 1971. Reprint, Stuttgart, Germany: United Bible Society, 1975.

———. and Michael D. Coogan, eds. *The Oxford Companion to the Bible.* New York: Oxford University Press, 1993.

Moltmann, Jürgen. *The Trinity and the Kingdom: The Doctrine of God.* Translated by Margaret Kohl. San Francisco: Harper & Row, 1981.

Morgan-Wynne, John E. "References to Baptism in the Fourth Gospel" in *Baptism, the New Testament and the Church: Historical and Contemporary Studies in Honour of R. E. O. White.* Edited by Stanley E. Porter and Anthony R. Cross. Sheffield: Sheffield Academic Press, 1999, 157-72.

Mortley, Raoul. *From Word to Silence.* 2 vols. Theophaneia 30, 31. Vol. 1, The Rise and Fall of Logos. Vol. 2, The Way of Negation, Christian and Greek. Bonn: Hanstein, 1986.

Moule, C. F. D. *Christ and Spirit in the New Testament.* Cambridge: University Press, 1973.

Mowinckel, Sigmund. "The Name of the God of Moses." *Hebrew Union College Annual* 32 (1961): 121-33.

———. *Religion and Kultus.* Göttingen: Vandenhoek and Ruprecht, 1953.

Mueller, J. Theodore. "Holy Baptism." In *The Abiding Word: An Anthology of Doctrinal Essays*, Vol. 2. Edited by Theodore Laetsch, 394-422. Rev. ed. St. Louis: Concordia Publishing House, 1975.

Murphy-O'Connor, Jerome. "Christological Anthropology in Phil., II, 6-11." *Revue Biblique* 83 (1976): 25-50.

Neusner, Jacob, William S. Green, and Ernest S. Frerichs, eds. *Judaisms and Their Messiahs at the Turn of the Christian Era*. New York: Cambridge University Press, 1987.

Newman, Carey C. *Paul's Glory Christology: Tradition and Rhetoric*. NovTSup 69. Leiden: Brill, 1992.

Nicholl, W. Robertson, ed. *The Expositors Greek Testament*, 5 vols. London: 1897-1910.

Nicholson, Ernest W. *God and His People: Covenant and Theology in the Old Testament*. Oxford: Clarendon Press, 1986.

Nickelsburg, George W. E. *Jewish Literature Between the Bible and the Mishnah: A Historical and Literary Introduction*. Philadelphia: Fortress Press, 1981.

———. and Michael Stone. *Faith and Piety in Early Judaism*. Philadelphia: Fortress Press, 1983.

Niles, D. Preman. "The Name of God in Israel's Worship: The Theological Importance of the Name Yahweh." PhD diss., Princeton University, 1974.

Norris, David S. "Creation Revealed: An Early Pentecostal Hermeneutic." Paper presented at the annual meeting of the Society for Pentecostal Studies, Duke University, March, 2008.

———. "No Other Name: A Socio-Historical Approach to the Argument of Luke-Acts." PhD diss., Temple University, 2000.

———. "Origins and Biblical Theology of Modalistic Monarchianism." Master's thesis, Palmer Theological Seminary (formerly Eastern Baptist Theological Seminary), 1991.

———. *Operation Daybreak*. Dover, DE: Halak Press, 1993.

———. "Response to Robin Johnston's 'Evening Light: The Development of Early Oneness Pentecostal Soteriology.'" Paper presented at the annual Urshan Graduate School of Theology Symposium, March, 2005.

Norris, S. G. *The Mighty God in Christ*. St. Paul, MN: Apostolic Bible Institute, n.d.

Nygren, Gotthard. *Das Prädestinationsproblem in der Theologie Augustins*. Göttingen: Vandenhoek and Ruprecht, 1956.

Obeng, E. A. "Abba Father: The Prayer of the Sons of God." *Expository Times* 99 (1988): 363-66.

Oberman, Julian. "The Divine *YHWH* in the Light of Recent Discoveries." *Journal of Biblical Literature* 68 (1949): 301-23.

Oegema, Gerbern S. *The Anointed and His People: Messianic Expectations from the Maccabees to Bar Kochba*. Sheffield: Sheffield Academic Press, 1998.

Ogden, G. S. "Time, and the Verb *hayah* in the Old Testament Prose." *Vetus Testamentum* 21 (1971): 451-69.

Onesti, Karen L. and Manfred T. Brauch. "Righteousness, Righteousness of God" in *Dictionary of Paul and His Letters*. Edited by Gerald F. Hawthorne, Ralph P. Martin, and Daniel G. Reid, 827-37. Downers Grove, IL: Intervarsity, 1993.

Osiek, Carolyn. *Shepherd of Hermas*. Edited by Helmut Koester. Minneapolis: Fortress Press, 1999.

Otto, Rudolf. *The Idea of the Holy: An Inquiry Into the Non-rational Factor in the Idea of the Divine and its Relation to the Rational*. Translated by John W. Harvey. New York, Oxford University Press, 1923.

Owens, Robert. "The Azusa Street Revival: The Pentecostal Movement Begins in America." In *The Century of the Holy Spirit: 100 Years of Pentecostal and Charismatic Renewal*. Edited by Vinson Synan. Nashville: Thomas Nelson, 2001.

Pagels, Elaine. *The Gnostic Gospels*. New York: Random House, 1979.

Parham, Charles. *Kol Kare Bomidbar: A Voice Crying in the Wilderness.* Baxter Springs, KS: n.p., 1902.2

Parke-Taylor, G. H. יְהוָה *Yahweh: The Divine Name in the Bible.* Waterloo, Ontario: Wilfrid Laurier University Press, 1975.

Pelikan, Jaroslav. *The Christian Tradition; A History of Doctrine and Development.* Vol. 1, *The Emergence of the Catholic Tradition, (100-600).* Chicago: University of Chicago Press, 1971.

Pentecost, J. Dwight. *Things to Come: A Study in Biblical Eschatology.* Grand Rapids, MI: Zondervan Publishing House, 1958.

Pettinato, G. "Royal Archives of Tell Mardikh-Ebla." *Biblical Archaeologist* 39 (1976): 44-52.

Pierson, A. T., ed. *The Inspired Word: A Series of Papers and Addresses Delivered at the Bible Inspiration Conference, Philadelphia, 1887.* New York: Anson D. F. Randolph, 1888.

Pink, Arthur W. *The Exposition of the Gospel of John: Three Volumes Complete and Unabridged in One.* Grand Rapids, MI: Zondervan, 1975.

Pinnock, Clark H. "From Augustine to Arminius: A Pilgrimage in Theology" in *The Grace of God, the Will of Man.* Edited by Clark H. Pinnock. Grand Rapids, MI: Zondervan, 1989.

Plastaras, James. *The God of Exodus: The Theology of the Exodus Narratives.* Milwaukee: The Bruce Publishing House, 1966.

Polhill, John B. *Acts.* Nashville, TN: Broadman Press, 1992.

Pollard, T. E. *Johannine Christology and the Early Church.* Cambridge: Cambridge University Press, 1970.

Pritchard, James B., ed. *The Ancient Near East: An Anthology of Texts and Pictures.* 2 vols. Princeton, NJ: Princeton University Press, 1958.

Pritz, Ray A. *Nazarene Jewish Christianity: From the End of the New Testament Until Its Disappearance in the Fourth Century.* Jerusalem: Magnes Press, 1988.

Pryor, Hattie E. "The Water Way" in *The Bridegroom Songs*. Edited by G. T. Haywood. Indianapolis, IN: Christ Temple, 1926.

Rad, Gerhard von. *Studies in Deuteronomy*. Translated by David Stalker. Chicago: H. Regnery, 1953.

Rainbow, Paul A. "Jewish Monotheism As The Matrix For New Testament Christology: A Review Article." *Novum Testamentum* 33 no. 1 (1991): 78-91.

Reed, David A. *"In Jesus Name": History and Beliefs of Oneness Pentecostals*. Dorset, UK: Deo Publishing, 2008.

———. "Oneness Pentecostalism" in *The New International Dictionary of Pentecostal Charismatic Movements*. Revised and expanded edition. Edited by Stanley M. Burgess, 936-44. Grand Rapids, MI: Zondervan, 2002.

———. "Oneness Pentecostalism: Problems and Possibilities for Pentecostal Theology." *Pentecostal Journal of Theology* 11 (1997): 73-93.

———."Origins and Development of the Theology of Oneness Pentecostalism in the United States." PhD diss., Boston University, 1978.

Reumann, J. "The Gospel of the Righteousness of God." *Interpretation* 20 (1966): 432-52.

Ridderbos, Herman N. *The Gospel according to John: A Theological Commentary*. Translated by John Vriend. Grand Rapids, MI: Eerdmans, 1997

Robeck, Cecil M. Jr. *The Azusa Street Mission and Revival: The Birth of the Global Pentecostal Movement*. Nashville, TN: Nelson, 2006.

Robertson, A. T. *A Grammar of the Greek New Testament: In the Light of Historical Research*. New York: Hodder & Stoughton, 1915.

———. *Word Pictures in the New Testament*. 1930. Reprint, Nashville, TN: Holman, 2000.

Rowe, C. Kavin. "Biblical Pressure and Trinitarian Hermeneutics." *Pro Ecclesia* 11 no. 3 (2002): 295-312.

———. "Luke and the Trinity: An Essay in Ecclesial Biblical Theology." *Scottish Journal of Theology* 56 no. 1 (2003): 1-26.

Runia, David. *Philo and the Church Fathers.* Vol. 32. Leiden and New York: E. J. Brill, 1995.

Sanders, E. P. *Judaism, Practice and Belief, 63 BCE to 63 CE.* Philadelphia: Trinity Press International, 1992.

———. *Paul and Palestinian Judaism.* Philadelphia: Fortress Press, 1977.

Sanders, Jack T. *The New Testament Christological Hymns: Their Historical Religious Background.* Cambridge: Cambridge University Press, 1971.

Schaff, Philip. *History of the Christian Church.* Vol. 2. Grand Rapids, MI: Eerdmans, 1950.

Schoedel, William R. *Ignatius of Antioch: A Commentary on the Letters of Ignatius of Antioch.* Edited by Helmut Koester. Philadelphia: Fortress Press, 1985.

Schoeps, Hans Joachim. *Jewish Christianity: Factional Disputes in the Early Church.* Translated by Douglas R. A. Hare. Philadelphia: Fortress Press, 1969.

Schürer, E. *The History of the Jewish People in the Age of Jesus Christ (175 BC-AD 135).* 3 vols. Edited by G. Vermes, F. Millar, Matthew Black. Revised edition. Edinburgh: T. & T. Clark, 1987.

Schwarz, Hans. *Christology.* Grand Rapids, MI: Eerdmans, 1998.

Scofield, C. I. *Plain Papers on the Doctrine of the Holy Spirit.* New York: 1899.

Segraves, Daniel. *Hebrews: Better Things. Vol. One. A Commentary on Hebrews 1–8.* Hazelwood, MO: Word Aflame Press, 1996.

———. "Reading Packet in Systematic Theology." For use in classes at Christian Life College, n.d.

Sexton, E. A. "The Bride of Christ." *The Bridegroom's Messenger* 3 (1 May, 1910).

Seitz, C. R. "Handing Over the Name." In *Trinity, Time, and Church: A Response to the Theology of Robert W. Jenson*. Edited by Colin D. Gunton. Grand Rapids, MI: Eerdmans, 2000.

Sharp, Granville. *Remarks of the uses of the definitive article in the Greek text of the New Testament containing many new proofs of the divinity of Christ, from passages which are wrongly translated in the common English version*. Philadelphia, PA: B. B. Hopkins, 1807.

Shotwell, Willis A. *The Biblical Exegesis of Justin Martyr*. London: SPCK, 1965.

Snook, Ivan. "Language, Truth and Power: Bourdieu's *Ministerium*." *An Introduction to the Work of Pierre Bourdieu: The Practice of Theory*. Edited by Richard Harker, Cheleen Mahar, and Chris Wilkes. London: MacMillan, 1990.

Soggin, J. Alberto. *A History of Ancient Israel*. Translated by John Bowden. Philadelphia: Westminster, 1984.

Stark, Rodney. *The Rise of Christianity: A Sociologist Reconsiders History*. Princeton, NJ: Princeton University Press, 1996.

Stephens, Randall J. *The Fire Spreads: Holiness and Pentecostalism in the American South*. Cambridge, MA: Harvard University Press, 2008.

Stevenson, James, ed. *Creeds, Councils and Controversies: Documents Illustrative of the History of the Church A. D. 337-461*. New York: Seabury Press, 1966.

Stone, Michael E. *Scriptures, Sects and Vision: A Profile of Judaism from Ezra to the Jewish Revolts*. Oxford: Basil Blackwell, 1980.

———, ed. *Jewish Writings of the Second Temple Period*. Philadelphia: Fortress Press, 1984.

Stronstad, Roger. *The Charismatic Theology of St. Luke*. Peabody, MA: Hendrickson, 1984.

Stuhlmacher, Peter. ed. *The Gospel and Gospels*. Grand Rapids, MI: Eerdmans, 1992.

Synan, Vincent. *The Century of the Holy Spirit: 100 Years of Pentecostal and Charismatic Renewal.* Nashville, TN: Thomas Nelson, 2001.

———. *The Holiness Pentecostal Tradition: Charismatic Movements in the Twentieth Century.* Revised edition. Grand Rapids, MI: Eerdmans, 1997.

Talbert, Charles H. "The Problem of Pre-Existence in Philippians 2:6-11." *Journal of Biblical Literature* 86 (1967): 141-53.

———. *Reading Luke: A Literary and Theological Commentary of the Third Gospel.* New York: Crossroad, 1982.

Tannenhill, Robert C. *The Narrative Unity of Luke—Acts: A Literary Interpretation.* 2 vols. Philadelphia: Fortress Press, 1986, 1990.

Tate, J. "Plato and Allegorical Interpretation." *The Classical Quarterly* 23 (1934).

Taylor, George F. *The Spirit and the Bride: A Scriptural Presentation of the Operations, Manifestations, Gifts and Fruit of the Holy Spirit in Relation to His Bride with Special Reference to the Latter Rain Revival.* Dunn, NC: The Author, 1907.

Theissen, Henry Clarence. *Lectures in Systematic Theology.* Revised by Vernon D. Doerksen. 1949. Revised ed., Grand Rapids, Eerdmans, 1986.

Theissen, Gerd. *The Religion of the Earliest Churches: Creating a Symbolic World.* Minneapolis: Fortress Press, 1999.

Thurston, Bonnie. *Spiritual Life in the Early Church.* Minneapolis: Fortress Press, 1993.

Torrey, R. A. *What the Bible Teaches: A Thorough and Comprehensive Study of the What the Bible has to say Concerning the Great Doctrines of Which it Treats.* 17th ed. New York, 1933.

Tov, E. "The Septuagint" in Mulder and Sysling (eds.) *Mikra: Text, Translation, Reading and Interpretation of the Hebrew Bible in Ancient Judaism and Early Christianity.* CRINT 2 no. 1. Philadelphia: Fortress Press, 1988.

Turner, Max. *Power from on High: The Spirit in Israel's Restoration and Witness in Luke-Acts.* Sheffield: Sheffield Academic Press, 2000.

———. *The Holy Spirit and Spiritual Gifts in the New Testament Church and Today.* Peabody, MA: Hendrickson, 1996.

Tyson, James L. *The Early Pentecostal Revival: History of Twentieth-Century Pentecostals and The Pentecostal Assemblies of the World, 1901-30.* Hazelwood, MO: Word Aflame Press, 1992.

Vermès, Geza. *Jesus the Jew: A Historian's Reading of the Gospels.* New York: Macmillan Publishing, 1974.

———. *The Dead Sea Scrolls: Qumran in Perspective.* Revised edition. Philadelphia: Fortress Press, 1977.

———. "The Use of בר נשא/בר נש in Jewish Aramaic." Appendix E in M. Black, *An Aramaic Approach to the Gospels and Acts.* 3rd ed. Oxford: Clarendon, 1967.

Vincent, Marvin R. *Word Studies of the New Testament.* 4 vols. 1887-1905. Reprint, Peabody, MA: Hendrickson, n.d.

Vondey, Wolfgang. "The Symbolic Turn: A Symbolic Conception of the Liturgy of Pentecostalism." *Wesleyan Theological Journal*, (36) No. 2. Fall 2001: 223-247

Vööbus, Arthur. "Liturgical Traditions in the Didache." *Papers for the Estonian Theological Society in Exile* (1968): 36-39.

Wacker, Grant. *Heaven Below: Early Pentecostals and American Culture.* Cambridge, MA: Harvard University Press, 2001.

———. "The Functions of Faith in Primitive Pentecostalism." *Harvard Theological Review* 77 (1984): 353-75.

Wainwright, Geoffrey. *Doxology: The Praise of God in Worship, Doctrine, and Life. A Systematic Theology.* New York: Oxford University Press, 1980.

Walker, James B. "Niceno-Constantinopolitan Creed." In *The Dictionary of Historical Theology.* Grand Rapids, MI: Eerdmans, 2000, 396-99.

Ward, A. G. *Soul Food for Hungry Hearts.* Springfield, MO: Gospel Publishing House, 1925.

Wenham, Gordon J. *Genesis 1-15.* Word Biblical Commentary 1. Waco, TX: Word Books, 1987.

Westermann, Claus. "Das Alte Testament und die Theologie." In *Theology—was ist das?* Edited by Georg Picht and Enno Rudolph. Stuttgart: Kreuz Verlag, 1977.

Wildier, N. Max. *The Theologian and His Universe: Theology and Cosmology from the Middle Ages to the Present.* New York: The Seabury Press, 1982.

Williams, J. Rodman. *Renewal Theology: Systematic Theology from a Charismatic Perspective. Three Volumes in One.* Grand Rapids, MI: Zondervan, 1996.

Williford, Don. "John 3:1-15—*gennethenal anothen*: A Radical Departure, A New Beginning." *Review and Expositor* 96 (1999): 451-61.

Winston, David. *Logos and Mystical Theology in Philo of Alexandria.* Cincinnati: Hebrew Union College Press, 1985.

Witherington, Ben, III. *The Christology of Jesus.* Minneapolis, MN: Fortress Press, 1991.

———. *The Many Faces of Christ. The Christologies of the New Testament and Beyond.* New York: Crossroad, 1998.

Wolfson, Harry Austryn. *The Philosophy of the Church Fathers.* Vol. 1, *Faith, Trinity, Incarnation.* Cambridge: Harvard University Press, 1957.

———. *Philo: Foundations of Religious Philosophy in Judaism, Christianity, and Islam.* 2 vols. 1947. 5th Printing, Cambridge: Harvard University Press, 1982.

Wordsworth, Christopher. *Six Letters to Granville Sharp, esq. respecting his Remarks on the uses of the definite article in the Greek Text of the New Testament.* London: J. Hodson, 1802.

Wuest, Kenneth. *Word Studies of the Greek New Testament.* 3 vols. 1959. Reprint, Grand Rapids, MI: Eerdmans, 1983.

Young, Edward J. *The Study of Old Testament Theology Today.* Westwood, NJ: F. H. Revel, 1959.

Zehnle, Richard F. *Peter's Pentecost Discourse: Tradition and Reinterpretation in Peter's Speeches of Acts 2 and 3.* SBLMS 15. Edited by Robert A. Kraft. Nashville: Abingdon Press, 1971.

Zeisler, J. A. "The Name of Jesus in the Acts of the Apostles." *Journal for the Study of the New Testament* 4 (1979): 28-41.

Zuck, Roy B. *Basic Bible Interpretation.* Wheaton, IL: Victor Books, 1991.

Subject & Author Index

Aaron, 15, 41, 233
Aaronic priesthood, 126-27
Abba,
   Jesus teaching about, 102
   as a metaphor for Christian initiation, x, 211-14
   Jesus' use in prayer, 118-19
Abel, 24, 253 n.62-63
Abraham, ix, 20-1, 37-8, 66, 70, 74, 109, 111, 246 n.25; 251 n.39; 257-8 n.41; 279 n.27; 280n.40
   and covenant initiation, 196-98, 303 n.40-46
Abramowski, Luise, 291 n.6
Adam (see also, "Jesus, typologically answering to Adam"), vii, 7-8, 12, 17-18, 22-23, 35-36, 39, 71, 82-83, 91-5, 97-8, 100, 108, 116, 120, 122, 127, 138, 169, 189, 211, 216, 248-9 n.10; 249 n.17, 19-21; 253 n.62; 258 n.4, 7, 9; 270 n.10; 272 n.9, 17; 274 n.40-41, 46
   created in the image of God, 17-19
   in covenant with Yahweh, 35-36
   restored covenant with Yahweh, 36
Adams, Christopher, as allegory of Jesus, 100-2
Adam and Eve, 8, 18, 22-3, 35-36, 39, 91-2, 249 n.17; 253, n.62; 258 n.7, 9
   creation in the image of God, 17-19
   in covenant with Yahweh, 35-36, 37-38, 42
Adonai, 30, 70, 102, 130, 141, 251 n.39; 256 n.26-27; 284 n.28; 311 n.51
Adoption, as a metaphor for entering into covenant, 212, 237, 270 n.12
Adoptionism, 88, 157, 239, 264 n.27; 272 n.16; 286 n.2; 290 n.66
Advocate (see also *Parakletos*), 117, 279 n.25
Alexandria (Egypt), 26, 29-30, 32, 164-66, 255 n.15; 255-56 n.18; 257 n.31, 35-36; 258 n.42; 288 n.41; 292 n.22; 294 n.55, 63; 297 n.35
Albright, William F., 19, 250 n.29; 251 n.39; 256 n.27; 267 n.21; 285-6 n.46

Allegorical interpretation, vii, 25, 28-30, 164-5, 172, 255 n.14-15; 257 n.29, 39; 258 n.43; 292 n.10
Ancient Near East, 26, 38-39, 259 n.30; 254 n.3; 269 n.2
Ancient of Days, 109, 134
Anderson, Robert Mapes, 221, 234, 308 n.1, 9; 310 n.37; 312 n.10
Anderson, James N., 267 n.32
Ankerburg, John, 240
Angel(s), 17-18, 21, 57, 76-7, 129, 131-2, 157, 166, 208, 248-9 n.10; 249, n.14, 16, 19, 22; 250-1 n.32; 257 n.37; 288 n.35; 294 n.49
Angel of Yahweh (the LORD), 250 n.32
D'Angelo, Mary Rose, 276 n.11
Anointing of Jesus at His baptism (see "Jesus, anointing of") 85, 87-90, 95, 114, 240
Anthropomorphism, zoomorphism, (Biblical) 21, 29, 252 n.43
   Hellenistic anthropomorphism, 25, 31-33
Anthropological understanding of Jesus, viii, 80-84, 250 n.23; 252 n.43; 270 n.13; 271 n.20-3; 274 n.48, 275 n.51
Apocalyptic imagery, 110, 133, 254 n.4; 273 n.24; 288 n.35
Apologists, second century, ix, 161, 163-65, 167, 172-3, 181, 268 n.36; 269 n.46; 290 n.57; 291 n.1-8; 292 n.9-23; 293 n.24-32
Apostolic (definition) 4, 8-9, 244 n.9
Apostolic hermeneutic, vii, 4-5, 8-9, 12, 47-8, 50-1, 53, 225-7, 244 n.9; 265 n.47; 280 n.3
Aquinas, 245 n.19
Aramaic, 253 n.59, 277 n.29, 31; 284 n.28
   as the conversational language of Jesus, 102, 118, 211, 275 n.10; 245 n.28
   as utilized by the earliest church, 193, 211-12; 307 n.61
Archer, Gleason, 248 n.2
Archer, Kenneth, 244 n.12

Aristides, 164
Aristotle, 27, 254 n.7-8; 255 n.11
Aristeas, 255 n.17; 255-56 n.18
Arius, ix, 181-82, 298 n.47, 49, 51
Arrington, French L., 307 n.49
Arndt, William F., 246 n.28
Assyria, 26
Atonement, Day of (see "Feasts/Holy Days, Jewish Day of Atonement")
Athanasius, ix, 152, 181-2, 297 n.26; 298 n.49, 51
Atkinson, William, 304 n.8
Attridge, Harold W., 294 n.60
Augustine, ix, 82, 152, 182-85, 254-5 n.9; 286 n.6; 295 n.10; 298 n.52, 54-5; 57-64, 66-9, 71-72
Aune, David, E., 307 n.74
Austin, J. L. (John Langshaw), 266 n.2-3
Ayers, Lewis, 298 n.54
Azusa Street revival, 219-20, 229-31, 234-35, 243 n.4; 308 n.18; 311 n.5, 9
Babylon, 26
Bacon, Francis, Baconian method, 217, 308 n.6
Bakken, Norman K., 94, 275 n.49, 51
Balentine, Samuel E., 253 n.58
Baltzer, Klaus, 272 n.5
Baptism by John, 87-91, 128, 190-2, 205, 273 n.22-24; 280 n. 15; 300 n.6-7
Baptism of Jesus, 58, 66, 85, 87-91, 98, 114, 121, 130, 191-2, 266 n.5; 272 n.8, 16, 18; 273 n.21-2, 24; 286 n.2
Baptism,
introduction of in New Testament, 190-2, 300-1 n.5-14
in Jesus' name, ix, 4-5, 12, 142-45, 155-9, 168, 189-90, 192-4, 196, 200, 208 213, 221-4, 226-7, 232, 235-7, 270 n.5; 276 n.13; 285 n.35; 288 n.30, 301 n.16; 302 n.16, 22, 24-5; 302 n.26-9; 310 n.36
and the modern Pentecostal movement, 218-27, 233-8, 243 n.1; 244 n.11; 244-5 n.13
as it relates to covenant initiation, ix-x, 189, 192-200, 206-9, 213, 232-3, 235 8; 272 n.13; 276 n.13; 288 n.30; 300

n.10; 301 n.11, 22, 24-5; 302 n.26-39; 312 n.15-6
as it relates to circumcision, 196-200, 302 n.43-51
as it relates to justification, 196-99, 302-3 n.40; 303 n.41-55; 304 n.54-5
as it relates to Spirit baptism, x, 189-196, 202, 204-11, 223-4, 232-238, 278 n.13; 307 n.71-2; 312 n.15-16
as it relates to the remission of sin, 190-3, 198-9, 237, 289 n.47; 300 n.8; 303 n.52-4
as it is interpreted as a triune formula, 59, 168, 171, 199, 223-4, 294 n.60; 301 n.16-17, 23
Baptism of the Holy Spirit, (see also "Holy Spirit, filling," etc.) x, 4-5, 12, 56, 128, 202-214, 218-220, 223-4, 232-238, 304-5 n.8-18; 305 n.18-35; 306, n.36-53; 307 n.54-75; 308-9 n.18, 309 n.23-32; 310 n.32-39; 310 n.47; 311 n.4-5; 311-12 n.14; 312 n.15
Bar Mitzvah (alleged) of Jesus, 86
Baron, Salo, 255 n.16
Barr, James, 275 n.11
Barrett, C. K., 93, 135, 254 n.7; 274 n.41; 282 n.37; 306 n.52
Basil, 182, 185, 300 n.77
Bath Qol, 273 n.21
Bauckham, Richard M., 48, 54, 114, 130-1, 145-6, 152, 163, 166, 169, 247 n.32, 37-8; 262 n.2; 264 n.25; 264 n.28; 266 n.7; 277 n.37, 41; 278 n.6-7; 281 n.19-22, 24; 284 n.31, 35; 285 n.36, 43-5; 285-6 n.46; 292 n.17-8; 294 n.50-1
Baumert, Norbert, 311 n.3; 311-12 n.14
Baumgartner, Walter, 246 n.28; 253 n.59
Bauer, Walter, 246 n.28
Baus, Karl, 289 n.45, 50
Beasley-Murray, G. R., 191-2, 300-1 n.5; 301 n.8, 14; 302 n.38
Begotten, Jesus as,
begotten of the Father, viii, 56, 65-7, 72-3, 77, 119, 266 n.6
begotten of the Spirit, 56, 66, 77

Subject & Author Index | 353

begotten from the dead, 66-67
"eternally begotten (allegedly)" 66, 297 n.33
Hippolytus's view of Noetus's understanding, 297 n.23
Beasley-Murray, G. R., 191-2, 300 n.5, 8; 301 n. 14; 302 n.38
Behm, Johannes, 274 n.47; 301 n.8
Beisner, Calvin, 240
Belleville, Linda, 305 n.25
Berchman, Robert M., 291 n.2; 297 n.35
Berkhof, Hendrikus, 47, 55, 68, 73, 83, 132, 183, 246 n.26-7; 264 n.26; 266 n.15; 267 n.26; 268 n.44; 271 n.26; 281 n.27; 282 n.8; 291 n.5; 293 n.32; 299 n.59
Berkhof, Louis, 244 n.6
Bernard, David K., xi, 71, 236-7, 244 n.11; 266 n.14; 267 n.33; 283 n.10
Benedictions,
  NT, epistles, 56, 58 (see also "Salutations in the epistles")
  OT, priestly, 41 (see also "Blessing, priestly")
Bethel Bible School (run by Charles Parham in Topeka), 219
Biblicism of Pentecostalism, 221, 308 n.4
Blasphemy against the Holy Spirit (see "Holy Spirit, blasphemy against")
Blessing, priestly 41-2, 58-9, 128, 139, 259 n.18
Blood,
  in Tabernacle/Temple rites, 41, 127
  of Jesus, significance of in atonement, 74, 107-09, 122, 127, 132-3, 160, 265 n.43; 290 n.61
Blumhofer, Edith L., 311 n.52
Boer, Harry R., 258 n.8
Bonsor, Jack A., 295 n.10
Borg, Marcus, 263 n.16
Bourdieu, Pierre (see also "Orthodoxy, as a sociological construct"), 153, 186, 286 n.10; 287 n. 11; 289-90 n.56; 300 n.80-1
Bousset, Willhelm, 262 n.11
Braaten, Carl E., 261 n.39
Braumann, G., 279 n.25
Brauch, Manfred T., 302 n.43
Brawley, Robert L., 274 n.38; 283 n.18
Brichto, Herbert Chanan, 252 n.41

Bride of Christ, 220, 222-4, 231, 235, 238, 309 n.25, 27; 310 n.32-33; 310-1 n.47
Bromily, G. W., 248 n.6; 252 n.43
Broshi, Magen, 255 n.16
Brown, Collin, 254 n.7-8; 255 n.10, 13-14; 298 n.36; 305 n.25
Brown, David, 260 n.26
Browne, Peter, 308 n.3
Brown, Raymond, 29-30, 49, 111, 131, 142, 245 n.21; 256 n.23-25; 262 n.1, 8-9; 277 n.38-40; 279 n.24; 279 n.32; 281 n.25; 284 n.32
Browne, Peter, 272 n.3
Bruce, F. F., 126-7, 145, 195, 275 n.5; 280 n.5, 10; 282 n.6; 285 n.41; 302 n.28, 34; 307 n.71
Brunner, Emil, 7, 245 n.18
Brueggemann, Walter, 42, 261 n.42
Buber, Martin, 15-6, 248 n.1
Buchanan, George Wesley, 280 n.14
Bultmann, Rudolph, 262 n.11; 283 n.9
Burgess, Stanley E., 243 n.2
Butler, Daniel L., 309 n.19; 310 n.45
Buttrick, George Arthur, 261 n.34
Cain, 24, 253 n.62, 64, 253-4 n.65; 254 n.66; 258-9 n.10
Calling on the name of Yahweh (see "Invocation of the name of Yahweh"),
  in Genesis 4:26, 36-37
  by the priests, 40-42
Calvin, John, 245 n.19; 246 n.24
Calvary (see also "Crucifixion of Jesus"), 107, 112, 125, 127, 211, 222
Camp, Ashby L., 199, 303 n.54
Carson, D. A., 50, 262 n.10; 268 n.34
Canon, canonization, 9, 49, 160, 170, 246 n.26; 247 n.34
Canonical criticism, 6, 8-9
Catholic Church,
  approach to salvation, 194
  approach to baptism, 194, 237
  approach to baptism of the Spirit, 237, 307 n.70; 312-3 n.15
  approach to church tradition, 5, 10, 32-3 161
  development of christology, 5-7, 9-10, 48, 52, 56, 79-80, 151-5, 164-7, 175-186
  perspective of the Reformation, 215

Centers (multiple) of divine consciousness, as a concept to be rejected, 77-8, 82-3, 89-91
Chadwick, Henry, 32, 257 n.38
Chaeremon, 28
Chafer, Louis Sperry, 245 n.22
Chance, J. Bradley, 283 n.18; 306 n.40
Charismatic movement, 3, 229, 243 n.2; 243-4 n.4; 311 n.3
Charlesworth, James H., 284 n.28; 293 n.43
Childs, Brevard, 8-9, 246 n.29; 246-7, n.30
Christiansen, Irmgard, 257 n.29
Christology,
 Adoption christology, 88, 157, 239, 264 n.27; 272 n.16; 286 n.2; 290 n.66
 Anathasius's christology, ix, 152, 181-2, 298 n.49-51
 Angel christology, 157, 288 n.35; 294 n.49
 Augustinian christology, 182-5
 Bauckham's christology, 48, 54, 114, 130 1, 145-6, 152, 163, 166, 169, 247 n.37-38; 262 n.2; 264 n.25; 266 n. 7 277 n.37, 41; 281 n.19-22; 284 n.31, 35; 285 n.43-5; 285-6 n.43-6
 Berkhof's (Hendrikus) christology, 55, 68, 73, 83, 132, 264 n.26; 266 n.15-6; 267 n.26; 268 n.44; 271 n.26; 281 n.27-8; 282 n.8
 covenantal christology, x, 233, 238-42
 critique of Creedal christology, 6-10, 58, 86, 154, 182, 186, 217, 222, 245 n.19; 246-7 n.30; 247 n.35; 299 n.73
 Dunn's christology, 145-6, 247 n.37; 267 n.25-6; 285 n.42; 274 n.35; 275 n.51; 285 n.46
 evolution of, 10, 12, 32, 47-48, 60, 84, 145 6, 151-73, 175, 264 n.35; 286 n.3-10; 287 n.11-28; 289 n.55-89; 291 n.1-8; 292 n.9-23; 293 n.24-34; 295 n.1-11; 296 n.11-24; 297 n.27-43; 298 n.44 64; 299 n.65-76; 300 n.77-81
 Ebionite christology, 158-9, 171, 288 n.42 4; 289 n.45-56
 Hippolytus's christology, 152, 154, 180, 287 n.16; 288 n.44; 294 n.56; 296 n.22-3; 297 n.33

 Ignatius's christology, ix, 160-1, 164, 179, 225, 285 n.45; 289 n.58; 290 n.59-68; 291 n.69
 Jewish christology, ix, 51, 59, 69-70, 73, 77, 8-1, 116, 130-1, 140-7, 154-9, 166, 192, 247 n.38; 262 n.11; 263 n.14; 267 n.23-30, 47-9; 270 n.5; 273 n.28; 274 n.47 276 n.12-15; 281 n.19 24; 283 n.21-6; 284 n.32-3; 285 n.46; 287 n.19-21, 25; 288 n.38-44; 289 n.45-56; 302 n.30
 Logos christology, 32, 152-4, 162, 165-8, 172, 175, 192-3, 286 n.9
 Modalist christology, ix, 4, 161, 170, 172, 175-181, 185, 187, 244 n.8; 270 n.16; 274 n.39; 285 n.45; 286 n.2, 9; 287 n.13, 24; 288 n.42; 290 n.66; 294 n.53, 55-59; 295 n.3
 Name christology, viii-ix, 69-70, 75, 104, 140-5, 155-158, 171, 192-3, 276 n.15; 283 n.21; 287 n.19-25; 288 n.38-40; 296-7 n.63
 Oneness christology, viii-x, 5-8, 11-2, 48, | 55-61, 63, 68, 75, 78-84, 139, 146-7, 151-3, 167-72, 175-86, 201-2, 215-6, 229-42, 244 n.8-10, 13; 246-7 n.30; 247 n.35-8; 268-9 n. 46; 270 n.16; 286 n.2, 4, 7-10; 287 n.15, 24-5; 290 1 n.66; 291 n.72; 294-5 n.63; 306 n.35; 309 n.19; 310 n.34
 Origen's christology, ix, 152-4, 166, 179 83, 286 n.3-4, 7; 287 n.15; 297 n.29 40; 298 n.37
 Praxean christology, ix, 156, 175-8, 270 n.16; 287 n.13-5, 25; 295 n.1-9, 12-3
 Tertullian's christology, ix,, 152-6, 176-8, 180, 270 n.16; 285 n.45; 286 n.3-4, 8; 287 n.13-15, 25; 295 n.2,4,7-11; 296 n.11-17
 Trinitarian christology, ix, 6-7, 9, 32, 58, 63, 66-9, 78-9, 83-4, 147, 152-4, 169 71, 175, 177-86, 264 n.35; 270 n.14; 274 n.42; 282 n.8; 286 n.3-10; 294 n.60; 298 n.54-63; 299 n.65-76; 300 n.77-81

Christological hymns (see "Hymns, chritological")
Church history, triumphalistic reading, 5,
    10, 151-5, 162, 186
Circumcision, 255 n.15
    as discussed at the Jerusalem council, 144
    Pauline perspective, 196-9, 303 n.50
Circuminsessio (see *Perichoresis*)
Civil War, 217, 308 n.7
Clanton, Arthur L., 309 n.19
Clanton, Charles E., 309 n.19
Clark, Gordon H., 298 n.53
Classical Pentecostalism, 3, 229, 243-4 n.4; 311 n.4
Cleanthes, 28
Clement (of Rome), 289 n.57
Clement of Alexandria, 164, 166, 180, 288 n.41;
    291-2 n.3; 292 n.22; 294 n.63
Collins, John J., 255 n.15
Commandments (ten), (see also "Decalogue"),
    29, 39, 285-6 n.3
Commodius, 156
Conception of Jesus (see "Jesus, conception of")
Constantine, 181-2, 289 n.45
Conybeare, Fred C., 301 n.16
Coogan, Michael D., 255 n.17
Cook, Glenn, 222-3, 235, 310 n.44
Cornelius, 208, 210, 306 n.47-8
Corwin, Virginia, 290 n.66
Covenant, God's covenant: vii-x,
    with Abraham ix, 20, 37, 196-99, 303 n.40-46
    with Adam and Eve, vii, 18-19, 23-4, 35-37
    related to baptism, ix, 189-200
    covenantal soteriology, x, 233-236
    covenantal christology, x, 233, 238-242
    covenantal worship, 12, 19, 23-4, 36-37,
        41-2, 78-9, 139, 201
    defined theologically, 5, 7-8, 13, 35-43
        (see also "Covenant, NT" below)
    covenant, OT, 11, 35-43
    covenant, NT, 5-7, 11-13, 60-1, 126-8, 189
        214
    in creation, 18
    Holy Spirit and covenant initiation, 201-14
    with Israel, 21-22, 25, 37-42
    Jesus as fulfilling covenant, vii-x, 11, 85
        95, 121-3, 125-36

prophesied for the Gentiles, vii, 42-3
    with Noah, 37, 253 n.63; 259 n.20-1; 259
        60 n.22; 260 n.23
    rediscovering the biblical understanding
        of covenant, x, 215-27, 233-442
Craigie, Peter C., 273 n.31
Crawford, F. L., 309 n.27
Creation, vii, 15-19, 21-3, 28, 107, 248 n.9; 274
    n.40; 292 n.5
    the Son and creation, 32, 68, 249 n.13;
        267 n.27; 268 n.35; 296 n.10; 297 n.33
    and the Prologue of John, 70-2
Cross, Frank M., 251 n.39
Cross, Terry, 4, 244 n.6
Crossan, John D., 263 n.19
Crouse, Robert, 298 n.55; 299 n.57
Cullmann, Oscar, 6, 52, 90-1, 115, 128, 213, 245
    n.16; 263 n.15; 272 n.8, 15; 273 n.25, 27,
    29, 33; 274 n.46; 277 n.26, 29; 278 n.5, 10;
    280 n.13; 302 n.39; 307 n.61; 308 n.74
Culy, Martin M., 199, 303 n.56
Crucifixion of Jesus (see "Jesus, crucifixion of,
    meaning of")
Cyprian, 192, 286 n.6
Dagon, 127, 249 n.14
Dahl, Nils, 54, 57, 59, 262 n.50; 264 n.23, 36;
    285 n.37
Daniel, 109, 110, 120, 134, 262 n.50; 269 n.2
Daniélou, Jean, 70, 140, 156-7, 171, 264
    n.28,;267 n.24; 269 n.46; 278 n.13; 283
    n.23; 287 n.21, 23, 26; 288 n.26, 31, 38,
    40-1; 290 n.66; 292 n.16; 294 n.62-3; 302
    n.30
Darwinism, 217
David, (King), 42-3, 74, 77-8, 109, 121-2, 144,
    233, 241, 261 n.44-7; 270 n.11; 27
    n.25; 280 n.3; 285 n.38
    Tabernacle of, 144, 261 n.45-7; 285 n.38
Davis, Carl Judson, 198, 205, 282 n.6; 303 n.52
Dayton, Donald, 307 n.1; 308 n.4, 7, 14-5; 309
    n.22
Death angel, 132
Debar (see "Word," *Logos*), 71, 167
Decalogue, 39, 256 n.22; 285 n.46 (see also
    "Commandments, ten")

Delitzsch, F., 250-1 n.32; 267 n.27
Denney, James, 212, 307 n.64
Denominationalism, early Pentecostal attitudes toward, 220, 310 n.29-30
Dillon, John 297 n.37
Diaspora, Diaspora Jews, 26, 28, 141, 143
Dikaiosune (see also "Justification"), 198, 302 n.43; 303 n. 46-7
Dispensational premillennialism, 219, 245 n.22; 248-9 n.10
Divine origins, Jesus' language about (see "Jesus, language about divine origins")
"Divine Person," Jesus as an (alleged) "Second Person" of God
Donum superadditum, 203
Doxa/doxazo/doxasthestai (see also "Jesus ascension, glorification, heavenly ministry of"; see also *kabod*), 70, 115-6, 267 n.22; 268 n.45; 278 n.14, 18; 281 n.19
Dorner, Isaake, 298 n.61; 299 n.65
Dorner, J. A., 295 n.3
Dove, at Jesus' baptism, 88-91, 240, 273 n.19-21
Driver, G. R., 250 n.28; 260 n.24; 261 n.38
Dunn, James D. G., 258 n.6; 272 n.9; 280 n.41-2
  on christology, 145-6, 264 n.22,28; 276 n.11; 285 n.42; 285 n.46
  on the Philippian hymn, 274 n.35, 40; 275 n.51
  on the Prologue of John, 267 n.25-6
  on Spirit Baptism, 203-10, 213, 247 n.37; 282 n.6; 304 n.8; 305-6 n.18; 306 n.31-2, 35; 306 n.39, 43-4, 46-8, 49 51; 307 n.54, 56, 69
Durham, William, 222-3
Durkheim, Emile, 250 n.28
Dwelling, of Yahweh,
  Heaven as the "abode" of Yahweh, 22-4, 72, 89, 107-8, 252-3 n.51; 253 n.52-7 268 n.40-1
  Yahweh dwelling (covenantally) where His name is applied, 69-70, 106, 140, 267 n.19, 22; 268 n.41; 269 n.47; 289 n.51; 302 n.30
  uniquely in Jesus Christ, 70-3, 78, 89, 104, 140-3, 155, 158-9, 161, 268 n.38, 42; 269 n.47
  inhabiting the cosmos, 89

Dynamic Monarchianism, 171-2, 185, 286 n.2; 287 n.24
Ebed Yahweh (Servant of Yahweh), 90, 93, 98, 100, 104-5, 114, 119, 130, 272 n.11; 273 n.29; 281 n.19
Ebionitism, ix, 158-9, 288 n.42-44; 289 n.45, 51, 53-4
Ecumenism, 229-32, 311 n.4
Eden, Garden of, 8, 18, 22-3, 35, 37, 39, 82-3, 201, 245 n.22; 248 n.9; 274 n.40
Ego eime, 30, 117, 119, 131, 137, 245 n.21; 251 n.36; 256 n.25; 277 n.37; 279 n.24
Egypt/Egyptians, 19-21, 26, 29, 38-9, 152, 165, 250 n.28; 251 n.39; 256 n.21; 257 n.36; 286 n.6; 298 n.35
Ehrman, Bart D., 291 n.70; 293 n.35-42
Eichrodt, Walther, 7, 22, 37, 197, 245 n.22; 246 n.23-25; 248 n.2; 253 n.54, 56; 260 n.23; 303 n.44
Edersheim, Alfred, 261 n.36; 271 n.1
Eis, 198-9, 301 n.25
El, 21, 274 n.40; 251-2 n.40; 269 n.2; 297-8 n.2
El Shaddai, 20, 251 n.39
El Elyon, 251-2 n.40
Elohim, 17, 21, 249 n.14, 16; 252 n.40-1; 269 n.2
Elohist, 251-2 n.40
Emotions, God, as having emotions/passion, 21, 29-30, 252 n.44
  view restricted by Hellenistic thinking, 184
  view gradually rejected by church fathers, 177, 183-4, 285 n.45
Epiphanius, xiii, 158, 178, 288 n.43-4; 289 n.47,49; 296 n.24; 297 n.27
Epistemology, shift in Christological understanding
  in the second and third century, 48, 84, 152, 163-193, 226, 247 n.38
  in the fourth century, 181-5
  leading to the advent of modern Oneness Pentecostalism, 223-4
Erickson, Millard, 244 n.6
Ervin, Howard, 306 n.49
Essenes, 233
Eternal Son, 63, 65-8, 72-4, 94, 109, 116, 130, 182, 274 n.43; 298 n.47

eternal generation of the Son/*Logos*, of being eternally begotten, 66, 179-82, 267 n.31-2 (see also *Logos*)
Eusebius, 153, 185, 192, 286 n.7; 289 n.53; 290 n.60; 298 n.47; 299 n.76; 301 n.16
Evangelicals/evangelicalism, 3-5, 194, 202, 217, 224, 230, 236-7, 244 n.5, 12; 245 n.22; 308 n.3; 308 n.8
Eve, 8, 18, 20, 22-3, 35-6, 39, 91-2, 249 n.17; 253 n.62; 258 n.7, 9
Eve, Raymond A., 308 n.6
"Evening time," 223, 234, 236, 310 n.44
Ewart, Frank, 4, 12-13, 222-3, 230, 235, 242, 243 n.3; 244 n.10; 244-5 n.13; 309 n.26; 310 n.44; 311 n.11
Exodus (from Egypt), 260 n.27
Face-to face relationship: God in covenant (see also *panim*), 19, 23-4, 35-41, 69, 120, 201, 203, 253 n.59-61; 253-4 n.65; 260 n.30-1
(alleged) of Father and Son in the Prologue of John, 71-2, 267 n.31-2
Faith:
and the Spirit, 202-3, 208
in conversion, 65, 190, 194-200, 203, 208, 213, 306 n.48
of Abraham, 196-7of Adam, 97
of Christians/people of God, Christian community, 9, 49, 144, 160-164, 216, 230-1, 278 n.5; 282 n.8; 289 n.52, 58; 291 n.1
of the church fathers, 180, 291 n.1; 298 n.54
of the Greeks/Plato/Platonists, 28, 166, 176, 298 n.54; 292 n.15; 296 n.10
of Jesus (see "Jesus, faith of")
of the Jewish people/covenant community, Israel, 26, 33, 144, 246 n.25-7; 252-3 n.51; 253 n.63; 258 n.4; 272 n.13; 285 n.46; 287 n.25
of the Pentecostal movement, 230
rule of, 177
statement (the Bible as faith statement), 50, 53
Fall of Adam (and Eve)/humanity, 7, 18, 35, 82, 91, 216

Fallen/sin nature, 82, 218
as it has been defined in contrast with Jesus, 82
Father, viii, 4-5, 55-59, 63, 66, 71-4, 77, 78, 82-4, 89, 102-8, 116-9, 127-9, 135, 138-9, 156, 161, 165, 167-71, 177-80, 182-4, 192, 211-2, 221, 223, 225, 238-40, 265 n.42-3; 45; 268-9 n.46; 270 n.12; 271 n.20-1; 272 n.5; 272 n.17; 275-6 n.50; 275 n.5; 276 n.11; 276 n.15; 278 n.15; 284 n.30; 286 n.7; 287 n.25; 290 n.64-66; 294 n.55; 296 n.13, 23-4; 297 n. 27-8, 33; 298 n.47, 54; 299 n.71, 75; 307 n.67
Jesus' language about the Father, viii, 86, 102-4, 107-8, 116-8, 127
name of the Father (see "Name" and related subjects), 193, 276 n.15; 301 n.19
related to the Prologue of John, 71-4
as suffering (see "Patripassianism"), 79 | 80, 160-2, 172, 177-8, 184, 291 n.61; 295 n. 64; 296 n.13, 24
Yahweh, as becoming a father through the act of paternity, 56, 74, 76-8, 136, 270 n.9-13
Faupel, D. William, 218, 220, 224, 307 n.1; 308 n.10-11; 309 n.25, 27-8, 32-3; 310 n.42; 311 n.49
Fausset, A. R., 260 n.26; 261 n.38
Feast(s), Jewish/Holy days
Day of Atonement, 40-2, 65, 127, 203, 280 n.37
of Tabernacles, 128
Passover, 65, 291 n.70; 302 n.26
Pentecost (Feast of Weeks), 143, 304 n.8
Fee, Gordon D., 135, 205, 212, 282 n.34; 301 n.22; 305 n.26, 28-9; 307 n.63; 311 n.2
Fellowship (see also *koinonia*)
of Jesus and the apostles as a source of doctrinal teaching, 9, 49, 54
modern Oneness Pentecostals with other groups, 224, 230-1
of the Holy Spirit, 58, 265 n.44-6
of the "eternal Son" with the Father, 63, 71, 267 n.31-3

First-begotten, firstborn, 68, 132, 167, 292 n.13
First-century church, 9-11, 48, 52-4, 55-6, 195, 199-200, 224, 237, 274 n.39; 289 n.55
First-century cultural understanding, 11, 50, 52, 58, 69-70, 76, 80, 139-40, 163, 189-90, 195, 224, 247 n.36; 276 n.23; 293 n.32; 304 n.8; 308 n.4; 311 n.5
First-century christology (see "Christology"), viii-ix, 8, 10, 54-6, 58, 60, 68-70, 73, 75-6, 80-4, 109, 139-40, 146-7, 151-60, 163, 170, 175, 186, 189, 264 n.28; 270 n.16; 276 n.15
Fitzmyer, Joseph A., 284 n.28 ; 300 n.51
Flesh (see also *soma, sarx*), 103, 210, 271 n.21-22
  as related to Jesus, 68, 72-4, 80-2, 108-9, 118-9, 122, 160-1, 178, 180, 238, 241, 269 n.47; 270 n.11, 13; 271 n.20-22; 277 n.24-5; 285 n.45; 286 n.7; 299 n.73
Flusser, David, 273 n.28
Foster, Fred J., 309 n.19, 310 n.34, 36, 38
Fox, Everett, 248 n.8; 249 n.11; 253 n.64; 253-4 n.65; 258-9 n.10
Fox, Norman, 193, 301 n.25
Form of God, 94, 274 n.47; 275 n.53
Frankfort, Henri, 254 n.3
Freedman, David Noel, 253 n.53
Frei, Hans, 6, 245 n.15
French, Talmadge, 222, 243 n.1; 309 n.19; 310 n.34, 41, 43-44
Frick, Peter, 257 n.31; 257-8 n.41
Frerichs, Ernest S. 246 n.26
Furnish, Victor Paul, 265 n.42
Garden of Eden (see Eden)
Gaston, Lloyd, 197, 303 n.42
Genetic material as related to Jesus, 77-8
Gilmore, S. Maclean, 304 n.8
Glueck, Nelson, 259 n.20
Gentrification of Pentecostalism, 229
Gethsemane, viii, 91, 118-9, 211, 271 n.20; 272 n.8
Gezera shava, 131, 281 n.20
Gibson, J. Monroe, 244 n.13
Gilmore, S. Maclean, 304 n.8
Gingrich, Wilber F., xiii, 246 n.28
Glory, 236,
  (of God) as applied to creation/God's mighty acts, 16-17, 248 n.6; 260 n.31-2; 265 n.43; 267 n.22; 304 n.6
  as an attribute/circumlocution for Yahweh, 49, 70, 143-5, 260 n.31-32; 267 n.22
  as an incarnational concept, 72-3, 155-6, 168, 184-5, 268 n.38, 41, 45, 268 n.46; 269 n.47
  as it relates to Adam, 17, 274 n.40
  as it relates to the cross, 114-117
  as used enigmatically of/by Jesus describing His identity and work, viii, 90, 99, 104, 109-10, 113-8, 126, 129-36, 159, 161, 269 n.46-7; 278 n.14-21
  as it relates to the ascension/eschaton, 90, 110, 113-7, 126, 129-36, 143, 280 n.2-5; 284 n.30; 299 n.73
  of Yahweh, 40, 143, 281 n.43
Glorification of Jesus (see "Jesus,ascension/ glorification/heavenly ministry of")
Glossolalia (see also "Tongues, speaking in"), 208, 211, 213, 230, 307 n.74
Gnostic/Gnosticism (see also "*Gospel of Thomas*"), 53, 158, 164, 176, 246 n.27; 262 n.11; 263 n.19; 271 n.4; 276 n.24; 289 n.54; 293 n.32; 295 n.7; 296 n.20; 297 n.28
Gnuse, Robert K., 251-2 n.40
Goff, James R., 308 n.18
Goiten, S. D., 250 n.28
Golden calf as evidence of broken covenant, 39-40
Golder, Morris, 309 n.19
Goldingay, John, 6, 7, 245 n.17
González, Justo L., 295 n.11
Gospel of Thomas, 53, 83, 263 n.20; 271 n.25
Gospels, 5, 49-51, 53, 56, 70, 76, 83, 99, 105, 109, 113-5, 118-9, 121, 125, 128, 138, 191, 202, 204-5, 245 n.21; 247 n.32; 263 n.12, 18-9; 265 n.49; 266 n.7; 267-8 n.34, 38; 268 n.35, 38; 268-9 n.46; 269 n.48, 50; 270 n.10; 271 n.20; 275 n.10; 276 n.14, 25; 277 n.25, 31, 37; 278 n.13; 282 n.2; 287 n.25; 288 n.33; 290 n.67; 292 n.6, 16; 293 n.32; 301 n.12-13, 22; 302 n.29; 305 n.24
  as providing historically accurate information/biography of Jesus, 5, 49-51, 53, 263 n.12, 18-19
  noncanonical, 53, 263 n.20; 271 n.25; 296 n.20

Goss, Ethel E., 310 n.36
Goss, Howard, 310 n.36
Goulder, M. D., 206, 305 n.34
Grace, 299 n.64
  covenant of, 245 n.22
  of Yahweh, 43, 259 n.20
  as it is utilized in the OT priestly blessing, 58, 265 n.43
  in the identity/life/ministry/work of Jesus, 120, 138-9, 161, 195, 312 n.15
  in the Prologue of John, 72
  in the salutations and benedictions of the epistles, 58, 139, 265 n.40
  as initiation into covenant, 195, 311-2 n.15
  of the Spirit, 297 n.27
  second work of, 218, 222, 308 n.15
Grant, Robert M., 257 n.34; 268 n.35; 288 n.33; 290 n.65, 67; 291 n.69
Graves, Brent, 139, 283 n.10
Grasping at divine prerogatives,
  in Adam, 94, 98
  Jesus not grasping at divine prerogatives, 94, 98, 110, 275 n.50
Greco-Roman period, 29, 216, 292 n.10
Greek, philosophical worldview, 26-33, 48, 175-87, 247 n.35; 254 n8; 254-5 n.9; 255 n.11-5; 257 n.38; 292 n.10,21
Green, Joel B., 245 n.17; 301 n.22
Green, William S., 246 n.26
Grillmeier, Alois, 274 n.42
Grosheide, F. W., 135, 282 n.36, 38
Grudem, Wayne, 51, 263 n.12
Gunton, Colin E., 293 n.25
Haber, Susan, 280 n.9
Haenchen, Ernst, 282 n.6
Hahn, Ferdinand, 59, 265 n.46
Hahn, Robert, 262 n.5
Hall, Mike, 283 n.11
Hamilton, Victor P., 37, 259-60 n.22
Harnack, Adolf von, 49, 154, 157-60, 167, 169-70, 172, 176, 180-1, 225, 262 n.7; 285 n.42, 45; 286 n.9; 287 n.16-8; 288 n.36; 288 n.42; 289 n.53, 55, 58; 290 n.59-60, 64; 291 n.71-2; 293 n.26, 31; 294 n.54, 56-9; 295 n.66, 68; 295 n.7; 297 n.39, 41, 43; 298 n.44-5

Harris, Elizabeth, 73, 269 n.48, 50-1
Harris, Murray J., 305 n.25
Harris, R. Laird, 248 n.2; 253 n.55
Harrold, Francis B., 308 n.6
Hartman, Lars, 191, 193, 199, 270 n.5; 272 n.14; 301 n.11, 24; 302 n.26; 303 n.55
Hasidim, 32
HaShem (see also "Name"), 70, 140, 155, 283 n.21
Hatch, Nathan O., 308 n.5
Hay, David M., 266 n.7; 280 n.2-5
Hays, Richard B., 272 n.7
Haywood, G. T., 4, 12-13, 222, 230, 238, 242, 243 n.3; 244 n.10, 13; 245 n.20; 310 n.41; 311 n.48; 311 n.12
Heart,
  as a component part of God (metaphorically), 18, 31
  as a component part of Israel's worship (metaphorically), 42, 81, 261 n.44
  as a component part of Jesus, 80-1
  as a component part of NT believers (metaphorically), 99, 128, 168, 171, 195, 212, 214, 295 n.8; 309 n.27
Heaven(s), 16, 18, 22-3, 47, 57, 67, 71-2, 78, 89-91, 94, 102-3, 107-10, 120, 123, 125-7, 129, 132-3, 143, 147, 168, 206, 212, 252-3 n.51; 253 n.51, 53, 55-57; 268 n.35, 41; 273 n.22, 24, 28; 275 n.50; 276-7 n.24; 277 n.25; 278 n.14; 280 n.42; 280 n.5; 281 n.29-30; 293 n.21; 299 n.68, 73; 308-9 n.18; 310 n.47
  as the dwelling place of God, 22-3, 72, 78, 89-91, 107-109, 252-3 n.51; 253 n.2; 252 n.57; 268 n.41
  as becoming the abode of Jesus Christ, 47, 125-136, 168
Hellenism, vii, 26-32, 254 n.5; 255 n.15; 262 n.11; 267 n.28; 268 n.42; 268-9 n.46; 293 n.32; 301 n.8; 302 n.29
  as it redefined Yahweh as absolutely transcendent, 11, 26-33, 237, 256 n.22, 26-27; 256-7 n.27; 257 n.35
  as it was represented by church fathers in their understanding of God, 80, 152-6, 247 n.38; 278 n.13

as it was represented by church fathers in their understanding of Jesus Christ, 80, 152-6, 162-7, 178, 181, 183-4, 226, 257 n.35; 289 n.56; 291 n.3; 292 n.13-8, 21
Helper (see *Parakletos*)
Hengel, Martin, 254 n.5; 266 n.9; 384 n.28
Heraclitus, 166, 254 n.7; 295-6 n.8
Herod, 115, 255 n.16
Hertz, J. H., 249 n.19; 270-1 n.19
Hesiod, 28
High priest,
  Jesus as typologically answering to a high priest, 127, 278 n.5; 283 n.21
  Jesus before the high priest, 119-20
  role in Jewish worship/culture, 40-1, 140, 203, 257 n.28; 261 n.36; 305 n.21
Hippolytus (see "Pseudo-Hippolytus"), 152, 154, 180, 287 n.16; 289 n.44; 294 n.56; 296 n.22-3; 297 n.25; 297 n.33; 301 n.23
Hittite suzerainty treaties, 38-9, 260 n.25
Holiness of God, 22, 248 n.2,
Holiness movement, 217-22, 309 n.12
Holman, Charles L., 305 n.30, 311 n.4
Holy Spirit,
  blasphemy against,105-6
  Jesus, language about, viii, 105-9, 117, 128, 303 n.2
  as defined by the Holiness movement, 18-9, 308 n.11; 309 n.17
  as defined in the epistles, 265 n.42; 305 n.26
  as defined by the advent of modern Pentecostalism, 219-34, 244 n.7; 308 n.18; 309 n.23, 27-32; 309-10 n.33; 311 n.1-2
  as portrayed by the church fathers and in other ancient literature, 156, 161, 168, 170, 177-82, 257 n. 37; 290 n.64; 294 n.55; 299 n.75; 300 n.3
  as related to baptism, x, 192, 221, 223
  as related to the dove at the baptism of Jesus, 273 n.19-21
  as related to covenant initiation, x, 4, 12, 128-9, 194, 201-14, 229-38, 244 n.11; 300 n.3-5; 304 n.8, 13; 304 n.18; 305 n.30, 35; 306 n.39; 307 n.49; 308 n.70-74; 301 n.3-5; 311 n.9; 311-12 n.9; 312 n.15
  as related to the Incarnation, 77, 270 n.7
  rejected as a "co-equal Person," 4, 12, 56-8
  identified as Jesus by NT authors, 138, 238
Homer, 28, 257 n.29
Honor, 255 n.15
  as affirming God's deity, 73, 133
  as applied to Jesus, 92, 115, 133, 136, 141, 190, 280 n.5, 14
Hooker, Morna D., 272 n.9
Horbury, William, 246 n.26
Horsley, Richard A., 263 n.17
Howard, J. Keir., 272 n.13; 300 n.10
Humanity,
  compared with angels, 249 n.19
  created in covenant, 7, 12, 15, 17, 22-23, 35-38
  fall of, 35, 82, 91, 216, 258 n.7
  in the image of God, vii, 7-8, 17-9, 93-5, 250 n.23-4; 258 n.8; 259-60 n.22
  of Jesus (see "Jesus, humanity of")
  philosophical view of, 27, 31
  redemption of, 91
  full restoration of, 116
Huperupsosen (see also "Jesus, glorification of")
Hurtado, Larry, 57, 247 n.37; 264 n.28, 34; 267 n.28; 268 n.45; 382 n.33; 283 n.27, 284 n.30-1; 285-6 n.46; 288 n.44; 294 n.60; 302 n.38
Hymns, christological, vii, 51, 56, 67-8, 70, 85, 93-5, 98, 119, 129-30, 136, 147, 160-1, 172, 225, 266 n.9; 268 n.39; 271 n.31; 274 n.39, 43-4; 275 n.49, 53; 275 n.5; 277 n.1; 279 n.30; 284 n.29; 289 n.58; 291 n.67-8; 292 n.69

I AM, vii-viii, 11, 147, 223,
  as an OT confession, 251 n.34-6
  as revealed to Moses, 19-21, 40, 76
  invoked over Israel/Moses in covenant, 38-42, 249 n.29-32
  prophesied to, spoken over the Gentiles, 42-3
  Isaiah's use of, 131-2, 277 n.37, 39, 41
  Jesus' use, vii, 47, 66-7, 74, 111-2, 117, 119-20, 131, 135, 137-9, 147, 223, 226, 245 n.21; 262 n.1; 278 n.15; 279 n.23-4, 26, 31; 282 n.2; 284 n.31

Philo's use of, vii, 32-33, 258 n.42
    in the eschaton, 131-2
    in the Septuagint, 29-30, 256 n.25; 292 n.19
Justin's use, 166-7 (see also "Justin Martyr," *I AM*)
Yahweh as "I AM," vii, 19-21
Incarnation, viii, 6, 47, 51, 55, 63, 66-7, 69-75, 77-84, 88-9, 94, 98, 107-8, 131, 133, 139-40, 147, 155, 158, 164-5, 181, 211, 226, 247 n.37; 264 n.37; 266 n.14; 268 n.38; 275 n.50, 53; 283 n.21; 284-5 n.33; 290 n.65; 297 n.33
"I-Thou" relationship (see "Yahweh, in 'I-Thou' relationship")
Ignatius, ix, 160-1, 164, 179, 225, 285 n.45; 289 n.58; 290 n.60, 62-7, 69
Image of God, humanity as created in the image of God, vii, 18-9, 94, 249 n.19; 250 n.23-4; 258 n.8; 259-60 n.22; 274 n.40; 274 n.46
    in the Philippian hymn, 93-4
    Jesus in the "image of God," 94-5, 98-9, 274 n.40; 275 n.5
Immanuel, 76, 80
Immutability of God in Augustine, 183, 298 n.61, 299 n.65
Incarnation, 55-66, 121-23, 218, 251, 316
Intercession, Jesus as Intercessor, 132
Intermediaries, the need for,
    in Philo, 31-2
    in the church fathers, 164-6
Interpenetration of persons/*circumincessio*/perichoresis, doctrine of, 56, 84, 185, 264 n.32; 299-300 n.73
Invocation of the name of Yahweh, vii, 12, 36-43, 58, 69, 128, 137, 139, 143, 145, 201-2, 259 n.11-20; 261 n.39; 265 n.43; 267 n.21; 285 n.40; 300 n.3; 304 n.5
Invocation of the name of Jesus, ix, 137, 140-5, 155-6, 159, 168, 171, 190, 192-4, 196, 198-200, 201, 203, 207-9, 213, 221-2, 226-7, 234-7, 243 n.1; 259 n.19; 261 n.36, 38, 39; 276 n.13; 285 n.35, 40; 288 n.30, 40; 302 n.25, 29; 310-11 n.47
Irenaeus, 152, 172, 179, 181, 247 n.34; 294 n.59; 297 n.28

Isaac, 20, 37, 198, 251 n.39; 279 n.27; 303 n.46
Israel/Judah (the nation), vii, 47, 152, 169, 245 n.21; 246 n.26-7; 251 n.39; 252 n.46; 252-3 n.51; 254 n.6; 258 n.4; 266 n.1; 269 n.2; 270 n.10; 272 n.17; 277 n.28; 284 n.32; 286 n.6; 294 n.49; 304 n.8
    called into covenant, vii, 7, 20-2, 24, 76, 201, 245 n.22; 246 n.25; 251 n.36; 259 n.19; 260 n.24, 27; 267 n.17
    influenced by Hellenism, 26, 30, 37-40, 80, 256n.20
    in covenant worship, 40-3, 63, 65, 81, 127, 132, 140, 146, 226, 250 n.25; 259 n.11; 260 n.30; 261 n.37, 42-44; 285 n.40
    in prophecy, 113-4, 278 n.2; 283 n.18
Jacob, 20, 37, 79, 111, 251 n.36; n.39; 279 n.27
Jacobsen, Douglas, 230, 243 n.3; 308 n.18; 311 n.48; 311 n.7
James (preeminent leader of the Jerusalem church), 49, 144-5, 284-5 n.36; 285 n.37-8, 40; 288 n.30; 306 n.38
Jamieson, Robert, 260 n.26; 261 n.38
Jehovah (see also "Tetragrammaton," "Yahweh," "LORD"), 5, 19, 223, 244 n.10; 244-5 n.13; 250 n.27
Jenson, Robert W., 6, 245 n.15; 293 n.25
Jeremias, Joachim, 273 n.22, 29; 275-6 n.11; 300 n.5
Jerusalem Church, 54, 284-5 n.36; 289 n.52
Jesus,
    Adam, typologically answering to Adam, 7, 35-6, 82-3, 84, 91-5, 97-100, 108, 116, 122-3, 138, 211, 272 n.9; 272 n.17; 274 n.40-1, 46
    anthropology of; viii, 5, 11, 77-84, 270 n.11
    apostles' teaching regarding, 5, 8-10, 49-50, 53-55, 137-47, 151-2, 162, 182-202, 204-13
    ascension/glorification/heavenly ministry of (see also *doxa*) viii, 43, 47, 66-7, 69, 90, 98, 103, 105, 107, 109, 112, 116-7, 118, 120, 123, 125-32, 137-8, 142, 145, 153, 169, 202, 206-7, 238, 266 n.8; 278 n.16-18; 279 n.19-21, 27; 280 n.1; 281 n.19, 21-2, 24-5; 284 n.29; 286 n.2; 304 n.13; 306 n.35
    at age twelve, viii, 11, 86-7

at the Last Supper, 56, 60, 105, 116, 118, 278 n.17
at Gethsemane/and tried before rulers, viii, 91, 118-121, 211, 271 n.20; 272 n.8
Baptizer of the Holy Spirit, 11, 56, 126-8, 202, 205-6, 213-4
baptism of, viii, 66, 85, 87-91, 98, 114, 121, 130, 141
birth of, 60, 75-80, 87, 142, 270 n.11
Christos (see also "Messiah"), 76, 85, 142, 262 n.11
conception of, 5, 56, 77-80, 270 n.11, 13
covenant partner of Yahweh, 11, 43, 47-8, 85-95, 97-100
crucifixion of, viii, 11, 51, 65, 75, 92, 103, 105, 107, 112, 113-7, 121-3, 125-7, 129, 132-3, 136-7, 139, 142, 184, 213, 234, 240-1, 247-8 n.38; 271 n.20; 272 n.15; 278 n.5; 278, n.18; 279 n.27; 282 n.2; 284 n.31; 299 n.73
faith of, 11, 87, 97-8, 104, 115-7, 121-2, 272 n.7, 9; 273 n.31; 278 n.5; 279 n.19
"first-born" of all creation, 68
genealogy of, 77-8, 277 n.25glory, relationship to the glory of God (see "Glory")
"historical Jesus"/revisionist reading of, 50, 52-5, 247 n.36; 262 n.11; 263 n.18-20; 271 n.4
incarnational language (see "Incarnation")
in the eschaton, viii, 65, 75, 91, 93, 99, 117, 120, 130-1, 132-6, 139, 280 n.43; 281 n.19
"Lamb of God," 64-5, 87-8, 90, 92, 95, 132-4, 281, 39 n.31
Living Bread, 108-9, 245 n.21; 276-7 n.24
Mediator, viii, 59, 68, 127-8, 132-3, 135, 146
Messiah, 11, 76, 87-93, 104, 111, 114, 135, 139, 159, 168, 191, 202, 233, 235, 246 n.26; 266 n.1; 271 n.20; 276 n.14, 23; 277 n.27, 29, 40; 279 n.23, 33; 280 n.35; 284 n.28; 285 n.38; 289 n.51; 293 n.20; 304 n.9
name of, etymologically meaning, 76 (see also "Name")
omnipresence of, 78, 106-7, 141
priesthood, Aaron, fulfilling typological priesthood/high priesthood after the order of Aaron, viii, 40-1, 126-8, 132, 135, 278 n.5; 280 n.9; 305 n.21
priesthood, Melchizedek, as fulfilling typological priesthood after the order of Melchizedek, 126-7, 251-2 n.40; 280 n.8
preexistence (alleged), viii, 11, 63-8, 70-4, 93-5, 109, 115-7, 131, 267 n.32; 275 n.50-1, 3
redemption by, 7-8, 58-9, 63-6, 70-4, 91-2, 113, 117, 119-23, 126-136, 138-9, 258 n.7; 265 n.45
temptation of, viii, 87, 91-95, 98, 272 n.8
victory over Satan, 122-3, 129-32, 135-6, 280 n.39-43
Yahweh incarnate (as the 'unique locale' of God"), 47, 55, 60, 66-7, 74, 76, 83, 88, 111-2, 117, 119-20, 135, 137-8, 146, 226, 245 n.21; 262 n.1; 278 n.15; 279 n.23-4, 26, 31; 282 n.2; 284 n.31
John the Baptist, 205-6, 287 n.25; 300 n.6; 306 n.38
Johnson, Luke Timothy, 245 n.14; 272 n.7; 285 n.38
Johnston, Robin, xi, 223, 244-5 n.13; 310 n.46-7; 311 n.11-12
de Jonge, Marinus, 257 n.37, 39; 264 n.22; 266 n.13; 276 n.23; 294 n.43
Joseph (husband of Mary), 76, 86-87, 271 n.3
Josephus, 284 n.28; 300 n.5
Judaism, 11, 26-8, 52, 212, 246 n.26, 29; 249 n.20; 250 n.31; 254 n.1, 5-6; 255 n.15, 17; 255-6 n. 18; 258 n.44; 262 n.5; 263 n.17; 273 n.29; 283 n.27-8; 285 n.46; 289 n.52, 57; 291 n.3; 293 n.30; 303 n.48
Judas Iscariot, 119, 271 n.23; 278 n.17
Juel, Donald, 109, 120-1, 211, 264 n.23; 266 n.7; 273 n.25; 277 n.27; 279 n.33, 35; 307 n.57
Justification (see also *Dikaiosune*), 194, 237
by faith, its biblical meaning, 65, 198-9, 303 n.46-9
justification and Abraham, 196-9, 303 n.46
linked with baptism and infilling of the Spirit, 204-9
Justin Martyr, ix, 168, 172-3, 183
critique of Oneness believers, 152, 167, 170, 180, 268-9 n.46; 287 n.22

on the *Logos*, 153-5, 165-6, 175-6, 179-80, 270 n.14
integration of his philosophy and view of God, 152-5, 164-6, 278 n.13; 286 n.8; 291 n.3, 13, 15-6, 20, 26, 29-30; 296 n.9-10; 297 n.28
Justinian, 180, 297 n.37
Kabod (see also *doxa*, "Jesus, ascension/glorification/heavenly ministry of"), 70, 267 n.22
Kai, its usage
in salutations of the epistles, 59, 139, 283 n.10
in John 3:5 to join water-Spirit, 305 n.25
Kenosis: as alleged "lowering" from a heavenly realm, 95, 274 n.42; 274 n.44; 275 n.53
as a mindset of Jesus in the Incarnation itself, 116
Kee, H. C., 169, 293 n.43
Keener, Craig, 311 n.2
Keil, C. F., 250 n.32; 267 n.27
Kelly, J. N. D., 153, 181, 287 n.12; 297 n.27; 297 n.42
Kelly, Vonelle R., 277 n.25
Keswick, England/Keswick Movement, 218-9
King,
Yahweh as a king/sovereign, 38-40, 258 n.1; 259 n.15; 260 n.26-7
Jesus as eschatological king/sovereign), viii, 90, 110, 122-3, 126, 132, 134-6, 168, 270 n.10; 273 n.25; 275 n.50; 279 n.34; 280 n.39; 280 n.16
Kistemaker, Simon J., 128, 281 n.14
Kittel, Gerhard, 70, 73, 116, 212, 248 n.6; 249 n.18; 267 n.23, 30; 268 n.43; 278 n.11, 14; 279 n.19, 21; 307 n.58, 62
Kloppenborg, John S., 263, n.18
Knee, every knee bent,
to Yahweh, 129
to Jesus, 129-31, 136
Koch, Glenn, 271 n.2; 288 n.42
Koch, Klaus, 254 n.6
Koester, Craig R., 269 n.47-8
Koester, Helmut, 262 n.11; 288 n.32; 290 n.66
Köhler, Ludwig, 249 n.12; 252 n.41; 258 n.2
Koinonia, 49
Kosmala, Hans, 301 n.16

Kraft, Robert A., 254 n.1; 306 n.36
Krazo, 212
Kugel, James, 271 n.19
Küng, Hans, 80, 270 n.18
Kurios, 140, 142,
as the translation for Yahweh, 76, 129, 132, 141-2, 270 n.5; 281 n.17; 284 n.28
as applied to Jesus, ix, 60, 129-30, 132, 141-2, 265 n.46; 270 n.5; 281 n.61; 284 n.30; 285 n.42; 290 n.61
as applied the Holy Spirit, 265 n.46
Ladd, George Eldon, 264 n.39
Lamb, Jesus as (see "Jesus, Lamb of God")
Land, Stephen J., 308 n.12
Language, as an argument, as controlled by the dominant group, 152-5, 186, 266 n.2-3; 286 n.10; 287 n.11; 289 n.56; 300 n.80-1
Larkin, Clarence, 248-9 n.10
Latter rain (see "evening time")
Law (see also "Torah"), 29, 38-9, 159, 201, 262 n.9; 272 n.9; 287 n.25; 304 n.8
(oral Law), 254 n.4
Lebreton, Jules, 286 n.7; 299 n.39
Levine, Lee I., 254 n.3
Lewis, Joe O., 268 n.38
Liddell, Henry George, 290 n.68
Life setting (*Sitz im Leben*),
of the church/Jesus, 51, 54, 142, 263 n.14
of Romans 10 as a baptismal setting, 196, 302 n.38
Lindbeck, George, 245 n.15
Lindars, Barnabas, 205, 305 n.24
Living bread, Jesus as (see "Jesus, as 'living bread'")
Locale, God as having, 22-3, 78, 89, 107-8, 252-3 n.51; 253 n.55
Jesus as the "unique locale" of God, 70, 72-3, 78, 104, 107-8, 267 n.24; 268 n.36, 38, 40-2; 269 n.47
Locke, John, 216, 308 n.3
The Logos, 83-4,
of Philo, 31-2, 257 n.35
in the Prologue of John's Gospel, 70-3, 267 n.26-33; 267-8 n.34; 268 n.35-45; 268-9 n.46; 269 n.47-55

its absence as a construct in the earliest Christianity, 155-8, 168
Logos christology, 32, 171-2, 175,
as adversely influencing Jewish Christian beliefs, 158-9
as evolving, 286 n.3-6, 9
as framed against Oneness christology, 153-4
of the church fathers, 152-5, 164-67, 172-3, 177-185
as developed by Athanasius, 181-2, 298 n.47-51
as ultimately incorporated and transformed by Augustine, 182-5, 298 n.52-63; 298-9 n.64; 299 n.65-73
as developed by Justin, 165, 292 n.13-16
as developed by Origen, ix, 179-80, 297 n.29-31
as developed by Tertullian, 176-8; 295 n.8-10; 296 n.12-18
Long, V. Philips, 280 n.11
Longenecker, Bruce W., 87, 272 n.9, 10
Longenecker, Richard N., 51, 54, 142, 155, 263 n.14; 264 n.24; 264 n.28; 276 n.14; 283 n.24; 284 n.33; 287 n.20; 289 n.54; 290 n.57; 293 n.30
Lord (see also *Adonai*)
LORD (see also "Tetragrammaton," "Jehovah," "Yahweh"), 19, 36, 63, 71, 92-3, 121, 125, 135, 142, 144, 146, 194, 244 n.10; 252 n.42; 256 n.20; 259 n.12, 15; 267 n.19; 311 n.51
Lüdemann, G., 282 n.6
Luther, Lutheran, 237, 245 n.19; 312 n.16
LXX (see "Septuagint")
Mack, Burton A., 255 n.17; 257 n.29-30, 36
MacQuarrie, John, 296 n.16
Malbon, Elizabeth Struthers, 263 n.21
Maloney, Francis J., 301 n.12; 305 n.23
Marcion/Marcionites, 170, 291 n.5; 294 n.53-4, 56
Marsden, George M., 308 n.8, 14, 16-7
Marshall, I. Howard, 270 n.10; 282 n.6
Martin, R. P., 274 n.39, 43; 275 n.50; 302 n.43
Martin, Walter, 240
Mary, mother of Jesus, 5, 56, 76-78, 86-87, 176, 270 n.11, 13
McAlister, R. E., 221-2
McDonnell, Kilian, 213, 307 n.70; 311-12 n.14

McIntyre, Luther B., Jr., 303 n.53-4
McGee, Gary B., 310 n.39
McGiffert, Arthur Cushman, 167, 178, 293 n.29; 296 n.18; 301 n.15
McGrath, Alister E., 164, 176, 185, 247 n.34; 286 n.6; 291 n.4; 295 n.6, 8; 299 n.72; 299 n.73-5
Mediator, Old Testament priests as (see also "Jesus, as Mediator"), 40-2, 126-8
Meier, John P., 262 n.9; 263 n.20
Melchizedekian priesthood (see "Jesus, priest after the order of Melchizedek")
Melito of Sardis, 161-2, 179, 225, 291 n.70, 72-4; 295 n.64
Menzies, Robert P., 209-210, 304 n.8, 16; 306 n.50-1; 307 n.54
Meslin, Michel, 301 n.23
Mesites, 128, 280 n.12 (see also "Jesus as Mediator")
Messiah (see "Jesus as Messiah")
Metzger, Bruce M., 255 n.17; 266 n.11
Mind,
as a component part of Jesus, 81-2
of God, as God's reasoning/God's proleptic purpose, 74, 82
Miqwah, 254 n.4
Modalism, 286-7 n.9; 288 n.42,
as an umbrella term, 170, 180-1, 185, 244 n.8; 290 n.66; 294 n.55, 58-59; 295 n.3
Noetus, Noetan modalism , ix, 176, 178-9, 239, 286 n.2; 296 n.23-4; 297 n.25
Praxeas, Praxean modalism, ix, 156, 175-8, 270 n.16; 285 n.45; 287 n.13-5, 25; 295 n.1-2, 4, 7, 12-13, 15; 301 n.23
Sabellius, Sabellian modalism, ix, 176, 179, 182, 185, 238-9, 286 n.2; 294 n.53; 297 n.26-7; 300 n.77
Moltmann, Jürgen, 295 n.64
Monarchianism,
Modalistic Monarchianism (see "Modalism")
Dynamic Monarchianism, 171-2, 185, 286 n.2; 287 n.24
Montague, G. T., 213, 307 n.70; 311 n.14
Montanus, Montanists, 170, 294 n.55-6
Moo, Douglas, 262 n.10

Moody, Dwight L., 218
Morgan-Wynne, John E., 301 n.13
Morris, Leon, 262 n.10
Mortley, Raoul, 257 n.33
Moses, 15, 19-21, 23, 31-3, 39-40, 47, 69, 72-3, 76, 111, 120, 139, 166, 176, 201, 248 n.8; 249 n.14; 250 n.30; 251 n.39; 257 n.37; 258 n.42; 259 n.17, 19-20; 260 n.26, 31; 267 n.17; 268 n.45; 269 n.49; 278 n.9; 295 n.10; 303 n.44; 304 n.6
Moule, C. F. D., 283 n.9
Mowinckel, Sigmund, 42, 250 n.30; 261 n.41
Mueller, J. Theodore, 312 n.15
Murphy, Roland E., 255 n.17; 257 n.29-30, 36
Murphy-O'Connor, Jerome, 94, 250 n.23; 274 n.45; 274 n.48; 275 n.51
"The Name" (see also *HaShem*),
 as a circumlocution for Yahweh, 69-70, 102,
 as a first century incarnational construct, viii-ix, 70, 76, 137, 140-5, 155-8
Nazareth, Jesus at, viii, 86-7, 92, 119
Neo-Platonism (see "Platonism, neo")
Neusner, Jacob, 246 n.26
New Birth, 222-4, 231-2, 236-7, 239, 244 n.11; 311 n.13
"New Issue," 223, 310 n.45
Newman, Carey C., 268 n.45
Nicea, Council of, 48, 163, 182, 267 n.24; 269 n.46; 287 n.23
Nicene-Constantinople Creed, 154
Nicholl, W. Robertson, 307 n.64
Nicholson, Ernest W., 258 n.1
Nickelsburg, George W. E., 254 n.1; 255 n.17-8
Niederwimmer, Kurt, 294 n.60
Niles, D. Preman, 36, 40, 42, 250 n.25: 259 n.11, 13, 16, 17; 261 n.35, 40; 262 n.48
Noah/Noahic Covenant, 37, 253 n.63; 259 n.20-1; 259-60 n.22; 260 n.23
Noetus (see "Modalism," "Noetus," "Noetan Modalism")
Norris, David S., works cited by, 100-2, 244 n.13; 256-7 n.27; 274 n.39; 275 n.6; 310 n.47
Norris, S. G., xi, 136, 252 n.49; 282 n.39
Notley, J. Steven, 273 n.28
Nygren, Gotthard, 299 n.68

Obeng, E. A., 212-3, 307 n.67
Oegema, Gerbern S., 304 n.9
Ogden, G. S., 251 n.33
Omnipresence (see "Jesus, omnipresence of," "Transcendence of God," "Yahweh, omnipresence of")
Onesti, Karen L., 302 n.43
Oneness christology,
 briefly defined, 5, 12, 77-80
 briefly differentiated from Trinitarianism, 55-60, 80-4
Oneness of God, see "unicity of God"
Oneness Pentecostalism
 history of Modern Oneness Pentecostalism, 1-3, 216-24
 definition of, 3-8
Origen, ix, xiii, 152-4, 166, 179-83, 286 n.3-4, 7; 287 n.15; 288 n.42; 291 n.2-3; 292 n.23; 297 n.29-31, 35, 37, 40
Ousia, 140, 167, 182, 184
Orthodox, orthodoxy,
 Oneness Pentecostal understanding of, 5, 8-10, 48-55, 151-5, 221-4
 as a sociological construct, 153-5, 186, 221-2, 234, 286 n.10; 287 n.11; 289 n.56; 300 n.80-1
Osiek, Carolyn, 288 n.32-5
Otto, Michel, 268 n.40
Otto, Rudolph, 15-6, 248 n.3-5
Pagels, Elaine, 296 n.20
Panim (see also "Face-to-face relationship"), 23, 69, 201, 253 n.61; 253-4 n.65
Parakletos, 117
Parham, Charles, 219-21, 234-235, 308 n.18, 309 n.21, 23, 32; 310 n.36
Parke-Taylor, G. H., 251 n.34; 259 n.15
Parsons, Mikeal C., 199, 303 n.56
Passover (see "Feast(s), Jewish/Holy days, Passover")
Patriarchs OT (see also "Abraham," "Isaac," "Jacob"), 20-1, 37-8, 246 n.25; 258 n.42; 260 n.30
Patripassianism (see also "Suffering of God, Father suffering"), 177, 285 n.45; 294 n.54; 296 n.13

Paul, apostle (see also the Scripture index)
  Abba (see "Abba, as a metaphor for Christian initiation"),
  baptism (see "Baptism")
  incarnation, as allegedly "creating" the incarnation, 50-1, 262 n.11
  equating Jesus and the Spirit, 56-7, 138-9
  conversion/Christian initiation (see also "Covenant, NT," and "Covenant, Holy Spirit and Covenant initiation,"), 190-2, 195-200, 204-6, 211-3
  faithfulness of Jesus (see "Jesus, faith of")
  hymns (see "Hymns, christological"), viii, 51, 67-8, 93-5, 119, 129-30, 136, 268 n.39; 274 n.39-48; 274-5 n.48; 275 n.49-53; 277 n.1
  unicity of God (see also "Unicity of God," *Kurios*), 72-3, 78, 142, 265 n.46; 284 n.29-31
Paul of Samosata, 185
Peace (see also "*Shalom*"), 41, 58, 139, 214, 240, 265 n.40
Pelikan, Jaroslav, 177, 180, 184-5, 264 n.27; 271 n.24; 291 n.71-2; 296 n.14; 297 n.40, 298 n.47-8, 51, 58; 299 n.67-8, 70; 300 n.79
Pentecost, J. Dwight, 245 n.22
Perichoresis (see also *Circumincessio*), 56, 84, 185, 299 n.73
Persons, historical evolution of the notion of "Persons in the Godhead" (see also ousia), 166-7, 177-8, 180-5, 291 n.71-2; 293 n.33; 296 n. 16; 299 n. 73; 300 n.74-80
Peter, the apostle (see also Scripture index),
  Christology/christological hymn, 68, 139, 142-5, 190, 226-7, 272 n.16; 276 n.13
  no distinction between Lukan Peter and historical Peter, 54
  teaching on Jesus' redemptive work, 64, 125, 128, 279 n.27
  teaching on conversion/initiation into covenant, 143-5, 190, 196-9, 206-10, 213, 226-7, 233-4, 276 n.13; 305 n.30; 306 n.36, 38, 42, 48; 307 n.53; 307 n.72
Peterson, Butch, in an allegory of Jesus, 100-2
Pettinato, G., 251 n.39
Pharisees, 32, 101, 233, 254 n.4; 276 n.12
Philip, the apostle, 104

Philip, the evangelist in Acts, 64, 208, 307 n.72
Philo, vii, 30-33, 255 n.15 ; 257 n.36, 39; 300-01 n.5; 301 n.8
  as a source for the church fathers, 164-7, 173, 179, 255 n.11; 258 n.42, 44; 291 n.3; 292 n.10; 297 n.30
  allegorical method of interpretation, vii, 30-2, 257 n.29
  "I AM," his reinterpretation, vii, 32-3
  view of God, 26-33, 257 n.31-2; 257-8 n.41; 258 n.42-44
  view of the *Logos*, 31-2, 257 n.35
Pierson, A. T., 308 n.10
Pink, Arthur W., 282 n.2
Pinnock, Clark H., 298 n.64
Plastaras, James, 40, 251 n.37; 261 n.33
Plato, 27-28, 31-3, 152, 155, 166, 181, 183, 254 n.7-8; 254-5 n.9; 255 n.10-11, 13-14; 296 n.10
Platonism/Middle Platonism/Neo-platonism, 254-5 n.9; 291 n.2; 297 n.35
  affecting Philo, 257 n.29
  affecting Athanasius, 181-2
  affecting Augustine, 182-5, 286 n.6; 298 n.54-5, 57
  affecting christology of the church fathers, 155, 164-7, 177-85, 286 n.3, 5
  affecting Origen, 179-80, 297 n.37
  affecting Justin, 152, 165-67
  affecting Tertullian, 176-8
Plotinus/Plotinian thought, 181, 183, 254-5 n.9; 286 n.3; 297 n.31
Plurality, language of (see also "Two-ness," "Threeness"), viii, 17-8, 55-60, 71, 82-4, 102-10, 132-6, 147, 176-7, 222, 249 n.14
Polhill, John B., 195, 302 n.33; 307 n.71
Pollard, T. E., 292 n.12
Polycarp, 160-1, 290 n.60, 62
Porphyry, 183, 298 n.57
Post-denominationalism, 230-2
Praxeas (see "Modalism," "Praxeas," "Praxean Modalism")
Preexistence of Jesus (see "Jesus, preexistence 'alleged'")
Priesthood of Jesus (see "Jesus, priesthood of")

Priestly blessing, invocation of Yahweh
Priscillian, 182, 185
Pritchard, James B., 254 n.3
Procksch, Otto, 105, 267 n.30; 273 n.21; 276 n.18; 282 n.5
Prophecies related to communication between the Father and the Son, 74,
Psalm 2:7, 65, 90, 121-2, 241, 273 n.25, 31
Psalm 22: 121-2, 241, 279 n.37
Psalm 110:64-6, 114, 125-7, 132, 135, 266 n.8
Servant Psalms of Isaiah, 64, 130-2, 256 n.25; 273 n.29-30; 281 n.19-24
Son of Man language in Daniel (see "Son of Man")
Protestant/Protestantism, 9, 215, 217, 225, 244 n.6; 247 n.33; 308 n.9
Pryor, Hattie E., 311 n.12
Pseudo-Hippolytus, 156
"Q" as a source for the Gospels, 53-4, 263 n.18-20
Quell, Gottfried, 140, 256 n.26; 256-7 n.27; 283 n.22
Qumran/Qumran Community/Qumran writings (see also in this index "Essenes"; see "Dead Sea Scrolls" in other ancient writings), 189-90, 285 n.38; 285 n.46; 300 n.1; 304 n.8
von Rad, Gerhard, 69, 140, 245 n.22; 246 n.25; 248 n.6; 252-3 n.51; 259 n.15; 260 n.32; 267 n.20; 283 n.19
Rainbow, Paul A., 146, 285 n.46
Reed, David A., 243 n.2; 283 n.21; 310 n.40
Reid, Thomas, 308 n.6
Reformation, the, 9, 194, 199, 215, 300 n.80; 310 n.39
Reumann, J. 303 n.47
Right hand of God, 66, 114, 120, 125-8, 161, 207, 266 n.7; 278 n.5; 280 n.2-5, 8; 281 n.22
Righteousness (see also *Dikaiosune*, "Justification"), 87-8, 136, 169, 195-8, 205, 237, 272 n.15, 302 n.40, 42-3; 303 n.47, 49
Robeck, Cecil M., Jr., 309 n.18
Robertson, A. T., 267 n.31; 303 n.54
Rowe, C. Kavin, 247 n.35; 269 n.4; 293 n.32
Runia, David, 258 n.42; 291 n.3
Sabellianism (see "Modalism," "Sabellius," "Sabellianism")

Sabin, Robert, xi, 107, 239-41, 275 n.2; 276 n.21; 279 n.37
Sacrifice, 23-4, 40-1, 69, 88, 107, 116, 118, 127-9, 132, 253 n.62-3, 259 n.21; 272 n.11; 280 n.38; 302 n.26
Sadducees, 32, 233
Salvation history, central events in, 75, 87, 112, 125, 135, 245 n.22; 306 n.45
Salutations in the epistles (see also "Benedictions, NT epistles," "Grace, in the salutations and benedictions of the epistles"), 56, 58-9, 138-9, 264-5 n.42
Samaria/Samaritan, 111, 193, 207-10, 277 n.40; 307 n.72
Sanders, E. P., 198, 246 n.26; 303 n.48-9
Sanders, Jack T., 67, 266 n.9
Sarx (see also "Flesh," *Soma*), 81
Satan, 18, 91-2, 98-9, 123, 230, 248 n.9; 248-9 n.10; 249 n.20; 253 n.64; 276 n.12; 280 n.39-40
Schaff, Philip, 297 n.26; 301 n.25
Scheppe, John, 221
Schoedel, William R., 290 n.66
Schoeps, Hans Joachim, 288 n.43-4, 51
Schwarz, Hans, 263 n.16; 295 n.9
Scofield, C. I., 219, 308 n.17
Scott, Robert, 290 n.68
Second work of grace (see "Grace, second work of")
Septuagint (LXX), 26, 29, 70, 255 n.17; 281 n.19, 23; 284 n.27; 293 n.24; 305 n.30
  as it facilitated the application of "Yahweh texts" to Jesus, 142, 270 n.5; 284 n.32; 285 n.40
  as it influenced Jewish understanding of Yahweh, 29-30, 32-3
  as it translated that Yahweh was not to be named, 29-32, 256 n.20
  as it relates to "I AM" texts, 32-3, 251 n.36; 256 n.25
Segraves, Daniel, 266 n.14; 283 n.10
Seitz, C. R., 166, 293 n.25
Seth, 36
Sexton, E. A., 309 n.27
Seymour, William, 219-20, 234-5, 311 n.9

Shalom (see also "Peace"), 41, 258 n.1
Shame, 114, 278 n.5
Sharp, Granville/Sharp's grammatical rule(s), 139, 265 n.45; 283 n.10, 12, 14
Shema, 59, 63, 81, 146, 222, 226-7, 262 n.11; 285 n.46
Shotwell, Willis A., 292 n.9-10, 13, 20
Sitz im Leben (see "Life setting")
Sinai, Mount, 38-40, 117, 260 n.31; 268 n.45; 269 n.48; 304 n.8
Socrates, 166, 291 n.7
Soma (see also "Flesh," *Sarx*), 81
Snook, Ivan, 300 n.80
Soggin, J. Alberto, 254 n.6
Son of man, 299 n.73
  Jesus' language about, viii, 105, 108-10, 120, 276 n.19; 277 n.28-31; 278 n.17; 282 n.3
  in Daniel/Revelation, 110, 113, 134-5, 137, 281 n.29
Sophia (see "Wisdom")
Soul, 32, 80-1, 122, 252 n.46; 271 n.20; 295 n.8; 297 n.31
Spirit as a component part of a human (see also "Holy Spirit"), 16, 31, 80-1, 161, 212, 271 n.21-3
Stark, Rodney, 230, 311 n.8
Stephen, in the Book of Acts, 143, 169
Stephens, Randall J., 309 n.18
Stevenson, James, 300 n.77
Stone, Michael E., 255 n.17; 255-6 n.18,
Stoic(s)/Stoicism, 28, 155, 166, 176, 179, 181, 254 n.7-8; 294 n.53; 295 n.8; 295-6 n.11; 299 n.73
Stronstad, Roger, 304 n.16
Stuhlmacher, Peter, 267 n.25; 270 n.10; 291 n.6
Suzerainty treaty, 38-9, 260 n.25, 27-8
Synan, Vincent, 220, 244 n.7; 309 n.13, 18, 23; 310, 29-30; 311 n.1; 311 n.5
Synod of Braga, 185
Synoptic Gospels, 81, 111, 266 n.7; 268 n.38; 271 n.20
Talbert, Charles H., 94, 245 n.14; 275 n.51; 275 n.53
Tabernacle/tabernacling (see also "Temple"), 65, 261 n.44; 269 n.47;
  as incarnational language, 72-3, 171, 268 n.38, 41; 269 n.47
  of David, 144, 261 n.45-6; 285 n.38; 310-11 n.47
Tannenhill, Robert C., 245 n.14
Tate, J., 255 n.14
Thurston, Bonnie, 194, 302 n.30
Tatian, 164, 172, 285 n.45; 295 n.65
Taylor, George F., 309 n.28; 310 n.28, 33
Temptation (see "Jesus, temptation of")
Temple (see also "Tabernacle"), 11, 25, 30, 32, 42, 69-70, 72-3, 86, 114, 119, 127, 140, 155, 159, 169, 190, 233, 254 n.1; 255 n.16; 261 n.36, 45; 262 n.48; 267 n.21; 269 n.47; 271 n.1; 272 n.5; 278 n.8; 283 n.18, 20; 285 n.40; 289 n.52; 302 n.26; 305 n.21
Tertullian, ix, xiii, 152-4, 156, 176-8, 180, 270 n.16; 285 n.45; 286 n.3-4, 8; 287 n.13-15, 23, 25; 288 n.44; 295 n.2, 4, 7-10; 295-6 n.11; 296 n.12-3, 15, 20; 301 n.23
Tetragrammaton (see also "LORD," "Yahweh," "Jehovah"), 19, 244 n.10; 248 n.6; 256 n.26; 256-7 n.27; 283-4 n.28
Theissen, Henry Clarence, 299 n.66
Theissen, Gerd, 264 n.22
Theogenes, 28
Theophilus, 164
"Threeness" in the New Testament, 56-57
Theophany, 23, 78, 89, 165, 253 n.58; 258 n.5; 269 n.48
Theophilus, 164
Throne, heavenly, 107, 113-4, 126, 130-6, 253 n.52; 278 n.5; 281 n.22; 294 n.49
Tongues, speaking with, x, 4, 202, 207-10, 213, 219-220, 229-31, 234-5, 304-5 n.15; 305 n.30; 306 n.35, 48; 307 n.70; 308 n.74; 309 n.22-3; 310 n.39; 312 n.9
Torah (see also "Law"), 9, 18, 20, 41, 49, 98, 103, 111, 139, 144-5, 158-9, 194, 256-7 n.27; 261 n.44; 280 n.9; 285 n.37
Torrey, Reuben, A., 218, 244 n.12
Tov, E., 283 n.27
Transcendence of God, 22-3, 31, 252-3 n.51; 253 n.52-5, 57
  as constructed by Philo, 32-3, 257-8 n.41; 258 n.42-4

Tree of knowledge of good and bad, 36, 92
Tree of Life, 133
Trinity, ix, 4, 7, 11, 56-8, 72, 89, 91, 94, 152,
    154, 167, 172, 177, 179, 182-5, 222, 225,
    230, 247 n.35; 257 n.39; 264 n.35; 268-9
    n.46; 269 n.4; 273 n.20; 278 n.13; 286 n.3;
    292 n.16; 293 n.25; 295 n.64; 297 n.37;
    298 n.53, 62; 299 n.73, 75; 301 n.23; 305
    n.25
Turner, Max, 245 n.17; 304 n.8; 311 n.2
"Two-ness" in the New Testament, 60
Tyson, James L., 309 n.19
Unicity (oneness) of God, 5, 8, 15-17, 30, 70-73,
    78-80, 100-2, 133-6, 146, 156, 227, 249
    n.12, 14; 251 n.36; 279 n.24; 282 n.7-8;
    283 n.9
Urshan, Andrew, 4, 12-13, 230, 242, 243 n.3;
    244 n.10; 311 n.48; 311 n.6
Vermès, Geza, 276 n.23; 277 n.31
Vincent, Marvin R. 212, 307 n.66
Voice at Jesus' baptism, 88-91, 121, 130, 240
Vondey, Wolfgang, 309 n.31
Vööbus, Arthur, 294-5, n.60
Wainwright, Geoffrey, 249 n.17; 252 n.50; 283
    n.9; 289 n.58; 302 n.38
Walker, James B., 299 n.73
"The Water Way," 235-6, 310 n.44; 311 n.12
Wacker, Grant, 221, 308 n.18; 310 n.35
Ward, A. G., 309 n.27
Wesley, John, 216-218, 245 n.19; 307 n.2; 308
    n.3-4
Westermann, Claus, 167, 293 n.32
Wheaton College, 239-40, 243 n.1
Wenham, Gordon J., 259 n.12, 21
Wildier, N. Max, 292 n.10
Williams, J. Rodman, 244 n.5
Williford, Don, 305 n.25
Winston, David, 257 n.35
Wisdom,
    evolution of the conflation of wisdom with
        the *Logos*, 32, 179-80, 184, 257 n.35-7;
        268 n.35; 296 n.15; 298 n.47; 299 n.58
Witherington, Ben, 51, 90, 212, 245 n.19; 263
    n.12-3; 263 n.19; 272 n.18; 273 n.24-6;
    307 n.68

Wolfson, Harry Austryn, 58-9, 152, 165, 167,
    172, 180-1, 258 n.44; 264 n.35; 265 n.40-1;
    286 n.3, 5; 291 n.8; 293 n.28; 295 n.67;
    296 n.17; 297 n.28-34; 298 n.46, 46; 299
    n.69, 71, 73
Word(s)
    as pertaining to God (*see also Logos,
        debar*), 31, 35, 57, 64, 66, 68, 89-90, 257
        n.37; 260 n.26; 266 n.14; 267 n.27, 29-30
    as applied by church fathers, 166, 183, 269-
        70 n.46; 292 n.21; 296 n.15; 299 n.73
    as pertaining to the Prologue of John, 71-2,
        268-9 n.34; 269 n.35
Wordsworth, Christopher, 265 n.47
Worship, 16, 254 n.3; 285 n.42-3
    covenant worship OT, 12, 19, 22-25, 36-7, 39,
        41-3, 69, 249 n.17; 250 n.25; 251 n.34; 253
        n.63; 259 n.11, 15; 260 n.29; 261 n.44-5;
        305 n.21
    covenant worship NT 78-9, 89, 92, 128, 134,
        136, 139-40, 145, 201, 229, 231, 242, 264
        n.22; 266 n.9; 284 n.29; 294 n.50
    worship in church history, 154, 160, 166, 169,
        177, 180, 249 n.17; 292 n.17; 298 n.49; 302
        n.39; 310-11 n. 47
Wuest, Kenneth, 280 n.40
Yahweh,
    alone in creation, 16-18, 63, 249 n.12, 14,
        19, 22
    in absolute identification with Jesus Christ,
        55, 60, 66-7, 110-11, 115-116, 118-119,
        148,166-67, 184, 208, 291 n.27; 296 n.45;
        298 n.5; 301 n.12; 306 n.13; 312 n.17, 19,
        23; 313 n.33; 316 n.29-30; 316-17 n.31;
        317 n.32; 339 n.30
    in covenant with Adam and Eve, 12, 18-9,
        23-4, 253-4 n.65; 258 n.4; 258 n.9
    in covenant with Israel, vii, 7-8, 37-43, 260
        n.24; 26-27, 30
    in covenant with the man Christ Jesus, viii,
        11, 67-68, 91-101, 103-106, 109-110, 228
    as Creator, vii, 16-19, 248 n.7, 9
    as equivalent to the Spirit, 17, 249 n.12; 265
        n.6; 270 n.7-9
    glory of (see "Glory")

as "I AM," vii, 19-22, 250 n.29-30; 250-1 n.32; 251 n.33-6, 39
invoked in covenant (see "Invoking the name of Yahweh")
in "I-Thou" relationship, 15-16, 22, 30, 37, 42, 120, 128, 248 n.1
known by name to patriarchs, 20-1, 251 n.39
name not to be spoken (after Jewish worship was Hellenized), 29-30, 69-70, 140, 256 n.20, 22, 26; 256-7 n.27; 257 n.28
represented by *Kurios*, 76, 129, 141-2, 283-4 n.27; 284 n.28-9
represented by *Soter*, 75-77, 269-70 n.
meaning of, 19-24, 69-70, 250 n.25, 28-30; 259 n.11-17
omnipresence of (see also "Transcendence of God"), 23, 253 n.57

Name represented in the name of Jesus, 75-7, 269 n.3
presence of, 22-24, 37-42, 69-73, 78-9, 128, 141, 143, 201-3, 250 n.30; 252 n.50; 253 n. 57; 253-4 n. 67; 254 n.68; 260 n. 30-1; 304 n.5; 305 n.21
Yahweh, Servant of (see "Servant of Yahweh")
Transcendence of (see "Transcendence of God")
Young, Edward J., 251-2 n.40
Yonge, Charles D., 257 n.32
Zehnle, Richard F., 207, 306 n.36-8
Zeiller, Jacques, 286 n.7; 297 n.39
Zeisler, J. A., 302 n.29
Zuck, Roy B., 255 n.14; 256 n.19

Scripture Index

Genesis 1	16, 17, 77, 249, 260 n.22, 267	Genesis 24:7	253 n.56
		Genesis 28:12	253 n.56
Genesis 1-15	259 n.12, n.21	Exodus 3	19, 20, 250 n.28
Genesis 1-17	259 n.22	Exodus 3:2	251 n.32
Genesis 1-3	93 274 n.10	Exodus 3:6	250 n.32
Genesis 1:1	16, 71, 249 n.10, n.14	Exodus 3:12	19
Genesis 1:2	16, 248 n.9, n.10, 249 n.11	Exodus 3:14	19, 20, 32, 76, 166, 250 n.29
Genesis 1:22	259 n.22	Exodus 3:15	256
Genesis 1:26	18, 184, 249 n.21	Exodus 6	20
Genesis 1:27	249 n.21	Exodus 6:3	20, 251 n.39
Genesis 2	17	Exodus 7:1	249 n.14
Genesis 2:4	251 n.39	Exodus 12:12	249 n.14
Genesis 2:7	249 n.15	Exodus 14-17	270 n.10
Genesis 2:17	36	Exodus 15:1	22
Genesis 3:8	258 n.5	Exodus 15:3	22
Genesis 3:22	18, 249 n.19, n.22	Exodus 19-20	38
Genesis 4	253 n.62, 258 n.10	Exodus 19:4	22
Genesis 4:6-7	253 n.64	Exodus 19:5	260 n.24, 270 n.12
Genesis 4:14	253 n.65	Exodus 19:8	39
Genesis 4:16	254 n.66	Exodus 19:11	253 n.56
Genesis 4:23-24	259 n.10	Exodus 19:16	304 n.5
Genesis 4:26	36	Exodus 19:18	39, 253 n.56
Genesis 5	260 n.22	Exodus 19:20	253 n. 56
Genesis 6	31	Exodus 20	38, 69, 259 n.19, 260 n.26
Genesis 6:2	249 n.20		
Genesis 6:6	31	Exodus 20:3	260 n.26
Genesis 6:7	31	Exodus 20:4	253 n.51
Genesis 6:8	259 n.20	Exodus 20:6	259 n.20
Genesis 6:9	37	Exodus 20:21-22	39
Genesis 8:8	273 n.20	Exodus 20:22	253 n.56
Genesis 8:21	259 n.21	Exodus 32:10	303 n.44
Genesis 9	253 n.63	Exodus 33	69
Genesis 9:1	259 n.22	Exodus 33:6	269 n.49
Genesis 9:2	259 n.22	Exodus 33:12	259 n.20
Genesis 9:6	18	Exodus 33:14	253 n.60, 259 n.20
Genesis 9:7	260 n.22	Exodus 33:16	259 n.20
Genesis 11:5	253 n.56,	Exodus 33:17	259 n.20
Genesis 11:7	249 n.22	Exodus 33:18	260 n.31
Genesis 15	197, 198	Exodus 33:19	40, 261 n.34
Genesis 15:6	196, 197, 302 n.40	Exodus 34:6	259 n.19-20
Genesis 15:8	251 n.39	Exodus 34:34	268 n.45, 284 n.30
Genesis 17:14	303 n.45	Leviticus 20:3	261 n.37
Genesis 18:21	253, n.56	Leviticus 21:12	261 n.37
Genesis 21:17	253 n.56	Leviticus 22:2	261 n.37
Genesis 22:11	253 n.56	Leviticus 22:3	260 n.30

Leviticus 22:32	261 n.37	Ezra 4:18	249 n.19
Leviticus 24:11	256 n.20	Ezra 6:12	294 n.62
Leviticus 24:16	256 n.20	Job 4:12	267 n.30
Numbers 6	259 n.18	Job 38:7	249 n.19
Numbers 6:23-27	41	Psalms 1-50	273 n.31
Numbers 6:24-26	265 n.41	Psalm 2	65, 90, 121, 266 n.6, 273 n.31
Numbers 6:27	41		
Numbers 21:8	278 n.6	Psalm 2:4	253 n.56, 268 n.41
Numbers 23:19	260 n.22	Psalm 2:7	65, 270 n.10, 273 n.25, 31
Numbers 25:12	258 n.1		
Deuteronomy 4:36	253 n.56	Psalm 5:5	21
Deuteronomy 4:37	253 n.60	Psalm 8:4-8	249 n.17
Deuteronomy 5:9	21, 252 n.45	Psalm 8:5	249 n.19
Deuteronomy 6:4	63, 285 n.47, 311 n.51	Psalm 18:6	253 n.56
Deuteronomy 7:2	258 n.1	Psalm 19:1	248 n.6
Deuteronomy 8:18	260 n.22	Psalm 19:10	261 n.44
Deuteronomy 9:5	260 n.22	Psalm 22	121, 122, 241, 279 n.37
Deuteronomy 10:15	250 n.28	Psalm 22:1	121, 122
Deuteronomy 10:20	274 n.37	Psalm 22:7-8	121
Deuteronomy 12:5	140, 267 n.19	Psalm 22:18	121
Deuteronomy 12:11	69, 140	Psalm 22:21	122
Deuteronomy 12:21	267 n.19	Psalm 22:22	122
Deuteronomy 17:6	103	Psalm 24:1	284 n.30
Deuteronomy 19:15	103	Psalm 24:8	248 n.6
Deuteronomy 26:15	253 n.56	Psalm 26:8	267 n.22, 268 n.41
Deuteronomy 32:35	284 n.30	Psalm 27:12	279 n.35
Deuteronomy 32:39	251 n.35	Psalm 33:6	71, 267 n.30, 268 n.35, 292
Deuteronomy 33:21	284 n.30		
Judges 3:9	269 n.4	Psalm 35	121
Judges 10:16	21, 252 n.46	Psalm 35:7	279 n.35
Judges 11:24	249 n.14	Psalm 35:11	279 n.35
Judges 12:3	269 n.4	Psalm 37:23	261 n.44
Judges 15:18	269 n.4	Psalm 37:24	261 n.44
Judges 16:23	249 n.14	Psalm 38:13-16	279 n.35
I Samuel 1:23	260 n.22	Psalm 63:2	248 n.6
I Samuel 3:12	260 n.22	Psalm 66:2	248, 260
I Samuel 4:4	268 n.41	Psalm 68:8	260 n.29
I Samuel 18:3	258 n.1	Psalm 69:21	121
II Samuel 5:3	258 n.1	Psalm 79:9	248 n.6, 260 n.32
II Samuel 6:2	268 n.41	Psalm 91:4	256 n.21
II Samuel 6:17	261 n.45	Psalm 94:2	284 n.30
II Samuel 7	73 n.25	Psalm 97:5	260 n.29
II Samuel 7:13	69	Psalm 100	266 n.7
I Kings 2:4	260 n.22	Psalm 103:13	21, 252 n.44
I Kings 3:2	69	Psalm 107:20	267 n.29
I Kings 8:27	253 n.57	Psalm 109:2	279 n.35
II Kings 11:17	258 n.1	Psalm 109:25	279 n.35
II Kings 13:23	260 n.30	Psalm 110	65, 114, 125, 126, 132, 281 n.22
I Chronicles 13:6	268 n.41		
II Chronicles 2:6	253 n.57	Psalm 110:1	66, 120, 126, 127, 266 n.8, 280 n.8
II Chronicles 6:18	253 n.57		
II Chronicles 23:3	258 n.1	Psalm 110:4	126, 135, 280 n.8

Psalm 113:5	253 n.52, 268 n.41	Isaiah 59:1	256 n.21
Psalm 114:7	260 n.29	Isaiah 61:3	261 n.38
Psalm 115:15–17	253 n.51	Isaiah 62:5	21, 252 n.48
Psalm 116:4	259 n.13	Isaiah 62:6	256 n.25
Psalm 116:12	259 n.14	Isaiah 63:9	21, 253 n.60
Psalm 135:21	268 n.41	Jeremiah 7:10	262 n.48
Psalm 138:1	249 n.14	Jeremiah 7:12	294 n.61
Psalm 138:5	248 n.6	Jeremiah 9:23-24	284 n.30
Psalm 139:7-8	253 n.57	Jeremiah 23:23	253 n.57
Psalm 147:15-19	71	Jeremiah 23:24	253 n.57
Proverbs 2:17	258 n.1	Jeremiah 29:10	260 n.22
Proverbs 8	181, 298 n.47	Jeremiah 31:31-34	202
Proverbs 8:23	298 n.47	Jeremiah 31:34	303 n.55
Isaiah 6	130, 131, 281 n.22, 23	Jeremiah 33:14	260 n.22
Isaiah 6:1	130	Jeremiah 34:18	260 n.22
Isaiah 6:8	249 n.22	Jeremiah 49:36	253 n.51
Isaiah 18:7	69	Lamentations 4:16	253 n.60
Isaiah 19:1	256 n.21	Ezekiel 16:63	303 n.55
Isaiah 28:11	284 n.31	Ezekiel 34:25	258 n.1
Isaiah 31:4	253 n.56	Ezekiel 36:24-28	43, 144
Isaiah 33:5	253 n.52	Ezekiel 37:4	267 n.30
Isaiah 37:16	268 n.41	Ezekiel 37:26	258 n.1
Isaiah 40:3	272 n.12	Ezekiel 43:7	294 n.62
Isaiah 40:13	284 n.30	Daniel 7	109, 110, 134, 277 n.29
Isaiah 41:25	248 n.7	Daniel 7:2	253 n.51
Isaiah 41:29	16	Daniel 7:7-14	110
Isaiah 42	90	Daniel 7:13-14	110,
Isaiah 42:1	90	Daniel 7:13	120
Isaiah 43:10	251 n.36	Daniel 7:14	134
Isaiah 43:13	251 n.36	Daniel 7:18	277 n.28
Isaiah 43:25	256 n.25, 277 n.37	Daniel 8:8	253 n.51
Isaiah 44:6	284 n.31	Daniel 11:4	253 n.51
Isaiah 44:24	16	Hosea 6:7	258 n.4
Isaiah 45:1	248 n.7	Hosea 6:7-11	258 n.1
Isaiah 45:5	295 n.2	Hosea 10:3-4	258 n.1
Isaiah 45:18	248 n.9	Hosea 13:4	256 n.25
Isaiah 45:23	129, 284	Joel 2:27	256 n.25
Isaiah 45:23-25	284 n.30	Joel 2:28–29	284 n.34, 305 n.30
Isaiah 46:4	251 n.36	Joel 2:32	284 n.30
Isaiah 46:11	248 n.7	Amos 1:9	258 n.1
Isaiah 48:12	251 n.36, 284 n.31	Amos 9	144
Isaiah 51:12	256 n.25, 277 n.37	Amos 9:11	285 n.38
Isaiah 52-3	130, 131	Amos 9:12	43, 262 n.48, 285 n.39
Isaiah 52:6	131	Micah 1:2	253 n.56
Isaiah 52:13	130	Zephaniah 2:11-15	43
Isaiah 52:14	130	Zechariah 2:6	253 n.50
Isaiah 53	64, 131	Zechariah 2:11	144
Isaiah 53:4	273 n.30	Zechariah 2:11-13	144
Isaiah 53:6	273 n.30	Zechariah 2:15	285 n.37
Isaiah 53:8	273 n.30	Zechariah 6:5	253 n.50
Isaiah 54:10	258 n.1	Zechariah 12:10	120
Isaiah 57:15	130, 281 n.21	Zechariah 14:3	284 n.30

Malachi 1:7	284 n.30		301 n.16
Malachi 1:12	284 n.30	Mark 1:2-3	272 n.12
Malachi 2:2-4	79	Mark 1:5	192
Malachi 2:9	79	Mark 1:8	264 n.33, 280 n.15
Malachi 2:14	258 n.1	Mark 1:11	273 n.23, 281 n.18
Malachi 3:6	79, 270 n.15	Mark 2:5	275 n.1
Matthew 1:18	270 n.8	Mark 2:28	277 n.34
Matthew 1:20	270 n.8	Mark 6:50	277 n.39
Matthew 1:21	76, 303 n.55	Mark 8:11-21	276 n.12
Matthew 1:23	76	Mark 8:31	277 n.23
Matthew 3	300 n.6	Mark 9:2	268 n.38
Matthew 3:3	272 n.12	Mark 9:31	277 n.72
Matthew 3:11	264 n.33, 280 n.15	Mark 10:17-8	99
Matthew 3:17	273 n.23, 281 n.18	Mark 10:37	278 n.3
Matthew 4:10	274 n.37	Mark 11:27-33	272 n.18
Matthew 6:9	103	Mark 12:35-7	266 n.7
Matthew 8:20	277 n.35	Mark 12:36	266 n.7
Matthew 9:6	277 n.33	Mark 14:36	118, 119
Matthew 11:28	307 n.75	Mark 14:38	271 n.21
Matthew 12:8	277 n.34	Mark 14:56-57	279 n.35
Matthew 12:32	105	Mark 14:61	120, 279 n.35
Matthew 14:27	277 n.39	Mark 14:62	120, 266 n.7, 277 n.39
Matthew 16	192	Mark 14:63-4	120
Matthew 16:1-12	276 n.12	Mark 15:24	121
Matthew 16:18	122	Mark 15:29	121, 279 n.35
Matthew 16:27-28	277 n.30	Mark 15:32	279 n.35
Matthew 17	192	Mark 15:36	121
Matthew 17:1	268 n.38	Mark 16:19	266 n.7
Matthew 17:12	277 n.32	Luke 1:17	306 n.38
Matthew 17:22	277 n.32	Luke 1:35	264 n.29, 270 n.7, 10
Matthew 18:20	79, 106, 279 n.26	Luke 1:42	270 n.11
Matthew 19:28	277 n.30, 278 n.2	Luke 1:68	306 n.38
Matthew 20:18	277 n.30	Luke 2	77, 86, 271 n.4
Matthew 20:20-7	278 n.3	Luke 2:11	76
Matthew 20:28	277 n.30	Luke 2:31-32	306 n.38
Matthew 21	276 n.12	Luke 2:48	86
Matthew 21:25	273 n.22	Luke 2:49	86, 272 n.5
Matthew 21:27	276 n.12	Luke 2:51	87
Matthew 22:41-46	266 n.7	Luke 2:52	275 n.3
Matthew 22:44	266 n.7	Luke 3	277 n.25, 300 n.6
Matthew 24:27	277 n.30	Luke 3:4-6	272 n.12
Matthew 24:37	277 n.30	Luke 3:16	264 n.33, 280 n.15
Matthew 24:44	277 n.30	Luke 3:22	273 n.23, 25, 281 n.18
Matthew 25:13	277 n.30	Luke 3:38	270 n.10, 12
Matthew 25:31	277 n.30	Luke 4:1	105
Matthew 26:2	277 n.30	Luke 4:1-13	270 n.10
Matthew 26:24	277 n.30	Luke 4:18-19	93, 105
Matthew 26:38	271 n.20	Luke 5:24	277 n.33
Matthew 26:41	271 n.21	Luke 6:5	277 n.34
Matthew 26:64	266 n.7	Luke 9	278 n.8
Matthew 28:19	57, 59, 192, 199, 221, 223, 245 n.13, 294 n.60,	Luke 9:22	277 n.32
		Luke 9:26	57

Luke 9:31	278 n.9	John 3:11	191
Luke 9:38	277 n.35	John 3:14	114, 278 n.6
Luke 9:44	277 n.32	John 3:16	108
Luke 9:51	278 n.9	John 3:22	192, 300 n.7
Luke 9:58	277 n.35	John 3:26	192
Luke 11:2	108	John 3:34	78, 83
Luke 11:11-13	202	John 4	111
Luke 11:13	276 n.17	John 4:2	300 n.7
Luke 11:16	276 n.12	John 4:10	276 n.17, 304 n.14
Luke 12:50	114	John 4:14	305 n.33
Luke 13:22	278 n.9	John 4:24	304 n.14
Luke 13:31-34	278 n.9	John 4:26	111, 277 n.41
Luke 13:32	115	John 4:10	202
Luke 13:33	115	John 4:24	304 n.14
Luke 16:22	280 n.40	John 5:41	278 n.12
Luke 17:11	278 n.9	John 5:44	278 n.12
Luke 18:31	278 n.9	John 6	81, 108
Luke 19:11	278 n.9	John 6:15	276 n.23
Luke 19:28	278 n.9	John 6:20	277 n.38, 41
Luke 20:41-4	266 n.7	John 6:35	277 n.38
Luke 20:42-43	266 n.7	John 6:51	109, 276 n.24, 277 n.38
Luke 22:30	278 n.2	John 6:58	109
Luke 22:69	266 n.7	John 6:63	271 n.22
Luke 22:70	277 n.39	John 6:66	109
Luke 23:46	271 n.21	John 7	202
Luke 24	276 n.14	John 7:18	278 n.15
Luke 24:36	277 n.39	John 7:37-8	128
Luke 24:47	301 n.22	John 7:37-39	276 n.17, 305 n.33
John 1	191, 300 n.6	John 7:38-39	202, 212, 276 n.16
John 1-13	245 n.21	John 7:39	304 n.13
John 1:1	71, 72, 73	John 7:42	277 n.25
John 1:1-18	275 n.53	John 8	103
John 1:14	72, 73, 264 n.29, 268 n.38, 269, 294 n.62	John 8:12	277 n.38
		John 8:24	277 n.38, 41
John 1:15	73	John 8:28	114, 137, 277 n.38, 41
John 1:17-18	72	John 8:39	268 n.34
John 1:17	269	John 8:41	103
John 1:18	73, 269	John 8:50	278 n.15
John 1:23	272 n.12	John 8:58-9	67
John 1:29	272 n.11	John 8:58	111, 277 n.38, 41
John 1:33	264 n.33, 280 n.15	John 9:5	277 n.38
John 1:36	272 n.11	John 9:24	115
John 1:41	235	John 10	104
John 2:11	278 n.18	John 10:7	277 n.38
John 2:19	56, 278 n.8	John 10:9	277 n.38
John 2:21	278 n.8	John 10:11	277 n.38
John 2:22	282 n.1	John 10:14	277 n.38
John 3	191, 204, 205, 301 n.11	John 10:30	55
John 3:1-15	305 n.25	John 11:4	278 n.18
John 3:3	204	John 11:25	277 n.38
John 3:5	191, 204, 276 n.17, 312 n.16	John 11:33	271 n.23
		John 11:38	271 n.23

John 12:16	278 n.16	Acts 2-3	306 n.36
John 12:23	278 n.17	Acts 2:4	210, 235
John 12:27	271 n.20	Acts 2:17	306 n.53
John 12:32-34	114	Acts 2:21	284 n.34, 35
John 12:33	114	Acts 2:22	272 n.16
John 12:38-41	130, 131	Acts 2:27	271 n.20
John 13:7	282 n.4	Acts 2:29	306 n.41
John 13:8	64	Acts 2:30	270 n.11, 277 n.25
John 13:19	117, 262 n.1, 277 n.38, 41, 279 n.24, 282 n.4	Acts 2:31	271 n.20
		Acts 2:33	128, 210, 305 n.35
John 13:21	271	Acts 2:33-35	266 n.8
John 13:31	278 n.17	Acts 2:34	266 n.7
John 14:6	127, 277 n.38	Acts 2:34-35	125
John 14:8-10	72	Acts 2:34	266 n.7
John 14:7-10	104	Acts 2:36	272 n.16, 303 n.54
John 14:16	56	Acts 2:38	191, 193, 198, 205, 207, 223, 224, 235, 236, 303 n.52,-4, 306 n.42, 312 n.16
John 14:16-18	106		
John 14:16	117		
John 14:18	57, 279 n.26		
John 14:20	282 n.4	Acts 2:39	306 n.42
John 14:26	56, 117, 264 n.32	Acts 3	306 n.36
John 14:28	55	Acts 3:13	272 n.16
John 14:29	282 n.4	Acts 3:13-14	279 n.27
John 15:1	277 n.38	Acts 3:19	272 n.16
John 15:5	277 n.38	Acts 4:12	143
John 15:26	117	Acts 5:31	266 n.7
John 16:12-13	282 n.4	Acts 5:32	138
John 16:13	276 n.13	Acts 5:41	283 n.25
John 16:13-14	280 n.1	Acts 7:55-6	266 n.7
John 16:23-24	282 n.4	Acts 8	93, 206, 207
John 17	116, 232, 279 n.21	Acts 8:16	207
John 17:3	60, 116	Acts 10	193, 206, 208, 210, 307 n.72
John 17:5	116		
John 17:17	268 n.24	Acts 10:38	272 n.16
John 17:18	279 n.22	Acts 10:44-8	208
John 17:22	279 n.20	Acts 11	208, 210
John 17:24	74, 116, 278 n.15	Acts 11:14	208
John 18:4-5	279 n.31	Acts 11:15	210
John 18:5	277 n.38, 41	Acts 11:16	264 n.33, 280 n.15
John 18:6	119, 277 n.41	Acts 11:17	306 n.48
John 18:8	277 n.41	Acts 13:33	266 n.6, 270 n.10
John 8:24	277 n.38	Acts 13:34	272 n.16
John 8:28	277 n.38	Acts 14	6
John 8:58-9	67, 277 n.38	Acts 15	43, 144, 158, 193, 262 n.6, 285 n.36, 288 n.30
John 13:19	277 n.38		
John 18:36	121	Acts 15:14	144, 306 n.38
John 18:37	279 n.34	Acts 15:16	285 n.38
John 20:28	283 n.9	Acts 15:17	302 n.29
Acts 1:5	210, 264 n.33, 280 n.15	Acts 16:6	138
Acts 1:8	209, 306 n.41	Acts 16:7	138
Acts 2	193, 206, 207, 208, 210, 306 n.48, 307 n.72	Acts 17	208
		Acts 18:8	199

Scripture Index | 377

Acts 18:26	235	I Corinthians 11:7	19
Acts 19	206, 208, 209, 210, 307 n.72,	I Corinthians 12	213
		I Corinthians 12:3	213, 307 n.74
Acts 19:6	209	I Corinthians 12:4-6	57, 59
Acts 20:28	290 n.61	I Corinthians 12:13	206
Acts 22:16	191, 198, 199, 312 n.16	I Corinthians 13:8	304 n.15
Acts 28:25	138	I Corinthians 14:21	284 n.31
Romans 1:3	55, 74, 270 n.11, 277 n.25	I Corinthians 15	123, 135, 136, 280 n.43
		I Corinthians 15:1	277 n.1
Romans 1:18-25	274 n.40	I Corinthians 15:22	93, 258 n.7
Romans 3:21-6	272 n.7	I Corinthians 15:24	135
Romans 4:3	196, 302 n.40	I Corinthians 15:24-28	135
Romans 4:4	311 n.65	I Corinthians 15:25	266 n.7
Romans 5	91	I Corinthians 15:45	273 n.34
Romans 5:14-19	258 n.7	II Corinthians 3-4	268 n.45, 279 n.21
Romans 5:14-18	273 n.34	II Corinthians 3:4	73
Romans 5:15	138	II Corinthians 3:6	282 n.5
Romans 6:4	264 n.30	II Corinthians 3:15-18	268 n.45
Romans 6:11	303 n.55	II Corinthians 3:16	284 n.30
Romans 7:7-11	274 n.40	II Corinthians 3:17	57, 138, 265 n.44, 279 n.26, 303 n.1
Romans 8	123, 213, 307 n.74		
Romans 8:1-11	282 n.7	II Corinthians 4:4	99
Romans 8:9-11	138	II Corinthians 4:6	99
Romans 8:9	195	II Corinthians 4:4-6	275 n.5
Romans 8:9-11	303 n.1	II Corinthians 4:6	99
Romans 8:11	264 n.30	II Corinthians 4:10	282 n.5
Romans 8:15	212	II Corinthians 5:19	72, 88
Romans 8:16	212	II Corinthians 10:17	284 n.30
Romans 8:19-22	274 n.40	II Corinthians 11:3	258 n.7
Romans 8:31-39	280 n.42	II Corinthians 12:9	282 n.5
Romans 8:34	266 n.7	II Corinthians 13:14	57, 58, 265 n.43
Romans 9:5	283 n.9	Galatians 2:15-21	272 n.9
Romans 10	196	Galatians 2:15-21	303 n.49
Romans 10:9	195	Galatians 2:16	87
Romans 10:13	195, 284 n.30	Galatians 2:20	272 n.9
Romans 11:13	284 n.30	Galatians 3:1-4:11	272 n.7
Romans 11:33	299 n.68	Galatians 3:5	213
Romans 12:19	284 n.32	Galatians 3:24	246 n.28, 266 n.4
Romans 14:11	284 n.30	Galatians 3:27	195
Romans 14:17	268 n.34	Galatians 4:6	212
I Corinthians 1:5	213	Galatians 4:11	272 n.7
I Corinthians 1:7	213	Galatians 4:25	268 n.34
I Corinthians 1:8	304 n.15	Galatians 5:25	282 n.5
I Corinthians 1:13	303 n.55	Ephesians 1:20	266 n.7
I Corinthians 1:31	284 n.30	Ephesians 2:6	266 n.7
I Corinthians 2:8	184	Ephesians 2:8	195
I Corinthians 2:16	284 n.30	Ephesians 2:14-16	266 n.9
I Corinthians 4:1-5	282 n.33	Ephesians 3:1-2	290 n.66
I Corinthians 6:11	191, 205, 303	Ephesians 4:8-10	123
I Corinthians 10:21	284 n.30	Ephesians 5:26	191
I Corinthians 10:22	284 n.30	Philippians 2	85, 279
I Corinthians 10:26	284 n.30	Philippians 2:5-11	274 n.39

Philippians 2:6-11	67, 93, 250	Hebrews 7:16-17	280 n.8
Philippians 2:6	55, 274 n.46	Hebrews 7:17	266 n.7
Philippians 2:6-11	274 n.39, 275 n.49, 51	Hebrews 7:21	266 n.7, 280 n.8
Philippians 2:7	94	Hebrews 7:25	132
Philippians 2:7-8	119	Hebrews 8:1	266 n.7
Philippians 2:9-11	129	Hebrews 8:6	128, 280 n.12
Philippians 2:10-11	284	Hebrews 9:14	122, 241
Philippians 2:11	272 n.16	Hebrews 9:15	128, 280 n.12
Philippians 3:9	198	Hebrews 10:12	132
Philippians 4:5	282 n.33	Hebrews 10:12-13	266 n.7, n.8
Philippians 4:13	282	Hebrews 10:22	191
Colossians 1-2	286 n.1	Hebrews 11	196
Colossians 1:15-20	67, 68	Hebrews 11:4	253 n.63
Colossians 2:9	72, 78	Hebrews 12:2	266 n.7, 278 n.5
Colossians 2:11	303 n.51	Hebrews 12:24	128, 253 n.63, 280 n.12
Colossians 2:11-12	303 n.50	Hebrews 12:35-37	266 n.7
Colossians 2:15	123	James 1:1	139
Colossians 3:1	266 n.7	James 1:17	270 n.15
Colossians 3:4	282 n.5	James 1:27	59
I Thessalonians 1:5	282	James 2:7	141, 194
I Thessalonians 3:13	57, 284 n.30	James 2:21	303 n.46
I Thessalonians 4:6	284 n.30	James 3:9	19
I Timothy 1:17	258 n.5	I Peter 1:1-2	58
I Timothy 2:5	59, 128, 145	I Peter 1:20	64
I Timothy 2:14	258 n.7	I Peter 3:18-22	67, 280 n.40
I Timothy 3:16	67, 68, 275 n.53	I Peter 3:21	303 n.51
I Timothy 5:21	57	I Peter 3:22	266 n.7
Titus 2:13	283 n.9	II Peter 1:1	283 n.10
Titus 3:5	205	I John 2:1	117
Titus 3:5-6	206	I John 4:12	258 n.5
Titus 3:5	305 n.30, 312 n.16	I John 5:7	57
Titus 3:6	206	III John 1	300
Hebrews 1	98	III John 7	141, 283 n.25
Hebrews 1-8	266 n.14	Revelation 1	134, 135
Hebrews 1:1-4	55, 68	Revelation 1:4	281
Hebrews 1:2	68	Revelation 1:8	284 n.30
Hebrews 1:3	67, 98, 99, 266 n.7, n.8	Revelation 1:13	281 n.29
Hebrews 1:4	131	Revelation 1:10	273 n.24
Hebrews 1:8	136, 283 n.9	Revelation 1:13	281
Hebrews 1:13	266 n.7	Revelation 1:14-15	134
Hebrews 2:4	213	Revelation 1:18	123, 284 n.31
Hebrews 2:14-15	122	Revelation 1:20	268 n.34
Hebrews 2:17	267 n.33	Revelation 2:7	264 n.31
Hebrews 4:15	91, 272 n.8	Revelation 2:11	264 n.31
Hebrews 5:1-10	55	Revelation 2:13	264 n.31
Hebrews 5:1	267 n.33	Revelation 2:17	264 n.31
Hebrews 5:4-10	280 n.6	Revelation 2:18	134, 281 n.29
Hebrews 5:6	266 n.7, 280	Revelation 2:29	263 n.31
Hebrews 5:7-8	118	Revelation 3:1	281
Hebrews 5:8	98	Revelation 3:6	264 n.31
Hebrews 6:5	213	Revelation 3:12	57
Hebrews 7:1-6	280 n.7	Revelation 3:13	264 n.31

Revelation 3:21	266 n.7	Revelation 14:14	281 n.29
Revelation 3:22	264 n.31	Revelation 19:6-9	309 n.32
Revelation 4:1-2	273 n.24	Revelation 20	135
Revelation 4:1	281 n.30	Revelation 20:15	136
Revelation 4:5	281	Revelation 21:1-3	273 n.24
Revelation 5:1-7	133	Revelation 21:6	284 n.31
Revelation 5:5-6	133	Revelation 22:1	133
Revelation 5:6	133, 281 n.30	Revelation 22:3	134
Revelation 10:1	273 n.24	Revelation 22:4	134
Revelation 12:11	133	Revelation 22:13	284 n.31
Revelation 13:8	64, 133	Revelation 22:16	264 n.31, 281 n.30
Revelation 14:13	281 n.30	Revelation 22:17	281 n.30

Index for Ancient Writings

Apocrypha

Baruch 2:15; 285 note 40
Baruch 2:26; 285 note 40
I Maccabees 7:37; 285 note 40
Wisdom of Solomon; 255-6 n. 18, 257 n. 36,
    10:17; 257 n.37

Other Ancient Writing

Pseudepigrapha
1 Enoch
    1:5; 303 n.55
    5:6; 303 n.55
    37–71, 282 n.33
    chapters 46, 48, 52, 62, 69, 71; 277 n.29
    48:10; 277 n.29
    52:4; 277 n.29

Philo
Allegorical Interpretation, vii, 2, 2:86; 258, n.43
On the Unchangeableness of God, 22; 31, 257 n.32
On Agriculture, 51; 257, n.39
On the Change of Names, xiii, 11; 281 n. 32, 257-8 n.41; 258 n.42 (*Mut Nom*) 121; 298 n.3
On the Life of Moses, 1-2; 258 n.42
On the Migration of Abraham, 120-1; 258 n.42
That the Worse is Wont to Attack the Better, 160; 258 n.42

Dead Sea Scrolls
4QFlor 1:12, 13; 285 n.38
Damascus Document
    XVI, 2–4; 300 n.1
    VII.16; 285 n.38
    XX.17ff.; 300 n.2
    II.53; 300 n.3
Genesis Apocryphon, 300 n.1

New Testament Apocrypha
Acts of Andrew, 168, 293 n.33
Acts of Christian Martyrs, 169

Acts of John, 168, 293 n.35
Acts of Paul, 168, 293 n.37
Acts of Paul and Thecla, 168, 293 n.37
Acts of Peter, 168, 294 n.41-2
Acta Pionii (*The Acts of* Pionius) 294 n.58
Apoc. Sophon.(*Apocalypse of Sophonias*) 294 n.58
Acts of Thomas, 168, 293 n.36
Infancy Gospel of Thomas 2:1-7, 271 n.25
Gospel of Thomas, 53, 83, 263 n.20
Kerygmata Petrou (*Kerygma of Peter*), 289 n.46
The Pseudo-Clemintines, 289 n.46
Pseudo-Hippolytus, *Paschal Homily*, 156

Testamentary Literature
Testaments of the Twelve Patriarchs, 169, 293 n.43
Testament of Asher, 169
Testament of Benjamin, 169
Testament of Dan, 169
Testament of Judah, 169
Testament of Levi, 294 n.49
Testament of Naphtali, 169
Testament of Simeon, 169
Testimonia, Jewish Christian, 169, 225

Church Fathers
Athanasius, *Contra Arius* 1.8; 298 n.49
Augustine
    City of God 50.11.10; 298 n.61
    Confessions; 183
        8.2.3; 298 n.52
    Enchiridion on Faith, Hope, and Love 38; 299 n.69
    On Christian Doctrine, II.xl.60–61; 286 n.6
    On the Gift of Perseverance 17.41; 299 n.67
    On the Spirit and the Letter 43.60; 299 n.68
    Quaestiones in Exodum 2.73; 298 n. 59-60
    The Trinity
        6.7; 298, n. 62, 63
        12.6.6–7: 299 n.70
Barnabas, Epistle of
    7:2; 291 n.71
Clement of Alexandria
    Excerpts from Theodotus 86.2; 288 n.41, 294 n.63
    Tutor (*Paedagogus*) 8.71.1; 292 n.22
1 Clement; 156,
    2:10, 285 n.45
    58.1; 156
    59.2, 156

Index for Ancient Writings | 383

    59.3, 156
2 Clement; 161, 291 n.71-2
    1:1–2; 161
Clement of Rome; 289 n.57, 291 n.71-2
Epistles of Cyprian,
    73:4, 16; 301 n.15
Eusebius,
    Recognitions 1:55; 289 n.47
    Historia ecclesiastica
        book 1. 286 n.7
        1.3; 299 n.76
        3 5.3; 289 n.53
        5.28.4–6; 290 n.60
The *Didache*,
    3; 294 n.60-1
    7; 171
    7.1; 301 n.16
    9; 171
    9.4; 301 n.16
Epiphanius
    Panarion; 297 n.24
        29.5.4; 288 n.44
        30.6.9; 289 n.47,
        30.14; 289 n.49
        30.27; 288 n.44
        62.1; 297 n.27
Hermas (*Shepherd of*), 156-7, 288 n.32-3, 289 n.57
    Vision. III,3:5; 157
    Similitude. IX, 14:5; 157
    Similitude. VIII, 10:3; 157
Hippolytus,
    Refutation of All Heresies
        5; 297 n.25
        7; 297 n.22-3
        9.6; 287 n.16,
        28; 297 n.25
    Apostolic Tradition; 302 n.23
Ignatius
    To the Ephesians
        Inscription, 290 n.60
        1:1, 290 n.60, 291 n.69
        3.2: 290 n.60
        7.2, 161, 290 n.67
        18:2, 291 n.69
    Magn. (To the Magnesians)

384 | I AM: A Oneness Pentecostal Theology

        6.1; 290 n.66
        8.2; 290 n.66
        3.2, 290 n.62
        8.3, 290 n.90
    To Polycarp, 160-1, 290 n.62
    To the Romans,
        6:3; 285 n.45, 290 n.60, 291 n.69
    Smryn.(*To the Smyrneans*)
        1:1, 290 n.60, 66
        6:1,10:1, 290 n.60
    To the *Trallians*
        7:1, 290 n.60
Irenaeus, *Against Heresies*;
    Against Heresies,
        4.20.3, 297 n.28
        Book I, 294 n.59
Justin
    1 Apology
        6; 166,
        53; 292 n.13
        58; 292 n.13
        59-60 296 n.10
        63; 293 n.20, 293 n.29
    2 Apology
        6; 292 n.14
        10.8; 292 n.7
    Dialogue with Trypho 128; 269 n.46, 287 n.22, 292 n.13; 293 n.27
Jerome, *De viris illustribus* 3; 289 n.53
Melito of Sardis
    Fragments 13-4; 161, 291 n.72
    Fragments 105; 161, 291 n.73-4
    On the Passover 75; 161, 291 n.70,
Origen
    Against Celsius,
        5.39; 297 n.29
        16.1; 287 n.15
    On First Principles
        1.2.4; 297 n.27
        1.3.6; 293 n.23
        4.4.1; 298 n.40
    On *Prayer* 24.2; 293 n.23
Porphyry (possibly)
    Commentary of the Parmenides) 299 n.57
Tatian, *Oration to the Greeks* 13, 285 n.45, 295 n.65
Tertullian
    Against Praxeas: 156, 176-8
        2; 287 n.13, 295 n.4
        3; 287 n.15, 296 n.12

5; 296 n.15
20; 295 n.20
22; 296 n.9
26; 302 n.23
29; 296 n.13
31; 287 n.14, 287-88 n.25
On Baptism; 302 n.23
Prescription against Heretics 7; 295 n.8
Modesty 21; 296-7 n.20

Miscellaneous Ancient Sources

Classical Greek: Plato, *Timaeus* 27–30; 255 n.13
Jewish Christian:*(De) Montibus*, 156, 288 n.25
Rabbinic: *b Pesach.*60a; 302 n.36
Sibylline Oracles; 300-1 n.5